SOCIAL RESEARCH
THE BASICS

SOCIAL RESEARCH
THE BASICS

MATTHEW DAVID AND CAROLE D. SUTTON

SAGE Publications
London • Thousand Oaks • New Delhi

SAGE Publications Ltd
1 Oliver's Yard
55 City Road
London EC1Y 1SP

SAGE Publications Inc
2455 Teller Road
Thousand Oaks, California 91320

SAGE Publications India Pvt Ltd
B-42, Panchsheel Enclave
Post Box 4109
New Delhi 100 017

British Library Cataloguing in Publication data

A catalogue record for this book is available from the British Library

ISBN 0 7619 7366 4
ISBN 0 7619 7367 2 (pbk)

Library of Congress Control Number is available

Typeset by M Rules
Printed in Great Britain at The Alden Press, Oxford

CONTENTS

PART IV PRESENTING RESEARCH FINDINGS

LIST OF FIGURES, TABLES AND BOXES

FIGURES

TABLES

BOXES

ACKNOWLEDGEMENTS

We would like to take this opportunity to thank the following friends and colleagues for their support. To Kevin Meethan and Malcolm Williams for their feedback on the book proposal. To Katharine Clarke, Danny Daniels, and Alison Green for their valuable comments on early chapter drafts. To Alison Anderson, Sam Regan de Bere and Mike Sheaff for their contributions to Chapter 5. To Alison Pilnick and Susan Child for their permission to reproduce in this volume extracts of their writing.

Particularly thanks are extended to Lyn Bryant, Tim May and Mike Presdee for their continued support and encouragement in the competitive world of academia.

Thanks to all the Sage editorial staff, in particular Chris Rojek, Kay Bridger, Ben Griffin-Sherwood and Rosemary Campbell, as well as to Solveig Gardner Servian. Thanks also to the anonymous reviewers for their helpful suggestions.

Screenshots from QSR NVivo 2.0 and N6 are reproduced with permission by QSR International Pty Ltd. Copyright QSR International Pty Ltd 2002. QSR can be contacted at www.qsr.com.au. Screenshots and output from SPSS v11.5 are reproduced with permission of SPSS Inc. SPSS can be contacted at www.spss.com.

Social research is all around us. Social researchers generate a wealth of data about the world in which we live, underpinning the activities of commercial, charitable and state funded services, the mass media, the workplace, in universities and elsewhere. One only needs to read a daily newspaper to be confronted by assertions and claims about the way we live, how things have changed, how things are better or worse either in the past or elsewhere in the world. These assertions are made by politicians and commentators keen to have us believe that they know 'best'. One fundamental role of social research is to put such assertions to the test. The ability to comprehend and critically interpret the social research of others is a powerful tool in enabling the making of informed choices. The ability to conduct social research takes this power to a higher level, not only enabling the researcher to make informed choices, but also influencing the choices made by society itself. In a complex, changing world, good quality social research skills are therefore an increasingly valued resource, for both supplementing the information society has about itself and for interpreting and applying it. As a result of what is sometimes called 'post-industrialization', as well as what others call 'globalization', there has been an increased demand for individuals capable of conducting social research in a variety of settings. This has blurred the distinction between the professional social researcher and others who carry out social research as a part of their professional practice.

This book provides the reader with a practical, balanced and comprehensive introduction to social research. The emphasis is on the application in the real world of social research, while outlining the intellectual debates which frame practical concerns. This text gives an equal weight to the qualitative and quantitative approaches. The structuring of the contents allows the researcher to use this book as a textbook or as a handbook. *Social Research: The Basics* includes comprehensive introductions to the data-analysis software packages NVivo2.0, N6 and SPSS v11.

What this book provides is a foundation and a framework that is in itself sufficient to carry out a final year social science undergraduate dissertation project. The text is accessible enough to be read by those with no prior knowledge or experience. At the same time, the book is comprehensive enough to allow the user to design, conduct and analyse research. To fine-tune a project in the direction the researcher wishes to take it will require reference to specialist texts in those areas of methodology. The book in your hands will give you a level of understanding and practical know-how that will allow you to comprehend and apply the specialist texts.

The language of social research is littered with jargon. The Glossary of key terms at the back of this book is designed to enable you to translate this technical language into plain English. The Glossary contains 365 terms that are commonly in use in discussions of social research, but which are not common in everyday language. Using the Glossary will help you clarify what you are reading and what you are thinking about doing with the knowledge you gain. The Glossary also makes the book easier to read in a non-sequential way. The reader who is using this book more as a practical handbook than as a textbook may want to jump straight to the chapter they need to follow. This will mean skipping over materials discussed in earlier chapters, and may result in missing out on definitions of concepts mentioned there. The Glossary is the first place to look if you approach the book in this way and come across terms you do not understand.

The first time any term contained in the Glossary appears in the text, it will appear in sans serif bold. The most important Glossary terms used in each chapter will be listed under the heading 'Keywords' at the end of that chapter.

This book is supported by a website containing links to a range of up-to-date electronic sources related to the conduct of social research. These include links to data-archives, professional and academic associations, software providers and sites offering substantive materials relating to research design. This website is located at: www.sagepub.co.uk/resources/davidsutton.htm.

This book is divided into four parts. Part I (Chapters 1 to 5) outlines the issues facing a researcher before they begin collecting and analysing data. Part II (Chapters 6 to 15) addresses research design and data collection, in both qualitative (Chapters 6 to 10) and quantitative (Chapters 11 to 15) forms. Part III covers data analysis for both qualitative (Chapters 16 to 19) and quantitative (Chapters 20 to 24) data. Part IV (Chapters 25 and 26) focuses upon presenting research findings.

Part I Chapters 1 to 4 focus upon initial stages in the research design process prior to data collection. Chapter 1 addresses the choice of research design and of a research question. Does the researcher have a prediction they want to test or do they have a question they want to explore? How can a research topic develop out of the search and review of existing literature? How is a literature search and review to be carried out? Chapter 2 outlines the ethical issues the researcher has to confront and how they solve, or at least address, these. Chapter 3 addresses the questions of whether the social researcher should collect their own data or analyse existing data. Questions of logic, cause and human action are discussed, alongside the forms of data that a researcher can collect. The issue of internal and external data validity is then discussed. Finally, the purpose of research is addressed in relation to evaluation research, participant action research and feminist methodology. Chapter 4 tackles the meaning and relationship between quality and quantity in social research. A range of different meanings, associated with the two terms, are set out and analysed in detail. The philosophical underpinnings of the division between qualitative and quantitative research are also detailed. However, this chapter also shows how quality and quantity underpin each other in all research.

Chapter 5 presents four examples of how qualitative and quantitative research were combined in the subject fields of: 1 Environmental issues in the media; 2 Education evaluation; 3 Health inequalities; and 4 Rural deprivation. Each example outlines the type of research that was undertaken, the types of questions that were asked and the research techniques used, each drawing on a range of methodologies and methods. The fields illustrate how qualitative and quantitative approaches are both complementary and divergent.

Part II Chapters 6 to 10 set out the logics of qualitative research design and data collection. These discussions are framed within a more general discussion of qualitative research design, induction, qualitative sampling and the ethics of qualitative research (Chapter 6). The process of interviewing, one-to-one and group based (Chapter 7), the conduct of ethnographic fieldwork and case study research (Chapter 8), textual data collection (Chapter 9), as well as ethnomethodology and conversation analysis (Chapter 10) are detailed.

Chapters 11 and 12 introduce the research designs associated with quantitative approaches to social research, the process of operationalization and the measurement of concepts. Chapter 13 details the different sampling techniques available. Chapter 14 focuses on the data collection methods associated with the self-completion survey and structured interview. Chapter 15 examines issues relating to the administration of a survey, the management of data collected and using existing quantitative data sources.

Part III Chapters 16 to 19 and 20 to 24 introduce a range of data analysis techniques associated with qualitative and quantitative data respectively. In these chapters the approach taken is practical, explanatory and hands-on. Step-by-step guidance in the software packages NVivo 2.0, N6 and SPSS v11 are given.

In Chapters 16 to 19 the process and practice of qualitative data analysis are set out. The relationship between data collection and analysis is discussed (Chapter 16) before moving on to discuss the specifics of a range of different qualitative data analysis techniques: in particular qualitative content analysis (Chapter 17), as well as discourse analysis and conversation analysis (Chapter 18). An illustrated step-by-step guide to the seven stages of data analysis is given using the NVivo/N6 qualitative data analysis software (Chapter 19).

In Chapters 20 to 24 the techniques for quantitative data analysis are discussed. The data analysis process starts with the data entry (Chapter 20) before moving on to the first data analysis phase that involves the describing of single variables (Chapter 21). The exploration of relationships between variables enables the researcher to address the original research question and hypotheses (Chapter 22). The use of inferential statistics enables the social researcher to make generalizations from the sample data to the population (Chapter 23). Finally, the various data management techniques that are available to extend the data analysis further are discussed in Chapter 24.

It is important to note that while SPSS and similar statistical computer packages are universal in the analysis of quantitative data, the use of computer software is still relatively controversial in the analysis of qualitative data. Only one of the three traditions of qualitative data analysis, that is, qualitative content analysis, is directly compatible with qualitative data analysis software, and much of qualitative content analysis is not carried out using computers. The organization of Chapters 16 to 19 and 20 to 24 reflect the different levels of computerization within the two fields.

Chapters 25 and 26 focus upon presenting your research findings. These chapters contain guidance on preparing written reports (Chapter 25) and oral presentations (Chapter 26). The key stages of report writing and presentations tailored to different types of audience are discussed.

The process of carrying out social research is like juggling! At first, trying to keep more than one thing in the air at the same time tends to lead to dropping everything else. The elements outlined above, and which are detailed more fully in the text to follow, may at first appear dislocated and complex. The process of actually doing social research is the only way that such complex processes can become familiar. From familiarity comes confidence, and the ability to experiment and develop innovative research strategies of your own.

PART I

STARTING YOUR RESEARCH

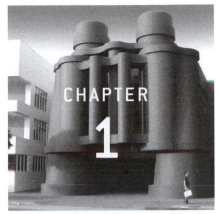

CHAPTER
1

GETTING STARTED:
THEORY, LITERATURE AND RESEARCH QUESTION

Chapter contents

By the end of this chapter you will be able to:

- Understand key elements in formulating a research question.

- Structure and begin a literature search.

- Carry out a literature review.

- Distinguish between deductive and inductive research designs, and be able to address the questions that social researchers need to ask when choosing which approach to adopt.

Getting into the water

This chapter, along with Chapters 2 and 3 set out issues that all social researchers need to think about, decide upon and carry out in order to begin an empirical research project. In some respects this is like getting into the water when going swimming. There is an advantage to just jumping in: the best way to learn is to have a go. But just jumping in without having learnt some basic things might lead to drowning, so here we offer some basic guidelines on what to do. These chapters are about 'getting into the loop'. Doing social research requires that you do a large number of things, seemingly at the same time. This, at first, seems confusing. Those who have been doing research for a while tend to take it for granted, and so they are not always aware of every aspect of what they are doing when they do it. This can confuse the beginner even more. Getting into the loop is about picking up the taken-for-granted routines of the more experienced, and practising them. Once you are familiar with the steps, processes and short-cuts you will no doubt develop your own style, your own routines and your own agenda. The way things are set out here is to help you get started. You will always have to bear them in mind, but after a while you may do things in your own way.

What is social research: science, theory and data collection

Social research has many forms, and this book seeks to introduce the reader to their basic forms and logics. Part I sets out the key questions that the social researcher must address when setting out to conduct a research project. In so doing, Part I will outline the basic properties of social research. While practical in nature, the first three chapters will highlight more abstract issues and debates, in particular the relationship between theory and the research process, both in conduct and in choice of **method**. These debates hinge around two questions:

- Is social research a science?

- Can humans be studied usefully in a scientific manner?

These two questions will be briefly addressed now, before moving on to the practical question of how to get started.

Science is, in the popular imagination, the experimental method. Experimental method is the establishment of **controlled conditions** in which the effect of **variables** on other variables can be measured. Regulation of inputs allows accurate estimation of causes in the variation of outputs. Experimental method requires an initial prediction about how variation of inputs will effect outputs such that this prediction can then be tested. This **prediction** is a provisional theory (or thesis). This is called a **hypothesis**. A variable is anything whose amount can vary, and which is defined in such a way that its variation can be measured (and in an experiment also controlled in this variation). A number of variables may be specified. In the classic experiment all identifiable variables are held constant (controlled conditions), bar two variables. These are the **independent** and **dependent** variables set out in the prediction/hypothesis. The hypothesis predicts that variation in the independent variable causes variation in the dependent variable. With all other things held constant, the experiment is designed to allow this hypothesis to be tested. The hypothesis is drawn from prior examination of research on the subject. As such the experiment is theory driven (in other words, the data collection is designed to fulfil a need for information required to answer a theoretical question). This approach to the relationship between theory and research is called deduction. Hence the experimental method is called **hypothetico-deductive**. The experiment is the stereotypical image of scientific method. Some social researchers use the experimental method. However, most social researchers do not!

It is important to note that much research in the physical sciences is not strictly speaking experimental. Much of geology, astronomy and biology deploy methods of **data collection** beyond the laboratory. Geological and evolutionary time, galaxies and eco-systems cannot be replicated in controlled conditions. This is also the case for many aspects of social life.

Science cannot be defined exclusively in terms of the classical experiment.

However, despite not always using the experimental method, much of the remaining physical science research does deploy another form of hypothetico-deductive research (that is, research where a prediction is tested through the variation of observed conditions). This may be through comparison over time or between locations. If different levels of a particular variable exist in different locations or at different times, it may be possible to measure the levels of other variables in those times and places to see if patterns (or **correlations**) exist. Whilst an element of control is lost, it may still be possible to show that variations in one factor go along with variation in other factors (even if what is causing what is harder to pin down). A hypothesis can be stated. The researcher can then go looking for the conditions **necessary** to test that hypothesis. Data can be collected and results analysed which will then support or challenge the hypothesis. This is still therefore hypothetico-deductive research.

A far greater amount of social research adopts this approach. Proponents of this type of social research tend to see themselves as scientists. However, some forms of social research are not hypothetico-deductive and pursue an **exploration**-based approach. Sometimes this is to identify what is going on when existing knowledge is insufficient to generate hypotheses. There are plenty of such examples in the physical sciences. Sometimes, this exploratory approach is adopted as a rejection of the hypothetico-deductive method, its predictive method and **causal** assumptions. This raises the question of whether scientific methods are appropriate to study humans, or whether humans possess qualitatively different characteristics to physical objects (most particularly consciousness and choice) that invalidate predictive forms of research and the predictive model of explanation which hypothetico-deductive research is based upon. These issues will be discussed later (see 'Testing or exploring' p. 11 and Chapter 4). These are questions that will recur throughout the research process, but ones that cannot be resolved at this stage.

Identifying a research question

While a hypothesis is a proposition to be tested, rather than a question to be answered, hypotheses are designed to focus attention within broader research areas or questions. While some research questions are very specific and others far looser in definition, the process of identifying a research question is always an essential first step in any project.

Social problems, political issues, personal motives?

A researcher may enter the process of identifying the research question at a number of different stages. Ironically, the student conducting a research project for their studies and the well-established research professor may have more in common here with each other than either may have with the majority of researchers in the middle. The privilege of starting from first principles, rather than being brought in in the middle or towards the end of the research problem identification process, is most often denied those neither well established or researching for study.

Identification of the research question may have many levels, only some of which will be within the researcher's power to alter, at least in the first instance. Issues may become 'ripe' for research in the minds of those able to fund such activities for a number of reasons. Bodies engaged in education, health care, law and order, social work, economics, urban planning, commercial and governmental administration and so on will, for various reasons, come to the view that research may help them address or more clearly identify problems. Research may be funded by charities on issues of concern to them so that findings stimulate awareness and debate about those issues. These bodies will form an opinion about what needs to be researched and such motivations play a crucial role in the identification of research questions.

However, even while such factors play a crucial role in directing research, the question of how such research is to be carried out requires the researcher to develop the identification process from an idea to a practical activity. It is here that the researcher's own interpretations of the 'problem', and the best way to research it, come into play. When the researcher can claim a degree of expertise in both the subject to be studied, and in the methods by which such a subject can best be studied, they are in a position to introduce their own definitions of themes and interpretations of 'problems'. To this extent the more developed researcher may become pro-active in regard to seeking funding from potentially interested parties for projects the researcher is personally motivated by. In this way the researcher may move 'up stream' in the question identification process. When a researcher's own previous research comes to define how potential research funding bodies perceive an issue, they may consider themselves to have become the source of the stream itself. Most researchers are not in such a fortunate situation, but, as Tim May (1997: 27) points out, the relationship between theories of what problems exist and methods applied to investigate their existence is always a two-way street, even if the density of traffic in each direction varies.

Whether contracted to research a particular topic, doing a project within or on behalf of an organization, bidding for funding from a public or private agency, or conducting research as a training exercise within an educational context, the first step in identifying the research question in a practical fashion is to identify what has gone before. Those interested in the intricacies of gaining funding, and in the politics of such processes, will find many interesting discussions (for example, Hammersley, 1995, 2000). Here we will move on to the question of researching the existing literature. We will then look at the two types of research question, hypothesis testing and exploratory investigation.

Researching the literature

One definition of a **literature review** is as follows:

> The selection of all available documents (both published and unpublished) on the topic, which contain information, ideas, data and evidence written from a particular standpoint to fulfil certain aims or express certain views on the nature of the topic and how it is to be investigated, and the effective evaluation of these documents in relation to the research being proposed. (Hart, 1998: 13)

This is all very well in theory, but it sounds a tall order. Researching the literature comes in two parts, although these parts feed into each other:

- Searching for literature. A **literature search** seeks to find materials related to a topic.
- The analysis of its content. A literature review seeks to analyse the content of that material in more depth.

Of course, what counts as part of the literature of interest depends upon its content, and knowing its content depends upon finding it first. The two parts

feed into each other. A chicken and egg scenario! So where to begin? As with starting a job, moving to a new town or learning any new skill, we are confronted with the novelty of what those more established there take for granted. The established researcher in a field knows who the key players are, what they have written, the journals to keep an eye on, as well as the conferences and presentations to attend. They are in the loop. Their social networks in the field are a crucial asset in keeping their fingers on the pulse. In one of the authors' own research for the British Library into literature searching (David and Zeitlyn, 1996; Zeitlyn, David and Bex, 1999), it was found that more established researchers were quite unlikely to use the technical literature searching services available to them, while younger researchers did. Just as an established resident is unlikely to use a map of their town, so the more established researchers drew upon experience and personal networks to find their way around. So how to get into the loop? This is where more technical searching services come in, but such searching services are only as good as the questions asked of them. Computers might be the answer, but what is the question? How do we identify the crucial themes, concepts and theories?

Searching the archives

Bouma and Atkinson (1995: 35) counsel that: 'A good librarian is the finest resource available to anyone undertaking social science research'.

Keefer (1993: 336) states: 'The basic "information problem" revolves around the fact that the inquirer knows enough to know that he or she needs information, but doesn't know enough to ask the "good" questions that would produce the needed information'.

Before searching the **archives**, it is essential to discuss your topic with peers, tutors and librarians. This is the best way to identify the **keywords** that are going to assist you in wading through the near infinite mass of literature that exists.

Once you begin to accumulate **texts** from within a field, new keywords may begin to stand out, initial ones may drop out, and others may take on additional significance. Keeping records of what you have read, and of the central arguments and keywords used within these texts, is therefore an essential task. Traditionally researchers would keep a card index of all texts read (usually ordered alphabetically by author, but sometimes ordered by other criteria). Nowadays, such indexes can be stored electronically, either in straightforward word-processing files or in more specific indexing software. Either way, it is essential to establish your own indexing system. This enables the streamlining of content, the storage of essential information, and allows for comparison. Another key consideration when developing an indexing system is how you are going to organize the content of each text's respective card or file (see 'Reviewing content' p. 10).

Once you have identified your provisional keywords, established how you are going to store the reference details of the texts you uncover and prepared some means of ordering and storing the actual materials you uncover (shelves, filing cabinets and piles on the floor are popular), you are ready to begin formal searching.

Searching for books, articles, theses, Web materials, newspapers and other materials   Most of us when we think about literature think first of books. However, in conducting an efficient literature search, it is often more productive to begin with journal articles, theses and reports from bodies concerned with the subject we are interested in. This is for a number of simple reasons. Articles, theses and reports are usually shorter than books, are more tightly focused, and so are more rapidly published and read. The latest journal articles, theses and reports will be more up to date and their bibliographies are likely to

be the best source of references for older research, and particularly the older research that has become core reading in the field in question. Reading the latest articles, theses and reports is therefore the fastest and most effective method of getting to grips with a field.

Almost all libraries now have Online Public Access Catalogues (OPACs) that enable the researcher to identify the volumes shelved in that library. Academic and research libraries often have these OPACs networked, allowing the researcher to search catalogues of libraries around the world via a networked computer. However, OPACs only catalogue volumes and not their contents. This means that OPACs are not the best vehicle for identifying journal articles. For this we must turn to other services.

Abstracts and indexes for articles, theses and reports
Abstracts and indexing services enable the researcher to search the content of articles, theses and reports (usually not books). This requires that the researcher identify keywords by which to search. The wrong keywords may lead you in the wrong direction. Keywords that are too general will generate references to too many texts, and the researcher will get swamped. Too specific keywords may not generate enough references. Keywords may be the names of authors, places, dates, names of journals, academic fields and disciplines or concepts (such as gender or crime). Discussion with peers, tutors and librarians is the key to getting past this problem of which keywords

---

David, Matthew (2002), 'Problems of participation: the limits of action research', in *International Journal of Social Research Methodology: Theory and Practice*, Volume 5, Number 1, pp. 11–17.

Abstract
Alvin Gouldner (1979) suggests knowledge is both culture and capital. Knowledge enables meaningful action. Capital is culture privatised. Culture is capital generalised. This raises the question of ownership in social research. Detachment in social research is praised as a virtue but also viewed as a source of difficulties epistemologically and ethically. Participatory action research offers a critique of detachment and advocates its opposite, 'commitment'. This may not necessarily involve 'political' advocacy. However, commitment to involve participants, and to further their goals through the conduct of research, does become a form of 'advocacy'. This paper draws on problematic experiences as a 'participatory action researcher' in social movement and evaluation research. Drawing of the recent work of Steve Fuller (2000), I will suggest, rather bluntly, that when asked 'whose side are we on', academics might be more bold and suggest we are on our own side.

Keywords: PAR, participatory action research, advocacy, detachment, instrumentalism, social movements, evaluation research, telematics, social exclusion, politics.

Figure 1.1   Example of an abstract with keywords that would be used in a search

to start with. Once you get going, additional (and sometimes better) keywords will present themselves. Authors are asked to specify the keywords that best reflect their piece (see Figure 1.1). In addition to keywords, the bibliographic details (date of publication, author name/s, title and journal title and so on) are also stored as keywords in the abstracts and indexing system. Your job is to second-guess these. The physical sciences have a more systematic process of allocating keywords than is found in the social sciences, so second-guessing in the social science abstracts and indexes is harder.

Traditionally **indexes** were large bound volumes organized alphabetically by author, title and keywords from the text. Each index would cover a specified academic field for a specified period. Specific indexes were devoted to either academic journal articles, academic theses or commissioned reports. A researcher seeking to find materials would search the relevant indexes for references to texts that might be of interest to them. Each entry in the index would then reference the location of an **abstract** of that article, thesis or report. An abstract is a short summary of the text, as shown in Figure 1.1.

By reading the abstract the researcher would gain a better idea of whether the text might be worth finding and reading in full. Bound volumes of abstracts relating to the bound volumes of indexes would usually be kept in the same section of the library and in some cases the abstracts and indexes would be within a single bound volume. This was a laborious process and was seen as one of the 'rights of passage' in 'becoming a researcher'. One of the most tedious aspects was cross-referencing between keywords. For example, if you were interested in women's use of illegal drugs you would want to identify all articles that refer to both. This would mean finding not only all the articles that had keywords related to 'women', but also all the articles that contained keywords related to 'illegal drugs'. There may be thousands of articles on each and so too many to read. You would want only those articles that contained both. This is an 'AND' type search. Sometimes you will want a 'BUT NOT' search, where you might request, for example, all articles about drugs 'BUT NOT' those relating to medication. Such 'AND', 'BUT NOT', 'OR' and other types of search are called Boolean searches, and form one strand of qualitative data analysis (see Chapters 16, 17 and 19).

It is essential to identify alternative keywords when searching for a particular theme. For example, if you were interested in poverty, many articles may be of use to you that do not have the term 'poverty' as a keyword. These articles may have terms like 'social exclusion', 'inequality' or 'deprivation' as keywords. While these words do not have identical meanings, their meanings cross over. In any keyword search it is important to think of as many such overlapping terms in order to conduct a comprehensive search. These terms can be generated by the researcher in advance, in collaboration with colleagues and others, or new keywords can be generated as the researcher goes along (looking at the other key terms used in the abstracts of articles found along the way). Once keyword searches point to potentially useful abstracts, these abstracts can be read and a decision made as to whether it would be useful to find and read the full article.

This narrowing down required seemingly endless trawling backwards and forwards, between pages within the abstracts and then between the indexes and the abstracts they referred to. Things have changed radically in recent years. Though some paper abstract and indexing services still exist, and may be useful, electronic services have now largely taken the place of paper. Electronic services allow searches that would have once taken days to be carried out in minutes. Of course, being easier does not ensure that searches done electronically are done better.

Electronic abstracts and indexing services have evolved rapidly. The earliest electronic systems emerged in the physical sciences (for example, Chemical Abstracts On-Line), Medicine (Med-Line) and Law (Lexus). They involved centrally stored databases that could be accessed on-line. These services charged for time on-line and were complex and expensive. Researchers would usually get a specialist (librarian or other) to do searches quickly on their behalf. The advent of the CD-ROM enabled the data to be held locally at a fixed price. This meant that researchers could do their own searches without per-minute costs. CD-ROMs are still a popular medium for abstracts and indexing services, but updating requires replacement each time. The next stage in the development of electronic abstracts and indexing was the rise of consortia which brought together numerous databases within a single search format, and then charged institutions (usually academic and research based libraries) fixed rates (usually per year) to access their service. This meant a high initial fee, but no per-minute charges. This enabled these institutions to give open access to these services to all their members (or end-users) without fear of excessive costs. In this way the 'liberated end-user' has access to the most up-to-date version of the database without their institution having to continually buy new CD-ROMs. The latest development has been the availability of many of these services through the World Wide Web, thus easing access and improving interface quality.

Pay-per-minute services, CD-ROMs and fixed fee based systems all exist, but, as a beginner, you are likely only to use the latter two. These systems are all fundamentally similar to the traditional paper services. You have to identify the keywords you want the system to search for, and then cross-reference, but electronic services offer increased scope, speed and range of peripheral services. Abstracts found electronically can be saved to word-processing files or sent as e-mails to the researcher's account. Journals store their articles in electronic format. Some journals allow these to be made available via the electronic search services, so in addition to an abstract you may be able to get the full text. This may sometimes be at no additional cost, but often you will be expected to pay for individual articles. You may prefer at this stage to go and find a paper copy of the text to read in the library (using that library's OPAC to locate the relevant volume). However, instant access may be something you are prepared to pay for, and not all journals are available in every library. You may find that your library is prepared to order copies of articles for you via inter-library loan, which is usually cheaper and sometimes free to you if the library has a budget for supporting this provision.

Similar services exist for newspapers and magazines. The search engines available to search for World Wide Web pages have a similar format. Each such system will have its own quirks, and not all will be available to you through your home computer or via the institutions you either work or study in. Once again your librarian is your best friend in this regard and it is they (not us) who can best advise you on what is available to you, and how best to access and use it. Technical networks do not replace social networks when it comes to doing social research, and especially when it comes to knowing how to ask a relevant question.

Reviewing content

Reviewing the content of literature gathered is a form of research in itself. It is a form of secondary **data analysis**, and as the content we are dealing with here is

textual, this form of secondary data analysis is a form of **qualitative** data analysis. All these themes are discussed in greater detail in Chapters 16 to 19. At this stage it is useful to suggest five possible sets of questions that can be addressed to the content of specific pieces of literature. These five approaches feed into each other and are drawn from the work of Hart (1998). As one becomes more confident as a researcher, these practices may become habits that take on a less formal quality. The more seasoned researcher may trust their 'instincts' and adopt a more holistic approach to reviewing texts. Whether this is healthy or just laziness is a matter for speculation, but the seasoned researcher can get away with it more easily, while the beginner cannot. As such it is best to start with some degree of formal ordering. When you are a famous social researcher you can do your own thing.

1   Defining parameters – how does the particular text define the field of study (what are the key elements included, what are the boundaries drawn around the topic, and what are the elements explicitly excluded)?
2   How are the findings of the work classified? What framework of categories is being used to define the objects identified in the research? What distinctions and variables are being used? What methods are being used?
3   Argumentation analysis: logic and argument. What is the argument being developed in the work? How is evidence used to build towards a conclusion? What are the conclusions drawn?
4   Organization and expression of ideas. What theoretical models are being used?
5   How best can the text's content be represented? Here the researcher may wish to use mental maps, flow diagrams and compressed summaries of the piece.

Once specific texts have been treated in this way it is possible to move on to the more synthetic task of evaluating the relationship between such texts. A firm grasp of the elements will enable you to ask the questions:

• What do some or all of these texts have in common?
• What do some or all of these texts contain that distinguishes them from each other?

These questions will return you to the five questions posed above. 1 How is the definition of the field established and/or disputed? 2 What are the key categories and variables being deployed and how far is their use agreed and/or disputed? 3 How is evidence used to establish or dispute findings? 4 What are the theoretical lines of dispute and agreement that operate within the field? 5 How best can such disputes and/or consensus be represented (here time-lines and mental maps are particularly useful in representing how disputes and/or agreements develop historically, within and between different theoretical traditions, and in different locations – localities, states and larger geographical areas).

In asking and seeking to answer these types of question, you begin to move away from cataloguing towards critical evaluation. In time and with regard to different fields of study you will come to develop your own interrogation strategies. The job of a literature review is to focus, find, catalogue and evaluate. Each step may turn up issues that require going back a step to widen, narrow or shift the direction of the review, but the aim is that of evaluation. It is only at this stage that the researcher can claim to have a grasp of their chosen (and to a degree self-generated) field. It is only at this stage that the researcher can claim to occupy a vantage point from which to identify the gaps and crucial lines of conflict which require further investigation. Even where research is contracted and comes with a high degree of pre-specification about its aims, the translation of these aims into practical research objectives requires the researcher to know what has gone before, if only to avoid reinventing the wheel, but also to enable the research meaningfully to contribute something new to the field.

Testing or exploring?

Researching the existing literature will have given you some sense of what has been said before, what the key findings and key disputes are, and perhaps will have left you with a sense of what is missing or still needs further investigation or clarification. Similarly, whether the original motivation for your research was personal, moral, political or intellectual fascination, or the interest of the organization funding the research, this will have given some focus and direction to the research, even if only to establish some of the initial keywords used in your literature search. So, your research will have some degree of focus already, but the degree and nature of that focus must now be clarified further.

At this stage you will need to ask yourself the following questions:

- Do I have a hunch (in other words a hypothesis) about what is going on here?
- Does that hunch/hypothesis suggest to me what the key causes and effects are?

You do not need to be sure. If you knew for sure that increasing amounts of X led to increasing amounts of Y, it would not be necessary to research it. The purpose of at least one type of research is to test hunches. Whether or not the hunches are supported in the final research, we have a result. Research that is based upon the idea of testing hunches is to be distinguished from research where we are setting out only to explore what is present in a particular situation.

Testing a hunch requires that we can state it in such a way that it can be compared with reality. This formulation of the hunch is then a **prediction**. This is not the same as a question. A question is open-ended, while a prediction states an expected outcome. What is open-ended, in the case of a prediction, is whether this expected outcome conforms with the actual outcome. Will the prediction be correct? A hunch is a theory that has not yet been supported with evidence. In research terms this is called a hypothesis. What distinguishes a hypothesis from other kinds of ideas is that a hypothesis is designed to be tested, and so must state clearly the elements involved (measurable categories of actions, objects or **actors**) and the nature of the relationship between them that is being predicted (cause, **mediation** or correlation). These practical matters will be dealt with in greater detail in Chapters 4 and 5. Here it is only necessary to be aware of the distinction between testing and exploring, and the logic behind choosing either one or a combination of both. So what is exploratory research and why choose not to test a hypothesis?

On completing a review of the literature you may feel that there is a reasonable case for suggesting that X has a relationship with Y, even that the relationship is a causal one. This may not have been actively tested in the previous research examined, or such testing may have been long ago or in a different location, thereby warranting your wish to carry out such tests. Alternatively, you may feel that the literature does not leave you with a hypothesis that can be tested, only a series of open questions about what is going on. If this is the case, it is not going to be possible to draw up a testable hypothesis. You have no tentative predictions, only questions. In this instance you will want to adopt an exploratory approach. Without a prediction to test, the design of exploratory research will be more open-ended. Because of this, exploratory research tends to collect more **qualitative** (interpretive) data, though this is not always true. Testing a hypothesis is more often associated with the use of **quantitative** (numerical) methods. Chapter 4 examines the qualitative/quantitative distinction in more depth.

The key to hypothesis testing is the belief that the existing literature is a reasonable source of predictions. Exploratory research tends to occur when such predictions cannot be gleaned from the literature. However, some argue that it is not just a question of 'if and when' the literature cannot generate reasonable predictions, but a question of principle, and that theory should not determine the structure of research in such a rigid way as is required for hypothesis testing. Such researchers argue that theory should be built up from exploration of reality, not used to predict it in advance. This is an **inductive** (as opposed to a **deductive**) approach to theory building and research. Here it is enough to say that all good research combines elements of prediction and exploration even without using the terminology. In using a literature review all researchers to some degree are guided in their work by predictions of what is useful to research, where and how to look and what to look out for. Even the most 'inductive' researcher cannot avoid this. Yet at the same time the use of some form of exploratory research is standard practice in even the most rigid hypothesis testing research. The **pilot** study, where researchers seek to explore the extent to which their methods and terminology are meaningful to those they seek to research, may take many forms. Some are more open than others, but all are forms of preliminary exploration (see Chapter 4). For now, suffice to say, while differences are great, they are not always as great as might first appear.

So then the question for the researcher is: should I generate a hypothesis or adopt a more exploratory approach? In part this will depend on what you have found in your review of the literature, but it will also depend on your stance concerning the nature of human action – causation or choice (see 'Causes, meanings and probabilities?' p. 25 and 'The deeper divide' p. 37.).

Summary

Social research takes many forms. The classical experimental method is rare in social research, but in other respects much social research adopts a scientific approach. Deductive research seeks to test a proposition, while more inductive research seeks to explore a research question or field. Hypotheses and research questions emerge from social, political and the researcher's own personal and theoretical motivations. However, research needs to demonstrate that its findings are the result of rigorous methods and not simply the motives of the researcher or those funding them. The search and review of existing literature enable a research question or hypothesis to be clarified and for appropriate methods to be identified.

Keywords

Abstracts and Indexes	Empirical	Method
Actors	Exploration	Necessary Conditions
Archival Research	Hypothesis	Pilot
Causality	Hypothetico-deductive Method	Prediction
Controlled Conditions	Independent Variable	Qualitative
Correlations	Induction	Quantitative
Data Analysis	Keywords	Text
Data Collection	Literature Review	Variables
Deduction	Literature Search	
Dependent Variable	Mediation	

Questions

1   What distinguishes deductive research and inductive research?
2   How far can social research motives be separated from research methods?
3   What is the relationship between empirical research, literature searching and literature reviewing?
4   To what extent should/can the social researcher seek to emulate the methods of the natural sciences?
5   How do social researchers come to study the issues they do?

Further reading

Hammersley, Martyn (1995) *The Politics of Social Research*. London: Sage.

Hart, Chris (1998) *Doing a Literature Review*. London: Sage.

Hart, Chris (2001) *Doing a Literature Search*. London: Sage.

Keefer, Jane (1993) 'The hungry rats syndrome: information literacy, and the academic reference process', *RQ*, 32 (3): 333–9.

CHAPTER

2

BEING ETHICAL

Chapter contents

By the end of this chapter you will be able to:

- Distinguish key ethical standpoints and draw practical conclusions about how to, and how not to, conduct research in an ethical way.

- Distinguish forms of consent, anonymity and confidentiality.

- Outline and comprehend the ethical issues confronting the social researcher at each stage of the research process.

- Relate ethical positions to more theoretical stances in the social sciences, and to the division between qualitative and quantitative approaches to studying the social world.

Sensitivity: being ethical at every stage – before, during and after

During the process of designing and implementing your piece of research you need to consider the **ethical** implications of undertaking the research. 'Ethics is the science of morality: those who engage in it determine values for the regulation of human behaviour' (Homan, 1991: 1). Collecting information about people raises ethical issues in the focus of attention chosen, the methods adopted and in the form and use of the findings. These three areas of concern are examined below.

Ethical issues in the decision to research

What should deserve our attention? Can the values that direct our attention towards some questions and away from others be warranted on objective grounds, or do they inevitably stem from particular biases and perspectives? Can values be based upon **facts**? Can good research help us decide what our values ought to be, or are facts and values fundamentally distinct?

It is generally believed that the success of the physical sciences lies in the separation of factual (**positive**) propositions and values (**normative** propositions) and the prohibition on the use of values in the evaluation of 'truth'. This separation of facts and values is said to enable objective research that is free of values (value freedom). It presumes the physical world is devoid of ethical content, and that the introduction of values constitutes an inappropriate projection of human sentiment. This position has been criticised, but that is not our business here. In the realm of social research, such an assumption that what we wish to study is devoid of ethical content is untenable. Researchers and the researched alike hold, attribute and claim ethical status. Ethical beliefs both motivate research and are one of the things researchers investigate.

So there is a tension here. Will values inevitably undermine factual research or should our choice of research reflect our moral concerns? What is the relationship between facts and values? Functionalists, Marxists and feminists hold the view that values can be derived from the facts of human nature and social life. To correctly understand what it means to be a society or an individual human allows us to judge whether particular conditions or practices are right or wrong. However, these theorists disagree over what the correct interpretation of social reality and human nature is. Those who adopt a more constructivist view of social order and human nature tend to suggest that humans are relatively plastic. There is, for constructivists, no fixed human nature and so no best social order in which they could all live. The ethical conclusion to draw here is that one cannot come to a single set of ethical conclusions about what is right and wrong from the facts of social life. Ironically, this is the same conclusion that is drawn by those social researchers keen to preserve the legacy of the physical sciences by suggesting that social research should avoid values and only deal with positive facts. The irony lies in the fact that such positivists (those that believe in the neutrality of science) and constructivists are otherwise diametrically opposed to each other in all other respects. So there is certainly no simple solution.

Nevertheless, whether or not the researcher believes that facts secure their values, it is still the case that however these values (and so their research priorities) are derived, they must still seek to conduct research in such a way that it will not be rejected by others as simply the projection of the presumptions that preceeded the research. This is especially true when funding comes from bodies with values and interests in the field. If the values of funders directly influence results, then the purpose of doing social research is lost. Max Weber (1949) distinguished value freedom and **value neutrality**. He suggested that while all social research is motivated by values (and so can never be value free) the researcher is obliged to conduct their research in such a way as to ensure that such values do not dictate the outcome. In other words, the methods chosen must be value neutral. This is an ideal, at least for many, but can never be fully attained. It remains a benchmark around which researchers can reflect and debate the merits of particular research projects. Does value neutrality prohibit the researcher from taking sides? No. However, it forces the researcher to defend their methods and reflect hard upon them. Honesty and reflection on these issues is the best policy as there is no magic formula.

Howard Becker (1967) argued that social researchers should seek to understand the outlook of those whose voices are under-represented. 'Underdogs' and 'Outsiders' are more prone to being misunderstood. Becker suggested that presenting a view of the world from the point of view of society's 'underdogs' will always draw the criticism, from those in authority, that the researcher has become biased, an advocate of those they seek to present. Whilst Becker advocated methods that 'got close' to the lives of those being researched, he rejected the claim that presenting an outsider view was the same as advocating it. Many took Becker to be suggesting that because the accusation of bias was inevitable, so bias itself was inescapable. Marxists and feminist researchers, alongside many who work with those they consider to be disadvantaged, exploited and/or oppressed, have advocated a **standpoint** approach to research. Standpoint approaches suggest there can be no neutral position from which to conduct research, and no neutral choice as to what to study or how to study it. Ethical decisions about what to study merge with political choices over how to study. In this view research is always a form of **advocacy**. Social research is seen as a political weapon to empower the 'underdog', not as a neutral science seeking to objectively 'map' them. This was not Becker's view. *Participatory action research* is one extension of the logic of advocacy (see 'Evaluation, participation and action research' p. 29).

Sensitivity in the conduct of research

Control, observation and interrogation are the hallmarks of science, but may have negative connotations when applied to humans. Respect for those you research can be diminished in the act of treating them as research material. The principle of informed consent is generally agreed to be the ideal mode of operation when enlisting others in a researcher's designs.

> Informed consent means the knowing consent of individuals to participate as an exercise of their choice, free from any element of fraud, deceit, duress, or similar unfair inducement or manipulation. (Berg, 1998: 47)

While there are occasions when researchers feel it is justified to deceive those they are researching, either with outright lies, in not informing them that they are being researched, or in not informing them fully of the purpose of the research, these circumstances are fraught with ethical difficulties and require substantial justification and scrutiny. The question of whether it is ever justified to proceed without the informed consent of those researched hinges around the question of whether the ends ever justify the means. Those who adopt a **consequentialist ethical** position suggest that if the greater good can be best served by research that is not explicit about either its intentions or even its very existence, then the ethical violation of those deceived is outweighed by the good that might flow from the research findings. This is the justification usually given for the double-blind trials of new medical drugs where half the test subjects are given the drug while the other half are given a placebo. The parallel here with social research lies in the possibility that knowing one is being researched, or knowing the objectives of the research, might lead those researched to act differently. As such, **covert** observation, or not giving a full account of one's motives, may allow the researcher to get a more accurate impression of real life. Those that adopt a **de-ontological ethical** position suggest that the benefit of the many does not justify the violation of the few. Such arguments have been used to successfully challenge the ethics of double-blind medical trials in both the US and parts of Europe (see Collins and Pinch, 1998, Ch. 7). It is suggested that once it is accepted that the benefit of the majority justifies the abuse of the few, there is no ethical boundary stopping those in authority doing whatever they like in the name of 'the majority'. The de-ontological ethical stance defends the ideal that human rights are universal and cannot be traded.

Laud Humphries' (1970) study of male homosexuals using public toilets to meet for sex was conducted without informing those observed that they were being researched. Humphries claimed that his research served to prove that those engaged in 'the tea room trade' were not perverts or child molesters, as was typically assumed in the media at that time. Covert research allowed Humphries to claim that his research avoided the possibility that those researched were hiding their true behaviour whilst being watched. As such, he claimed that deception served the greater good in the long run. Nigel Fielding's (1981) research into the racist National Front political party in the UK was partially covert in that Fielding sought to give the impression of sympathy for the organization upon entry and then did not fully disclose his researcher role to most of those he encountered during his fieldwork. Exposing the racism within that organization could be said to justify such a limited openness. However, would we support such methods if the organization being researched, and which might lose a significant amount of credibility as a result, was one we had more sympathy with? For a more developed account of consequentialist and de-ontological views, see Malcolm Williams and Tim May (1996).

While this dispute over the basic principles of social research ethics is of great importance, it should not worry you unnecessarily at this stage. If you are just starting out, and especially if you are doing a research project as part of a training or educational programme, you should stick rigorously to the principle of **informed consent**.

Second, it is important to recognise and respect the privacy of those you are researching. In so far as you are following the principle of informed consent, you will need to gain the permission of those researched for you to 'invade' their privacy. In addition it is essential that you protect that privacy in the storage and use of any data collected. This can be either by means of anonymity or confidentiality. **Anonymity** refers to the situation where you do not know or do not record the personal details (that is, name, address and so on) of those researched. **Confidentiality** refers to the situation where that information is known and recorded by the researcher, but is not revealed. In line with data-protection protocols and laws, it is essential that if any personal details that could identify an individual are to be stored by the researcher (electronically or on paper), this information is kept separately from other data collected. This is best achieved by assigning research participants an identifying code. This **code** is used in the filing of data, while a separate list is kept linking real names with their assigned code reference. In this way the likelihood of those researched being personally identified is kept to a minimum. It is often essential that those researched are assured that their confidentiality is maintained, and it is your responsibility as a researcher to do your utmost to ensure that this confidentiality is maintained.

Third, it is essential to be aware of the sensitivity of many topics researchers are keen to investigate. Research may become damaging to the research participant's sense of self if sensitive topics are pushed without consideration. If sensitive topics are to be addressed (and it is important to remember that what is sensitive may be understood differently by the

research participants than it is by the researcher), the research subject's right to withdraw must be respected. This needs to be explained in advance as part of the process of gaining informed consent. It is best practice to introduce the themes of the research prior to its conduct to forewarn the research subject and so to allow the choice to withdraw. In the conduct of more open-ended observation or interviewing, these issues become more complex. Further guidance can be found in a number of useful books (for example Lee, 1993; Renzetti and Lee, 1993). At the end of an interview, experiment, questionnaire or observation it is important also to 'debrief' participants, to explain issues that were raised and to ask if there are questions the participant wants to ask you about the motives, content or intended outcomes of the work they have contributed to.

In addition, it is important to be aware of the ethical codes of practice that have been established by various professional bodies involved in social research. If your research takes you beyond the bounds of these codes of practice you could easily get yourself into trouble, either with those you are researching, those that are supervising your research, the professional bodies themselves, the law, or any combination of them. As a beginner, it is easy to make mistakes, so it is all the more important that you are aware of the boundaries of good practice and stick well within them. Before undertaking a piece of research it is strongly advisable to consult with the professional organization most closely associated with your topic area. Most organizations have a website where their ethical statements can be accessed. For example: British Sociological Association (www.brit-soc.org.uk); American Sociological Association (www.asanet.org); Market Research Society (www.marketresearch.org.uk); British Psychological Association (www.bps.org.uk).

In addition, conducting research in large organizations will often require the researcher to submit the project proposal to an ethical approval committee and may involve the completion of specific forms. For example, health-related research undertaken in the UK National Health Service requires the completion and submission of ethical clearance forms to the appropriate Primary Health Care Trust. The process can be time consuming, especially as the ethical approval committees may meet at certain fixed times in the year, and this needs to be accounted for when planning the project.

If you are conducting a piece of research as part of an educational course you may also be required to complete an ethical clearance procedure in addition to any external organization's requirements. You should seek advice from your project supervisor as to the exact process at your institution. For a more in-depth discussion of the ethical and legal issues in social research, see Dawn Burton (2000: Part II).

Another extension of the principle of informed consent arises from the level of involvement the researched have in the direction of the research. Researchers who adopt a principled stance on the use of inductive methods of exploratory research argue that **hypothetico-deductive** research adopts a position of superiority over those being researched, in so far as it fails to involve the researched in defining the issues as they experience them. To research people in the way you would research things may be considered in itself unethical. Researchers from a more deductive tradition (one more at home with the claim that human actions can best be explained in terms of causes and effects, even to the extent that those effected are not always aware of the causes of their behaviour and/or circumstances) would respond by suggesting that it is not that they do not respect human beings, only that they understand human beings differently. They might even suggest that if people are sometimes victims or products of forces they are not fully aware of, it would be unethical to address only those things those people were aware of as if the hidden forces did not exist. As you may well have gathered, those using deductive forms of research (grounded in a **causal** approach to social life) are more likely to adopt a consequentialist approach to research ethics. Inductivists (who are more likely to account for events in terms of intentional actions and beliefs) are more likely to adopt a de-ontological approach. The former will accuse the latter of a superficiality that fails to get to grips with the unseen influences which shape the lives of individuals, and of being ethically complicit with the continuation of those hidden forces. The latter will accuse the former of using claims of unseen social forces to justify an image of ordinary people as hapless dupes incapable of making up their own minds. There is no simple solution to this dispute, so the best advice is to be aware of it and to reflect upon the role you think you are performing when you conduct social research yourself.

Sensitivity over the use of social research findings

Deductive researchers are more prone to believe that the purpose of research is to identify causes not always visible to those they are researching. One consequence of such research findings might be the call for interventions that seek to address these unseen causes. These calls may come from the researchers themselves, from those who funded the research, or from other interested parties. More inductive researchers tend to the view that their research serves more of a translator's function, seeking to understand those who are different from ourselves rather than seeking to explain their actions in terms of causes beneath their own intentions. Nevertheless, publication of such research may be used to argue for interventions and policy changes, again not always from the researchers themselves. Once research is published it may be taken up and used for a variety of purposes. The researcher must be aware of the potential for their work to be used in ways that are not their own. It is therefore essential that the researcher writes up their work in such a way that:

- those researched are protected from personal identification, and
- they are responsible about the claims they make.

Whilst it is not possible to fully control the way a published work will be used or interpreted, the social researcher must reflect on how their work might be used and guard against abuses. In the decision whether to take on certain forms of research, or to take funding from certain agencies, these questions must be asked. Whilst certain topics may be interesting for a researcher to investigate, sometimes it is better not to research or publish at all rather than risk abuse. Sometimes a researcher must resist the temptation to publish interesting materials they have worked hard to collect and analyse if there is a significant risk of harm. For example, research into work may show that workers who feel themselves to be underpaid or overworked or both may sometimes take extra breaks, slow down the pace of work deliberately, or even steal from their employer. The desire to show that this goes on may come from the researcher's desire to show that such actions are a legitimate response to bad conditions, but may result in those conditions becoming worse for those workers, and may even result in them losing their jobs. For a more in-depth account of this danger, and for a useful set of examples, see Roger Homan (1991: 140–59).

To conclude, it is essential to bear in mind that ethical considerations influence all aspects of the research process and that there are no magic formulas. In so far as social research is a part of the same social world it seeks to research, and that this social world is deeply divided both materially and ethically, social research becomes political. Yet the systematic attempt to clarify and reflect upon its methods and its motives may give social researchers some additional capacity to understand the world, do so in an ethically informed way, and aid in the making of ethically sensitive and socially responsible decisions.

Summary

Research involving human subjects needs to be ethical in its selection (design), conduct and in the use/distribution of its findings. Ethical approaches to research connect with fundamental understandings of what makes society and individuals what they are.

Keywords

Advocacy
Anonymity
Causality
Codes
Confidentiality
Consequentialist Ethics

Covert Research
De-ontological Ethics
Ethics
Facts
Hypothetico-deductive Method
Informed Consent

Normative
Positive
Standpoint
Value Freedom
Value Neutrality

Questions

1   In what ways might social research be similar to the natural sciences, and in what ways might it be different?
2   Is it ever appropriate to mislead people in the conduct of social research?
3   What distinguishes anonymity from confidentiality; and what are the practical and ethical grounds for choosing between them?
4   Can social research goals and the role of being an advocate for the particular social group being researched be combined successfully?
5   How does the adoption of a consequentialist or a de-ontological ethical stance alter what the researcher considers to be acceptable methods of researching humans?

Further reading

Homan, Roger (1991) *The Ethics of Social Research*. Harlow: Longman.

Humphries, Laud (1970) *The Tea Room Trade*. London: Duckworth.

Lee, Raymond (1993) *Doing Research on Sensitive Topics*. London: Sage.

Renzetti, Claire M. and Lee, Raymond M. (1993) *Researching Sensitive Topics*. London: Sage.

Williams, Malcolm and May, Tim (1996) *Introduction to the Philosophy of Social Research*. London: UCL.

DATA AND DATA COLLECTION

Chapter contents

By the end of this chapter you will be able to:

- Distinguish primary and secondary data, and be able to critically evaluate their relative advantages and disadvantages.

- Identify logical fallacies that recur in research and in everyday life, and which distort understanding.

- Comprehend the basic elements of sampling.

- Understand key elements of data validity..

- Outline the debate over researcher detachment from and attachment to those they research.

Primary and **secondary sources**

The process of social research outlined in this text focuses predominantly on the designing, processing and analysing of data collected by the researcher, known as **primary research**. Depending on the area of research and research question, it may be appropriate to consider using and searching for existing data. This data can then be examined and analysed, a technique called secondary analysis.

It is worth taking a few minutes to discuss what exactly is defined by **secondary data analysis**. Compared to primary research, much less has been written on secondary analysis. Hakim provided the traditional definition of secondary analysis, defining it as 'any further analysis of an existing data set which present interpretations, conclusions of knowledge additional to, or different from, those presented in the first report on the inquiry as a whole and its main results' (1982: 1). Dale et al. (1988) suggest that secondary analysis is a more broad term that simply entails data being analysed by someone else other than the original researcher. Historically in the UK, secondary analysis emerged during the 1960s and 1970s as a product of the large surveys undertaken by government departments and agencies. These developments were paralleled in other industrial societies across the world. Surveys such as the General Household Survey, Family Expenditure Survey, British Crime Survey, British Social Attitudes Survey, and the 10-yearly Census were conducted by government to inform economic and social policy. The UK government did, of course, collect data on the population before this date. The first Census was in 1801. Since the 1960s, the number of surveys and coverage of the surveys have broadened considerably and the availability of data for secondary analysis has been improved through the development of websites detailing the original survey and data, for example, the ESRC (Economic and Social Research Council) Data Archive at Essex University (www.data-archive.ac.uk).

The decision to undertake primary or secondary analysis should be determined by the theoretical and conceptual nature of the research question. Beyond this, secondary analysis can often be restricted by the availability and quality of existing data. Given the historical nature of secondary analysis, with its roots in government surveys, the majority of data available is quantitative, numerical data, derived from questionnaire and structured interview based surveys. There are current on-going initiatives being undertaken to redress the balance through funding for a qualitative data archive (www.qualidata.ac.uk) which aims to collect interview transcripts, diaries, participant observation notes and so on.

Causes, meanings and probabilities? Logic, relationships and people

A naïve or simple conception of causation suggests that when X is said to cause Y, what is meant is that X makes Y happen. This implies a mechanism at work, and this idea of mechanisms is not accepted by many in the social sciences who suggest human action is either too complex or qualitatively distinct from physical events which seem more easily reducible to mechanistic accounts. Are these objections legitimate? Statements like 'X causes Y' seem to suggest either that every instance of Y is the result of a prior instance of X, or that every instance of X will result in the production of an instance of Y. The first is a logical fallacy. The second is false on the grounds that no singular action is ever 'sufficient' to explain an outcome. First, it is logically incorrect to say that because X causes Y all Ys must result from Xs. Exams cause stress but not all stress is caused by exams! Second, in conditions of complexity (reality) it is incorrect to assume that because X causes Y then all incidents of Xs will lead to Ys. Exams cause stress but not all exams are experienced as stressful because intervening factors can influence the outcome in some cases.

The first example is an instance of a logical fallacy: the fallacy of reversal. Just because something may cause another thing to happen does not mean it is the only possible cause. Other logical fallacies are those of 'composition' (that is, if one woman can become prime minister then all women can, or if one is bad all in that group must be bad), and 'association' (that is, if storks nest before babies arrive, storks must cause babies to arrive). Logical errors of this sort characterize much of everyday consciousness and political rhetoric as well. Social researchers are not immune, so care must be taken to avoid such logical pitfalls when posing a hypothesis or in deciding whether to pursue a causal hypothesis. For further discussion of logical fallacies, see Sayer (1992).

The second example (where a causal agent does not lead to the same effect every time) is a manifestation of complexity, and raises the issue of **necessary** and **sufficient conditions** of causation. Sometimes when a light switch is flicked the light comes on. Sometimes it does not. It is not enough to say that flicking the switch causes the light to come on, although it is a part of the causal process at work. There are other links in the chain, and if any of these are out of place the sequence is not completed and the effect does not happen. Necessary conditions are those that are required for an event to occur, but no single one of them is sufficient on its own. As such, causation in conditions of complexity never operates by means of single links where X will always cause Y. The weather is a complex set of interacting systems and sub-systems. Because of the extent of its complexity it is not possible to predict with absolute certainty what certain conditions will lead to. Causation is too complex to map outcomes with absolute certainty. Within such complex systems prediction is not always possible, even where a fairly clear idea of the causal factors and mechanisms has been developed. Open systems defy absolute prediction, but this is not because they are beyond causation.

Tendencies are one way of describing the existence of forms of causal association that are never absolute because of the complex interaction of many necessary conditions. There is a tendency for class background to affect educational performance, but this is never absolute, as there are many factors in an individual's life that may alter their chances, even if these factors are largely stacked in favour of those from more affluent backgrounds. Intervening factors are often called **mediations**. Tendencies can be expressed in the form of probabilities rather than in terms of absolute causation. Modern statistical techniques were largely developed to aid researchers in the human sciences deal with the fact that complexity never allows for singular causal agents to have 100 per cent outcomes.

So far, then, the objection to simplistic (X makes Y happen) causal explanations of human action can be accepted on the grounds that reference to mechanisms may imply too simplistic a set of causal processes than are in fact at work. However, if we avoid logical fallacies of causation and recognize complexity, while limiting the scope of prediction and prohibiting the use of simple mono-causal models, these objections are defused. Are there other grounds for resisting causal explanations in social research?

One suggestion is that human action is intentional, and that intentions are future orientated. Can a future state that motivates a present action be called a cause? As causes must come before effects the future cannot cause the present and so, it is argued, intentional action is best not understood in causal terms. This is a logical error, as it is not the future that causes an intentional action, but the intention itself, which can be firmly located prior to the intentional act. Another suggestion is that causes refer to external forces acting upon an object. Human actions emerge from the workings of inner states. It is suggested that it is meaningless to suggest that something caused itself. Could this argument be applied to a video-recorder? Having a complex inner mechanism a video-recorder acts upon itself. Causal mechanisms operate inside the box. A third suggestion is that beliefs and meanings are linguistic entities rather than physical ones. Whilst language may have rules, structures and even devices and mechanisms, these are not the same as physical rules and mechanisms. As such, using the term 'causation' to describe the influence of an idea or the strength of a belief may be misleading. Certainly, using the kinds of mechanism appropriate to physics to explain language would be unduly reductionistic. Many biologists would say the mechanisms in physics are not sufficient to explain biological phenomena. It may be that language is simply another level of causation that has its own set of mechanisms. Perhaps it is fundamentally distinct? It is not really important to decide here whether language, human consciousness and intentionality really transcend causal logic and explanation. Language and conscious intentionality can be seen either as mediations in the causal process or as something distinct from causal mechanics. Either way, language and conscious intentionality play a part in the outcome of social affairs, even if the extent to which this is the case is open for dispute. Whether you reject causation as key to understanding social life or accept it, there will always be a role for asking people what they think is going on, even while it may well be the case that other important processes operate 'behind their backs' as it were. A false belief as much as a true belief, and a caused belief (if such a 'thing' exists) as much as a freely chosen belief (if such a 'thing' exists) have implications for the behaviour of the believer and their social world.

Data: asking, looking, reading and recording

What is **data?** While there is a great deal going on beyond that which researchers record, what goes on 'out there' is not data. Data is not what is out there to collect. Data is what is actually recorded by the researcher. As such, data is not naturally occurring 'stuff', it is in a very important respect what researchers manufacture in their work as researchers. Why make this distinction? Well, fundamentally it is to remind you that what the researcher records is not reality itself, but a 'reflection' of that reality, shaped by the tools they use to generate and record it. This is important to remember. It is nice to imagine that the camera or the human eye gives a 'picture' of the world that never lies. This is not true. The camera must be pointed in one direction rather than another. The human eye (and the sensory system of which it is a part) is selective. How the researcher chooses to direct and select will shape the data they collect. How they choose to record what they collect will involve classification, and this classification also shapes the data that is collected. How they choose to **sample** will affect what it is they collect. How they choose to frame their questions or structure their observations will influence the form and content of their data. In this respect, data is a product of research and not something that researchers simply collect. Data is the output of research, not the input. Research is in many respects therefore a kind of manufacture, and requires all kinds of tools and apparatus. This may also be called a form of technology. These tools may be physical objects (such as cameras, tape-recorders, computers, or in the case of the physical sciences microscopes and spectrometers). Tools refer also to forms of structured interactions, such as the **interview** or the **observation**. The survey questionnaire and the experiment are tools that fuse both physical and social elements (a carefully structured text on paper or a controlled laboratory). All of these tools (or technologies) act to stimulate and filter events and actions so as to generate materials that can then be recorded as data. Even the most naturalistic forms of research (such as an ethnographic field trip where the researcher lives with a community to observe their everyday lives) involve complex designs and tools (choices over where to visit, how to live, how to ask questions and how to record findings). There is no such

thing as the totally unstructured interview or observation, even if some forms of research adopt far less pre-emptive structuring than others.

As will be discussed in the following chapters, all forms of social research involve a lot of planning. All **data collection** requires the development of tools and technologies of both a physical and social kind. While social research can be divided in terms of the type of data collected and the degree and form of structure imposed in the collection and recording of that data, all data is manufactured. The types of data are observational based, question asking, and the collection of **'textual'** materials (these materials may be diaries, letters, photographs or receipts and so on). The degree of structure refers to the deductive and the inductive forms. This allows the generation of six ideal typical forms of primary data collection:

1   The deductive observation: such as the **experiment**.
2   The inductive observation: such as the **ethnographic study**.
3   The deductive questioning: such as the survey questionnaire.
4   The inductive questioning: such as the **in-depth interview**.
5   The deductive textual study: such as quantitative newspaper **content analysis**.
6   The inductive textual study: such as qualitative content analysis or **discourse analysis**.

Research projects may adopt a combination of methods to achieve specific ends. This is often called **triangulation**. Observation records what people are doing at the point of observation. Interviews and questionnaires record what people say or write at the point of response. These two things are different. Your choice of method needs to reflect whether you are more interested in action or talk, or your best judgement as to what method will best give insight into an issue. It should always be borne in mind that what people do and what they say they do are not always the same thing. Similarly, what people say and do and what people say and do when they are being observed are not always the same things.

What, and how much, is good enough? Validity, reliability and generalizability

Spending a large amount of time observing or interviewing a small number of people offers greater opportunity to know them better. Spending less time with each person or group, and so allowing the research to involve a larger number of people, offers greater opportunity to claim that what one finds is not idiosyncratic. This tension cannot be washed away with a single formula. What is to be done? This tension is often described as one between **validity** and **generalizability** (or between internal and external validity).

Validity refers to the closeness of fit between data and reality. Is your data really showing what is 'out there'? Validity can be divided into two parts. The first part refers to the fit with those you actually studied. Does your data actually express the reality of their lives and beliefs? This is what is called **internal validity**. The second part refers to the fit with the wider world. Does your data really show the reality of the wider **population** from which your sample was selected? This is **external validity** (sometimes called generalizability). (A more detailed discussion of 'validity' can be found in 'Reliability and validity' p. 171). Population does not refer to everybody. Population refers to everybody in the group you claim to be researching. If you claim to be studying the French, then your population is everyone who is French. We do not need to worry too much about this here, but defining such a group, or any group, is not a straightforward exercise. If you claim to be researching the homeless in Plymouth, your population is every homeless person in Plymouth. What counts as homeless and Plymouth requires interpretations that can be practically measured and defended as accurate. This is not always easy; especially when the group researched is not readily identified. Criminals and racists are not always forthcoming to be recorded, so these populations are largely hidden (see 'Reliability and validity' p. 171 for more detail about types of validity).

In-depth interviewing and long-term observation allow for greater internal validity (though do not ensure it). Inductive approaches may also allow greater depth of understanding as the researcher is freer to allow the researched to dictate the direction of the research. However, the downside to this is that time spent focused on a small group limits scope for a greater number to be included. This may lead to a loss of external validity. In addition, inductive forms of research that do not impose a strict order on interviews and observations generate problems of **reliability**. If each interview is different, each interviewee may have greater scope to develop their own interpretation of reality, but it becomes harder to compare one interview with the next. A structured observation or interview/questionnaire allows clearer comparison. Deductive researchers tend to emphasize the value of reliability (or uniformity) in generating comparable results. They also place greater emphasis on the need to gain a sufficient number of respondents to allow reasonable claims about the whole population concerned. Both these concerns hinge around an emphasis on external validity. Inductive forms of research tend to emphasize internal validity. In so far as inductive research is less concerned with testing a hypothesis than it is with exploring a field, it is less concerned with making generalizable claims.

Gaining external validity is not just about getting as large a number of respondents as possible. A well-chosen but relatively small sample is far more useful than a larger but badly-chosen group of respondents. A **census**, where every member of a population is researched, may sound ideal, but it is rare to have the opportunity and as rare to have to time to analyse all the data that would be generated. So what counts as a well-chosen sample? A well-chosen sample seeks to mirror the population the researcher is interested in. The first question here is whether it is possible to say who the members of a population are? It is far easier to say who the prison population is than it is to say who the criminal population is. Even if we could define what a criminal is (do you count all those who have ever broken a law?), they are not a group who openly advertise their identity. The most valid sampling method is called the **random sample**. This requires that the whole population have an equal chance of being chosen, and this requires that we can identify them all. A **sampling frame** is a list (or even a hat) containing the names of the whole population from which a sample can then be drawn in such a fashion that all have an equal chance of being chosen. This is the meaning of 'random' in a random sample. Random in this context does not mean stopping the first person you meet on the street. A school register is an ideal sampling frame if your population are the children at that school. Other such lists exist for other populations. But many populations do not have such records, or where they do exist you may not always be allowed access, and in such cases random sampling (strictly speaking) is not possible. Researchers have devised numerous approximations of the random sample to deal with different situations, and these will be discussed in more detail as the book develops (see Chapter 13 for a full account of sampling methods).

Here it is only necessary to mention the extreme opposite of the random sample. This is the **snowball** sample. Where a population is hidden and not much is known about who is and who is not a member, it may be suggested that exploratory/inductive methods be best used. The snowball sample is highly inductive. Where no sampling frame exists and so where a more pre-structured selection of sample members cannot be achieved, the researcher may use their first respondent's personal networks as a means of gaining access to other members of the population. This raises many serious questions about external validity, but in an exploratory research project it may be the only way to generate a sample.

Finally, how big does a sample need to be in order to be a good sample? As was said above, size is less significant than good selection methods, but having enough respondents to fulfil the purposes you require is still essential. This will be discussed in more detail in Chapters 6 and 13.

Evaluation, participation and action research

Evaluation research seeks to measure performance. In social research this will usually involve the evaluation of an organizational strategy or the delivery of a service. Performance may be measured in terms of objective indicators (increased sales, declining absenteeism, or the reduction of crime in an area), or in terms of more subjective perceptions (customer satisfaction, employee contentment or perceptions of safety). Evaluation research is more interested in practical objectives rather than purely theoretical motives, but of course it is the researcher's job to design the best method, and this will involve consideration of past research and theory in the area being researched. As such, evaluation research follows the same processes as other forms of research. In so far as evaluation research tends to start with a clear sense of what is of interest, it will tend to be more deductive in nature. However, especially with regard to the more subjective indicators of performance (which may be less easy to establish in advance), more inductive and exploratory forms of research may be adopted to investigate perceptions and experiences. For more detailed discussions of evaluation based research, see Rossi et al., 1999; Pawson and Tilley, 1997; and/or Clarke and Dawson, 1999.

Participatory research takes two basic forms,

though a combination of these two creates a third. In the first, the researcher seeks to participate in the everyday practices of those researched in order to gain a better understanding of their life and experience. Such observation by participation is generally led by the routines and practices of those researched. It therefore tends to be inductive, but more deductive forms of participant observation can be used. **Participant observation** is an extension of the classic ethnographic method of non-participant observation. However, a researcher may take up the role of participant observer with a pre-structured set of questions they want answered, but which they feel can best be investigated by means of observation in natural settings rather than via questionnaires or surveys. Participant observation may be **overt, covert** or partially covert. It can be claimed (on 'consequentialist' ethical grounds, see 'Sensitivity in the conduct of research' p. 18) that not telling those being observed that their fellow participant is a researcher may be justified. This may, in certain situations, be true. However, as a first-time researcher it is not advisable to choose a topic (such as researching the cultural practices of international gunrunners) where revealing your identity as a social researcher may undermine the validity of the research (and the viability of your health).

The second form of participatory research involves the recruitment of those researched in the conduct and even the construction and evaluation of the research. Involving participants in this way may allow insights not available at the outset, and is a logical extension of inductive principles. Nevertheless, just as inductive methods can sometimes be used at the start of a research project to get a sense of the field prior to the development of a more deductive design, so the initial involvement of participants in developing the research agenda can give way to more deductive forms of participatory research. Such research is almost always overt.

A combination of these two strategies may be adopted. Here the researcher participates in the routines of the researched and the researched participate in the routines of the researcher.

Action research is an extension of **evaluation research**. Action research is designed to facilitate the development of the goals of an organization rather than simply to measure the level of success in achieving such goals. Such a form of research presumes the goals of the organization are both clear and are ones the researcher feels are appropriate for them to become involved in promoting. Where funding is involved this may lead to pressure on researchers to accept goals as defined by those in the organization in a position to offer the funds. It should be remembered that organizations are not homogeneous and those at the bottom may not see things in quite the same way as those at the top (David, 2002).

One particular brand of research is **participant action research**. This is the combination of action research with a form of participation (Whyte, 1991a, 1991b). The researcher seeks to facilitate the goals of those they are researching. This is the meaning of the term 'action research'. The researcher also seeks to participate with those being researched and to recruit the researched into the process of **research design** and conduct. This is the meaning of participatory research. Participant action research is a form of advocacy research and assumes the legitimacy of the **standpoint** of those being researched. If the researcher aims to facilitate the goals of those researched, there must be a presumption that these goals are legitimate. This fusion of research and advocacy parallels many debates within feminist research over the most appropriate research methods to take forward feminist intellectual and political goals.

Is there a 'feminist method'?

First-wave feminism fought for formal equality, such as the gaining of the vote for women. Second-wave feminism in the 1960s and 1970s demanded more substantive equality and questioned the meaning of equality. Was it enough to demand equality with men, or was it important to demand recognition that women were different and that they might want different things out of life? Second-wave feminism not only questioned the under-representation of women in science (social and physical), it also questioned the nature of scientific method. In the social sciences this debate hinged around the value of quantitative and qualitative **research methods**. Feminist researchers (Oakley, 1981; Stanley and Wise, 1983) argued that the quantitative methods of science were tools of objectification, pacification and domination. These methods were condemned as part of a 'malestream' model of science that enforced a hierarchy of power and detachment. Feminist researchers such as Oakley advocated the in-depth interview as both more egalitarian (allowing a more balanced and democratic

dialogue between interviewer and interviewee than is the case in a pre-structured questionnaire schedule) and more in tune with a feminine mode of data collection. Feminist standpoint theory suggests that women are better able to listen to others than are men. Men are said to be more prone to want to take control of an interaction, while women are less concerned to take power. From this perspective, women are better interviewers and the in-depth interview is a better method for achieving feminist research goals (understanding women's experience, enabling shared consciousness raising and overcoming/avoiding modes of domination). Feminist standpoint **epistemology** (epistemology meaning 'way of knowing') is logically associated with methods that avoid the view that detachment is the best route to knowledge. For a time, many feminist writers rejected quantification. More recently, debate has shifted. Increased recognition of the diversity of women's experience has undermined the view that women either share a common experience or are naturally capable of relating to and understanding others. Recognition of difference between women challenged naïve assumptions about empathy as a research method. However, feminist researchers are keen to highlight that in many ways women do face common experiences as women, even if these experiences are never identical. Identifying the continued patterns of shared experience, such as lower average incomes and higher average expectations in the distribution of child care, have led some feminists to re-claim the value of certain forms of quantitative research (Oakley, 2000). While some feminists maintain the standpoint perspective, those who have re-claimed the value of quantitative methods might best be called 'feminist empiricists' (see Harding, 1986). Feminist empiricism suggests that the value of feminist insight in science does not lie in the rejection of existing scientific methods, but in their appropriate application. Feminist insights into the weaknesses associated with quantification allow a more reflexive and modest use of numbers in the research process. In this model, feminism improves science; it does not reject or replace it.

Sandra Harding (1986) suggests a third feminist epistemology (in addition to standpoint and empiricist). This is feminist postmodernism. Feminist postmodernism rejects the hierarchical claims of malestream science and the claim to superior knowledge made by standpoint feminists. Postmodern feminists reject all claims that there is a 'best' way to the truth, and often reject the idea that there is a single truth to be found. Postmodern feminists do not tend to carry out primary research and focus more on textual analysis of other theories (in the style of the discourse analysis to be discussed in Chapter 18).

There is certainly no singular **feminist method**, though it is reasonable to argue that feminism has made a significant contribution to recent debates on research methods.

Summary

Are human beings 'free' agents, or 'social' beings? Answers to such questions shape the kinds of question we might want to ask and the hypotheses we might formulate, as well as the level of prediction/explanation we might expect our accounts of society to give us. Social life is never fully predictable. 'Data' is what the researcher collects – either by asking questions, observing situations or reading human records. Validity, reliability and generalizability are all criteria by which the 'truth' of research can be judged. The quality of the selected sample in relation to the population in question, as well as the quality of the data collection instruments, will determine the depth and scope of the findings. Some research seeks not only to know the world, but also to help change it. This approach raises certain ethical and validity questions. Such approaches offer their own solutions as well as limitations.

Keywords

Action Research	In-depth Interview	Sample
Census	Induction	Sampling Frame
Content Analysis	Interview	Secondary Data Analysis
Discourse Analysis	Mediations	Secondary Research
Covert Research	Necessary conditions	Secondary Sources
Data	Observation	Snowball Sampling
Data Collection	Overt Research	Standpoint
Deduction	Participant Action Research	Structured Interview
Epistemology	Participant Observation	Sufficient Conditions
Ethnography	Population	Tendencies
Evaluation Research	Primary Research	Textual
Experiment	Random Sample	Triangulation
Feminist Method	Research Design	Validity (Internal/External)
Generalizability	Research Methods	

Questions

1   Is the unpredictability of human action evidence that humans are outside the scope of causal explanation?
2   What is the difference between internal and external validity?
3   Should the researcher assume a degree of critical distance from those they research, or is attachment or even advocacy sometimes more appropriate?
4   How might logical errors lead to faulty conclusions being drawn from empirical work?
5   What is data?

Further reading

Becker, Howard (1967) 'Whose side are we on?', *Social Problems*, 14: 239–47.

Dale, Angela, Arber, Sara and Procter, Michael (1988) *Doing Secondary Analysis*. London: Harper Collins.

David, Matthew (2002) 'Problems of participation: the limits of action research', *International Journal of Social Research Methodology: Theory and Practice*, 5 (1): 11–17.

Hammersley, Martyn (1995) *The Politics of Social Research*. London: Sage.

Oakley, Ann (2000) *Experiments in Knowing: Gender and Method in the Social Sciences*. Cambridge: Polity.

Sayer, Andrew (1992) *Method in Social Science*. London: Routledge.

Whyte, William Foote (ed.) (1991a) *Participatory Action Research*. London: Sage.

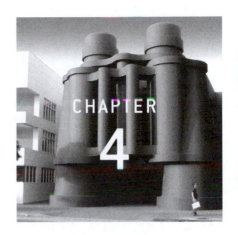

CHAPTER
4

THE QUALITATIVE AND THE QUANTITATIVE IN SOCIAL RESEARCH

Chapter contents

By the end of this chapter you will be able to:

- Comprehend the multidimensional distinctions made between qualitative and quantitative research designs, data and analysis.

- Distinguish different and fundamental ontologies and outline the methodological and epistemological consequences that flow from such positions.

- Identify common features that unite quality and quantity in all social research.

- Outline the strengths and limitations of mixed methods research.

Beyond the wars of religion?

The terms 'quality' and 'quantity' in social research have come to mark a distinction. This distinction has led to passionate arguments over the nature of social research and social life itself. The force of this divide has led some to suggest that it represents a fundamental ideological split within social research, one that cannot be resolved by facts and arguments, as each side is not prepared to accept that the other side's 'facts' and 'arguments' stand up. At one level this distinction is relatively easy to identify. At another level it actually becomes quite hard to pin down exactly what is being meant when the distinction is employed. It is the case that the terms are used to mark out a distinction, but exactly what is being distinguished is not as clear cut as it may first appear to be.

- Qualitative research usually emphasizes words rather than quantification in the collection and analysis of data. As a research strategy it is inductivist, constructivist, and interpretivist, but qualitative researchers do not always subscribe to all three of these features. (Bryman, 2001: 506)
- *Qualitative methods*: Methods of social research that employ no quantitative standards and techniques; based on theoretical and methodological principles of symbolic interactionism, hermeneutics and ethnomethodology. (Sarantakos, 1998: 467)
- *Qualitative observations*: Scientific observations that are not recorded in any standardized coding format. (Ellis, 1994: 377)
- *Qualitative data*: Data which express, usually in words, information about feelings, values and attitudes. (Lawson and Garrod, 1994: 218)
- Quantitative research usually emphasizes quantification in the collection and analysis of data. As a research strategy it is deductivist and objectivist and incorporates a natural science model of the research process (in particular, one influenced by **positivism**), but quantitative researchers do not always subscribe to all three of these features. (Bryman, 2001: 506)
- *Quantitative methods*: Methods employing quantitative theoretical and methodological principles and techniques and statistics. (Sarantakos, 1998: 467)
- *Quantitative observations*: Scientific observations that are recorded in a numeric or some other standardized coding format. (Ellis, 1994: 377)
- *Quantitative data*: Data which can be expressed in numerical form, for example, numbers, percentages, table. (Lawson and Garrod, 1994: 218)

A number of lines of distinction can be seen at work here. One is between numbers and meanings. Another is between deduction and induction. A third is between objectivism and what can variously be called **constructionism** or **phenomenology**. A fourth is between **generalizability** and **depth validity**.

Numbers and meanings

Quantitative data refers to things that have been or which can be counted and put on a numerical scale of some kind. This requires that these things can be specified in such a way that they can be counted and scaled. Reality has to be viewed in such a way that elements within that overall reality can be specified as individual units, whether this means people, plates or television sets. The number of such units present can then be recorded (for example, centimetres in a person's height or portions of fruit in a person's daily diet). Qualitative data refers to the collection of materials in a linguistic form, a form that has not been translated into a location on a numerical scale. Numbers require that the world can be broken down into units. Attention to meaning raises the question of whether beliefs can similarly be broken down into units. It is perfectly possible to ask people about beliefs in a fashion that can be measured in units. *Do you believe in organized religion? Yes or No.* That is quite easy. The qualitative researcher is more interested in the fact that meanings come in packages, wholes, ways of life, belief systems and so on. Attention to 'meanings' in this sense is a reference to the 'holistic' fabric of interconnected meanings that form a way of life and which cannot remain meaningful if they are extracted and broken down into seperate units outside of their meaningful context. What organized religion means may be very different from one culture to the next, or even in the opinion of different individuals.

Deduction and induction

As was discussed in Chapter 3, deductive research sets out to 'test' a hypothesis, while inductive research sets out to explore a field. As such, deductive research requires a greater degree of pre-emptive structure in the data collection process. If you are seeking to test a hypothesis you will want to measure the relationship between **variables**. Does the increase in variable X go hand in hand with the increase in variable Y? A variable, as you will recall from Chapter 1, is any class of event or thing (height, shoe size, likelihood of voting) that can be different (across time, between places, or in different people). Variables require some method of measuring variation and that requires counting and numbers. Inductive methods are exploratory, seeking to build accounts of what is going on from the data collected. This does not require the establishment of pre-set measures and methods of counting. In fact, it is often the case that the researcher chooses **exploration** over hypothesis testing precisely because they do not know what the 'right' measures might be. Quantitative research is associated with the deductive approach, while qualitative research is associated with the inductive approach. However, some exploratory research is quantitative (identifying and developing units and measures as one goes along, rather than in advance), while some qualitative research starts from the formulation of a hypothesis. In some respects this blurring is always the case. Things are never cut and dried. As will be suggested below, this last fact raises some serious questions about what is really at stake in the distinction between quality and quantity.

Objectivism and constructionism/phenomenology

Quantitative research is associated with a belief in the **objectivity** of the social world, and the idea of causation in social processes. This is linked to the belief that social research can draw on the methods of the physical sciences, in particular the use of numbers to measure the relationship between 'things'. The notion of the objectivity of the social world is associated with this view that the social world is

populated with 'facts', 'things' and 'objects'. While different from those that exist in a physical sense, objectivists and realists argue that **social structures** and social mechanisms constrain and enable those who live within them. Qualitative research tends to be associated with the idea that social life is the product of social interaction and the beliefs of **actors**, that the social world is not populated by things, but by relationships and actions. The focus on meaning reflects this emphasis on the subjective and the constructed nature of events. Objectivism is associated with the notion of social structure as key cause of social reality and key site for understanding, while subjectivism or constructionism places a greater emphasis on micro-interactions as the source from which to gain information about the creation of social life. Measuring the relationships between large things or large numbers of things requires the use of numbers. Attention to the relationships between individuals may not. The distinction between macro and micro focus is often associated with that of quantity and quality.

Generalizability and depth

As the above quotes suggested, quantitative research is associated with the use of standardized methods of data collection and data analysis, while qualitative research is associated with less structured formating. As was pointed out in Chapter 3, quantitative researchers tend to emphasize the need for research to be reliable and generalizable. Given a tendency to believe in macro-patterns and social causation, quantitative researchers will tend to be more interested in establishing generalizations than are qualitative researchers, who are often less interested in macro-patterns and causal explanations. As such, quantitative researchers are more keen to be able to claim that results from their limited sampling can apply to the population from which the sample was drawn. The use of **standardized questions** that can be answered in a numerical fashion, as well as the use of random samples, allows statistical methods to be used. These enable the researcher to evaluate the likelihood that their results came about by chance. When the relationship between the variables is strong enough, it is possible to claim that the likelihood of that result being by chance alone (such as throwing 100 heads in a row with a coin) is remote enough to be discounted. To conduct research in such a fashion requires a great deal of ordering. Questions must be structured and repeated without deviation. Laboratory conditions must be superficially contrived to achieve control over all possible deviations. Such conditions are highly artificial. Qualitative research is often associated with the critique of such conditions. Will such conditions not distort responses? Can such standardized questions get at the particularity of individual experiences? Does fitting people's lives into the researcher's pigeonholes give any real understanding? Qualitative research is associated with the prioritization of depth validity over generalizability. This can be linked to the discussion of deduction versus induction, and is also associated with debates over the macro and the micro. If you believe that people are the product of social conditions, you will need a macro focus and therefore you will need a generalizing approach, which will more often than not need to be deductive in nature. If you believe that people are the producers of social conditions, you will need a micro focus and may be less interested in generalization.

Problems and complexities

As we have seen above, the distinction between qualitative and quantitative research is not simply between meaning and numbers as such. Simple meanings, such as yes and no answers, can be quantified. What qualitative research is interested in is meaning as something holistic from which elements cannot merely be broken off and measured out of context. This is said to set qualitative data apart from things that can be broken down into discrete units of measurement. Yet, as we have seen, quantitative research is associated with objectivism, the belief that social structures have a causal influence on individuals, while qualitative research is associated with a more subjectivist (or micro) approach that looks at the actions of individuals and small groups as key site of social construction. This seems curiously at odds at first glance. Qualitative research seems interested at one level in micro-interactions and personal meanings, while at another level it seems interested in what cannot be broken down and detached from context. Quantitative research on the other hand seems interested in breaking things down in order to get at the big picture.

The question of induction and deduction maps onto these apparent tensions. While induction allows the researcher to explore the wider context from the actor's point of view, does the qualitative focus upon the holistic nature of meaning, and the belief that the actor's own beliefs represent the best route to understanding social life, constitute a hypothesis in itself? Conversely, to what extent can the deductive researcher escape from the fact that they, as researcher, and those they research are engaged in a constant negotiation of meaning between themselves, interpreting questions, observations and responses in the micro context of the questionnaire, experimental or interview situation?

The deeper divide: it's not just about how to research people, it's about contrasting beliefs over what makes people what they are!

As can be seen above, there are a number of themes around which the distinction between qualitative and quantitative research hinges. These themes are a mix of **methodological** questions about how best to find out about people and **ontological** questions about what it is we are looking at in the first place (what does it mean to be human?). As has been pointed out above, there are compromises in every choice that has to be made when conducting research. A larger sample may increase generalizability. However, increasing the number sampled decreases the amount of time that can be spent with each person or group. **Structured questions** or **observations** that are repeatable and which generate answers that are quantifiable make it easier to conduct comparison and generalization. However, the rigidity of the questions may act to distort the recording of individual lives and experiences that are not best categorized within the prescribed pigeonholes of the researcher. On the other hand, more **open-ended questioning** or observing, in a more inductive style, gives the advantage of openness to the specifics of individual lives and their general context, but such a method is hard to generalize from, with the results from each interview or observation hard to compare with the next. Large-scale research that seeks to identify macro patterns in society might be helpful in showing the existence of **correlations** (things that seem to go together), but their meaning is hard to pin down when data is only recorded in numerical form. For example, to say that X per cent of the population has experienced stress over the last 12 months, or that this figure is up or down relative to previous years, tells us little about what stress actually feels like or whether that experience is the same for any two people.

At one level it would seem rather obvious that the solution is to conduct research of both a qualitative and quantitative kind, either as separate projects or as an integrated whole. While this seems to be very good common sense, it is not always what happens. Why is this? Well, it is because a great many social researchers are committed to a particular kind of research approach (either qualitative or quantitative) for more than just methodological reasons. The choice of seemingly 'pure' qualitative or quantitative research (though appearances are deceptive as will be shown below) often reflects the researcher's fundamental beliefs about the nature of human beings. Beliefs about how best to know people will depend on what it is you think they really are. The most basic opposition in the social sciences is between a numerical ontology and a phenomenological ontology.

Numerical ontology

For Pythagoras the universe was made of numbers. Beneath surface appearances reality seemed to follow a series of patterns which could only be represented in numbers. Earth, wind, fire, water and spirit were seen to be merely the three-dimensional manifestations of numerical patterns (pure forms). Modern science comes close to the view that the universe is made of numbers and patterns. Whether in the work of Newton, Galileo, Einstein or Hawking, there is a sense that numbers speak the language of the universe because the universe is somehow fundamentally numerical. The world is a matrix of numerical relationships that create patterns. The development of science in this sense is the development of a method for mapping numerical patterns beneath the qualities of surface appearance. Just as the universe is a code waiting to be cracked, so the social world is a code. Beneath the surface of words and actions there are patterns that are not always apparent. Only through mapping those patterns will the truth be revealed, a truth that can only be told in numbers. People are not always aware of the influences upon them, or even of the patterns their own actions are a part of. To the extent to which people are the product of patterns and routines they do not control, and of which they are not always aware, the role of the social researcher is to go beneath everyday understanding, language and action, to identify the big picture. For this approach science is the search for patterns beneath appearances, and these patterns are revealed through numerical relationships. For those in the social sciences who

adopt this approach, social research can and should adopt methods that are similar to those in the physical sciences, even if these similarities are never absolute.

Emile Durkheim's (1952) classic sociological study of suicide is based upon a presentation of numerical differences between countries, regions and social groups. While it may appear obvious that people commit suicide because of their personal sadness, loss or failure, Durkheim sought to show that this is not true, and that social forces operate above the level of individual experience to generate patterns of behaviour in social groups. The fact that women are more regularly diagnosed with depression, but are many times less likely to commit suicide, suggests that there is something at work beneath the level of personal experience. Erik Olin Wright (1997) draws together research from across the world to suggest that social inequality displays systematic patterns, patterns that are not fundamentally altered by the attitudes and beliefs held in different societies about whether or not inequality is high/low or good/bad in that country. The Black Report (see Whitehead et al., 1992) shows that poor people die younger than the more affluent, and that this is not the result of the choice to live an 'unhealthy lifestyle'. Cigarettes kill and so do poverty and discrimination whether you are aware of it or not, or so the parallel runs.

Phenomenological ontology

The basic premise of phenomenology (Schutz, 1972) is that for humans at least reality is not something separate from its appearance. The way that humans think about themselves is fundamental to what they are. Humans are conscious beings and their consciousness shapes their reality. While a stone is what it is and has no conception of itself, a human being is shaped by his or her conception of themselves. Phenomena, the appearance of things, and nomena, things as they really are, might be separate in the physical realm (a stone is a stone regardless of whether it is perceived), but in the realm of humans phenomena and nomena are intimately linked together. Self-perception, an awareness of one's self, is not a perception of something separate, it is the fusion of appearance and actuality. A human who is not aware of her or his own existence would not be human in the full sense of the term. In the realm of human life beliefs are not abstractions from the real, they are part of the reality of being human itself. To some extent humans are what they think they are. This leads to the suggestion that to understand humans it is best to discover what they think and how they behave, rather than to dig deeper for some hidden truth that lies beneath action and awareness.

Max Weber's study of Protestantism's 'elective affinity' with the early capitalism of Western Europe (1905) makes the case that beliefs played a crucial part in driving people towards radical social change, just as beliefs play a key role in the maintenance of social roles, institutions and relationships. Weber's (1949) methodological writings defend a **verstehen** approach, which means the attempt to see the world from the point of view of the person or group being studied, as their outlook is an essential element in understanding why they do the things they do, even while Weber retained the need to study social 'structures' in a more objectivist fashion to complement the *verstehen* approach. Schutz's phenomenology sought to extend the *verstehen* approach, using Husserl's (1962) phenomenological philosophy, to the point where institutions were understood as a set of relationships held together by actions and beliefs held in common and taken for granted by groups and individuals. This attention to the 'life-world' is to the exclusion of assumptions of structure. This is taken furthest in the work of Ethnomethodologists (see Chapter 10), while Goffman (1968, 1990) likens his work on stigma and the career paths of the institutionalized to focusing attention upon the grass growing through the cracks in the social order. Goffman's dramaturgical metaphor likens social action to role-play on a stage, though Goffman extends his studies to the role-play that goes on 'back-stage' as well as in the public arena. While Goffman attends to the maintenance of order enabled by the actors' performances, he leaves the analysis of the stage (the structures in which performance takes place) open for a more structural analysis (which he does not do himself and which more pure phenomenologists would reject the need for).

So, at one level we might suggest that different methods for conducting social research are just different ways of getting to the reality of human life, but at another level there is a dispute over the very nature of social life. This is what has given the debate over qualitative and quantitative research methods their passion. This debate has become polarized between philosophical extremes. Below it will be suggested that this polarization ignores a fundamental fact. This is the fact that all social research relies upon qualitative and quantitative aspects. All social research requires some form of **classification**. All social research requires some form of measurement to identify the existence and prevalence of those things that have been classified. Classifications register the existence of distinctions. These distinctions can be called qualities. Some qualities of an orange, for example, would be that it is round and that it is orange. Measurements register the existence of quantities. But quantities have to be quantities of something, and these somethings are qualities. At one level this may simply be to note the existence of a quality (one rather than none). It may, however, register the degree of its existence (large or small, high or low and so on). It may register this existence in a more exact numerical form (in 25 per cent of cases, half the time, 25 individual cases, 1 meter 60 centimetres and so on). The dispute between quality and quantity in social research obscures the fact that there is always a degree of quantification in any form of qualitative research and that there must always be a qualitative dimension in any attempt at quantitative research. All research is qualitative and quantitative.

The qualitative inside all research: classification

To ask a research question or to make a set of observations requires the capacity to make and record distinctions. The most simple distinctions are binary in nature: Yes or No, present or not present, black or white, X or not X. More complex distinctions may have many more gradations, classes or types. However complex a set of distinctions might be, they all require one basic capacity, that is the capacity to identify the boundaries between the gradations, classes or types. Classification requires the capacity to identify the qualities that make a particular response; action or object go into one classification rather than another. The capacity to make such qualitative distinctions is the basis upon which any subsequent quantification can take place. It is impossible to measure the amount of something if you cannot specify how to identify the presence of that something, in other words to distinguish it from other things. Two important factors enable the identification of qualities. One is **internal homogeneity** and the other is **external discretion**. Internal homogeneity is the requirement that all members of a particular category share something, in some sense (if not in every sense) they are the same. They have a common quality. External discretion is the requirement that if a certain quality is what makes those with that quality into a meaningful category, this quality must be theirs alone. For example all human males have warm blood. This is a quality they all share. In this sense all human males are the same. This is internal homogeneity. However, having warm blood is not sufficient to distinguish human males from human females, who also have warm blood. Warm blood is not sufficient on its own to make the category of human males externally discrete. While having warm blood would be a sufficient quality to distinguish humans from reptiles, other qualities would be needed to distinguish meaningful classifications within the human species.

The formulation of such classifications of qualities has led to great controversy within the human sciences. To pursue deductive forms of research, where one is seeking to test a hypothesis, requires that classification occur prior to the collection of data. This allows the data to be collected in such a way that it can be used to test the relationships the researcher believes are important. More inductive forms of research seek to allow classifications to emerge through the course of the **data collection** process. There are advantages and disadvantages here. Those who seek to classify their qualities prior to data collection can be accused of imposing their own priorities, while those who seek to allow classifications to emerge during the research process are thereby unable to use the data collection period to test their subsequent theories. They too can then be accused of imposing their own priorities because it is hard to confirm or disprove their interpretations as no 'testing' has been done.

As will be pointed out in the discussions of quantitative and qualitative research, it is always essential that any classification scheme that is developed is evaluated prior to its application. This may mean the conduct of a set of pilot surveys in a more quantitative research format, or in the conduct of open-ended cumulative interviews/observations in qualitative research. In either case the purpose is to evaluate the validity of the qualities one has identified as the key indicators of difference.

A second aspect in the controversy over classification in the human sciences is over the objectivity/subjectivity of human qualities. In what sense are the qualities of interest to social researchers real objects? To what extent are any of the classifications of interest to social researchers externally discrete and internally homogeneous? Attempts to classify humans into economic classes, races, nationalities and ethnic groups have all run into

very significant difficulties. While it is presumed that the objects in the physical world are relatively stable (this may be less so than is often presumed), those in the social world are prone to modification and dispute, not least by those classified. When does a person without a home of their own become 'homeless'? When does a person without official and/or paid employment become 'unemployed'? When does an impairment become a 'disability', and when does that 'disability' make the person with it 'disabled'? When does a person become an 'adult'? When does 'love' become 'abuse'? These are not just questions for researchers. These are the kinds of questions that are asked and fought over in everyday life.

Those who adopt the position of phenomenological ontology (discussed above) argue that we cannot assume that such things as class, race, unemployment and abuse 'exist' outside of our beliefs about them, and that these beliefs are generated and sustained though the interactions between people. As long as we take these things for granted we can go on believing that the relationships our actions sustain are in fact objective realities. For social research to look for the true classifications by which human actions can be mapped and predicted would only be to repeat the everyday misconception; that is, the search for explanations for our actions outside of those actions. For those who start from phenomenological ontology (we are what we think we are), the task is to study how people come to construct the routines, practices and meanings of their lives through action and interaction with others. *Researchers seek to map the maps used by actors.*

For those who adopt something closer to the numerical or realist ontology (which suggests the existence either of patterns or mechanisms beneath the level of consciousness that are the frameworks which individuals and groups are required to act within), social reality does contain limits that can best be understood as objective constraints. These limits affect the life chances of individuals differently depending upon their 'race', 'ethnicity', 'class' and/or 'gender'. While social realists might generally dispute the existence of objective 'races', many would point out that 'institutional racism' operates against those not classified as 'white'. By 'institutional' it is suggested that discrimination operates in many countries through institutional structures and rules that are not necessarily reducible to the conscious actions of individuals (see Box 4.1).

Likewise the operation of markets, bureaucracies, states, the law and other institutions (such as the family

BOX 4.1 INSTITUTIONAL RACISM

The concept of institutional racism emerged in the US in the 1960s in order to challenge the idea that racial inequality was merely the result of the attitudes of a few, pathologically prejudiced, white people. It aimed to draw attention to the systematic, structural character of racism that had its roots in the organization of societies like the UK and the US. In practice, the term is used in a variety of ways, some of which stress intentionality and some of which discern the effects of institutional racism in any pattern of disadvantage which affects people who are not white. For useful discussions see: Carmichael and Hamilton (1968); Gillborn (1990: 9–10); Mason (1982); and Williams (1985). [After the collapse of the Stephen Lawrence murder trial, the Macpherson (1999, para 6.34) inquiry concluded that institutional racism is] 'The collective failure of an organization to provide an appropriate and professional service to people because of their colour, culture or ethnic origin. It can be seen or detected in processes, attitudes and behaviours which amount to discrimination through unwitting prejudice, ignorance, throughtlessness and racist stereotypes which disadvantage minority ethnic people.'

David Mason (2000: 9)

or the school) form frameworks that are not controlled by individuals, that establish routines to which the individual must adapt, and so act as external constraints upon their lives. Rosemary Crompton's (in Crompton et al., 1996) work with large **data sets** from more than one country is designed to identify patterns of employment and non-paid domestic work that may inform the choices of individual women. While many women make personal choices to have children, and pursue less ambitious careers to fit around this, these choices are made within conditions where alternatives (such as good quality and affordable childcare, or a culture where men take an equal responsibility for raising children) are limited. For the realist (such as Crompton) it is essential that the researcher develop classifications that capture the underlying reality. They seek to identify the manifest qualities (the surface appearances) by which such hidden realities can best be identified. *Researchers seek to map the realities that shape actors.*

As can be seen here, the dispute between quality and quantity is not between those who focus on qualities and those who do not. All research focuses upon the qualities by which the world can be classified, even if there are significant differences in how such qualities are sought and understood.

The quantitative inside all research: measurement

The fact that all forms of social research use forms of quantification, in other words measurement is

unavoidable. As will be discussed in Chapter 12, there are various **levels of measurement**, these being nominal, ordinal, interval and ratio levels. Elements of all these levels of measurement are deployed in both qualitative and quantitative research, though 'qualitative' research more typically deploys the former two types, while the latter are most often the preserve of 'quantitative' research. **Nominal** level data refers to things that have no necessary numerical order, for example, hair colour, style of clothing, country of birth. **Ordinal** data can be put in order, but not in a more sophisticated numerical scale, which allows the size of the differences between levels to be registered. An example of this might be a scale between very happy and very unhappy. While happy might be less happy than very happy, it is not possible to say by how much. If one song is at number eight in the music charts and another is at number twelve, we can see which has sold the most, but such ordinal data does not tell us by how much. **Interval** data is data that is ordered and where a scale exists whereby one can say 'how much' the difference is between different points on the scale. An example of this might be shoe sizes or temperature. **Ratio** data is data that is ordered and which has numerical intervals, but to be ratio level data the scale must pass through a zero that registers complete absence of the thing being measured (even if no actual zero results are recorded). Height is a good example. Nobody is zero centimetres tall, but because height can be measured on a scale in which zero equals no height, it is possible for different heights to be measured in a ratio form (that is, two metres to one metre is a ratio of 2:1). As has been pointed out already, quantitative data allows for the use of statistical methods of calculating the probability that observed results could have come about by chance, and the strength of the relationships between variables. **Statistical** analysis can be conducted on data at any of the four levels of measure. The more mathematical the level of measure (the least being nominal and the highest being ratio level), the greater the scope for statistical analysis, yet data collected at any level of measure is open to mathematical manipulation. Of course, the units of analysis (areas of residence, levels of belief, temperature or wealth) all require qualitative definition before the incidence of that particular quality can be measured.

It is often suggested that qualitative research is not open to statistical analysis. This is not true. What is true is that qualitative data is not usually collected with the primary purpose of applying statistical techniques. However, qualitative research collects data that is usually nominal or ordinal in nature, and this requires some mode of measurement. In the case of nominal level data, it may simply be a matter of registering the existence or non-existence of a particular variable. Noting whether the person interviewed or observed is male or female is to record a nominal level piece of data. Identifying the characteristics of a group or setting in the conduct of ethnographic research involves noting what is present and perhaps what is absent. This is often a form of nominal data collection. This may become ordinal or even interval data collection if the researcher identifies or records the existence of levels of belief, or loose accounts of differences in the incidence of certain actions, attitudes or rewards. In recording the talk and interactions of others, the researcher will be collecting many instances of the research subjects' own classification systems, evidenced either in words or in action, which will most often be of nominal or ordinal level. The ways in which a racist divides up the world, or how a sexist male classifies women, or how a middle class teacher classifies working-class students are fundamental to the organization of their own lives and may have profound effects upon those so classified. The qualitative researcher may wish to explore (inductively) the meanings at work in the classifications being used in everyday life, rather than impose a classification scheme of their own in order to (deductively) test it (as is said to characterize more quantitative approaches). However, the qualitative researcher must still engage in measurement at either the nominal or ordinal levels just to be able to record

whether particular qualities are present (nominal) or are greater or lesser in their presence, intensity or longevity and so on (ordinal). If the qualitative researcher notes that household X spent twice as much on electricity as household Y, they are engaging in ratio level data collection. This is a less significant part of the routines of qualitative research, but the use of measurement at the nominal and ordinal levels is inescapable.

Quality and quantity: distinctions and parallels

Once again it is necessary to point out that the boundary between qualitative and quantitative research is not simply between the use of numbers and the use of meanings, or between the use of measures or the use of qualities. The distinction between qualitative and quantitative research methods involves a number of blurred distinctions, none of which are absolute. The distinction between quality and quantity sustains neither internal homogeneity nor external discretion. All forms of research involve the construction and recording of qualities and quantities. The distinction is best defined in terms of a tension that is both practical and philosophical. Those who adopt the more numerical approaches tend to give greater practical emphasis to reliability and generalizability. This tends to flow from the philosophical belief that fundamental characteristics of human life lie in the influence of often hidden macro 'structures' or 'processes' upon individuals and groups. Those who adopt the more phenomenological approach tend to give more practical emphasis to issues of **depth validity**. This tends to flow from the philosophical belief that the social world is not external to the actions and beliefs of actors, and that it is the product of human interaction. When it comes to the generation of classifications (qualities) and measurements (quantities), there is a tendency for the former to adopt a more inductive approach, while the latter tends towards a more deductive approach. This maps onto the distinction between exploring and testing, and that between an anti-causal understanding of human actions and causation in the social world.

It remains the case that within the social sciences disputes rage over the broad philosophical question of 'causation' versus 'freedom' in human action. Human beings display behaviour that is at one level predictable (to some degree). This level is that of overall averages.

BOX 4.2 CRITICAL REALISM: THE ATTEMPT TO MOVE BEYOND NUMERICAL AND PHENOMENOLOGICAL ONTOLOGY

Sam Porter (2002) presents an attempt to move beyond crude physical conceptions of social structure and approaches that deny the existence of patterns and mechanisms of constraint/opportunities. The extension of phenomenological ontology to the denial of any external realities constraining thought and action has led to a postmodern strand of social theory and qualitative research that is more concerned with questioning any attempt to know the world than with explaining, or even describing, what is 'really' out there. The work of Clifford (1986) is exemplary in this regard. While useful as criticism of the arrogance of any claim to provide a complete 'truth', such work '. . . does so at the cost of abandoning the very *raison d'être* of ethnographic [or any other] research' (Porter, 2002: 59). Porter suggests a post-postmodernism that accepts the limits of any claims to depth and/or generalizability, but does seek to justify more modest claims to knowledge. Attentive to the meanings people attach to their lives, critical realism also seeks to identify the patterns of constraint and opportunity that shape such lives. Drawing on the work of Roy Bhaskar, Porter suggests that while dependent upon human action for their existence and being less enduring than physical objects, social relationships that take on institutional forms nevertheless display an endurance and an influence on human actions and opportunities that are essential to explaining the way people live and the choices they make. Porter notes the parallel between the 'theory of structuration' proposed by Anthony Giddens (1984), which also seeks to move beyond the dualisms of structure and agency, and of positivism and phenomenology. Porter suggests that critical realism is distinct from structuration theory in the key respect that structuration theory sees individual action and social institutions as mutually creating each other's conditions for existence in a moment-by-moment process, such that social institutions are really little more than the co-ordinated actions of all actors acting at any one moment in time. Critical realism highlights the enduring and pre-existing reality of institutions (the actions of past generations) in creating conditions into which new generations are born and have to work with. While both approaches place greater emphasis upon language and meaning than did more positivistic and objectivist forms of structural sociology, structuration theory is closer to phenomenology while critical realism is closer to traditional structural sociology. Although the gap is narrower, and the unhelpful extreme opposition between positivism and both postmodern scepticism and phenomenological individualism is bypassed, differences of emphasis remain.

The children of the more affluent gain, on average, higher educational qualifications. Women in Europe are, on average, less likely to commit suicide, than men. Divorce rates in some countries are systematically higher than divorce rates in other countries. These 'facts' suggest that there are 'macro' processes at work that influence the choices and actions of individuals. Some might choose to use the term 'causal influence'. However, while averages show the existence of patterns, individual behaviour displays a level of complexity that makes **prediction** hard. Individuals in seemingly similar situations react differently. The same situation can be interpreted differently by two individuals and their reactions differ accordingly. Perhaps all we can say is that the terms of our understanding must be, in some fundamental sense, flawed. Modern physics faces the apparent paradox that light appears to behave as both a wave and as a particle. Depending upon the test being conducted,

light seems to be one thing or the other. It might be concluded that light is both particle and wave, but to suggest this is only to force the question, what is it that can be both? Fundamentally, it must still be concluded that light is in fact neither a wave nor a particle but something else, and that we have simply been looking at light in two equally flawed ways until now. This is widely understood, but nobody has yet come up with such a qualitatively new concept. The same is perhaps true in social research. Human behaviour is not identical to that of objects without consciousness, yet neither does it escape causal influence. Much energy has been expended by those who seek to emphasize the subjective and phenomenological variation, just as there has been much energy spent by those who wish to highlight the existence of predictable patterns. Real innovation in social research will come from those who seek to overcome the distinction, not merely to mechanically repeat the practices and beliefs of one side or the other (see Box 4.2 for a discussion of critical **realism** and structuration theory as attempts at such an overcoming). This requires a capacity to utilize and critically evaluate the qualitative and the quantitative dimensions of social research.

Mixed methods, pluralism and triangulation

The above discussion has already made clear that there can be no absolute separation between the qualitative and the quantitative in social research and that the boundary between qualitative and quantitative research is not set by any single or agreed set of principles. Yet, as has also been pointed out, the prioritizing of depth validity or generalizability, and the philosophical principles that stand behind such prioritizing, lead those who tend towards the former priority to a more inductive, naturalistic and less mathematical approach to **research design** and data collection, while the latter tend to more deductive, structured and mathematical approaches.

Nevertheless, all research is both qualitative and quantitative. There are advantages to be had in both the inductive and the deductive approaches. **Induction** allows for exploration and a greater insight into the lives of those studied, while **deduction**, due to a tighter focus, allows for greater reliability and generalizability. To combine the benefits of both emphases is, of course, therefore attractive. Malcolm Williams (2002) suggests that all research must claim some degree of depth validity and generalizability if it is to be called research, rather than art. As such the inevitability and the necessity of combining qualitative and quantitative research leave room only to ask how such a combination is best effected in particular circumstances and in reference to particular questions. Williams concludes:

> Indeed Weber (1975) speaks of nomothetic and ideographic approaches, not as scientific versus non-scientific modes of inquiry, but both as forms of scientific inquiry. The nomothetic Weber equates with the abstract generalizable law like statements, whereas the ideographic he regards as the science of *concrete* reality, of specific instances. Moreover, he expressed the view that with the exception of pure mechanics and certain forms of historical inquiry all 'science' requires each mode of inquiry . . . The view that sociology (or any other social science) can be

only ideographic would therefore be antipathetic to Weber (and of course the opposite would be true). While Weber did not go on to recommend methodological pluralism, this seems to be an inevitable conclusion if we can accept that sociology has a nomothetic and an ideographic dimension. (2002: 139)

When (quantitative) survey researchers conduct a pilot survey with follow-up interviews, they are attempting to get a better sense of how their prospective respondents think and live. The researcher here is trying to gauge what their questions might mean to those they hope will answer them. There is no point asking people questions they will not understand. Even if respondents think they understand a question, if that understanding is not that which the researcher intended then the answers may be misunderstood in return. The quantitative researcher may wish to carry out a deductive hypothesis testing exercise, but would be wise to do some inductive exploration first. Piloting one's questionnaire is an essential first step. Alternatively, the survey researcher may wish to conduct a short spell of ethnographic **fieldwork**, living with those they seek to survey, in order to improve the kinds of questions they will ask. Of course, the survey researchers may not wish to carry out such work themselves. Different researchers with different skills may be employed to carry out different aspects of a research project, or, the researcher may consult secondary sources (using the existing literature). Similarly, the researcher may begin with the collection of statistical data concerning the field they wish to research. The data once collected may give rise to questions that the researcher feels can best be explored using a less mathematical form of data collection.

In reverse fashion a researcher who has conducted in-depth interviews may find that certain patterns exist in their data and set out to clarify their findings with a more numerical questionnaire. Alternatively, at the end of a survey the findings might be made available to some of the researcher's sample and a focus group discussion might be held. This would allow for some in-depth feedback that might help the research team clarify their findings or iron out any misinterpretations (or at least highlight any differences in interpretation that might otherwise not have been noted).

Such approaches can be called **mixed methods**, **pluralism** or **triangulation**. While all research is both qualitative and quantitative in nature, specific methods exist along the spectra of induction/

deduction, linguistic/ numerical, depth/generalizability, naturalism/control and so on. The use of mixed methods is the explicit attempt to gain some benefit from different methods from across the different spectra. It is an attempt to get the best of all the available options. The use of mixed methods is not just about the balance of quality and quantity. An experiment may be combined with a survey to gain two different takes on a theme. Both 'takes' in this case sit on the quantitative end of the spectrum. Ethnography may be combined with in-depth interviews to give a triangulation of qualitative methods. While the use of mixed methods is often cited as a means of getting the best of both worlds (quality and quantity), it is not always used for that purpose and is not a guarantee of success. How the results of mixed methods can be compared or rendered compatible is often profoundly challenging and may be no less problematic, or rewarding, than trying to cull the existing literature for suitable concepts and usable measures.

Summary

The distinction between qualitative and quantitative approaches to social research has many meanings and many dimensions. The distinction has become a central point of contention within the social research community. While much energy has been expended defining the value of one approach over the other, as much energy has been expended seeking to overcome the divide. The dispute hides the fact that all research has a qualitative dimension, that of identifying conceptual categories that are meaningful units, and a quantitative dimension, that of measuring the scale or incidence of such units (even if only to register presence or absence in some cases). The deeper divide lies between those who hold to an objectivist view of the social world, one which sees social institutions and 'structures' as 'fact' like constraints shaping the lives of human beings, and those who hold a more **social constructivist**/phenomenological view, in which it is social actors who create the patterns of social life through their beliefs and actions. The selection of research methods often reflects these deep-seated ontological beliefs.

Keywords

Classification	Interval	Prediction
Constructionism	Level of Measurement	Ratio
Correlations	Methodology	Realism
Data Sets	Mixed Methods	Research Design
Deduction	Objectivity	Social Structures
Depth Validity	Observations	Standardized Questions
Exploration	Ontology	Statistic
External Discretion	Open-ended Questions	Structured Questions
Field Research/Fieldwork	Phenomenology	Triangulation
Generalizability	Pilot/Piloting	Variable
Induction	Pluralism	
Internal Homogeneity	Positive/Positivism	

Questions

1   What are the range of meanings given to the distinction between qualitative and quantitative methodology in social research?
2   What are the fundamentals of objectivist and constructivist/phenomenological ontologies?

3   What is the relationship between generalizability and depth in social research?

4   All research is both qualitative and quantitative. Discuss.

5   What are the advantages and limitations of mixed methods (that is, triangulation)?

Further reading

Bauman, Zygmunt and May, Tim (2001) *Thinking Sociologically*. Oxford: Blackwell.

Bryman, Alan (1988) *Quantity and Quality in Social Research*. London: Routledge.

Porter, Sam (2002) *Critical Realist Ethnography*, in Tim May (ed.) *Qualitative Research in Action*. London: Sage. pp. 53–72.

Williams, Malcolm (2002) *Generalization in interpretive research*, in Tim May (ed.), *Qualitative Research in Action*. London: Sage. pp. 125–43.

Williams, Malcolm and May, Tim (1996) *Introduction to the Philosophy of Social Research*. London: UCL.

CHAPTER
5

WHAT IS SOCIAL RESEARCH?
EXAMPLES FROM THE FIELD

Chapter contents

By the end of this chapter you will be able to:

- Identify a range of quantitative data collection and research design strategies.

- Identify a range of qualitative data collection and research design strategies.

- Outline the ways in which mixed methods can be used to strengthen social research findings.

This chapter contains four examples of social research topics where the combination of **qualitative** and **quantitative** data collection and analysis complement each other in providing a better picture of reality than could be achieved by either one approach or the other. These examples can be read individually or as a set. Read as a set, the four examples bring to light the range of issues that form the substance of this book.

Doing social research involves becoming familiar with a wide range of issues, techniques and choices. A common trap is to learn one technique and stick to it. This often leads the researcher to becoming either a qualitative or a quantitative researcher, when the benefit of combining the two is by far the best way, even if it may take a little more effort. This should encourage you to approach research from a balanced perspective.

The four examples will introduce you to many issues, such as selecting primary or secondary data, choosing or relating qualitative and/or quantitative methods, mixing methods and triangulation, working on theoretical problems or more policy- or evaluation-based projects, reviewing the existing literature to clarify a topic for research, and choosing between theory testing and exploring a new area. The examples cross a range of data collection methods, from surveys and interviews, questionnaires and content analysis to forms of discourse analysis and beyond. Questions about sampling and the ethics of social research are also addressed.

In the first example it should be noted that the term content analysis refers to quantitative forms of content analysis, and not to more qualitative forms of content analysis, which are discussed in Chapters 16–19.

Social Research Topic Example 1: Mass media and environmental risks

*Alison Anderson**

The mass media play a central role within contemporary society. It is therefore of signal importance that research is conducted to examine their impact upon our everyday lives, our beliefs, lifestyles, sense of identity, and the ways in which we interact with one another. In recent years there has been growing sociological interest in the social construction of environmental issues in the news media. It has long been recognized that news media portrayal does not mirror 'reality'. News is not the product of a series of random events; it is the outcome of a number of routine organizational processes and taken-for-granted assumptions. Coverage of environmental risks tends to be highly 'event' centred. As such, risks that are relatively rare, such as those connected with unexpected dramatic disasters, tend to be over-reported. Researchers have focused upon the following kinds of question:

- How do the news media define the 'environment' as a distinctive category of news reporting?
- Which issues tend to gain most coverage and why?
- Which environmental news actors gain the most prominence in news reporting?
- How do the news media ideologically position news sources as a way of framing the debate?

Context

Content analysis of hierarchies of access among news **actors** has focused upon empirically mapping the number and type of sources used for each news item (for example, pressure groups, government sources, industry sources and so on). Researchers have also coded the medium through which news actors gain access to the media (for example, conference, press release, un-staged event), and the different forms of

*Dr Alison Anderson is Principal Lecturer in Sociology in the University of Plymouth School of Sociology, Politics and Law

knowledge (for example, experiential versus rational) that sources provide (see Anderson, 1997; Ericson et al., 1991; Schlesinger and Tumber, 1994).

In what follows I outline one study that has been selected to illustrate the ways in which particular mass communication research methods are appropriate for addressing specific research questions. The chosen study focuses on the ways in which environmental issues are constructed by television news. It is concerned with the representation of environmental issues rather than with the effects of such coverage on public attitudes. One cannot make any inferences about the impact or influence of the media purely on the basis of **textual** analysis; these kinds of question would need to be approached through other research techniques such as **interviews**, **focus groups** or a **survey**.

At the outset it is important to mention that for many decades the sociological study of the media was heavily dominated by quantitative methods. However, during the 1980s this field of study underwent a 'qualitative turn' and the distinction between so-called qualitative and quantitative methods is no longer regarded as rigid. Indeed, these methods are seen as increasingly complementary.

Illustrative study

Simon Cottle, *TV News, Lay Voices and the Visualisation of Environmental Risks* Reported in Allan et al. (1999)

This piece of research sets out to empirically map the extent and nature of lay or 'ordinary' public access to television news. Lay voices are defined as 'the voices of the institutionally, organisationally and professionally, non-aligned' (1999: 33). Cottle is interested in examining not simply the prominence or lack of prominence of lay views, but how these views are packaged by the news media in the symbolic representation of the 'environment'. In particular, the study focuses upon how lay views are positioned in relation to 'expert' views. Cottle examines which types of news actors are most likely to be presented in which kinds of news formats (for example, live studio interview, news visual, news reference, news quotation). Some news formats are far more restricted than others, in terms of their constraints on opportunities for news actors to get their views across.

Choice

The study is based upon a systematic content analysis of a **sample** of 40 news programmes drawn from a two-week period. The programmes were taken from eight television news outlets between 25 January and 5 June 1995. Such a sampling strategy seeks to ensure that variation in media content over different days of the week, and seasonal differences, is taken into account (for a useful discussion of sampling strategies, see Hansen et al., 1998). The research that is reported here is based upon a sub-sample drawn from the wider study of news access. Content analysis within media studies involves counting the frequency with which words, phrases or themes occur in a text and measuring the amount of space devoted to particular topics or views over a set period. The classic definition describes it as '. . . a research technique for the objective, systematic and quantitative description of the manifest content of communication' (Berelson, 1952: 147). Thus content analysis is a research tool that seeks to examine the manifest (surface level, observable), as opposed to the latent (deeper level) content of media texts. As Hansen et al. note:

> . . . during its long history of use it has repeatedly been criticised, *inter alia*, for its quantitative nature, for its fragmentation of textual wholes, for its positivist notions of objectivity, for its lack of a theory of meaning . . . (1998)

While one should view claims about 'objectivity' with caution, content analysis is a very useful method for identifying overall trends in media content; it allows one to gain a glimpse of the 'big picture' in terms of broad patterns across media texts (see Deacon et al., 1999: 117). As Deacon et al. argue:

> To use quantitative content analysis effectively, you need to be clear from the beginning what it is that you are interested in investigating. Content analysis is an extremely directive method: it gives answers to the questions you pose. In this regard the method does not offer much opportunity to explore texts in order to develop ideas and insights. It can only support, qualify or refute your initial questions – which may or may not be pertinent. Furthermore, it is better at providing some answers than others. (1999: 118)

Process

Having defined the research problem, considered the appropriateness of the chosen methods and selected the media and sample, the researcher must give careful consideration to defining analytical categories and how the material is to be **coded**. Since the categorizing of media content is time consuming, it is crucial to ensure that the coding schedule includes only those dimensions of texts that can be expected to yield information of relevance to the research questions (Hansen et al., 1998). In order to be able to draw up analytical categories it is necessary to immerse oneself in the textual material to gain familiarity with its content and overall structure. This allows the researcher to gain a feel for the subtleties of the text. Standard categories include identifying the medium (for example, the newspaper or television channel) the date, type of item (for example, news report, editorial, feature, reader's letter, photograph) or genre of item (for example, advert, documentary, news, film), its length or duration, and its position (for example, page or scheduling order). The analytical categories will vary considerably depending upon the nature of the project and the specific research questions. Many content analysis studies include the classification of themes or subjects in the textual material, types of vocabulary used, and the identification of the number and type of news sources (including the context in which they appear, and the type of knowledge that they offer). Researchers often develop evaluative categories to assess the overall message of the textual material. For example, in a study of environmental reporting, this may involve coding statements in terms of positive or negative framing. This can be problematic, since there is considerable scope for subjective interpretation. As Hansen observes:

> Perhaps the main problem with evaluative categories is that they generally require a considerable degree of interpretation by the coder – they can rarely be deduced on the basis of single words or sentences, but require the coder to consider the 'overall' tone of a newspaper article or broadcast item. Unless very clear interpretation guidelines are laid down, content analysts often find it difficult to achieve a high degree of coder-agreement in the coding of evaluative categories. (1998: 115)

As discussed below, it is important to acknowledge that subjective factors potentially enter into each stage of the research process.

Analysis

Cottle's decision to use content analysis allows him to provide an overview of differential source access to television news over a given period. The data suggest that ordinary voices gain the highest percentage of coverage on television news. In purely **statistical** terms, then, the content analysis suggests that lay views gain far more prominence that do the views of any other news actor category such as pressure groups, government, professionals/'experts', scientists, industry or royalty. However, when we look at the formats in which ordinary voices appear, a rather different story emerges. What Cottle finds is that ordinary views are most likely to appear in 'restricted' formats. In other words, lay views tend to be represented through a brief comment that refers to them or through a photograph/image (news references, news actor references, news visuals or through a news attributed statement). By contrast, government and politicians are often referenced by the news media and, at the same time, are more likely to gain access through electronic news gathering (ENG) video interview. In this way they gain a rather more extended opportunity to get their message across. Indeed, video interviews were found to account for 27 per cent of all news entries for the category 'UK government/local administration'. The most common opportunity presented to news actors to present their views is the 'expansive' format. According to Cottle, this '. . . entails either live or full interview inclusion in which the interviewee is allowed to develop his or her point of view at some length, perhaps in engaged debate with the opposing view' (1993: 156). However, Cottle's research found that gaining 'extended' or 'expansive' entry through, for example, live interviews or editorial control, was very rare in his sample of television news.

The research also statistically coded the types of knowledge provided by the news sources. Cottle wanted to explore the question of the extent to which different news actors drew upon rational/analytic or experiential/sensory knowledge, and public/private forms of address. As Cottle puts it:

> Accessed news speech can be defined as 'public' if explicitly addressing the world of public affairs and/or collective concerns; 'private', if explicitly addressing an individual's own circumstances or familial world of home and/or personal relationships. Speech can also be characterised as

'analytic' if advancing a rationally engaged form of argument or point of view; 'experiential', if based on an account of experience or response that is emotionally charged. (1999: 35)

The content analysis found that ordinary people tended to be used to illustrate the human side of environmental news stories. An overwhelming majority (83 per cent) of ordinary news actors gave voice to experiential knowledge. Such accounts often retold their personal lived experience as victims of environmental problems, or described what they saw as first-hand witnesses of disasters. They were also much more likely to use private rather than public forms of address. By contrast, in the vast majority of instances, politicians and scientists were found to provide analytical/public forms of knowledge.

It is very important to give careful thought to the kinds of questions that one seeks to answer through quantitative content analysis. Had Cottle simply examined the frequency with which news actors appeared in television news, he might have been led to conclude that lay views considerably inform environmental news. However, immersing oneself in the textual material before developing a coding schedule makes the task of identifying themes and codes considerably easier. One of the most common potential difficulties with content analysis is to not give sufficient regard to the need to ensure that what is counted relates directly to the specific research questions. As Hansen et al. (1998) note, it is all too easy to get carried away with counting characteristics of texts that do not bear any direct relevance to the research question in hand.

The selection of a sample, together with the codes and themes of analysis, requires the researcher to make subjective value judgements as to what is considered important. However systematically the content analysis is carried out, subjective elements inevitably impinge upon various stages in the research process. One must therefore be wary about drawing sweeping conclusions on the basis of the 'factual' evidence. Moreover, it is imperative that the researcher is explicit about how they have selected the sample, operationalized the key variables and developed their coding scheme (Deacon et al., 1999).

A key limitation of quantitative content analysis is that it glosses over the complexities of meaning within media texts. It is poorly suited to uncovering the 'latent' levels of meaning that lie beneath the surface content. Content analysis is an inappropriate tool for

studying in-depth questions about the ways in which issues and arguments are ideologically constructed within news media discourse. These kinds of questions need to be studied through qualitative approaches that involve detailed textual analysis. Rigid statistical techniques do not reveal the micro-scale nuances of media texts. While content analysis tends to fragment media texts, qualitative textual analysis allows for a more holistic approach.

For these reasons Cottle supplements his content analysis with a discursive analysis of the ways in which different news actors are portrayed in television news. This provides a deeper understanding of precisely how it is that different news actors are symbolically represented within television news coverage of environmental affairs. Content analysis, by itself, does not reveal how meanings are created within media texts. An in-depth analysis of the language and visuals within a small selection of news stories reveals the ways in which ordinary views are used to symbolize the world of everyday experience. It highlights how particular images are carefully juxtaposed to represent our 'unspoiled' natural heritage versus an environment that is contaminated by human activity and under threat. Various writers within the critical linguistics tradition have shown how media texts often present dominant discourses as 'natural' and 'common sense' (for example, Fairclough, 1995). Discursive approaches are ideally suited to exploring the question of how these discourses 'work'; how arguments are ideologically constructed and rhetorically developed. **Semiotics**, or the 'study of signs', identifies the ways in which particular metaphors draw upon deep-seated imagery that resonates with, for example, fears about the unknown, or with nostalgic images of idyllic rural life in a bygone age. Cottle provides the example of an environmental story that was the lead item in a BBC 1 news bulletin in April 1998. Through a brief analysis of the language and visuals, Cottle demonstrates how ordinary voices are symbolically positioned to show the human effects of the toxic waste leak from an industrial reservoir in southern Spain. He shows how the choice of words ('choked', 'devastated', 'despair', 'disaster', 'ruin') and images (for example, 'the dead fish', 'belly up') serve to anchor the piece in terms of a wider set of concerns relating to the environment 'under threat'.

One of the main drawbacks with these qualitative forms of media analysis is that they are based upon relatively small numbers of items. As Deacon et al. observe, 'In the past claims about frequency, or the lack of it, have often been made in qualitative analyses of media content. Such claims emphasise the need for co-operation between quantitative and qualitative approaches' (1999: 133). Additionally, these approaches are often criticized as being particularly open to subjective interpretation. One has to be very careful to select cases that do not simply reinforce your own pre-existing assumptions. Yet at the same time it is important to acknowledge that media texts are open to being interpreted in a variety of ways; media sociologists refer to this as **polysemy**. As such, it is important to present your analysis as one possible interpretation rather than the definitive meaning of the text.

Dissemination

The findings of this piece of research were presented in a textbook aimed at undergraduate/ postgraduate level students and researchers. The discussion is based upon a sub-sample of a wider study of news access. The author chose to illustrate key findings through drawing upon a few well-chosen illustrative excerpts of television reports to draw out some broader themes about how the media frame 'expert', 'counter-expert' and 'lay public' definitions of environmental risk.

Ethics

One of the advantages of secondary analysis is that it does not involve human participants as subjects. Accordingly, many of the **ethical** considerations that have to be taken account of in other forms of research do not apply. Nevertheless, ethical considerations and the role of **values** in the research process are inextricably bound. It is necessary to be mindful of how values inevitably impinge upon topic choice, aims and objectives, the data collection process, analysis and the use made of the research findings.

Conclusions

This brief discussion has illustrated how quantitative and qualitative approaches are essentially complementary and can usefully be combined within media analysis. Both types of analysis have their own particular strengths and weaknesses. There is considerable value in using both research methods together. For example, we have seen how content analysis in media studies usefully reveals patterns of representation in media content over time, whilst critical linguistics and semiotics examine how a limited number of texts work at a deeper level. When employed singly, each of these research techniques provides an inevitably partial account. But, when they are combined, the rich data produced from detailed micro-level textual and visual analysis is accompanied by an account of the 'big picture' of overall trends in patterns of representation. Therefore, not only is it important to consider which is the most appropriate method for answering your chosen research questions, but also what benefits may be gained by combining research methods to produce a more rounded assessment of the area.

Social Research Topic Example 2: Evaluation

S. Regan de Bere*

As with all social research, it is the object of study and what we seek to find out about it that should direct our **methodological** approaches. In the past, evaluation methodologies have been largely unimaginative, based on traditional experimental approaches to examining cause and effect relationships. They have tended to be based on pseudo-scientific models of experimental design and, for this reason, many social scientists have not considered evaluation as an equal contender in the 'rigorous research' stakes. However, in recent years, debates have focused on the need to use evaluation methods more flexibly, in order to access data about educational programmes that give us a 'bigger picture' or a more holistic view of their impact.

An example of this change in perspective can be seen in the nature of Educational Evaluation Reviews. The criteria for evaluation methodologies have traditionally been narrow, and have commonly

*Dr Sam Regan de Bere is a Research Fellow at the University of Plymouth Peninsula Medical School and Associate Lecturer in Sociology in the University of Plymouth School of Sociology, Politics and Law.

included only randomized controlled trials (RCTs), controlled before and after studies (CBAs) or interrupted time series (ITSs). All of these are quantitatively-based experimental designs. Recently, however, more inclusive reviews have acknowledged the role of various evaluation methodologies, including quantitative (before and after measures and surveys) and qualitative (longitudinal, pre-, mid- and post-event opinion studies, action research) designs that capture valid evidence ranging from reactions and learning to behavioural and organizational/practice changes. This section demonstrates how using different research methods for evaluation can lead to the development of very different ideas about what is happening in educational programmes, as well as the nature of their impact on students and educators. It is based on an actual study that used both qualitative and quantitative data, within a **mixed-method** approach to educational evaluation.

Context

In reviewing the educational literature, it becomes clear that the term 'evaluation' has been used to encompass a wide variety of activities, conducted for a variety of purposes. Evaluation remains an elusive concept, and one that prompts much theoretical debate. The central questions are:

* What counts as evaluation?
* How far must this conform to acceptable standards of valid research?
* When does evaluation merit little more than recognition as a monitoring process?

Further questions spill into the field of methods themselves:

* What methods can acceptably be used for collecting valid data in educational evaluation?
* How far can they be combined to provide us with a fuller understanding of processes and outcomes?

These latter concerns fuel the discussion presented here.

Part of the 'research rigour' debate has been contention over the relationship of evaluation models to their methodological bases. This has commonly been presented in terms of the alleged quantitative/ qualitative divide, and the drive to capture evidence of either structural influences or human agency. Whilst

traditional methodologies based their quantitative models on the requirement of assessing outcomes for summative accountability or formative policy guiding, others have opted for more qualitatively-based paradigms, employed primarily to understand the learning 'experience'.

More recent contributions have developed an eclectic use of different methodologies. They have demonstrated the relevance of both quantitative and qualitative approaches, of multi-method data collection, and of applied and **action research**. They have also highlighted the importance of political context and the interplay of various multi-level influences on education and learning – influences that should be incorporated into the focus of evaluation research, but not interchangeably, and not without taking great methodological care.

Constructing evaluation methodologies that capture 'valid' evidence of change relating to education is far from simple. It is difficult to provide multi-dimensional measures of the many influences on learning and, importantly, its transference to practice (since much educational evaluation is related to learning for work or organizational purposes), within a single evaluation framework. Contributions to both educational and professional literature commonly acknowledge the need for multi-dimensional evaluations that involve the examination of personal, professional and organizational influences on education, and vice-versa.

However, there is still no clear consensus on the suitability of various indicative measures of processes and outcomes in evaluation research. The following example of an actual evaluation is presented in order to illustrate the ways in which we can respond to these complex issues, and to explore the implications of using different methods for our potential research findings.

Example: evaluating interprofessional education in relation to understanding improvements in health and social care

The evaluation was developed for a programme of Interprofessional Mental Health education (see Regan de Bere et al., 2000 for details). It does not represent a definitive or archetypal evaluation model: as previously stated, different evaluation strategies must be shaped by the different types of interprofessional collaboration and education involved. However, it does illustrate some of the methodological challenges already outlined.

The problems targeted by the educational programme were deficiencies in interprofessional collaboration[1] and service user involvement[2]. Programme developers and course providers sought to challenge barriers to improvement in these areas, and to facilitate positive change through learning shared amongst different occupational and professional groups. Obviously, such a complex remit requires a clear and comprehensive methodological framework. In reading this text, you will become aware of the importance of careful and competent **operationalization** of abstract concepts (and possibly theories) into 'workable' definitions, indices and measures. However, it is not possible to describe these processes in detail here: should you wish to read more about them, see Regan de Bere (2003), which includes a step-by-step outline.

To summarize briefly, intervention and change were assessed on several levels. Before and after reflective accounts of personal, professional and organizational priorities, as well as more technical processes, and their impact on actual experiences, were invaluable. For the purposes of our own evaluation, attitudes, behaviours and practical experiences were identified and charted by comparing data collected from different stages in the life of the educational programme (as well as some time afterwards). Outcomes were then measured against baseline data, as well as the original aims of the programme. Such a theoretical framework meant that these measures could also be analysed in terms of the interplay between personal, professional and organizational discourses (and their implications for compatibility or conflict) in order to identify potential and actual gateways or barriers to improvement in practice.

Choice

For the purposes of our evaluation, overall emphasis was placed firmly on the subjective and interpretative processes of individuals, occupational groups and organizations in formulating and sustaining or transforming discourses about mental health care

practice. This located our methodology primarily within a family relationship with theoretical perspectives based on constructionist, pluralist and interpretative paradigms. However, in addition to this, we were interested in identifying patterns in attitudes and actual behaviours (relating to discourses and their practical consequences). We required such data for description and exploration, and also to examine how emerging patterns changed as education progressed.

In short, the evaluation was based primarily upon qualitative research, involving data that were subjective (often based on people's interpretations of, and opinions about, their experiences). It also used more objective and factual data about processes and practices, and some basic quantification. Data collection was conducted in a flexible manner, within a **multi-method** approach, in order to access different types of data to complete the required 'picture' of educative and working practices.

Process

Qualitative (in-depth interviews, observation, discourse analysis of documentary data)

Two sets of interviews were conducted with each programme participant: **baseline** interviews at their induction, with follow-up interviews (to measure change) six months after completion. Interview schedules were semi-structured and covered a number of issues, including: formal/informal education processes; recruitment and marketing; course materials; administrative and library support; staff/student relations; group dynamics; service user involvement; organizational/professional body and other external support networks and so on.

Interviews[3] with programme staff, both academic and administrative, added depth to the analysis, as did regular observation of some classes and curriculum development meetings. Discourse analysis of course documents, minutes of course team meetings and learning material provided for thorough assessment. Documentation was derived from source organizations, together with occupational details of

---

1 Interprofessional collaboration refers to the process of collaborative working between different professionals, in this case mental health care workers with different professional backgrounds (such as nurses, psychiatrists and psychologists, occupational therapists, GPs, forensic workers and so on).

2 Service user involvement refers here to the involvement of service users in discussions regarding the best care for those with mental health problems or issues.

3 Using the same interview schedules, modified where appropriate.

participants: these were used to explore organizational aims, objectives, processes, accountability, stakeholder involvement, professional aims and objectives, ethics and so on.

Quantitative

Questionnaire data were collected in order to measure change and chart specific relationships, correlations and points of change. Course participants were asked to fill in identical questionnaires at three stages: prior to, mid-way through and following education. Question areas included:

- Personal details. For example, gender, age, location.
- Occupational, professional and organizational roles and responsibilities. For example:
  - What is your i) job, ii) profession, iii) organization.
  - Please rate, in order of importance, how these inform your sense of identity.
  - Please rate how much each one of these impacts on your day-to-day work.

- Current and potential levels of collaboration. For example:
  - What approximate percentage of your time is spent working collaboratively with the following professions: social work, medicine, nursing, psychiatry/psychology, occupational therapy, the police, judiciary and so on?
  - What percentage of time, in your own view, should be spent working collaboratively?
  - What problems, if any, have arisen from interprofessional collaboration?
  - What successes, if any, have arisen from interprofessional collaboration?

- Attitudes towards own and other professions and organizations. For example:
  - On a scale of 1–10, please indicate how well you relate to the following professions: social work, medicine, nursing, psychiatry/psychology, occupational therapy, the police, judiciary and so on.
  - On a scale of 1–10, please indicate how often

you think it is desirable to work with practitioners from these professions?
  - On a scale of 1–10, how i) easy, ii) problematic do you find working with practitioners from these professions?
  - What are the i) benefits, ii) disadvantages in relation to working with these other professions?

- Attitudes about interprofessional education and education more generally. For example:
  - What in your view, is interprofessional education?
  - On a scale of 1–10, how important is interprofessional education?
  - What, in your view, are the merits of interprofessional education?
  - What, in your view, are the problems of interprofessional education?
  - Has your experience of interprofessional education changed your views on interprofessional education?
  - Do you have any i) professional, ii) organizational support for your involvement in interprofessional education?

Analysis

The interview data collected for the evaluation were subjected to systematic qualitative analysis, this process being facilitated by the use of the qualitative data management package – NUD*IST N5.[4] All of the qualitative data collected were explored in the context of identifiable individual, professional, organizational and educational discourses. This process enabled us to establish what attitudes and behaviours had been brought together in education and how they influenced, and were influenced by, educational intervention.

The raw data from the quantitative questionnaires were analysed using Statistical Products and Service Solutions (SPSS) software. Simple statistical testing (frequencies and **cross-tabulations**) provided us with measures of attitudes and behaviours, and the potential relationships between these and the various features of the educational programme. This allowed us a certain 'breadth' of information, providing a

---

3 Using the same interview schedules, modified where appropriate.
4 This has, since writing, been upgraded to NUD*IST N6. A similar package is also available: Nvivo.

framework in which to contextualize the more 'in-depth' findings from the qualitative **fieldwork**.

One benefit of combining quantitative and qualitative analyses was that it took us beyond uni-dimensional explanations. It provided for the development of a **conceptual** and methodological framework through which dynamic processes of change could be illustrated. The **discourse analytic** approach, based primarily on our qualitative data, but framed by the quantitative findings, enhanced our ability to analyse the impact of our education programme on participants, educational staff and service users, as well as the organizations from which participants originated. This allowed for consideration of difference within and between the learning and practice experiences of professionals.

Qualitative interviews facilitated the exploration of the rather more complex influences that informed, affected and constrained change – those elements that are often more difficult to tie down, but are nevertheless important in terms of their implications for the experience and merits/shortfalls of education. The questionnaire data provided a framework within which we could measure specific patterns and analyse change as the education progressed.

Analyses of qualitative data firstly identified the different systems of meaning attached to various people and things, and uncovered significant features of those discourses. We then explored the ways in which different individuals or groups, in different contexts, drew upon these discourses, and how other (educational, organizational and professional) discourses influenced people's reference to these discursive frameworks.

Rather than simply providing a snapshot, we were able to map answers from the three questionnaires and the interviews against time, charting any changes in patterns that took place along the way. Therefore, we were able to observe these personal, professional and organizational discourses by the method of a **longitudinal analysis** of these discourses before, during and after education.

Understanding existing discourses and their impact on professionals' attitudes and behaviours in practice

Quantitative analysis identified key points of different personal, professional and organizational attitudes that appeared to have implications for the motivation and experiences of participants in the programme. Qualitative analysis then allowed us to explore them in

more detail. Personal discourses were varied, generally based on vocational aspirations, moral attitudes, a sense of social responsibility and also personality traits. Professional discourses were more standardized, drawing on professional ethics, codes of conduct and the discourses of governing bodies.

Combined quantitative and qualitative analyses illustrated that, in general, people were able to draw simultaneously on both personal and professional discourses: they tended to complement one another. They also appeared to be compatible with, and amenable to, educational discourses. However, we were able to understand, through interviewing, how different discourses involved various attitudes towards 'others' within an 'us and them' context, some of which led to initial conflict of opinion between different professions:

> I'm an OT through and through. It's kinda through me like a stick of rock. The words 'Occupational Therapy' . . . Yeah, it's very much a part of me and what I do, and who I am . . . and, I mean, it's a particularly OT way of looking at things, this breaking down activities into their component parts, and see how people gradually acquire different bits of the skill. So even to parenting my own children, and relating to other people, I look at it in a very OT kinda way.

> Health care professionals use a preventative model, in contrast to social workers' who refer to a crisis model – it just makes it difficult for us to work together and see things the same way.

The qualitative data demonstrated that organizational discourses were more diverse still, and more problematic, than was initially apparent from the questionnaire data. Problems arose out of the different goals and policies of specific institutions, including political priorities and the more practical considerations of budgets, caseloads and time management. Unlike the former two types of discourse, organizational imperatives were often viewed as hindering improvement, especially in terms of education and collaboration:

> I don't identify with the organization . . . I'm not terribly loyal to my employer . . . because they don't have the same values as I do towards mental health, or towards Social Work . . . just budgets . . . although some managers are OK.

My own views and objectives are somewhat hampered by my work situation . . . the organization I work for, and its own outlook on things . . . generally budgets and managers' preferences.

In addition, questionnaire data highlighted the impact of organizational attitudes on recruitment to education, where discourses may clash before students even reach the classroom or lecture theatre. It identified organizational managers as powerful **gatekeepers**, posing an additional layer between promotion of the programme and uptake of course places. The educational status of interprofessional training, the accreditation of courses and the potential of work-related projects all played an important role in negotiating the support of service managers.

This is unsurprising perhaps, as it tells us that managers had their own agenda. But it doesn't tell us very much about those agendas. The facility to 'probe' in our qualitative interviews, however, enabled us to reveal attitudes of organization managers that lurked beneath the surface of a more seemingly pro-education veneer. We were therefore able to explore in detail the ways in which managerial attitudes towards education represent additional (organizational) discourses that interacted with interprofessional learning.

Qualitative analysis revealed some other motivations that were not originally detected by analysis of the questionnaire data. It demonstrated how driving forces behind participant registration on the programme were not concerned solely with improving interprofessional collaboration. Different recruitment and promotion styles appeared to have implications for motivational factors, as well as for attitudes towards interprofessional education. This was related to specific emphasis in the presentation of educational courses. Analysis revealed that those modules with explicit interprofessional emphasis (informed by interprofessional discourses) encouraged collaborative improvements far more successfully than clinically focused modules, where interprofessional emphases and discourses were more implicit. This despite the fact that all modules contained learning methods conducive to collaborative improvement.

Identifying the emergence of more collaborative discourses and their implications for practice

Comparison of questionnaire 'before' and 'during' data sets on SPSS facilitated comprehension of how participants began to develop a deeper understanding

of the roles and expectations of other professions as the course progressed. Attitudes became increasingly based on interprofessional ideas (before education, 38 per cent of attitudes supported interprofessional collaboration; during education, 70 per cent; and on completion, 77 per cent). Furthermore, in terms of behaviour patterns, positive collaborative ventures increased as the course progressed (before education, 22 per cent of working practice; during education, 59 per cent; and on completion, 62 per cent). Interview data supported this view:

It improved my knowledge about others and this has definitely affected my prejudice.

Having this wider viewpoint challenged my assumptions.

The multi-professional angle has increased awareness and made us focus on the importance of working together. As well as having positive outcomes for working practice and collaboration, it has led to better or fuller practice and us using more useful and relevant information in our work. Generally, I think we all agree that the material provided by [the course leader] provided a wider view of interprofessional work than we had imagined.

Such comparison enabled us to examine how far such change appeared to be related specifically to the education intervention, and how relationships had changed over time. To briefly summarize, the introduction of interprofessional education resulted in a situation whereby the somewhat more antagonistic professional discourses became gradually centralized around the principles of collaboration, and the various strategies that could be employed to achieve it. Although other differences remained, these more conducive elements were utilized as gateways to improved collaboration. Some participants perceived this as total change – an abandonment of 'old' discourses.

However, qualitative interviews revealed how personal, professional and organizational discourses had not been abandoned altogether. Instead, their varying elements had been adapted, or modified, to fit a new interprofessional discourse based on an underlying generic mental health care discourse. The development of this new approach was less straightforward than the questionnaire findings originally suggested. The emerging interprofessional mental health discourse retained some of the character of professional discourses. However, with their features combined in slightly different ways, it appeared to have facilitated both education and collaborative practice and helped align professionals in protecting their common interests:

> We all realized that it was always there, that we didn't have to change radically – if you think of it in terms of a Venn diagram – our major experience was within more uni-disciplinary learning and practice – but this interprofessional stuff brought us all together and affected the way we're now thinking about things, more interprofessionally so we haven't changed completely.

Exploring the suitability of various approaches to teaching/learning interprofessional education

Analysis also highlighted how academic discourses appeared to present their own problems. Questionnaires provided information on the general advantages/disadvantages of formal teaching methods. But interviews also allowed participants to point out how academic staff tended to naturalize and normalize more 'academic' models of interprofessional education, when they felt that its principles could be presented to equal effect in less of a 'textbook' fashion. Mixed-method evaluation therefore demonstrated how the use of academic models and rather more abstract and conceptual terms resulted in what the evaluation team came to view as 'discursive mystification', whereby academic convention served to mystify elements of an overall goal that participants felt should be more clearly linked to practice. We were thus able to feed back the information to curriculum developers for consideration and action.

Revealing the potential of interprofessional education for service user/practitioner conflict

Multi-method analysis enabled us to reveal more implicit obstacles that arose out of the very interprofessional discourses which had facilitated collaborative thinking. Officially, professional and educational discourses had encouraged service user involvement: this view is evident in questionnaire answers. But through interviewing and **observation** we were able to reveal a different picture. Qualitative analysis highlighted a quite covert process whereby service users had become marginalized. Whilst participants began to identify themselves less with traditional professions, there was some evidence that they nevertheless constructed their 'sameness' as mental health care professionals against the non-professional status of service users. Service users on the course lamented their relatively low status, within a 'them and us' relationship with other participants.

Examining the sustainability of interprofessional learning, and the implications for working practice

The questionnaire-based aspects of our evaluation were designed in order to chart the influences of specific elements of interprofessional education on various personal, professional and organizational attitudes/behaviours over an extended period of time. Analysis of the questionnaire data made clear how the transference of learning to the work situation was no straightforward process. However, it was the interview-based data that highlighted specific problems. These included organizational issues and priorities, financial constraints, managerial particularism, individual biases and bureaucratic procedures, all of which were bolstered through organizational discourses that prioritized their importance.

The relevance of this to our discussion is that the specific features of organizational discourse were not picked up by the pre-formulated questionnaires. However, they did come up time and time again in **in-depth interviews**. The opportunity to allow participants to raise issues that they felt were important (rather than imposing pre-selected categories on them) was crucial to these significant findings.

This line of enquiry led the evaluation team to a fundamental question: do problems arise exclusively from professional differences, or is conflict more often the result of inter-organizational, or inter-agency, collaboration? The questionnaire data, when analysed, highlighted changes in attitudes and behaviours during and at the end of the education. These attitudes remained relatively constant following completion and beyond (from 77 per cent on completion to 72 per cent after six months). However, actual collaborative working was not sustained: collaborative ventures began to decrease as practitioners returned to work (from 62 per cent on completion to 46 per cent six months after completion).

These patterns appeared to illustrate a negative impact in the period following education, when professionals returned to work and were no longer participating in the interprofessional education. It was the interview method that allowed us to access data that could help us understand why this might be the case. Analysis of the qualitative data demonstrated that, whilst motivation for collaboration remained relatively high, it became increasingly difficult for professionals to maintain actual collaborative practice without the support of the educational team (including academic staff and other professionals enrolled). It transpired that senior managers were rather less than enthusiastic about increased collaboration once practitioners had completed courses, and that professionals found themselves isolated in their efforts to sustain collaborative projects they had begun during their education. Extracts from interviews illustrate:

> The course was great, actually, but I've given too little time for it since leaving because of balancing other commitments at work and dealing with the organizational prejudices that remain.

> I would have liked to have had more time and support for applying all I've learned, but I'm not sure my changed view suits my manager's or the institution.

> Too many barriers have resulted from people's own agendas affecting their commitment to putting into practice what I've learned. In some ways it's worse, because I can see it clearly now . . . it's very frustrating.

Therefore, both methods provided us with evidence that participants were increasingly able to overcome professional differences through their mutual interests in improving mental health care, but that frustrations continued to arise out of inter-agency working once back in the workplace due to a lack of support and the absence of interprofessional discourses that could otherwise support interprofessional learning and its transference to practice.

Conclusions

The above example of an existing evaluation demonstrates the importance of paying rigorous attention to methodological issues, and carefully selecting appropriate quantitative or qualitative methods or, as we have demonstrated here, a multi-method approach. Its many findings, some of which have been very briefly outlined here, would not have been evident

had we simply employed traditional experimental approaches. Illumination of both the human and structural issues surrounding education and learning was only made possible by employing different methods: together they enabled us to access different types of data that provided us with a detailed and well-rounded understanding of a complex situation.

Social Research Topic Example 3: Health inequalities and research methods

Mike Sheaff*

Clear and systematic differences in the health status of different social groups have long been recognized. One of the more consistent findings is that people who are financially disadvantaged tend also to suffer poorer health, and to die younger. In the UK, where infant mortality rates are relatively low by international comparison, the risk of an infant dying before reaching the age of 12 months is twice as great for those whose parents are unskilled manual workers compared to those with professional parents.

Why should this be so? The question has prompted considerable debate, and not all research points convincingly in the same direction. This should not be surprising. Causes are complex, and different research approaches will focus on these differently. To illustrate this, two types of study are described in what follows to provide a comparison between a quantitative and qualitative approach. The two studies are selected as both focus on a similar theme, the relationship between insecurity and health: one concentrates on employment insecurity, and the other on an aspect of housing insecurity.

Quantitative study – privatization, job insecurity and health

Reported in Ferrie et al. (2001)

This research is part of a much larger piece of work, known as the 'Whitehall II' study, a longitudinal programme instigated with the aim of monitoring the health of all London-based civil service office staff. It

*Dr Mike Sheaff is a Senior Lecturer in Sociology at the University of Plymouth School of Sociology, Politics and Law.

looks particularly at experiences of coronary heart disease.

At its outset in 1985, information was collected about the employment, lifestyle, and health status of all respondents, including a clinical examination and a self-administered questionnaire. Subsequent changes in health can be tracked from this baseline, potentially indicating what factors are most closely associated with differential outcomes.

This choice of method reflects an acknowledgement that social science cannot directly replicate the methods of many natural sciences. For the latter, **experimental** situations can often be constructed in ways designed to control the environment. A chemical reaction, for example, may be studied in differing circumstances, with factors such as temperature, air pressure or lighting being manipulated by the experimenter. This should, in principle, enable the independent effect of these influences to be assessed, because they can be measured separately from the influence of other factors.

In social research, experimental control of this kind is not generally available (for practical as well as ethical reasons). Data must be collected in situations where there are many extraneous influences beyond the researcher's control. The school someone attended, the parents who brought them up, the friends they mixed with, and much else, may all have influenced a person's health-related behaviours and health status.

When it is not possible to control these influences in ways sought in laboratory experiments, alternative means can be sought. In particular, gathering data about a range of potentially relevant factors, with statistical control being used to isolate the independent effects of each one. This was the approach adopted in this study, which achieved a high response rate, involving 10,308 participants, working across 20 government departments.

During the course of the study, one of the departments, the Property Services Agency (PSA), was privatized, prompting the researchers to examine the health experiences of 666 staff working within the sample who worked in that particular environment. Between April 1990 and July 1991 the PSA was split into six separate businesses, one of which (where most of the staff in the study sample worked) was sold to Tarmac PLC in December 1992.

Data was collected 18 months following privatization, with attention paid to the degree of job security that individuals felt themselves to have. Staff who remained employed were differentiated between those who described their employment as 'very secure' or 'secure', and those who regarded it as 'insecure' or 'very insecure'. Those who were not in employment were divided between those who said they were seeking alternative work, and those who were not. Thus there were four categories: secure re-employment, insecure re-employment, unemployment, and permanently out of paid employment.

The authors of the study describe their aim as being 'to determine whether change in morbidity [illness] between baseline and follow-up differed between respondents in the four categories of employment after privatization. In the absence of a control group who had not experienced privatization, we used participants in the most favourable category in the labour market (secure re-employment) as the reference group.'

Of the 666 staff in the original baseline study, 81 per cent responded, with 539 providing usable data. The proportions in each of the four employment categories were as shown in Table 5.1:

Table 5.1 Proportion of employment categories after privatization

Employment status	Number	%
Secure re-employment	165	30
Insecure re-employment	155	29
Unemployment	101	19
Permanent exit from labour market	118	22
Total	539	100

Several health variations between groups were found, including:

- those who were unemployed or insecurely re-employed were more likely to have consulted a general practitioner or experienced minor psychiatric morbidity in the previous year. These differences were statistically significant.
- those who were permanently out of paid employment were much more likely to have experienced longstanding illness. This difference was statistically significant.

How might such differences be explained? Could it be, for example, that the healthiest staff were more likely to gain secure re-employment? In other words, health (rather than employment status) represents the **independent variable**.

It is for this kind of question that a study of this type can be valuable, because it produces 'baseline' data, and as the authors report:

> In general, respondents with less favourable employment outcomes had greater morbidity and poorer psychosocial profiles and health related behaviours at baseline . . . . However, analyses of health outcomes after privatisation adjusted for the baseline values of all the health measures and all the potential explanatory variables were similar to the results presented. (Ferrie et al., 2001: 3)

In other words, the scale of the observed differences does not appear to be explained by previous health status and behaviours. However, this does not mean that it is necessarily the experience of privatization that is responsible. It could be that those who experienced the least secure employment were worse off financially, and it was this experience that generated emotional and health problems.

The study's authors attempt to test for this, employing statistical analysis to explore the contribution that different influences make to the observed differential health outcomes. Unsurprisingly, it finds an association between unemployment and financial strain, although this explained only 9 per cent of the association between unemployment and minor psychiatric morbidity. Several other factors are identified as having effects upon health, including the amount of exercise taken and the level of decision-authority enjoyed by individuals in subsequent employment.

Quantitative studies such as these are an important means of highlighting these issues, seeking to substitute statistical control for the kind exercised in the laboratory. But this tells us little about the actual experiences of those involved. Here we are dealing with the more subjective feelings and emotions of the individuals involved, and how they interpret and explain what is happening around them. For this, qualitative methods can provide a deeper and richer source of data.

Qualitative study: health consequences of losing your house

Reported in Nettleton and Burrows (2000)

This study looks at another form of insecurity and its relationship with health, in this case experiences of mortgage repossession. The context for this was the almost half a million households (containing an estimated 1.3 million people) experiencing mortgage repossession in the UK between 1990 and 1998.

Housing insecurity, and specifically mortgage repossession, had been the subject of an earlier statistical study (Nettleton and Burrows, 1998) that had investigated the relationship between mortgage debt and health status. This had been based on data from the British Household Panel Survey (BHPS), a nationally representative sample of over 5,000 households that are tracked over time. From this data, the researchers found that the onset of mortgage indebtedness could invoke poor mental health and an increase in the use of primary health care services.

As was indicated in the preceding account, statistical associations are important, and quantitative studies have helped to provide important insights into the relationship between health status and social factors. But people are not simply passive victims of circumstances. Quantitative studies are not able to tell us very much about how individuals manage and negotiate social and personal changes within their specific environments. For this, qualitative methods can be more appropriate, as illustrated in the following study.

At the outset, the authors acknowledged that isolating the contribution of an individual factor is very difficult:

> The onset of mortgage problems can be the product of a complex set of factors many of which may themselves be related to a change in health status and/or subjective wellbeing. Our task is to disentangle the independent impact, if any, that the onset of mortgage problems have on subjective wellbeing. (Nettleton and Burrows, 1998: 178).

However, drawing from the quantitative study already conducted around these issues, the authors felt confident in concluding:

> . . . the relationship between difficulties with mortgage payments and poor mental health does appear to hold even when other variables (such as household income, employment status and physical health) are held constant. (Nettleton and Burrows, 1998: 184–5)

The aim of Nettleton and Burrows, however, was to go beyond establishing the existence of this statistical association, to explore this relationship further and hopefully reveal more about the individual and personal accounts beneath it. They wanted to:

> . . . systematically listen to and analyse people's own personal accounts, stories and narratives of this stressful and emotional experience and to make the link better between understanding how the structural determinants of health and the lived experiences and behaviours of individuals mesh together. (Nettleton and Burrows, 1998: 465)

For this to be achieved, a qualitative study was instigated, involving 30 families with children who had experienced mortgage repossession and had subsequently been rehoused in the social rented sector. Semi-structured interviews were conducted with 44 adults from these families, and with 17 children and young people. Some couples, and several of the children, were interviewed together.

It can be very difficult to summarize qualitative data, and here just a few of the key points will be highlighted. The stressful nature of the episode was emphasized by many people, with repeated reference being made to the fact it felt like a 'complete nightmare'. People described experiences such as anxiety, breathlessness and sleeplessness, with several commenting on what they felt could be negative consequences for the immune system from this kind of stress.

The emotional significance of the event was constantly referred to, with one mother of five children responding to the question 'What would you say was the biggest impact of losing your home?' by saying:

> Just the emotional side of it really, that's what I can say got us all, at the time.

Another respondent, a lone father, described how he felt:

> Broke, broken. Not broke money-wise, but broken. Absolutely devastated . . . I don't know, it's a feeling I would never wish on anyone. It hit me in the morning when I was waiting for the furniture people and the eviction people, I just sat there and cried; sat with my dog and cried.

The emotional impact, often accompanied by references to a feeling of 'loss', could sometimes be associated with feelings of isolation, and a desperate need to talk to someone. However, contact with the financial institutions involved is frequently described as being highly impersonal. A number said they felt they were simply 'figures' on the books. One father described how he was 'taken aback at just how black and white and cold it was, I think that really, there was *no human element* in there at all.'

All of these aspects – the emotional stress, a sense of loss, feelings of isolation, and impersonal contact with financial institutions – could come together to generate a feeling that the individuals could no longer control what was happening. One lone mother, whose husband had left and failed to contribute financial support, explained:

> I just felt that it was all out of my control, you know, there was nothing really that I could do. I was just sort of helpless, it's the only way I can describe it and knowing that with just that quick instant decision from the judge I would be on the street.

Nettleton and Burrows note that 'the feeling of not being in control left some people with an emotional legacy of enduring insecurity'. One couple, when asked what had been the biggest impact of losing their home, answered:

> *Husband:* Security.
> *Interviewer:* In what way?
> *Husband:* The loss of it in terms of being out of control where you are going to live.
> *Wife:* I feel very insecure, that's one thing I do feel, it's the one thing that's affected me more than anything else.

Many other issues were mentioned in interviews. These included the changed social status that went with being a 'renter' rather than an 'owner'. People often felt ashamed and embarrassed, and a recurrent theme was that this represented failure, with negative consequences for feelings of self-confidence and self-esteem. The stigma that people felt (and also experienced) could have its own results in terms of affecting people's social relationships and networks.

These accounts can help to explain the nature of the relationship between mortgage repossession and health status. That there is one had been signalled in the preceding quantitative study, and the qualitative study was not conducted with the purpose of re-establishing that this association existed. Instead, the objective was to explore in a different way how this association appeared, what were the important mediating processes, and how were these experienced by the individuals and families involved.

Each of these studies sought to examine an important feature of contemporary British society, whether in the context of employment or housing, and look at what impact these might have upon the health of individuals, and how these processes might operate.

For addressing this type of question, they should not be viewed as alternative so much as complementary approaches. The important point is to be clear about the form of question being asked, and to adopt a method most likely to generate appropriate data.

More than this, it is important to approach the problem with some conceptual framework within which the relationships are understood. Not only does this reduce the likelihood of identifying bizarre associations between unconnected factors, it can help clarify areas where most attention is needed.

This, in turn, can assist in developing explanations which may account for observed statistical associations. There is considerable data to show that insecurity can have negative consequences for health, as illustrated in the studies considered here. Both quantitative and qualitative techniques can contribute to research that moves beyond description, to develop a fuller understanding of how these associations develop.

The complexities of the relationships involved between social changes and personal insecurity make this task a difficult one. But the significance of this relationship for human wellbeing makes it an extremely valuable and important task. The utilization of a range of research methods can help generate more systematic empirical data, which needs to be accompanied by developments in the way the relationships are conceptualized and understood.

Social Research Topic Example 4: Researching rural deprivation

Carole Sutton*

The research on deprivation and social exclusion informs government policy and the targeting of funding initiatives to areas of greatest need. The research outlined in this section is centred on a study that examined the experience of rural deprivation within the boundaries of a district council in England. The research undertaken contributed to various policy decision-making processes within the district council.

Context

England is divided into administrative areas known as local authorities, county councils and district councils. Within each of these administrative areas there is a further geographical division into electoral wards. Quantitative data about the population is often collected at ward level by various administrative bodies and organizations. Data is occasionally available at a parish level. Parishes are smaller administrative areas mostly organized around local towns and villages.

Poverty and deprivation are concepts that have received considerable interest from social scientists for many years. They are concepts that are used to discuss the social condition that individuals find themselves in. Governments have been interested in defining poverty in order to address the needs of the poorer members of society. Definitions have focused on economic requirements to meet basic needs (Rowntree, 1901; Beveridge, 1942) through to a wider definition of relative deprivation (Townsend, 1979). Outhwaite and Bottomore state that:

> People are relatively deprived if they cannot obtain, at all or sufficiently, the conditions of life – that is, the diets, amenities, standards and services – which allow them to play the roles, particularly in the relationships and follow the customary behaviour which is expected of them by virtue of their membership of society. (1993: 504)

Rural deprivation refers specifically to the requirements and needs of the disadvantaged in a rural setting. While similar to those disadvantaged in urban centres, individuals in rural locations have additional issues to address.

Households and individuals that experience deprivation in rural areas are faced with a number of additional difficulties that are not experienced by those

---

*Carole Sutton is a Senior Lecturer in Sociology at the University of Plymouth School of Sociology, Politics and Law.

who live in poverty in urban areas. Payne (1995) and Giarchi (1999) highlight a number of specifically rural issues. For example, a lack of employment opportunities and affordable housing particularly for young people, access to and provision of local services particularly in relation to geographical distances from central facilities which tend to be urban based (The Countryside Agency, 1999, 2000, and Mullins et al., 2001). In addition, geographical distance can also bring about information deprivation (David, 2003), a particular issue for elderly people and low-income families who do not know of the economic support and social support services available to them. These factors can bring about feelings of increasing isolation and lack of social support networks especially for older members of the population.

A further issue regarding rural deprivation is that it is often hidden by national measures and indices. The reasons for this are varied, but centre on the way in which quantitative data is measured across fixed geographical areas, normally at electoral ward level, and that rural populations are spread over a wider geographic area. The difference in levels of affluence in rural areas, particularly with urban populations increasingly relocating to rural areas, results in small areas of deprivation and poverty being 'cancelled out' and hidden by the more affluent households. This can also occur where wards are located in the travel-to-work area of an adjacent town or city that is administered by a different council. These wards, adjacent to the town or city, will have a higher level of affluence that again cancels out deprivation in other ward areas across the district council. The quantitative data available at ward level can also hide smaller populations of deprivation at a parish level.

Choice

Research aims

The aim of the research project was twofold. The first was to build a detailed statistical picture within the district council boundaries to describe and analyse the extent and characteristics of rural deprivation. The second, and main, focus of the study was to gain an understanding of individuals' experiences of rural economic deprivation and their access to networks of support. The research adopts both deductive and inductive strategies.

The nature of the two aims generated different research approaches, thus making the use of mixed methods appropriate. The first aim of building a statistical picture involved the collating and analysis of secondary quantitative data. Much of this data was already in the public domain and was supplemented by data provided by the council's own information department utlilizing geographical information systems (GIS) software at both an electoral ward and a parish council level. In addition, a limited amount of data on household incomes was anonymously accessed through a local voluntary support group that helps households in financial crisis.

Given the critique of the use of quantifiable **indicators**, in the way in which they can mask areas of deprivation and fail to convey an understanding of the experience of deprivation, a qualitative methodological approach was also adopted in order to meet the second aim. This involved the collation of some of the existing qualitative research on rural deprivation, at both a national and local level, together with information gathered through interviewing key local people who have expert knowledge of the issues. In addition, primary data was collected through face-to-face interviewing at a household level to gather data on the experiences of deprivation and the effects on household members of distance from a variety of services and facilities. The data gathered from the interviewees also included data on all members of the household. The interviews also provided 'rich insights into people's experiences, opinions, attitudes and feelings' (May, 1997). A **self-completion** postal **survey** would not have resulted in the same depth of data, nor allowed for the interviewer to gain additional knowledge about areas not previously considered of importance by the research team. A semi-structured **interview schedule** was used with the specification of questions based on the key issues highlighted from the existing literature and research. The semi-structured nature of the interviewing freed the interviewer to ask follow-up questions appropriate to the concerns expressed by the interviewee.

Process

Quantifying and measuring deprivation

The first stage in the research process was to undertake a literature review of existing research. From this review existing measurement tools and indicators were identified. There have been many measures of deprivation developed over the years;

each has been refined and developed as understanding of deprivation has been expanded. The main measurement tool used to assess the deprivation of different areas in the UK, normally at ward level, is an indices of multiple deprivation (IMD).

The quantitative measurement of deprivation

National IMDs have provided uniform measures across all types of geographical area. These indices have been developed and refined over a number of years. The most recent development is the Indices of Multiple Deprivation 2000 (DETR, 2000). The IMD 2000 is a measurement that enables policy makers to assess the relative deprivation of one area compared to another. The smallest area at which the IMD is calculated is at UK ward level. The IMD 2000 is based on six domains of deprivation:

* income;
* employment;
* health deprivation and disability;
* education, skills and training;
* housing; and
* geographical services.

For each of the six domains appropriate indicators were selected. These indicators are measurable and could be combined to provide an overall domain value. There are a total of 32 indicators across the six domains. The indicators are drawn in the main from official government department figures and government surveys. For example, in the income domain (DETR, 2000) three of the eight indicators were official figures for 'Adults in Income Support Households for 1998', 'Children in Income Support Households for 1998' and 'Adults in Disability Working Allowance Households for 1999'(source: Department of Social Security). In the health deprivation and disability domain (DETR, 2000), three of the five indicators were 'Comparative Mortality Ratios for Men and Women at Ages under 65, 1997–1998, at Ward Level' (source: National Statistics Office), 'Proportion of people who receive Attendance Allowance or Disability Living Allowance in 1998' (source: Department of Social Security) and 'Age and Sex Standardised Ratio of Limiting Long-term Illness' (source: 1991 Census, National Statistics Office). In the geographical access to services domain (DETR, 2000), two of the four indicators were 'Access to a Post Office for April 1998' (source: General Post

Office Counters) and 'Access to Food Shops 1998' (source: Data Consultancy). The latter is an indicator taken from a non-government survey. Each domain is given a weighting. Income and employment are weighted at 25 per cent, health deprivation and disability, education, skills and training at 15 per cent, geographical access to services and health are weighted at 10 per cent.

The resulting IMD **score** is calculated for each electoral ward. National, regional and local tables are produced with both the scores and ranking positions of Wards. The major difficulty with these **tables** is that they compare urban and rural wards and thus make judgements about relative deprivation. Payne (1995) suggests that it is problematic to talk about the 'most deprived' county or district as it fails to address the dimensions of rural deprivation.

While some indicators relating to rural issues were contained within the access to services and health domain, it received relatively low weighting, at 10 per cent, in the overall calculation of IMD. The indicators selected were narrow and could have been expanded to include items like access to regular public transport, access to secondary schools, and access to library services. The data is collected at ward level and again this can have the effect of masking the smaller pockets of need in geographically spread populations.

Primary qualitative data collection

The topic areas covered by the interview schedule were determined by existing literature, previous research, summary data findings from analysis of the quantitative data, and interviews with active members and leaders of the local communities. The main areas covered in the interviews were: employment, including access to work, choice and opportunities; economic support, including access to housing; education and training, access and needs; social life, activities, leisure and recreation; family networks; young people; access to all services and to transport. In addition, the semi-structured interviews allowed issues not covered in these main areas to be discussed with the researcher.

Interview locations and sample size

The selection of households with which to carry out interviews needed to take account of the location of the household. The sample needed to reflect the rural elements of the district and the experience of deprivation. It was also considered important to identify locations where relative affluence and deprivation co-existed in close proximity, since one of the criticisms of the index of domains calculated at ward level was that deprivation becomes masked by affluence in such areas. Other considerations were the distance from centres and services. The basis of the sample selection was an examination of the quantitative deprivation data. This data was mapped onto a geographical area profile of the district. Ward boundaries, population density and location of domestic properties were mapped. This provided a geographical framework upon which a sample could be selected. Households were selected according to their distance from a population centre or town. The team selected wedge-shaped geographical areas that spread from these centres. The areas to be targeted were agreed in consultation with the council. The council then used the electoral role to randomly select households in each of these areas. A letter was sent to the sample households asking them if they would be willing to participate in the study. Willing participants contacted the research team to arrange interview times. The final sample size was 55 households. The initial target number was set at 40 households, this number having been decided upon partly because of time restriction but also because in the view of the research team this number of households would be sufficient to achieve **saturation** (that is, no new items being introduced by the respondents). The additional 15 interviews were undertaken as more households than had been expected agreed to be interviewed and, in the event, time allowed for their completion. The interviews were taped and transcribed for the purposes of analysis.

Analysis

The quantitative data

Analysis was undertaken of both the IMD and each of the six domains that make up the indices. At a national level each ward is assigned a ranking for each set of scores in the index. There are 8,414 wards in England and in terms of the scores the most deprived ward is ranked as 1 and the least deprived ward is ranked as 8,414. The ranking of wards within the district boundaries showed considerable variation. Only 6 of the 32 wards fell into the second half of the English rankings, with a ranking of 4,200 or higher. These wards could be identified as areas that had boundaries with the travel-to-work areas of the nearest city, or in

areas considered desirable for retirement which had attracted in-migrants (internal migrants as distinct from overseas migrants) from more affluent areas. Of the remaining wards, 10 had a ranking of 3,000 or less and one ward had a ranking that placed it in the top 15 per cent of the most deprived wards in England. There was some variation in the ranking of the wards within the council boundaries for each of the six domains. A more detailed analysis of the data is contained in the full research report.

The qualitative data

Fifty-five households agreed to participate in the qualitative research and a total of 66 individuals from these households participated in the interviews. Over half of the participants were male and almost a third had children under the age of 18 years. Almost half of the participants had lived in the council area all their lives. Owner occupation accounted for almost three-quarters of the sample.

A summary of the results from the interviews has been divided into a number of themes. It is not possible to report all the findings here, and the focus will be on employment and transport issues only. Issues of restricted work opportunities for people in rural areas were highlighted in the interviews. The low-wage economy was particularly emphasized, with even highly-skilled employment being paid at relatively low rates. One respondent commented that hourly rates for a skilled electrician were only a quarter of the hourly rate they would expect to be paid in the southeast of England. Many respondents commented that the majority of jobs they saw advertised were only offering the minimum wage and those that were working for this wage had to work long hours to earn enough money to survive. The situation was compromised further by structural changes in the local economy with the decline of farming and farming-related businesses, and the prevalence of seasonal work.

Opportunities were further compromised by transport issues, including poor access to public transport and the associated costs of car ownership in a low-wage economy. Indeed, transport and access to services was a major issue for the majority of households. Three-quarters of households owned a car, but low wages and high rates of unemployment meant that many people struggled to afford the running costs. For retired people (over half the sample), concerns were expressed about future transport requirements if they became unable to drive because of ill health or extreme old age. For those without access to cars, lack of public transport and problems related to the frequency and routes of public transport were of concern. Many respondents expressed worries about access to support services, particularly hospitals, for both routine appointments and for Accident and Emergency, while for children and young people the transport timetables inhibited participation in after-school activity clubs, thus restricting the opportunities to build and maintain social networks.

These findings from the interviews, which revealed the depth of the concerns about transport access, were reinforced by the quantitative data. The mapping of the public bus routes and frequency of services within the council boundaries showed that in some areas there were no bus routes, or routes with a frequency of less than three services on a weekday with none at weekends.

These findings support research undertaken by Halliday (1998) and Shucksmith et al. (1996) who highlighted that poor transport infrastructures for rural communities not only lead to physical isolation, but also serve to reduce an individual's personal, occupational and social mobility. With increasing numbers of the population choosing to retire to rural areas, access to transport will continue to be a major concern. This group is increasingly likely to have family and social networks living at a distance and have a greater dependence on personal transport to maintain these important social links.

Dissemination

The research was presented to the district council in a report format. The report was structured to present the background literature, the profile of the rural deprivation measures across the geographical area of the district council, and the findings from the semi-structured interviews. The findings from the mixed methods were then drawn together in a detailed discussion and included the implications for a variety of policy initiatives. The council was then able to present the report to appropriate committees and meetings responsible for deprivation-related issues.

Ethics

The research was carried out in accordance with the ethical procedures of the University of Plymouth and was approved by the ethical clearance committee. The existing secondary data was already anonymized. Additional care was taken not to inadvertently map sensitive data onto a map where the potential to 'second guess' the property that the data applied to could occur. For example, some of the data was available at postcode (zip) level. In areas of low property density, such as in rural areas, it would be possible to map the count of benefit claimants to an area containing two or three properties. Due to the small number of participants in the primary data collection, the interviews and the nature of the subject matter, issues of anonymity and confidentiality needed to be addressed. Only the interviewer knew the contact details of the respondents. Once the interview was conducted, the interviewee details were removed and after the interview was transcribed, the original contact details and the audio tapes were destroyed. Only a reference number then identified the interview. Care was taken in the analysis and report writing stage not to identify individual households in any way. Personal names and place names were removed. In addition, care was taken not to identify individuals by inference.

Conclusions

The research undertaken provides an excellent example of how different methodological approaches taken can result in the collection of different levels of data. The quantitative secondary data analysis provided a statistical context for the interviews. The critique of the quantifiable deprivation indicators illustrates some of the difficulties with collating data across a geographical area. The interview data revealed the complexities of rural living, and the everyday difficulties and challenges faced by household members. In the case of access to public transport, it was also possible to link the comments made by interviewees with the statistical data.

General issues

The four examples highlight the range of issues faced by social researchers. These issues are complex and overlapping, but for the purposes of getting to grips and understanding the basics of social research, the following six themes have been identified. Every social researcher needs to think about all six themes when starting and developing a research project.

Induction versus deduction

Deductive research designs allow the researcher to define in advance what it is they are going to look for. All four of the quantitative studies were deductive, as was the health inequality interview design. Cottle's qualitative discourse analysis was deductive in the choice of data, though the analysis was less prescriptive and more exploratory. Sutton and Regan de Bere's qualitative studies are also a mix of deductive and inductive strategies. Based upon review of the literature, including existing research data, catagories can be clearly operationalized within deductive research. This enables questions to be designed that are robust and which can be fully piloted. Deduction also enables the sampling to be rigorous, as the group to be investigated can be specified in advance. Results can thus claim a high level of **external validity**. The value of more inductive designs was shown in the ability to identify issues that had not been apparent to the researcher at the beginning of the research (such as the significance of inter-organizational differences, rather than just interprofessional ones, in Regan de Bere's work).

Primary versus secondary data collection and analysis

Primary research involves the researcher undertaking the data collection themselves. It allows the researcher to determine the research design, the conceptual framework, the sampling technique, the research method and measurement tools. Regan de Bere's work involved only primary data collection. This was appropriate as it was specifically focusing on the experiences of course members. Two studies undertook a mix of primary and secondary (health inequality and rural deprivation). One study collected broadcast media for analysis. This is primary data, as the specific data set had not been collected and researched before. Secondary data involves the researcher identifying an existing data set that has been collected from a previous study. The analysis of secondary data needs to be understood within the context and conceptual framework of the original study. This issue was particularly highlighted in the discussion of existing deprivation indicators and their appropriateness as a measure of rural deprivation. Measurements of health were based on biological indicators taken from medical records.

Secondary data enables the researcher to analyse data from larger samples than would be possible within the financial and time restrictions of their own research project (the health inequalities and rural deprivation research example particularly highlight this point). While the project documentation setting out the aims and objectives of the programmes under evaluation in Regan de Bere's research were primary data (not being a previously generated and researched data set), the use of such data, to get at the ideas and decisions made in the past, is often the reason that secondary data is collected.

Ethics in the choice of topic, conduct of data collection, analysis and presentation

Ethical considerations should be understood by the researcher. The researcher needs to critically reflect upon the motivations for researching a particular topic area, especially where it is framed by a policy directive, and to be sensitive to the needs of those whom they wish to research. This should apply equally to both quantitative and qualitative research.

During the data collection process care must be taken to ensure confidentiality and anonymity (where appropriate), and that participants understand the nature of the research and have given informed consent. The health inequality research was a particularly sensitive area as it involved approaching respondents at a stressful time in their lives. The data collected in the education evaluation required the course members to reveal opinions on other professional organizations involved in interprofessional collaboration that could be both of a sensitive and political nature. This research was linked to a policy directive that encouraged interprofessional collaboration. At the data analysis and presentation stages of the research process, care needed to be taken to ensure that confidentiality and anonymity were maintained. This is a particular issue with small-scale research. Cottle's research on the media raises an interesting debate on the ethical position of a researcher who analyses a data source that exists in the public domain, since the original news actors did not consent to being included in the study. In all the four examples, issues of anonymity in the report presentation had to be considered.

The value of numbers and textual data

Large quantities of numerical data can be easily presented in a range of tables and graphical forms.

Such data can also be easily manipulated using statistical techniques for the purpose of identifying patterns within the data. This can be seen in Anderson's discussion of quantitative content analysis and in Sheaff's discussion of health inequalities. Because there are generally accepted methods of evaluating the strength of statistical relationships and the **validity** of samples, results from previous studies can be easily specified and used in generating new indicators or in testing the utility of existing ones in different contexts (such as in Sutton's discussion of deprivation indicators). Collecting numerical data makes comparison between groups and across time relatively straightforward (as in Regan de Bere's discussion). However, the reduction of social life to numerical measures to enable comparison and contrast may distort and hide the reality it seeks to measure. All four textual studies were designed to show the weaknesses of purely numerical measures. This is particularly the case in the studies discussed by Anderson and Sutton, where it is not just the possibility that the quantitative data are missing something, but that there is a danger that such data would get things totally wrong if not qualified with more in-depth data. However, the ease of numerical measurement does enable data to be collected from larger samples, and this is not something easily achieved in more textually-based research.

The value of large-scale data collection and small-scale (in-depth) research

Research projects that involve large-scale data collection allow the researcher to gather data from across a wider population. Sutton's account of rural deprivation used data from across a district council area as the basis for developing deprivation indicators. In Sheaff's account of health inequalities, data was initially drawn from over 10,000 civil servants. Anderson's account of how experts and lay people are presented in news coverage of environmental issues involved a relatively large sample of news programmes. The larger sampling units allow the researchers, subject to appropriate sampling techniques being employed, to undertake statistical testing to generalize their findings to the wider population. The data gathered from small-scale research cannot be subjected to the rigour of statistical testing. However, it may offer a greater scope for insight or depth when qualitative research methods are applied. As in the cases of research into health inequalities and into rural deprivation, large-scale data collection can provide the framework for undertaking small-scale, in-depth, research that seeks to provide greater understanding, while the fine-grain/small-scale research enables weaknesses in large-scale and deductive research to be brought to the researcher's attention.

The value of mixed methods

Each study discussed above had advantages and disadvantages. The value of mixed methods may be in allowing the best of both worlds. However, it is not a solution to every problem to suggest the use of mixed methods in every case. In some ways all good research employs mixed methods. The review of existing research prior to an empirical study is archival research (which may be qualitative discourse analysis or the secondary analysis of existing quantitative data, or both). Piloting a quantitative data collection instrument will often involve a qualitative dimension (asking respondents to describe what the questions meant to them). As piloting involves an inductive moment (the alteration of research questions and maybe even an original hypothesis in the light of data collected), even a typical hypothetico-deductive project usually involves a mix of induction and deduction. However, the choice to carry out two or more data collection exercises within the same project (such as was the case in all four of the examples in this chapter) is not universal. Resources may not always be available. Also data from different sources are not always compatible, so contrasting results cannot be used to refocus one method or the other. A researcher may simply wish to replicate and retest an earlier study, so mixed methods are not necessarily appropriate. Nevertheless, time and resources permitting, the use of mixed methods is an advantageous mode of conducting social research.

Summary

All four field examples showed how qualitative and quantitative studies complement each other across a range of specific issues (as outlined in the preceding six themes). All too often social researchers come to specialize in either qualitative or quantitative methods. This may reflect the perception amongst first-time researchers that one approach is either easier or superior to the other. While it is often the case that individual researchers do relate more easily to one approach (numbers or words), it is not true that one approach is superior. It is the intention of this chapter, and of this book as a whole, to encourage every reader to explore both approaches. Each approach can make a valuable contribution to the understanding of any social setting. The skill of the researcher lies in determining how best to approach a particular problem. This requires that they understand all the available options, and can thereby make the right choice and put it into practice.

Keywords

Actors	Gatekeeper	Quantitative
Action Research	Independent Variable	Questionnaire
Baseline	In-depth Interview	Sampling
Coding	Indicators	Saturation
Comparative Analysis	Interview	Score
Concept	Interview Schedule	Self-completion Survey
Content Analysis	Literature Review	Semiology/Semiotics
Cross-tabulation	Longitudinal Design	Statistic
Discourse Analysis	Methodology	Survey
Ethics	Mixed Methods	Tables
Evaluation Research	Multi-method	Text/Textual
Experimental Research	Observation	Validity (External/Internal)
External Validity	Operationalization	Values
Field Research/Fieldwork	Polysemy	
Focus Group Interview	Qualitative	

Questions

1   Why should poverty be measured differently in rural, as distinct from urban, areas?

2   How might mixed methods help in highlighting the difference between what people say and what they do?

3   How have health researchers sought to investigate the potentially two-way street between job insecurity making you ill, and illness making you more job insecure?

4   How have media researchers highlighted the importance of an integration of qualitative and quantitative research methods?

5   How might evaluation researchers use mixed methods to explore organizational tensions over the meaning of 'effectiveness'?

Suggested further reading

Anderson, Alison (1997) *Media, Culture and the Environment*. London: UCL.

Barr, H., Hammick, M., Koppel, I. and Reeves, S. (1999) 'Evaluating interprofessional education: two systematic reviews', *British Educational Research Journal*, 25 (4): 533–45.

Bryant, Lyn, Evans, Julie, Sutton, Carole and Beer, Julian (2002) *The Experience of Deprivation and Exclusion*. Plymouth: Social Research and Regeneration Unit, University of Plymouth.

Burgess, Robert (ed.) (1993) *Education Research and Evaluation: For Policy and Practice?* London: Falmer.

Cottle, Simon (1999) 'TV News, lay voices and the visualisation of environmental risks', in S. Allan, B. Adam and C. Carter (eds), *Environmental Risks and the Media*. London: Routledge. pp. 29–44.

David, Matthew (2003), 'The politics of communication: information technology, local knowledge and social exclusion', in *Telematics and Informatics*, 20 (3): 235–53.

Ferrie, J., Martikainen, P., Shipley, M., Marmot, M., Stansfield, S. and Davey-Smith, G. (2001) 'Employment status and health after privatisation in white collar civil servants: prospective cohort study', *British Medical Journal*, 322: 1–7.

Murphy, Roger and Torrance, Harry (eds) (1987) *Evaluating Education: Issues and Methods*. Buckingham: Open University Press.

Nettleton, Sarah and Burrows, Roger (1998) 'Mortgage debt, insecure home ownership and health: an exploratory analysis', in M. Bartley, D. Blane and G. Davey-Smith (eds), *The Sociology of Health Inequalities*. Oxford: Blackwell.

Nettleton, S. and Burrows, R. (2000) 'When a capital investment becomes an emotional loss: the health consequences of the experience of mortgage possession in England', *Housing Studies*, 15 (3): 463–79.

Norris, Nigel (1990) *Understanding Educational Evaluation*. London: Kogan Page.

Regan de Bere, Sam (2003) 'Evaluating the implications of complex interprofessional education for improvements in collaborative practice: a multidimensional model', *British Educational Research Journal*, 29 (1): 105–124.

Regan de Bere, Sam, Annandale, Stephen and Nattrass, Howard (2000) 'Achieving health improvements through interprofessional learning in south west England', *International Journal of Interprofessional Care*, 14 (2): 161–74.

PART II

RESEARCH DESIGN AND DATA COLLECTION

CHAPTER

6

INTRODUCTION TO THE PROCESS
OF QUALITATIVE RESEARCH

Chapter contents

By the end of this chapter you will be able to:

- Distinguish a number of different forms of qualitative data collection methods.

- Identify issues specific to qualitative research when selecting a sample.

- Outline the range of different approaches to research design emerging from choices over induction, deduction and grounded theory.

- Specify crucial ethical issues that must be addressed by the qualitative researcher.

Induction and exploration

As has been suggested already, the distinction between **qualitative** and **quantitative** research is at best hard to define, and at worst can be positively misleading. It is best to use the distinction with caution. In what follows the research methods described will be those which give emphasis to the collection of primarily non-numerical data, that is, thick descriptions of events, **in-depth interviewing** and the use of written/recorded records and **artefacts**. What has come to be understood as qualitative research involves more than simply the lack of emphasis on quantification. Qualitative research is also strongly associated with **induction** and **exploration** in research, rather than in the more **deductive** testing of preconceived theories. Induction and exploration imply that the researcher sets out with a more tentative idea of what is important. The researcher attempts to be more sensitive to the priorities held by those whom they will interview, observe or whose texts/artefacts they will attempt to 'read'. As such, the process of **research design** involves the deliberate attempt to leave a certain degree of openness in the structuring of the research questions, in the formulation of the research **sample**, and in the design of interview questions/ observational schedules and so on. In 'From literature review to a research question' p.78, this openness is examined in the movement from literature review to research question and then on towards research design, conduct and analysis. This movement is, crucially, not a one-way street. The relationship between literature, question formation, **data collection** and theory building in qualitative research often involves on-going modification, with data collection leading to emergent theories which themselves redirect the data collection process. It is important to examine the relationship between induction and prior literature. While induction and exploration are key elements within the qualitative tradition, this tradition is itself carried forward within the background literature each researcher carries with them as they enter the field. To what extent can the qualitative researcher suspend such theoretical baggage, and to what extent should they do so? This fluid relationship between theory and data collection is examined in 'Degrees of grounded theory

and sampling in qualitative research' p. 79, with particular reference to the notion of **grounded theory**. Grounded theory offers a particular approach to theory building in the conduct of qualitative research. While formal processes of qualitative data analysis will be examined in Chapters 16 to 19, this chapter outlines how on-going data analysis during the conduct of data collection has become a near standard practice within much qualitative research. 'Ethics of qualitative research' p. 81 addresses the specific ethical issues raised by qualitative research.

Primary data collection or secondary sources?

In the past, and still today, critics of qualitative research have argued that one of the major limitations of such methods is the difficulty other researchers have in getting hold of the original 'data' of qualitative researchers. The relatively open **methodology** characteristic of qualitative research leaves little in the way of a transparent trail and so is harder to replicate. To a degree this is changing with the advent of large capacity computer archives; however, it is in the nature of qualitative research that it will rarely generate the kind of uniformity and transparency characteristic (or at least idealized) in quantitative forms of data collection. Having said this, it should be pointed out that in so far as qualitative research is about the collection of primarily non-numerical data for the purpose of linguistic analysis (the search for interpretive patterns rather than statistical patterns), evaluation of previous qualitative research and the data presented in such work constitutes a form of secondary qualitative analysis. Many of the techniques of qualitative data analysis parallel those of literature reviewing (discussed in 'Reviewing content' p. 10). Likewise, in archival forms of qualitative data collection the methods deployed are very similar to those employed in the conduct of a literature search ('Searching the archives' p. 7). Whether it be ethnographic **monographs**, media discourse analyses, the writing up of interview-based research or any other form of qualitative research, attempting to locate and decode the qualitative research findings of others constitutes a form of qualitative research in itself. Of course, one may wish to go deeper and seek access to the researchers' original field notes, interview transcripts and other texts/artefacts. While rare in the past, this is becoming increasingly possible (see 'Researching rural deprivation' p. 64)

Interviews/observations/archives

Interviews, observations and archives are types of data collection, each of which take many forms (as was seen in the four examples discussed in Chapter 5). This diversity will be described in further detail as this chapter develops, while Chapter 7 will deal with the two fundamental forms of the qualitative interview, first the more traditional one-to-one interview and then the **focus group**, or group **interview**. Each approach has its advantages and disadvantages. You will need to evaluate these in relation to the research you wish to carry out and the resources/experience you have at your disposal. Chapter 8 examines the ethnographic method. Here the researcher spends time with a group of people, observing a way of life. Ethnography will usually also involve interviewing and often the collection of artefacts for analysis. Given the attention to interviewing in Chapters 7 and 8, it is the observational element of ethnography that will receive most attention. Sociologists often prefer to use the term 'participant observation' to describe what anthropologists have traditionally called ethnography. The distinction is porous, but examining it will allow some important themes to emerge (such as between participation and 'passive' observation, and between covert and overt observation). The term case study can apply to any research that is not comparative in nature, that is, where there is only one case. This case may be an individual, an organization or an entire community/culture. Interviews, observations and the collection of text/artefacts may be used. 'Case studies' p. 111 addresses how such techniques are used in the particulars of biographical, life history, organizational and community studies, sometimes ethnographically, but sometimes not. Chapter 9 examines the collection of textual data. The term 'text' has come to mean any artefact that contains or has been given meaning by a culture. From the collection of straightforward printed texts (such as newspapers, government reports, diaries and letters), textual data has come to include television programmes, photographs, art works and so on. As will be seen in Chapter 18 concerning qualitative data

analysis, discourse analysis and 'semiotics' have opened the field of textual interpretation and **hermeneutics** (the study of meaning) to all things human. Ethnomethodology (addressed in Chapter 10) has developed a number of data collection methods to draw out the methods by which people generate and sustain a sense of 'order' in their interactions. Conversation analysis (CA) (see Chapter 10, p. 126) can be seen as a fusion of innovative observation and textual analysis techniques, being the unobtrusive recording of naturally occurring talk for purposes similar to those of ethnomethodology. Both ethnomethodology and CA challenge mainstream social research to work in radically different ways and to different ends.

From literature review to a research question – degrees of closure

As has been pointed out already, qualitative research tends towards a more inductive and exploratory form. This need not be the case. Research that is designed to collect non-numerical forms of data, whether by means of interview, observation, or by the collection of archival materials or artefacts, may be deductive. It is perfectly possible for a researcher to formulate a research question that takes the form of a hypothesis (a prediction that can be tested) and to then seek to test that hypothesis by collecting qualitative data. For example, a researcher might, on the basis of a review of existing literature, hypothesize that male and female students attach different meanings to their education. By interviewing male and female students the researcher may seek to test that hypothesis. The researcher may choose in-depth (that is, qualitative) interviews if they feel that this may offer the best means of identifying the 'meanings' held by students. Other forms of qualitative research methods may be similarly employed to investigate a hypothesis if they are deemed most useful. The reason qualitative research tends to be associated with more inductive and exploratory (that is, non-hypothesis driven) research projects is because the kinds of depth which qualitative methods are said to enable allow the researcher to explore issues by following the priorities and actions of those they are researching. Conversely, quantitative research methods require the researcher to have a well-defined hypothesis so as to enable them to identify exactly what it is they need to measure. Quantification does make testing simpler, as what counts as a positive or negative result is more easily identified in numbers. However, simplicity is not always best. On the basis of a review of existing literature the researcher may be left with a very strong sense of what needs to be measured, a weak sense of the general area that needs to be investigated, or something in between. All empirical research requires the researcher to identify the basic issues and locations they need to investigate. In the loose sense of the term, all researchers start with a 'hunch' of some kind, even if many of these 'hunches' would not be sufficiently precise to be called 'hypotheses'. Where a hunch is not precise enough to be 'tested' (and the researcher may deliberately choose to avoid such precision in order to remain open to new 'leads'), the researcher should adopt a more inductive approach.

Inductive research seeks to build theory on the basis of empirical research (see 'Deduction and Induction' p. 36). This means that the relationship between literature review and data collection will be less prescriptive. There is a greater degree of openness. This, however, does not mean that such forms of qualitative research fail to build upon rigorous foundations within the existing literature. It may well be the case that it is precisely the findings of past research in the particular field in question that suggest to the researcher the need to adopt a more open and exploratory approach. This may be through particular findings or the lack of them. The choice of a more open research design may also flow from existing literature at a higher level of abstraction. The researcher's choice may stem from general theoretical commitments (recall 'The deeper divide' p. 37) developed through that person's career as a social scientist and itself grounded in their past reading, rather than simply their evaluation of research related to a particular topic. In this regard research is never fully inductive, just as it can never be fully open. As was suggested above, openness and closure are the opposite ends of a spectrum. All research sits somewhere between these extremes.

Returning to the example of male and female students and the meaning they attach to their education, the suggestion that males and females may differ in this regard constitutes a very weak hypothesis in itself. If this proposition were bolstered by more precise predictions (such as predictions about the nature of those differences, their manifestations in expressed attitudes, beliefs and behaviours, and their strength), this prediction would begin to take on the characteristics of a fully formed and so testable

hypothesis. If not, then the weak prediction is best not called a hypothesis at all, and may best be called a research question. The former is more open to numerical data collection. The latter is best suited to a more qualitative approach.

It should, however, be recalled (see Chapter 4) at this point that even the most precise hypothesis cannot be translated into a testing instrument without being piloted. Piloting in deductive research (testing the test) will often involve a degree of reformulation. This is usually at the level of the questions to be asked or the observational measures to be taken, rather than of the hypothesis to be tested. However, piloting may throw up new insights that force the researcher to reconsider their hypothesis. As such, this represents an inductive moment (the generation of theory on the basis of empirical observation) even within the most rigorous forms of deductive research (the use of empirical research to test a pre-specified, but as yet tentative, theory). In qualitative research the tendency is to extend this moment by means of more fully inductive data collection techniques. These techniques are what will be explored in this chapter.

Degrees of grounded theory and sampling in qualitative research

The term grounded theory has taken on an almost mythic status in qualitative research. Barney Glaser and Anselm Strauss's (1967) *The Discovery of Grounded Theory* sought to demonstrate how theory could be built through the conduct of qualitative research. By theory Glaser and Strauss mean concept formation. While the conduct of deductive and quantitative research requires that the researcher operationalize their **concepts** (identifying how abstract concepts can be turned into measurable categories/variables) prior to then 'going out' and measuring the incidence and/or levels of them, grounded theory offers a methodology for allowing concepts to be generated in the course of empirical research. **Emergence** refers to the way in which the researcher seeks to formulate and clarify a picture of the world they are studying by identifying categories that capture what is going on. Through various forms of qualitative data collection (and even the collection of numerical data), the researcher seeks to identify patterns. They then seek to formulate concepts that capture such patterns, in other words which *best* describe what is going on in the data. Best is not a static term. On reflection, after initial investigations the researcher formulates what they think are strong **descriptive** tools, concepts that seem to capture the situation. The researcher then needs to further investigate the power of such descriptions through further research. This will often require that initial concepts be reformulated or even abandoned. New or refashioned concepts may then emerge to face a new round of examination. Grounded theory thereby seeks to build a picture of events that best fits that situation. Grounded theory is an explicit reaction to the kinds of deductive research that seek to apply 'grand theory' empirically by means of hypothesis testing. It should be noted, however, that grounded theory is not simply a form of inductive theory building. A straightforwardly inductive form of theory building would conduct data collection and then seek to build theories afterwards. Grounded theory seeks to fold induction into deduction back and forth, collecting data, formulating tentative theories and then seeking to test these with new data collection and analysis, which itself may lead to more than just testing (as it may lead to the generation of new concepts). This cycle of data collection, theory building, testing and reformulation carries on (ideally) until the point of **saturation**. Saturation refers to the point at which the currently held set of concepts seems reasonably able to describe and even predict the situation they seek to theorize. Of course, no theory can fully predict every aspect of a situation or field, and likewise, no research project can go on forever. As such the researcher must make a judgement about the validity of their theory relative to the resources they have available to continue their research.

Whilst grounded theory is not the only approach to qualitative research, it does highlight a more general characteristic of qualitative research, which is the fluid relationship between data collection and data analysis. Whilst piloting in quantitative research often involves the reformulation of how research questions are to be posed empirically, it is less common that the research question, and the basic concepts and categories being used, are reformulated. This is precisely what grounded theory seeks to facilitate. In grounded theory, data collected at each stage requires analysis prior to moving on to the next round of data collection. Whilst forms of qualitative data analysis are to be discussed in more detail in Chapters 16 to 19, it is important at this stage to point out that data analysis is an essential stage in the development of more grounded forms of data collection.

Sampling

The conduct of quantitative data collection requires a clear and pre-emptive specification of the key concepts and their translation into measurable categories/variables. Qualitative research more often seeks to retain a degree of openness such that data collection enables the formulation of such concepts rather than their testing. As such the process of sampling in qualitative research design tends to differ in its aims and its method from sampling in quantitative research. Qualitative research tends to be exploratory. One aspect of exploration may be exploring the identity of those you are seeking to research. It is often not possible to specify in advance exactly who you are interested in. Research into issues such as homelessness, racism and alcoholism does not present the researcher with target groups whose members are 'registered' or even easily identifiable. Part of the exploratory process may be to find these people. It is not possible in such cases to draw a random sample, as there is no sampling frame (a list of all members) from which to randomly select (see Chapter 13 for a discussion of formal sampling methods). Of course, a non-random sample group can be researched using a quantitative questionnaire, just as a statistically random sample group can be researched using qualitative interviews. How one generates a sample does not dictate the subsequent research instruments used. However, the use of qualitative data collection methods may be useful in the generation of subsequent members of a snowball sample. In-depth interviewing or participant observation and so on may enable the researcher to identify where to look next or who to talk to next. In the same way that responses to **open-ended questions** may generate theoretical insights, so they may offer new leads in the identification of research subjects. As such, qualitative research is often associated with exploratory, or snowball, sampling. In such situations, where a sample is built up through information provided in the last stage of data collection, the same principles of validity and saturation (discussed earlier in this section) apply as they did in the case of concept formation and theory building. A sample would be sufficient when the current round of theory building provides sufficient insight such that subsequent sample members' identities and responses/behaviours are predictable. Even in the conduct of a case study, where one organization or group is chosen, and so, in terms of statistical sampling theory, the results cannot be readily generalized from, it is still possible to sample respondents within that group or organization in a formally random fashion if a sampling frame can be devised or found. It is essential that the social researcher choosing qualitative methods understands quantitative techniques, and vice versa. This is not only true in cases when using mixed methods (as highlighted in Chapter 5), but even when one approach is selected. A choice based on understanding is far better than doing only one because you don't understand the other. Regarding sampling, it is therefore essential to read Chapter 13.

Ethics of qualitative research

As has been discussed in Chapter 2, social research requires ethical consideration at all stages; in the decision to research one topic over another, in choosing one method over another, in the conduct of data collection and analysis, and in the dissemination of findings (as well as in limiting the dissemination of such identifiers as might damage research participants). Qualitative research offers advantages, but also presents difficulties at each of these stages in the research process.

The traditions of qualitative research arose largely as a reaction to the positivism of quantitative social research and its attempts to replicate the methods of the 'natural' sciences. Many qualitative researchers see their methods as an active attempt to avoid the reduction of their participants to the status of objects. The more inductive approach favoured in much qualitative research is said to give more of a voice to those being researched, allowing them a greater power to direct the flow of the research. The use of more open-ended forms of data collection enables the words of the researched to come through, rather than for their beliefs, values and behaviours to be tightly filtered and boxed through the deductive researcher's prescriptive categories and scales.

Perhaps the most famous (if very often misunderstood) article published on the subject of the ethics of qualitative research is Howard Becker's 'Whose side are we on?' (1967). As noted in 'Ethical issues in the decision to research' p. 17, Becker suggested that by researching society's 'underdogs', and in unearthing their way of looking at the world by means of in-depth interviewing, participant observation and so on, those in authority will inevitably accuse the researcher of being biased in

favour of those they have researched (the accusation of 'going native'). Presenting 'their story' from 'their point of view' will often be taken to be advocating rather than simply representing. However, many subsequent researchers have taken Becker to be suggesting that the researcher cannot be neutral and so must choose to use their research to support either authority or the underdogs. Qualitative research is seen as ideally suited to the task of demonstrating the validity of ways of life and belief that may be otherwise misunderstood. Forms of participant observation allow the researcher to combine research with involvement within an organization or movement they feel is worthy of their support. Participatory action research (PAR) involves the researcher conducting research in order to actively forward the goals of an organization (Whyte, 1991a, 1991b; see also 'Evaluation, participation and action research' p. 29 and 'Evaluation' p. 53). As such the researcher is involved with the goals of the organization and the members of the organization are actively involved in shaping the direction of the research. Many qualitative researchers investigating new social movements (such as feminism, ecology and so on) have argued that the role of advocate is not at odds with the role of social researcher (Harries-Jones, 1991). They suggest that the idea of value freedom is a myth and that the detachment of researcher from the researched simply allows the researcher to become a social engineer, researching in order to better manage society's troublesome misfits and outcasts. However, not all feminist writers accept that only qualitative forms of research can fully grasp the truth about women's lives in a manner that does not distort or even oppress (Maynard, 1998; Oakley, 2000). Similarly, not all qualitative researchers are comfortable with the idea that social research needs to abandon any commitment to standards of objectivity and neutrality in the conduct of research. Becker himself was keen to assert that while qualitative research was always likely to be accused of bias in favour of those being researched, it was still the job of the researcher to present that way of seeing/way of life in as truthful a fashion as possible (Hammersley, 2000; David, 2002).

This raises the ethical question of 'truth'. While the qualitative researcher may wish to claim greater depth validity, more quantitative researchers often claim that their ability to deliver greater reliability and generalizability offers 'more' truth. This is a thorny dispute that cannot be resolved here. It is only possible to note the importance of truth as an ethical criterion in social research. It is questionable as to whether social research would be worthwhile if truth were not a goal, even if one that could never be fully achieved (Hammersley, 2000; David, 2002).

While advocates of qualitative research have tended to advance the virtues of depth as both a means of gathering data and of retaining an ethical relationship with those who are being researched, it is important to note that there are ethical difficulties with such an approach to data collection. The conduct of in-depth interviews, ethnographic observation and so on gives a greater opportunity for those researched to expose themselves to harm by revealing damaging or threatening facts and opinions. This may, in the first instance, be to the researcher. However, the smaller sample size characteristic of qualitative research makes it harder to hide the identity of respondents in subsequent dissemination of research findings. Where the respondents to a written questionnaire may be able to avoid personal disclosure, the face-to-face interview offers less protection. The researcher in such situations must be all the more conscious of the dangers involved in researching sensitive topics (Lee, 1993). Likewise, the qualitative researcher must be doubly conscious of the need to protect the confidentiality of those they research, both from the wider audience and from other participants in the research. This latter task is particularly problematic as it is in the nature of qualitative research to offer depth, whilst at the same time the researcher needs to prevent such depth insight rebounding negatively upon those researched. It is not possible in the context of a focus group interview to avoid disclosure to other participants what is disclosed to the interviewer. It is

therefore not advisable to deal with highly-sensitive subjects using focus groups.

Finally, there is the issue of consent, which raises some particular problems for certain forms of qualitative research. The qualitative interview (whether one-to-one or in a focus group format) offers the researcher plenty of opportunity to clarify issues with the interviewees. However, forms of archival research and observational research are more problematic. The classical experimental form of observation has been criticized as often the research subject is not told the purpose of the research until debriefing, giving them no opportunity to withdraw. Forms of overt participant observation, where the researcher is open about their role as researcher, allow a greater dialogue. However, even the most overt participant observer may find it hard to inform everyone they meet in the course of their research about their researcher role. As such, not everyone is able to give informed consent. This is, of course, all the more true in covert forms of participant observation where the researcher does not disclose their researcher identity. Quantitative archival data will tend to be in a format that does not identify individual respondents. However, qualitative archival materials, whether these are primary sources such as diaries and letters, or secondary sources, such as field notes and interview transcripts, may contain more explicit personal identifiers. Often the advantage of archival materials is that the authors are not otherwise accessible (the older the archives, the more likely this is to be the case). Whilst this makes the archive a useful source, there is still the question of whether it is right to unearth personal details about people who have not consented to this taking place.

Summary

Qualitative research design is commonly associated with more exploratory and descriptive forms of research design, though this need not be the case. Forms of grounded theory, where inductive exploration precedes more deductive forms of testing theories emerging from earlier exploration are also common, and some forms of qualitative research test hypotheses and/or seek to identify causal relationships. Qualitative forms of research have been advocated on the grounds that the more open-ended forms of data collection are ethically (as well as empirically) advantageous, giving those researched a stronger voice and say in the direction of the research. However, qualitative data collection techniques and the data itself also generate greater scope for intrusion upon privacy, non-informed consent and exposure to harm through the revelation of potentially damaging personal information either at the point of data collection or in subsequent publication/presentation.

Keywords

Artefacts	Grounded Theory	Open-ended Questions
Concept	Hermeneutics	Qualitative
Data Collection	In-depth Interview	Quantitative
Deduction	Induction	Research Design
Description	Methodology	Sample
Emergence	Monograph	Saturation
Exploration		

Questions

1   Why is qualitative data collection most often associated with exploratory and descriptive research questions?

2   How do qualitative researchers seek to avoid premature 'closure' in their data-collection, what does this mean, and why do they seek to do it?

3   In what ways are the practical advantages of qualitative research also the sources of significant ethical dangers?

4   What is grounded theory?

5   What issues have led some qualitative researchers to use non-random sampling techniques, and how do such sampling methods differ from random sampling?

Further reading

Becker, Howard (1967) 'Whose side are we on?', *Social Problems*, 14: 239–47.

Berg, Bruce L. (1998) *Qualitative Research Methods for the Social Sciences*. Needham Heights, MA: Allyn and Bacon.

Glaser, Barney and Strauss, Anselm (1967) *The Discovery of Grounded Theory: Strategies for Qualitative Research*. Chicago, IL: Aldine.

Hammersley, Martyn (2000) *Taking Sides in Social Research: Essays on Partisanship and Bias*. London: Routledge.

Lee, Raymond (1993) *Doing Research on Sensitive Topics*. London: Sage.

Whyte, William Foote (ed.) (1991a) *Participatory Action Research*. London: Sage.

Whyte, William Foote (1991b) *Social Theory for Action: How Individuals and Organizations Learn to Change*. London: Sage.

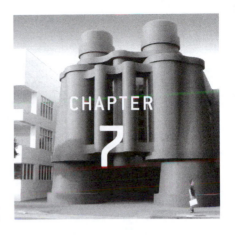

CHAPTER
7

QUALITATIVE INTERVIEWING:
ONE-TO-ONE AND FOCUS GROUPS

Chapter contents

By the end of this chapter you will be able to:

- Identify the advantages and disadvantages of interview-based data collection methods.

- Distinguish the value and limitations, in relation to particular research questions, of one-to-one and group-based interviews.

- Outline key elements within the design of interview questions and interview schedules.

- Specify the range of choices that exist, and the reasons for choosing between them, when sampling for focus groups and for the composition of individual groups.

- Understand the difficulties involved, and the steps required to minimize difficulties, when recording and transcribing interview materials.

Qualitative interviewing

Interviewing involves asking people questions, but it is equally about listening carefully to the answers given. Not all questions are best answered by means of an **interview**. In some cases, observations or records may be better. The qualitative (or in-depth) interview takes many forms. Such interviews may be one-off and one-to-one, as used by Sutton and Sheaff, and discussed in Chapter 5. Alternatively, interviews can be cumulative (returning to the same person a number of times), as was the case in Regan de Bere et al. (discussed in Chapter 5), or group based (to be discussed in this chapter). They may be a combination of the above. Qualitative interviewing may be combined with observational and archival research. Ethnography and case study research often involve qualitative interviewing. Qualitative interviews are most often face-to-face, but may be carried out over the telephone or by computer. The thing that makes an interview qualitative lies in the formatting of the questions and the scope made available for the interviewee to answer. We can distinguish structured and unstructured interviews, as well as standardized and unstandardized interviews. Structure refers to the degree to which the form and order of questions asked are kept identical from interview to interview. The structured interview seeks to maintain high levels of reliability and repeatability. The more unstructured interview seeks to emphasize the depth validity of each individual interview; the attempt to let the interviewee tell their story and so determine to a greater extent the flow of the dialogue. Standardization refers to the level of closure placed around the answers interviewees can give. Closed answers allow greater scope for quantification. Open answers allow for greater depth and personal detail, but are harder to compare numerically. The qualitative interview is that which tends towards the unstructured and the unstandardized, though the spectrum from semi-structured to unstructured, and between semi-standardized and unstandardized is a broad one. Some interviews are formally arranged and timetabled as interviews. Other kinds of interviewing may be less formal and almost spontaneous (for instance, an unscheduled exchange that occurs between a participant observer and an informant). The more informal, unstructured and unstandardized an interview is, the more the interviewer needs to work during the conduct of the interview. Berg (1998, Ch. 4) refers to the drama of the interview. The interviewer is performer, audience and choreographer. When the script is flexible, the qualitative interviewer must be all the more prepared for the role they are to perform.

Designing open-ended questions and semi-structured interview schedules

So what is it that you want to know? Whilst a qualitative interview is unlikely to start from the desire to test a specific hypothesis, it is still necessary to start with an outline of what you are seeking to investigate. This reflection allows the researcher to draw up a list of key themes around which interviews can be built with varying degrees of structure and standardization. These reflections will be, in part, on the background literature you have identified and your own interpretations of this material. Reflections may also be on previous data collection, whether in the form of interviews, observations or archival materials. It should be remembered that grounded theorists recommend that the qualitative researcher should shift the emphasis of their questioning as they go along, based on their previous rounds of data collection. Once a set of key themes has been identified, the researcher will then want to take each key theme one at a time and identify specific questions that may allow them to probe that theme in more detail. In the course of an interview the researcher may choose to follow the set of themes and sub-questions in a relatively structured fashion. However, they may prefer to keep the set of themes and sub-questions as an **aide-mémoire**, from which to return during the course of the interview, but which does not dictate the order. In highly unstructured interviewing (such as where a participant observer engages in spontaneous conversations with informants) the value of the setting out of key themes and sub-questions in advance lies in giving the researcher a sense of order from which to draw questions from unplanned encounters. Even when no written record of such questions is to hand, the

BOX 7.1 SEMI-STRUCTURED INTERVIEW *AIDE-MÉMOIRE*

Training, strategy, information and local knowledge: a study of small and medium sized enterprises in Cornwall, Devon and Somerset

Dr Matthew David, Senior Lecturer in Sociology, University of Plymouth

1 Brief introduction to you and the business.
2 Issues of size, number of employees, types of employee (age, qualifications, geographical recruitment and so on)
3 How do you identify the skills that people need to work here?
4 How do you expect/encourage those who work here to gain the skills required?
5 How do you find out about training provision, if at all?
6 How do you gauge the success of your 'on-the-job' training?
7 For 'off-the-job' training, what are the issues that you have come up against when trying to set training needs against other needs?
8 What support have you been able to get in promoting staff development?
9 Does your company have a formal training strategy? If so, how is this strategy identified and put into effect?
10 Does your company have a training manager? If so, how does their job fit within the overall management of the enterprise?
11 Does your company have a training budget? If so, how is this calculated and allocated?
12 Do you or your company have 'networked' computing facilities (most particularly the ability to access the World Wide Web on your computer/computers)? If so, who uses them, how did they get trained, do others working here learn from them, and what is it that these machines are used for?
13 If you were able to ask for tailor-made training, what is it that you would ask for, and how would you like it to be delivered?
14 When you need to know something about training, who are the people you talk to (for example, friends, people you work with, local agencies, government bodies, local and national associations)?

process of reflection in advance aids the researcher's sense of clarity. In this sense even the most seemingly unstructured interview involves a degree of structure. This element of structure is what distinguishes an interview from a casual conversation. An interview is a conversation with a purpose (Burgess, 1984). The purpose is clarified in the act of setting out themes and sub-questions, even if these do not become a formal interview schedule (or a questionnaire). The questions set out in Box 7.1 could be asked one after the other in exactly the form written, or the questions could be used as prompts to be ticked off in any order they may best be fitted into a less structured discussion.

Question types

Questions may be of a number of different types. Warm-up questions seek to establish trust and rapport with the respondent. Demographic questions elicit factual data about the respondent (age, sex, occupation and so on). Core questions address key themes of the research. Prompts and probes seek to elicit additional information about a core question (for example, 'Can you say a little more about that?'). Clarifying questions seek to check the meaning of a response (for example, 'What do you mean by that?'). Clarifying questions may ask a different question that approaches the same theme from another angle. Practising the generation of core, clarifying and probing questions and so on increases the ability of the researcher to react creatively to the answers they are given. Just as in music, practising the elements better enables the performer to play 'spontaneously' and in tune with those around them.

Piloting

Once the researcher has generated a set of questions relating to each of the key themes, it is necessary to pilot these questions. These questions are the basis for the researcher's interaction with their interviewees. Questions are a bridge between the two sides. Faults in the questions may lead to faulty information passing between the two sides. The first step in the piloting process will involve showing your provisional themes and questions to colleagues and experts in the field for their critical review. Second, it is important to interview a small number of people from your target population. Language is the key to the interview. It is the medium through which data is collected/generated. It is essential that questions be asked in a language that the interviewee can make sense of, and which is understood in the same sense that the interviewer intends. An essential part of the piloting process is to conduct the interview and then talk over with the interviewee what (if anything) they understood by each question. If you are interested in what people believe, rather than their behaviour, it is important that this be clearly communicated. If you are interested in what people do rather than what they say, you have another serious issue. This concerns motivation. What motivates an interviewee to answer questions? How can the interviewer put their respondents at their ease, win their trust and gain their interest and enthusiasm? Piloting may highlight hidden resentments and resistances. Questions may give rise to offence. Asking people about social status, money, sexuality, religious beliefs, the success (or failure) of their children at school and so on all require the greatest tact and sensitivity.

Understanding the question and wanting to answer are not the only potential weak points in an interview. It is possible that questions may address things that the interviewee is unable to answer. A respondent may not have access to certain kinds of information, even about themselves. Interviewing people about their own lives is not always able to generate all the detail you might wish for. People's own lives are not entirely transparent even to themselves.

Finally, it is essential to ask pilot respondents whether they felt the interview was leading or biased in any way. Of course, the purpose of the interview directs it to some extent, but it is important to ask the pilot interviewees how they experienced the interview. Did they feel they were able to express their point of view effectively? Did they feel the questions asked addressed the core features of the area as they see it? There is a great danger that questions contain built-in bias. Feedback from experts, peers and pilot interviewees should be directed to this issue. Also, the tendency to introduce bias in prompts and probes is something which, at least in part, is the result of inexperience. In everyday conversation we seek to support or disagree with the person we are talking to. Whether it is in body language or in words we often encourage or discourage lines of discussion without really knowing we are doing it. It may be necessary to learn to avoid saying Yes or No, or 'That's right!' when an interviewee comes to the end of an answer. It may be necessary to learn to say more neutral things, such as 'That's interesting', or 'Can you tell me more about that?'. Piloting may be an opportunity to learn about yourself in relation to the topic at hand and the people you will be interviewing, and to confront your own biases and preconceptions. Piloting also allows the researcher to gain a reasonable idea of how long interviews are likely to take. This is important when arranging interviews as locations, interviewees and interviewer need to be co-ordinated and informed (and in some cases booked).

The conduct of qualitative interviewing

As has been already mentioned, the interview situation is itself a social interaction. Both parties in an interview are playing roles in a situation loaded with many potential meanings. The notion of **interviewer bias** does not simply refer to the way in which questions might be asked and how answers are responded to. Interviewer bias refers to the whole character of the interviewer and the impact this may have on the responses of the interviewee. The sex/gender, class/status, ethnicity and appearance/behaviour of the interviewer may impact on the interviewee's sense of the interview situation. This in turn may impact on their 'talk', or lack of it. The sense of social difference or distance may create tension and defensiveness. Depending upon the nature of the questions to be asked it may be more or less possible (for example) for women to interview men, middle-class interviewers to interview working-class respondents, or for white researchers to interview black interviewees successfully. Such interactions may generate talk that is as much the product of the dynamics of the interview situation as it is a reflection of the interviewees' everyday lives. Postmodern social theorists have suggested that all data is only ever the product of such dynamics. Others seek to identify methods of reducing such bias. One such method might be to use more than one interviewer (male and female for example). This would enable comparison of

BOX 7.2 TEN COMMANDMENTS OF INTERVIEWING

On the basis of extensive practice as a qualitative interviewer, Berg (1998: 87–8) suggests Ten Commandments of interviewing:

1   Never begin cold: always warm up with light, chatty conversation.
2   Remember your purpose.
3   Present a natural front.
4   Demonstrate aware hearing: be attentive and be seen to be so.
5   Think about appearance.
6   Interview in a comfortable place.
7   Don't be satisfied with mono-syllabic answers: use probes and prompts.
8   Be respectful.
9   Practice.
10   Be cordial and appropriate.

results to identify interviewer effects. Having more than one interviewer raises serious issues about interviewer training, but these are not directly relevant to this text. As beginners, you are unlikely to be asked or able to recruit your own team of interviewers.

The setting and timing of an interview may have similar implications. The researcher needs to take all these things into account when setting up interviews. It is important for the researcher to identify a time and place where the interviewee is going to feel comfortable and where the interview itself can be conducted without interruption. This may create a tension. Naturalistic settings, such as in the interviewee's home or workplace, may have advantages of comfort and security for the interviewee (this may not always be the case). However, they are also prone to interruption. In addition, the use of recording equipment, whilst highly recommended in terms of capturing the fullness of the interaction, may be off-putting to the interviewee. Professional actors train long and hard to avoid drying up when confronted with an audience or a recording device, yet it still happens. The impact of such things on interviewees should not be underestimated. All these factors make the interview a situation which the researcher has to work very hard to manage. Making the interviewee feel comfortable requires confidence, experience and sensitivity. These things can only be developed through practice. See Box 7.2 for some useful guidelines.

Any interview will be 'bracketed' by what goes before and what comes after. Contacting potential interviewees, identifying yourself, exploring the suitability of the potential participant, explaining the purpose and time requirements of the research, asking for participation, arranging time and location and so on, are all performances designed to win trust, display integrity and establish rapport. It is as well to set out an *aide-mémoire* for the recruitment process, as this interaction is very similar in nature to the interviewing it pre-empts, and is prone to many of the same pitfalls. It is essential that the right to withdraw from research, the right to informed consent and to **confidentiality/ anonymity** are explained to potential interviewees in advance (see 'Sensitivity in the conduct of research' p. 18). When recruiting an interview **sample** from a sampling frame it is often the case that contact is made by letter (paper or electronic) when requesting participation. This letter should outline the above information clearly (for a further discussion of the construction of covering letters, see Chapters 14 and 15).

In this sense, warming up starts long before the microphone is switched on. Creating the interview situation may involve booking rooms, arranging soft drinks and snacks (preferably non-crunchy ones, which challenge even the best tape-recorders), getting to locations in good time, having functioning recording equipment (check and check again), having all the necessary paperwork (prompts, interview schedule or *aide-mémoire*, identification documents and/or any explanatory materials you may need to clarify issues with the interviewee) to hand. Maintaining all this while appearing unflustered is something that requires plenty of practice and a good bag.

In the case of informal interviews, such as

conversations that crop up in the course of participant observation, all the above preparation cannot be set in motion in advance of the encounter. Nevertheless, establishing a strong sense of what you are interested in and of how to ask questions in a manner meaningful to the other person and which are not biased allow even the most spontaneous encounter to generate fruitful data. In such situations one may ask if it is possible to record the interaction (either on audiotape or on paper). However, when this is not possible it may be necessary to write extensive notes on the encounter immediately after it occurs. Once again your good bag is essential, in which to keep tape-recorder and/or paper and pencil/pen.

Once an interview gets underway the interview schedule or set of prompts/*aide-mémoire* should allow you to set the course of the conversation without forcing the pace or direction of the talk unduly. As a beginner, you may feel more comfortable with fully-scripted questions, but with practice you will gain more confidence. Confidence is most fully expressed in the ability to keep silent, or to gently encourage the respondent to carry on with what they are talking about. Being attentive to both the interviewee's talk and your own themes requires a level of skill that comes only with practice. Having a go and making mistakes is part and parcel of becoming a researcher. Don't expect to get it right first time. Your first few interviews will teach you more about yourself than about the person you are talking to. Luckily, piloting offers some scope to practice before formal data collection.

The length of qualitative interviews (even with the same set of questions) may vary considerably. Take spare tapes and batteries. Try to book a time and space that will allow for a degree of spill-over. Nevertheless, it is respectful to avoid pushing the respondent to go beyond a loosely agreed time limit. It is useful to give an estimated time limit when arranging an interview, but suggest the need to be flexible in advance. It may be the case that you will want to speak to the same respondent again after an initial interview. This may be part of a design for cumulative interviewing, or it may be something that turns out that way. Be flexible, grateful and polite. If you find a particular respondent fascinating, tell them so at the end. If you found them deadly boring, it is better not to tell them.

Once an interview is over and the tape-recorder is switched off, ask the interviewee what they felt about the interview. This may elicit very valuable material, both about the subject being researched and the handling of the interview itself. Both types of information may be more freely given once the tape-recorder is turned off, and you may want to ask if you can take a few notes. If this request is made in terms of how useful the interviewee's comments would be to the research, and to the researcher, it is usually not a problem, but this is not always true and consent should never be taken for granted. After thanking the interviewee, and separating, it is essential that you write down your own experiences of the interview. This gives you the chance to reflect upon the strengths and weaknesses of your own practice, and allows you to identify things that might be improved upon, as well as emerging themes to build into future data collection. It is also insurance against a faulty tape-recorder.

The recording, transcribing and storage of qualitative interviews

All forms of data collection are prone to complications. One of the key features of qualitative interviewing is that the direction and duration of the interview is relatively open. As such the interviewer needs to be prepared for an interview that may go on for longer than initially expected. Always take additional tapes if you are going to record an interview. Also, as has been mentioned, check your recording equipment (see Box 7.3).

Transcription of interview data is time-consuming and often highly taxing. Even with a good transcribing machine it is still likely to take between three and six times as long to transcribe an interview as it took to record. If there is a lot of background noise or if the voices are not clear on the tape, you can add extra time. It is possible to get transcription done for you by a professional typist, but this is expensive and takes you one step away from your own data. The hours of listening required to transcribe a tape are often the best way of gaining a fine-grained knowledge of your own data. While software can now assist you in qualitative data analysis it cannot bypass the need to have a feel for the talk, which only time can provide.

Always keep in mind that in-depth interview data is rich in the personal details of those from whom it is collected. As such there are ethical implications to be considered when storing it in a form that others may be able to access. It is worth recalling that it is best practice to ensure that personal identifiers are separated from other data and stored in a separate format (see Chapter 2).

BOX 7.3 ALWAYS CHECK YOUR RECORDING EQUIPMENT!

As a researcher, one of the authors was once asked to carry out a set of interviews. The project director was confident that his tape-recorder was very sturdy and reliable. It had been up mountains, into swamps and through forests and thickets. In the event the first interview, when played back, sounded as though the interview had been conducted in a combination of all the above locations. A new tape-recorder was immediately acquired.

The same person conducted a focus group interview. It took some time to arrange. Sadly, it was forgotten that the microphone had a separate on/off switch in addition to the record button on the tape-recorder itself. Apart from handwritten notes of the event, the discussion was lost. It is always a good idea to take some written notes during an interview and to write up your experiences as soon as the interview is over. It is an even better idea to turn your microphone on. Best of all, do both!

Focus group interviewing

Some research questions can best be 'asked' (or addressed) by actually asking people questions directly (in interviews or questionnaires). Other topics may be better suited to more unobtrusive or observation-based methods. When asking questions directly, it may not always be best to ask these questions in a one-to-one interview format. Sometimes asking a group of people to discuss a question, or a set of questions, may generate more useful and interesting data. An example of a focus group interview prompt sheet is given in Box 7.4.

Form and function

The **focus group** is a group **interview** rather than the more stereotypical one-to-one interview. Formally developed in the social sciences in the 1940s, the focus group method of data collection was taken up mainly in market research in the decades that followed. The focus group has become more popular again in the social sciences only since the 1980s. The focus group takes a number of forms. While this diversity has led some to argue over what should and should not be counted as a focus group, David L. Morgan (1997) argues that such debate is not helpful and it is most useful to reflect on what form best suits the research you want to carry out. Focus groups may be relatively highly structured to generate data that can easily be compared with that from other focus group interviews (with different types of interviewees). This enables strong comparison between the groups selected to participate. Focus groups may be relatively unstructured to enable **exploration** rather than strict comparability. Those selected to participate in the interview may be experts in their field. Such interviews are designed to elicit debate at the cutting edge of that particular field. Such focus groups are called **Delphi groups**. Other groups consist of non-experts. Such groups may be made up of individuals with certain common characteristics (age, gender, ethnicity or class for example). This enables the researcher to compare the characteristics of such groups with reference to the issues being discussed by comparing the discussions in different groups. Alternatively, the groups may be made up of individuals with a diverse array of characteristics. This may enable the study of how such differences play off against each other in the individual group interviews. Groups may vary in size. Groups may be made up of strangers or of people who already know each other. Groups may be assembled by the researcher, or the researcher may 'take advantage' of naturally occurring group interactions, which they may either intervene in or observe more passively. Of course, presence in a group may have an effect, therefore no observation is totally passive.

The purpose of focus groups is to use the interaction between a group of interviewees to generate discussion about a topic. This discussion, it is hoped, will be more detailed and wide-ranging than would result from a one-to-one interview. Focus group interviews also hold out the possibility of giving the interviewees greater control of the talk as they bounce off each other, rather than simply with the interviewer. The focus group then works by means of creating a group dynamic. This dynamic (people feeding off each other) may be a means to an end, a way of generating more data on the topic being discussed. Alternatively, the group interview may seek to study group dynamics as a social phenomenon in itself. How do individuals

BOX 7.4 FOCUS GROUP INTERVIEW PROMPT SHEET

Dr Mike Sheaff, School of Sociology, Politics and Law, University of Plymouth, UK.

Interview schedule

Headings and questions in bold indicate the main themes and focus for the discussion at each stage. Subsequent questions in parentheses are illustrative follow-up questions.

Introduction

Focus of project on inter-professional relationships within multi-disciplinary team working in the field of learning disability – discussions being conducted in three locations.

Interest in work relationships and systems – not inter-personal relationships. Project organized through the University of Plymouth on behalf of the South West Association of Learning Disability.

Confidentiality and right to withdraw.

Informal, semi-structured, discussion.

Experiences

What difference has the co-location of teams meant for your own work?
(Do you think client experiences have changed?)
(What have been the positive and negative aspects of the change?)
(Have there been differences within the team – for example, between different professional/admin groups?)

Relationships

What impact has the changed system had on work relationships within the team?
(Are professional boundaries and roles less clearly defined?)
(What changes have occurred in communication and understanding within the team?)
(What have been the benefits and difficulties in having a single manager across disciplines?)

Change process

What involvement did you have in the process of change?
(Was any involvement as an individual or as a team?)
(Were there any particular problems or issues that arose?)

General

How would you assess the changed working arrangements overall?

react to others? How might consensus or conflict emerge in a group? What is the role of leaders in group opinion formation? These are fascinating questions. However, group dynamics in focus groups tends to be the means to other ends (getting data about topic X), rather than being the subject of study in itself. This is unfortunate, as much of the debate over the value of focus group methods hinges on whether group dynamics generates depth or bias.

The focus group is used in a number of ways. It may be used as a piloting device to explore a topic area or to investigate the **validity** of a survey that is being prepared. It may be used as a **post-primary** research tool, to clarify results generated by other means.

Alternatively, the focus group may be used as a part of a multi-method approach. Also there is the use of the focus group to study group dynamics (as mentioned above). Finally, focus groups can be used as a means of consciousness raising; here research is designed not simply to increase the researcher's knowledge of the group being studied, but to increase the group's understanding of themselves (see Chapter 3). It can be argued that the focus group is democratic and participatory, giving more power to the interviewees. The ethics of focus groups are discussed in the next section along with the advantages and disadvantages in general.

The advantages and disadvantages of focus groups: ethical and practical

The longstanding and extensive use of focus groups in market research, and their more recent adoption by political parties looking to tailor their language and policies to 'key' voter groups (those most likely to switch their votes), has led many to suspect focus groups of being a cheap and superficial device, open to abuse in:

- selecting participants;
- directing discussion; and
- interpreting responses in a biased fashion.

All three abuses exist, and it is not in the power of textbook authors to change the motives and manipulations of those who would abuse research for economic or political advantage. That similar abuses can be effected in the design of public opinion and marketing questionnaires (through the use of leading questions, unrepresentative samples and selective interpretation of results) does suggest that the problem is with the user, not with the method used.

While focus groups offer the ethical advantage of giving the participants greater control over the direction of the discussion, the ethical downside is that given the group nature of the talk, the researcher is unable to offer the degree of confidentiality available in a one-to-one interview format. This may have more than just ethical implications, as members of the group may not give full accounts of sensitive issues in such a setting, thus weakening the depth validity of any data collected.

As mentioned above, the group interview offers the advantage of allowing the talk of members of the group to stimulate other members of the group.

However, there is the danger that dominant individuals within a group may come to dominate the discussion, either in terms of setting the tone or in terms of the amount of time they spend talking. This may lead to a discussion in which less dominant individuals either don't say very much or tend to go along with the views of more vocal participants. This possibility requires that the focus group leader (often referred to as the facilitator or moderator) works hard to counter the dominance of particular individuals in the group. It may be the case that the facilitator can use the strong opinions of one participant to draw out alternative views from others. This requires that the facilitator be prepared to intervene. Just as in the one-to-one interview where the use of prompts and probes can be used to keep a fairly open-ended dialogue within the broad boundaries of the researcher's remit, so even a fairly unstructured focus group may require a strong degree of management. This involves setting ground rules before the discussion gets under way so that the group can, in part, manage itself. Degrees of self-management/facilitator intervention vary. The need for ground rules does not (Box 7.5 on p. 97 for a basic set of such rules). The focus group is not an open forum.

Another related issue is the way different groups may generate different responses. If the group know each other this may have effects on what they say or don't say. There is evidence that men say different things about women if there are women in the group, and vice versa (Wight, 1994, cited in Morgan, 1997: 12). A group of people brought together as members of a particular group are more likely to conform to stereotypical characteristics that are associated with that group (Morley, 1980). The tension between a group dynamic that encourages group identification and one that encourages differentiation cannot easily be resolved. The next section on group composition and size will seek to address the issue in more detail.

Once the focus group facilitator recognizes the need to 'manage' the group dialogue, they must confront the danger of the group tending towards pleasing the facilitator in their discussion. While the facilitator may wish to avoid letting dominant individuals in the group enforce a pre-emptive consensus, they must also avoid the tendency of imposing their own 'correct' responses, even as they still seek to set the broad framework for discussion. This requires a high degree of preparation in setting out prompts and probes that are stimulating but which do not direct the group to one opinion or another. Just as with any research instrument, designing good questions is as important as getting them answered.

Focus groups are not a cheap and quick data collection method. They require a great deal of preparation and organization. Data is also hard to record, transcribe and analyse. However, such groups do offer a way of talking to a number of people at the same time, and getting them to interact may stimulate insights. One hour spent with eight people (group size will be discussed shortly) may generate more data than one hour spent with one person. However, one hour spent with eight people in a focus group does not generate as much detail as eight one-hour interviews with eight individuals. Fern (1982) found that a focus group generated only about 70 per cent of the 'original ideas' that were generated by a set of one-to-one interviews with the same number of individuals. Of course, this still means that one focus group interview generates more ideas than a single one-to-one interview, but a focus group with eight participants is not the equivalent to eight separate interviews.

Composition and size

The central questions around focus group composition are:

- Strangers or existing groups?
- Homogeneity or heterogeneity?
- Naturalistic or researcher constructed?
- Group size?

Strangers or existing groups?

If a focus group is made up of people who know each other already, there is the possibility that existing knowledge of each other will enable members of the group to feel comfortable with the group environment and so feel at ease when talking. This may make the discussion easier. However, there is always the danger that such a group will take each other for granted. In one sense this is an advantage, as members will not have to take time to 'settle in' to the discussion. The danger is that members will be 'too settled'. This may lead to a conversation where too much is taken for granted and so not expressed. While being confronted with strangers may at first be a challenge to individual members, it is this very challenge that encourages exploration of assumptions and beliefs. Such a challenging environment requires careful management by the facilitator, but is generally regarded as a more productive environment for data collection. The facilitator must encourage participants to feel comfortable, but not so comfortable that they feel they have nothing to add. Another factor that might inhibit open discussion is the desire not to disclose sensitive information to people you know, and who may pass such revelations on to others in the participants' social networks. As already mentioned, this is an ethical as well as a data collection issue. Once again it is generally agreed that 'stranger' groups offer less fear of embarrassment and so are a richer and more ethical means of data collection. This is not to say that groups who know each other cannot be useful, especially in the context of case-study research and ethnography, where the focus of the research is a particular group and where focus groups might be adopted as a means of supplementing other methods. In expert focus groups (Delphi groups) it is harder to bring people together who are not in some way already known to each other (as being an expert in a field usually entails an awareness of other experts). In such situations it is essential that the researcher reflects on the dangers and difficulties outlined above in order to minimize both the ethical and methodological weaknesses. Again, this will often involve setting ground rules and creating a non-confrontational environment. One such ground rule would be for participants to sign up to an agreement to respect the confidentiality of other participants (see 'Structure, organization and location' p. 96).

Homogeneity or heterogeneity?

The dynamics of a group will be affected by the degree to which participants are selected as representatives of a particular category of people. However, these effects are not fully predictable. Set in a group of women, a single male may adopt a less masculine tone than might be the case if he was in an all-male group. However, the reverse may be true, as being the only male may encourage him to take a more 'masculine' tone. Morgan (1997: 12) cites Wight's findings that young males expressed more 'macho' attitudes towards women in all-male groups than was found in mixed groups. Is it the case that one of these results is true, while the other is false? Does one of the group compositions get to the real, while the other encourages the men to disguise their true feelings? Perhaps these young men have mixed feelings! Perhaps such beliefs are context specific and not fixed outside social interaction. David Morley's (1980) study of

95

audience interpretation of the UK news and current affairs programme *Nationwide* used relatively homogeneous focus groups to represent different social groups (for example, separate groups for trade unionists, managers and Afro-Caribbeans). While the groups appeared to interpret the same programmes in very different ways, were these expressions as much the product of the group identity given to them in the interview situation as the product of their 'true' beliefs? Does such a group environment realistically capture the everyday dynamics of opinion formation? Are people's everyday lives and communities so homogeneous? If young males spend most of their time interacting with other young males, a focus group of young males may best capture the everyday social dynamics of opinion formation. If young males spend most of their time in mixed groups, then a mixed group may be more appropriate. In this regard the question of homogeneity or heterogeneity in focus group composition is one of naturalism, does the group come close to the everyday dynamics of interaction or is it artificial? If you feel the issue at hand is one that is likely to be highly open to peer pressure, you may prefer one-to-one interviews, or you may use focus groups to study consensus formation and pressure to conform. In this latter situation, the data you would be interested in is not the attitudes expressed, but the processes of interaction that led them to be said. The question of naturalism takes us on to the use and usefulness of self-generated groups.

Naturalistic or researcher constructed?

If it is advantageous for a focus group's composition, at least in part, to reflect the composition of everyday interaction, it might seem obvious that naturalistic focus groups (where the researcher arranges to conduct their focus group interviews with pre-existing groups) would be the ideal focus group form. Naturalistic focus groups do not require the researcher to create the group, and members will usually be easier to bring together than would a group of strangers. Members are familiar and so will find it easier to talk to each other. The researcher is not imposing an identity on the group. The group has already identified itself. The boundary between naturalistic focus groups and ethnographic observation is highly porous. Attending group meetings (whether these be, for example, in the study of social movements, patient self-help groups or sports supporters) and addressing questions to those groups, rather than to individuals,

comes close to naturalistic focus group interviewing. However, as has been noted, there are ethical and validity difficulties in interviewing groups who already know each other. These difficulties need to be weighed against the potential bias that may be introduced by the artificial construction of a group. Such a balancing of ethical, practical and methodological issues is inevitable. There is no one blueprint to fit all situations.

Group size?

David Morgan (1997: 34) suggests that, in the conduct of social research, groups of between 6 and 10 people work best. Market researchers have tended to use larger groups (8–12). It is generally suggested that the more group members know about or are motivated by the topic at hand, the smaller the group needs to be. Expert focus groups (Delphi groups) may have only four participants, but are likely to have a lot to say and are likely to be able to feed off the comments of others more readily. Groups of consumers discussing their experience of a new product may have less to say, so a larger group, if well managed, may be better. Smaller groups are more challenging to participants as there is greater pressure to contribute, while larger groups offer greater opportunity to sit back and not say much. The latter case requires that the moderator acts to involve all participants and to avoid individuals coming to dominate the discussion (unless the research is more concerned with group dynamics and leadership in opinion formation than with individual opinions).

Structure, organization and location

The conduct of effective focus group research requires well-organized sampling, a well prepared interview guide or *aide-mémoire*, clear instructions for the participants, and an environment (both physical and social) that will enable dialogue and recording. Sampling methods will depend upon the nature of the subject groups you wish to recruit. If a random sample can be drawn, this has many advantages (see Chapter 13). However, this is not always possible and the whole range of alternative sampling methods, used in social research generally, are equally applicable in the context of focus group research. If you wish to recruit a group with a particular range of characteristics, you will need to use a stratified sampling method (whether random or not). The choice will depend upon the goals of the research, the nature of the groups sought, and the practicalities of the particular situation. Wilkinson (1998) suggests the precautionary principle of over-recruitment, due to the added complexity in group interviewing of getting all members of the group to arrive at the same location at the same time. If you are hoping to conduct a group interview of seven people, it is best to recruit eight or even nine to be safe.

Again as in other forms of interview-based research, the production of an interview schedule/ guide or *aide-mémoire* is essential, and again as in qualitative interviewing more generally, the extent to which this is structured or relatively unstructured will depend on the interest of the researcher. The extent to which the moderator wishes to structure the flow of talk will determine the nature of the schedule/guide. Where the researcher sits in on naturalistic group discussions and hardly intervenes at all represents an extreme. However, this may not be considered a focus group at all by many. It may better be described as straightforward ethnography. The inexperienced focus group moderator will tend to require a tighter hold on events, as they have developed fewer of the subtle interview management skills that come with practice. As such, the inexperienced focus group moderator is best advised to have a relatively well structured interview schedule, even if they should be careful not to use such a security blanket too dogmatically. Experience enables flexibility.

In addition to a well thought out interview guide, it is often useful to prepare 'stimulus materials'. These may include video materials, paper-based materials, objects, photographs or even spoken presentations. Where participants cannot be expected to be highly informed and/or highly motivated about the topic of interest to the researcher, it is often useful to provide some introductory background to the issue to generate interest and reflection. Of course, this requires attention to the danger of bias in the material presented. Often it is advisable to present material explicitly as a range of perspectives, rather than to give the impression that these are 'the facts'.

Clear instructions to participants are essential. This has been mentioned already with reference to the ethics of confidentiality, but it is essential that the participants be given certain ground rules that will enable the discussion to run smoothly, and to allow recording (see Box 7.5).

These instructions need to be clearly outlined in advance. This will aid greatly in encouraging the group to regulate itself. This leaves the moderator with less need to intervene, except in introducing the research themes.

Setting ground rules is essential in the creation of a positive environment in which participants feel comfortable in expressing their views. Also essential in the creation of a positive environment is the choice of interview location (and timing). Not only is it essential to secure a location that is quiet, it is also important to identify a time and place that are convenient to those whom you wish to participate. This requires some level of background research into the routines and commitments of those you seek to recruit, or of those you have provisionally recruited. Morgan (1997: 55) makes the useful reminder that a table, which everyone can sit around, is an essential aspect in the choice of location. Finally, it is often useful to lay on soft drinks and snacks. If you are conducting organizational research and wish to interview a group of people from a particular organization, it may be useful to use lunch breaks as a time when groups can get together. In such situations you may want to provide a light lunch to compensate. It is best here not to lay on crunchy food as this may interfere with recording.

BOX 7.5 BASIC GROUND RULES FOR FOCUS GROUP PARTICIPANTS

1 Only one person should speak at a time.
2 No sub-group discussions.
3 Allow others to speak.
4 Respect the right of others to express views that are not your own.
5 Speak clearly.
6 Respect the confidentiality of other members of the group.

(Adapted from Berg, 1998: 115)

Conduct and management

How long should a focus group be? Focus groups vary in duration from around 45 minutes to 90 minutes, though the more open-ended discussions may last for up to two hours. The greater the number of themes and the more open-ended the form of discussion, the longer the focus group will tend to be. When recruiting participants and securing the location it is important to have a clear idea of how much time will be needed. Preparation, outlining the ground rules and dealing with any issues that might need to be dealt with at the end of the session all add to the required time. When conducting focus groups for the first time it is usual to opt for shorter sessions. For a 45-minute discussion it is realistic to inform participants that they will need to 'give' you around 90 minutes of their time. It is advisable to book your location for a longer period again.

Once a group has been constructed and brought together, the tape-recorder has been set up, turned on and checked, and once the purpose and ground rules of the discussion have been outlined, the moderator has to manage the event itself. It is useful to have a second researcher who takes charge of recording and takes a second set of notes on the proceedings, as this frees the moderator to engage fully with the group. However, this is not always possible. Moderator involvement with the group takes a number of forms and serves a number of purposes.

The first question is the level of moderator involvement. If the research is primarily interested in the dynamics of group interaction and influence, it is likely that the moderator involvement will be kept to a minimum. If the primary aim is to elicit the opinions and experiences of the individual participants, it is likely that the moderator will take a more active role in encouraging all to speak and in curbing the more dominant participants. The researcher needs to ask themselves where on the spectrum between individual expression and group process their interest lies.

The moderator needs to listen carefully in order to identify where the discussion is going, both in order to take notes on what is being said and to direct the flow if necessary. Careful listening will often allow the moderator to direct the flow of talk along the broad lines they are interested in by picking up on comments and feeding these back to the group. This avoids the need for blunt re-directions. Of course, the flow of talk will not always present the moderator with such opportunities, but the more attentive the listening, and the better the note-taking, the greater the likelihood

that such opportunities will not be lost. The degree to which such opportunities are taken advantage of will, of course, depend on the degree to which the research seeks to follow a relatively narrow focus (with the need to keep things on track) or wishes to keep things open. This will depend on the research question being asked and the way it has been formulated.

How are questions to be asked? The best advice is to ask about experiences and opinions rather than about facts. Questions should encourage reflection and exploration. This may best be elicited by asking about the context in which certain experiences occurred and where certain opinions developed. The moderator may highlight contrasts in the accounts given and ask the group to reflect upon these. The moderator needs to be careful here not to give priority or support to one opinion/experience over another. It is important in this context for the moderator to avoid playing the part of an interviewer. This means avoiding one-to-one discussions between the moderator and individual participants (though single questions can be directed towards specific individuals).

The flow of the discussion can best be set in motion with icebreakers and warm-up questions. These need to be easy and everyone needs to be brought into the process of 'getting to know each other'. From such easy questions it is then possible to move towards general themes. From these, it is hoped that leads may emerge that the moderator is then able to re-introduce to the group at a later point. The movement from general themes to particular issues is important, as the reverse may close off debate or direct it too readily in one direction rather than another.

Drawing a focus group to a close is best facilitated with a round-up, where each person is asked to contribute their experience of the session and the things they feel have emerged. This is a useful data collection device: it brings the event to a close and it allows the participants a sense of closure. It is also an opportunity for the moderator to identify any last points that may need elaboration before things are wound up.

How many focus groups are needed? Morgan (1997: 43) cites the arguments of Zeller (1993) for social science research and Calder (1977) in marketing. Both claim that more than five focus groups with similar members rarely generate more significantly new data than can be generated by three to five groups. The variation between three and five will depend upon the composition of the group and the level of structure.

The more diverse the group composition and the more open-ended the structure, the greater the number of groups required. The three-to-five rule of thumb applies to research into one segment of the population. Of course, many research projects will seek to compare the beliefs and experiences of different segments of the population (such as between older and younger people or between men and women). In such instances it would be ideal to carry out three to five focus groups with each segment. Some research would seek to use mixed groups, rather than homogeneous groups. In the case of researching the attitudes of males and females, one could opt for either five mixed groups or six single-sex groups (three male/three female). Perhaps in this case it would be best to conduct three male, three female and two mixed, if resources allowed. If one was interested in age and gender, one would need more groups still as the number of segments starts to multiply once you introduce more variables. Just dividing 'age' crudely into 'young' and 'old', and crossing this with male and female, would generate four segments (young male, young female, old male and old female), and this would require at least 12 focus groups if Morgan's formula were applied dogmatically. However, for practical reasons, this multiplication is rarely fully adhered to. Morgan (1997) cites Calder's (1977) suggestion that the number of focus groups actually carried out should not be determined strictly by a formula. Rather, the researcher should apply the grounded theory method of gauging *saturation* as they move from one focus group to the next (see 'Degrees of grounded theory and sampling in qualitative research' p. 79). Saturation is the realization that after so long the researcher begins to be able to predict what will come out in the next group. Once the researcher comes to hear nothing significantly new from one session to the next, the purpose of continuation starts to diminish.

Recording and transcription

Good quality tape-recording is essential, but it is also important to write notes during the conduct of the sessions, for both the management of the discussion and to enable immediate reflections after the group has ended. Good notes and a written summary of the researcher's experiences and reflections immediately after the session enable the researcher to transcribe more easily (especially where parts of the dialogue are unclear on the recording). When the moderator is not the person transcribing, such notes and comments can be equally useful. **Transcription** is a very time-consuming process. A professional transcriber may require at least three times the duration of the session to transcribe it, and a non-professional may take twice as long again. As is the case with one-to-one interview recording, the temptation to get a professional to do the transcription (to save time) should be tempered by the fact that time spent transcribing is a very useful way for a researcher to 'get close' to the data. Knowing every word of the conversation is a great advantage when it comes to qualitative data analysis.

Summary

Interview techniques (whether one-to-one or group based) seek to draw inferences about social life from talk generated in research-driven encounters. The nature of qualitative interviewing requires the researcher to pay great attention to the nature of the questions they ask and the place and time in which they set their interactions. This attention is to ensure a balance between the researcher's focus of attention and the priorities and interpretations of those being interviewed. The ability to ask open questions and to create an open environment in which respondents feel comfortable to answer is a difficult and complex set of achievements.

Keywords

Aide-mémoire
Anonymity
Confidentiality
Delphi Group
Ethics
Exploration

Facilitator
Focus Group Interview
Interview
Interviewer Effect/Interviewer Bias
Moderator
Multi-method

Naturalism/Naturalistic
Post-primary Research
Sample
Transcription
Validity (External/Internal)

Questions

1   What are the relative merits and limitations of one-to-one interviews and focus group methods of data collection?

2   What are the epistemological limits of interview-based data collection?

3   What are the ethical grounds upon which a researcher might choose between one-to-one and focus group interviews, and how do such grounds relate to the questions they are seeking to research?

4   What issues need to be considered when deciding upon how to sample and structure the participants within focus groups, and how do these factors affect the researcher's choices for focus group composition?

5   What issues need to be addressed when designing interview questions and interview schedules?

Further reading

Berg, Bruce L. (1998) *Qualitative Research Methods for the Social Sciences*. Needham Heights, MA: Allyn and Bacon.

Burgess, Robert G. (1984) *In the Field*. London: Allen and Unwin.

Fern, Edward F. (1982) 'The use of focus groups for idea generation: the effects of group size, acquaintanceship, and moderator on response quantity and quality', *Journal of Marketing Research*, 19: 1–13.

Morgan, David, L. (1997) *Focus Groups as Qualitative Research*. London: Sage.

Morgan, David L. (1998) *The Focus Group Guidebook*. London: Sage.

Morley, David (1980) *The 'Nationwide' Audience: Structure and Decoding*. London: British Film Institute.

Wilkinson, Sue (1998) 'Focus groups in feminist research: power, interaction and the co-production of meaning', *Women's Studies International Forum*, 21 (1): 111–25.

CHAPTER
8

ETHNOGRAPHY AND CASE STUDY RESEARCH

Chapter contents

By the end of this chapter you will be able to:

- Define ethnography and identify its historical roots.

- Identify the key stages in the conduct of ethnographic research.

- Specify the strengths and limitations of ethnographic and case-study based research.

- Understand the relationship between ethnography and related research designs.

- Understand the relationship between the range of different data collection methods that can be deployed within the broader ethnographic methodology.

What is ethnography?

Berg (1998: 120) cites a range of definitions of **ethnography**: 'unfettered or naturalistic enquiry' (Lofland, 1996: 30); 'cultural description' (Wolcott, 1973); 'thick description' (Geertz, 1973); and 'subjective soaking' (Ellen, 1984). Hammersley (1998: 2) suggests five central aspects of ethnography:

* The study of people's behaviour in everyday contexts.
* Largely based upon informal observation and conversation.
* Being relatively unstructured.
* Using a small number of cases.
* Offering more description than causation.

John Brewer writes:

> Ethnography is the study of people in naturally occurring settings or 'fields' by methods of data collection which capture their social meanings and ordinary activities, involving the researcher participating directly in the setting if not also in the activities, in order to collect data in a systematic manner but without meaning being imposed. (Brewer, 2000: 6)

Ethnography is based upon a belief in the value of **naturalistic** methods of data collection in natural settings. Ethnography involves time spent 'within' a culture or group. This location 'within' leads to it often being referred to as field research. Ethnography often involves living with those the researcher is studying, and this living may involve the researcher living as a participant within that field. As such, some ethnography is called **participant observation**. Not all field research/ethnography involves the researcher in taking a role as participant, though the line between participation and non-participation is often, perhaps always, blurred. Not all ethnographic data collection is based upon **observation** (participant based or not). Ethnographic data collection may involve **interviews** and the use of documentary sources. As such the term 'ethnography' covers a wider range than the term

'participant observation', which may be one aspect of an ethnographic project.

Ethnography can be **deductive** (designed to test a specific **hypothesis**), but tends to be **inductive** (theory building in the course of data collection). Being in the field offers great scope to explore a culture or group 'way of life'. This focus on a 'way of life' means that ethnography tends to be 'holistic' rather than 'mechanistic'. This combination of **exploration** and holistic interest means that the ethnographer tends towards description over **causal** theories as the aim of their research. The word 'ethnography' is used to describe both a form of data collection (that is, field research) and a form of written account (the monograph or account of fieldwork and analysis).

Origins of ethnography

The term 'ethnography' originates in anthropology and referred to the conduct of 'fieldwork' within 'cultures' other than the anthropologist's own. This tended to mean research by white Europeans within the European colonies in Asia, Africa, Australia/New Zealand, the Pacific and the Americas. In the late nineteenth and early twentieth centuries, such research was largely carried out by colonial administrators and geographers, and focused upon what were seen to be small-scale and geographically specific 'cultures'. Such research rarely involved living as a part of that 'culture'. Bronislaw Malinowski (see Kuper, 1973: Ch. 1) established the modern ethnographic tradition in the early years of the twentieth century with his suggestion (though not always in his practice) that to live with and within a culture was the only way to really understand it.

Within sociology a similar strand of research method developed in the 1920s. The Chicago School of Sociology popularized methods of researching urban life by means of time spent with people, learning about their lives, routines and experiences. This type of research paralleled early studies of urban life (for example, Henry Mayhew's studies of the life of London's poor in the late nineteenth century (reprinted 1961), but built upon it. Such research did not involve living in a far away 'field', but did emphasize and develop field-based empirical data collection methods (Bulmer, 1984).

Finally, the tradition of **community studies** fed into the development of 'field research'. The community studies tradition sought to research specific towns, cities or regions as organic entities. Research involved time spent in the specific location, building a picture of life in that place, by means of interviews, observation work and the collection of documentary sources (Bell and Newby, 1971).

The pros and cons of ethnographic methods: ethical and practical

The same ethical issues (both advantages and disadvantages) which were raised in Chapters 6 and 7 apply to ethnographic methods.

Not all 'fields' are open to the ethnographer. Some are only accessible if the researcher enters covertly (pretending to occupy a non-research role), and this presents problems. Not all aspects of life are open to routine observation (the bedroom and the past being two examples). Nevertheless, ethnography offers a powerful means of data collection and theory building. 'Being there', on location, on the inside, offers a range of opportunities which are not available to those using other methodologies such as the interview or the experiment. Field research offers the chance to see what people 'really do', not just what they say they do, or what they do in artificial situations. Of course, this assumes that people will behave naturally in their everyday circumstances, even when in the presence of a researcher. It is dangerous to overly romanticize ethnography as being a royal road to 'how things really are', yet the possibility of the researcher having an effect on the data they collect is common to all research strategies. Martyn Hammersley (1998) offers a useful summary of the pros and cons of ethnography. He suggests there have been three defences of the ethnographic method against those who argue that field research lacks the control, reliability and transparency of experimental forms of observation. First, naturalistic methods can be said to be more valid than methods dependent upon artificial situations when researching humans. Second, field research offers a greater scope for exploration. Finally, ethnography is useful for describing specific cases in detail and should not be criticized for not generating comparisons and generalizations if that is not its aim. Hammersley argues that the sacrifice of **generalizability** for depth is a legitimate trade-off as long as the loss involved is not ignored. The inability to prove causation in the complexity of field situations may be regarded as problematic if one sees physics as the only model for good science (though proving **causation** even in laboratory physics is highly problematic). Description may be a legitimate goal as long as description is not then falsely passed off as explanation. If one wants to investigate the possibility of a specific causal relationship, there are other methods, though ethnography may still have a part to play even in them. Interestingly, as Hammersley suggests, there are critiques of ethnography that suggest it is too scientific. The idea of naturalism as a means of getting to the truth of what is really going on can be criticized. The idea that the ethnographer can see the truth and then report it may be too simplistic. Paul Atkinson (1992) has pointed out how much ethnography relies on a naïve belief that things can be seen as they really are if you just spend enough time looking. He also points out the **genre** styles that characterize ethnographic writing, and which are used to convince the ethnographic monograph's reader of the researcher's account. The ethnographer is forced to use story-telling (narrative) devices and metaphorical (re-description) devices to both construct their own 'experience', and to convey that 'experience' to the reader. This always involves selection and interpretation. The truth of a culture, group or way of life cannot simply be passed directly into another culture's (the ethnographer's own) words, and there are almost always competing claims as to what is important, and how things are to be understood even within the group being researched. Even identifying the boundaries of 'the group' or 'culture' to be studied requires selection. To talk of cultures or groups as objects with discrete boundaries is to copy the language of physics, and this is highly misleading. Ethnography, while a powerful social research approach, should not be assumed to be unproblematic. We should not be naïve about naturalism! Porter's (2002) discussion of critical realist ethnography (see 'Quality and quantity: distinctions and parallels' p. 42) outlines one, perhaps two, attempts to balance extremes, but such views are by no means universally accepted.

BOX 8.1 A RATIONALE FOR ETHNOGRAPHY

Dr Sue Child, School of Sociology, Politics and Law, University of Plymouth, UK.

Within the archetypal domestic banking branch, staff engage in a multiplicity of jobs; for example, cashier, customer service officer, branch manager, with each role demanding certain behaviours and competencies. In order that my research would not simply end up as a 'compare and contrast' adjudication between the experiences of cashiers and other categories of workers to newly imposed working regimes, I chose to focus my research on just one 'category' of staff – cashiers. However, researching within an organization like Bank UK, where not only is one job heavily dependent upon input from another, but where there is also an increasing requirement for staff to be flexible, and able to 'multi-task' by competently undertaking jobs other than their own, cashiers simply could not be researched 'in a vacuum'. Other staff were key players to the way that cashiers experienced revised working regimes and increased working hours, thus the experiences of these staff also form a key part of my analysis and conclusion (see Child, 2003).

To answer questions of this nature, I used a variety of classic ethnographic data gathering techniques, for example, participant observation, interviewing, oral life histories and focus groups. Ethnography is not a particular method of data collection but 'a certain style of research distinguished by its objectives to understand the social meanings and activities of people in a given field or setting' (Brewer, 2000: 11), traditionally encompassing '. . . some amount of genuinely social interaction in the field with the subjects of the study, some direct observation of relevant events, some formal and a great deal of informal interviewing, some systematic counting, some collection of documents and artefacts; and open-endedness in the direction the study takes' (Fielding, 1995: 157).

'The value of adopting an ethnographic approach to workplace relations is that it can illustrate and begin to explain the complexity of social change to a degree which other research techniques cannot' (Scott, 1994: 29). Thus: 'This choice of research method may be seen as my response to the self-interrogative: "If I want to understand what it is like working under JIT [Just-in-time management] and TQM [Total quality management] shall I sit in my office and mail out questionnaires or shall I go and observe it, experience it, and ask people about it first hand?"' (Delbridge, 1998: 15).

Over a 16-month period from May 2000 to August 2001, I endeavoured to record every aspect of a cashier's working life, both business and social, through the adoption of a variety of ethnographic research methods: completion of field diaries, participant observation, oral life histories, increasingly focused individual and group interviews, and participation in 'out of work' social activities. In order to be in a position to explain events within the context in which they occurred, I chose to 'go native'. In quintessential 'Chicago School – esque' ethnographic style, I went out and 'got the seat of my pants dirty in real research' (Park, cited in Bulmer, 1984: 97). By wearing the uniform and working alongside other cashiers, enduring continuous, unwarranted public rudeness and frequent, unpleasant male sexual advances in response to the 'flirtatious' expectations of selling – all simply part of 'just doing business' for Bank UK – I strove to integrate myself as a 'useful part' of the social fabric of all my research sites. I ensured that I adopted and continuously used the dual languages of both 'bank-lingo' and the strong local colloquial language of the area, both of which served not only to demarcate those 'inside' and 'outside' the organizational culture, but also those considered 'inside' and 'outside' local social culture. In classic ethnographic style, I needed to cement relationships with people in whose natural environment I was researching, and I needed to show trust by using their language, speaking as they speak and doing as they do (Brewer, 2000: 85).

In order to capture 'hidden' data not apparent from the mere physical side of working, I 'bitched' and 'gossiped' in 'the ladies' – going 'backstage' with members of the team, where audiences could not see us, often ridiculing the audience in a way that was inconsistent with the face-to-face treatment normally reserved for them (Goffman, 1959: 169). I sat in various staff rooms, joining others in the escapism of lunchtime 'soaps' and dissemination of holiday brochures. Alongside fellow workers, I endured relentless sales and service directives from Head Office, and subjected myself to individual performance-related assessment through participation in a variety of sales-related activities, appearing to require a combination of both selling and flirting skills.

Preliminary rounds of semi-structured interviews enabled the testing of early data analysis, and as the ethnographic study developed and findings were progressively analysed, increasingly structured questions tested emergent hypotheses.

Stages in the ethnographic method

John Brewer (2000: 58) suggests a checklist for enabling open and reflexive **fieldwork research**:

1 Outline aims and objectives.
2 Justify choice of site and cases.
3 Identify resources and needs (time, money and so on).
4 Identify sampling scope (time, people and places).
5 Identify gatekeepers, contacts and access issues.
6 Negotiate role.
7 Identify analysis methods.
8 Exiting strategies.

These elements may shift during the course of field research, but it is useful to monitor all these elements to map change in the research strategy over time. These issues are addressed below, though not in the sequence outlined by Brewer.

Choosing a topic

In so far as ethnography tends towards inductivism, holism and naturalism, the nature of the research topic could be the exploration of the particular group, 'culture', community, organization and so on without further pre-emptive specification. Nevertheless, ethnography, like any other form of social research, draws upon past work in the formulation of the 'who' and the 'how' as well as the 'why' questions about a research project. Choosing to engage in a 'pure' form of exploration by means of ethnographic fieldwork is slightly misleading. To choose such an approach is, in some ways, to follow in the footsteps of an established tradition and body of work, itself contained within a wealth of existing ethnographic monographs (books

that detail particular fieldwork projects). The written ethnographies of earlier researchers are often what the new ethnographic researcher starts from when developing a research topic. These texts will contain details about duration of fieldwork, accessing issues, role issues as well as discussions of findings, theories that emerged and conclusions about the group studied and similarities/differences with the findings of other researchers.

Ethnographers do not always choose strictly inductive and exploratory approaches in which the topic of the research is to explore the life of one group or **case** without further specification or focus. A researcher may choose to study a group for specific reasons. They may be funded to research particular issues within a particular organization. This may be a form of **action research**, where the researcher interacts and assists the organization in addressing an issue it sees as problematic. The researcher may be keen to research a particular group because they wish to test a theory or compare particular characteristics with those found in another group, or by means of a different research method. These approaches are more deductive and specific. Ethnography is not always inductive and holistic.

Selecting cases

The selection of cases for research is intimately bound up with the nature of the topic the researcher wants to research. It is also bound up with the question of access. To a degree the selection of cases depends upon their suitability for researching the researcher's chosen topic, but the reverse is also sometimes true, that is, that the topic may be changed to fit the characteristics of the case or cases the researcher actually managed to gain access to. Brewer (2000: 76) refers to Stake's (1998: 88–9) suggestion that there are three types of case selection:

- *Intrinsic cases* are selected and studied for their own sake, without the intention to generalize from the results.
- *Instrumental cases* are selected to represent a set of similar settings. It is believed that it is possible to generalize from the findings of such cases.
- *Collective cases* are selections from different settings designed to allow comparison.

Of course, it is not just a question of choosing whom you would like to study and then going and studying them. The issue of access is highly problematic. Ernest Gellner (1992) went so far as to suggest that the debate within anthropology over whether ethnography was worthwhile given the difficulties of translating the reality of one culture in such a way that it would be genuinely understood by another culture, has its origins in the increasing difficulty anthropologists found in getting visas to visit other societies once those societies were no longer colonies. Being unable to gain access to other cultures, many anthropologists seemed to decide that it was not really useful going there anyway. Ethnographers have found it very hard accessing elite groups in their own society, while those lower down the social scale have often been easier to gain access to. This may be said to have biased the nature of ethnographic research. Ethnography has also tended to focus upon small-scale 'places' rather than larger regions, countries and even continents. This is because it is possible to access a small location, while it is hard to observe a large space. This may lead the ethnographer to give more emphasis to micro interactions rather than to interactions that occur over long distances. Once again, access may bias the orientation of the ethnographer. It is important to balance the advantages of ethnographic method with an awareness of its limitations.

Getting in

The nature of the field determines the nature of the researcher's entry problems. Going to live in a village in the Amazon rain forest will present a different set of entry problems than becoming a participant observer in a car factory, or spending time with a street gang. Is the place you wish to enter a public space or a private space? Do you need formal permission to be there? Formal permissions must be sought from authorities of various kinds and this requires a degree of tact and negotiation. Organizational leaders may want to recruit you to do research for them. You need to retain a degree of independence, though you may agree to show them your finished research findings. If you do, it is essential that the confidentiality of other contacts is upheld, and that you make it clear at the start that you are not prepared to breach that confidentiality. If you are suspected of being a management spy, your data collection will be much diminished, as people will not be so willing to talk to you.

In such instances, the first-time researcher should ask the advice of someone more experienced either with research or with the particular organization whose 'private' space you want to enter. The latter group are called **gatekeepers**. These may be people in the organization or location whose help and consent will enable your research to develop. They may be people from outside the group you are interested in, but who have connections within. Some gatekeepers are official gatekeepers, such as ethics committees and public relations managers. Others are semi- or unofficial, that is, community/organizational/gang leaders.

Many public spaces are effectively privatized through the practices of groups and cultures. While you may not need permission to go to a particular village, hang out on particular street corners, or attend a particular religious building, your uninvited presence may not grant you much access to the lives of others present. A stranger may be shunned or ignored. Suspicion may lead people to act differently in the presence of a stranger. Real life may be conducted in the private spaces hidden within the public realm, while the stranger is treated to a front. Access to a culture is more than just spending time in a place. Contacts are important. Gatekeepers might be met in the course of conducting prior or preliminary **fieldwork** in public settings or they might be cultivated in advance.

Beyond the gatekeepers are the guides and informants whose advice will enable the researcher to get a deeper kind of access, often by means of **snowball sampling**. At this stage it is only important to recall that the point at which you start will affect where you end up. Consent at one level of an organization or from one set of people within a community may make contact at other levels or with other groups harder (David, 2002). Cultivating relationships is always a balancing act, and this balancing act begins with the cultivation of your first contacts and gatekeepers.

Roles

One way to short-circuit a number of access and gatekeeper problems is to assume the role of a member of the group you are interested in and conceal your researcher role. This is more realistic in some situations than in others, and raises a range of **ethical** and methodological questions. **Covert research** involves deception. Can this be justified, ever or in particular cases (see Chapter 2)? Covert research cannot employ **overt research** techniques such as formal interviewing or even certain kinds of observation without arousing suspicion. Fieldnotes, the record of the researcher's observations and conversations, cannot be written up in public. These limitations may weaken the research. Alternatively, the covert researcher may gain access to locations unavailable to an overt researcher. Those being researched may react more 'normally' in the presence of a covert researcher, thinking the researcher is 'one of them'. As such there is always a trade-off. Nevertheless, as a first-time researcher it is highly advisable not to be covert. Being honest and avoiding situations that require deception makes life a lot easier and potentially a lot safer.

Martyn Hammersley and Paul Atkinson (1995: 104) refer to Junker's (1960) elaboration on Gold's (1958) fieldwork role spectrum. Four points on a spectrum are set out:

1 *The complete participant:* Here the researcher researches from the position of a full participant – for example, a teacher conducting ethnographic research on school life or a police officer on police work.
2 *The participant as observer:* Here the researcher assumes the role of a member of the group they are interested in and lives as a member for the duration of their research. An example would be of a researcher becoming a research assistant in a chemical laboratory to study the construction of scientific knowledge.
3 *The observer as participant:* Here the researcher spends time and may even live with a group, but is never really a full-time participant, though they may get involved in certain rituals and events. An example of this would be the anthropologist who goes to live in a village in Papua New Guinea for two years and is invited to participate in a variety of customs and everyday activities.
4 *The complete observer:* Here the researcher is not a participant. Of course, just being around may have an effect and so all researchers participate in the situation they are present within, but in this case the researcher does not formally take up a role within the group other than that of being a researcher. An example of this might be from more traditional forms of ethnography where the anthropologist observed from the sidelines and did not seek to take part in the 'native' way of life.

The complete participant role offers scope for being covert, though the role does not require a covert approach in most cases. Moving along the spectrum towards the complete observer involves an increasing necessity for an overt researcher status. In any research project it is likely that the researcher will move back and forth across the spectrum at different times unless, of course, they are completely covert and so must stick to their participant role. The researcher's role as insider/outsider requires the constant management of marginality (Hammersley and Atkinson, 1995: 109).

It is important to remember that any researcher role involves some degree of performance or even theatricality. This is all the more manifest in the case of ethnography. It is important for the researcher to fit in even if they are not trying to pretend to be someone they are not, or not to be someone they are. Choice of clothes and appearance (suit or jeans, high-heels or trainers, long hair or short, make-up and so on) may all play a part in establishing whether you fit in. Trying too hard (trying to be too fashionable, or trying to give the impression of being too interested/ knowledgeable or impressed) may be as bad as not making an effort at all. The researcher is there to learn, not to judge. It is not necessary to compete with members of the group to see who has the most local knowledge or street credibility.

Data collection

Watching, doing, listening, reading, asking, thinking. The ethnographic researcher may build towards an understanding of the social situation they are in through participation. They may observe passively. They may ask questions. These questions might be in the form of informal conversation or more formal interviews (usually fairly unstructured, but not always). Interviews may even take the form of focus groups. The ethnographer may use written sources (diaries, letters, local newspapers, organizational communications and so on). The ethnographer can draw upon a range of methods for collecting data. Ethnography is a broad umbrella, referring to the presence of the researcher for an extended period within, for example, a community or organization. What the researcher does when in the location varies depending upon what works and what is possible. We have discussed interviews at length in Chapter 7. The use of existing written materials will be the topic of Chapter 9. Here, therefore, the focus will be upon observation in fieldwork research.

Field-based (or naturalistic) observation

The experiment is observation in highly-controlled conditions. Naturalistic or field-based observation sacrifices control for the hope of greater **internal validity** (the belief that behaviour observed in natural settings is less likely to be changed by the research process). However, it is important to appreciate that field observation is not totally unstructured. The selection of fields for the conduct of research already involves choices about sampling. Once in the field the observer needs to organize the when, where, who and how of observation. They also have to devise a method of identifying what they are looking at (**classification**) and what they are looking for (focus). Also they must identify methods of recording their observations. One cannot observe everything that is going on even at one moment in a relatively small space. One cannot record in full even the things that one is able to observe. Perception involves selection. Becoming reflexive about selection is important. Once in the field, and even beforehand when negotiating access, it is important to reflect upon the range of times and locations that exist within a field. Schools are different places at different times of the day and night. What goes on at the front desk of a police station is not the same as what goes on behind locked doors. Fieldwork observation requires access to the range of

when and wheres. Time and place needs careful consideration. This is a form of sampling that may be organized before and/or during the field research period. Likewise, the researcher may want to observe (or interview and so on) a range of different people. Initial gatekeepers and contacts are not necessarily typical and may give a one-sided impression of the scene. Others may present themselves, or need to be sought out.

Recording observations involves the use of classification. This may be in the generation of lists or in the writing of detailed descriptions. Classification is the process of distinguishing things and defining what makes some things go together and what separates some things from others. Classification may draw from prior reading of the literature, or from established classifications (such as male/female). Alternatively, a more inductive form of classification can emerge from time spent in the field. Starting out without clear classificatory schemes, the researcher may come to see patterns after a while spent in the field. These they then explore, sometimes elaborating, sometimes rejecting, as they steer through the field according to what emerges as they go along. This issue of steering, the choice of where to go, what to look for/at, who to talk to and what about, is the question of focus. Once again this will in part derive from the researcher's survey of existing literature (the desire to study gender relations in the police force may motivate the researcher to conduct an ethnography inside and around a police station), yet the focus will develop during the course of the fieldwork.

Finally, there is the question of recording field observations. Fieldnotes are a written record of the ethnographer's observations, as well as of their other data collection methods. The traditional advice to the anthropologist, that they should keep their hard-bound notebooks inside biscuit tins to protect their writings

---

BOX 8.2 A CHECKLIST FOR TAKING FIELDNOTES

Berg (1998: 147–8) suggests a five-point checklist for fieldnotes:

1   Record people's keywords and phrases in the field.
2   Make notes about the sequence of events as soon as possible.
3   Limit time spent in the field as the ratio of field time to writing up may be 1:4.
4   Write up 'full' notes immediately after exiting the field. Exiting means at the end of each day/session and at the end of each period of fieldwork. Fullness means an account of events/people and the relationships between them.
5   Get notes written up before showing them to others.

from insects and moisture, may not always apply, but the writing and preservation of field notes still presents many problems. The covert participant observer cannot take notes easily in view of others. This may lead to a great many visits to the toilet to scribble down notes, or to a loss of valuable data as things get forgotten between events and the next convenient writing-up time. It is advisable to write up events as soon after they happen as possible, and always on the same day. Building time into your fieldwork schedule to take notes is essential, even if this is hard. The more inductive approach makes planning hard as the researcher may find themselves following unexpected routes at any moment, but making time to write up field notes is essential Box 8.2 provides a useful checklist.

The regular writing-up of fieldnotes offers the researcher the opportunity to reflect upon what they have found. This reflection encourages elementary theorizing, thinking about the connections and the interesting new issues that have arisen. From such reflection the researcher may derive new ideas about what is important in their research, and about the location they are researching. They may begin to think they can see what is really going on. This is where data collection links into inductive forms of theory building.

Building theory

As will be discussed in greater detail in Chapters 16 to 19, and as has been mentioned in Chapter 4 and in Chapter 6, the processes of data collection and data analysis are not separate in many forms of qualitative research. The inductive approach to theory building, where theory develops out of the conduct of empirical research, rather than being developed in advance for the purpose of 'testing' by means of empirical research, may leave theorizing till after the data collection has been done. However, given that inductive approaches do not specify so rigidly in advance what their focus is going to be, the selection of topics and the **sampling** of events, people, places and times develop as the research moves along. As such, choices as to what is important and what is not are made during the course of the research. Such choices express emerging theories, theories that flow from the research and begin to move it in particular directions. This is what grounded theorists call theoretical induction. Ethnography tends towards the use of such an approach to theory building. Ethnography is best suited to such an approach as being in the field provides the greatest number of opportunities to be struck by the unexpected, those things that may or may not lead you in directions not previously thought of. The theory building process of theoretical induction requires that the researcher can be highly reflexive. Well-written and full fieldnotes are an essential foundation for this. Howard Becker (1986: ix; in Brewer, 2000: 133) suggests that 'writing is thinking'. As can be seen from Berg's set of reminders for writing fieldnotes, the process of building from initial descriptions of events, times and places to a more developed description of the processes involved,

---

BOX 8.3 BUILDING THEORY FROM FIELDNOTES

David Fetterman (1998: Ch. 5) identifies a range of strategies for building theory out of fieldnotes:

1 Content analysis (what categories are contained in the data). The distinction between quantitative and qualitative forms of content analysis will be discussed in Chapters 16 and 17.
2 Noting patterns (what keeps happening in different places and or times?).
3 Common use of language (note similarities and differences in use and context).
4 Interpreting key events in terms of the routine and the extraordinary in that field .
5 Maps (plot the space between people and events that create a sense of 'place').
6 Flow charts (plot the time lines and gaps between events in the field).
7 Organizational charts (plot the lines and relationships that bind people together).
8 Matrices (draw up cross-tabulations between types of people and/or events and other types of people/events – see Chapter 17).
9 Statistical analysis of the instance of key variables (the move beyond matrix diagrams towards more sophisticated mathematical examination of the data).

parallels the development of theoretical induction (see Box 8.3). All of these methods of data analysis will be discussed in greater detail in Chapters 16 to 19.

An important point to note is that theoretical induction can never be pure induction. This is intimately bound up with the nature of perception, language and writing. To take fieldnotes presupposes we have a language that can describe the things we see. This language will reflect our established ways of seeing. We bring existing systems of classification to novel situations. Are such ways of dividing and labelling appropriate to describe cultures and settings different from our own? Ethnographers struggle with the question of how to write about other cultures. Can we see the world as others do? How would we know if we were doing so? The **grounded theorists** argue that through saturation in the life of others we can begin to build a picture of the world that maps the 'native' experience. However, the researcher can never be totally grounded, they can never start at some base level of raw experience without theoretical expectations. There will always be theories the researcher brings to the field. The best that can be expected is that the researcher uses their confrontation with difference to reflect upon the weakness of their existing ways of thinking to capture the experience of others. Reflexive fieldnote writing is part of that process. Reflecting on one's experience is one way of telling when it is time to leave the field. Other factors (time, access and finance) also play a part.

Getting out

A more deductive research strategy will set out in advance the data required to address the question being asked (or the theory being tested). More inductive forms of research cannot specify in advance what and how much data will be sufficient to complete the research. How, then, should the ethnographer decide when to leave the field? One key factor is time. Research funds and access permission have their limits. These constraints may set external limits. Internal criteria can also be developed. As with other forms of inductive research, data collection may be said to be sufficient once a level of **saturation** has been reached. Saturation refers to the situation the research reaches when new data only acts to confirm what the researcher already predicted would be the case based upon their prior research. Once the theories that have developed through the course of data

collection and reflection become powerful predictors of future data, there is little reason to carry on collecting data. As has already been noted, in the section on focus groups ('Conduct and management' p. 98), what would be sufficient predictive power for one researcher might not be sufficient for the next. There are no agreed procedures for evaluating how predictive is predictive enough. This creates scope for variation. At the end of the day it is likely that in most cases the external constraints of money and time will arrive sooner than the internal constraints of indisputable theoretical saturation.

Leaving the field requires careful management of relationships established during the course of the research. Trust relations that have been set up need to be respected and participants in the research need to be reassured that they will not be abused, misrepresented or exposed to potential harm by the researcher's use of the data. Contacts are often retained for the purposes of subsequent clarification or in the event of subsequent research. Sometimes relationships are maintained because time together has developed into friendship.

Case studies: life histories, auto/biography, community and organizational studies

Case studies are in-depth studies of specific 'units'. Units may be individuals, organizations, events, programmes or communities. Case studies are distinguished from experiments in that they are not conducted in controlled conditions and are not specifically designed for comparison. Case studies are distinguished from surveys in that they are primarily designed to investigate specific cases in depth. Case studies may draw upon a range of methods, such as interviews and questionnaires, focus groups, observation (participant and non-participant), document and artefact collection and analysis. In this regard case studies share many characteristics in common with ethnography in particular. The two terms are often used to mean the same thing. With regard to the study of organizations and communities, case study and ethnography often mean the same thing. Case studies, however, are not the same as ethnography in all cases. In-depth analysis of particular events, organizations, individuals and communities may be carried out in ways other than the ethnographic **field research**. We have already discussed focus groups, interviews and documentary sources. Here the focus will be on the life history and **biographical** approach.

Case studies may involve a range of methods, a range of purposes and a range of sampling techniques. Robert K. Yin (1994: 1) suggests that case study research can seek to explain an individual, outcome, event or community situation; it may seek to explore, or it may seek to describe. Explanatory case studies tend to be more **quantitative** and **deductive**. Exploratory and descriptive case studies tend to be more **inductive** and **qualitative**. Methods of design, data collection and sampling will be chosen accordingly. Case studies in the physical sciences tend to be explanatory, as they are in economics and psychology. In the social sciences there is greater variety.

Individual **life histories** use a biographical approach to understanding particular individuals and the times they lived in. Life histories offer insights that may be either theoretical or therapeutic. Freud's psychoanalysis is often referred to as 'the talking cure', a reference to the suggestion that talking about one's life, in particular early traumatic events, offers the chance to bring to consciousness hidden anxieties and conflicts whose unconscious existence causes psychological illness. Once brought to the surface such issues can be addressed and overcome. This is a therapeutic form of case study research.

Robert Atkinson (1998: 4) refers to Erikson's studies of the lives of Gandhi and Luther. These texts sought to explore both the person and their social context through the study of their lives. Ethnographers often rely upon key informants in their **fieldwork** and it is often the case that extended interviews with these key informants about their lives enable the researcher better to understand the field in which that person lives as well as the relationship their

key informant has with that situation. The Chicago School of Urban Research pioneered the use of life histories as ways of exploring social life (Bulmer: 1984).

Yin (1994) suggests that the **case study method** is best applied to the study of contemporary events by methods that are naturalistic in form (that is, which gather data in natural settings or via relatively open-ended interview/observation techniques). While this might be true, the use of documents and life histories allows the case study researcher to explore past events through the study of key events, key individuals or through the recollection of ordinary lives.

While the life history, biographical interview shares many characteristics in common with other interview forms, Robert Atkinson (1998: Ch. 3) offers a number of useful suggestions as to the topics that may shape the course of a life history interview. These include birth and family origins, cultural settings, up-bringing and traditions, family, friends, siblings, schooling, media experiences, hobbies and interests, love and work, relation to and recollection of historical events, retirement, inner life and spirituality, major life themes (gifts, decisions, learning, mistakes, difficulties, disappointments, relationships, influences, achievements and fears) and visions of the future. To this might be added political beliefs, actions and affiliations. These themes need to be narrowed or broadened to take in the person being interviewed. As such they are only suggestions and not instructions. Catherine Kohler Riessman (1993) suggests that what distinguishes the **narrative** focus of life history research as a method is a **research design** that gives the respondent as much time as they need to tell their story. This requires open-ended questions and a degree of flexibility in the questioning (see 'Designing open-ended questions' p. 87). Life history as a form of case study research may draw also upon the use of textual data sources such as diaries, biographies and letters (see the first section of this chapter).

Summary

Ethnography seeks to identity holistic patterns of belief and action within the 'culture' of small-scale communities, groups or organizations. It is important to recall that field research (ethnography) may draw upon the techniques of interviewing and textual/non-intrusive data collection in addition to forms of naturalistic observation and participation. The same is true of community and organizational case study research. What makes ethnography/case study research distinct is the primary focus upon one site, rather than the primary concern with comparison. The intimacy of fieldwork relationships can be the greatest advantage of ethnography, but it is also the source of its greatest ethical difficulties. Insight may also represent invasion of privacy.

Keywords

Action Research	Ethics	Life History
Biographical Method	Ethnographic/Ethnography	Naturalism/Naturalistic
Case	Exploration	Observation
Case Study/Case Study Method	Field Research/Fieldwork	Overt Research
Causality	Gatekeeper	Participant Observation
Causation	Generalizability	Sample
Classification	Grounded Theory	Saturation
Community Studies	Hypothesis	Snowball Sampling
Covert Research	Induction	Validity (Internal/External)
Deduction	Interview	

Questions

1   Is biography a useful resource for or topic of social research? What does this distinction mean?

2   Can covert forms of fieldwork ever be justified ethically or practically?

3   What are the advantages and disadvantages of ethnographic/case study focus upon single groups, rather than upon comparisons between groups?

4   In what different ways is the relationship between data collection and theory building managed within ethnographic research?

5   How might observation-based data collection be supplemented in ethnographic fieldwork, and how might the ethnographer's role assist or hamper such attempts at mixed methods research?

Further reading

Atkinson, Paul (1992) *Understanding Ethnographic Texts*. London: Sage.

Atkinson, Robert (1998) *The Life Story Interview*. London: Sage.

Brewer, John (2000) *Ethnography*. Buckingham: Open University Press.

Hammersley, Martyn (1998) *Reading Ethnographic Research* (2nd edn). London: Longman.

Hammersley, Martyn and Atkinson, Paul (1995) *Ethnography: Principles in Practice* (2nd edn). London: Routledge.

Kohler Riessman, Catherine (1993) *Narrative Analysis*. London: Sage.

Yin, Robert K. (1994) *Case Study Research: Design and Methods* (2nd edn). London: Sage.

The journal *Sociology* Volume 27, number 1, special issue on Auto/Biography in social research is also particularly helpful.

CHAPTER
9

COLLECTING TEXTUAL DATA (INCLUDING VISUAL 'TEXTS'): MASS MEDIA, PUBLIC, PRIVATE, PERSONAL

Chapter contents

By the end of this chapter you will be able to:

- Define the meaning of the term 'text' as it is used in social research.

- Identify a range of types and sources of 'textual' data.

- Evaluate the strengths and limitations of 'textual' data.

- Engage with ethical debates concerning the use of 'textual' data.

Textual Data

The great value of textual data lies in its abundance. Written materials, and those that can be 'read' as a text, are all around us. Some of this material is already well archived and available for researchers even after their authors are long dead, or otherwise unavailable. However, not all archived materials are readily accessible or well ordered. In addition, whether in archives or not, available textual material may be either unrepresentative or invalid, or both.

Purpose and varieties of textual data

Textual data refers to any form of meaning-laden objects that the researcher can collect for the purposes of analysis. There are a range of sources and forms (recall Anderson's discussion of Cottle in Chapter 5, p. 50). The term **text** is used to refer to anything that can be 'read'. This has allowed images (paintings, photographs, postcards and so on) and other traces of meaningful human activity (such as buildings, clothing and furniture) to be used as 'textual' data. Here discussion is restricted to words and images. For a more wide ranging discussion of 'unobtrusive methods' (that is, reading artefacts rather than directly researching people), see Lee (2000). For a detailed introduction to **visual data** in the social sciences, see Emmison and Smith (2000), Banks (2001) and/or Pink (2001).

Why collect textual data? Textual data provides what John Scott (1990: 3) calls 'mediated access' to the lives of those who produced the texts. Why would we wish to use mediated access as opposed to directly accessing people by means of interviews, observations or other methods? Scott suggests two reasons. First, textual data often outlives its producers. Historians have long relied on textual records of the lives of people no longer available for interview. Second, textual data is 'non-reactive'. Whereas humans react to the fact of being researched, texts offer less reaction. Such documents may open a window to parts of life that the researcher would otherwise not have access. The minutes of corporate board meetings, the discussions of government officials, or the diary of a drug addict may offer insights otherwise unavailable.

There are many types of textual data. Scott (1990: 14) offers a system of classification based upon authorship and access. Scott identifies modes of authorship:

* Personal;
* Private (for example, business/media/charities and so on); and
* State.

He then outlines four levels of access:

* Closed;
* Restricted;
* Open (archival); and
* Open (published).

A diary may be written for a closed readership of one, or for a restricted readership (as are personal letters). However, a diary may be written with an eye to being made more widely available later (via an archive or by publication). Diary and autobiography merge at this point. A letter to a newspaper is intended to be more openly accessed than a letter to a best friend. An official letter to or from a bank or government department will be recorded institutionally. Postcards and birthday cards are sometimes kept and sometimes thrown away or lost. Private and state bodies keep records of routines and of special events. These are sometimes made available (via archives or publication) but are sometimes closed, restricted, lost or even destroyed. Written documents are not the only forms of material that people and institutions keep. Individuals keep photographs and films (cine, video and so on). Institutions also may keep photographic or film archives (surveillance video footage, for example). The media (television, radio, print and new media) generate huge quantities of textual (word and image) data, which is often easy to access, record and thereby analyse.

Raymond Lee (2000: 66–81) offers an array of interesting examples of how textual data can offer insights into social life. The choice of children's names over the years is recorded in registers of births and religious initiation. Personal advertisements may tell us a lot about the way we live. How obituaries are written in different times and places may offer comparative and longitudinal insights. Radio and television schedules may offer insights into changing lifestyles and attitudes. Job descriptions, advertisements and representations of work in the media all contribute to an understanding of social life. Lee cites fascinating research that draws upon school yearbook entries, personal curriculum vitae, published autobiographies and suicide notes. Many will be familiar with 'reading' other people's holiday postcards and photographs for 'clues' of things we might feel it would be rude to ask bluntly about. Lee (2000) devotes particular attention to the Internet as a new source of unobtrusive data. Whether it be e-mail, chat rooms or the World Wide Web, Internet activity leaves a textual trail that the researcher can follow and record. It should be remembered that such activity is not evenly spread throughout the population and this raises the question of **sampling** and selection. Surveillance of the Internet is currently an ethical hot topic. However, the **ethical** issues relating to using the Internet to collect textual data (often from people who are not aware that they are being researched) are in many respects the same as those raised by social research more generally. The ethics of documentary research will be touched upon after the next section.

Sampling

Sampling tends to refer to the selection of materials such that the selected group is 'representative' of the population the researcher is interested in. John Scott (1990) identifies four criteria for selecting and evaluating the usefulness of textual materials:

- Authenticity;
- Credibility;
- Representativeness; and
- Meaning.

Authenticity relates to

- whether the 'text' is what it claims to be (that is, that it is not a forgery), and
- that the author of the text is whom we think it is.

Credibility refers to the level of trust we can place in the contents of the 'text'. Is it trustworthy? Is the source reliable? Was the author sincere and/or accurate? The question of representativeness refers to how typical the text is, and how typical the author is.

Not all texts survive and not all that do are made available. As such, those texts that the researcher gains access to may be highly unrepresentative. At the same time, certain texts are more likely to be produced about or produced by certain types of people. Diaries in seventeenth-century England were mainly written by the middle and upper classes. Police surveillance today is more heavily concentrated on the less powerful. 'Meaning' refers to what the text actually says. Scott (1990: 36) points out that the meaning of a text can be used as either a resource or as a topic. The contents of a diary may be an accurate portrayal of the life and world of the writer. If so, the diary is a resource, a window to the life it was a part of. Alternatively, reading Victorian cookbooks may tell us little about the real diet of people in the nineteenth century, but it might tell us a lot more about the attitudes and beliefs of their middle-class authors. Here the text is a topic in itself. Much analysis of mass media content focuses on what the texts (words and images) are seeking to convince us of. It is rarely assumed that such coverage is itself 'credible' as a resource. All textual material is generated within the author's framework of 'moral accounting', whether this be a diary, a letter, or a government's record of births and deaths. Texts will always reflect the context of their production. Whether they accurately represent the world they seek to record is a more complex question. For a wide-ranging and insightful discussion of the value of **auto/biographical** work as a research resource and as a topic in the social sciences it is worth reviewing the collection of articles contained in Volume 27, Number 1 of the journal *Sociology* (1993), edited by Liz Stanley and David Morgan.

The actual selection and collection of textual materials varies according to text type and research context. Materials may be accessed directly from those being researched or from **archives**. Personal texts (such as diaries, letters and photographs) may be sought directly from those being researched or from archives. The books, magazines, newspapers, music recordings and videocassettes which an individual accumulates constitute a personal archive that may speak volumes about them. The letters, birthday cards and bills they choose to keep may also constitute a revealing personal archive. Museums and libraries often contain specialist collections of personal documents. Formal texts from private or public institutions will more usually have to be accessed from archives, though the type of archive might vary. Some institutions keep archives of their own textual production, which the researcher may seek permission to access. Other materials (such as mass media production) may be archived by other institutions, such as libraries or research institutes. Accessing archive materials may constitute the first stage of a research project, as a parallel to a **literature review**. It may constitute the main substance of a research project. Alternatively, in more **ethnographic** research the researcher may accumulate textual material in a more grounded fashion from those they observe, participate with and interview. Asking for personal materials (diaries, letters, photographs and so on) may be built into an interview schedule or questionnaire. Research projects relating to education, health or the law may wish to draw upon institutional records of individuals or groups. These materials can then be compared to the experiences and personal archives of students, patients and those enmeshed within the legal process (such as lawyers, police officers, criminals, those accused, witnesses, jurors and those convicted). Media researchers may wish to compare media output with the experiences of audiences, or the practices of those involved in the process of media production (journalists, actors, producers and editors, owners and shareholders, as well as pressure group and institutional actors who seek to influence media content). Historical records in all these areas can be used to compare the past with the present.

The ethics of documentary research

The use of textual materials raises some serious ethical issues (as briefly mentioned earlier). To begin with, there is the problem of consent. Gaining consent from an archive to research the materials held there is one thing. It is another to claim that such an institutional consent represents the consent of those whose materials are contained within that archive. Materials written by or written about the dead raise the ethical problem of whose consent should be sought. Does death annul all ethical obligations? Were the documents meant for circulation beyond a limited circle? How were the documents acquired by the archive, and with what provisos concerning their use? The researcher is obliged to address these questions. If authors or people mentioned by an author are still alive, should the researcher seek to gain their consent to use the material? Health, education, employment,

tax and legal data are protected by law. Is it enough to retain confidentiality, or should formal and informed consent be sought? For legal as well as moral and methodological reasons researchers should seek guidance about the specifics of any proposed use of archival materials. Academic and professional associations in different countries offer guidance tailored to specific contexts. These should be investigated (see Chapter 2). Regarding personal materials gained by researchers directly from those they research, it is easier to ask for informed consent and this should be done, once again, in accordance with the ethical guidelines of the relevant professional and/or academic association.

Recording and storage

Notes taken from, or transcripts of, written materials can be recorded and stored in the same way as one would take notes from any other source in a **literature search**. Some archival materials may be available electronically and may be recorded and stored as such. Other archival materials may be available on loan or have to be noted from within the archive itself, as is the case with much library reference material. Such material may or may not be reproduced (via scanning or photocopy). Personal documents and images may be viewed, borrowed and even reproduced with consent. In a field context, storage of artefacts is problematic and recording (either in text or via photography, scanning, video or photocopy) raises all the problems encountered in the earlier discussion of taking field notes ('Data collection', p. 108). In an archival context, storage issues are those discussed in the context of doing a literature review (Chapter 1). In each case, the purpose of recording and storage is to allow subsequent analysis. As **qualitative** analysis is based upon the analysis of meaning, recording and storage needs to facilitate subsequent access to meaning. This requires the recording of the text and its 'context' (that is, source: time and place, author and other information that will locate the text in the social conditions of its production and retention in either a personal or formal archive). Just as it is essential to record the demographic details of people interviewed (age, sex, social position and so on), it is similarly important to record the corresponding characteristics of texts.

Summary

Primary text based data collection generates data by **non-intrusive data collection** methods that do not primarily involve direct interaction with the producers of the texts collected (though accessing such materials may involve such interaction). While avoiding many of the practical and ethical difficulties involved in interviewing and field research, textual data collection presents the reverse difficulties of distance and detachment. The questions of source reliability, validity and representativeness are the same as for all research methods, but lack of access to the producers of texts may limit the researcher's ability to provide answers. This is balanced against the greater scope to cross reference different texts and to be able to access sources where their producers may be either dead or otherwise unavailable. Whether textual materials offer a window on reality, or only into the minds of their producers, is another question that must be addressed by the researcher.

Keywords

Archive/Archival Research
Autobiographical Method
Biographical Method
Case Study/Case Study Method
Deduction
Ethics
Ethnographic/Ethnography

Field Research/Fieldwork
Genre
Induction
Literature Review
Literature Search
Narrative
Non-intrusive Data Collection

Qualitative
Quantitative
Research Design
Sampling
Text/Textual
Visual Data

Questions

1   When might primary textual data collection be used either instead of or in addition to other forms of qualitative data collection?
2   How does the question of consent complicate the ethical status of textual data collection?
3   On what ground should a reflexive researcher question the validity of any textual data they collect?
4   What different sorts and sources of textual data exist?
5   With regard to issues of sampling, what are the advantages and disadvantages of textual data?

Further reading

Banks, Marcus (2001) *Visual Methods in Social Research*. London: Sage.

Emmison, Michael and Smith, Philip (2000) *Researching the Visual: Images, Objects, Contexts and Interactions in Social and Cultural Inquiry*. London: Sage.

Lee, Raymond (2000) *Unobtrusive Methods in Social Research*. Buckingham: Open University Press.

Pink, Sarah (2001) *Doing Visual Ethnography*. London: Sage.

Scott, John (1990) *A Matter of Record: Documentary Sources in Social Research*. Cambridge: Polity Press.

The journal *Sociology* Volume 27, Number 1, special issue on Auto/Biography in social research is also particularly helpful.

CHAPTER
10

ETHNOMETHODOLOGY AND CONVERSATION ANALYSIS

Chapter contents

By the end of this chapter you will be able to:

- Outline the theoretical underpinnings of the ethnomethodological and conversation analytic challenge to social research.

- Understand the practical and methodological basis by which these two approaches seek to study human interaction.

- Identify and comprehend a number of key studies which highlight how both approaches operate in practice.

- Critically evaluate the practical strengths and limitations of both approaches.

- Engage with the ethical issues raised by both approaches.

Ethnomethodology: 'qualitative experiments'

Sociology, but not as sociologists know it!

Ethnomethodology, according to Graham Button (1991: 1) represents 'a foundational respecification of the human sciences'. It may be seen as sociology, but not as sociologists know it. **Ethnomethodologists** refuse to get to grips with what has traditionally been seen as 'the problem' and have adopted methods appropriate to dealing with 'their' respecification of the problem. Ethnomethodology seeks to find the methods used by 'members' in everyday interaction which achieve the sense of order often called 'society' (hence 'ethno' – methods). Ethnomethodology's focus upon the achievement of a sense of order through the actions of participants in that interaction requires an empirical focus upon the micro-processes of everyday life. Ethnomethodology does not seek to explore macro patterns of social 'structure' and seeks to exclude from its 'explanations' of events all attributions of prior or unobservable 'social processes and forces'. In drawing upon external 'causal explanations' from beyond the **data** at hand to the researcher, the conventional social researcher stands accused by ethnomethodologists of engaging in a deception.

Harold Garfinkel and a circle of students and colleagues in California founded ethnomethodology in the 1960s. Garfinkel's *Studies in Ethnomethodology*, published originally in 1967 (reprinted in 1984), represents the definitive founding text. Garfinkel's early work on suicide and mental illness set his approach on a collision course with the founder of sociological method, Emile Durkheim, whose use of variations in suicide statistics represented perhaps the most influential foundation of sociological method. Garfinkel adopted a number of innovative research strategies in order to explore the methods actors, in everyday interaction, use to build and sustain the sense of social order commonly perceived to pre-exist the interaction. Durkheim used suicide statistics as a resource for exploring the social forces 'causing' suicide. Garfinkel wanted to know how the statistics were put together. Garfinkel suspended judgement over any relationship between the figures and a supposed 'real' level of self-inflicted death. Such was the nature of Garfinkel's challenge to conventional social research, both as an institution and as a set of methods. Ethnomethodology still generates extreme reaction. In some quarters it is a heretical non-sense, while in others it has achieved an almost cult like status. With its own agenda, language and methods of practice, ethnomethodology still appears 'strange' to those schooled in other ways of researching. This, combined with a certain insularity amongst its core adherents, means that the insights gained within ethnomethodology are poorly communicated. Here, it is attempted to show how ethnomethodologists work.

Key concepts

Emerging from the tradition of **phenomenology** (see 'Phenomenological ontology' p. 38), Garfinkel's ethnomethodology was to reject the value of 'grand theories' of social structure in favour of a focus upon the practices of participants. As such the key concepts within ethnomethodology refer to forms of action, not to forms of social structure/institution. It is the exploration of forms of action that directs ethnomethodological research. The key nexus of actions hinges around what Garfinkel referred to as 'indexicality' and 'reflexivity'. The two combined make up what Garfinkel called 'the documentary method (or accounting)'.

Indexicality refers to the way explanation is often offered in terms of illustration. Indexing, in its crudest form, involves pointing at something and saying, 'That's what I mean'. Indexicality involves an appeal to something tangible and shared when engaged in clarifying some point of dispute. Abstract issues require grounding in concrete examples. It is in agreeing about the correct examples that a sense of agreement over more abstract ideas is generated.

Reflexivity refers to the way specific things or events are explained with reference to 'general patterns'. In its crudest form, reflexivity involves saying, 'Ah, what you are looking at there is an example of X'. Particular events and objects are thus rendered meaningful by placing them within categories, locating them within our general theories of the world. Things are made to make sense this way.

A chicken-and-egg situation is thereby revealed. Clearly, if indexicality and reflexivity are brought together, what is created is a circular process. If particular events and objects are explained by members in terms of the general theories held to be shared by members, while at the same time the members' 'general theories' are being held up through indexing particular events and objects as examples of those theories, it becomes clear that each is dependent upon the other. Members sustain the sense of an order through such circular processes. This is what Garfinkel calls the documentary method. This is the members' method (an ethno-method). Garfinkel's research, and that of other ethnomethodologists, highlights the active nature of such accounting in sustaining the sense of social order.

Why is this significant to the conduct of social research? Garfinkel suggests that social researchers are not that different from everybody else when it comes to the use of the documentary method. Social researchers, Garfinkel suggests, use examples to justify their theories, and theories to explain their data (that is, their examples). This applies to the quantitative researcher who justifies their prescriptive **categories** on the basis of the very data such categories structure the creation of, and which are then used to explain their results. The accusation also applies to the qualitative researcher whose selection of quotations and descriptions will be driven by what they think they have found, even while what they think they have found is said to have emerged from their quotations and descriptions. In each case appearances are claimed to show what lies beneath, while at the same moment appearances are explained in terms of what lies beneath.

The ethnomethodological method

Garfinkel sought to step out of this trap. To do so he proposed a stance of indifference towards the truth claims made by members and, furthermore, he proposed that the study of members' methods would study the uniqueness of particular interactions, rather than seek to prove overall patterns behind all such interactions. These two dimensions map onto the questions of **depth validity** and **generalizability**. Indifference towards the truth value of claims made by members, whether lay members or professional sociologists, made such claims a topic for research rather than a resource. Such claims did not take us beyond the interactions they were a part of. What is of

interest to Garfinkel is how such claims are 'achieved' and 'sustained', not whether they are true. Garfinkel is not interested in whether members' knowledge is valid. He seeks to describe how it happened. Of course, we should be concerned as to whether Garfinkel's data has depth validity. Garfinkel (and others) developed an array of tactics in their attempt to achieve this end. As regards the claim that ethnomethodology seeks only to describe the unique nature of each particular creative achievement they research, there is scope for dispute. Ethnomethodologists do seek to make generalized claims about the nature of social interaction based upon specific research, itself driven by particular theoretical motivations. Ethnomethodologists use experiments, **participant observation**, **interviews** and **case studies** along with other techniques in their own way and to their own ends. Outlined below are some empirical techniques used by ethnomethodologists to explore members' methods.

The fake student counsellor 'experiment'

Garfinkel used a number of experiments to explore actors' methods of sense making. In one such experiment 10 students were asked to pose questions to a supposed student counsellor by means of an intercom system (Garfinkel, 1984: Ch. 3). Each question was answered either Yes or No. The student was then required to turn off the intercom and write their interpretation of the answer they had been given. The Yes or No answers were, in fact, random, yet in each case the students managed to interpret the response in a way that was meaningful to them. Drawing upon the transcripts of the students' responses, Garfinkel sought to show the work that each student put into the interpretation. Sense making, or reflexive accounting, requires an active attempt to bring order to the situation. The students appeared naturally disposed to the creative use of such methods. Each student felt they had 'understood' the intentions of the counsellor, despite the fact that there were no 'intentions' to be understood.

Enough is enough: working with the taken-for-granted

In parallel 'experiments' (Garfinkel, 1984: Ch. 1 and 2) students were asked to insist on clarification in a number of exchanges with others not party to the instruction. If asked 'How are you today?', students would reply: 'What do you mean exactly?' or 'Can you clarify that question for me?'. The result was confusion and often anger. Garfinkel highlights the sense of expectation that is violated in such an exchange, as well as the sense of something shared but unspecified that underpins such expectations. Without formal agreement people have a sense that they all know what X means. Even if 'How are you today?' can be read in different ways, to deviate from the impression of 'something understood' is to open up the whole fabric of social order, this fabric being the fiction that everyone really does know what everyone else means when they ask 'How are you today?'. Similarly, when students were sent home to act as lodgers in their homes, the resulting confusion and anger was said to highlight the taken for granted, yet unspecified, and in an important sense un-specifiable, 'rules' that were assumed to govern normal home life. When challenged, the rules could not be clearly specified. Garfinkel (1984: 70) draws a parallel with Wittgenstein's claim that no rule contains within itself the rules of its own interpretation. We think there are rules we all agree to, but as no rule can ever be fully and exhaustively set down such that no divergence can emerge over interpreting it, we are forced to rely on the assumption of a common understanding. The repair work done in day-to-day life, which sustains this illusion of solid foundations and rules, is exposed in these experiments. Garfinkel called such experiments **breaching**.

Passing: the case of 'Agnes'

Based on over 30 hours of interviews, Garfinkel researched the sexual identity of 'Agnes', born with male genitalia, but who at puberty developed breasts and later had reconstructive surgery in order to have a vagina rather than a penis. Garfinkel was keen to explore the social reconstruction that Agnes had had to undergo in order to take on the public role of a woman. Agnes asserted that she had always been a female, and had always known that her identification as a boy was a mistake premised upon having a penis. Garfinkel was not interested in whether Agnes had or had not always been a female. For him, what Agnes performed was the work necessary to maintain the social status of female. Before and after reconstructive surgery Agnes had to consciously take on the female role. The rituals and the routines of maintaining the binary distinction of masculine and feminine involve much more than simply having a penis or a vagina. Garfinkel is interested in the social actions involved in 'passing', managing identity. For him Agnes reveals much about the nature of managing gender. Garfinkel

suggests (1984: 180) that Agnes 'Highlights how normal sexuality is accomplished through witnessable displays of talk and conduct', not simply by means of hidden biological facts. Agnes is the doer of the accountable person who is Agnes. Such effort illustrates the surfaces by which supposedly biological identities are attributed.

The social organization of juvenile justice

One of Garfinkel's collaborators, Aaron Cicourel (1968), used a comparative study of two areas, using a mix of secondary sources and interviews, to investigate how classification of young offenders impacts upon the construction of criminal statistics. Cicourel wanted to investigate the process by which criminal statistics were generated. How were rules interpreted? What would be the consequences? What Cicourel showed was that the processing of a 'crime' involves a series of interpretive filters. Was the event observed? If so, was it interpreted as a crime? If so, was it reported? If so, was it recorded? If so, was it investigated? If so, was someone 'caught'? If so, were charges pressed? If so, did it come to court? If so, was there a conviction? If so, was there a custodial sentence? If statistics on the composition of juvenile criminals are based on so much interpretive work, can we trust that the figures give us the 'truth'? Cicourel is suspicious of using 'truth' as a benchmark. What he is able to highlight is that in the more affluent area particular events are less likely to progress through all the stages. At each stage there is a greater rate of 'dropping the case' in the more affluent area. Rules are interpreted more harshly in the poorer area, and there are higher conviction rates there.

Some comments on methods in ethnomethodology

As can be seen in the above examples, ethnomethodology, while often associated with forms of **naturalistic** experiment, has involved a range of data collection methods: interviews, case-study work, comparative analysis, and secondary data analysis. Ethnomethodology can also be carried out by means of **ethnography** (Zeitlyn et al., 1999). In this sense, ethnomethodology is not a method in itself; it is an investigative orientation towards members' methods. However, while not a singular method, ethnomethodology has challenged the conventional assumptions about what social research should investigate. Garfinkel's naturalistic experiments offer insights into how such a reorientation of focus can be taken up empirically. Taking up these insights has led to innovations within more traditional methods, such as interviews and ethnography.

However, it is important to point out that many of Garfinkel's experiments would be considered unethical today. Other experiments of his involved secretly taping the deliberations of juries in criminal trials and recording conversations with people telephoning suicide prevention lines. Often Garfinkel's experiments involved deception. There is an argument that deception is essential in any experimental method involving human subjects. Others suggest the value of qualitative research lies in its avoidance of the experimental deception, regardless of whether the experiments are in a lab or in everyday contexts (see 'The qualitative inside all research: measurement', p. 39).

It is worth noting that in pointing to the income differences between the neighbourhoods in his study of juvenile justice, Cicourel deviated from the orthodox ethnomethodological premise of looking only at what is present in data collected in observed interactions. Cicourel's use of externally produced theoretical models to locate his data and to structure his choice of sites is a classic instance of reflexivity. Such a violation of orthodoxy may lead some to reject the attribution that 'affluence'/'poverty' is a **causal** factor in accounting for juvenile conviction rates and only retain the observation that rates vary because interpretations vary. Others may take Cicourel's

deviation from the orthodox ethnomethodological prescriptions as proof of the need to abandon such a dogmatic school of social research. Perhaps the most useful interpretation is that social researchers can learn from each other, and that the gulf between ethnomethodology and other forms of social research is not as absolute as it is often said to be.

Conversation analysis: fine-grain recording of naturally occurring talk

Taking advantage of small-scale cassette recording technology, **conversation analysis** sought to revolutionize social research with a refocusing of attention upon the mechanisms at work in, and the achievement that is, everyday naturally occurring human conversation.

Harvey Sacks' mission

Harvey Sacks (1992) created conversation analysis (not to be confused with content analysis – see Chapter 16 and particularly Chapter 18) from within and yet beyond ethnomethodology. The two approaches share many fundamentals, but conversation analysis (CA as it is often called) developed a particular formal approach to the examination of everyday interaction, the search for 'machinery' which generates the natural organization of talk. CA seeks to replace general theory with a general methodology (see Box 10.1).

BOX 10.1 BASIC PRINCIPLES OF CONVERSATION ANALYSIS (CA)

David Silverman (1998: Ch. 4) outlines a set of basic CA methodological principles:

1 Avoid summary representations – provide detailed transcripts to the reader (such that they can examine your claims about the data fully).
2 Pursue data sets which allow study of fine detail (that is, tape recordings).
3 Question reliance upon interview data (seek naturally occurring talk).
4 Address the most basic details of interaction rather than relying upon 'glosses' (appeals to supposedly taken-for-grantedness). Make common sense a topic, not a resource.
5 Be hyper-scientific, and behaviourist (study only what can be seen, avoid the tendency to attribute meanings and motives that cannot be seen).
6 Don't introduce theoretical concepts and constructs: seek out the real members' categories, the machinery that actors actually use.
7 Focus on the routine, not the unusual.

BOX 10.2 FEATURES OF TALK

This list of features is taken from Silverman (1998: Ch. 6).

1 People talk one at a time.
2 Speaker change recurs.
3 Sequences that are two utterances long and are adjacently placed may be 'paired' activities.
4 Activities can be required to occur at 'appropriate' places.
5 Certain activities are 'chained' (sequences of expectation ensue).

Actors generate order within and through interaction. Sacks sought a method of capturing those methods. This involved the taping of conversation and then the analysis of what were often tiny fragments of that talk to demonstrate the complexity of the interplay.

From adjacency pairs to the general machinery of expectation

The most basic facet of conversation is the fact that one person saying something to someone else will often contain an expectation of a response. Call and response expectation establish what Sacks calls **adjacency pairs**, basic units of naturally occurring talk. The first part of the pair creates a conversational space which the second party to the conversation is expected to fill. It is not the case that the first person compels the second to respond, or that the nature of the response is determined by the first part of the pair. As Silverman points out (1998: 99), it is possible to ignore someone if they say hello to you, though it is interesting to note that it is not as easy as one might think to do so. If, however, one does choose to reject the request contained in an invitation to respond, this is likely to be taken as an insult. The fact that offence may be taken from a 'snub' lies in the force of the expectation. Butting into a conversation or speaking out of turn are morally regulated in the action of conversation. Silverman (1998: Ch. 6) highlights a range of sequential features contained within conversation (see Box 10.2)

Once again it is important to note that the machinery is not what makes people do what they do. The machinery is what the people use to do what they do. Expectations can be broken, but they are nevertheless expected.

Trivia?

Sacks was keen to argue that it is precisely the seeming triviality of talk that makes it so important. It is the bedrock of social life and yet it is so often taken for granted. The fine-grained analysis of talk allows for the micro-machinery upon which all else is built (in Sacks' view) to become available to us. Recording natural talk allows very mundane things to take on a great significance precisely because they at first seem so obvious. The example of putting a 'Hm!!' into a conversation allows for the study of **turn-taking**, and the general requirement to be oriented to the other within a conversation that is essential to the maintenance of social action. Benson and Hughes (1991) highlight the fact that for Sacks it was not a question of generating large samples, but of identifying the machinery in every individual interaction. In so far as a set of general themes emerged, these were always to be subordinate to the need to ground all claims in the particular data (and the ability to defend any such claims by recourse to a full and detailed transcript of the talk). Hyper-detailed transcription, published alongside any analysis, is the foundation upon which CA seeks to identify and justify claims concerning the machinery at work in talk.

Transcription notation

Sacks began the process of developing a system of **transcription notation** that would allow the process of conversation to be formally represented. However, this work was taken up by his collaborator, Gail Jefferson. It is Jefferson's version of CA transcription notation that has formed the basis for most subsequent CA work, though there have been many adaptations and additions to take into account novel

---

BOX 10.3 CONVERSATION ANALYSIS TRANSCRIPTION NOTATION IN PRACTICE

Example of CA transcription notation in use, from Alison Pilnick (2002: 341):

```
204 C:    If it was (.) shown that you definitely (.) have the gene for °Huntington's°=
205 Cl:   =Mmhmm
206 C:    Ehhm (.) that would open up the possibility of testing an unborn [baby
207 Cl:                                                                      [Mmhmm
208 C:    by a test which could be carried out on (.) at around about tw- (.)
209       eleven to twelve weeks [°of your pregnancy° and it would
210 Cl:                          [Mm (.) can check that
211 C:    involve removing a very tiny piece of the placenta (.) by a
212       well established technique which involves passing a very fine
213       catheter (.) through the birth canal °into the placenta° (0.2) and
214       pulling out a little piece and sending it off to the lab (.) [and then
215 Cl:                                                                 [Mmhmm
216 C:    testing for DNA (.) genetic material in that placenta=
217 Cl:   =Mmhmm
218 C:    and if you get (.) a good result that's great (0.2) if you get
219       a result back that's uhh bad (.) the::n you know (.) that
220       they have inherited the gene for Huntington's disease (.)
221 Cl:   [Mmm
222 C:    [and you then are faced with this awful decision of what to
223       do (.) and that's your business=
224 Cl:   =Mmhmm=
225 C:    =we'll support you whatever you [decide
226 Cl:                                   [yeah
227       (2.0)
```

interactional situations (such as human computer interaction). CA has developed a descriptive capacity through which the complexity of talk can be captured for the purposes of fine-grain analysis. For an example see Box 10.3.

This system is best summarized by J. Maxwell Atkinson and John Heritage (1984: ix–xvi). Here only the key notations are outlined and a number of examples are given, based upon Atkinson and Heritage's account.

1   *Simultaneous utterances:* where two people begin to speak at the same time. Here a pair of square brackets is placed at the start of the lines of transcribed conversation indicating that the two lines of talk occurred at the same time (see Box 10.3, lines 221 and 222).

2   *Overlapping utterances:* where a second speaker starts to talk while the first speaker is still talking. Here

the square brackets are placed at the point in the first speaker's talk where the second speaker begins. Both speakers' talk is then written one above the other after the square bracket. The square bracket is closed at the point at which one speaker stops talking while the other continues (see Box 10.3, lines 214 and 215).

3   *Contiguous utterances:* where there is no gap between one person's talk finishing and another person's talk starting. Here the equals sign is placed at the end of the first speaker's talk while another equals sign is placed at the beginning of the second speaker's transcribed talk (see Box 10.3, lines 223–225).

4   *Intervals within and between utterances:* where there is no talk. Here the time interval in tenths of a second is placed inside round brackets, that is, (0.8) or (3.4). This may be either in the line between two speakers or within the transcribed talk of one speaker

depending whether the continuation of talk comes from a second speaker or from the same speaker as last spoke. Very brief pauses are indicated with a dash, that is, – or a dot in brackets (.) (see Box 10.3, lines 218–220).

5   *Characteristics of speech delivery:* here it is the character of the speaking that the transcription seeks to highlight. A falling tone, intonation, rising inflection, animated tone and abrupt cut-off or stammering are indicated by full stops, commas, question marks, question marks with a comma rather than a stop at the bottom, exclamation marks and dashes respectively. Upward and downward arrows are used to indicate intonation, underlining is used to show a tone of emphasis in the talk, capital letters identify louder than usual speech, while elevated circles indicate quietness. A stream of similar formal notation devices has been developed. A word stretched will be written out with a series of ::: marks to indicate its elongation (for example, hel::::lo).

6   *Transcription doubt:* where the transcriber is unsure what has been said exactly. Here the whole portion that is in doubt is placed in parentheses (round brackets). Sometimes alternative possibilities are presented one below the other.

Analysis of data in CA is addressed in Chapter 18.

The value of CA

It may seem that the value of a conversation analytic approach is to highlight the creativity of everyday interaction and to thereby demonstrate the significance of the micro-interactional competence of people, as distinct from the drive to show how people are the unknowing products of macro-structural forces. Nevertheless, it is important to note that it was Sacks' intention to use CA to build a general methodology for discovering the machinery of human interaction. CA has been used to show how and when breakdowns occur in everyday interaction, and how repair work is carried out. It has also been used to show how humans interact with machines (see Zeitlyn et al., 1999; Turkle, 1996; Button, 1990). This often leads to interactional breakdowns because humans transfer the conversational expectations they have of other humans to machines that do not operate according to the same machinery. As a method of recording talk, CA has great significance. As a challenge to conventional assumptions about inference, CA can also be questioned. To the extent that CA suggests it is possible to study talk with no reference to the motives of speakers or the context in which speech occurs, it has set for itself operational limits that are almost never fully adhered to. To focus only on what is manifest in the talk itself, with no attempts to infer to or from motive or context may be impossible. However, the call to pay attention to what and how people talk should be heeded.

Summary

Ethnomethodologists and conversation analysts seek to identify general practices within micro-level social interaction. While sharing common origins and much else in common, conversation analysis has sought to develop a far more formal approach to recording micro instances of naturally occurring talk (talk that is not generated by a researcher-driven interaction), while ethnomethodologists have pursued an approach that is less formal in its recording of data, but which is more interventionist in selecting, intervening in, and even setting up the micro-interactional situations they wish to study. Both approaches seek to highlight how 'social order' is achieved by the interaction of people, rather than order being the framework within or stage upon which action takes place.

Keywords

Adjacency Pairs
Breaching
Case Study/Case Study Method
Categories
Causal
Conversation Analysis

Data
Depth Validity
Ethnographic/Ethnography
Ethnomethodology
Generalizability
Interview

Naturalism/Naturalistic
Participant Observation
Phenomenology
Transcription Notation
Turn-taking

Questions

1   How and how far can ethnomethodological and/or conversation analytic techniques be integrated with other forms of qualitative data collection?

2   In what ways do ethnomethodology and conversation analysis differ, and to what extent are they compatible?

3   In what ways do ethnomethodology and conversation analysis challenge the validity of other forms of social research data, and is such a challenge itself valid?

4   What are the ethical strengths and weaknesses of conversation analysis and ethnomethodology?

5   Are the things that ethnomethodologists and conversation analysts study trivial?

Further reading

Atkinson, J. Maxwell and Heritage, John (1984) *Structures of Social Action: Studies in Conversation Analysis.* Cambridge: Cambridge University Press.

Button, Graham, (ed.) (1991) *Ethnomethodology and the Human Sciences*. Cambridge: Cambridge University Press.

Garfinkel, Harold (1984) *Studies in Ethnomethodology*. Cambridge: Polity.

Psathas, George (1995) *Conversation Analysis: The Study of Talk-in-Interaction.* London: Sage.

Sacks, Harvey (1992) *Lectures on Conversation*. Oxford: Blackwell.

Silverman, David (1998) *Harvey Sacks: Social Science and Conversation Analysis*. Cambridge: Polity.

Zeitlyn, David, David, Matthew and Bex, Jane (1999) *Knowledge Lost in Information*. London: British Humanities Press.

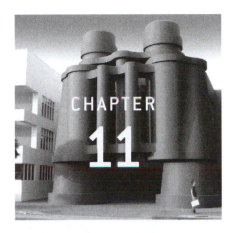

CHAPTER
11

INTRODUCTION TO QUANTITATIVE RESEARCH DESIGN

Chapter contents

By the end of this chapter you will be able to:

- Understand what is meant by the term 'research design'.

- Distinguish between experimental and non-experimental designs.

- Outline the different types of quantitative research design available to the social researcher.

- Understand the difference between primary data collection and the use of secondary data.

- Consider ethical issues associated with research including confidentiality, anonymity and informed consent.

Research design

Quantitative **research design** is based within the positivist traditions of the natural sciences. The purpose of a research design is to provide a framework for the collection and analysis of data. In the natural sciences research is often performed using experiments that are designed to control for all known factors that could influence the data collection. These experimental designs are concerned with controlling and manipulating a specific characteristic, called a variable, and measuring any changes that occur as a result of an external stimulus being applied. For example, applying heat to a container of ice and measuring the change in the state of the water from solid ice to liquid water.

In social research the quantitative research design ideally should stay within the traditions of **positivism** and **naturalism**. However this is problematic, as it would be almost impossible to manipulate characteristics in a social setting. For example, in a study that wished to investigate changing political opinions at different ages, the researcher could record an individual's political opinion but would be unable to change their age to then record any change in that political opinion. The natural passage of time would have to elapse before recording political opinion at an older age.

In some incidences it may be possible to adopt the techniques of the natural sciences, but to do so would raise serious **ethical** issues. For example, randomly placing children into two separate groups and allocating them into different educational settings where one group is more disadvantaged than the second group.

In response to the difficulties of the experimental design, social research has developed alternative non-experimental approaches that focus on collecting data from already occurring groups in social settings. Statistical analysis techniques are used to compare the data from these different groups. The best known of these non-experimental designs is the **cross-sectional design**. The logic of the experiment with its focus on analysing the relationships between characteristics is maintained. In the experimental design the change in one variable as a result of the application of a stimulus is measured, whereas in the non-experimental design data on a number of different characteristics, or variables, is collected and analysed to explore the possible relationships and associations between them. The main method of collecting this data is the self-completion survey or structured interview.

There are a number of experimental and non-experimental designs available. This chapter will detail the main experimental and non-experimental designs. Chapter 12 will discuss variables and the testing relationships between variables, and the key stages in the research process and the development of a research question, hypotheses and operationalization. Chapter 13 discusses various sampling techniques for selecting participants in a study. Chapter 14 concentrates on the two main research methods in quantitative research, the self-completion survey and structured interview; key issues in question development, format and sequencing, piloting, data collection and preparing question responses for analysis by a computer are discussed.

Primary data collection or secondary sources?

The main emphasis in this chapter is on the collection of primary data. This is research where the researcher undertakes all the stages in the research process, from research question to final data analysis. In many cases this is the most appropriate method for the topic under investigation. There may be some topic areas that can be researched and explored further using existing data that has been collected, coded and entered into data files. The use of such sources is called secondary data analysis. The decision to undertake either primary research or to use secondary data sources will ultimately be determined by their availability and appropriateness for the research area.

Research design: experimental and non-experimental

Research design provides the logical framework upon which the research project is conducted and enables the researcher to gather evidence that will enable the research question to be addressed.

The function of a research design is to ensure that the evidence obtained enables us to answer the initial question as unambiguously as possible. Obtaining relevant evidence entails specifying the type of evidence needed to answer the research question, to test a theory, to evaluate a programme or to accurately describe the phenomena (de Vaus, 2001: 9).

Research design is often confused with **research method**. Both are intrinsically linked but are distinct from each other. Research method refers to the actual techniques of data collection, for example, the self-completion survey, interviews, focus groups and participant observation. **Experimental research** designs are based upon the natural sciences. **Non-experimental** research designs have been developed to take account of research undertaken in social settings. Frequently used non-experimental designs include the case study design, the cross-sectional design, the longitudinal design and the **comparative design**.

The classic experimental design

The **classic experimental** design involves randomly allocating subjects into two groups, the experimental group and the control group. Observations of the characteristic to be measured, known as a dependent variable, in both groups are undertaken at the start of the research, often referred to as the pre-test. The experimental group is then subjected to the manipulation or stimulus, known as the independent variable, while the control group is not subjected to the stimulus. A second set of observations of the

measured characteristic are then taken from both groups, often referred to as the post-test (see Figure 11.1). Pre-test and post-test observations of both groups can then be compared and analysed.

There are variations on this experimental format: see Black (1999) for a detailed discussion. There are a number of issues to be considered in relation to the experimental design. The first is the application of such a design in the social world. It is often not possible to be able to allocate subjects randomly into two groups, and even where possible, there is an issue of other external factors influencing the measured observations. The second issue is that introducing a manipulation or stimulus can be very difficult.

Quasi-experimental design

In situations where a classic experimental design cannot be achieved, the researcher may decide to use a **quasi-experimental design**. While not adhering to all of the characteristics of an experimental design, it endeavours to meet certain characteristics of the approach and is often applied in situations where subjects cannot be allocated to an experimental or control group. There are many variations on the quasi-experimental design. The main feature of a quasi-experimental design is that the subjects are allocated to groups according to already occurring features and are not randomly allocated by the researcher. The two main types of quasi-experimental design are **non-equivalent control group** designs and before-and-after designs (Schutt, 2001: 185). Non-equivalent control group designs have experimental and control groups that the subjects naturally belong to. The same process of pre-test and post-test is undertaken and the experimental group is subjected to the manipulation of the independent variable. **Before-and-after** designs differ in that there is no control group. Subjects are measured pre-test, subjected to the manipulation of the independent variable, and measured again post-test.

Groups	**Observation 1**	*Experiment stage*	**Observation 2**
Experimental group	Pre-test	Experiment performed	Post-test
Control group	Pre-test	No experiment	Post-test

←——— Compare and analyse ———→

Figure 11.1   The classic experimental design

Case study design

A **case study** design is concerned with the detailed examination of a single case. It is commonly associated with qualitative research techniques (see Chapter 8), though it can be used in quantitative approaches. The case study can seek to explore a topic where there has been little prior knowledge or understanding. It can also involve following one case over a period of time, for example, researching an individual's life history. The key element here is the definition of the term 'case'. A case could be an individual, an organization, an institution, an event or a geographical area.

One of the difficulties of case study design in quantitative research is defining the case. There are occasions when a research project may be described as employing a case study design yet the defining characteristics of the case are not the key objects under study. For example, the case study may be identified as a work organization, though the focus of the research is the individual employee. Yin (1994) provides a full discussion of undertaken case study research, including the design, case selection, data collection and analysis of results.

Cross-sectional design

A cross-sectional design is the most recognizable research design in social research. It is concerned with collecting data on more than one case at a single point in time and is often referred to as the 'social survey design'. Take care not to confuse this term with the term social survey that is used to refer to the self-completion survey, which is a method of data collection.

The researcher is concerned with selecting cases on the basis of variation in identified characteristics, known as variables. For example, selecting individuals or households by geographical area. Data recording different characteristics is collected from each case and is used to describe and explore relationships through the detecting of associations between the characteristics. For example, a questionnaire survey records a respondent's age and income. The association between age and income can then be described and analysed using a variety of statistical techniques.

The case studies from Chapter 5 on health inequalities, rural deprivation and evaluating inter-professional collaboration in education based the

research on a cross-sectional design. In the health inequalities research, the original health, lifestyle and employment data was collected from employees. Relationships and differences between the employee characteristics and health variables could then be explored. In the evaluation case study, the quantitative element of the research involved collecting personal details, occupation and professional data. This data was then used to explore relationships and differences between different groups and their responses to the attitudinal and collaboration questions. Both the health inequalities and evaluation case studies included a **longitudinal** aspect to the research design (see next section). In the rural deprivation study, both the quantitative and qualitative research elements involved a cross-sectional design. The quantitative data was collated for different geographical areas that could then be compared. The semi-structured interviews included biographical questions that allowed the researchers to examine the data for relationships.

In cross-sectional design the exploration of relationships and associations between variables needs to be carefully thought through. In experimental design the independent variable was that attribute which was being manipulated to measure variability in the dependent variable. With cross-sectional design there is no pre-test/post-test measure to compare, as the data is collected at one point in time. Instead the researcher has to use the knowledge gained, through an extensive literature review and prior experience, to determine the independent and dependent variable(s). In many instances the independent variable will be a characteristic of the case, for example sex, marital status and age. Changes in the dependent variable, for example income, can be explored by examining the differences between men and women, or plotting the variation in income by age. Variables and the testing of relationships are discussed in more detail in 'Variables and levels of measurement' p. 144.

Longitudinal design

Longitudinal design involves collecting data over time and is particularly useful when studying social change. The design will involve data collection from the same sample at two or more points in time. The data from each collection period can be compared to assess social change. Longitudinal studies are financially more expensive and time consuming, and consequently are not frequently undertaken by individual researchers. They tend to be conducted by government-based organizations and use self-completion surveys or structured interviews as the method of data collection.

The design of the longitudinal study tends to be a cross-sectional design. The Longitudinal Study, established in 1973, was designed to collect information on a randomly selected sample of half a million individuals in England and Wales. This was about one per cent of the entire population. Information is collected on these individuals from a variety of official sources. The National Health Service Central Register (NHSCR) is used to identify and track individuals. Data from the vital statistics indexes (births, marriages, deaths) and census data are linked using the NHSCR register (Marsh, 1988). Studies that involve surveying representative samples at two or more points in time are known as **panel studies**. A high level of consistency between the questions and representative samples will allow the researcher to analyse the data for changes over time or time trends (Ruspini, 2000). Studies that involve returning to the sample participants are known as **cohort studies**. For a fuller discussion of the issues relating to longitudinal design, see Hakim (2000), de Vaus (2001), Marsh (1988) or Menard (1991).

Two of the case studies in Chapter 5 involve a longitudinal design. The quantitative health inequalities research involved using original baseline data on health, lifestyle and employment of employees. The employees from one privatized department were then approached to participate in a follow-up survey. A response rate of 81 per cent was achieved. The data from both surveys was then used to explore relationships between changing employment situations, health and lifestyle measures. The evaluation research involved the same course participants completing a questionnaire at three stages during the education course, before, mid-way and following. This allowed the researcher to identify relationships and change over the period of the course duration.

Comparative design

Comparative research design has been developing and growing in recent years. The focus of comparative research is to identify differences and similarities between different groups, for example, **nation-states**. A research project could examine the similarities and differences in deprivation experienced by rural populations in different countries in the European Union. The growth in comparative research has taken place at a time of increasing globalization and the development of mass communication systems. Information and data on a variety of aspects, particularly nation-states, are more widely available through the development of government sponsored surveys and censuses. Other organizations that also collect data are corporate businesses and non-government organizations.

The ethics of quantitative research

A general discussion of ethical issues in social research can be found in Chapter 2, 'Being Ethical'. The following highlights the central ethical issues when undertaking quantitative research.

Confidentiality and anonymity

Confidentiality refers to the researcher ensuring that no one outside the research team will be able to identify the participants in the study and that responses of individuals are not directly repeated to others. **Anonymity** refers to the practice of ensuring that no one will be able to identify the participants in the study. Anonymity is the more challenging ethical issue to address. The process of confidentiality begins with the contacting of the sample, which should be undertaken by the research team, although administratively this is not always possible. Care needs to be taken during the data collection process to record sensitive data, such as names and addresses, separately from the question responses. The normal practice for confidentiality is to allocate each participant a unique identifying code.

The researcher does need to be aware that even these procedures do not always ensure anonymity, as an individual with specific knowledge of the sampling frame may be able to identify individuals through the careful scrutiny of the final research report. For example, in an organization it may be possible to identify individuals through other characteristics, for example, position in the company, sex and length of service. In these cases the researcher needs to give careful consideration as to how the research findings are reported.

Informed consent

It is the duty of the researcher to provide the potential participant with information on the nature and purpose of the research to be undertaken. In obtaining **informed consent** the participant should be given enough time to consider their participation in the research. Ideally details should be given before the completion of the data collection. In the case of a mail survey, this can take the form of a covering letter. For research involving face-to-face interviews, participants should be sent a covering letter prior to the interview and the interviewer should check that the respondent has received this and understood the research before starting the interview. In the case of interviews, it is also important that documentary evidence is obtained to confirm that informed consent has been obtained and this usually takes the form of signing an agreement. This is increasingly important to avoid any future litigation issues. For surveys, completion and return of the questionnaire can be taken as evidence of consent.

There is an issue of how much detail to pass on to the respondent. This is difficult to stipulate, as it will vary according to the nature of the project. It may also be necessary to obtain informed consent from 'key others' who may act as a gatekeeper to access. For example, a study involving school children completing a questionnaire survey may involve the informed consent of the headteacher, the classroom teacher, the parents/guardians and the school children themselves.

Conduct of the researcher

The researcher should at all stages in the research process conduct themselves in a professional manner.

Privacy of data

The researcher should accurately record the data and process the data accordingly. The fabrication of or falsifying data is a serious misconduct offence. In order for the researcher to ensure confidentiality and anonymity, the privacy of the data collected needs to be protected. The data should be recorded anonymously. If data is recorded with respondents' personal information, it should conform to the Data Protection Act legislated in the country you are working in. Details of the United Kingdom Data Protection Act (1998) can be found at the Information Commissioner website (http://www.dataprotection.gov.uk/). Details on privacy legislation in the US can be found at the Federal Trade Commission (www.ftc.gov).

Ethics and Internet-based research

In addition to the ethical issues that have already been discussed so far, using the Internet for research raises some specific issues that need to be considered. The first issue is that of anonymity. Respondents who e-mail completed surveys back to the researcher can be identified by the reply e-mail address. Surveys based on websites can record the Internet Protocol (IP) address of the computer that is accessing the Web page. It is technically possible for this address to be located. Websites can also set cookies – requests for information – which can gather additional details about the user's computer. Respondents who use computers in public access areas, Internet café's or libraries, reduce the technical possibility of being traced. An additional concern to the researcher is the issue of ensuring confidentiality through not disclosing data collected to any third parties. This is subject to the security software system installed on the Web server. Security could be breached by hackers who could access and corrupt data files.

Summary

Quantitative research design provides the framework for the social researcher to undertake a research project based on the positivist traditions of the natural sciences. This chapter has detailed both experimental and non-experimental designs that are available for the collection of primary data. The adoption of an experimental design would follow most closely those adopted in the natural sciences. However, the social researcher needs to consider both practical and ethical issues as to the feasibility, or indeed the desirability, of adopting such a design. The majority of quantitative researchers maintain their theoretical position within positivism and naturalism by adopting non-experimental research designs. The most commonly used design is that of the cross-sectional or social survey design. Cross-sectional designs and longitudinal designs are adopted in the large government-based surveys that researchers use to undertake secondary data analysis.

Keywords

Anonymity	Cross-sectional Design	Non-equivalent Control Group
Before and After Design	Ethics	Non-experimental Research Design
Case Study/Case Study Method	Experimental Research	Panel Studies
Classic Experimental Design	Informed Consent	Positive/Positivism
Cohort Studies	Longitudinal design	Quasi-experimental Design
Comparative Design	Nation-state	Research Design
Confidentiality	Naturalism/Naturalistic	Research Method

Questions

1   What is the difference between primary data and secondary data?

2   What are the main features of an experimental design?

3   Describe the different types of experimental and non-experimental quantitative research designs.

4   What are the ethical issues associated with quantitative research?

Further reading

Black, Thomas (1999) *Doing Quantitative Research in the Social Sciences: An Integrated Approach to Research Design, Measurement and Statistics*. London: Sage.

Robson, Colin (2002) *Real World Research: A Resource for Social Scientists and Practitioner-Researchers* (2nd edn). Second Edition. Oxford: Blackwell.

Sarantakos, Sotirios (1998) *Social Research* (2nd edn). Basingstoke: Macmillan.

Aldridge, Alan and Levine, Ken (2001) *Surveying the Social World: Principles and Practice in Survey Research*. Buckingham: Open University Press.

May, Tim (2001) *Social Research: Issues, Methods and Process* (3rd edn). Buckingham: Open University Press.

CHAPTER

12

HYPOTHESES, OPERATIONALIZATION AND VARIABLES

Chapter contents

By the end of this chapter you will be able to:

- Understand the key stages in the hypothetico-deductive process.

- Describe what is meant by the terms hypothesis and concept.

- Understand the process of operationalization.

- Distinguish between independent, dependent and control variables.

- Describe the four different levels of measurement.

Formation of the research question: theory, hypotheses and operationalization

Formulating a research question involves stating clearly what the researcher wants to find out. The research question will be a product of theories drawn from the literature review, discussions with professionals or experts in the area of study, and the 'hunches' or theories of the researcher. A full discussion of this process can be found in Chapter 4. The key factor in formulating the research question is that it must clearly state what exactly is to be researched. It is often the hardest aspect for the new researcher to grasp, as it requires a level of focus that is not initially easy to find. The development of a research question is the first stage in the research process.

The hypothetico-deductive research process is summarized by a number of stages (see Figure 12.1). At the first stage the literature review and knowledge gathered from other sources allows for a theory to be developed, and from the theory a hypothesis may be constructed which can, in turn, be tested. A hypothesis states the expected causal relationships between concepts. A **concept** is a unit that allows a researcher to organize an idea or observation. For example, the concept of the family or healthy lifestyle. Before the hypothesis can be tested the concepts need

to be **operationalized**, requiring the development of an operational definition and measurable indicators. Without an operational definition of the concept it would not be possible to collect data to accept or reject the relationship stated in the hypothesis. For example, if a project were examining family structures, how would the concept of family be defined? If a project were going to explore variations in healthy lifestyle amongst different social classes, the concepts of both healthy lifestyle and social class would need to be defined.

The next phase in the hypothetico-deductive model is the collection of data. After data collection, the data can be analysed to explore the relationships stated in the hypothesis. From the analysis the initial hypothesis can then be accepted or refuted with subsequent alterations to the initial theory made.

The research process as shown in Figure 12.1 is an idealized model. The reality for the social researcher is that the research process is frustrated by the complexities of the social world. As Bryman states:

> Quantitative research is invariably much more messy. It tends to involve false trails, blind alleys, serendipity and hunches to a much greater degree than the idealization implies. Nor does the idealized model take sufficient account of the importance of resource constraints on decisions about how the research should be carried out. (Bryman, 1988: 21)

However, the idealized model of the research process does provide a valuable structure and rigour for the researcher. The importance of addressing the issues at each stage in the research process should not be underestimated.

Operationalization: measuring concepts and developing indicators

Concepts need to be operationalized through the development of an operational definition and **measurement tools**. Operationalization is the process of turning abstract theoretical concepts into observable and measurable entities. Some concepts are easier to provide an operational definition for than

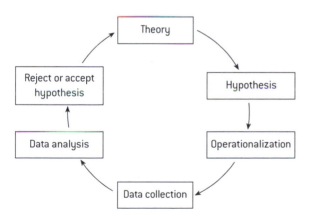

Figure 12.1 The research process in a hypothetico-deductive research model

others that are more abstract and difficult to 'pin down'. The key issue for the researcher is that there is often no consensus on the definition of concepts and the measurement tools or **indicators** developed for them. The literature review should provide the researcher with information on how previous research conducted in a particular subject area defined and operationalized the concepts used. This can be used as a foundation for the development of the measurements in your own research.

De Vaus (2001) provides a framework for developing the measurements called the 'ladder of abstraction'. The first step is to define the concept; one or more definitions may already exist and the researcher will need to decide which one to use or to develop their own definition. In either instance, a clear rationale for the decision needs to be stated. The next stage is to decide on the different dimensions through which the concept can be measured. Within each dimension subsequent sub-dimensions may exist. The next stage is then to devise an operational or working definition of the dimension that can be observed and measured. Through the operational definition of the dimension, the development of appropriate indicators can be achieved.

Where a concept has more than one dimension, multiple indicators can be developed. The issue for the researcher is then what indicators to use and how many of the indicators to include in the data collection and analysis stages. Many indicators already exist and have been developed amongst academic and professional researchers over many years. It makes sense at both the practical and methodological level for the first-time or student researcher, with limited experience, to make use of existing indicators. Use of these indicators, where appropriate, will also allow the researcher to make comparisons between their own research findings and those of others. Where new indicators are developed, with slightly different definitions, comparisons become problematic. Indicators exist in a wide range of fields and particularly in relation to areas that are strategic to government policy decisions. These indicators are likely to have been developed from their application in government sponsored surveys, such as the General Household Survey and the Family Expenditure Survey. The UK government statistical services provide a handbook detailing the main indicators used in these and other surveys. This is a very useful resource for the social researcher. Refer to Government Statistical Service (1998) *Harmonised Concepts and Questions for Government Social Surveys: Update December 1997*.

Example of a process of operationalization

Students, grades and paid work

Some people suggest that students undertaking paid work during their studies gain valuable experience that enhances both their future employability and their academic performance. Others argue that paid work interferes with study and leads to reduced academic performance and hence has a detrimental effect on future employment prospects. In order to investigate this issue it is essential to operationalize the concepts of 'student', 'paid work', 'academic performance' and 'employability'.

By 'student' we would need to clarify whether we were referring only to undergraduate degree students or whether we also wished to include other groups, such as pre-higher education students, those on other kinds of higher educational studies, and/or post-graduate level students. In addition, we would need to clarify whether we wished only to focus upon full-time students, or whether we would also want to include those who study part-time. What would count as full- and part-time then becomes a key issue. It may be important to consider whether different institutions of learning adopt different definitions of full- and part-time study, which might affect the comparability of the data.

By 'paid work' we would need to decide whether we were only interested in work carried out during academic term time/semester time, or whether work during holidays/vacations would also be taken into account. The time of day at which work takes place may alter the effect it might have on studies, so this may be a factor. Should work carried out at weekends be recorded, or are we only interested in work that took place during the week, when students might otherwise be attending to their studies? The type of work carried out may also be significant: The question of how to classify different kinds of work would require serious attention. The number of hours spent at work may be more difficult to record than might be imagined, and the rate of pay should also be recorded as poor pay may influence quality of life and hence performance.

By 'academic performance' do we only mean formal grades, or are there other elements to be taken account of? How might these be measured? Frequency of attendance, contribution to tutorials and seminars, involvement in student-centred self-support groups, and fulfilling deadlines and performance targets may all be affected by time spent in paid work.

Should we measure these, or simply measure final grade outcomes? Should we record students' self-perception regarding grades and other indicators, or seek institutionally held secondary data?

Post-study employability is, of course, something that happens some time after a student's study time. How long should one wait to test the relationship between study, grades, paid work and future employment? Would it be better to measure current students and wait till they graduate, or might it be best to approach those already in employment and trace back their educational performance and employment record while they were students. And, what criteria should be applied to 'measuring' employment success? Is it enough simply to measure income, or are other factors significant? What might these be and how might they be measured?

Before any quantitative data can be collected, the issues raised around the above four concepts need to be resolved. Each concept needs to be operationalized into a measurable data collection tool.

Variables and testing relationships

A **hypothesis** is a statement that expresses the proposed relationship between two variables, an independent variable and a dependent **variable**. There are three different types of variable in the describing and testing of relationships set out in the hypothesis. A variable is defined as a characteristic, attribute or single unit of information collected on a case. A **case** is the individual respondent, for example, a person, a business or an educational institution. If the case were

an individual, some of the variables would contain data that describes their attributes, for example, age, sex or marital status. Alternatively, if the case were a business some variables would contain characteristics that would describe the company, for example, the business sector, number of employees and annual financial turnover. Additional variables would also contain data that related to the topic area to be studied.

To establish a relationship between two variables, as stated in a hypothesis, requires the use of statistical techniques to establish **causality**. Variables can be placed into three different roles depending on the complexity of the hypothesis or model of the relationship: these are an **independent variable**, **dependent variable** or **control variable**. The hypothesis represents what the researcher proposes as the relationship between the variables. Variables can take on one or more of these roles according to the relationship that is being described and tested.

The independent variable, also referred to as the cause, is assumed to be the variable that is influencing a second, dependent variable. The independent variable is presented as the X variable in mathematical notation. The dependent, also referred to as the effect variable, is the variable that is being influenced by the independent variable. The dependent variable is presented as the Y variable in mathematical notation. In many instances there is a time order associated with the independent variable and dependent variable relationship. The relationship between the independent and dependent variables is shown in Figure 12.2.

The control variable is a variable that the researcher 'suspects' is influencing the relationship between the independent and dependent variables. The exact nature of the influence may not be understood. It is often presented as the Z variable in mathematical notation. Figure 12.3 shows the possible influences that the control variable can have on the relationship between the independent and dependent variables. The control variable can have a direct influence on the independent variable, X. Alternatively, the control variable may intervene or mediate in the relationship between the independent, X, and dependent, Y. Both of these are shown in Figure 12.3 as **a** and **b** respectively.

The process of analysing the relationship between an independent and a dependent variable controlling for the effects of a third, control, variable is referred to as 'elaboration'. When the relationship between the independent and dependent variables disappears as the

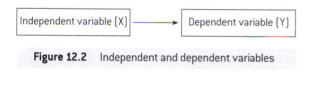

Figure 12.2   Independent and dependent variables

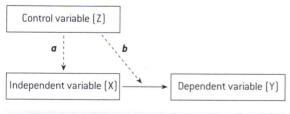

Figure 12.3   Control variables

result of the introduction of a control variable, the relationship is said to be spurious.

While it is possible for the researcher to undertake analysis of all possible relationships between all variables in their data set, it is not a recommended or efficient practice. Attempting to embark on such a task will result in too great a volume of results that are unmanageable and ultimately meaningless. Instead the strategy should be to collect data relevant to the original model of the relationships and to map out the relevant relationships between variables.

In mapping out relationships between variables, care must be taken to assess the time order of the variables. You need to avoid exploring relationships between two variables where the independent variable naturally occurs in time after the dependent variable. For example, an analysis of a relationship between income and sex has a time order of sex occurring in time before income. The individual is born with a specific sex, the independent variable, and income, the dependent variable, can only occur once the individual is a working adult. Likewise, in the relationship between number of years of formal education and income, the time order is formal education years, the independent variable, and income, the dependent variable. Chronologically the individual should complete some schooling before entering the labour market. Assessing the time order is a useful technique at the data analysis stage.

Of course, when the researcher reaches the data analysis stage, the idea of setting out a formalized relationship between two variables may seem abstract to the real social world where many factors or variables will influence particular outcomes. For example, one only needs to think of the wealth of literature and research that has been undertaken on widening access and participation in higher education. The focus of much of this research has been on the choices potential students make and how these choices are 'infused with class and ethnic meanings' and different individuals' biographies and 'opportunity structures' (Ball et al., 2002: 51). Reducing the analysis to a simplistic cause-and-effect relationship between two variables would hardly seem sufficient. The data analysis would need to reflect the range of factors identified from the literature review. The use of a cause-and-effect relationship model, though, does provide a useful structure at the data analysis stage.

Variables and levels of measurement

Variables can be defined into four different **data types**, known also as **levels of measurement**, according to the particular features of the data. The four data types are **nominal**, **ordinal**, **interval** and **ratio**. It is important that the researcher is able to distinguish between them as the data type or level of measurement will influence the type of statistical analysis techniques available at the data analysis stage.

Interval/ratio

Interval and ratio variables contain data that is measured on a continuous scale. They are also referred to as quantitative variables, since the data can be subjected to mathematical operations. Both interval and ratio variables can be placed in rank order of importance and the distance between observations is known and can be calculated. Interval variables have no **true zero point**. They include measures such as time and temperature. Ratio variables have a true zero point; examples include measures of length, height, weight, age and number of persons in household. For convenience, interval and ratio variables are often referred to as simply interval or scale variables. It is important to note the difference between interval and ratio levels of measurement at the analysis stage, particularly if the researcher decides to manipulate the original data.

Ordinal

For ordinal data, response categories can be placed in a rank order. No calculation can be made as to the distance between the different categories, though it is possible to judge one category to have a higher order than a second category. A common example of ordinal data is a scale measuring attitudes; for example, a 5-point scale of strongly agree, agree, neutral, disagree, strongly disagree.

Nominal

Nominal or categorical variables result from questions that ask a respondent to select a response category from a list of named items. For example, a question asks the respondent to select the newspaper that they read on a daily basis from a list of 10 different newspapers. The response categories cannot be placed in any order and no judgement can be made about the relative size or distance of one category to another. Consequently, no mathematical operations, addition, subtraction, multiplication or division can be performed on these variables. In the literature nominal variables are sometimes referred to as qualitative variables because they have no mathematical properties. Variables that have only two responses, for example, Yes or No, are known as dichotomies.

Hierarchical order with levels of measurement

Nominal, ordinal and interval/ratio variables can be placed into a hierarchical order. Nominal variables are the lowest, ordinal variables are in the middle, and interval/ratio variables are the highest. This is an important hierarchy to remember, as it is possible to re-code, or adjust, the data. Interval/ratio variables can be re-coded into ordinal variables or nominal variables. Similarly, ordinal variables can be re-coded into nominal variables. However, lower order variables cannot be re-coded to a higher order variable. Ordinal variables cannot become interval/ratio variables and, likewise, nominal variables cannot become ordinal or interval/ratio variables.

When developing survey questions it is important that the researcher considers the data type of the question response and the likely analysis to be undertaken. For example, a question that asks for last week's salary to be recorded to the nearest whole pound, euro or dollar, can be analysed using an array of techniques appropriate for interval/ratio data. It can also be manipulated into an ordinal or nominal variable at a later stage if required. A salary question that has response categories of salary ranges and is therefore ordinal data can be analysed using ordinal techniques and can be manipulated into wider salary range categories or into nominal data. The researcher needs to balance the analysis techniques available for different levels of measurement against the appropriateness of questions and responses. In the earlier example of salary, would asking someone to specify his or her salary for last week be more likely to result in a refusal to answer than being asked to tick an appropriate salary range?

Summary

In the hypothetico-deductive research process, the research moves through a number of defined stages from knowledge gathering, development of a theory, construction of a hypothesis to the operationalization of concepts, data collection and analysis. The operationalization process turns concepts into observable and measurable entities that are then stored as variables for the purposes of analysis. The subsequent analysis undertaken involves exploring relationships between different variables that requires independent variables, dependent variables and control variables to be identified.

Keywords

Case	Hypothesis	Nominal
Causality	Independent Variable	Operationalization
Concept	Indicators	Ordinal
Control Variable	Interval	Ratio
Data Type	Level of Measurement	Variable
Dependent Variable	Measurement Tools	

Questions

1   What are the key stages in the process of operationalization?
2   Give three examples of variables that a researcher may construct to record information about an individual person.

3   Describe the main characteristics of a nominal, ordinal and interval/ratio variable.

4   Why is it important to consider the level of measurement of the data collected?

5   What is the relationship between an independent variable and a dependent variable?

Further reading

Black, Thomas (1999) *Doing Quantitative Research in the Social Sciences: An Integrated Approach to Research Design, Measurement and Statistics*. London: Sage.

Bryman, Alan (1988) *Quantity and Quality in Social Research*. London: Routledge.

Fielding, Jane and Gilbert, Nigel (2000) *Understanding Social Statistics*. London: Sage.

Balnaves, Mark and Caputi, Peter (2001) *Introduction to Quantitative Research Methods: An Investigative Approach*. London: Sage.

CHAPTER
13

SAMPLING

Chapter contents

By the end of this chapter you will be able to:

- Describe the terms population, sampling frames, sampling technique and sample size.

- Understand the difference between probability and non-probability samples.

- Outline the different sampling techniques available.

- Understand the factors that will influence sample size selection.

This chapter discusses the issues of deciding who will participate in the research project. It will cover the issues of **population, sampling frames**, a variety of **sampling** techniques and **sample size**.

If the group to be studied is small it may be possible to survey the entire group, otherwise a selection of the group will be surveyed which must be representative of the entire group. The first stage in this process is to define the population that is to be surveyed; depending on its size the researcher will then take a **sample**, a selected number of cases from the population to survey. Consideration of how the cases are selected and the appropriate number of cases to select need to be addressed.

Population and sampling frames

A population is simply every possible case that could be included in your study. It will be defined by the nature of your enquiry. For example, in a study of first-year student debt the population would all be first-year students. If the research question were then further refined to focus on two degree programmes, BSc Geography and BSc Sociology, the population would then be defined as first-year students on BSc Geography and BSc Sociology. In this example the population refers to individuals, though this is not necessarily always the case. The individual units within a population will be defined by the research question and could be companies, households, or where quantitative content analysis is being undertaken, policy documents, media news coverage or minutes of meetings.

When the population is too large to undertake a **census**, that is, survey every individual case, then a representative group, called a sample, needs to be selected. As long as the sample is representative of the population, surveying only a fraction of the entire population can still yield results that would, on the whole, be found if the entire population was surveyed. In order to select a sample, a sampling frame needs to be drawn up.

A sampling frame contains every unit in the population and the subsequent sample is drawn from it. The units that are selected are known as **sampling**

units. The main issue facing social researchers is whether they are able to define and locate the population. In the above example, the educational institution should have a definitive list of students enrolled at stage one on either the Sociology or Geography programmes.

There is a practical distinction that can be made between a population and sampling frame. While the population is every individual case, the sampling frame is inevitably defined by specific criteria and has the possibility of being out of date (Black, 1999: 119). For example, the list of enrolled students is established at the beginning of the academic year. Students who leave their course of study prematurely may not be accurately recorded and removed from the list.

Defining the population for research purposes in some areas may not be so apparent. For example, a research project wishes to compare the leisure activities of the over-75s that live in rural and city locations. The population would be defined as the over-75s that live in city and rural locations. The first stage would be to define 'city' and 'rural' and from this locate all over-75s within each. This sounds straightforward; however, in reality it is extremely unlikely that a definitive list of all over-75s in rural and city locations exists. The researcher will have to access other sources to build a list, perhaps gaining access to local doctors' lists or contacting support organizations that have contact with over-75s. While these may allow a list of individuals who are over 75 years of age to be established, it will be a list of over-75s who *also* have contact with these organizations and *not* all over-75s.

Types of sampling

One of the key requirements of sampling is that the selected sample is not biased by either over- or under-representing different sections of the population. Consideration of the different characteristics within the population need to be included in this process. In the earlier example of research into first-year student debt, the researcher may want to ensure that they have a sample that represents the different social backgrounds of first-year students. For example, students who attend university straight from school or college, older students returning to study after a period away from education, students who have parental responsibilities or students who have to travel significant distances to attend lectures on campus.

The different sampling techniques available can be divided into two classifications. **Probability samples** are based on each case in the population having an equal chance of being selected. Non-probability samples are used when it is difficult to identify all potential cases in the population. There are a number of sampling techniques available within probability and non-probability techniques, each of which will be examined in the subsequent sections.

Probability sampling

There are four main types of probability sample:

* simple random sampling;
* systematic sampling;
* stratified sampling; and
* cluster/multi-cluster sampling.

The decision as to which technique to use will depend on:

> … the nature of the research problem, the availability of good sampling frames, money, the desired level of accuracy in the sample and the method by which the data are to be collected. (de Vaus, 1996: 61)

Simple random sampling

Simple **random sampling** involves randomly selecting individual units from a sampling frame. The term 'random' refers to a selection based on a mathematical formula that will consistently give all units an equal chance of being selected – it is not just a matter of a researcher randomly selecting units from a list! The mathematical techniques are also employed at the analysis stage and form the basis of inferential statistics and parametric tests (see Chapter 23).

There are a number of defined stages in undertaking a simple random sample (Black 1999; Fink, 1995b). The first stage is to obtain a complete sampling frame. For example, a list of all first-year degree students. The second stage is to assign each unit, in this instance a student, with a unique number. The third stage is to randomly select the appropriate

amount of random numbers. There are several ways of achieving this. One can make use of random numbers generated through a computer or use random number tables. Random number tables contain rows and columns of random numbers. An extract from a random numbers table is shown in Table 13.1

Table 13.1   Extract from a random numbers table

29	32	95	99	57	98	08	36	97	08
12	11	80	16	17	01	03	97	59	73
87	58	22	25	55	35	72	79	28	15
02	92	42	87	57	53	53	34	55	75
69	28	63	73	98	45	61	10	43	20

Source: Kmietowicz and Yannoulis (1988)

A systematic selection of random numbers across the table should be until enough random numbers have been selected for the total sample size required. Deciding on the required sample size is discussed in 'Sample size' p. 153. The final stage is to match the random numbers with the number of each unit in the sampling frame. The units that match the selected random numbers are selected for inclusion in the final sample.

Simple random sampling works well as a sampling technique when there is a large population with a quality sampling frame. There are some practical considerations to include when deciding whether to employ this technique. The most obvious and practical issue is linked to the method employed. If the population is large and spread over a large geographical distance, how feasible is it to conduct face-to-face interviews? A mail survey may be more practical in these circumstances, although this then brings in the other issues specific to this method.

Systematic sampling

Systematic sampling is an easier technique for sample selecting than the simple random sampling technique. Again the first step is to define the sampling frame. The next stage is to decide upon the sample size and to work out what fraction of the total sampling frame this represents. For example, if there were 1,000 first-year students and the sample size was to be 100, then this represents 10 per cent of the population. The first unit would normally be selected by random numbers and every subsequent tenth unit would then be selected.

Systematic sampling is a quicker technique than simple random sampling; however, there is one inherent weakness. It can be easy to inadvertently select units with 'like' characteristics, for example, in a sampling frame of first-year students the student records may have been arranged into a male then female order. If the sample size required you to select every fourth unit and if the randomly selected unit were male, all subsequent case selections would also be male (see Figure 13.1). This can be overcome by careful checking of the characteristics of the sampling frame prior to sample selection.

Stratified sampling

Stratified sampling is designed to produce more representative samples. The sampling frame is constructed according to a characterizing variable. This variable is also referred to as the 'stratified variable', for example, sex or social class, age group or ethnicity. The selection of the variables will be determined by the characteristics required for survey. The sampling frame is then organized according to these variables. For example, in the survey of first-year students we want to select a representative sample based on sex. The first-year students would be organized into two groups, male and female. The next stage is to determine the proportion of male and female students to select. In the population of 1,000 students the percentage of men is 60 per cent and percentage of women is 40 per cent and the sample size is to be 100. Sixty per cent of the sample size should be male and 40 per cent female, thus we need to select 60 male students and 40 female students. A systematic sampling technique can be used to select the male and female students. More complex stratified sampling techniques can be adopted to sample across more than one stratified variable; for a more detailed explanation, see Moser and Kalton (1971).

Cluster and multi-stage sampling

A **clustered sampling** technique involves selecting a sample based on specific, naturally occurring groups within a population. For example, randomly selecting 20 universities from a list of all universities in England, Wales and Scotland. Cluster sampling is a convenient sampling technique often used when the geographical spread of the population is large and where time and cost issues are of importance. **Multi-stage sampling** refers to a technique where cluster sampling is repeated at a number of different levels, from general to more specific groups. For example, rather than sample all first-year university students in England, Wales and Scotland, the sampling procedure would be staged. The first stage would involve randomly sampling universities according to different regions in England, Wales and Scotland. The second stage would then be to randomly sample students from each selected university.

Non-probability sampling

Non-probability sampling can be used when there are no convenient sampling frames of the population available or time/cost restrictions make the surveying of a widely dispersed population impractical.

Convenience, availability or opportunity sampling

Convenience, availability or opportunity sampling is simply a sample that is selected for ease of access. For example: conducting a survey involving stopping pedestrians in a city centre; stopping students as they walk around a university campus; or magazine or newspaper surveys that asks their readers to complete and return a survey. They are useful when the population is unknown or when a researcher is exploring a new research setting (Schutt, 2001: 130). The disadvantage is that they are not generalizable to the population, making analysis beyond simply describing the sample problematic.

F	**M**	F	M	F	**M**	F	M	F	**M**	F	M	F	**M**
	1st case				2nd case				3rd case				4th case

Figure 13.1   Systematic sampling

Quota sampling

The **quota sampling** technique involves selecting cases, by opportunity based selection methods, according to some pre-defined characteristics of the population. These pre-defined categories are referred to as quotas. The quotas can be selected in order to reflect the population's profile. For example, in the earlier example of a survey of first-year students, if the researcher was unable to obtain a student list from the university they could ascertain from university central reports the proportion of the current new student intake that is male and female. If the proportions were 60 per cent male and 40 per cent female and our sample size was to be 100, then we would need to select 60 male and 40 female first-year students.

The sample selection could be defined further with the introduction of a second quota, for example age. If the university profile of the student population age indicates that two-thirds are 21 years or under and one-third over the age of 21, the selection of male and female students could reflect this. In the sample of 60 men, 40 men should be 21 years or under and 20 men over 21 years. In the sample of 40 women, 27 women should be 21 years or under and 13 women over 21 years.

The difficulty with a quota sampling technique is that the sample is selected according to specified characteristics used in the quotas and excludes other population characteristics, for example, ethnicity and social class. This can be further complicated by not knowing the full population characteristics. Unlike availability sampling, quota samples do at least allow the researcher to establish characteristics that provide for a sample that will allow for comparisons between different groups within the population to be made, for example, comparing men to women.

Purposive or theoretical sampling

In **purposive or theoretical sampling**, the units are selected according to the researcher's own knowledge and opinion about which ones they think will be appropriate to the topic area. For example, in a study on rural poverty the researcher decides to sample key individuals within local communities, for example, local councillors and voluntary group leaders. These individuals are judged by the researcher to hold specific knowledge on this issue. The sample selection is based entirely on their opinion of who are the most appropriate respondents to select.

Snowball sampling

Snowball sampling is a particularly useful technique when a population is hidden and thus difficult to identify. It involves the researcher making contact with one appropriate case from the population who, in turn, is able to put the researcher in contact with other 'like' cases. Snowball sampling is based on social networking and provides an informal method of accessing the required population (Atkinson and Flint, 2001).

The difficulty with snowball sampling is that the technique will inevitably result in a biased sample. The researcher is reliant on others to make appropriate contacts. The sample is self-selecting and will reflect the social networks of those that choose to participate (Griffiths et al., 1993). Since the population is hidden, its characteristics are likely to be unknown and it will be virtually impossible for the researcher to make a judgement as to its representativeness. The sample characteristics will reflect only those that agree to participate and will fail to reflect on those cases who refused or were not approached to contribute to the study. Lee (1993) provides a detailed discussion on the different strategies for sampling rare or deviant populations.

Sampling and the Internet

Sampling in Internet-based surveys brings with it its own set of issues. As with many other areas in the social sciences, there is a problem in being able to define the population and consequently the sampling frame. Adopting a sampling technique is immensely problematic, as there is no definitive list of e-mail addresses. Even if such a list existed, there is scope for sampling bias towards those who have regular access and usage of the Internet. The popularity of the Internet has risen steadily in the UK. Regular home Web users have risen to 16.5 million users, with an estimated total of 30 million people who access the Internet from home or other connections (*Guardian*, 2002).

Adopting a snowball sampling technique can be an effective strategy to build a sample. The researcher can e-mail topic-appropriate newsgroups and bulletin boards, inviting interested parties to access a Web address that contains the self-completion survey. As detailed discussion of sampling issues and Internet-based surveys is beyond the scope of this text, see Mann and Stewart (2000) and Coomber (1997).

Sample selection in the case studies

The sampling strategies used in each of the four case studies (social research topic examples) in Chapter 5 varied according to the different research requirements. Anderson reports on Cottle's study of the content analysis of television news coverage of environmental risks. The selection of television coverage was based on a multi-stage sampling strategy selected according to a number of parameters. These parameters were the seasonal and weekly variations in media content and the number of television news outlets. Seasonal and weekly variations were accommodated by selecting two one-week periods in January and June. In Regan de Bere's evaluation of interprofessional education, the nature of the project required all course participants to be involved in both the quantitative survey and qualitative interviews. This is a census of all course participants. Sheaff's account of researching health inequalities using quantitative methods also involved a census of all employees for the original baseline health, lifestyle and employment survey. The subsequent follow-up survey involved approaching all employees in one privatized department. The second account of researching health inequalities involved a qualitative approach. The focus of the sample was families with children who had experienced mortgage repossession and been rehoused in the social rented sector. Details of the number of households and individuals are provided, but no information as to how they were selected is provided. Sutton's account of researching rural deprivation involved interviewing a sample of households. The sample needed to reflect individuals' different experiences of rurality, the distances that households lived from centres and services, and the mix of relative affluence and deprivation that can exist geographically close to each other. The sample selection was based on target geographical areas identified through analysis of the quantitative data. These geographical areas were wedge-shaped areas that spread out from population centres or towns. The research team did not posses a readily available sampling frame. The research team requested that the council, who hold the electoral roll of individuals registered to vote at each household address, randomly select and contact by letter households within these areas. A total of 55 households responded and were subsequently interviewed. Time restrictions limited the number of households interviewed.

In each of the case studies the sample selection was based on specific requirements for the research. Sampling techniques, particularly probability sampling, are most often associated with quantitative approaches to research. There is no reason, however, for research taking a qualitative approach not to consider using these sampling techniques. Clearly there are restrictions to the use of these techniques as a sampling frame, or approximation of a sampling frame, may not exist or be extremely difficult if not impossible to build.

Sample size

Sample size is an issue that often provides the most concern to first-time researchers. The question is often one of 'How large should my sample be in order for it to be representative?' The answer is not simply 'the larger the better' as the representativeness of the sample is a product of the sampling technique and the size of the population. A smaller sample size, with careful attention to sampling technique, may be more representative than a larger sample selected without consideration to the sampling frame and sampling technique. Determining the adequate sample size is dependent on how much error you are prepared to accept in your sample.

There is a complex mathematical formula available to calculate an adequate sample size. It is based upon assumptions of the normal distribution curve, the amount of variation in the characteristic being measured in the population, confidence intervals and significance. A more detailed discussion of these terms can be found in chapter 23 'Inferential Statistics and Hypothesis Testing'. The basic notion is to select a sample size that will allow you to state, with a certain level of confidence, that the sample findings would also be found in the population. The sample size required minimizes the difference between the true population value, called a parameter, and the sample value, known as the **sampling error**. While the larger the well selected sample the smaller the sampling error, beyond a certain point a large increase in the sample size does not translate into large gains in the reduction of the sampling error. The general formula used for calculating sample size is based on the central limit theorem and confidence intervals. A detailed discussion of the various calculations available for obtaining an optimum sample size can be found in Moser and Kalton (1971: 146) and Fink (1995b). One version of the formula is shown below:

$$n = \frac{s^2}{(S.E)^2}$$

s is the standard deviation of the population characteristic

S.E is the Standard Error

n is the sample size

Selecting the sample size is dependent on the researcher knowing the amount of variation, as defined by standard deviation, in the measured characteristic in the population. The standard error relates to how much difference between the true population value and the sample value the researcher is willing to accept. Most research involves collecting data on more than one characteristic, for example, age, and marital status creating difficulties as to which characteristic to base the sample selection on.

Another consideration in determining sample size is the level of analysis required. A general analysis involving a few key variables will require fewer cases than a detailed analysis that involves the examination of more complex relationships and interactions.

A number of statistical tests require a minimum number of expected cases. Expected cases are calculated from the observed cases. The researcher therefore needs to ensure that the sample of observed cases is sufficient to meet this requirement. The chi-square test, a frequently undertaken hypothesis test, requires a minimum expected observation of five in each cell of a table (see 'The chi-square test for categorical data' p. 316).

From the discussion of these main issues in relation to sample size, the question still remains 'How big should my sample be?. If you do not know the variation in a population characteristic, then the mathematical calculation of a sample size is problematic. An alternative is to use some of the rough rules of thumb. Basically, a sample size should not be less than 30. Beyond basic description it would be difficult for the researcher to undertake more complex statistical analysis, as most of these analyses require a minimum sample of 30. Ideally the sample size should be greater than 30, otherwise the observations when exploring relationships between two variables will be small. One suggestion is to look at the variables derived from the survey questions and to look at the relationships you wish to explore. Since many of the variables are likely to be nominal or ordinal, the sample size could be based on the minimum expected observations of five required for the chi-square test (an appropriate test for two categorical variables – see Chapter 23). A two by two (2x2) relationship of sex by work full-time or work part-time would require a minimum sample of 20, though 30 should ideally be the minimum. A minimum sample of 20 would be five expected observations for each relationship: male and working full-time; male and working part-time; female and working full-time; female and working part-time. Examination of the number of categories in other categorical variables will allow you to extend this principle. For example, examining the relationship between age, grouped into six age categories, and a variable recording the daily newspaper read, containing nine different newspapers, would produce a 6x9 table requiring a sample size of 270 units (54 cells in the table times minimum value of 5). If this relationship were going to be explored further, by controlling for sex, then the sample required would ideally be 540. Others have suggested alternative minimum observations for each category in an independent variable. Sapsford (1999) suggests 20 and Aldridge and Levine (2001) suggest 50. There are other factors to consider in determining sample size. The two main factors are time for the conduct of the research project and the associated financial costs of the data collection method.

Summary

Sampling refers to the process of deciding who will participate in the research project. When the population is known and is small enough, it may be possible to survey the entire group. However, for the majority of research the population is either too large or is unknown at the outset of the research. In these instances a small group or sample will be selected for the research study. Where the population can be identified and a sampling frame drawn up, it is possible to select individual sampling units using a probability sampling technique that will seek to represent the population. In instances where the population is hidden, difficult to locate or access, non-probability sampling techniques are employed. Probability sampling techniques aim to reduce the sampling error, this being the difference between the true population data findings and the sample data findings. Determining sample size is a complex issue that is determined by a number of factors including the level of acceptable sampling error, the size of population, the variability in the characteristic to be measured, and time and cost considerations.

Keywords

Availability Sampling	Probability Sampling	Sampling Unit
Census	Purposive Sampling	Random Sampling
Cluster Sample	Quota Sampling	Snowball Sampling
Convenience Sampling	Sample	Stratified Sampling
Multi-stage Sampling	Sample Size	Systematic Sampling
Non-probability Based Sampling	Sampling	Theoretical Sampling
Opportunity Sampling	Sampling Error	True Zero Point
Population	Sampling Frame	

Questions

1   Why is it important for the social researcher to consider the most appropriate sampling technique for a particular research project?
2   Describe the difference between probability and non-probability sampling.
3   Define these terms: Population, Sampling Frame, and Sampling Unit.
4   What factors should be considered when determining the sample size?

Further reading

Fink, Arlene (1995b) *The Survey Kit: How to Sample in Surveys*. Thousand Oaks, CA: Sage.

Lee, Raymond (1993) *Doing Research on Sensitive Topics*. London: Sage.

Moser, Claus A. and Kalton, Graham (1971) *Survey Methods in Social Investigation* (2nd edn). London: Heinemann.

Sapsford, Roger (1999) *Survey Research*. London: Sage.

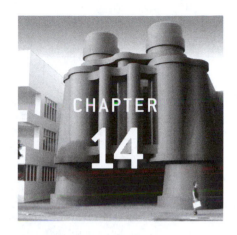

CHAPTER
14

SURVEY DESIGN

Chapter contents

By the end of this chapter you will be able to:

- Understand the advantages and disadvantages of conducting research using a self-completion survey or a structured interview.

- Distinguish between different types of survey questions.

- Identify the key issues relating to the structure and organization of survey questions.

- Understand issues of reliability and validity in relation to the development of survey questions and indicators.

The Survey: The Self Completion Survey and Structured Interview

The two main traditional methods of data collection when adopting quantitative research are the **self-completion survey**, also known as the **social survey** or **questionnaire survey**, and the **structured interview**. Both approaches require the respondent to complete a series of questions that have been designed by the researcher.

The delivery and return of the self-completion survey can be undertaken using a number of different methods. The researcher may or may not be present. When the researcher is present, there will be little or no dialogue between the two parties beyond asking questions and recording answers during the completion of the questionnaire. The traditional and most widely used approach is to send the self-completion survey through the postal service, when it is known as the **mail survey** or **postal survey**. In recent years the growth of the Internet has seen a rise in its use to conduct survey-based research, particularly by market researchers. **Internet-based self-completion surveys** can be distributed and returned via e-mail, or at a site on the World Wide Web.

The **structured interview** involves an interviewer asking questions and recording the responses from the respondent being interviewed. Where the interview is conducted in person with both the interviewer and interviewee, or respondent, present it is called a **face-to-face interview**. An alternative method is to conduct the interview by telephone, known as **telephone interviewing**.

The general advantages and disadvantages of using self-completion surveys and structured interviews for data collection are detailed in the following section.

Self-completion survey: advantages and disadvantages

There are a number of different types of self-completion surveys. A postal or mail questionnaire involves distributing the questionnaire by post with a covering letter and normally a pre-addressed postage paid envelope for the respondent to return the questionnaire. A follow-up letter to boost response rates may be required; sometimes the questionnaire may include incentives to return the questionnaire, such as entry to a prize draw. New technologies, especially the growth in the Internet, have enabled the distribution of questionnaires by e-mail or via Web pages.

Postal or mail survey

The first advantage of the postal or mail survey is that the relative costs associated with its completion are lower than with other methods. The main costs are the reproduction of the questionnaire, envelopes, postage costs and data entry costs. Time and resources committed to data entry can be reduced by the use of closed-ended questions that can be pre-coded, allowing for easier data input. Specialist software applications are also available to automate all or part of the questionnaire design and data entry phase. The second advantage is that data from a large sample, possibly distributed over a wide geographical area, can be surveyed within a limited time span. It would be difficult to gather data from such a sample using a face-to-face interview method unless the research team consisted of a large number of interviewers with a sufficient timescale. In this situation the issues of interviewer effect and bias would require specific focus to ensure consistency between interviewers. The third advantage is that there are no interviewer effects. The responses given by the interviewee can be affected by the presence of the interviewer, who influences the replies made by the manner in which questions are worded, tone of voice, mannerisms or general characteristics of the interviewer (age, gender, ethnicity). The fourth advantage is that a self-completion survey may be a particularly useful tool when collecting data on sensitive topics that the respondent may otherwise be too embarrassed or reluctant to respond to. Other advantages often mentioned include that the respondents can complete the questionnaire at a time convenient to themselves, and that questionnaires can be completed and returned anonymously by the respondent.

The main disadvantage of a mail survey is the often low response rate obtained. A response rate of 50 per cent or less can be the norm. Reasons for this low response rate are varied and can include factors such as 'the subject matter of the survey, the target population under study, the recipients' perception of its value, and the ease of completion of the questionnaire' (Simmons, 2001: 87). However, good question development and layout, together with clear instructions on the nature of the study and why it is important to complete and return the questionnaire, can dramatically improve response rates.

Response rates are also difficult to assess as they are related to the sampling technique used and knowledge about the target population. 'Response rates will be underestimated if questionnaires have been sent to people who are not part of the target population or who have moved address' (Aldridge and Levine, 2001: 52). The issue for the researcher is that it is not possible to distinguish between non-response due to a refusal and a non-response due to an inappropriate sampling unit, such as the wrong individual being selected. See 'Non-response' p. 181 for further discussion of factors that effect non-response.

There is also an implicit assumption made with self-completion surveys that the targeted respondent's literacy level is sufficient to provide written responses. The advice to restrict the structure of individual questions (that is, simple, not cumbersome, short, not too many **open-ended questions**, careful use of contingency questions to direct respondents to specific questions according to set criteria) can restrict the data that is collected and depending on the nature of the research a questionnaire may simply not yield the information required for the research.

Other disadvantages often cited include the inability to control the context within which the questions are completed; respondents may jump between questions and not complete in the intended order. The researcher is also unable to determine if the targeted sampling unit, for example, a named individual, was actually the person who completed and returned the questionnaire.

Internet-based surveys

Developments in computing technology and software have enabled surveys to be distributed by electronic mail (e-mail) and on the World Wide Web. The advantage to Web-based questionnaires is that the data can automatically be placed in a data file that in turn can be imported into a suitable analysis package. The Web-based questionnaire can be written in such a way

that the accidental selection of an inappropriate number of categories or failure to respond can be avoided; for example, when a question states tick one response only, or failure to complete all the questions in the survey can be brought to the attention of the respondent by displaying an alert message directing them to the incomplete questions.

Questionnaires can also be distributed via e-mail or respondents e-mailed and invited to complete a survey at a website. As with paper-based questionnaire surveys, inducements to complete the questionnaire can be offered, such as entry into a prize draw.

The disadvantages of Internet-based surveys are that the researcher needs to acquire the technical expertise in the area of distributing e-mails, Web page construction and on-line databases. Alternatively, technical personnel need to be employed on the research project. In addition, appropriate hardware and software need to be purchased and maintained. As with telephone interviews, there is also the issue of excluding certain social groups from the sample as they do not have access to the relevant hardware/ software or user skills for the World Wide Web. For a fuller discussion of the issues associated with using Internet-based surveys, see de Vaus (2001) and Mann and Stewart (2000). For an interesting discussion of issues about using Internet-based surveys to access difficult to reach groups, see Coomber (1997).

Structured interviews: advantages and disadvantages

Face-to-face interviews

One of the biggest advantages of face-to-face structured interviews is that there can be a greater use of open questions and the interviewer can provide additional explanation, if required, to aid the respondent's understanding of the question. Prompting can be included with the questions and if a question is inappropriate, data on why no response was made can be recorded. This enables the question sequencing to be more complex, if required, and greater use of routing or funnelling questions. This can be seen by examining interview schedules from large government sponsored surveys, such as the UK's General Household Survey or the USA's General Social Survey. Instructions for prompting by the interviewer are included in the questionnaire schedule. Additionally, the use of show cards, containing the response categories for closed-ended questions or other visual aids can provide an accurate and swift completion of the questions. The non-verbal cues of human interaction can also be recorded, such as facial expressions.

The advantages of face-to-face interviews have to be balanced against the disadvantages. Obviously in a face-to-face interview the issue of anonymity no longer applies, though the interviewer can make assurances of **confidentiality**. There is also the potential for both interviewer effect and interviewer bias. The age, social background and whether the interviewer is male or female are all interviewer effects that could influence the responses given by the interviewee. The general awareness, prior experience and communication skills of the interviewer at making the interviewee feel comfortable, willing to participate and talk honestly will be key factors in limiting the potential interviewer effect. Interviewer bias can occur through both the verbal comments and non-verbal cues made by the interviewer.

Telephone interview survey

The telephone interview survey can be a favoured method when funding is sufficient to cover telephone costs. As with the mail survey, it is also possible to obtain a large sample over a wide geographical area. Some of the issues of interviewer effect are removed, as there is no visual contact, although the tone and pitch of the interviewer's voice may introduce some interviewer bias.

The disadvantages of the telephone interview are that the guidelines for self-completion questions must still be adhered to. Questions should be short, simple and the number of response categories specified must not be too great as the interviewee will be unable to remember all the list items from which to choose. Open questions can be included, though not too many, to enable the respondent to express their responses in their own spoken language and terminology.

Undertaking telephone interviews also introduces an element of bias in the sampling as it will automatically exclude those without a telephone and if using publicly available directories those that are ex-directory. Furthermore, people are often unwilling to participate in cold-call telephone interviewing, raising questions about the quality of data that is collected (Thomas and Purdon, 1994). This can be overcome by approaching respondents initially to participate in the research and to arrange a suitable time for the telephone interview to be conducted.

Developing survey questions

The development of questions is a time-consuming process that requires sufficient allocation of time and effort. At first the development of questions for a questionnaire or interview schedule will seem relatively unproblematic; however, a researcher who thinks like this seriously underestimates the complexity of the process. The questions must be carefully thought through in a systematic manner, piloted, then reviewed and edited before the full survey commences. A rushed, ill-thought through set of questions will inevitably fail to collect the data required. This will result in the researcher being unable to explore relationships or test the hypotheses from the original research question. Once the survey is conducted there is no possibility of revising badly worded questions or questions that fail to collect data relevant to the research question.

The following section provides an overview of the process of developing questions and the main issues to consider.

Getting started

The purpose of developing questions is to enable the researcher to collect data in order to investigate the research question through the exploration of hypotheses. The data collection process requires the development of survey questions and measurements. Some of the questions will be open-ended, enabling the respondent to provide their own written or spoken responses, while other questions will be in a closed-ended format with specific responses, also known as categories, to select from. The development of these categories will be undertaken in conjunction with topic-specific knowledge of appropriate responses and also different measurements.

From the literature review a range of concepts and indicators for measuring these concepts will have been developed in relation to the research question. It may also be appropriate to conduct some limited fieldwork by interviewing key individuals in the area to be studied. For example, in a survey of the integration of women into naval sea service (Bryant et al., 2000), appropriate personnel responsible for sea training programmes were interviewed to gather information on what they felt the key issues relating to sea service were.

From existing literature or your own hunches you may have developed one or more hypotheses about how the **indicators** may vary between different groups and are influenced by other factors. For example, in a study of rural and urban poverty and deprivation you may have developed an indicator defining rural and an indicator defining urban. A variety of indicators for measuring deprivation may include household income, number of waged earners, income from state benefits or deprivation indicators for not just economic but also those relating to access to services, location of post offices, location of food supermarkets, distance to bus stops, frequency of bus routes, location of banking services and so on. The case study on researching rural deprivation detailed in Chapter 5 used the indices of multiple deprivation as a quantitative measure for deprivation. The indices were calculated from existing data that were identified as appropriate from the operationalization of the concept deprivation. These then formed the background framework for the questions asked in the interviews.

Background details about the respondent, which could be an individual or a family or a company, also need to be collected in order for comparisons to be made between the indicators and different respondent groupings. For example, is access to local services restricted to those who own a car?

Types of questions

There are a number of different types of questions and question formats. A combination of these is likely to be used in a survey. The questions can be classified into three broad groups. Questions can be factual, concentrating on a behavior or knowledge. Questions can focus on gathering attributes about the respondent; for example, an individual's age or marital status. These questions are primarily concerned with collecting background information on the respondent

for the purposes of classification and comparison at the data analysis stage. Questions can also be concerned with gathering data on opinions, beliefs and attitudes; for example, in a survey of knowledge about and use of local bus services there could be a series of questions (see Figure 14.1).

Development of survey questions needs to be understood within the framework that the potential participant will respond in. Background information on the topic area needs to be thoroughly researched in order to develop questions that are appropriate and clearly worded with a logical layout in order for the participant to interpret and respond accordingly.

Closed-ended or open-ended questions?

The format of a question can be **open-ended** or **closed-ended**. Open-ended questions, also known as **un-standardized questions**, enable the respondent to enter a response in their own words. Closed-ended questions, also known as standardized questions, require the respondent to select from a range of stated answers. The advantages of closed-ended questions are that with a clearly stated question they enable the respondent to provide a quick response. Respondents are generally more willing to complete a series of questions if the response time is minimal and requires less effort in completion, though the issue of false data being collated can then become a concern. Another useful aspect is that closed-ended questions are simpler for the researcher to deal with when it comes to the data entry and analysis stages. Fixed answers are easier to code, and pre-coding the answers can save time once the completed survey is returned for data entry and analysis.

There are a number of disadvantages that must be

Factual – Behaviour: 'In the last week, have you used local bus services?'

Factual – Knowledge: 'How frequent is the bus service to your nearest town?'

Opinion: 'Do you think that bus services should be operating in this area?'

Attitude: 'How would you rate local bus services?'

Personal attribute: 'Are you male or female?'

Figure 14.1   Example of different types of questions

considered when developing closed-ended questions. The main issue relates to the fact that they can force the respondent to select one of the responses when, in fact, they would not have spontaneously offered either any response or that particular response. For example, an individual responds to an attitudinal question expressing an opinion that they do not necessarily hold.

The concerns of potential false responses with closed-ended questions may influence the decision to make use of open-ended questions. Open-ended questions enable the respondent to express their response in their own words and allow for the possibility of issues arising that the researcher had not previously considered. There is the issue with open-ended questions that they are reliant on the respondent being sufficiently interested in or knowledgeable of the question to provide an answer and being able to express in a written format their response. Open answers are also more time consuming for the researcher to code and analyse as they require post-coding (see 'Coding for open-ended questions' p. 183).

Ultimately, the choice between closed-ended and

open-ended questions is dependent on the area being researched, the type of question, background considerations on the motivation of respondents and how and where the survey is administered. A self-completion survey will be completed in a different environment to a structured interview.

Format of closed-ended questions

When developing closed-ended questions you will need to decide upon the format of the response categories. The development of these need to be considered in relation to the data type or level of measurement of the data to be collected. There are four types: nominal, ordinal, interval and ratio (as outlined in 'Variables and levels of measurement' p. 144). At the analysis stage the data type determines the statistical techniques available. How a question is worded will determine the response given and so in turn the level of measurement of the data. It is worth spending a few minutes to consider this point with an example.

In the example in Figure 14.2, the researcher wishes to ask a question about an individual's age. Three different ways are displayed in which the question could be asked, together with the respective responses. The format of the responses will impact on the statistical analysis available.

In Version 1 the age question requires the respondent to select one of two categories, under 21 or 21 or over. Beyond this the question response will not allow the analysis to distinguish between respondents of different ages within each of those categories. Consequently, if in the subsequent analysis the researcher wanted to focus on responses made by those aged 71 or over, this would not be possible as they did not collect the age data in a format that allowed them to identify this sub-set of the sample. The level of measurement is nominal and since there are only two categories it is referred to as a **dichotomy**. In Version 2 there are seven age categories available. The categories can be placed in rank order of ascending age and the data type is ordinal. Each category must be mutually exclusive, also known as **externally discrete** which means that the age ranges do not overlap. This version of the age question would allow the researcher to distinguish at the data analysis stage between a respondent who was 71 or over and one who was aged 31–40 years. However, within each category the researcher would be unable to determine the actual age of the respondent. In Version 3 the question is open-ended with the respondent being

---

Version 1

How old are you? Please tick one response only:

Under 21   ☐

21 or over ☐

Version 2

How old are you? Please tick one response only:

Under 21   ☐

21–30   ☐

31–40   ☐

41–50   ☐

51–60   ☐

61–70   ☐

71 plus   ☐

Version 3

Please enter your current age, in years:

——————— years old.

Figure 14.2   Three formats for asking a question on age

asked to enter their actual age in years. Here the data is interval/ratio. With interval/ratio data a greater range of statistical analysis techniques are available. The hierarchical order of the levels of measurement means that an interval variable, for example, age in years, can be re-coded or collapsed into an ordinal variable, for example, categories of age ranges, or into a nominal variable, two age categories (a dichotomy). While collecting the respondent's actual age, in years, can offer the greatest flexibility at the data analysis stage, it must be balanced against the difficulty that this can be a sensitive issue which may result in a large number of non-responses. A trade-off between issues of sensitivity and the restrictions on the range of analysis techniques available needs to be considered by the researcher. The majority of questions asked by researchers when investigating the social world have response categories that are of a nominal or ordinal level.

Developing closed-ended question responses

The development of question responses should consider the guiding principles of exhaustiveness, exclusiveness and balancing categories (de Vaus, 2001: 100–101).

Exhaustiveness refers to the need to ensure that an appropriate range of responses is made available. The question would fail if relevant responses were omitted, resulting in the respondents not responding to the question. While every effort should be made to ensure that the list of responses is exhaustive, it is common practice for questions that list a number of responses to include a final category that allows the respondent to indicate that none of the listed categories were appropriate. A final response of 'other' with a qualifying 'please state' can be used. Sometimes it may be more appropriate to include a response stating 'none of the above'. For attitudinal responses, a category of no opinion or neutral should be included.

Exclusiveness means that response categories are exclusive in the sense that respondents can select only one of the categories. In the earlier example of the respondent being asked to select the age category there are no overlaps in the age categories. For example, if a researcher had wrongly set the first two age categories as '21 and under' and '21–30', the 21-year-old respondent would fall into both categories. In this example the issue of exclusiveness is easy to deal with; however, questions that have a list of responses from

which to choose and the respondent could select more than one need to be given more consideration and thought.

In the following example there is a question about mode of transport used to get to work.

How did you travel to work this morning?

Car   ☐
Bus   ☐
Coach   ☐
Taxi   ☐
Train   ☐
Other   ☐

There is the possibility that a respondent may use more than one mode of transport. For example, train and bus. There are a number of ways in which you can deal with this. The first would be to create mutually exclusive category combinations, for example, car only, bus only, coach only, taxi only, train only, car and bus, train and bus and so on Where there is a long list of categories and potential combinations this can be inappropriate. When there are only two categories the inclusion of a third category 'Both' would suffice. The second, if appropriate to the research, is to reframe the question to focus on the main mode of transport used, for example, 'What was the main mode of transport that you used to get to work this morning?'. However, in this example you are requiring the respondent to define the term 'main mode'. The third option is to alter the format of the question to allow for multiple responses, where the respondent ticks all categories that are applicable. The fourth option is to split the original question into a number of separate questions with responses of Yes and No. For example, 'Did you use the Bus to travel to work today?', 'Did you use the train to travel to work today?'.

Balancing categories refers to simply ensuring that when using a series of categories that can be placed in a rank order, for example, attitudinal scales, that the categories are balanced with equal numbers of positive, or high, and negative, or low, categories. More categories at one end of the scale could distort the responses given. The scale is normally balanced by including a neutral category in the middle position. For example, on a scale of importance the categories should run from Very Important, Important, Neutral, Unimportant, and Very unimportant.

Different formats of closed-ended question responses

In this section some of the common formats used for closed-ended question responses are outlined.

Questions with only two responses

One question format is to ask questions that have only two response categories, known as dichotomies. Such questions can be useful when gaining basic factual information or to provide structure to a questionnaire by directing respondents to complete certain sections of a questionnaire (see 'Routing questions and funnelling respondents' p. 171). Beyond this their use should be carefully considered, especially in relation to questions asking about a respondent's opinion as the nature of the dichotomies may force the respondent to express a view that is greater or less extreme than their true view. For example:

Do you think that degree students should pay tuition fees?

Yes ☐

No ☐

How would a respondent answer this question if they felt that the payment of tuition fees should be subject to parental income? The respondent may also not have considered this issue before and have no immediate opinion. Consideration of the inclusion of a 'Do not know' category should be made.

Questions with a list of responses

These questions list a number of responses, or categories, from which a respondent can select. Clear instructions need to be included with the question as to whether one or more of the responses can be selected.

Figure 14.3 contains two examples of the format and listing of questions that have a list of responses. Both questions asked the respondent to state the daily newspaper that they read. In Example 1 there is a specific instruction that states 'Tick *one* only' to indicate that only one of the listed categories should be selected. In Example 2 the instructions accompanying the question state 'Please tick all applicable' to indicate that the researcher is allowing for respondents who read more than one newspaper a day. When more than

one response can be selected the questions are **multiple response**, requiring special attention at the coding and data entry phases.

Additional categories have also been included at the end of the list. The inclusion of an 'Other' category allows the respondent to enter a newspaper that is not included on the selective list provided by the researcher. In addition, the final category of 'Do not read a daily newspaper' has been included. This category could have been omitted by the introduction of a preceding routing question that asked if the respondent read a daily newspaper, which would have filtered out those that did not, and only those that reply Yes would then complete the full newspaper question. More details can be found in 'Routing questions and funnelling respondents' p. 171.

When listing the categories it is important that the researcher spends time considering what the relevant categories are. For questions on individual attributes, consider spending some time looking at existing survey examples such as those undertaken by the large government surveys where such surveys focus on data collection for mainly social policy decisions and thus contain many questions relating to various aspects of the individual, for example, income, health, education, employment.

Piloting of the survey questions may reveal additional categories not considered by the researcher and can be included in the final survey. In order to fulfil the requirement of exhaustiveness it is wise to include a final all-encompassing 'Other' category followed by an open response of 'Please state'.

Attitudinal or opinion question responses

Questions that seek to gather data on a respondent's opinion will make use of a **rating scale**. A number of different rating scales have been developed and can be used to develop formal **scales** to measure concepts by combining responses from a multitude of statements. This section will first examine some of the frequently used rating categories and second describe the application of **Likert scales**.

Rating question responses

Rating question responses are simply response categories that are presented in a rank order between two extreme positions, normally positive and negative. The number of categories in the scales can vary, with

Example 1: Selecting only one response

Which of the following daily newspapers do you normally read?

Tick *one* only:

Financial Times ☐

New York Times ☐

Washington Post ☐

Melbourne Age ☐

Times of India ☐

South China Morning Post ☐

Le Monde ☐

Other ☐   (Please state) _____

Do not read a daily newspaper ☐

Example 2: Selecting one or more responses (multiple response)

Which of the following daily newspapers have you read in the last week?

Tick all applicable:

Financial Times ☐

New York Times ☐

Washington Post ☐

Melbourne Age ☐

Times of India ☐

South China Morning Post ☐

Le Monde ☐

Other ☐   (Please state) _____

Do not read a daily newspaper ☐

Figure 14.3   Questions with a list of response categories

three and five categories the most common. Rating questions with three categories could be Less, Same or More. Rating questions with five categories are shown in Figure 14.4.

The 10-Point and 100-point numerical scales

These scales involve presenting a numerical scale with extreme positions at both ends. The respondent then circles the number that most closely represents their position on the continuum. They are similar to the five-point scale except that labels are not applied to each of the numerical points on the scale, leaving individual respondents to decide where their position is on the scale.

A frequently used scale is the 10-point scale, which will run from 1 to 10, or from 0 to 9.

An extension of this scale is to increase the range of points on the scale. Occasionally questionnaires may ask individuals to position their response on a 100-point scale, which may be represented as a thermometer with a scale from 0°C to 100°C

Very important	Strongly agree
Important	Agree
Neutral	Undecided
Unimportant	Disagree
Very unimportant	Strongly disagree

Figure 14.4   Examples of five-point scales

Bad	0	1	2	3	4	5	6	7	8	9	Good
Dull	0	1	2	3	4	5	6	7	8	9	Fun
Low	0	1	2	3	4	5	6	7	8	9	High

Figure 14.5   Ten-point scale

Semantic differential scales

Semantic differential scales are used to assess individuals' responses to particular statements that have been developed to measure one or more concepts. Responses would be made by circling the numerical position on the scale that most represents the respondent's feelings, attitude or belief to a particular item under study (see Figure 14.5). Each end of the scale represents an extreme position, Bad to Good, Dull to Fun, Low to High. Its application is particularly useful in research that involves comparing the attitudes of one group of individuals to another. For example, employees rating of line management or supervisory staff.

Likert scales

They are a convenient method of collecting data on a concept from a number of different approaches (Oppenheim, 1992). They also allow the researcher to obtain more information of a respondent's opinion or feelings on a particular topic that is beyond simply asking a Disagree/Agree or Yes/No response.

The structure of the Likert scale is to write a number of statements, known as scale items, each with the same standard set of responses. The scale items will consist of a mix of positive and negative statements. The responses would be on a rating scale with two extreme positions, positive and negative, at

either end of the scale. A Likert scale consists of the five points strongly agree, agree, undecided, disagree, strongly disagree (see figure 14.4). Each of the response categories is given a score from 1 to 5. Scale items (statements) that are positive require response categories that are scored 5, strongly agree, to 1, strongly disagree. Scale items (statements) that are negative require response categories that are scored 1, strongly agree, to 5 strongly disagree. An example of four scale items and the scores assigned to each of the respective response categories is shown in Figure 14.6. Scale items (1) and (2) are positive statements. Scale items (3) and (4) are negative statements.

Once the respondents have completed the scale items, the next stage would be to enter the individual scores into a data analysis package (see Chapter 20). The final stage is to calculate a final score by the addition of all of the scale items. Taking the example in Figure 14.6, a respondent who has answered for statement (1) Agree, scored as 4; statement (2), Agree, scored as 4; statement (3) Disagree, scored as 4; and statement (4) Agree, scored as 2. The total score for this respondent would be 4+4+4+2=14. The computation of the total score is easy to complete in the data analysis package SPSS, using the compute new variable commands (see Chapter 24).

One of the difficulties with the computation of a total score is that the process of aggregation makes it difficult for the researcher to interpret scores that are in the middle range. Are they slightly disagreeing or slightly agreeing? A further difficulty is that the total score can be reached by a wide range of differing responses. Look again at Figure 14.6 and consider how many different combinations of responses could be used to obtain a total score of 14. In addition to computing a total score, the analysis of responses to each of the individual statements can reveal further information to the researcher.

Specialist texts are available on design scales for specific purposes. For example, there are a number of complex scales that have been developed in relation to measuring health and quality of life. These include the Short-Form 36 General Health Survey Questionnaire, SF-36 (Ware and Sherbourne, 1992), Sickness Impact Profile, SIP (Bergner et al., 1981) and Quality of Life Index, QL-Index (Spitzer et al., 1981).

For a general text on measuring health and medical outcomes see Jenkinson (1994) and McDowell and Newell (1996).

	Strongly agree	Agree	Neutral	Disagree	Strongly disagree
(1) I have enjoyed studying this module.	5	4	3	2	1
(2) The aims and objectives of the module were clear to me.	5	4	3	2	1
(3) It was difficult to access the student portal for course related materials.	1	2	3	4	5
(4) Access to university computers outside of workshops was difficult.	1	2	3	4	5

Figure 14.6 Example of a Likert scale

Ranking question responses

Ranking question responses are used when the researcher wishes to collect data on how respondents rank a list of items in relation to each other. This could involve ranking the importance of access to public services or a range of environmental issues. Ranking questions can be structured in two different ways. The first is to list a series of items and ask the respondent to rank all of them in order of importance from 1 to the maximum number of items listed. The item of most importance should have a 1 entered next to it, the item of second importance would have a 2 entered next to it and so on until all items have been ranked.

The second is to list a series of items and ask the respondent to rank only the top three items of importance from 1 to 3. Items not deemed of sufficient importance do not have a numerical rank entry entered for them. Figure 14.7 has an example of both approaches. Each of the questions contain detailed instructions for their completion.

Multiple response questions

Multiple response questions are simply any question that requires the respondent to indicate more than one response or answer. These would include questions that require all relevant categories to be selected from a list and also the ranking questions mentioned in the previous section. It is important that the researcher recognizes when they are asking a multiple response question as it will impact on how the data will be coded and analysed. The key to multiple response questions is that enough variables have to be created in the data set to accommodate the maximum number of question responses made by an individual case. In the second example of a ranking question, Figure 14.7, the respondent was required to rank their top three items in order of preference and hence would require three variables in the data file. More information on coding multiple response questions can be found in 'Coding for multiple response questions' p. 182.

Matrix question structure

Where there are a large number of rating questions it can be appropriate to organize them into a **matrix question** structure. It is advisable to organize the rating questions into specific related areas and make use of more than one matrix question if there are a large number of rating questions on a variety of different topics. Separate matrix questions should be used if the rating scale is different for some questions. The advantage of matrix questions is that they allow for a large number of questions or statements to be condensed into a smaller area in the questionnaire. An example of a matrix question is shown in Figure 14.8.

Developing the wording of questions

The development of the question needs to be carefully assessed and scrutinized before conducting the main survey. The formulation of the questions will often precede the decision as to whether questions are open- or closed-ended.

The first steps in survey question construction would be to identify the key areas for data collection. These areas will be identified from the process of operationalization. The literature review may have revealed some questions used in previous studies that

Example 1

Below is a list of local facilities that could be improved. Enter a number, from 1 to 9, in the box next to each of the faciliites listed to rate the importance of improving each of the facilities. The most important facility to be improved should be given a value of 1, the second most important a value of 2, repeat this until you get to the value 9 for the least important facility for improvement.

Indoor sports facilities	5
Outdoor sports facilities	3
Children's play centres	4
Swimming pools	1
Libraries	7
Local parks and green spaces	2
Cinemas	8
Theatres	9
Local Community Centres or Halls	6

Example 2

Below is a list of local facilities that could be improved. Select the three most important facilities that in your opinion should be improved upon. Place these three into order of importance, 1 for most important, 2 for second important and 3 for third important.

Indoor sports facilities	
Outdoor sports facilities	3
Children's play centres	
Swimming pools	1
Libraries	
Local parks and green spaces	2
Cinemas	
Theatres	
Local Community Centres or Halls	

Figure 14.7 Example of two ranking questions

	Strongly agree	Agree	Neutral	Disagree	Strongly disagree
The module aims were clearly stated.	☐	☐	☐	☐	☐
The course materials accompanying this module were clear and easy to follow.	☐	☐	☐	☐	☐
It was easy to gain access to university computers outside of formal sessions.	☐	☐	☐	☐	☐
I have enjoyed studying this module.	☐	☐	☐	☐	☐

Figure 14.8   Example of a matrix question structure

you could include, with or without modification, in your questionnaire. An excellent source of questions can be found at the ESRC-funded Question Bank at <www.qb.soc.surrey.ac.uk>. These can be particularly useful for selecting questions on socio-economic backgrounds as they contain copies of many UK government sponsored survey questions.

General guidance on question construction concentrates on the following areas:

- *Clear question wording:* The wording of questions needs to be clear, direct and simple. There should be no ambiguity.
- *Question length:* Questions that are too long are likely to put off the respondent. Questions can also be too short and fail to provide adequate guidance and information on the data required from the respondent.
- *Terminology.* Avoid terms where there is not one universal definition or a term that not all respondents may be familiar with. Equally one needs to ensure that the question itself cannot be interpreted in more than one way. For example, do you have a car? Does this mean have your own car? Have access to a car? Have a company car? Is the issue one of car ownership or usage of a car?
- *Double questions:* When first constructing questions it is very easy to word a question that is in fact asking two questions. For example, 'How would you rate the frequency *and* cleanliness of local bus services?'. It is important to avoid such occurrences.
- *Leading questions:* Question wording needs to avoid bias and leading the respondent to give a particular response. The wording of the question may hint at the 'correct' or 'desired' response.

- *Questions that require a very specific memory recall:* Respondents may not always be able to remember exact events, particularly frequency of events, over a specified timescale. For example, asking the question 'How many times have you used the local bus services in the last year?' is unlikely to result in an accurate response. In these instances the time period can be shortened, for example 'How many times in the last week have you used the local bus services?'. Although there is then the issue of defining 'last week': does this mean the previous seven days or the previous working week? An alternative method of dealing with these types of question is to replace the open response of actual frequency with a series of closed responses. For example:

  Everyday
  4–6 times a week
  2–3 times a week
  Once a week
  Never

Survey layout

The presentation and layout of the self-completion survey and questions need to be considered carefully. Failure to allow time for this in your planning schedule could result in a poor completion rate for a mail survey and confusion for the telephone interviewer or face-to-face interviewer. It is important that the survey is professionally presented to convey a sense of importance to the respondent who in turn will, hopefully, be more willing to complete and return the document. A survey that fails to convey this is unlikely to receive the response desired.

Organization and order

The organization of the questions needs to be carefully considered. It is important that the questions are organized by similar topic areas. This makes it easier for the researcher to visualize and manage the relationship between the questions and measurement tools used for each question and the original questions and hypothesis. At the development stage it may be useful to sketch out the relationship between these two using a simple organization chart.

Routing questions and funnelling respondents

Routing or funnelling questions are a convenient method of directing or funnelling respondents to particular sections of questions. They are appropriate to use when it is known that some groups of questions will not be applicable to specific respondents. For example, in a survey of healthy lifestyles, a series of questions on participation in sporting activities undertaken would be not applicable to those who do not participate in any sporting activity.

Directing respondents away from completing questions that are not applicable to them will reduce completion fatigue; ticking 'Not applicable or relevant' to a series of questions can become very tedious! The use of routing questions can reduce the time required to complete the overall questionnaire. Routing questions also have the advantage of making the researcher think through carefully why they are asking particular questions and how they relate back to the original research question.

Routing questions typically place the respondent into a particular category. The question will normally consist of a Yes/No or tick all applicable responses followed by clear instruction to then progress to a particular set of questions. Two examples are given in Figure 14.9.

Reliability and validity

The use of indicators and tests raises issues of **reliability** and **validity**. Reliability is the degree to which the indicator or test is a consistent measure over time, or simply, will the respondent give the same response if asked to give an answer at a different time. The importance of accurately measuring an indicator is that it will allow for the detection of differences, or variance, between different groups of cases. It is inevitable that the data collected in a measurement tool, or indicator, will consist of the true measure plus an error measure. The reliability of a measure is measured by consistency in response and the limitation of the error measure. It is not possible to totally eliminate error. Even when taking measurements in the natural sciences errors will occur. For example, measuring a length of string will always be an estimate according to the skill of the scientist, the accuracy of the rule and the number of decimal places used in the length unit. Reliability is an important issue as a large error or unreliability will impact on the analysis of relationships between the variables.

'When a measure has low reliability, some of the differences in scores between people which it produces are spurious differences, not real differences' (Punch, 1998: 100).

The only way of assessing the reliability of the measurement tool or question is the test-retest method where the respondent is asked the same question at different intervals. Correlation techniques can then be used to assess the consistency in the answers given. A correlation coefficient of 0.8 or higher is taken as an indication that the question is reliable (de Vaus, 1996: 55). The difficulties with the test-retest method are that it is often not practical to ask the questions to the same sample on two or more occasions and respondents may remember their previous response. The test-retest can then become a measure of respondent's memory and not reliability of the measurement tool. Reliability can be improved by the careful construction and piloting of the questions, making use of existing questions from reputable surveys. For structured interviews the skill of the interviewer is important, particularly where two or more interviewers are used. The use of multiple indicators can also improve reliability.

Validity refers to the degree to which a measuring instrument actually measures and describes the concept it was designed to. Validity is a more complex issue to understand as it is separated into a number of sub-divisions.

Criterion validity involves the researcher undertaking some initial analysis of the measure to check that it performs in the way that it would be expected to. For example, a measure has been devised to measure an attitudinal difference between men and women. The measure fails to show any difference in attitudes between the two groups. This suggests that either the measure is not performing as expected or that there is no measurable difference between men and women. If existing surveys suggest those differences between the attitudes of men and women do exist, then this would

---

Example 1: Yes/No response

In a survey at a GUM clinic respondents were asked if they used self-treatments.

Q.1   When you first had the symptoms did you try to treat yourself?

Yes   ☐   If YES go to Q.2
No   ☐   If NO go to Q.4

Q.2   What did you use? Please give as much details as possible
[more space was provided in the original questions]

‑   _____

Q.3   Did it work?

Yes   ☐
No   ☐
Partly/Yes for a short time   ☐

Q.4   Did you consult your Doctor?

Yes   ☐
No   ☐

Example 2: Tick all applicable, followed by directions to different sections of the survey.

Have you suffered from any of the following conditions? (Please tick all applicable)

Thrush/Yeast infections   ☐   Please complete Section 2
Cystisis   ☐   Please complete Section 3
Herpes   ☐   Please complete Section 4
Genital warts/Papilloma virus ☐   Please complete Section 5
Vaginitis   ☐   Please complete Section 6
Vulvar vestibulitis   ☐   Please complete Section 7

Source: Sutton (1994)

Figure 14.9   Examples of routing questions

suggest, perhaps, that the measurement tool is not measuring the variation. However, this is based on the existing measurement being accepted.

Predictive validity involves a time lag between the research itself and its prediction for future findings. If the predicted findings are measured at a later date, then the measure has predictive validity.

Face validity refers to the assessment of whether the measure is a suitable measure of the concept. This assessment should be undertaken by the researcher, a

critical self-evaluation and by referring the measure to identified experts in the area.

Content validity is concerned with assessing how well the measurement claims to measure all of the different dimensions of the concept. For example, in the measure of religiosity, a measurement tool that only collected data on ceremonial attendance would have poor content validity as it would not take into account the other dimensions of religious belief.

Construct validity involves assessing how well the

measurement conforms to the theoretical model. The assessment of construct validity is dependent upon the strength of the original theory.

Two other validity terms that are more general in nature are **internal validity** and **external validity**. The internal validity needs to establish that there is no evidence that other factors, on which data may or may not have been collected, are responsible for the variation in the dependent variable. The sampling technique and the measurement tools used for data collection can compromise internal validity. Establishing internal validity is a difficult process. Some data analysis techniques for performing limited internal validity checks can be found in 'Elaboration and spurious relationships' p.306. External validity is the extent to which the research findings can be generalized to larger populations and applied to different settings. It is determined by the representativeness and size of the sample from which the findings are derived.

Summary

The questions the piece of research attempts to answer and the geographic location of those to be surveyed will be major factors in the decision to conduct a self-completion survey or structured interview. There are advantages and disadvantages to both methods that the social researcher will need to consider. Both methods require the development of survey questions. The literature review will identify appropriate concepts and indicators from which survey questions can be developed. The survey questions are the data collection tool that will enable the researcher to investigate the initial research question and hypothesis. Depending on the nature of the study, it may be appropriate to use existing survey questions from established large-scale repeated studies. Survey questions seek to obtain factual information, personal knowledge and attributes, beliefs and opinions. The format of the survey question can be open-ended or closed-ended, depending on the type of data to be gathered. Attention needs to be given to the structure, wording and format of the questionnaire survey and structured interview schedule.

Keywords

Balancing	Face-to-face Interview	Rating Scales
Closed-ended Questions	Indicators	Reliability
Confidentiality	Internal Validity	Routing or Funnelling Questions
Construct Validity	Internet Self-completion Survey	Scale
Content Validity	Likert Scales	Self-completion Survey
Criterion Validity	Mail or Postal Survey	Semantic Differential Scales
Dichotomy	Matrix Questions	Social Survey
Exclusiveness	Multiple Response Questions	Structured Interview
Exhaustiveness	Open-ended Questions	Telephone Interview
External Validity	Predictive Validity	Un-standardized Questions
External Discretion	Questionnaire Survey	Validity
Face Validity	Ranking Questions	

Questions

1   Under what circumstances would a self-completion survey be preferable to a structured interview?
2   How can the categories selected for closed-ended questions restrict the subsequent data analysis?
3   What issues should the researcher consider when wording questions and deciding on question order?
4   What do you understand by the terms 'reliability' and 'validity' and how do they relate to question construction?

Further reading

Aldridge, Alan and Levine, Ken (2001) *Surveying the Social World: Principles and Practice in Survey Research*. Buckingham: Open University Press.

Belson, William A. (1981) *The Design and Understanding of Survey Questions*. London: Gower.

Cicourel, Aaron (1968) *Method and Measurement in Sociology*. New York: Free Press.

Fink, Arlene (1995a) *The Survey Kit: How to ask Survey Questions*. Thousand Oaks, CA: Sage.

Fowler, Floyd (1988) *Survey Research Methods*. London: Sage.

Fowler, Floyd (1995) *Improving Survey Questions: Design and Evaluation*. London: Sage.

Jenkinson, Crispin (ed.) (1994) *Measuring Health and Medical Outcomes*. London: UCL.

McDowell, Ian and Newell, Claire (1996) *Measuring Health: A Guide to Rating Scales and Questionnaires*. New York: Oxford University Press.

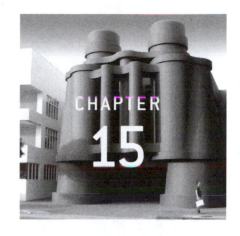

CHAPTER

15

COLLECTING AND CODING DATA

Chapter contents

By the end of this chapter you will be able to:

- Understand the importance of piloting a survey.

- Understand the administrative aspects of conducting a survey.

- Identify issues associated with non-response.

- Construct a code book appropriate for different variables and types of question.

- Identify potential sources of secondary data.

Piloting

The **piloting** stage of the survey questions is concerned with assessing the main elements of the **data collection** process. The survey questions should be piloted on a test group of cases from the target population. It is important that this test group reflect the characteristics of the actual sample cases. For example, a survey that is intended for distribution to final year undergraduates should be piloted on a small group of students from their final year.

The piloting of a self-completion survey will allow the researcher to gather information on the appropriateness of the questions, the pre-defined response categories for each question, and how the overall survey format and structure actually function. Aldridge and Levine (2001: 91) suggest that the following 'warning signs' are an indication of problems with surveys that will need to be addressed:

- multiple answers to questions where only one was required;
- only one response is given to a **multiple response** question;
- ranking question inadequately completed;
- uniformity of answers;
- no answers given to a question; and
- completion time is lengthy.

Incorrect completion of questions suggests that the instructions for completing the question are inadequate. Failure to answer suggests that either the question is inappropriate or the question needs rewording. Sometimes respondents will write comments over survey questions to indicate the difficulties they experience in completing the question and prove a valuable resource in determining how to reword the question or in deciding to remove the question entirely.

In structured interviews similar issues as for self-completion surveys may occur. The skill of the interviewer will play an important role in teasing out difficulties and problems. Where questions are inappropriately answered, the interviewer can make specific follow-up questions to ascertain the reasons why. This is of particular value where questions are unanswered. The interviewer is in a position to assess the wording of questions and appropriateness of pre-defined categories, prompting the pilot respondent for other more appropriate categories.

Administering the survey

Administering a survey is an important stage in the research process, requiring the researcher to ensure that a number of related matters are addressed. Once the survey questions have been developed arrangements need to be made for their reproduction. For mail surveys envelopes need to be purchased, together with postage stamps or franking. The mail survey will need to include an introductory letter explaining the nature and purpose of the study. Consider including a pre-paid return envelope to maximize the potential response. Another consideration is the use of a follow-up or reminder letter to be sent a few weeks after the initial survey to remind those sampled of the importance of returning the survey.

Covering letters

A **covering letter** is a short piece of text that introduces the nature and purpose of the study. The purpose of the letter is to:

- identify who is undertaking the research;
- explain the aim of the study;
- stress the importance that as many people as possible should participate in the study;
- give assurances of confidentiality;
- confirm that the study has been approved by an ethical clearance protocol;
- provide contact details should additional information be required;
- include completion and return details (self-completion survey only);
- include details of the interview date/time and location (structured interview only);
- convey the importance of the completion and return of the survey.

Address:
Date:

We are part of a research team based at the University of Plymouth undertaking a study of the prevalence of chronic vaginal discomfort in the general population and attempting to establish what causes this distressing condition. As part of the research we are comparing information gathered from those who have suffered chronic vaginal discomfort with information from a sample of women in the wider population. This wider sample is being drawn from women attending Family Planning Clinics in the Plymouth area. The research has been approved by the Hospital Trust Ethical Committee and the University of Plymouth's Ethical committee.

You have been randomly selected for inclusion in this study. The enclosed questionnaire seeks to gather all relevant information on vaginal discomfort and asks specific questions about your personal life, such as methods of contraception, sexual activity and personal hygiene. The GUM clinic or Family Planning Clinic has kindly forwarded this questionnaire on our behalf.

All the information that is gathered from the survey will be treated with the utmost confidentiality. Your personal details are not recorded on the questionnaire and it is to be returned directly to the research team at the university. The individual responses given cannot be traced back and will not be passed on to anybody else.

We would appreciate it if you could complete and return the enclosed questionnaire in the pre-paid reply envelope as soon as possible. The information collated will enable us to understand this painful condition in more detail. If in the meantime you would like to speak to someone about any medical concerns that you have, please speak to your doctor or nurse at your practice or contact one of the services available on the enclosed help sheet.

If you would like more information about the research you can contact Carole Sutton at the University of Plymouth (Tel: Plymouth 1234567).

We thank you for your participation in this survey and look forward to receiving your completed questionnaire.

Yours sincerely

Carole Sutton
Research Officer

Figure 15.1   A covering letter for a self-completion survey (taken from Sutton, 1994)

Figure 15.1 contains an example of a covering letter that would be sent out with a self-completion survey. Figure 15.2 contains an example of a covering letter that would be sent out to interviewees.

Internet-based surveys

Administrating a survey that is based on the Internet involves a number of different stages. Where the survey is to be distributed via electronic mail, the questions need to be placed into a suitable file that is attached to the message or included within the main body of the e-mail message. The e-mail message should also contain the same information as in the covering letter for a mail survey, plus technical details on how to complete and return the completed survey questions. The e-mail is then sent to the addresses in the sample or, in the case where a snowball sampling technique is adopted, to bulletin boards or newsgroups inviting people to participate in the survey.

Date:

Dear

Thank you for agreeing to participate in this study. Your interview will take place at _____ on ____ day day/month/year. We would like to provide you with some background information about this project and if you have any questions before your interview please feel free to contact me.

We are part of a research team based at the University of Plymouth undertaking a study of the prevalence of chronic vaginal discomfort in the general population and attempting to establish what causes this distressing condition.

As part of the research we are comparing information gathered from those who have suffered chronic vaginal discomfort with information from a sample of women in the wider population. This wider sample is being drawn from women attending Family Planning Clinics in the Plymouth area.

In order to ensure that all relevant information is gathered it will be necessary to ask specific questions about your personal life, such as methods of contraception, sexual activity and personal hygiene. All the information that is gathered in the survey will be treated with the utmost confidentiality and, for the purpose of this investigation, only a number will identify you.

The research has been approved by the Hospital Trust Ethical Committee and the University of Plymouth's Ethical committee.

It must be emphasized that your participation remains voluntary throughout. You can stop the interview at any time and at the end of the interview, if you are not happy, you can ask for the information not to be included in the study.

If you would like more information about the research you can contact Carole Sutton at the University of Plymouth (Tel: Plymouth 1234567).

Yours sincerely

Carole Sutton
Research Officer

Figure 15.2 A covering letter for a structured interview

Where the survey questions are going to be placed on the World Wide Web, the first stage is to transfer the questions and response categories in a suitable file format, for example, html (hypertext mark-up language), onto a Web server. This is likely to involve the support of local technical staff who will need to ensure that not only can the survey be viewed on the Web, but also that responses made are collected into a suitable data file. Any technical difficulties need to be addressed during the pilot phase. An e-mail can then be sent to the addresses of those in the sample and should contain the same information as for a mail survey covering letter. Where a snowball sampling technique is adopted, an e-mail can be sent to newsgroups and bulletin boards inviting participation in the survey.

Structured interviews

In structured interviews the interviewer is available to answer any concerns about participation directly,

Instruction to Interviewee

Thank you for agreeing to participate in this study. My name is_____.
The study is examining the prevalence of chronic vaginal discomfort in the general population and attempting to establish what causes this distressing condition.

As part of the research we are comparing information gathered from those who have suffered chronic vaginal discomfort from the GUM clinic with information from a sample of women attending Family Planning Clinics in the wider population. In order to ensure that all relevant information is gathered it will be necessary to ask specific questions about your personal life, such as methods of contraception, sexual activity and personal hygiene. All the information that is gathered in the survey will be treated with the utmost confidentiality and you will only be identified by a number.

Your participation in this interview is voluntary. You can refuse to answer particular questions, stop the interview at any time, and if you are not happy request that the information is not included in the study.

Are you happy to participate in the study? Do you have any questions?

Could you please sign the consent form (see attached sheet)

Consent Form

I have had the details of the study explained to me.
I understand that all the information gathered will be held in strict confidence. I am aware that I may withdraw from the study at any stage.

Signed (participant) _____

Signed (Researcher) _____

Date: _____

Figure 15.3   An introductory statement read at beginning of the interview

though if possible a written introductory statement should be sent to the participant prior to the interview to allow the respondent time to decide on participation and consider any arising matters.

Figure 15.2 contains a copy of a covering letter sent to interviewees before the interview. It is the same research project as used in the covering letter for the self-completion survey. You can see the slight difference in wording since the researcher will be meeting the participant. In addition, Figure 15.3 contains an example of the introductory statement read by the interviewer at the beginning of the interview and a consent form which may be a requirement of the local ethical committee. The

participant is required to sign the form before the interview can start.

Finally, ensure that the interviewer has enough survey forms if conducting more than one interview on a given day, together with spare pens and pencils.

Should you track participation?

The issues of confidentiality and anonymity have been raised in Chapter 11. During the administration and access of the sample you need to consider if you are going to track those that have responded to a request to complete a self-completion survey or structured interview. Keeping track of those that have responded allows the researcher to monitor response rates and to target those who have not responded with a follow-up letter reminding them to return the survey form or respond to a request to participate in an interview. For postal or mail surveys, questionnaires can be numbered before distribution with a note kept of the corresponding name of the recipient. The difficulty with this is that it would enable the researcher then to link the returned questionnaires to a respondent, thereby breaking issues of anonymity. For purposes of both anonymity and conforming to issues of data protection, care must be taken to ensure that the two sets of information (contact details and returned survey forms) are kept separate. An alternative strategy is simply to send a follow-up letter to all respondents in the sample even though this does incur additional financial expense.

Non-response

Non-response is defined as the failure to collect data from a sampling unit. The response rate is calculated as the ratio of the actual sample size obtained divided by the total sample size selected. For example, in a sample 75 individuals were surveyed from a total sample size of 100. The response rate was 0.75 or 75 per cent. Alternatively, this could be specified as a non-response rate of 0.25 or 25 per cent. Non-response is important as it affects the representativeness of the research results and introduces an error or bias into the findings (Fink, 1995b).

Decisions as to how to proceed with the issue of non-response will be constrained by the timescale of the research project. It is difficult to estimate the level of non-response that you may get; even large government-based surveys with their resource base experience non-response. The non-response rate for the General Household Survey (2000–2001) was 33 per cent and for the Family Expenditure Survey (1999–2000) it was 37 per cent (National Statistics Office).

Arber (2001) identifies two main sources of non-response, refusals and non-contacts. Refusals are from respondents who simply do not wish to participate in the study. They may consider the study as uninteresting, do not perceive the study as important or as having legitimacy. In the case of interviews, non-response can be influenced by the skills of the interviewer, and in mail surveys by the quality of the questionnaire design and explanation in the covering letter. Non-contacts occur when the respondent is not

at home when the interviewer calls, the respondent cannot be interviewed due to illness or communication issues, or in the case of a named respondent that they have moved home. Non-contact rates can be improved by the interviewer 'calling back' or the researcher providing follow-up letters encouraging completion and return of the questionnaire. Depending on the study the offering of an incentive, for example, entry to a prize draw, may improve rates. Where the respondent is non-interviewable it may be appropriate to arrange an advocate or proxy to help complete the survey or interview.

Arranging for proxy interview is particularly important in surveys of very old people, because the needs of the most frail would otherwise be under-represented. It may also be important to employ interviewers who speak appropriate languages or interpreters, otherwise the sample would be biased against those with least fluency in speaking English (Arber, 2001: 75).

Once measures have been put in place to limit the rate of non-response, there is little that the researcher can further do to enhance data collection. The next step is to assess the impact that non-response has on the overall representativeness of the sample. Take the key characteristics of the sample, for example, age, sex, occupation, and compare the proportions of each with the population characteristics. The population characteristics can be found from census data or other large, often government-based, surveys. In the UK, with the exception of the 10-yearly census, government surveys do not survey the entire population. For example, the General Household Survey 2000–2001 surveyed 19,266 individuals in 8,221 households (The UK Data Archive, 2002). Sophisticated sampling techniques are employed in these surveys to represent the population. Where differences in proportions are found, for example, a particular group is underestimated in a sample survey, weighting techniques can be used to multiply by an appropriate ratio; see 'Using SPSS to compute a new variable' p. 327. The assumption of employing this technique, however, is that there is uniformity between those cases that responded from the group and those that did not.

Developing a code book

You have already been introduced to the concept of levels of measurement in Chapter 12. There are four levels of measurement: nominal, ordinal, interval and ratio. Interval and ratio are often combined together and referred to as just interval in the literature as they have similar properties. A **code book**, also called a coding frame, provides the framework of how the responses given to survey questions are prepared for analysis in a computer package. A code book needs to be developed for all methods of quantitative data collection. For closed-ended questions it is possible to include the codes next to the response categories on the actual survey itself. This will aid data entry by increasing the likely speed of data entry and decreasing the likelihood of a data entry error. In addition, the coding of closed-ended questions before the survey is administered allows the researcher to check that the level of measurement of the data will be appropriate for the envisaged analysis.

Coding for nominal variables

Nominal variables are coded numerically. The starting code is normally 1. The categories can be coded in the order that they are listed in the questionnaire. Codes for subsequent categories are simply incremented by 1 on the previous category. Since there is no order to the categories, one could code in any order; however, the norm is to code in order of appearance. This makes intuitive sense and is likely to reduce the potential for coding errors at the data entry stage. Dichotomies are sometimes coded as 0 and 1. The following shows three examples of coding for nominal variables.

Variable: Sex
Coding: 1 = Male; 2 = Female

Variable: Have you read a newspaper today?
0 = No; 1 = Yes

Variable: Which newspaper did you read?
Coding: 1 = Financial Times; 2 = New York Times; 3 = Washington Post; 4 = Melbourne Age; 5 = Times of India; 6 = South China Morning News; 7 = Le Monde; 8 = Other.

Coding for ordinal variables

Coding ordinal variables is similar to that for nominal variables. Coding will normally start at 1 and increase by a count of 1 for each category. The categories should be coded in rank order to maintain the hierarchical order. The coding can run in either direction. In the first example below, the code for very

important is 5 to reflect that it is more important than 1, very unimportant. However, remember that it is not possible to make a statement that very important is 5 times the size of very unimportant. In the second example, the coding is in reverse order where 1 is the highest educational qualification and 6 the lowest educational qualification.

Variable: Importance scale
5 = Very important
4 = Important
3 = Neutral
2 = Unimportant
1 = Very unimportant

Variable: Highest Educational Qualification
1 = Degree or higher
2 = Diploma HE
3 = Certificate in HE
4 = A Levels
5 = AS Levels
6 = GCSE

When coding attitudinal questions, the coding can be reversed where question statements run in opposite directions; for example, in a list of statements there is a combination of negative and positive statements. For the positive statements it would be appropriate for the strongly agree to be given a higher value of 5, whereas in the negative statements it would be appropriate for the strongly disagree to be given a higher value of 5. Assigning values in the appropriate direction is a particular issue for psychologists who may wish that the responses to a list of statements are combined together into one total, or index, for analysis purposes (see 'Different formats of closed-ended question responses' p. 165).

Coding for interval/ratio variables

Coding for interval and ratio variables is simply to enter the data value. For example, if a respondent is 23 years of age, the value of 23 will be entered in the data file. If the number of persons in a household were 3 this value would be entered in the data file.

Coding for multiple response questions

The coding of multiple response questions requires the researcher to identify the maximum number of responses that any one individual could potentially give to the question. Below are the responses to a question asking the respondent to indicate which of the daily newspapers they read. Potentially a respondent could tick all of the responses.

Most questions in a survey require only one response to be given. Where one response is made, only one variable is needed to contain the data in the data file. Multiple response questions produce many responses and therefore require more than one variable in the data file. The easiest method of coding multiple response questions is to treat each category in the list as if it were a single variable. Responses for each variable, in this example each newspaper, are then coded as a dichotomy of 1 = 'Yes' and 2 = 'No'. The response 1 (Yes) states that they have ticked that newspaper and 2 (No) states that the newspaper has not been ticked.

Financial Times ☐
New York Times ☐
Washington Post ☐
Melbourne Age ☐
Times of India ☐
South China Morning Post ☐
Le Monde ☐
Other ☐
    (Please state) _____

Coding for ranking questions

Ranking questions requires the respondent to place two or more categories into a rank order, see Figure 14.7, p. 169, for an example. These questions are also multiple response questions and require additional variables. Two or more variables, according to the number of categories to be ranked, need to be allowed for and the code for each variable would be the entered rank value.

Coding for open-ended questions

The coding of open-ended questions, also known as **post-coding**, is determined by the nature of the question and the variation and depth of the responses given. Where responses are short with some uniformity, within a given range, it can be possible to place the responses into 'like' categories and for these categories to be coded in turn. The level of measurement and coding would be nominal. However, one of the difficulties with coding open response questions is that the responses may not be appropriate for

categorization and that the in-depth self-expression contained within the respondent's answer is removed by this process, thus removing the very rationale for including such a question in the survey. An alternative strategy for dealing with the responses from open-ended questions is to record in the data file a variable that indicates that a response was made and to record the actual response within a separate word-processed document. Included with the actual response should be the unique identifying number for that case, as this would allow for the response to be matched to the other data for that case at the analysis stage. The layout of such a document can follow the format for transcribing interviews, and the subsequent analysis of the open response could employ techniques used within qualitative analysis (see Chapters 16 to 19).

Coding for non-response

During the construction of a code book, consideration needs to be given to how you will deal with non-response, as it is missing data. Respondents may not provide responses to all of the questions because they either choose not to respond or do not have to respond because the question is not applicable to them. In most data analysis packages it is possible to simply leave a blank entry for all data that is missing. The problem with doing this is that it will not allow for the researcher to distinguish between the two types of missing data at the analysis stage. This could be important if question responses have a large proportion of non-responses. Failure to answer the question could signify problems with the question. A common coding strategy for non-response is to divide the different types of non-response into discrete categories and assign a code that is remote from the positive response codes. Some researchers prefer to code using a negative number. For example, –9 = Did not respond, –8 = Not applicable. These codes can be set at the data entry stage to be excluded from the results (see 'Defining a new variable' p. 263).

Locating and assessing secondary quantitative data

The analysis of existing, secondary, data can prove a valuable resource for a research project. Depending on the nature of the research, analysis of an existing data set can form either, or both, background information or the main focus of the project analysis.

Consideration of the inclusion of **secondary data** sources in a research project will be influenced by the theoretical and conceptual nature of the research project. Secondary data is available in a number of different formats. Dale et al. (1988) categorize these into three different groups: **aggregated data**, sample survey and cohort studies. These distinctions provide a useful framework for deciding when and how to incorporate secondary data into your research project.

Aggregated data is probably the easiest data to access and incorporate into research. It is data that has already been manipulated and condensed into summary tables. The pre-defined format allows the researcher to then present the data as tables or charts in a report. Often the aggregated data is derived from one or more sources, and is available on a wide range of topic areas. For example, economic indicators, vital statistics – births, marriages and deaths, national and regional crime statistics, and environment issues to name but a few. Aggregated data from government sponsored surveys, often referred to as **official statistics**, has increasingly been made more freely available via the Internet. In the UK this is via the National Statistics Office website (www.statistics.gov.uk), for the European Union this is via the Eurostat website (www.eurostat.com) and for the US this is via the Federal Statistics website (www.fedstats.gov). The level of public access varies at each website, with access to some aggregated data sets requiring registration as a user.

Sample survey data refers to the data from specific, often government initiated, surveys. Many of the surveys are undertaken on an annual or biannual basis, though one-off surveys are also included within this group. Examples of UK-based sample surveys include the General Household Survey (GHS), Family Expenditure Survey (FES) and Labour Force Survey (LFS). The data collected can be accessed as anonymised individual records, enabling the researcher to manipulate the data in a statistical and data analysis package, such as SPSS. The data can be analysed to specific geographical areas (in the UK to Ward or Postcode area), enabling the data findings to be compared to other statistical sources.

Cohort studies are a very specific type of study in that they are concerned with taking repeated measures from individuals over a longer period and are used within a longitudinal research design. In the UK two well-known cohort studies are the National Child Development Study (NCDS) and the British Household Panel Study (BHPS). The NCDS started in 1958 and took approximately 17,000 individuals from all those born between 3 and 9 March 1958 who lived in Great Britain. There have been five subsequent waves (1965, 1969, 1974, 1981, 1991). The data collected is multi-disciplinary covering the physical, educational, social and economic development of these individuals. Patterns of change over time can be described, controlling for age and historical events, and detailed analysis of relationships between variables undertaken. Complex data analysis can be undertaken that takes into account the developmental, age and historical events of an individual's life course.

Advantages and disadvantages of secondary data

There are a number of issues to be considered when deciding to use secondary data. The survey data should not be viewed as being free-standing as it is a product of the subject area that the original study focused on. This is of particular concern in one-off surveys that have a specific focus and is less so for government-based surveys that have a wider coverage. When considering specific data the sampling technique, sampling frame, research design and method of data collection should be considered together with the conceptual framework. How were concepts operationalized? What measurement tools were used? How were they defined? How were question responses coded?

The advantage of using secondary data is that its use has been established within the social sciences. Examples include the use of official suicide statistics by Durkheim (1952) and the use of socio-economic and health data in 'The Black Report' on poverty and inequalities in health (see Whitehead et al., 1992). In the UK, working within a higher-education setting allows the researcher to have privileged access to such data through the Data Archive. The search catalogues are easy to use and data access is mostly cost-free. In relation to government sponsored surveys and subsequent data sets, the National Statistics Office has developed a high level of data and statistical expertise, and the data is subjected to test and re-test methods for validity. The data sets generally contain a much larger and broader sample than could be realistically obtained by a researcher on their own, particularly if the research forms part of a course of study. In turn, the financial costs associated with the secondary analysis are much lower than for primary data collection, with no data collection, coding or data entry to be undertaken.

The disadvantages of using secondary data are,

first, that its use will be dependent upon the availability and applicability of existing data sets to the area of your study. While catalogue search engines are easy to use, it may take some time for the exact data file you require to be located; indeed, such a data set may not exist. The time saved in not undertaking primary data collection will instead be spent on the time-consuming task of downloading the data sets or subsets of data, familiarization with the data and the coding used. The conceptual frameworks used as the basis for the original data collection may be different to your current project. If using more than one secondary data source, there may be differences between the studies. It is important that time is spent examining the original purposes of the study, the questions and categories coded. Depending on the exact nature of the data analysis to be undertaken, it may require a higher level of technical, data handling and statistical expertise. This is particularly the case when using cohort studies for longitudinal analysis where issues such as missing cases need to be dealt with. Additional difficulties with using secondary data sources are well documented within the literature on using official statistics and the different methods of measurement (Atkinson, 1978).

Accessing data sets in the UK

The main route for searching and obtaining data for secondary analysis in the UK is via the Economic and Social Data Service (ESDS), funded jointly by the Economic and Social Research Council (ESRC) and the Joint Information Systems Committee (JISC). This website service (www.esds.ac.uk) integrates the data services between four centres of expertise. The UK Data Archive (www.data-archive.ac.uk) and the Institute for Social and Economic Research (ISER) are both based at the University of Essex. The Manchester Information and Associated Services (MIMAS) and the Cathie Marsh Centre for Census and Survey Research are (CCSR) are both based at the University of Manchester. The UK Data Archive website contains an on-line catalogue to search by topic and year for available data sets. Details on registering and applying for data sets are also given. The Office for National Statistics (ONS) website also provides social and economic data, mainly aggregated into table format, for the UK. Like the ESDS, much of the National Statistics data is available for free download.

Summary

Collecting and coding survey data are both key stages in the research process. Piloting a survey enables the social researcher to identify the appropriateness of the survey questions and to make subsequent amendments to these questions as required. Once the main survey is undertaken there is a certain amount of administration which accompanies this process, for example, the production of covering letters and introductory statements. If undertaking a structured interview, show cards containing the response categories for closed-ended questions enable the interview to be conducted smoothly and with clarity. A key stage in the research process is the development of a code book that details how the collected data is going to be transferred, mainly in a numerical code format, into a computer for analysis by a statistical package. As has been shown, the level of measurement of the data collected determines the coding of these responses. This data is stored as variables in the final data set. The number of variables needed varies according to the question structure, with multiple response questions requiring more variables. Development of the code book provides a structured concise framework for the data entry phase of the research process.

Keywords

Code book
Coding
Covering letter
Data Collection
Interval

Multiple Response Questions
Nominal
Non-response
Official Statistics
Ordinal

Pilot/Piloting
Post-coding
Ratio
Secondary Data

Questions

1   Why should you pilot survey questions?
2   What factors can influence non-response, and how can you take steps as a social researcher to minimize non-response?
3   How would you code nominal, ordinal and interval variables?
4   How do you code non-response?
5   What factors would you need to consider if undertaking secondary analysis of an existing data set?

Further reading

Aldridge, Alan and Levine, Ken (2001) *Surveying the Social World: Principles and Practice in Survey Research*. Buckingham: Open University Press.

Dale, Angela, Arber, Sara and Procter, Michael (1998) *Doing Secondary Analysis*. London: Unwin Hyman.

Fielding, Jane & Gilbert, Nigel (2000) *Understanding Social Statistics*. London: Sage.

Gilbert, Nigel (ed.) (2001) *Researching Social Life* (2nd edn.) London: Sage.

PART III

DATA ANALYSIS

CHAPTER

16

INTRODUCTION TO QUALITATIVE DATA ANALYSIS

Chapter contents

By the end of this chapter you will be able to:

- Identify the variety of qualitative data sources and their relationship to the diverse array of qualitative data analysis techniques.

- Distinguish qualitative content analysis and discourse analysis.

- Specify the significance of direction and purpose in the conduct and organization of qualitative data analysis.

- Outline key steps and guidelines for the conduct of qualitative data analysis.

Doing qualitative data analysis

In this chapter it will be suggested that the two dominant and competing forms of qualitative data analysis, **content analysis** and **discourse analysis** require each other and are combined in one way or another in all forms of qualitative data analysis. Qualitative data analysis (QDA) is often mentioned but rarely specified. Those involved in qualitative research or those pursuing mixed methods are inevitably engaged in some kind of QDA. Those also engaged in forms of quantitative research are conducting forms of QDA in the act of interpreting prior literature, and in identifying the concepts and **categories** that will structure their quantitative data collection instruments (questionnaires, observation schedules or experimental designs). Any attempt to draw meaning from the world is a form of qualitative data analysis even when it is not formally given that name. Likewise, much of what is carried out in the act of collecting qualitative data is QDA, even if it is not formally classed as such. In this sense, as has already been mentioned on a number of occasions, the distinction between qualitative **data collection** and QDA is not so clearly defined as is often the case in forms of quantitative research. As such, data collection and data analysis often fold into each other in exploratory forms of qualitative research. This form of folding is most often associated with **grounded theory** (see 'Degrees of grounded theory and sampling in qualitative research' p. 79). However, even those who adopt elements of a more **deductive** (see Chapter 4) or prescriptive data collection process agree that the value of qualitative research lies in the ability to **constantly compare** one's latest findings with the tentative explanations generated from the last round of findings. In this process the researcher may change the emphasis of the research and in so doing change the focus of the next round of data collection.

Having pointed out the more fluid and cyclical tendency in qualitative data collection and analysis, the question still remains as to what such analysis actually involves. Fluidity has often generated the impression that QDA is a rather *ad hoc* process of cumulative impressions. How the results emerged from the data is often obscure. It is true to say that such vagueness is commonplace, but it is not the task of this volume to explore, critique or explain this. Here it is intended to offer guidelines on good practice, transparency and reflexivity.

In this chapter the diversity of qualitative data will be highlighted, but its common features will also be highlighted. In Chapters 6–10 **interviews** and **observation**-based data collection were distinguished from data collection based on collecting existing **textual** materials. However, because all qualitative data can be and usually is 'transcribed' into a text form, all QDA is a form of textual analysis. In this sense at least, the text of an interview, a research diary and the contents of a series of newspaper articles are the same. While the more experienced researcher may want to explore the subtle differences in more detail, the beginner may rather acquire the general tools that allow basic analysis of all that can be qualified as 'textual' data. Basic characteristics of qualitative analysis and a set of 'rules of thumb' are given to guide the research process. **Inductive** and **deductive** approaches and their mixing are then outlined. This raises the issue of whether QDA should best be carried out by means of content analysis or discourse analysis. The distinction between content analysis and discourse analysis will be made.

Types of qualitative data – diversity and unity for purposes of analysis

While there is a diversity of forms of qualitative data, for the purposes of an introduction to data analysis, it is possible to identify a sufficient degree of unity to allow a fairly general outline. What defines qualitative data is the ability to extract meaning from its content, as distinct (though not exclusive from) the extracting of numerical relationships between elements of the data. As such, the process of data analysis is the attempt to identify the presence or absence of meaningful themes, common and/or divergent ideas, beliefs and practices. A number of issues arise at this point concerning the nature of the data to be analysed and the relationship between such data collection and its analysis.

The cyclical process

As has already been pointed out, qualitative data can be gathered in a number of ways. **Ethnographic fieldwork** will generate a large quantity of fieldnotes, observations and reflections, narratives and descriptions alongside attempts to provide provisional explanations of events to which the researcher has been exposed or has been a part of. Fieldnotes will also contain records of events and accounts of the researcher's own strategies and research plans, which will almost inevitably change over the course of a period in the field. Such notes are themselves a form of qualitative data, and can be analysed as such. However, the data in this case is the most explicit example of the on-going process of analysis within the data collection process itself and in the resulting data. The researcher's fieldnotes are always selective accounts of events, and selection will depend upon the researcher's choices of where to go, what to observe or participate in and whom to talk to. Such choices will be based upon the interpretations the researcher makes about the situations they have already been party to. Not only are such fieldnotes dependent upon the researcher's on-going analysis of the situation (just as the survey researcher's questionnaire is the result of prior analysis of existing literature and provisional piloting), so such notes will, or should, contain explicit analytical accounts and comments. The ethnographer or **participant observer** should maintain a separate account of such analytical reflections, often in a separate book or computer file. A clear linking by date, location, participants, event and so on should be maintained. This is to enable clearer reflection on the process when later rounds of analysis take place. Depending on the nature of the fieldwork situation, the field researcher needs to take time to maintain a record of this cyclical process of data collection and provisional analysis, and subsequently re-focused data collection.

Due to the nature of fieldwork data collection, where a large part of what is collected as data are the researcher's own notes, the researcher's influence upon such data is more explicit than in other forms of data collection. The fact that such data is more explicitly filtered through the mind of the researcher before being 'recorded' (on paper) is a constant reminder of the 'analytical' input that goes into what is recorded, and how this content then influences what the researcher does next, where they go and who they interact with. This cyclical process is a common feature in most of what counts as qualitative data.

Notes and transcriptions

Ethnography usually involves talking to people as well as observing and interacting/ participating in other activities. These may be informal conversations or formal interviews. If such talk is not recorded verbatim (for example, on audio-tape), the question of what gets 'saved' in the form of written notes again raises the question of analysis in the act of data collection. Just as interview schedules may be more or less structured, so what is to be noted down is also. In most cases, barring the most informal of conversations, or where recording would not be possible, full recording combined with written notes is the best approach.

However, the process of transcription itself involves a degree of analysis that is often underestimated or even ignored. This is particularly true when transcription is parcelled out to audio-typists to save time. Listening to recordings involves a degree of interpretation and selection and so involves an element of analysis. The transcripts of the same interview made by different transcribers can contain significant differences for this reason.

In addition to this aspect of transcription analysis, the sequential nature of interviews means that thoughts generated during prior interviews may come to influence the conduct of subsequent interviews. This may be more or less explicit. Just as in the case of field note-taking, so in interviewing the qualitative researcher needs to keep a record of their provisional interpretations of interviewee responses. Given the more **open-ended** nature of qualitative interview questions and **schedules**, it is rarely the case that such interviews will follow the same sequence from one interview to the next. It is important for the researcher, therefore, to keep a record of what they take from each interview as a means of identifying what it is they are bringing to the next.

In the case of **conversation analytic** research, the process of transcription takes on an added significance, as it is the attention to the fine-grain detail of talk (sequences of interaction, pauses and overlaps) that provide conversation analysis with the material they seek to analyse. Specific attention will be paid to this in 'Doing conversation analysis' p. 218.

Texts and secondary sources

The use of text as a source may be of two types:

- Primary texts – texts not produced for the purposes of research; that is, newspapers, diaries, letters.
- Secondary sources – texts generated by previous researchers.

In both cases selection for the purposes of the current research represents a set of prior analytical choices, and the texts once selected require further analysis.

The use of text as a qualitative data source highlights a number of general issues about QDA as well as having qualities of its own to contend with. The transformation of a variety of experiences (talk, observations, memories and so on) into text is a near universal step in the process of qualitative research. It is not usually the first step as encountering these sources precedes recording them, and recording such experiences may or may not be in text form in the first instance. Nevertheless, transformation into text, the transcription of experience into units of communicative meaning (that is, words and sequences of words) is itself both an act of analysis and often the pre-requisite for subsequent forms of qualitative analysis.

Images as texts

Can images be reduced to textual accounts of them or, more importantly, can this be done without losing much of the image's content? The same question can be asked of music and much else in human behaviour that is non-verbal. The relationship between words and images has generated a significant debate within qualitative research. This debate over the content of images has shifted away from art-history towards a more sociological approach to the meanings given to images by those who use them in various ways. As such, we might reasonably say that attributing meaning to images is the same as attributing meaning to text. Both are problematic, but they may not be fundamentally different. A number of the most recent computer software packages designed to assist in the process of QDA make explicit attempts to facilitate the analysis of images.

Texts and actions

While transcriptions of interview data directly relate to the production of words by those being researched, fieldnotes seek to record other forms of action as well as just talking/writing. Descriptions of actions other than talk, whether these are the descriptions given in talk by interviewees or descriptions made by the researcher of the actions of others, the relationship between **text** and other actions is a complex one that cannot be reduced to simplistic forms of representation. In the process of QDA the researcher needs always to bear in mind the difference between an account and the action itself. The researcher's interest may be in seeking to gain a true account of non-verbal events, or they may be more interested in the meanings given to such events by respondents. Alternatively, the researcher may be more interested in the ways respondents seek to represent events, which may not be the same thing as what they themselves think or believe, let alone what they actually did.

These differences between action, interpretation and representation may be resolved through the choice only to focus upon the representations themselves, as acts of storytelling or accounting. The attempt to give a picture of the world may be interesting in itself. The fact that some people seek to tell their stories in certain ways may tell us a great deal about the resources they have at their disposal and the strategies they believe will be successful. The differences in strategy adopted by different groups and individuals may be a sufficient focus of attention for the researcher. Alternatively, the researcher may want to analyse the relationship between accounts and the reality of people's behaviour. In this case they may wish to adopt forms of **triangulation**, such as a combination of interviews and observations. In this way the choice of data collection methods will depend upon what it is that the researcher wishes to analyse.

Analysis of data collected individually or by team research

Because QDA and data collection are very often interlinked in the cyclical process outlined above, it is important for the process to be made clear thoughout. This is highlighted in the case of team research, but is no less true when the data is collected and analysed by a single researcher. The act of team research simply forces the reflexive process into one of open communication. What the individual researcher needs to keep a track of, in the context of team research, requires that the members of the team regularly update each other on the on-going process of interpretation emerging and feeding into each other's conduct. This allows for co-ordination as well as deepening the process of reflection by which new insights from current rounds of data collection are fed into subsequent rounds.

Some rules of thumb and advice on process and practice

David Silverman suggests six rules for the conduct of QDA:

1   Don't mistake a critique for a reasoned alternative (highlighting tensions and even contradictions in the accounts and actions of those being researched does not in itself demonstrate irrationality or the need for those being researched to change).
2   Avoid treating the actor's point of view as an explanation (how someone describes their reality is not necessarily the same thing as the reality itself as explanations have purposes).
3   Recognize that the phenomenon always escapes (no account of accounts is ever total).
4   Avoid choosing between all polar oppositions (either/or is rarely an adequate account of complex realities and is more likely to mislead than to clarify).
5   Never appeal to a single element as an explanation (while axial themes may emerge, focus upon a single core is more likely to distort analysis than to provide insight).
6   Understand the cultural forms through which 'truths' are accomplished (if respondents say the same thing, this may say as much about shared ways of presentation as it does about any underlying reality).
    (1993: 197–208)

Silverman identifies four ways to develop the analysis of qualitative data within a developmental sequence where data analysis begins at the same time as data collection and where the two develop hand in hand. These four aspects are:

1   Focus on data which are of high quality and are easiest to collect.
2   Focus on one process [at a time] within those data.
3   Narrow down to one part [at a time] of the process.
4   Compare different sub-samples of the population. (2000b: 140)

What Silverman is suggesting here is how to start the ball rolling. By focus upon a rich stream of initial data

the researcher can develop ideas in provisional analysis that can then be compared with other research sites and groups. Initial judgements may emerge from the first rich source, but any such initial analysis is to be critically challenged in subsequent rounds of data collection. The choice of a rich initial source allows for relatively robust initial findings, but this robustness is for the purpose of heavy later challenge, not as a taken-for-granted basis for interpreting what will be encountered next.

Bruce Berg (1998: 226) points out that the act of 'deciphering' text is essential in all qualitative data. The term 'deciphering' refers to the fact that words do not always mean the same thing, while at the same time different words can be used to mean the same thing in other situations. As such it is never enough to say 'look' here is the same word or phrase and therefore here is a connection or a shared meaning. The researcher has to justify their claims to have identified connections and their claims to have identified differences in talk, just as they have to justify claims to have identified the 'meaning' of single texts. Berg suggests, in the first instance, that any claim to have identified a meaningful pattern must be demonstrated with at least three examples. One of the prime criticisms of qualitative research is the use of choice quotes to promote particular conclusions. The use of a minimum of three examples for each alleged finding at least forces the researcher to demonstrate what they mean by a pattern, both in terms of its incidence and its content. Such evidencing also helps avoid the equating of the researcher's way of seeing with the ways in which respondents see events, as the researcher has to show what it is that they are basing their claims upon. Such evidencing acts to make analysis more accountable and also more reflexive. Conversation analysis disputes the necessity of such 'exampling', but for specific reasons that will be discussed in Chapter 18.

Miles and Huberman (1994) adopt the expression 'think display' as their motto in the conduct of QDA. This is not only a suggestion to think about how best qualitative data can be represented, but also the suggestion that it is in the act of representation that analysis is actually achieved. By means of **visual reduction** the complexity of qualitative data can be rendered comprehensible in rather the same way that quantitative data is rendered comprehensible by means of **tables**, **graphs** and **statistical** procedures. More will be said about Miles and Huberman's approach to QDA in Chapter 17, but here it is useful to identify the range of displays they suggest. These authors identify **matrix displays** (grids) and **network diagrams** (flows and links) as the two most useful representational devices. They go on to identify forms of display that operate to describe and explore single cases or the comparison between cases. They also identify methods of representation that facilitate analysis at the level of **explanation** and **prediction** either within **cases** or between cases.

All the above authors give a great part of their accounts of QDA to the question of **coding**, and this is not surprising. Coding is perhaps the single most significant act in the process of qualitative analysis. Coding involves the identification of common themes (words, phrases, meanings) within the data being analysed. Every time the same theme is mentioned it is tagged (electronically or otherwise). Then all instances where the tag (code) has been made can be compared. Alternatively, the cross-referencing of two such tags can be used to highlight the incidence (or lack of incidence) of cases where the two themes occur together. These codes allow links to be made and are a form of data reduction, the highlighting of key points within the vast mass of the overall data. More quantitative forms of content analysis seek to count the number of times a theme is coded or the number of times a pair of codes occur in close proximity. More qualitative forms of content analysis use coding not just to count the number of occurrences, but also to allow exploration of what is going on when such occurrences happen. Various things can be selected for coding. Miles and Huberman suggest the following list of basic coding prompts:

- themes;
- causes/explanations;
- relations among people; and
- emerging constructs.

Some coding is predefined; a set of codes is developed and applied to the data. Another form of coding is called **open coding**. Glaser and Strauss' *grounded theory* is associated with the open coding approach, though Strauss (Strauss and Corbin, 1990) has been more willing than Glaser (1992) to suggest initial prompts to act as initial code selecting devices. Examples might be a set of questions like, who, what, where, when, why? Every time a name appears in the text this can be coded as an example of a 'who?' code and so on. Some see this as pragmatic, while others see

it as prescriptive and distorting. Fielding and Lee offer four tips for open coding (generating the codes to be used in the act of reading through the data, rather than generating the codes in advance):

1 Constantly question the data.
2 Data selected for coding must be treated microscopically (that is, in detail).
3 Coding should immediately generate memos of theory building.
4 Analytic import of categories must always be shown, not assumed.
   (1998: 33)

Advocates of discourse analysis often accuse other researchers of adopting too mechanistic an approach to coding. Discourse analysts suggest that more depth can be achieved by detailed analysis of singular cases or small **samples** than from systematic coding of larger amounts of textual data. However, even such an in-depth approach involves selection and analysis of elements within the materials selected. Both require forms of coding. This may be informal, but it is a form of coding nonetheless.

Fielding and Lee (1998) mention memos. Memos are notes that researchers leave for themselves as they go through the data assigning codes to segments. If they come across an interesting extract they may wish to make a note that this phrase or description seems to relate to other extracts in a new way or that it seems to link or challenge an established theory. Memos can be notes in the margins of a page, sticky labels attached to transcripts or sub-files within a computer package. Memos will be discussed in more detail in Chapters 17 and 19.

Two key dimensions of qualitative analysis: direction and purpose

The most important decisions in qualitative analysis are how to integrate analysis with the data collection process and what it is the research seeks to achieve. Qualitative data collection involves the accumulation of large quantities of mainly textual material, and a significant part of the data analysis process involves the attempt to reduce this volume by means of selection and organization. Data collection itself involves selection and organization of whom to observe, interact with or speak to, what to record and when. As such, the process of narrowing down occurs prior to any collection and the choices about how to focus research once data collection begins continue this process of reduction by selection.

Direction of research

To what extent should the research process be open to redirection in the light of on-going analysis throughout the various rounds of data collection? If each interview or day in the field were to be followed by a period of reflection over the meaning of the new data collected, and if these new tentative conclusions were then used to restructure the next interview or day in the field, it is possible that if these early interviews were unrepresentative then these encounters would move research away from other valuable insights that would have occurred if a steady course had been maintained. Alternatively, the choice to pursue a course of continuity may lead to other opportunities to pursue 'hot' leads being missed when they present themselves. The danger of redirecting the research too early on all too often lies in the willingness of the researcher to trust hunches that they feel the data is telling them, while the reverse danger lies in trusting your initial hunches even in the face of contrary evidence from early encounters. Keeping a reflexive record, via memos and a research diary, allows the researcher to confront these dangers and to seek a balanced response to these competing pressures.

There is no simple solution to this problem, but in the process of learning the ropes for the first time two rules of thumb may be drawn upon. The first can be taken from Chapter 6 (on qualitative data collection), that of data saturation. When thinking about how much data is enough in the context of qualitative research, it is not possible to draw easily on the sampling theories used in quantitative research. The grounded approach therefore uses the predictive ability of emerging theories as a yardstick to measure their usefulness and the usefulness of continuing to collect new data on that question. If a tentative explanation suggests itself, and this explanation suggests a change of research focus, it may be useful to continue along the same track as before to see if the next few encounters lead to the same conclusion. If so, follow the new direction. If not, carry along the existing line of data collection. Of course, the use of **data saturation** was initially suggested to show when research might reasonably come to an end. The level of saturation that might be reached after a

considerable amount of time is going to be far greater than that which might be reached in the early stages. If a new question arises early on in the data collection process, it is unrealistic to believe that it could draw upon the amount of supporting evidence that may be available to a researcher much further down the track. How much evidence might be needed to support a provisional conclusion such that it would justify a change of course? Here we might draw upon Berg's earlier rule of thumb concerning the evidence needed to support a tentative theory. Recall that Berg (1998: 226) suggests it is best to be able to show at least three independent examples of what you feel is evidence in favour of a conclusion before you can realistically suggest that it justifies a change of research direction. Early on in the research process this rule of three may act to balance the tension between an overly rapid change of course and too rigid a continuation with a preconceived research focus.

Purpose of research

Before the cycle of data collection and analysis can begin, the researcher needs to be clear what their analysis is actually aimed at achieving. Some important distinctions are worth repeating. Is it the intention of the researcher to describe, compare, explain or predict? Similarly, with reference to these possibilities, what is it that the researcher seeks to describe, compare and so on? Is it to be the accounts given by respondents? Is the researcher more interested in the beliefs of those they seek to research or is the research to be aimed at behaviour and action – what people actually do, as distinct from what they say or believe? When designing a research question, the researcher needs to have identified which of these options they are aiming for. It may very well be the case that in the course of conducting research the emphasis of the research will change. Choice to focus attention upon action, belief and/or expression is distinct from the issue of deduction and/or induction regarding the substance of the research, but the two are related.

The process of reduction and organization that makes up data analysis is not simply the attempt to boil down the data collected to a manageable size. That manageability can be done in a number of ways. Reduction by the use of certain codes, chosen to highlight certain features of the data, will act to reduce the visibility of other aspects of the data. Clear identification of what the researcher seeks to achieve may at least reduce the risk of reduction, hiding what may be of significance to their project, but which was not identified early enough.

As has been pointed out already, the act of analysis early on may act to redirect the research. Similarly, the act of coding redirects the attention of the researcher from certain themes within the data towards others. Clarity of purpose allows greater reflection upon the inherent dangers involved in data reduction.

Content analysis versus forms of discourse analysis

The classic example of the clash between content analysis and discourse analysis can be found in discussions of mass media (see Anderson in Chapter 5, p. 49). At one extreme there are those who seek to identify the quantity of space given to certain things in different newspapers or the quantity of time given over to certain themes within different broadcast programmes. It may be found, for example, that 20 per cent of news coverage is devoted to stories about crime. That would be an example of highly quantitative content analysis. On the other extreme, there are the attempts to identify the construction of an individual crime story. How are the players in the story represented? Who and what are included and/or excluded from the coverage? How are images and words brought together to create the impression of fear, sympathy, security or mystery? This would be an example of discourse analysis. The two approaches have come to represent the ends of a spectrum, with much passion being expressed about the validity or weakness of each extreme.

Within qualitative research there is a fierce debate over the value of forms of content analysis. Content analysis assumes that it is possible to identify content in terms of units: one unit of data being an example of one thing, while another unit of data is either an example of the same thing or it is not. Article one is a crime story, while article two is not a crime story, for example. Once you have been able to identify which units of data belong to which categories, it is then possible to count them to see how many or how much of each type there are/is. To some qualitative researchers this attempt to reduce social reality to a bunch of things that can be counted is a misguided attempt to turn qualitative research into quantitative research in the quest for respectability. To others the attempt to identify units within a large amount of data such that differences and similarities can be identified is essential to any thinking.

Those who oppose what they see as the imposition of quantification into qualitative research prefer to use forms of discourse analysis. Discourse analysis covers a wide range of things, from **semiotics** to **narrative analysis**. What these forms of analysis have in common is a resistance to mechanistic reduction of meaning to measurement (in numbers).

Berg (1998) identifies himself with those who seek to develop qualitative forms of content analysis. It is not necessary to fall into the traps that constrained researchers who adopted simplistic quantitative forms of content analysis in the past. The common accusation levelled against quantitative forms of content analysis was that they relied on classifications that were often deeply flawed. If you were analysing crime coverage in the media and simply assumed a consensus notion of what a crime story is, you would potentially ignore a great deal of diversity. The coverage of military killings might not be included on the grounds that such killings were not defined as crimes by the journalists. But does that mean that they were not crimes? Who is to define? Some news media might report certain terrorist actions as crimes, others as acts of war. The fact that there is a difference of definition may be significant. Does the researcher use the definitions adopted by the different media or should they adopt their own classification? On what basis should such an alternative model be devised? Berg's claim is that forms of content analysis in these instances are not flawed because they seek to count and measure the level of certain things. Rather, the fault lies in the construction of the units they seek to add up. There are better ways of constructing such units. Interestingly, what Berg is suggesting here is that what makes qualitative research qualitative is not the absence of counting, but the more inductive form of data collection and data classification. Classification achieved by more grounded methods allows the researcher to explore and develop more valid systems of coding.

Berg (1998) suggests that while he is a qualitative researcher who still believes in the value of content analysis (and therefore the whole coding enterprise), others do not see things the same way. He cites David Silverman as a qualitative researcher who rejects content analysis and counting in favour of more discursive and narrative based forms. While it is true that Silverman advocates forms of data analysis that do not fit with mainstream content analysis (especially his advocacy of conversation analysis), this is not to the exclusion of content analysis. Silverman's (1993)

discussion of the works of Miles and Huberman and his accounts of QDA software (all of which is built around forms of content analysis) show that, while more sceptical than Berg, he still accepts the use of counting and coding for certain analytical ends. The divide is not as great as is often made out.

In the next chapters, the logic of qualitative forms of content analysis will be looked at. Chapter 17 first hinges around the practice of coding, then addresses the attempt to use coded data to develop more sophisticated forms of analysis than simply coding and showing the incidence of coded themes. Chapter 18 deals with forms of narrative, semiotic, deconstructionist and conversation analysis. Chapter 19 outlines how to use the QDA softward packages NVivo 2.0 and N6.

Summary

The relationship between qualitative data collection and QDA may be deductive or inductive. However, quite often it can be a cyclical combination of both. While the *purpose* of research will have emerged at the literature review stage, early rounds of data analysis may shift the *direction* of research, that is, the way in which the purpose is interpreted and pursued.

A useful point can be made here. Those using qualitative content analysis believe it avoids both the reductionism of quantitative content analysis and the limited attention to generalizability of discourse analysis. They claim that a greater understanding of the data is acquired by 'coding up' from the data rather than imposing codes upon the data ('coding down'). This is said to increase the validity of the codes chosen. This requires a more in-depth reading and re-reading of the data prior to coding. This process is, in many respects, similar to what discourse analysts seek to achieve. While suggesting that a more holistic encounter with the data allows the best impressions to be formed, qualitative content analysis still suggests the need for such impressions to be examined through formal coding and comparison. This resembles the formality of quantitative analysis. However, the deductive code generation that guides most quantitative content analysis and the more inductive (or in fact cyclical) forms of code generation that guide qualitative content analysis is an essential distinction. The separation between discourse analysis and qualitative content analysis is not as clear-cut as it might appear once such distinctions within content analysis are taken properly into account.

Keywords

Case	Field research/Fieldwork	Prediction
Categories	Graphs	Sample
Coding	Grounded Theory	Schedules
Constant Comparison	Induction	Semiology/Semiotics
Content Analysis	Interview	Statistic
Conversation Analysis	Matrix Display	Tables
Data Collection	Narrative Analysis	Text/Textual
Data Saturation	Network Diagram	Trianglation
Deduction	Observation	Visual Reduction
Discourse Analysis	Open Coding	
Ethnographic/Ethnography	Open-ended Questions	
Explanation	Participant Observation	

Questions

1   What is the difference between direction and purpose in the conduct of qualitative data collection, and what is the relationship between both these and the process of qualitative data analysis?

2   What distinguishes qualitative content analysis from quantitative forms of content analysis?

3   What is discourse analysis?

4   How might each of the rules of thumb suggested by David Silverman help the would-be qualitative researcher avoid misinterpretation of their data?

5   What characteristics unite the diverse variety of data that can be analysed by qualitative means?

Further reading

Berg, Bruce L. (1998) *Qualitative Research Methods for the Social Sciences*. Needham Heights, MA: Allyn and Bacon.

Fielding, Nigel and Lee, Raymond (1998) *Computer Analysis and Qualitative Research*. London: Sage.

Glaser, Barney (1992) *Emergence vs Forcing: Basics of Grounded Theory Analysis*. Mill Valley, CA: Sociology Press.

Glaser, Barney and Strauss, Anselm (1967) *The Discovery of Grounded Theory: Strategies for Qualitative Research*. Chicago, IL: Aldine.

Silverman, David (1993) *Interpreting Qualitative Data*. London: Sage.

Silverman, David (2000b) *Doing Qualitative Research – A Practical Handbook*. London: Sage.

Strauss, Anselm and Corbin, Juliet (1990) *Basics of Qualitative Research: Grounded Theory Procedures and Techniques*. London: Sage.

CHAPTER

17

CODING QUALITATIVE DATA (QUALITATIVE CONTENT ANALYSIS)

Chapter contents

By the end of this chapter you will be able to:

- Specify the range of coding methods available to the qualitative researcher.

- Identify the deductive and inductive features of qualitative coding.

- Comprehend the significance of content analysis as a field of tension between qualitative and quantitative approaches to data analysis.

- Move beyond simple coding to the development of more sophisticated methods of analysing qualitative data.

Content analysis has a long tradition in quantitative research, and has been strongly criticised in this form by qualitative researchers (see Anderson's discussion in Chapter 5). However, there is also a tradition of qualitative content analysis which has sought to bridge the divide between deductive forms of quantitative content analysis and the more inductive and small-scale research of discourse analysis. This tradition of qualitative content analysis seeks to draw upon the advantages of both of the other traditions and to overcome their weaknesses. This chapter provides an account of qualitative content analysis, centred around the core theme of coding in qualitative research, and goes on to outline an array of techniques for, and types of, coding in the analysis of quantitative data.

Coding

Coding is the process of applying codes to chunks of text so that those chunks can be interlinked to highlight similarities and differences within and between texts. Codes are keywords, themes or phrases that may or may not correspond to actual terms in the text being analysed. If a set of interviews that investigated people's ideas about democracy was analysed, some codes might be words such as 'democracy', 'voting' and 'participation'. These words may be the words the interviewees used themselves, or the terms the researcher chooses to use to sum up or represent a range of similar findings that the researcher feels 'go together'. Similarly, in the analysis of fieldnotes or texts taken from other sources, the choice of codes may draw upon a number of sources, within and beyond the texts themselves.

Coding enables **data reduction**. By flagging up those chunks of text where key themes seem to recur, the researcher is able to narrow their focus of attention from the whole of a text to just those areas they feel are significant. By identifying whether there are patterns between the chunks coded for a particular theme, the researcher can test the strength of potential accounts, descriptions and/or explanations. Descriptions, explanations and so on are forms of reduction. They are attempts to give a brief summary or **model** of a much larger set of phenomena. Data collection is an attempt to streamline a complex set of events into a set of manageable things for the researcher to analyse. Coding is the most common subsequent step in the attempt to organize that data so as to allow further reduction in the process of analysis.

Coding is not just about the application of codes to chunks of text. Codes not only need to be selected. Codes also need defining so that the researcher is clear what it is that they are claiming whenever a code is applied. Common sociological **categories** such as 'family', 'class', 'ethnicity' cannot simply be applied. The researcher needs to produce clear definitions of what these categories are being used to mean, either prior to coding or in the process of coding itself. Of course, these definitions may change in the course of the research, but a record of these changes needs to be kept, so the initial usage needs to be recorded. Memos are the most common method of recording these ideas about coding.

A brief history of coding in qualitative research

Coding is an integral part of quantitative research. The capacity to identify any kind of numerical relationship, whether that be simply identifying the number of times something occurs or the strength of the link between one thing happening and another thing happening, depends upon the ability to identify those things and to record them as such. Coding is the foundation of quantitative research. If you can't code it, you can't count it. Coding is also a crucial element within qualitative forms of **content analysis**. While content analysis can be rigidly quantitative, forms of content analysis have been developed to allow the mapping of patterns within qualitative data in a way that avoids reducing meaning simply to the number of times a particular **textual** term occurs within the texts being analysed. Nevertheless, there is always the danger that coding – the application of codes to segments of text for the purpose of mapping patterns – may lead to meanings being fragmented and coded segments being abstracted from the context which gives that text its meaning. Those who pursue a **discourse analytic** approach argue that this is the greatest weakness of **content analysis**, however much the researcher tries to avoid the failings of quantification.

Fielding and Lee (1998: Ch. 2) provide an account of the development of 'formal' methods of qualitative data analysis (QDA). Analytical induction emerged as an attempt to develop systematic qualitative methods of case study analysis which sought to generate 'universal' claims without resort to large-scale samples and statistical inference (the attempt to claim generality on the basis of a 'sufficient' and well-selected sample). Developed by Florian Znaniecki in the 1920s and 1930s (Fielding and Lee 1998: 21–3), analytical induction involves the formulation of a research question and a tentative hypothesis. This is then tested in relation to a single case study. Does the hypothesis fit? If yes, then retest the same hypothesis. If no, then reformulate or reject the original hypothesis, and test the new one. Eventually, a robust defensible thesis will emerge by means of continual reformulation. Critics point out that such an approach is as **deductive** as it is **inductive** (testing reformulated predictions), and that it is not explained how each single case is 'analysed' so as to say whether the original hypothesis is either supported or challenged.

It was around this time that researchers from the Chicago School of Urban Social Research began using a range of techniques that we today would recognize as 'coding'. Segments from interview transcripts containing similar themes or phrases would be grouped together for comparison, and researchers conducting field studies would draw up summary sheets identifying the key events and themes of a particular encounter or interaction (Fielding and Lee, 1998: 23–4). Others engaged in open-ended interviewing from a number of academic and commercial fields also had to develop methods for teasing out the key themes from large volumes of textual data. Under a range of different names what would now be called coding developed apace.

Fielding and Lee (1998: 25) identify the work of Becker and Geer (1960) and Becker et al. (1961), in relation to research into the training of medical students, as the first sustained discussion of the value of coding. In the context of research into medical and scientific training, the perception that qualitative research was only capable of generating anecdotal accounts of events needed to be overcome. The desire to demonstrate a degree of rigour in the movement from data to conclusions led to a more systematic account of coding. Fielding and Lee conclude that while it was Becker and Geer who 'mainstreamed' coding, it was Glaser and Strauss (1967) who made it popular in their account of grounded theory.

Generating a coding frame

A **coding frame** is a catalogue that identifies all the codes to be applied to the data in order to identify patterns within the data. Just as in quantitative research, the development of a coding frame may come before the analysis of the data or through the process of analysis itself. The development of a coding frame involves a number of choices and approaches. These are discussed below.

Types of coding

If coding is the act of identifying a series of 'tags', which are attached to, or emerge from, chunks of text in order to allow links between those chunks to be

highlighted and explored, how are codes to be identified? A number of methods and types of coding can be identified.

Latent and manifest codes

Manifest codes refer to specific terms that recur within the text data collected. Manifest codes are terms that are in the data itself. **Latent codes** are terms or themes that the researcher identifies beneath the surface of the text. Terms like 'lonely', 'isolated' and 'unfriendly' may recur in the text. The researcher may feel that, having read the full transcripts or because of their prior review of the literature, these three terms are all referring to the same thing. Rather than having three codes, the researcher may feel that beneath the surface there is sufficient commonality to mean that a single common code should be applied to all instances where any one of these three terms is used, even where there is no common terminology in the text itself.

Sociological and in vivo

In vivo codes refer to terms that are in the language of those either interviewed or observed, or who wrote the texts being collected by the researcher. This is in many ways the same thing as what was referred to above as manifest codes. However, the distinction being drawn here is slightly different. **Sociological codes** are themes drawn not from the language of those being researched, but instead from the language of the researcher's theoretical background. Just as in the above case, where three terms used by interviewees might be identified by the researcher as meaning the same thing, so the researcher might conclude that what a series of interviewees are touching on in their talk (or in whatever other form of text source the researcher is using), the surface talk can be linked together through the use of a more theoretical term. This is similar to the notion of symptoms and diagnosis. What a number of different patients describe in different ways may appear to the doctor as symptoms of a common condition. The doctor classifies these things in terms of their theoretical account of the surface symptoms rather than in terms of the range of surface appearances or descriptions given. While *in vivo* codes remain true to the diversity of self-description/experience, sociological codes seek to identify underlying commonalities. The danger of *in vivo* codes lies in becoming lost in multiple terms for the same thing. The danger of sociological codes is to rush too quickly into reducing diversity to already existing theoretical pigeonholes. The researcher must seek to balance this tension as best they can in the particular conditions of the research they seek to carry out.

Deductive and inductive (and open) coding

Deductive coding involves the production of a list of **categories** by which data is to be coded prior to the collection of the data itself. In so far as there is always an element of selection in any form of social research, and in so far as the researcher is always influenced by their culture in how they see the world they research, there is always an element of deductiveness about coding. Inductive forms of coding involve the generation of codes after the collection and initial reading of the data itself. This may be at a number of stages in the data collection process. Either the first round of data collected is read to allow the researcher to generate a list of initial codes from which to give provisional conclusions, or the coding process is left until the data has all been collected. Early use of inductive coding becomes the basis for subsequent deductive forms of enquiry. This cyclical process is the basis for both analytical induction and grounded theory, though it is the latter that is more commonly practised (in broad terms). In the context of grounded theory the initial process of inductive coding is referred to as 'open coding'. Most texts on qualitative research suggest it is important to engage in forms of analysis from the very beginning of the data collection stage. However, it is also commonly announced that it is not good to be too pre-emptive in the kinds of coding that are done in early rounds of the cycle. This raises another set of questions about the types of code that can be generated.

Summary codes and pattern codes

Summary codes are often also called first level codes. These codes are ones that focus on general characteristics of a population, situation or encounter. The most elementary of these might be the what, where, when, how, and who type questions that allow the researcher to get a basic hold on what they have generated. This grasping applies in the case of individual interviews, notes on specific fieldwork encounters or from a single text (such as a newspaper article or letter). However, once such basic information has been coded, these summaries can be used to enable quick and easy comparisons between single cases. Summary codes are generally considered relatively non-distorting. In other words, such summaries do not seek to impose a particular agenda on the text. Fear that early coding may lead the researcher to become too focused too soon on one set of issues rather than another is offset by the belief that summary coding is not seeking to identify specifics. On the whole, summary codes are prescriptive and do not derive from the text itself. Wanting a record of who, what, when and so on is seen as a general interest. However, the specifics of a particular research project may lead to the formulation of some general summary questions which relate specifically to the project at hand. A study of undergraduate students may wish to record the stage at which the student is in their degree, for example. This will allow for some provisional organization of the data being collected. As has been pointed out earlier, it is not uncontroversial to use summary coding. Barney Glaser (1992) argues that even elementary codes used for initial organization of early rounds of data collection are too prescriptive and that all codes should develop from the data itself. This view is not widely shared and many would argue that it is not possible. Nevertheless, the dangers of **prescriptive coding** should not be ignored, and the use of summary codes rather than **pattern codes** may not be enough to avoid the dangers of substantive or pattern coding being developed too early.

Pattern coding is also called specific coding or depth coding and moves beyond what is called summary coding. Pattern coding seeks to highlight the existence of underlying patterns within the data. It is designed to get to the heart of what is going on in the data, or at least what is going on in terms of what the researcher is interested in, or what the researcher becomes interested in through the course of data collection and initial forms of analysis. This creates a tension. One cannot identify patterns without looking, and where and how does one look to see what is supposed to be beneath the surface? The initial application of summary codes will have involved the researcher in a preliminary scanning of the text. This should breed a degree of familiarity with the text's content without focusing the researcher's attention in one direction or another. The development of provisional pattern codes emerges from this familiarity, but a more detailed reading of the text may be required at this stage (whether this occurs after the first round of data collection, the second round or at the end of the data collection process).

While summary codes seek to map the content of

the text in terms of general characteristics, pattern codes are designed to enable the investigation of relationships within the specific content. This usually involves the identification of specific recurrent themes within the text, themes that can then be investigated, both for their relationship with particular summary code characteristics (that is, male/female, age, location and so on) and between themselves.

Axial codes and systematic codes

Axial codes are codes that the researcher selects to represent and to highlight what they perceive to be the core issues or themes within the text they are analysing. Whether the researcher is generating such axial (or 'meta', that is, higher order) codes in a preliminary form applied to early rounds of data collection, or where these axial codes are being developed in a more final sense after all the data has been collected, it is the case that axial codes imply a hierarchical ordering of codes. What this means is that axial codes highlight large units of meaning within which there will be lower level codes. In a study of student activity a series of axial codes may be developed such as classroom time, private study time, paid work time and leisure time. This first level coding could be said to apply a single first level code called 'time', which then leads to a series of sub-codes. Within each of these sub-codes there may need to be a set of further sub-codes. This creates a series of pyramids or cascades. The principle behind axial coding is that through the selection of a core set of themes, coding can allow the most significant underlying issues to be made more manifest. The idea is that the most important (or axial) issues are shed light on while other issues are placed in the background.

Systematic coding involves the attempt to go through the text to be analysed and to identify all the emerging themes that the researcher can find. Rather than making a choice as to which is the key theme or set of themes, systematic coding attempts to be less pre-emptive, and to allow selection and reduction to occur more slowly and after initial coding has taken place rather than during initial coding. Only after the data has been coded in this way is it possible to test the significance of potential links between codes in a systematic way. There is a danger with axial coding that the researcher simply feels that there is a significant factor at work in their data, they then code for it. This process highlights the instances in the text where that factor arises, while other factors not coded for are overshadowed. The researcher is then in danger of

making their prediction appear to come true. Systematic coding seeks to avoid this situation by starting with the more modest aim of marking as many themes as the researcher thinks they can find, only to select and reduce at a later stage. Axial coding may be developed in subsequent rounds, if this is seen as appropriate.

The counter-argument to the above point is that it is never possible to code for every theme within a text as there are likely to be a near infinite number of potential themes that could be selected, especially when there is a significant amount of text to analyse. As such, it can be pointed out that a selection process is inevitable between themes the researcher thinks are important and those they do not. In the end, therefore, there will always need to be a pragmatic balance between the 'principles' of axial and systematic coding. This does not mean that a researcher cannot choose to move closer to one ideal or the other. It only means that they can never achieve either ideal.

Individual or group coding

It is a good idea, whenever possible, to seek some form of collaboration when engaged in the selection of codes. If the researcher is working with others as part of a research team, it makes sense for all members of the team to engage in an initial reading of a selection of the data collected. Each member of the team then needs to identify what they think the core codes are that need to be applied, or which 'emerge'. The team can then meet to discuss the schemes each has identified and, with luck, this process should lead to a more developed coding scheme. Alternatively, the researcher can ask people whom they were researching to collaborate in identifying the core themes. When it is possible, the research may benefit from follow-up interviews that pursue this aim. Colleagues, fellow students and academic staff are alternatives, or might simply offer valuable additional insights.

Culling and refining: expansion and reduction

The common advice, that there should not be too many codes and not too few, in addition to the advice that one should not start too late in analysis, while at the same time avoid being too pre-emptive in rushing to analytical conclusions, may seem to offer very little concrete advice about when and how to proceed. This is truly a grey area, one that the researcher needs to reflect upon and seek to clarify in their practice.

Perhaps the best advice to the beginner is to start with a very rough sketch of as many potential themes as seem to emerge from a reading of the texts in front of you. Code for these. From these it should be possible to make links and connections between the wealth of themes. In so doing some themes will stand out, while others will come to appear less significant. Some themes will drop out; others will be merged together. This refinement process will allow a degree of reduction without eliminating potentially valuable themes. Make a note of the themes that have been tied together in this process. In your revised coding scheme you will need to give definitions of the codes you have selected and these definitions will need to include mention of the other themes that have been incorporated. It may be the case later that some of these incorporated themes may prove more significant and will need to be extracted and made into separate codes, so keep your records precise. Depending upon how you choose to mix the data collection and the data analysis, the process of refinement and expansion will vary.

Higher forms of code-based analysis: matrices and network diagrams

Matthew Miles and A. Michael Huberman (1994) provide a wealth of illustration on the art of presenting qualitative data in ways that facilitate analysis. Their motto is 'Think Display'. They suggest two main forms of representational device: the matrix and network displays. A **matrix display** is a table with rows and columns. By placing one or more variables in the columns and one or more variables in the rows, it is possible to create a grid into which cross-tabulations can be placed (that is, the results of each cross-over between rows and columns). Data entries might be numerical figures, quotations, categorical responses, keywords or coded **values** depending on the nature of the **variables** being cross-tabulated (see Table 17.1 and Table 17.2). Once data has been reduced by means of coding it is possible to extract specific aspects of the data to fill the spaces created within a matrix. Once information is presented in this way patterns may become easier to identify and certain links between themes may present themselves for further analysis. Content in the intersections can be either textual or numerical.

Network displays seek to represent flows and processes of connection. While matrices show content of a situation, **network diagrams** focus upon sequences and relationships more explicitly.

A network display may seek to depict the flow of events in a singular instance, or the variety of options taken by different individuals or groups (see Figure 17.1). This may be an individual or a group. A network diagram may seek to only describe a set of events or it may seek to map critical incidents or even **causal** processes. Network diagrams can depict a wide variety of phenomena, not just time. Flows of ideas, money, information and relationships between people can all be mapped using network diagrams (see Figure 17.2).

Miles and Huberman suggest four distinct ways in which such representational devices can be used in the

Table 17.1 Table of individual characteristics			
Sample characteristics	Age	In paid work Y/N	Attitude to study
Student A Student B Student C	(Numerical figure.)	(Categorical response.)	(Point on ordinal scale, quotation, keyword or coded value.)

Table 17.2 Table of group characteristics by gender			
Attitude to change	Nurses	Doctors	Managers
Male Female	(Summary of findings.)		

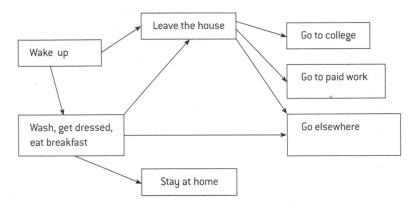

Figure 17.1   Starting the day: network diagram

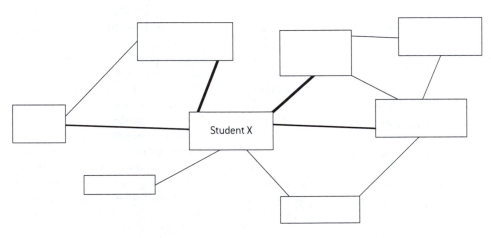

Friends (thick lines) and acquaintances (thin lines). Thickness of lines could be used to represent 'level' of friendship (by whatever measure one wished to use).

Figure 17.2   Network diagram of association (friends and acquaintances)

process of QDA. The first level is what they call **within-case displays**. Here data from one case is presented. A case may be an individual or an organization or one location within fieldwork. There are two types of within-case displays. The first seeks to explore and describe the characteristics of a case. The second seeks to highlight processes and causes at work within the case. The second level of display is what Miles and Huberman call **cross-case displays**. Cross-case displays seek to highlight similarities and differences between cases. Cross-case displays can also be focused upon exploration and description or causation and prediction.

Some rules of thumb in the construction of matrix displays

Miles and Huberman (1994: 239–42) provide a series of rules of thumb and questions for the researcher to ask themselves. The first set concerns the content and purpose of the display device:

1   Descriptive versus explanatory.
2   Are the categories in your rows and columns in a sequence or not?
3   Are you seeking to present the sequence of events or what is going on at a particular time?

4   What are your categories/variables: people, groups, things or actions?

5   How many levels of connection are you seeking to make?

6   What are your units to be made up of (numbers, quotes, ratings and so on)?

7   Single case versus multiple case data.
    (1994: 240–41)

The next set concerns designing a matrix:

1   What data does your research give you to play with?

2   Get colleagues to read through and suggest themes

3   Produce a sheet with all matrix possibilities.

4   Don't put too many variables in any one table.

5   Keep revising and expect so to do.

6   Re-order (put some rows in columns and vice versa to see what emerges).

7   Stay open to the option of adding new variables.

8   Balance between fine-grain and losing yourself in the detail.

9   Any one question may need many matrices.
    (1994: 241)

Rules of thumb for matrix data entry are:

1   Be clear about level of data (individuals, families, organizations and so on).

2   Remember that all data display is a reduction.

3   Use codes to locate key material.

4   Keep a clear record of reduction process for future checking.

5   Explain process in legend.

6   Show missing data clearly in matrices.

7   Don't lock up data matrix too early.

8   Use text and numbers.

9   Be careful with scaling.

10 Get colleagues to review from start and throughout.
    (1994: 241–2)

Content in any box within a matrix display may be numbers of incidents, it may be a description, or it may be a key quote as illustration.

Finally, the rules of thumb for drawing conclusions from matrix data are:

1   Squint analysis at the outset.

2   Read through to notice and make note of apparent patterns.

3   Write text (memos) on emerging conclusions as you spot them.

4   Use content analysis summary tables to avoid over-reduction.

5   First conclusions always need revision.

6   Seek to verify, triangulate, contrast and gain feedback.

7   Always check cases before moving to cross-case comparisons.

8   Illustrate conclusions, but be representative, don't pick just juicy quotes.

9   Beyond empirical verification, seek to confirm theoretical models.

10 Document conclusion-drawing procedures and ask colleagues to comment.

11 Ask what data the reader will need to confirm your account.
    (1994: 242)

Within-case displays: exploring and describing

Miles and Huberman (1994: 90–142) identify a wide range of representative devices by which to facilitate description of complex qualitative data. These can be organized into six broad types, as detailed below. Data to be presented in such a visual form may have different levels of ordering. Miles and Huberman distinguish between ordered and partially ordered forms of display. For example, data organized along a time-line, or which is presented in relation to age, would be called 'ordered'. Partially ordered displays present coded themes that emerged within a case study, but not in any sequential order (for example, types of work: building, teaching, administration, sales). A checklist table allows the content of a situation to be examined.

Context charts/checklist matrices

A context chart is a network diagram that seeks to show the range of groups, or individuals or topics that made up the 'situation' being studied. It is a map of what was going on and whom the players were, with lines to show relations between them. A checklist matrix is a grid into which a similar array of information is presented without the attempt to give it an order. A checklist matrix seeks to list all the key codes/categories that emerged from the case.

Time ordered displays

Time ordered displays include event listing, critical incident charts, activity record, decision modelling, growth-gradients and time ordered matrices. The use of time as an ordering scale of matrices, or network diagrams, allows for the production of representations that show how events or ideas unfolded. An event listing and an activity record are similar to a checklist with the added dimension that events are listed in time order. Decision modelling is a network diagram that moves across a time line. This form of network diagram is often referred to as a flow chart.

Role ordered displays

Here in the case of matrix displays one axis of the grid is made up of a listing of the key roles of participants in the case being studied, while the other axis lists other significant categories that relate to the different roles (level of commitment, level of training, level of funding, for example). The intersection would contain quotes, the researcher's summary of the responses or keyword/coding values that related to the intersection of that role, and category of data. In this way it is hoped that the differences between roles, or those that perform those roles, can be more easily identified.

Role-by-time matrices

The ordering of both axes allows one dimension of potential difference to be matched to a second. For example, did teachers change their overall view about a particular class over the course of a year, while their view of other classes stayed the same? Role by time is only one potential pair.

Conceptually ordered displays

This includes thematic conceptual matrix, folk taxonomies and cognitive maps. A thematic conceptual matrix seeks to highlight links between theoretically interesting themes coded for in the data analysis. Folk taxonomies seek to map how participants view their worlds. How do those researched categorize their environment? What do they see going together and what things are seen as separate? Folk taxonomies can be represented either within matrices or in network diagrams. **Cognitive maps** are representations of how people view their space, or how they understand change. What things go

where? What routes do which people follow? What and where are the boundaries? How do boundaries change? Who belongs and who is an outsider? What and who led to a particular outcome? If these themes are coded for within each interview or observation, the results can be drawn out in matrix or network diagrams.

Effects matrices

Where a cognitive map seeks to show via network diagrams how a person or a group understands a situation, and some of these situations will be 'outcomes' emerging over time, an effects matrix seeks to highlight how different groups or individuals see the same event or set of events. One axis is used to represent different players, while the second axis sets out dimensions of the change process or perception of the outcome. The grid then allows comparison of different groups' perceptions of an outcome and their accounts of how it came about.

Within-case displays: explaining and predicting

While not making generalized explanations, within-case displays may seek to highlight the process of causation in specific cases. Identifying a cause involves three levels:

- Identification of a sequence of events that leads to an outcome.
- Identification of 'constant conjunction' (the recurrent nature of a 'sequence' leading to an outcome).
- Identification of the 'mechanism', the way in which the sequence actually leads to the outcome.

Causally oriented matrices or network diagrams have a time-based dimension. A case dynamics matrix '. . . displays a set of forces for change and traces the consequential processes and outcomes. The basic principle is one of preliminary explanation' (Miles and Huberman, 1994: 148). One axis sets out preceding factors and the other axis sets out a series of outcomes. How often do the preceding factors lead to instances of the outcomes listed? The grid can be filled with numbers or descriptions. 'A causal network is a display of the most important independent and dependent variables in a field of study . . . and of the relationships among them . . . The plot of these relationships is directional, rather than solely correlational. It is assumed that some factors exact an influence on others. X brings Y into being or makes Y larger or smaller' (Miles and Huberman, 1994: 152–3). Exploratory matrices/network diagrams may lead the researcher to design case dynamics matrices.

Cross-case displays: exploring and describing

Cross-case displays are similar to within-case displays. Partially ordered displays (which use the same categories for each case) can be used to draw out potential similarities and differences, whether made in the form of numerical charts or content analytic summary tables.

Case-ordered displays are matrices in which along one axis are arranged the cases being examined and along the other axis are arranged one or more key variables emerging from the data. By so doing it may be possible to identify particular characteristics about cases that allow all cases to be arranged in some kind of rank order. Such rankings may be in terms of outcomes (degrees of success or failure, for example), time taken to achieve an outcome, size of organization, number of a particular type of incident, and so on. By developing such rankings the researcher may identify common and divergent features between cases. Two variable case ordering matrices, contrast tables, **scatterplot** diagrams and **time-ordered** displays develop this logic of comparison. Comparative decision tree modelling again uses the methods of single case analysis to produce a number of network diagrams that can then be compared (see Miles and Huberman, 1994: Ch. 7).

Cross-case displays: ordering and explaining

The methods for cross-case displays that aim to enable explanation build upon the earlier forms discussed. This is both in development of plausible variables to test against one another and in terms of the displays best suited to bringing out causal processes, constant conjunction and explanatory mechanisms (Miles and Huberman, 1994: Ch. 8).

Summary

Qualitative forms of content analysis involve the selection of codes and their application to sections of the textual materials under analysis. Patterns can then be identified between the coded segments and the location and incidence of certain codes can be mapped in relation to other codes (and by association, with the producers of those texts/those the texts were produced about). Coding may serve to identify patterns within or between cases, and can be used to map descriptive and/or causal relationships. Coding forms the basis for the production of tables and network diagrams. Content analysis can be conducted 'by hand', or using qualitative data analysis software (such as NUD*IST).

Keywords

Axial Codes
Categories
Causality
Coding
Coding Frame
Cognitive Maps
Content Analysis
Cross-case Displays
Data Reduction
Deductive Coding

Discourse Analysis
In Vivo Codes
Inductive Codes
Latent Codes
Manifest Codes
Matrix Display
Model
Network Diagram
Pattern Codes/Specific Codes
Prescriptive Coding/Pre-emptive Coding

Scatterplot
Sociological Codes
Summary Codes
Systematic Codes
Text/Textual
Time-ordered Displays
Values
Variable
Within-case Displays

Questions

1   What is the scope and what are the limits to causal explanation as an output of qualitative forms of data analysis?
2   What distinguishes a matrix display from a network diagram?
3   What is qualitative about coding in qualitative data analysis?
4   How do some dispute the claim that content analysis can never be truly qualitative?
5   Identify the range of coding methods available to the qualitative researcher?.

Further reading

Berg, Bruce L. (1998) *Qualitative Research Methods for the Social Sciences*. Needham Heights, MA: Allyn and Bacon.

Fielding, Nigel and Lee, Raymond (1998) *Computer Analysis and Qualitative Research*. London: Sage.

Glaser, Barney (1992) *Emergence vs Forcing: Basics of Grounded Theory Analysis*. Mill Valley, CA: Sociology Press.

Miles, Matthew and Huberman, A. Michael (1994) *Qualitative Data Analysis*. London: Sage.

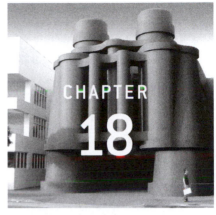

SEMIOTIC AND NARRATIVE FORMS OF DISCOURSE ANALYSIS AND DOING CONVERSATION ANALYSIS

Chapter contents

By the end of this chapter you will be able to:

- Distinguish between a range of non-content analytic forms of qualitative data analysis.

- Conduct forms of semiotic analysis.

- Conduct forms of deconstructive analysis.

- Conduct forms of narrative analysis.

- Conduct forms of conversation analysis.

This chapter outlines the principles and practical techniques involved in those forms of qualitative data analysis which do not adopt the formal techniques of coding that are associated with qualitative content analysis. The traditions of semiotics, deconstruction and narrative analysis, collectively referred to as discourse analysis, share with conversation analysis a rejection of what they see as the imitation of quantitative methods within qualitative content analysis. It is important, however, to note that, despite the rhetoric, qualitative data analysis in practice is more typically a mix of content and discourse analysis.

Semiotic and narrative forms of discourse analysis

The contrast between **discourse** and content analysis has become a site of polarized debate within **qualitative** research and between qualitative and quantitative forms of data analysis. The distinction is not as clear-cut as passionate advocates often make things seem. The two forms of analysis more often than not fold into each other in the process of qualitative data analysis, and claims to be doing one or the other tend to reflect variations within a family of similar processes rather than polar opposites. Of course, as has been pointed out above, qualitative forms of content analysis should be distinguished from more deductive forms of quantitative content analysis.

Jonathan Potter and Margaret Wetherell suggest that what distinguishes discourse analysis (DA) from forms of content analysis is that while **coding** represents a fundamental part of analysis in content analysis, coding only represents a provisional part of data preparation in DA. They argue that '. . . unlike the sorts of coding that takes place in traditional content analysis, the coding [in DA] is not the analysis itself but a preliminary to make the task of analysis manageable' (1994: 52). It should be noted that Potter and Wetherell are discussing DA of a large quantity of interview, text and field recording data here. In this case, they argue that it is useful to carry out forms of content analysis to identify key themes. In other contexts, where the researcher is seeking to analyse only a relatively small quantity of text, formal coding for the purposes of reduction may not be seen as useful. Even where coding is applied, DA gives a priority to overall themes and meanings within the **data**, and not to the incidence of particular words or phrases as such.

Jonathan Potter elsewhere (1997: 155) argues that the aim of DA is to identify the meaning of talk and text in general terms and that this often involves the identification of surface themes recurrent in the text. However, it is not the purpose of DA to remain at the level of surface characteristics. Its aim is depth exploration rather than the counting of examples. This gives greater emphasis to the singular and analysis of one phrase, or one advertisement, may require less attention to its generality within all talk or all advertisements.

Outlined below are two forms of DA, **semiotics** and **narrative analysis**. Potter (1997) highlights the fact that there are many research traditions that call themselves discourse analysis. Here we will focus upon the analytical methods employed by the two dominant forms in the social sciences. Semiotics addresses the analysis of meaningful objects at a fixed moment in time. Narrative analysis addresses the analysis of change and movement across time

Semiotic analysis

Semiotics or semiology is the study of signs. Signs are physical things (lines of ink, objects on the sides of the road or vibrations in the air) that carry meaning. How are such objects to be analysed? Semiotic analysis starts from the premise that anything that contains meaning, or which can be given meaning by an interpreter, can be called a 'text'. A text is anything that can be 'read', and 'read' means the act of taking a meaning from the thing being read. As such, the principles of textual DA can be applied not only to the written and/or spoken word, but also to all forms of readable objects such as music or film or television or fashion. What are these principles?

How to read a sign!

Within semiology, or semiotics, a **sign** is read as a combination of elements. A sign must have three elements:

- A **signifier**.
- A **signified**.
- The sign itself.

A signifier is a physical thing that has been given a meaningful content. A word is a physical sound or the physical combination of lines on a page or screen. A word is the signifier or carrier. Note that the same meaning will be carried by a different word in different languages, so the signifier has no necessary link to the meaning it carries. The signifier may be an image or object of any kind, as long as it has been given the role of conveying a certain meaning through its use. A signified is the meaning (concept) that is carried by the signifier. The sign is the combination of the signifier and the signified.

The final element in this equation is the referent (the thing to which a meaning might be said to correspond to in the real world). The word 'cat' may be a signifier for the idea of a certain type of animal. It might be assumed that the idea is equally bound to real things out there in the world. However, the link between sign and referent is much more complex than one of correspondence. Semiotics is concerned with how signs, signifiers and signifieds link together in texts (of all kinds) to create meaningful systems. It is less concerned with the link between words and things beyond language.

A common theme in semiotic analysis is to highlight how texts operate through the creation of oppositions within the text itself. Oppositions can be created through the combination of certain concepts under one unifying theme and then distinguishing this unity by setting up an opposite, which again unifies a certain set of themes.

Semiotic analysis involves the examination of texts to identify the relationships within and between signs. Within signs there is the creation of unity. Between signs there is the creation of opposites. Creating the impression that something is black or white, in other words that it is either one thing or the other, or that a situation involves the clash of one unity against another unity, is a common characteristic of texts. This may be seen as creating impressions of the world that serve to reinforce certain ideas about what is true, good and beautiful. The task of the semiotician is to identify the mechanisms by which such impressions are manufactured.

At one level it is enough to identify the use of certain signs within texts and to identify how certain signs are built up and set against each other to create a 'representation' of reality. However, the most significant aspect of semiotic analysis lies in the study of **myth** (Lévi-Strauss, 1979 and Barthes, 1967, 1973) and difference (Derrida, 1972, and for very useful introductions to Derrida and Deconstruction, see Norris, 1982 and 1987).

The concept of myth in DA refers to the situation where a sign becomes a signifier. This sounds odd and not in line with our common understanding of what a myth is. For example, the word SNAKE acts as signifier for the signified concept of SNAKE (reptile with no legs). So the SNAKE sign is the combination of the signifier SNAKE (word) and the signified SNAKE (concept). But the snake sign can be used for more than just recalling the concept of a legless reptile. In many cultures the snake stands for evil: in this case the SNAKE sign has come to stand for the concept/idea of EVIL. Here, then, the SNAKE sign is no longer the combination of a SNAKE signifier word and a SNAKE signified idea/concept. The SNAKE sign acts as a signifier for a new signified concept, EVIL. In myth the sign has become a signifier for something else below the level of the ordinary sign. What on the surface might mean one thing may stand for something else at a deeper level. This depth can best be identified by attending to the complex play of meaning within a text and not just the distribution of surface signs as may be the tendency in forms of content analysis.

It is not just in the study of classical mythic terms like 'snake' that we should look for mythic language. The study of advertising images highlights the way men and women, children and adults, suntans and shoes, dogs, hats and cars all come to take on the power of mythic signs, being filled with deeper meanings than just what is on the surface. Newspapers create mythic representations of criminals, which are constructed through images and language that build upon one sign to carry the meaning of another. Reading text and images for myths is one core dimension of semiotic forms of DA. News coverage, advertising, talk and text of all kinds can be 'read' for their mythic constructions.

The concept of difference focuses attention also on the construction of myth-like combinations of meanings, but in a slightly different way. Derrida's method of **deconstruction** involves the identification of tensions within texts over the meaning of key terms. Rather than identifying the incidence of certain terms and concepts to highlight their associations and significance, the deconstructive method seeks to show that where the same term is used on a number of occasions in a text, that term often carries very different meanings. While, again, certain parallels with content analysis exist, such as the search for recurring terms, the purpose of deconstruction is to show how such terms are rarely able to contain themselves (being loaded with different meanings in different places – or sometimes with divergent meanings at the same time). While content analysis highlights recurring language to identify connections, deconstruction highlights disconnections within recurrent use of the same language.

The deconstructive method is to read text in fine detail and to focus analysis upon a very small number of details where it can be shown that the meaning of the text contradicts itself or overflows. It is Derrida's contention that the words we use are not ones whose meaning we choose ourselves. As such, words do not correspond to a set of pre-existing mental feelings in our heads. For example, the term 'love' is one we use to express what we think is our inner feeling. We might have an inner feeling and believe that love is the word that best expresses the feeling we already have. But when we use the term 'love', we soon find that it is a word with so many meanings. For Derrida words never express things or capture them. Words are always linked to other words and not directly to things. Words do not correspond to the world and are at best metaphors. A metaphor is one sign, which stands for another sign. Looking at a text we can highlight the use of metaphor. Often a metaphor is presented as though it were a concept that really mapped onto reality in a direct way. But for Derrida language can never be a mirror on the world beyond language. Just as 'rose' is a word that can signify love, so 'love' is a word whose meaning is made up of links with other words. Trying to say what words really mean usually involves spirals or metaphor, simile and connection/comparison. All words carry the baggage of their links to other words and their metaphorical character always imports surpluses of meaning that add to, change and open the terms up to mean more than they might at first appear to.

Myth and metaphor are in many respects similar and highlight the core of the discourse analytic method. It is to seek out the methods by which meanings are constructed within the text itself, how a sense of reality and order is maintained and presented through textual material (images, objects as well as words).

Manning and Cullum-Swann (1998) and Potter and Wetherell (1994) provide useful hints for the use of DA semiotics (see Box 18.1 and Box 18.2). These are hints that can be applied generally. Other specific themes will emerge from particular texts and combinations of texts once these initial steps are undertaken. Once again, it is useful to stress that in order to achieve these, a degree of coding of data may be useful if there is a large amount of text. This coding will be very similar to the open forms of inductive coding carried out in grounded forms of content analysis. The gulf between qualitative content analysis and DA should not prevent pragmatic use of useful tools as long as such tools do not become an end in themselves.

BOX 18.1 APPLICATIONS OF SEMIOTICS

Peter Manning and Betsy Cullum-Swan (1998) highlight the possibility of applying semiotic approaches to the study of McDonald's fast food restaurants. This could be through the study of the restaurants' menus (the organization of items into groups that reflect certain cultural values). It could be through a study of the experiences of those who go there (which could be based upon interviews of ethnographic participation and observation). Alternatively, it could be through an account of the company's attempts to manage its representation through advertising (by means of textual data collection and analysis).

BOX 18.2 COMBINING DISCOURSE ANALYSIS WITH OTHER QUALITATIVE METHODS

Potter and Wetherell (1994) combine ethnographic, interview and textual materials in their discourse analysis of a television programme about cancer care. They provide a five-point list of themes for the discourse analyst. The list develops elements of the above discussion of signs and metaphors:

1 Using variation as a lever.
2 Reading the detail.
3 Looking for rhetorical organization.
4 Looking for accountability.
5 Cross-referencing discourse studies.

Narrative analysis

Semiotics focuses attention upon what is called the 'synchronic' aspect of language. This means the structure of language at a given moment in time, the way signs are organized around each other to create a symbolic world of meaning. This means that it has paid less attention to what is called the 'diachronic' aspect of language, that is, how language changes over time. The meaning of signs can be studied either in terms of their relation to other signs at a given moment or as they change over time. The focus upon time and change is addressed more fully in forms of narrative analysis, although it should be pointed out that much of narrative analysis focuses upon stories recounted in the present of events and lives that occurred in the past. As such they are not solely focused upon changes in the use of language, but in the way language is used to describe change. Narrative analysis is also interested in the constructions of meaning given at the point of telling. The relationship between the version of events as told now and the process of a life that such a story might seek to tell is a controversial one.

Catherine Kohler Riessman (1993) outlines a set of core analytical approaches to narrative in social research. Narrative analysis requires that the researcher collects data that is open-ended in terms of the storyteller's account of events. This may be either in the form of open-ended interviews or textual data such as diaries, letters or autobiographical material. As Kohler Riessman was once told by an interviewee whom she had asked to explain a particular aspect of their life: 'Well, you know, that's a really long story . . .' (1993: vi). To allow the analysis to focus upon this long story the data must be open-ended.

Analysis involves more than just a focus upon the content, a chronology of events. The focus of narrative analysis is less on the events as on the way the events are described and located together in a meaningful account. While content may not always be disregarded, attention should also be paid to the telling. Kohler Riessman suggests three analytical foci: life stories, critical events and the **poetics** of telling. Although each is given a different priority in the work of different researchers, all three in fact combine in the analysis of all storytelling.

Themes for the researcher to attend to are the elements within a story, the sequence in which the elements are combined, the relationships drawn between the elements, and the plot devices and genre styles in which the stories are put together. All these elements can be analysed by means of the semiotic approaches discussed above, but the overall aim of narrative analysis is to give a sense of the storytelling itself.

Analysis may also focus upon the coherence of an account, and tensions can be examined within particular accounts or between different accounts of the same event. Criteria by which stories are evaluated may be both those of internal validity, the coherence of the account, and external validity, the degree to which one account matches or differs from others.

Summary comments

David Silverman (2000a: 824–5) suggests five questions that any researcher should ask themself about their DA. He is discussing DA of interview data, but the list could be easily applied to the analysis of other forms of qualitative data, such as textual data, images and fieldnotes.

1   'What status do you attach to your data?' Do you think of it as a window to the world beyond the talk or as a performance to be analysed as a social event in itself?
2   'Is your analytic position appropriate to your practical concerns?' Are you obscuring more than you are revealing with the conceptual models you bring to the data?
3   'Do interview data really help in addressing your research topic?' Would other data collection tools give you better access?
4   'Are you making too-large claims about your research?' What can you really justify?
5   'Does your analysis go beyond a mere list?' Have you moved beyond content to a sense of the underlying meaning in the discourse?

Doing conversation analysis

Conversation analysis requires recordings of naturally occurring talk (conversation between at least two persons). Conversation analysis transcription involves a much more elaborate set of indicators to identify the length of pauses, tones of voice, interruptions and simultaneous talking and so on than would be required in other forms of analysis (see Chapter 10). Because conversation analysis is based upon the examination of very small 'units' of conversation rather than the contents of large amounts of materials, the first question is how do sections of talk get selected for such detailed treatment? The second question is what does the analysis in conversation analysis amount to? These two questions are in reality interlinked as the selection of fragments is in large part dependent upon the analytic concerns of conversation analysts. Identified below are the themes which conversation analysts seek to highlight within talk and which they then seek to identify and explore through detailed transcription and further examination.

John Heritage (1997: 161–82) outlines six themes that constitute the focus of attention for conversation analysis.

1   *Turn-taking organization:* Conversation displays an orderliness that demonstrates the orientation of participants to each other and their shared expectations about how turn-taking is to be managed. Focus upon turn-taking highlights the shared norms that participants bring to interactions and which they negotiate in the course of their interactions. Despite occasional breakdowns and disruptions, participants generally manage their own repair work and both order and repair activities highlight this. Studies of talk in particular settings highlight that there are general organizing principles and expectations that participants bring to interactions as well as specific principles and expectations that operate in certain situations (such as in schools, hospitals, doctors' surgeries and so on).

2   *Overall structural organization of the interaction – in specific cases:* The management of conversation involves the application of general expectations and orientations to unique encounters. The study of particular conversations highlights that people are not merely reciting scripts, but are creatively managing unique situations through the deployment of general principles.

3   *Sequence organization:* Conversations have beginnings and they conclude. Rather than focusing upon the intentions brought by participants to their conversations, something that is not directly manifest in the talk itself, conversation analysts are interested in the movement within a conversation from introductions, through the interaction towards a completion and cessation of the talk. How do the parties to the conversation establish themselves, identify themselves, negotiate the presentation of information or requests for it?

How do the parties to the conversation negotiate their exits? How are outcomes arrived at? Such processes highlight conventions and expectations which participants deploy and respond to.

4   *Turn design:* When someone responds to the last speaker they are following certain expectations and are demonstrating an orientation to the speaker. When a question is asked, or when someone speaks in a certain way, a reply is expected. In replying, the person replying is responding to the expectation. However, the way in which they respond is not determined by the question being asked, even if certain expectations are present. A reply may take a number of forms and move the conversation in a number of different directions.

5   *Lexical choice:* What words are chosen and how are they used? How might such choices influence the course of the conversation and what effects might they have?

6   *Epistemological and other forms of asymmetry:* Parties to a conversation do not bring the same resources or interests to the interaction. While such things as power, resources and motives are not the focus of conversation analysis as such, they become of interest in conversation analysis when they are manifested in talk itself. A number of asymmetries draw attention to such differences:
   – Asymmetries of participation occur when the shared expectations within a particular interaction mean that one party is given priority to either speak without being spoken back to or speak with little response from the other parties.
   – Asymmetries of interactional and institutional know-how or routine occur when one party to a conversation demonstrates that they are practised in the discussion of the topic, while the other party demonstrates a lack of experience about the topic. Alternatively, parties may manifest different levels of interest in the conversation, or different levels of awareness or even consciousness.
   – **Epistemological** caution and asymmetries of knowledge occur when those granted a certain status within the conversation seek to avoid commitment to a particular course of action or account of events. This may involve the use of distancing devices, technical language or claims to particular forms of privacy.
   – Rights of access to knowledge are contested within talk, both in the form of requests for or

denials to access and in the deployment of illicit forms of access, such as reference to secrets, invitations to secrets and the sharing of gossip.

Through attention to these themes by means of applying forms of content and discourse analysis to small segments of naturally occurring talk which have been transcribed in ultra-fine detail, the conversation analyst seeks to discover the complex order creating activities that occur within talk. George Psathas sets out seven principles for the conversation analyst. While Heritage's above list sets out the kinds of surface phenomena that are looked for within talk, Psathas provides an outline of the deeper processes which conversation analysts claim can be identified through theorizing the surface phenomena:

1   Order is produced order . . .
2   Order is produced by the parties in situ . . .
3   The parties orient to that order themselves; that is, the order is not an analyst's conception . . .
4   Order is repeatable and recurrent . . .
5   The discovery, description, and analysis of that produced order is the task of the analyst . . .
6   Issues of how frequently, how widely, or how often particular phenomena occur are to be set aside in the interest of discovering, describing, and analysing the structures, the machinery, the organized practices, the formal procedures, the ways in which order is produced.
7   Structures of social action, once so discerned, can be described and analysed in formal, that is, structural, organizational, logical, atopically contentless, consistent, and abstract terms.
    (1995: 2–3)

The goal of conversation analysis, then, is to demonstrate that talk displays a set of mechanisms and expectations whose application in various situations is specific, but whose nature is universal to talk. Conversation analysis is not interested in large-scale comparative samples as it seeks to generate a catalogue of specific analyses or how specific pieces of talk operate. Each such study should be published alongside the transcribed outline of the piece of talk being studied. Accumulation occurs over time and not in particular studies. While each study seeks to show the principles and expectations operating in that piece of talk, general principles emerge from the accumulation of specific **case studies**.

Given these orientations, the selection of pieces of

text for detailed transcription and analysis may occur in one of two ways. Either extracts of talk are selected at random or the researcher carries out provisional forms of either content analysis or discourse analysis to identify the issues they are interested to examine in more detail. In principle, any selection should be as good a choice as any other as there is no attempt to have a representative **sampling** method. Given that all extracts of talk are talk, and all talk (as conversation) is assumed to display principles and expectations on the part of the participants, any piece of conversation should do. However, studies of particular organizations or issues by conversation analytic means (such as studies of doctor–patient interactions or parent–child interactions) may require attention to those types of conversation. In reality, conversation analysts engage in forms of selection that usually amount to informal content and discourse analysis and are sometimes formally so.

The question of what constitutes a piece of talk is an interesting one. How long is a bounded unit of conversation? Of course, we might reasonably suggest that at the minimum level a unit of conversation would be a matched pair of talk–response. Much attention has been paid to adjacency pairs (call–response pairs in which the call successfully – in most cases – generates an 'appropriate' response). Examples of adjacency pairs are many. Greetings tend to elicit a return greeting. Questions tend to elicit answers. Closing a conversation tends to elicit a counter closure. Invitations tend to elicit replies. Complaints tend to elicit apologies or justifications. Beyond pairs the amount of conversation that constitutes a sequence is determined by the closure effected by the participants. This does not require that a sequence is always the length of the conversation it is a part of. Shorter sequences of talk that have their own boundaries can be identified within longer conversations. Conversation analysts seek to identify segments that display their own boundaries.

David Silverman (2000a: 831) provides guidance on how to do analysis in conversation analysis:

How to do conversation analysis:

1   Always try to identify sequences of related talk.
2   Try to examine how speakers take on certain roles or identities through their talk (for example, questioner/answerer or patient-professional).
3   Look for particular outcomes in the talk (for example, a request for clarification, a repair, laughter) and work backwards to trace the trajectory through which a particular outcome was produced.

Common errors in conversation analysis:

1 Explaining a turn at talk by reference to the speaker's intentions (except in so far as such intentions are topicalized in the conversation).
2 Explaining a turn at talk by reference to a speaker's role or status [for example, as a doctor or a man or a woman].

3 Trying to make sense of a single line of transcript or utterance in isolation from the surrounding talk.

Summary

Whilst discourse analysts are critical of the content analytic reduction of qualitative data to tables and charts via coding, discourse analysts often use coding techniques to contextualize the more detailed analysis they seek to carry out on either single texts or small sub-samples of material. Discourse analysis can be pursued in a number of different ways, each with a distinct focus of attention. Semiotic analysis focuses on the construction of associations and differences within signs. The analysis of 'mythic' signs seeks to identify the way in which particular texts (words and/or images) carry deeper connotations than are manifestly denoted within surface content. Deconstruction focuses attention on the multiple meanings at work within seemingly coherent and singular textual productions (words or longer segments). Rather than looking for the deeper meaning, deconstruction seeks to show the absence of a deeper meaning below a surface level riven with, often contradictory, meanings. Narrative analysis seeks to identify the devices by which a text seeks to construct such elements as time, genre, sequence, cause, content and context. If we take someone's life story literally (as a true picture), we might overlook the literary devices at work within their storytelling.

Conversation analysis has its own rules for the presentation and analysis of naturally occurring talk. Most importantly, what is sought is an account of the machinery at work within the talk that relies neither on assumptions about the context beyond the talk nor the assumed motivations of the talkers. Conversation analysis seeks to analyse the talk itself.

Keywords

Case Study/Case Study Method	Epistemology	Sampling
Coding	Induction	Semiology/Semiotics
Conversation Analysis	Myth	Sign
Data	Narrative Analysis	Signified
Deconstruction	Poetics	Signifier
Discourse Analysis	Qualitative	

Questions

1 What is a 'myth' in semiotic analysis?
2 What makes conversation analysis so distinct from other forms of qualitative data analysis?
3 What aspects of language are of principal interest in deconstruction, and how are these analysed in this approach?
4 What aspects of language are of principal interest in narrative analysis, and how are these analysed in this approach?

5   To what extent can such divergent approaches as semiotics, conversation analysis, narrative analysis and deconstruction be used together, or with forms of content analysis?

Further reading

Barthes, Roland (1967) *Elements of Semiology*. London: Cape.

Heritage, John (1997) 'Conversation Analysis and Institutional Talk: Analysing Data', in David Silverman (ed.), *Qualitative Research: Theory, Methods and Practice*. London: Sage. pp. 161–82.

Kohler Riessman, Catherine (1993) *Narrative Analysis*. London: Sage.

Norris, Christopher (1982) *Deconstruction: Theory and Practice*. London: Methuen.

Potter, Jonathan and Wetherell, Margaret (1994) 'Analysing Discourse', in Alan Bryman and Robert Burgess (eds), *Analysing Qualitative Data*. London: Routledge. pp. 47–65.

Psathas, George (1995) *Conversation Analysis: The Study of Talk-in-Interaction*. London: Sage.

Silverman, David (2000a) 'Analysing talk and text', in Norman K. Denzin and Yvonna S. Lincoln (eds), *Handbook of Qualitative Research* (2nd edn). London: Sage. pp. 821–34.

CHAPTER
19

USING COMPUTER SOFTWARE:
WORKING WITH NVIVO/N6

Chapter contents

By the end of this chapter you will be able to:

- Create and manage data files within NVivo/N6 project folders.

- Code files by creating and organizing nodes.

- Display results of coding.

- Create and use memos, attributes and models.

- Conduct a variety of simple and complex data searches within projects.

Using the software

Nigel Fielding and Raymond Lee (1998: 13) discuss what they called the '**epistemological** suspicion' which many qualitative researchers have in relation to 'computer-assisted **qualitative data analysis (QDA)**' (CAQDAS). This fear is expressed in terms of the dangers of transforming QDA into quantitative data analysis. This rejection is, in many respects, the same as the rejection of content analysis by some qualitative researchers. However, as has already been pointed out, this rejection of **content analysis** is often over-played. Qualitative content analysis seeks to allow **categories** to emerge from the **data**, rather than being imposed in advance of **data collection**.

The use of computer software to assist QDA is advocated on the grounds that it speeds up the process of searching data, highlighting relationships, coding, modelling and building theory from the data. CAQDAS can be challenged for precisely these reasons, as many advocates of qualitative research believe that qualitative analysis should take time and is a craft. Such critics would question the view that doing things faster is always an advantage.

The use of computer software in quantitative data analysis is now more or less taken for granted, but the same criticism can be raised against statistical packages as are raised against qualitative data organizing software. Making it increasingly easy to store and analyse large amounts of data has led many researchers (beginners and more advanced) to ask meaningless questions. Lack of contact with the data itself and a lack of understanding of the actual process of analysis leads to the production of meaningless outputs. Garbage in – garbage out. Of course, this can be achieved with or without computer software, but the less time spent with the data itself, the easier it is to ask meaningless questions. As such, software packages for anything have their dangers, but the advantages should not be ignored. It is not the intention of this chapter to tell the reader that they should or should not adopt CAQDAS. However, it is the case that without having tried it, it is not possible to judge. It is better, therefore, to understand the options and then decide.

There is a wide range of CAQDAS software available. These have emerged in recent years from simple text managers to more advanced and integrated packages that allow for coding, memoing, modelling and exploration of relationships. By far the most popular software currently available is QSR NVivo, with the second most popular its stable-mate N6, formerly QSR NUD*IST (which stood for Non-numerical Unstructured Data * Integration, Structuring and Theorizing). These software packages will form the basis for the following discussion, though some attention will be given to a number of other specialist software packages that social researchers may want to be aware of. It is important to note that **NUD*IST** has undergone a number of updates, and that **NVivo** is an entirely separate program. **N6** is the decendant of NUD*IST and NVivo is now in rev 2.0. The following introduction seeks to enable the user of either to get started. If you have an older version of either package, the instructions below are still applicable. At the basic level, the up-grades have not involved significant change. However, what the programs do at the higher levels and how they present it will appear different from earlier versions. If you are using an older version of the software, you will have to remember this. If the exact name or location do not appear, then have a look around the window and in the menus. In the case of button name changes, the correct option should be fairly clear, though you may need to root around a little. If you have neither package to work with, it is possible to download free demonstration versions of either or both packages by going to the QSR website at www.qsrinternational.com. This will enable you to follow the instructions below and to test each package if you are still undecided as to which to use or whether to use them at all.

The most confusing initial aspect of either/both NVivo and N6 is the range of options and the specific terminology and commands needed to operate within the system. The three most important ways of operating within both NVivo and N6 are its **menu bars** – along the top of each window, the **toolbars** – below the menu bar in most cases but sometimes at the bottom of the window, and the **context menus**. Context menus are opened by holding down the right mouse button. Context menus offer options relevant to the window you are in at any given time. Specific commands can also be executed using the function keys, but this option will not be discussed here as all these commands can be achieved by the first three methods outlined above. With more experience and with reference to the online Help you may wish to explore this option further.

Both N6 and NVivo provide extensive on-screen Help and Tutorial advice online. This outline seeks to get you to the point where you can explore and use the package yourself with a reasonable degree of confidence. For more comprehensive and advanced information other sources are available. If you acquire a personal copy of the NVivo2.0 or N6 software, the user guide and reference guide provide detailed explanations of every aspect of the package. Note that, if you are using N6 or NVivo under an academic or other site licence, you may not have direct access to these guides. If this is the case, then the user guide is available separately (Richards, 2002a, 2002b). Another useful text is Pat Bazeley and Lyn Richards (2000) *The NVivo Qualitative Project Book*, which comes with a CD-ROM that allows the reader to practise with examples on a no-save version of the software even if they do not possess the full package themselves.

This introduction takes you through the key aspects of QDA using NVivo. It should be noted that N6 is in many ways a simpler package than NVivo, designed for simpler analysis of possibly larger databases. It does not contain the capacity for presenting coding stripes as NVivo does, nor assigning **attributes** or making **models**. In the discussion below, each section starts with an outline of NVivo 2.0. The differences that exist in N6 are then outlined in indented blocks of text.

1   Creating a project
2   Documents and document management
3   Coding: nodes and links – stripes and reports
4   Attributes
5   Memos
6   Models
7   Searching

Note that all of what will be discussed relates to what has already been said about the nature of QDA. The software is designed to facilitate processes discussed in previous chapters. Of course, it is important to recall that no qualitative software will do 'analysis' quite in the sense that the term 'analysis' is usually used in quantitative research. What NVivo/N6 is able to do is allow the researcher to organize and clarify a large

amount of information so as better to see the connections that exist and discount those that may appear superficially to be present. Software allows the researcher to explore options and connections more easily. It does not do the thinking for you! The researcher is still the one who has to do the interpretation and the analysis. This should not be forgotten.

Creating a project

Before creating a NVivo/N6 project you will need to clarify a few things about the textual data you are going to be working with. The data might be interview transcripts, newspaper transcripts, fieldnotes or notes taken about archival materials. If you want to follow this guide to using NVivo/N6 but do not have any data to work with, it will be a good idea to generate some. For the purpose of practice this material might be some newspaper articles downloaded from the Internet, or some notes you have typed up from a book or article. Any textual material will do. If it is not currently in a computer text format you can type the material directly into NVivo/N6 files (as will be explained shortly). Once you have some textual material, in electronic form or not, you can proceed to opening the **Launch Pad**.

On opening NVivo2.0 you will be presented with the Launch Pad (see Figure 19.1). You have four main options: to create a project; to open an existing project; to open a tutorial; or to exit the package. A project is one set of files and the analysis you carry out on them. You will need to create a project in order to then import or create textual files within it, which you can then analyse.

Click once with the left mouse key the option you require. If you want to create a new project, click the **Create a Project** button. You will be presented with the **Project Wizard** window. The term 'wizard' refers to a pre-made set of windows that ask for particular information in order to 'wizz' you through the process of setting up, in this case, a new project. Other wizards exist for other tasks. The first wizard menu asks you to choose to create a 'typical' or a 'custom' project. Choose 'typical' by clicking the button next to the word 'typical'. You may wish to explore 'custom' projects at a later date. Click **Next>**. You are then asked to give your project a title and a description. Do this and click **Next>**. You are then presented with a window that outlines the characteristics and file location of the project you have just created. Click

Figure 19.1   NVivo Launch Pad window

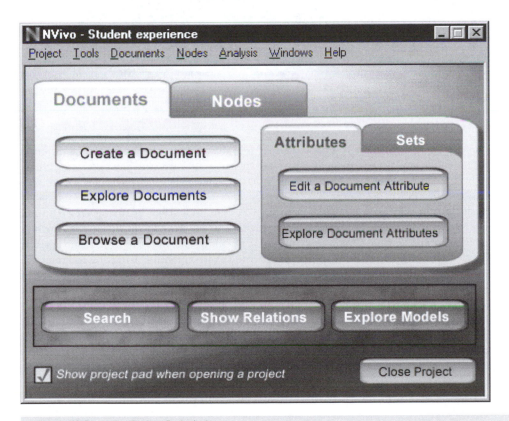

Figure 19.2   NVivo Project Pad window

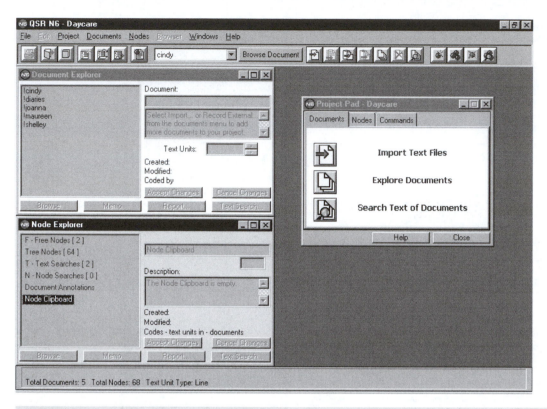

Figure 19.3   N6 Project window containing the N6 Project Pad

Finish and you will be presented with the **Project Pad** for your new project. If you have already created a project and are going back to it, then click the **Open a Project** button when you first open the **Launch Pad**. You will then be asked to choose the project and go to where it is currently stored, using the down arrow in the text box presented in the **Open a Project** window.

Documents are the files containing textual materials you have collected. This might be interview transcripts, fieldwork notes, observations, media texts, letters and so on. It is best to keep specific texts as separate documents. If you have a series of fieldnotes written at various times, keep each one as a separate document. If you have a series of interviews, keep each interview as a separate document. You can organize these documents into groups and hierarchies inside NVivo/N6 as we will see.

Documents can be imported into NVivo/N6, or they can be created in NVivo/N6. If your textual material is in non-computer form, then you can create a new document and type in the content

yourself (see below). If you have your textual materials in word processing software files, you can create copies of the materials as NVivo/N6 documents. However, you will have to save copies of your existing files in Rich Text Format (.RTF) before importing them into NVivo 2.0 (Plain Text Format for N6). This allows the software to read and convert content into NVivo/N6 files. To save a document as Rich Text Format, open the document and select **Save As** from the **File** menu. Then, in the **Save As** window, select Rich Text Format using the down arrow and scroll bar in the **Save as type** text box at the bottom of the window. Give the new copy a new name and select where it will be saved before clicking the **Save** button. The new .RTF document will be created and the original will also remain. With your textual materials ready to type up or with a copy of each file converted to .RTF, you are now ready to create NVivo/N6 documents.

Figure 19.2 shows what the **Project Pad** looks like. The project we will be working with here has been named 'Student experience'. You will want to give

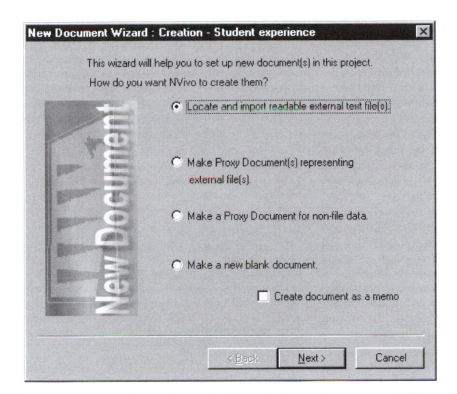

Figure 19.4 NVivo New Document Wizard window

your project a name suitable to what you are working on. As you can see, the **Project Pad** is set out with two virtual filing cabinet folders, one tagged 'Documents', the other tagged 'Nodes'. **Nodes** refer to the coding of documents and we will examine that process shortly. First we will look at the importing, creating and organizing of documents within a project.

N6 has the same four options on its **Launch pad**, only the names and visual presentation are slightly different. When creating a new project there is no project wizard to go through, as was the case with NVivo. You are only required to verify or identify the name of the new project, where the project files are to be located and to give your name (as N6 allows for groups of researchers all entering files within a project). Returning to an existing project is the same as in NVivo. Either procedure will take you to the **Project Pad** window which, in N6, is located within a project window that places the **Node Browser** and **Document Browser** 'up-front' alongside the **Project Pad** (see Figure 19.3).

Documents and document management

From the **Project Pad** window (with the **Documents** tab highlighted) click on **Make a Project Document** with the left mouse button. The **New Document Wizard** window appears (see figure 19.4). If you want to create a copy of an existing non-NUD*IST text file (remember to have saved a version of that file in Rich Text Format), click on the top option **Locate and import readable external text file(s)**. Then click on **Next>**. You will then be offered a search window in which to locate the file you want to import. The next window asks for the title you wish to give the new NVivo file. The file is then imported.

If you want to create a blank NVivo document, which you will then type the data directly into, choose the **Make a new blank document** option within the first window of the **New Document Wizard** and follow the wizard windows to name and create it.

Proxy documents are NVivo document files that summarize existing files which are either too large or of the wrong format to allow importing into NVivo or which summarize materials not available in any electronic format. A picture file might be an example of the former. Proxy documents create files that the researcher can then fill with relevant ideas about what it is they cannot directly import into the software. As will be seen, links can be made between NVivo files and other files such that the researcher can jump in and out of their project materials to check their ideas.

Note the square box towards the bottom of the first screen of the **New Document Wizard**, next to the words: **Create document as a memo**. Ticking this box makes the new document into a memo. A **memo** is a note the researcher makes to themselves, either in the data collection process or in the analysis process. Memos are then linked to documents or passages within documents, or to codes that the researcher develops. Linking memos to other documents will be discussed later in this chapter.

New documents (either created or imported) are initially arranged alphabetically in the **Document Explorer** (see Figure 19.5). To view the **Document Explorer**, click the **Explore all Project Documents** button on the **Project Pad** (or choose the **Explore Documents** option in the **Documents** menu on the **Project Pad**). Documents can either be kept in this alphabetical form or they can be reorganized into Sets.

If you have a large number of documents already, or if meaningful Sets already suggest themselves to you, create Sets now. You can always rearrange them later. Otherwise, you may wish to leave documents in the **All Documents** folder for now. Sets allow the researcher to organize documents into groups that are meaningful in terms of the research process or its emerging key concepts. To create a set, select **New Document Set** in the **Tools** menu of the **Document Explorer**. This will create an un-named set, which the researcher can then name. With the new set created, pointers to existing documents can be placed there by 'click and drag' (holding down the left mouse key over the file and then moving the mouse cursor over to the **Set** icon required and then releasing the mouse key). Note that the file is still present in the **All Documents** file in the **Documents** (left) pane of the **Document Explorer**, but its icon also appears in the **Set** selected. By this means it is possible to locate a document in more than one set. This may be desirable, but it can be problematic, so beware not to do this if it will lead to confusion.

In addition to creating **Sets** through the **Document Explorer** window, it is also possible to create and edit existing sets through the **Document**

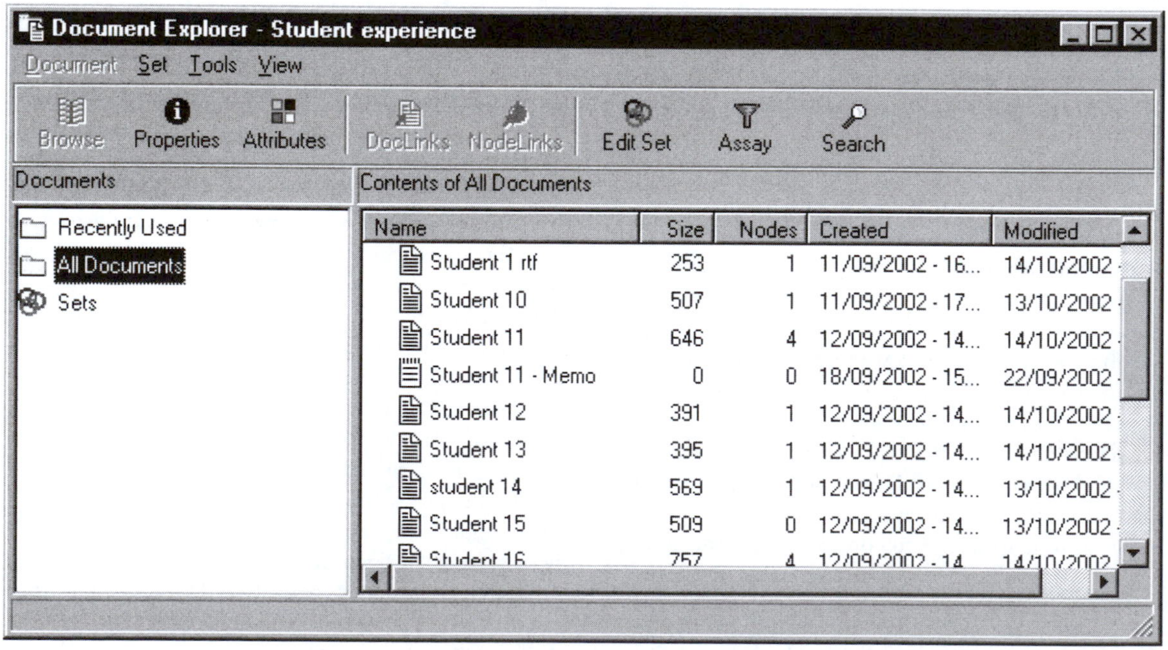

Figure 19.5   NVivo Document Explorer window

Set Editor (see Figure 19.6). This window is accessed through the **Project Pad** by selecting **Edit a Document Set** (which becomes visible when the **Sets** tab on the right hand side of the **Project Pad** window is selected from the **Documents** folder – as distinct from the **Nodes** folder). Within the **Document Set Editor** the left pane allows you to view the existing documents and sets. You can choose which to view by means of the **Documents In** text box above the left pane (click on the down arrow to view the menu of existing sets and all document options). The right pane allows you to build or edit sets using materials selected from the left pane. Using the **Documents In** text box above the right pane you can select which set to edit or create a new set as a **Working Set** (which can then be named).

Once a document is highlighted in either the left or the right pane (the active set has a white background), the middle function buttons become operational. These buttons allow you to copy or remove documents into or from a new or existing set. The

buttons below allow you to filter according to characteristics of the documents or their coding.

New sets can be named through the **Save As** option on the toolbar, while existing files and documents can be renamed in either the **Save As** or the **Set Properties** dialog boxes. Note the **Search** and **Browse** option buttons on the tool bar. These relate to the content of documents and the links that can be made between content in documents. This leads us from the construction and organization of documents to the coding and searching of those documents. In addition to saving documents and projects, it is useful to back up projects, that is, create dated copies that can be returned to if subsequent problems arise. This is achieved by selecting **Backup Project . . .** from the **Project** menu in the **Project Pad** window. If you have more than one project to choose from you will need to select the one you wish to back up, and then click **Backup . . .** and give your back-up a name and location.

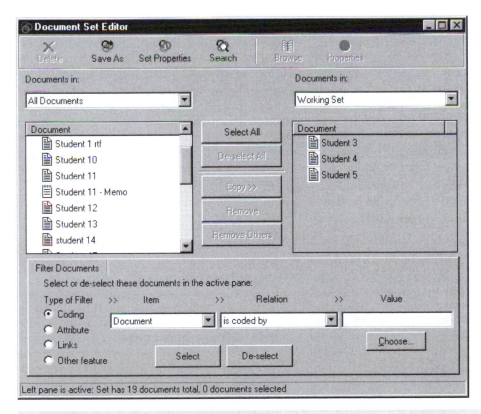

Figure 19.6   NVivo Document Set Editor window

Documents can be imported into, but would not usually be created within, N6 since it does not have the rich text editor of NVivo. The first significant difference between NVivo and N6 is that imported documents have to be saved in a Plain Text Format, such as Text Only, rather than into Rich Text Format (which N6 cannot read). The process of copying and saving existing files to this new format is the same, only the different format option is selected. On the **Document** tab on the N6 **Project Pad**, select **Import Text Files**. This opens up a file search and selection window, in which plain text files can be selected for import. Materials cut or copied from external documents can also be pasted into either existing or new N6 files by means of the options in the **Project** window **Documents** menu. New N6 files can be created from the **Project** window's **File** menu. With both the node and document explorer windows 'up-front', it is not necessary to search these out. Both windows have **Browse, Memo, Report** and **Search** buttons 'up-front'. These are addressed in the following sections of the discussion. N6 does not allow for the organization of **Documents** into **Sets**. A very important difference to NVivo is that when a document is imported into N6 it must be decided at that point how the text is going to be divided into what are called 'Text Units'. There are three possible options: lines, sentences or paragraphs. When it comes to coding text to nodes (see next section), N6 will store references to the units of text you select for coding. Once a document has been created you cannot change its units (though you can change the setting for subsequent documents), so think about what the most meaningful and useful units would be when setting up your documents.

Coding: nodes and links – stripes and reports

Within NVivo documents can be coded through the creation of nodes and the linking of words, passages and whole documents to those nodes. Other kinds of links can also be made between documents. As has been discussed before, **coding** is the basis of content analysis and can be either **deductive** (the application of prior codes drawn from theory to textual data) or **inductive** (codes being drawn from the texts themselves). Both NVivo and N6 allow either top down or bottom up coding, and any combination of the two. The researcher creates nodes to hold categories for thinking about their data, and if they wish, coding of documents. These may be terms that

emerge from the texts being analysed, or ones that the researcher generated from prior literature. Coding is done (see below) by the researcher reading through all documents within their project, placing references (as will be explained below) at the node to all relevant items of text. This is the electronic equivalent of going through paper documents and marking text with a highlighter pen, using a different colour for each code. Then it is possible to 'ask' NVivo/N6 (using various techniques to be explained below) to show references and patterns that may exist between the themes coded for.

Bottom up coding is where the researcher generates their codes during or after reading their texts. Top down coding is where the researcher sets up their codes by creating nodes in advance of reading their texts. Once nodes have been created, references to other segments of text can be added. Nodes can be reorganized, internally and externally. Coding stripes make patterns more visible. All these options are discussed below.

Coding up from the text

With one or more documents in place it is possible to **Browse** them, that is, open the file to read the contents. Within the **Project Pad** (on the **Documents** tab) click on **Browse a Document**. This opens the **Choose Document** window (see Figure 19.7).

From the **Look in** text box choose **All Documents**. Highlight the specific document you want to view and either double-click on it with the mouse or click OK at the bottom of the window. You can then read through the text in the **Document Browser** (see Figure 19.8).

Coding may develop in a number of different ways (recall Chapter 17). The researcher may seek to code for interesting themes that emerge as they browse texts or they may wish to read through a number of documents before deciding what codes to choose and what segments of text to code.

Within NVivo and N6, nodes are organized either as free nodes or into 'trees' and 'sub-trees' (directory metaphor) which are also called 'parents' and 'children/siblings' (family metaphor). At first we will look at free nodes, which are not organized in any hierarchical or meaning-based way. Later we will look at the creation of nodes in the areas of trees and cases. Text can be coded up from the data in two main ways: by using the word(s) in the text (*In-Vivo*) or by typing in the researcher's chosen name for the node.

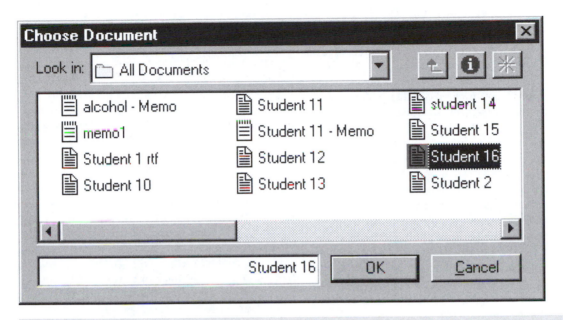

Figure 19.7   NVivo Choose Document window

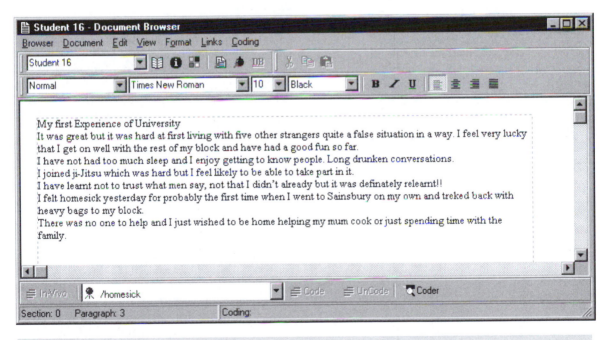

Figure 19.8   NVivo Document Browser window

Along the bottom of the **Document Browser** window there is a toolbar with various options including the **In-Vivo** coding button. This toolbar is called the 'speed coding bar'. In Figure 19.8 the word 'homesick' is highlighted. This is a term actually used by the student being asked about their experience of starting university. *In-Vivo* coding uses selected words in the text as the nodes. By highlighting a word or phrase and then clicking on the **In-Vivo** coding button, a node is created and the selected text is also coded at that node. Once a node has been created, other segments of text in the same or in other documents can be coded at that same node.

Alternatively, nodes to be created can be given names the researcher generates, not the terms in the text itself. Once a segment of text has been identified about which a new node is to be created, the researcher needs to give the node a name by typing that name into the speed coding bar text box (in the space between the **In-Vivo** button and the **Code** button), and clicking on the **Code** button. A new node is created. Now other segments of text can be coded at that node.

Figure 19.9   NVivo Coder window

Coding from the top down

It is perfectly possible to create free nodes, tree structures and sets prior to coding the data itself within NVivo or in NVivo/N6. Whether this is because the researcher has a prescribed list of codes they want to use or because they have begun to analyse their data 'by hand' prior to using the software is not important here. If the researcher chooses, they can create nodes, trees, cases and sets which have no initial content. This is achieved in the **Node Explorer**, which is accessed from the **Project Pad** by clicking on the **Explore Nodes** button. In NVivo click once on the icon in the left pane for the type of node you wish to create. If you want to create a free node, highlight the **Free Node** icon and select **Create Free Node** in either the context menu or the **Tools** menu. A new free node is created. Click once with the left mouse button on the highlighted free node and type in the name you wish. The same process operates for creating other types of node. With the different levels within tree node structures you need to create the first level tree or parent node first, then create children as discussed earlier.

NVivo has another way of linking a document to an idea. From inside the **Document Explorer**, highlight a document. Clicking on the **NodeLink** button opens the **Top Level NodeLinks** window for the highlighted document. Select the node you want to link to. This window can also be accessed to link any place in the text to a node, using the **NodeLink** button on the toolbar at the top of the individual document window.

Coding text at existing node/codes

To do this in either N6 or NVivo, the researcher usually needs to have the document open in the **Document Browser** window. Then they need to highlight the word, phrase or segment of text they wish to code at the existing node. Once the text is highlighted, the options on the speed coding bar become operational. First it is necessary to select the node you want to have the new item of text coded at. If the node you want to code at is one of the last ten nodes used, you can select it using the down arrow next to the text box on the speed coding bar (between the **In-Vivo** and the **Code** buttons). If not, it can be selected in the **Coder** (see Figure 19.9). Click the **Coder** button on the speed coding bar to bring up the **Coder** tool. Using either method, and with the text you want to code still highlighted in the **Document Browser**, highlight the node you wish to code the text at (in either the text box containing recently used nodes or in the **Coder**). From within the **Coder** route it is necessary to open the Free, Tree, Case or Set folder in which the desired node is located in order to highlight it. Then press the **Code** button (on the **Coder**). If you want to remove a text selection coding at a node simply highlight the text already coded for and click on the **UnCode** button on the speed coding bar. Repeat this process throughout the document(s) if there is more than one link that needs un-coding.

Note that within the **Coder**, if the **Show** box has **All Nodes, Explorer Style** selected, then nodes that are in bold are those with coding in the current document. Alternatively, if the **List All Nodes with Coding** option is selected in the **Show** box only the nodes coding the current document (or section) are displayed. Change the view using the **Scope of Coding** drop-down list. Use the down arrow to the right of the **Show** box to select options.

Once nodes have been created and segments of text have been coded at those nodes, it becomes possible for the researcher to examine this coding. Using either the **Explore Nodes** option on the **Project Pad**, or the **Browse a Node** option, it is

possible to show all the text coded at any particular node. Using the **Explore Nodes** route, the **Node Explorer** (see Figure 19.10) opens up and the researcher has to navigate in the left pane to locate the node they are interested in browsing. In Figure 19.10 it was necessary to click on the **Free Nodes** icon in the left pane to display the range of nodes held there. Double-click on the right pane node icon to browse that node. Using the **Browse a Node** route from the **Project Pad** takes you to the **Choose Node** window. This route allows much the same options, but with a different format. There are differences, but at this stage these are not important.

In the **Node Browser** (see Figure 19.11) we can see a part of the report of those passages coded at the node 'Homesick'. Note that the dark text is the coded material and the lighter text is the surrounding paragraph. Using the **Passage Contents Display** option in the **View** menu of the **Node Browser** the researcher can choose a variety of display formats: either only showing the coded text or also showing the surrounding text. The **Passage Contents Display** option allows a choice of degrees of context, showing either the surrounding sentence, paragraph or wider still. The researcher can choose whichever option suits their purpose best. Viewing the materials linked to any

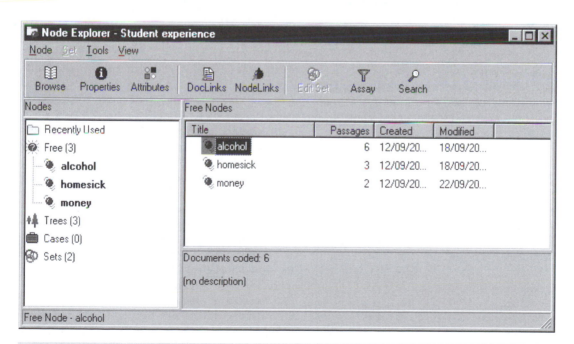

Figure 19.10   NVivo Node Explorer window

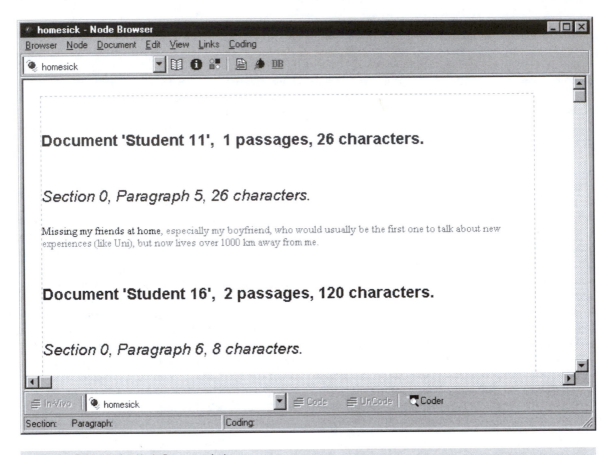

Figure 19.11   NVivo Node Browser window

particular node is one way to check for connections and dis-connections within materials selected. This process of checking may lead the researcher to change their mind about their codes and/or the content of their nodes.

If you are coding up from the text you may generate a large number of nodes that are not organized in any particular fashion. These are free nodes. This accumulation of codes may lead to two things. The first is the realization that the content of your nodes needs reorganizing. The second is the realization that the nodes need to be placed in a more structured order.

Re-organizing the contents of nodes

We have already seen how to de-code a passage or word in a document. Simply highlight the coded text and de-code it using the **UnCode** button on the speed coding bar. To delete a node altogether, it is necessary

to highlight the node in the right pane of the **Node Explorer** and using either the context menu (gained by holding down the right mouse button) or the **Node** menu, select **Delete Node**.

In order to merge two nodes together, in the right pane of the **Node Explorer** highlight the node to be merged (called the 'source') and then select **Cut** (or **Copy**) from either the context menu or the **Node** menu. Then using the left mouse key highlight the node that you wish the first node to be merged with (called the 'target'). Then, from the context menu or the **Tool** menu on the menu bar, select **Merge Node**. In the **Merge Node** window tick the **Merge** box and the **Add source's Links to the target** box. The option to merge attributes is also available at this point. The question of what attributes are will be dealt with in the next section of this chapter. In addition to the coding, any hyperlinks from the source node will be added to those of the target node under the target node's name.

If it is felt that some of the current coding at a particular node is better removed, or coded to another node, it is necessary to go through the text. In each instance select the coded text in the **Node Browser**, code it to the more suitable node and then uncode it via the **UnCode** button on the speed coding bar.

Re-organizing the management of nodes (trees and sets)

Trees Free nodes are the usual first step in coding up from the text. However, once a number of nodes/codes have been set up, it may become clear that some nodes/codes are subsets of others. For example, missing friends back home might be one subset of homesickness, while missing family might be another. Missing family could, of course, be broken down into further subsets. The organization of nodes/codes into trees allows for such a hierarchical organization of nodes/codes.

Within the **Node Explorer** window, clicking on the **Trees** icon (see Figure 19.12) once with the left mouse key enables the creation of a tree node by selecting **Create Tree Node** from either the **Tools** menu or from the context menu. Once a new tree is created it should be given a name. If you wish to replicate an existing free node and make it into a tree node, then hold the left mouse key down over the node icon you

wish to copy and move the node icon over the tree icon and release the left mouse key. This creates a first level tree node (that is, a parent node) with the title of the previous free node, while there will still be a free node remaining with that title.

To create branches for trees (otherwise known as children from parent nodes) it is necessary to have already created the first level tree or parent as explained above. Highlighting the chosen tree/parent node from which branches/children are to be subsets, by clicking upon it once with the left mouse button select the **Create** option from either the context or the **Tools** menu. The **Create** menu then offers the options either to create a **Sibling Node** or a **Child Node**. Siblings are nodes that all stem from the same parent. For example, 'Family' and 'Friends' (children of a parent node 'Homesick') are siblings in relation to each other (they are both children of the same Homesick node). When creating the first child/branch node within a tree structure, select **Child Node** from the **Create** option in the **Tools** menu. Once one **Child Node** is created it is possible to create further child nodes by highlighting the prospective parent node and selecting another **Child Node** as before, or highlighting the existing **Child Node** and selecting to create a **Sibling Node** from the **Create** option on the **Tools** or context menu. The result is the same.

If you wish to move an existing free node to

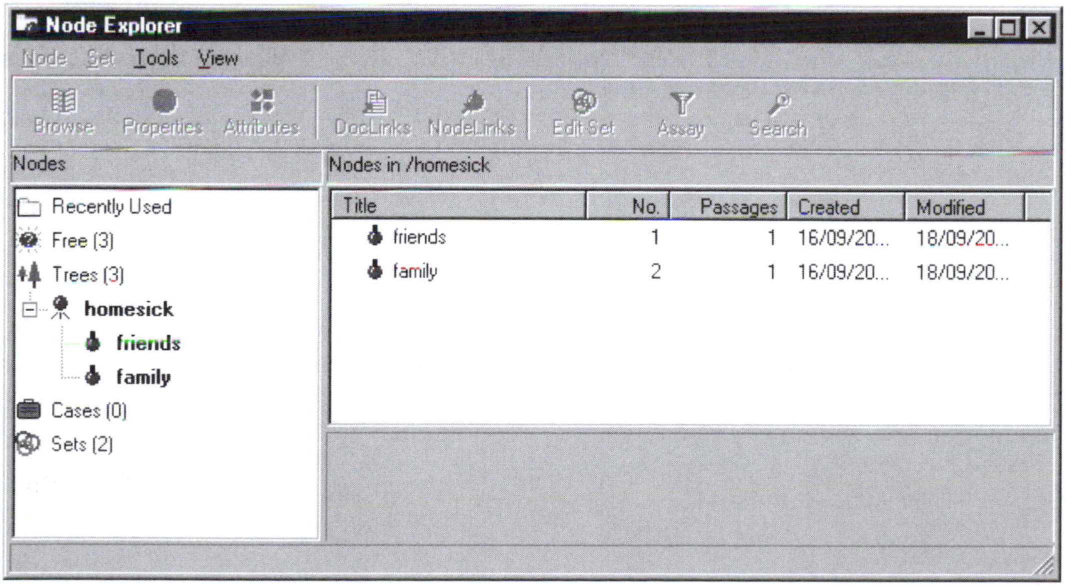

Figure 19.12   NVivo Node Explorer window: with tree with branches/parent with children open

become a child of an existing tree node, the process is much the same as the 'click and drag' process discussed earlier for the movement of a free node to create a first level tree node. Simply click and drag the free node to its new parent node, then release the mouse button.

Once a new node has been created, text can be coded to it in the normal way using the speed coding bar in the **Document Browser**. If an old free node has been moved to become a child within a tree, then its existing coding to documents and text will be retained. Sometimes the contents of the newly located node can be left as it is. However, it will often be the case that in creating a tree structure the text coded at a node moved into the new tree structure will need to be split up between the siblings. For example, in creating the sub-categories of '**Friends**' and '**Family**' within the general category of '**Homesick**', the links to the '**Homesick**' node will need to be split between the sub-categories. Browsing the '**Homesick**' node's coding (using the **Node Browser**) allows the researcher to re-code relevant passages to each of the child nodes. A record can be made by highlighting the icon of the relevant tree within the left pane of the **Node Explorer**. With the tree's top icon highlighted in the left pane, the next level within the structure will then be shown in the right pane. If this is the level you wish to view, simply double-click on the right pane

icon you wish to view and a **Node Browser** window will open containing all the coding at that node. From there it is a case of going through the individual documents highlighting the linked text and, using the speed coding bar, **UnCode** and **Code** accordingly.

Node sets allow for the organization of nodes in groups that are not sufficiently hierarchical to be located in a tree node structure. It is important to recall that the structure of the **Node Explorer** is such that the icons for a particular node can be placed in a number of different places. After clicking and dragging the icon of a free node into a tree node structure, or into a set or a case node folder, that icon will now appear in both places. 'Click and drag' is equivalent to copying and pasting an item, as distinct from cutting and pasting. It is possible to highlight a node in the **Node explorer**, then to select **Cut** from either the context menu or from the **Tools** menu, and finally relocate that node using the paste option. Either option can be used when creating and building trees and case folders. When you create a set, it will hold an alias to each node you drag it into. Materials that the researcher thinks may have some connection can be placed in a set without having to create an elaborate tree structure, and without having to remove existing forms of structure or free ordering. Sets can allow for provisional explorations of connections without excluding future possible reordering work.

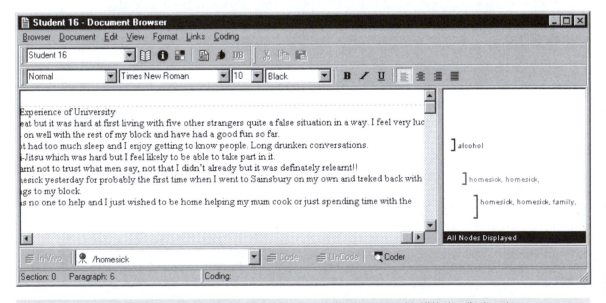

Figure 19.13   NVivo Document Browser with Coding Stripes sub-window open with All Nodes displayed

Case nodes are a special form of ordering nodes that code everything about a case. These will not be discussed here. Once you are familiar with free, tree and set ordering, you can follow the software tutorials and help packages to get to know about cases in more detail.

Coding stripes

Having coded your text, one initial method of looking over the content of your codes, the context in which your coded material is situated, and the relationships between the materials coded within a text, is to use coding stripes. Coding stripes are a graphic device to show what areas of text have been coded at which nodes. Stripes are coloured brackets running the length of coded passages (see Figure 19.13).

Once you have opened the **Document Browser** for the document you are interested in, you select **Coding Stripes** from the **View** menu (see Figure 19.13). You hide **Coding Stripes** in the same way. The default option is to display stripes for all the nodes coded for in the text being displayed. Each node is highlighted in a separate colour. You may wish to only look for the stripes of particular coded nodes to look in particular at the instance of that node or for the cross-over between two or more nodes. To select which nodes will be displayed in the **Coding Stripes** window, first ensure that **Coding Stripes** is already selected from the **View** menu. Then select the **Select Coding Stripes** option from the **View** menu.

Choosing **All Nodes** within the **Choose Node** window (see Figure 19.14) means that coding stripes for all nodes coded within a displayed text will be shown. Alternatively, you can go through the **Free**, **Tree** and other node menus and pick out the nodes you wish to display.

With the **Node Browser** and **Document Browser** 'up front' in the N6 Project window, the user can more directly move around when coding up or down. N6 has a speed coding bar at the bottom of each document window, as has NVivo. Highlighting a word or phrase in the document activates the **In-Vivo** coding button. Clicking this creates a new node located initially in the **Free Node** section of the **Node Browser** and also links that node with the text unit from which the word/phrase was selected. The other functions of the N6 speed coding bar are also the same as in NVivo. Within N6, nodes can only be **Free** or in **Tree** structures. There are no special places for **Cases** or **Sets**. Creating and moving nodes, as well as the creation of Tree structures, is achieved using the options on the **Nodes** menu. The **Make Free Node** option creates a free node that needs to be named. Highlighting an existing node and then selecting **Copy** from the **Nodes** menu enables that node to be duplicated elsewhere. This is achieved by highlighting the node that the copied node is either to be merged with or made a sub-branch of, and then choosing the **Attach With ***** or the **Merge With ***** options from the **Nodes** menu respectively. Coding with existing nodes in N6 is similar to NVivo (apart from NVivo not having prescribed text units). However, in N6 the 'up front' **Node Explorer** does the job of the

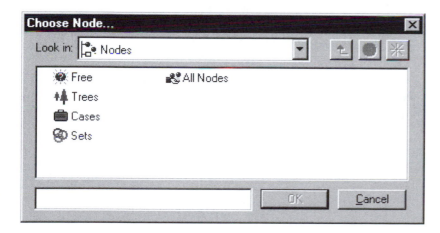

Figure 19.14   NVivo Choose Node window

Coder in NVivo, acting as the site where nodes are sought and selected for linking. Simply highlight the text unit to be linked and then either select from the **Node Explorer** or the speed coding dialog box (for the last 10 nodes used). Finally, press **Code**.

Uncoding is also the same as in NVivo. N6's 'up front' format allows the user to see all text linked to the node they choose to highlight, by using the **Browse** button on the **Node Explorer**. N6 does not have the same coding stripes graphical form that is found in NVivo. Alternatively, in N6 one of the **Report** options (accessed by pressing the **Report** button on the **Document Explorer**) is to request coding stripes. In N6 the user is then asked which segments of the document they wish to view, and which nodes they wish to view for. The resulting window lists each selected text unit and the nodes linked to it. Text units are assigned numbers, while nodes are assigned letters. The dots and strings of

letters running down the right-hand side of the page do in letters what NVivo does in colour.

Attributes

Attributes are characteristics that apply to 'objects' (people, places, events and so on). People have attributes such as age, residence, income, attitude towards politics and so forth. The application of attributes to 'objects' in NVivo has two forms. Attributes can be applied to documents or to nodes. Attributes are characteristics that the researcher chooses to pay particular attention to. Attributes are assigned a range of **values** (for example, age values, values for the number of rooms in that person's home, or the number of times each week they exercise). Each document or node is assigned one of the values attached to each particular attribute. For example, in the case of the **Student experience** project, each

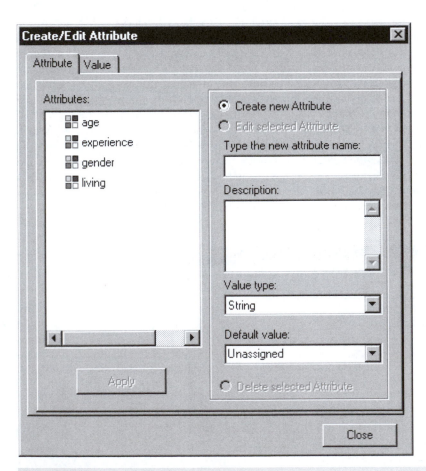

Figure 19.15   NVivo Create/Edit Attribute window

student document (each student's response being recorded in one document) was assigned values for the attributes, age, gender, experience and living (in other words, type of accomodation). For age the values would be numbers. For gender the value would be categorical (either male or female). For experience the value options were positive, negative or both. For accommodation the value options were student housing or family home. Giving each document or node attribute values enables the production of attribute **matrices** (see discussion of Miles and Huberman in Chapter 17). Attribute matrices highlight the variation within the group according to the attributes selected. The basics of attribute creation and matrices production are outlined below. The NVivo help menus give extensive explanation of the more advanced use of attributes, and these processes will not be discussed here. Here we will explore the production of document attributes. The process of creating node attributes is the same.

Creating attributes and values

From the **Project Pad**, with the **Documents** folder to the front, and with the **Attributes** sub-folder also to the front within the **Documents** folder, click on the **Edit a Document Attribute** button. This opens the **Create/Edit Attribute** window (see Figure 19.15).

To create a new attribute, click the **Create new Attribute** button. Then give the new attribute a name and description. Value type refers to the kind of values to be made available to assign to each document in the case of each particular attribute. The main options are String (a string of written text), Boolean (true or false) or Numerical (for example, age). In the Student experience project, age has numerical values, while living (with family or in student housing), experience (positive, negative or both) and gender (male or female) are string-based values. Once these three steps are completed, click on **Apply**. This creates the new attribute. Then, click on the new attribute icon and select the **Value** tab (towards the top left hand side of the **Create/Edit Attribute** window) to create values for the new attribute. Note that three pre-assigned values will already exist for the new attribute. These are **Unassigned**, **Unknown** and **Not Applicable**. These are the values to be assigned to various kinds of missing data. When creating a new attribute with string (that is, name-based) values, it is necessary to create and name each value required. In effect, such attributes

are at the nominal or ordinal level of measurement. Within the **Value** folder for the new attribute, select the **Create new value** button and assign a name before clicking **Apply** to create it. Create the required number of values in this way. To delete a value simply select the **Delete . . .** button and scroll down using the down arrow to locate the value to be deleted.

Assigning attribute values to each document

Attribute values can be assigned, created or edited in the **Document Attribute Explorer** (see Figure 19.16), which can be accessed either from the **Project Pad** (by clicking **Explore Document Attributes**) or from a set of individual documents by clicking the **Attributes** icon on the document toolbar (this icon is a square made up of four smaller coloured squares). The former's default is to bring up a display table of all documents set against all attributes, whilst the latter's default is to bring up a table of just the selected document set against all attributes. The default table format is to show each document as a row and each attribute as a column. The boxes formed at the intersection of the rows (for each document) and columns (for each attribute) contain the values given (that is, attributed) for each attribute in the case of each document.

Attribute values can be assigned to a group of documents *en masse* if an attribute is created after documents have been created. Alternatively, if attributes are created before the creation of one or more new document(s), attribute values can be assigned to each new document one document at a time via the **Attributes** button on each **Document Browser's** toolbar. The **Document Attribute Explorer** window in Figure 19.16 has already had the values inserted at the intersection between each document and attribute. This was achieved by highlighting each cell and clicking on the **Value** menu. All the available values for the column (attribute) which the highlighted box is a part of are displayed and it is necessary only to select the correct value for the document, which the highlighted box represents. In the case of the cell highlighted above (being the intersection of the document **Student 6** and the attribute **living**) the values available from the **Value** menu are those of the attribute living (that is, family, student housing and the three missing values). Student 6 lived in a student hall of residence so the correct value was **student housing**. Whether attributes are created before or after the creation of documents, and

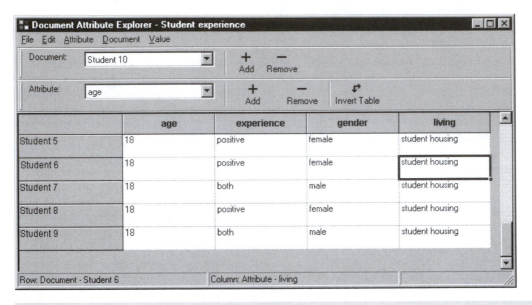

Figure 19.16   NVivo Document Attribute Explorer window

whether assigning attributes is done one document at a time or all together, are options the researcher can choose for themselves. The software enables any combination of approaches.

Attribute tables constitute one form of the matrix diagrams discussed earlier in relation to the presentation of qualitative research data (see Chapter 17). Various options exist for the editing of tables created in this way. This will involve some degree of either editing down when selecting from the **Explore Document Attributes** route and editing up when starting from the **Attributes** icon of a particular document. Rows and columns can be selected or deselected, values edited and formatting changed to create made-to-measure tables, which can then be exported into other software formats (for example, word processing or statistical packages). More detail can be found using the NVivo help pages.

In N6 attributes are handled by coding nodes which are made for the attributes, and 'child' nodes for the values, and the relevant text is coded at the value node. Thus, if a document is an interview with a woman, it will be coded at the node gender/female. As with NVivo, this information can be imported from a statistics package or table software. However, it is possible to create the equivalent of attributes by using the **Annotation** function of N6 (discussed below).

Memos

Memos are notes to oneself, or an audit trail of ideas emerging in the course of research. Memos can be linked to either nodes or documents. Node memos are documents where the researcher can record the process by which a node emerged and changed over the course of the analysis. Document memos record additional information the researcher may feel they want to record about the text. Memos are not the 'data' texts, and when it comes to searching the data using the **Search Tool**, texts that are marked as memos can be excluded from the scope of the search, or specified as included. This allows the researcher to input their comments without those comments becoming a part of the data.

To create a new memo, select **Create a Document** from the **Project Pad** (with the **Documents** folder highlighted). From here the process is the same as for creating a normal document, only you tick the **Create document as a memo** box located towards the bottom of the first wizard screen. The new document will have a memo icon as distinct from a standard document icon. Memos are displayed in the **Document Explorer** alongside all other documents.

One can link a document to an existing memo. Remember that a memo once created can be added to and re-worked as much as the researcher feels is necessary, and this does not change the links to it.

Alternatively, one can create a new memo at any time and link it to the document one is working on at the time. To link a document to a memo, first open the document browser for the document you want to make the link from. Using either the context menu (via the right mouse key), or the **Links** menu, or the **Make/Inspect DocLinks** button on the toolbar below the menu bar of the **Document Explorer** window, select the **DocLink . . .** option. The **DocLink** window is thereby opened (see Figure 19.17).

Figure 19.17 is entitled **Top-Level DocLinks**. This refers to the fact that in this format the link being created will be between a memo and a whole document. The alternative would be to link a memo to a segment of text rather in the way that a node might be. Note the two top buttons in the **DocLink** window (see Figure 19.17), which enable selection between creating/searching for **DocLinks** linked to a whole document (top-level DocLinks) and adding/searching for **DocLinks** linked

to specific pieces of text within a document (selected text position). If the latter option is selected, the window name changes to **In-Text DocLinks**. To make a link, it must first be decided which of these two types of link is most appropriate, and the chosen option selected. All existing documents are displayed in the left pane. You can either choose an existing document by highlighting it in the left pane and clicking the right arrow between the left and right panes, or create a new memo. Deselection of a **DocLink** is made by highlighting an existing link in the right pane and clicking the **Remove Document** button. **DocLinks** made to specific passages within a document will generate the DocLink icon at the end of the text selected.

To link a memo to a node involves similar processes. From either the **Node Explorer** window or from the **Node Browser** window of a particular node it is possible to select the **DocLink . . .** option in the same way as it is within the **Document Browser**

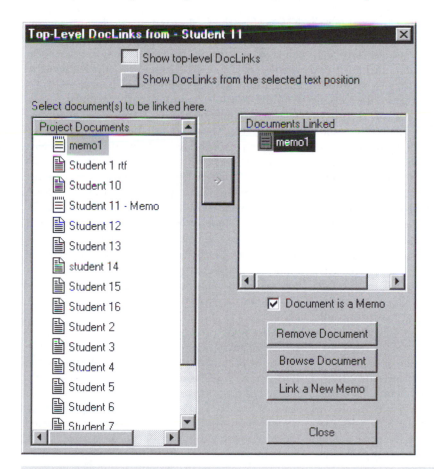

Figure 19.17 NVivo DocLinks window

(described above). In the **Node Explorer**, of course, the particular node you wish to make a memo link to has to be highlighted before the **DocLink . . .** icon becomes active. In the **Node Browser** window of a particular node, this is not necessary because there is only one node active to choose from (that is, the node currently being browsed).

DataBites – external links and proxy documents

DataBites are in-text links, but not to documents within NVivo. DataBite links can be created from an NVivo document or memo file by means of the **DB** (**DataBite**) button on the document browser toolbar. By creating such links the researcher can 'jump' between NVivo files and materials in other formats (image, sound or graphically-based files). This enables greater freedom to explore hunches and clarify relationships even where all the data cannot be held within the NVivo software.

As has already been mentioned, it is possible to create similar links using the **Proxy Document** option. While **DataBites** create links between specific text within an NVivo file and other sorts of electronically stored data, proxy documents are whole documents designed to 'stand in' for materials, which cannot be imported into NVivo itself. A proxy document is a summary of what it stands in for, and the researcher fills in that content themselves. To create a proxy document, simply follow the first steps in creating a new document. In the first **New Document Wizard** window, choose either to **Make Proxy Document(s) representing external file(s)** or to **Make a Proxy Document for non-file data**. Both choices create files that the researcher has to fill with content, summing up the materials that cannot be imported directly into the software. The difference is that the former creates a link to the file in which the non-importable materials are held, while the latter does not. The latter should be used for materials that are not in any computer-readable format.

In N6 memos are created, read and/or modified by selecting the node or document desired, and then by clicking on the respective **Memo** button. This opens the **Memo** window for that document or memo, or creates it if one has not already been created. The memo can then be edited or read. Only one memo can exist for any one node or document, unlike in NVivo. Annotations are additions to the text of particular documents and appear in double diamond brackets within the text (<< . . . >>). These are read as a part of the document itself and so can be used to input the kinds of demographic and other material that would be placed as attributes in NVivo. Annotations can be created by selecting the text unit within a document that you wish the annotation to appear below. Then, select the **Add Annotation** option from the **Browser** menu in the **Project** window. Follow the guidance to input in the relevant materials you wish to add. Then close the Annotations window and click the Yes button when asked whether you wish to save the recent changes. The newly annotated materials will appear in diamond brackets below the chosen text unit. All annotations within a project are held together within the **Annotation Node** in the **Node Explorer**. As such, it is possible to code other segments of text under this node.

Models

NVivo offers the facility to create visual representations of relationships and patterns that begin to become apparent as the researcher explores the links between various texts, nodes and cases. From the **Project Pad** click on the **Explore Models** button or select the **Explore Models** option from the **Analysis** menu. This opens up the **Model Explorer** window (see Figure 19.18). The left pane of the **Model Explorer** allows you to select existing models (if any have already been created within the project), create new models and/or to name files. To create a new model, select **New** from the **Model** menu in the **Model Explorer** window. The new model will initially be called New Model, but can be renamed as required. The model can be constructed within the right pane of the window. Here it will be explained how a simple model can be put together. With more experience you should be able to develop more sophisticated models, but a grasp of the basic ideas is sufficient here.

In the model presented in Figure 19.18, three nodes are shown linked by one directional arrows. Node icons can be selected from the **Model Explorer** toolbar. Click on the **Add Node** icon on the toolbar (run the mouse cursor slowly across the toolbar icons to see the name of each icon). This brings up the **Choose Node** window from which the required node can be selected. Once imported into the model building space (that is, the right-hand pane of the **Model Explorer** window), the icons can be moved around using 'click and drag' via the left mouse button. Creating arrows or lines is

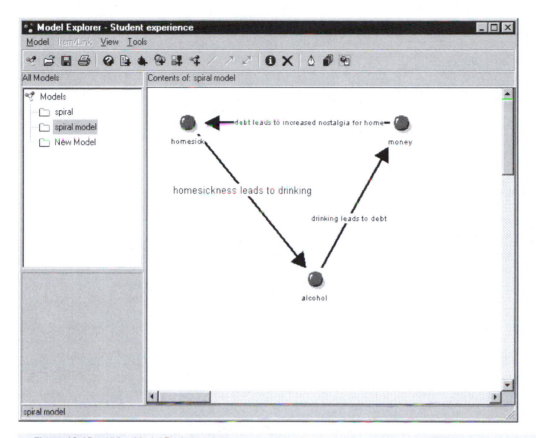

Figure 19.18   NVivo Model Explorer window

achieved by first clicking with the left mouse button on the icon you wish to begin the arrow or line. Then, with the chosen node still highlighted, click once using the left mouse button on the choice of arrow or line you wish to put into the model. These option buttons are located on the **Model Explorer** toolbar. Then click once on the destination node to which the line or arrow is to lead. The arrows are assigned labels by highlighting an arrow or line (with one left mouse click), then selecting **Properties**, either from the **Model** menu in the **Model Explorer** window or by clicking on the **Properties** icon on the toolbar.

Highlighting any item within a model and bringing up the **Properties** window enables that item to be modified in a number of different ways to achieve whatever visual effect the researcher feels is best for them.

Note that as items are added to the model, so they are catalogued in the left pane of the **Model Explorer**. At the bottom of the **Model Explorer** there is a space for the researcher to record their impressions and ideas.

Models can be made far more sophisticated and incorporate a number of sub-models, images and linkages within a singular display.

N6 does not provide modelling options. However, N6 is designed to allow materials to be exported into more graphically sophisticated packages. Node trees can be graphically represented within N6, using the **Node Tree Display** option in the **Nodes** menu.

Searching

Searching a project allows the researcher to identify patterns or connections between elements within the data. The search tool allows the building of theory by means of five different types of search operation. The **Search Tool** window (see Figure 19.19) is accessed from the **Project Pad** by clicking on the **Search** button towards the bottom left of the window. The **Search Tool** window contains three sections, the top, middle and bottom. The top section allows the selection of search type. The middle section allows the

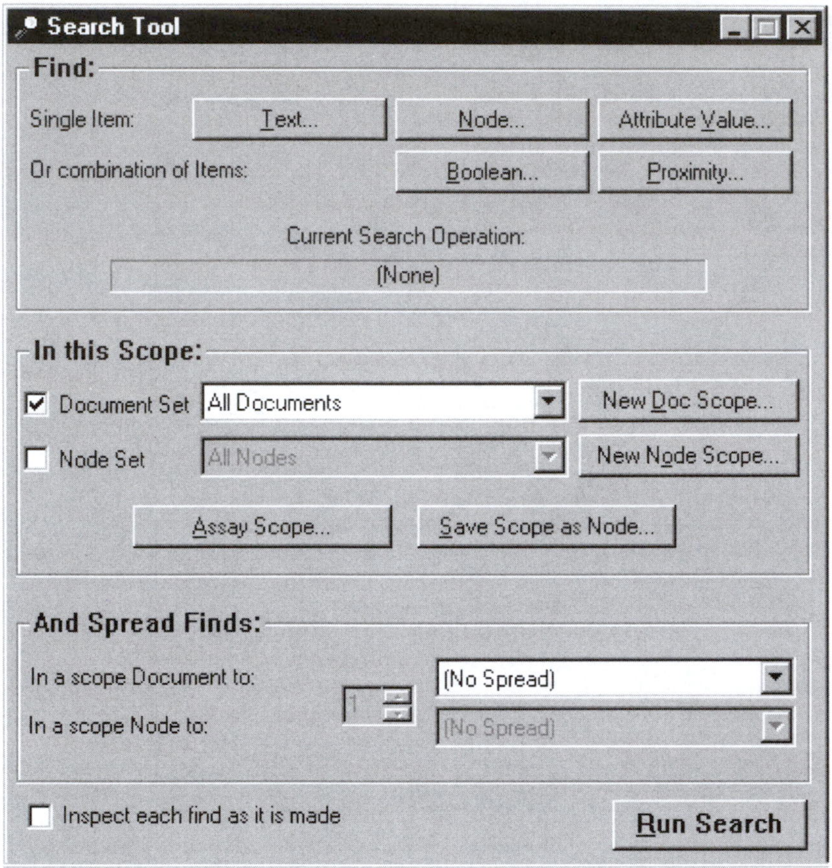

Figure 19.19   NVivo Search Tool window

researcher to select whether they want to search the whole database or selected files and/or sets; this is called selecting the search 'scope'. Finally, the bottom section of the window allows the researcher to choose the manner in which the results will be displayed. The finds can be presented independently or embedded in degrees of the surrounding text in which they were located; this is referred to as 'spread'.

Types of search

There are five search types within NVivo. Three search types involve searching for a single item; within NVivo these are referred to as 'basic searches'. The two remaining search types involve cross-referencing between two items; within NVivo these are referred to as 'advanced searches'. The first three (basic) search types are as follows:

1   **Node Lookup:** This search type allows the researcher to choose a node and search for instances of it. This is almost the same as if the researcher used the **Node Browser**, as has already been described. The only difference is that with the **Node Lookup** search type the researcher can select and deselect the documents and sets to be searched so as to customize the search.

2   **Attribute Lookup:** This search type allows the researcher to collate all files containing a particular value from a particular attribute (for example, all students living with family, or all students aged 20). Clicking on the **Attribute Lookup** search button at the top of the **Search Tool** screen calls up the **Attribute Value Lookup** window (see Figure 19.20).

Within the **Attribute Value Lookup** window it is necessary to select the required node attribute

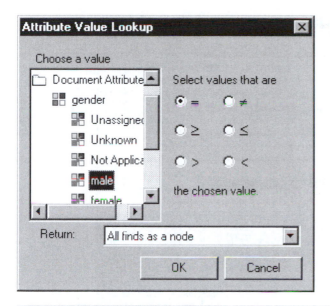

Figure 19.20   NVivo Attribute Value Lookup window

or document attribute folder in the left-hand text box. In Figure 19.20 it is the **Document Attribute** folder that has been opened. All the document attributes are then displayed. From these highlight one. In Figure 19.20 it is the gender attribute that has been chosen. All the values associated with that attribute are then displayed. Once the desired value is selected (in Figure 19.20 the male value has been selected), it is necessary to specify which results are desired. The right-hand side of the window gives a range of options. Selecting the equals sign (=) instructs the programme to extract all files where the value of the gender attribute is 'male'. Alternatively, it is possible to ask to see only files where the value of the gender attribute is not equal to male. For numerical values it is possible to ask to display values that are equal to, greater than, smaller than, greater or equal to, or smaller or equal to the value selected.

3 **Text Search:** This type of search allows the researcher to bring together all documents containing a particular string of text, numbers or specialist characters (see Figure 19.21). As all searches are automatically saved as new nodes, the **Text Search** option allows for the autocoding of new text searches. Of course, this presumes that single text strings will all relate to the same underlying theme, but it is possible to use **UnCode**,

Merge and manual coding to supplement and edit coding after an initial autocode.

In Figure 19.21 it should be noted that while a text search is referred to as a basic search, advanced options exist within it. In Figure 19.21 the **Advanced Options** 'Use this method' text box is set to 'Approximation Search'. The default option is a 'Regular Search', which searches only for exact matches to the string of text the researcher chooses to look for. Approximation searching allows a specified number of 'mismatches' (that is, different characters). The number of mismatches to be accepted is selected at the bottom of the **Advanced Options** section of the window. Making the search 'case' sensitive (that is, sensitive to capital and lower-case lettering) is an option in either regular or approximation searching. The use of wildcards is only available for regular searches. Wildcards are a form of special match characters, which specify additional match criteria. These characters can be selected from the **Add Special Character** menu towards the top of the window. These wildcards can be explored when the researcher is a little more familiar with the software.

Advanced search types allow cross-referencing of different kinds. This allows for the combination of the previous three types of search operands (that is, nodes, attributes and textual materials).

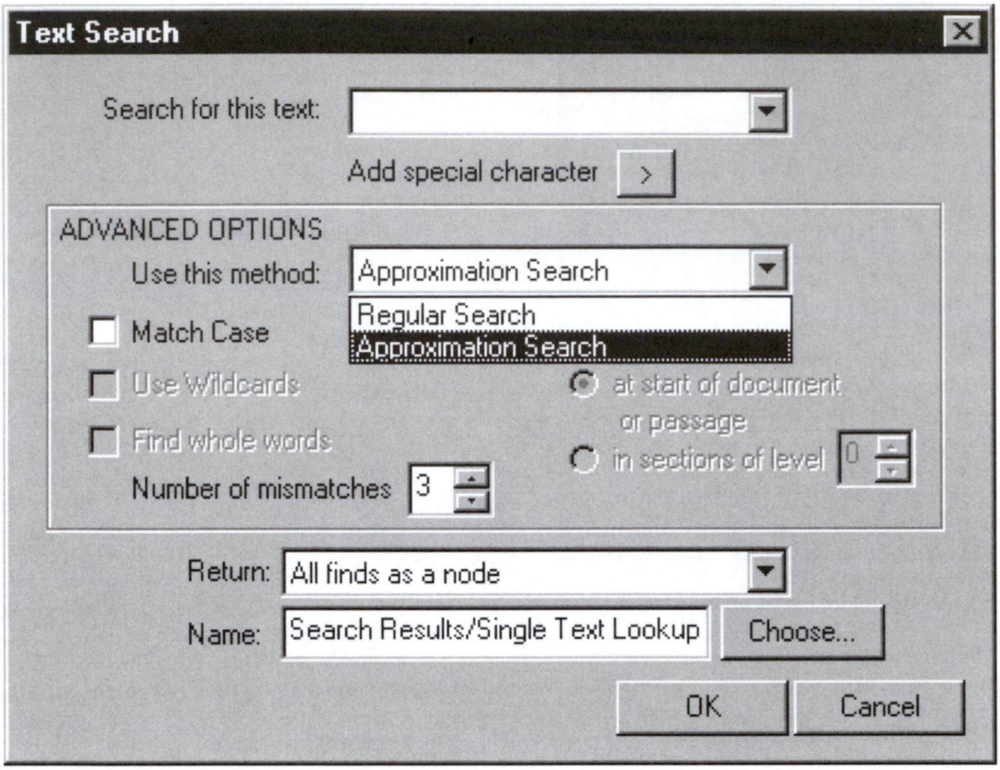

Figure 19.21   NVivo Text Search window

4   **Boolean Searches:** This type of search (see Figure 19.22) requires at least two operands (selected nodes, attributes or text etc.) to be cross-referenced. A number of different types of Boolean operations can be effected. The text box at the top of the **Boolean Search** window offers a range of Boolean search forms. Intersection [And] searches collate all document texts where the selected items are all present. Only text referenced by all the selected operands will be selected. Union [Or] searches bring together all text referenced by any one or more of the selected operands. There is no need for all the selected operands' references to overlap. Negation [Not] searches collate all text not referenced by any of the one or more operands selected. Difference [Less] searches have two panes rather than one into which one or more operands can be entered. The search returns only text referenced by the operand(s) in the top pane but which are not referenced by the operand(s) in the bottom pane. An example would be all students in student housing minus all those under 21.

Intersection, union and negation search windows have only one pane, while difference and matrix windows have two identical panes. There are two Matrix Boolean search forms (matrix intersection and matrix difference). In both instances, what is produced is a table identifying the number of instances when the selected operands either intersect or differ as specified in the search request. Right-click on any of the cells with results to browse the nodes containing the text for that particular cross-tabulation.

A Boolean matrix intersection search allows cross-referencing between three or more operands. One or more operands can be entered in the top pane, and one or more operands are entered in the lower pane. The outcome is a series of paired results. The first operand in the top pane is cross-referenced with each of the operands from the lower pane to produce a series of outputs. If there are other operands in the top pane, these are then also cross-referenced against each of the lower pane operands.

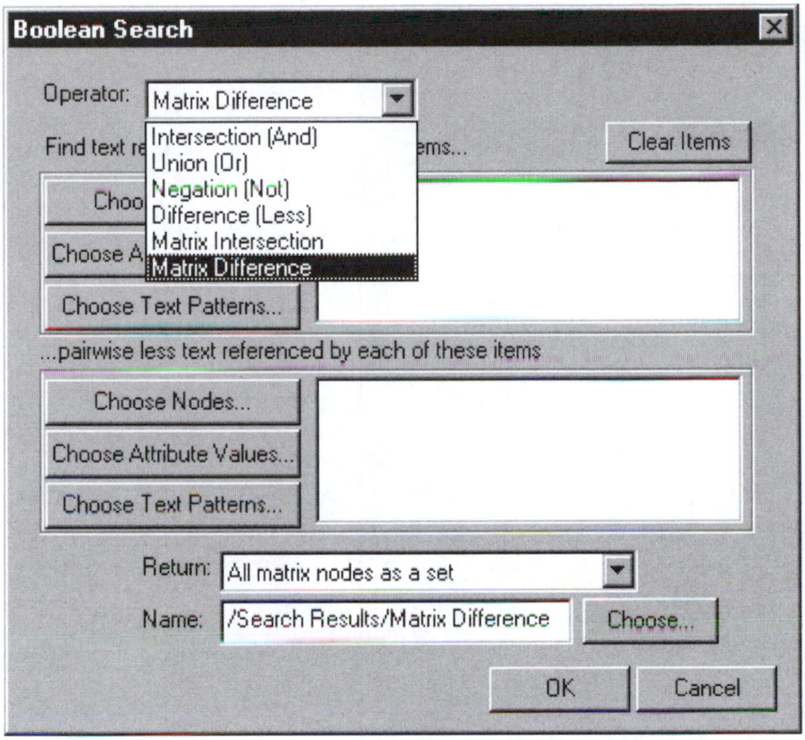

Figure 19.22 NVivo Boolean Search window

A Boolean matrix difference search requires at least one operand in the top pane and at least one in the lower pane. Text referenced by items in the top pane but not referenced by items in the lower pane is collated, then the cross between the first top pane operand and the next lower pane operand is collated and so on.

5 **Proximity Searching:** This type of search (see Figure 19.23) enables the researcher to collate passages in which text referenced by two operands (whether these are nodes, attributes or text) occurs within a specified distance of each other. The nature of the relationship being sought can be specified using the **Operator** text box (co-occurrence [Near], sequence [Preceding] or inclusion [Surrounding] and three matrix search options of the preceding kind). The operands to be used are selected in using upper and lower panes (choosing between nodes, attributes and text). The permitted distance between instances that the researcher considers close enough to count as 'proximity' (within each scope item) is

selected separately for documents and for nodes towards the bottom of the **Proximity Search** window. Finally, you can choose whether to include the text referenced by the first operand, by the second operand, the text in-between them, or any combination of these.

Defining search scope

Once the type of search to be conducted has been selected and the search content specified, you have the opportunity to specify exactly where the search will be conducted – the 'scope' of the search. This is done in the middle section of the **Search Tool** window. As has already been mentioned, the default option is to search all documents and/or nodes, but it is in this section of the window that it is possible to edit the search scope to the researcher's specifications if necessary.

Assay

The **Assay Scope** function accessed from the **Search Tool** window allows the researcher to find

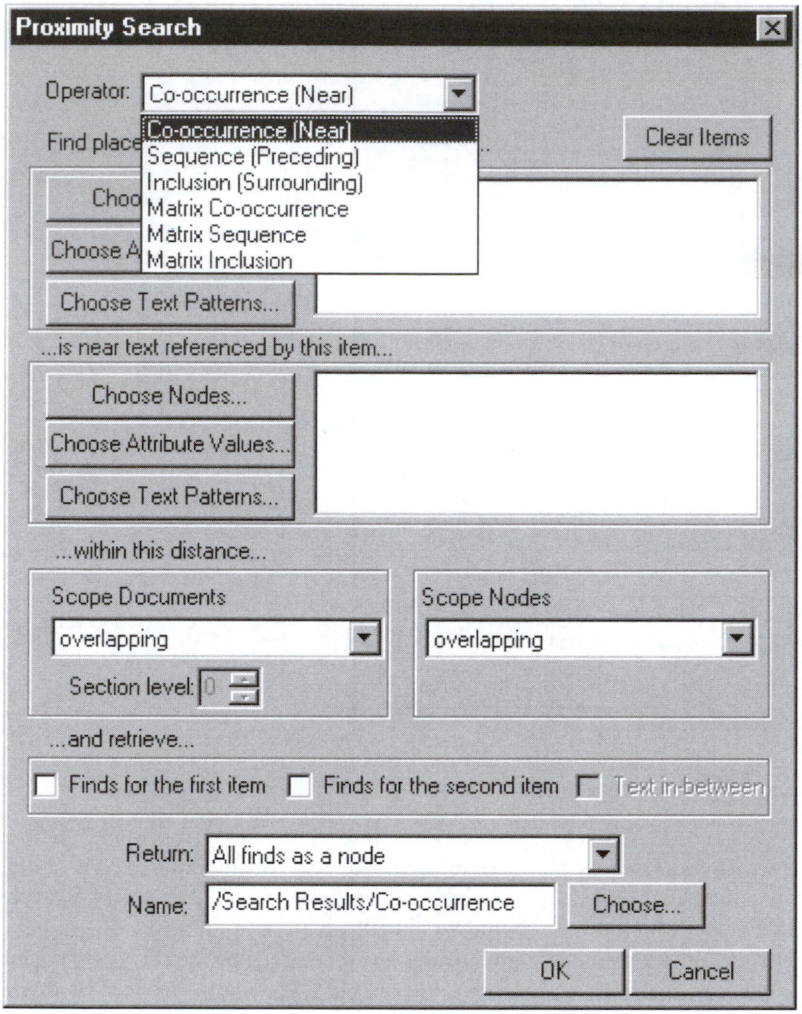

Figure 19.23   NVivo Proximity Search window

the characteristics of any scope. It is possible to make a profile matrix diagram showing the extent to which references exist between selected operands (nodes, attributes and/or textual materials) and scope items. Highlight those operands in the left pane of the **Assay Scope** window and you will see the number and proportion of the document that have that characteristic. Move them to the right pane by means of the **Item** button in the central column of the window. Finally, click the **Make Assay Profile** button. The consequent matrix diagram will show results with scope items as rows and **assay** items as columns. The number or empty space displayed in each intersection represents the presence or the non-

presence of the selected assay (column) item within that document (row).

How results are displayed

Once the search form, the search operands and the search scope have been selected, one last thing should be specified before it is possible to click the **Run Search** key. This is to specify 'spread'. Spread refers to the degree of context to be displayed around each operand. If a node is searched for, how much of the text surrounding each instance does the researcher want to be presented? Options available range from no context to the surrounding paragraph through to the whole document. The default format is to save the results in node form. A single node, attribute or text item search will generate a single node containing all the results. This will be saved to within a tree structure called **Search Results**. The researcher is required to assign names to the files. In advanced search forms, where more than one operand is being crossed with others, the results are saved as a set under the title **Search Results Set**. For matrix operations the results are saved as a tree structure containing nodes for each cross-tabulation. A range of custom display options exist. These can be explored as the researcher becomes more familiar with the software.

N6 contains very much the same range of search operators. Text, node, Boolean (simple and matrix form) and Proximity searches are all directly available. As N6 does not support the creation of Attributes, searches are of coding of text. Recall Figure 19.3. The N6 **Project Pad** contains three folders (Documents, Nodes and Commands). With the **Documents** folder highlighted, clicking the **Search Text of Documents** icon opens the **Text Search** window. This is in all major respects the same as that in NVivo. It should, however, be noted that what NVivo refers to as 'wildcards' (and sometimes as 'special characters') is only referred to as 'special characters' in N6. Node searches can be carried out from the **Node Explorer** window. To conduct Boolean and Proximity searches, click on the **Search and Compare Nodes** in the **Node** folder of the **Project Pad** (see Figure 19.24). Figure 19.24 shows the Boolean folder highlighted. The Boolean folder offers the same four search types as are available in NVivo, plus an **Overlap** search option (the same as an intersection search, but which displays the coded text of intersecting nodes rather than just that part of the text that intersects). It is also possible to conduct a single node search from this folder (using the **Just-one** option). Highlighting the **Proximity** folder in the **Search and Compare Nodes** window provides a range of proximity search options. The **Near** search options is like that described for NVivo above. The **If-inside** and **If-outside** options parallel the search form that NVivo refers to as a **Surrounding** search. The **Followed-by**

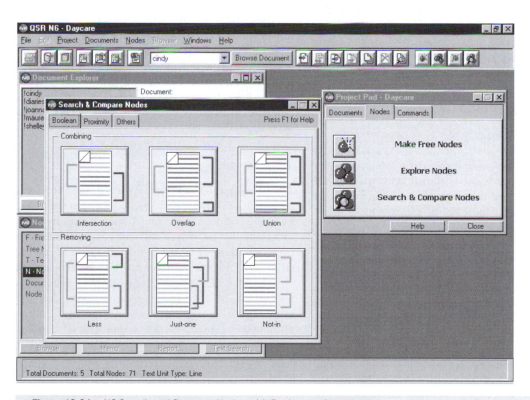

Figure 19.24   N6 Search and Compare Nodes with Boolean option selected

search option in N6 parallels the **Preceeding** search option in NVivo. In addition, N6 offers an **At-least** search option that allows the researcher to search for clusters of references where a specified number of references to a defined range of options is searched for. For more guidance select an option and press the F1 key for details from the help menus. Matrix searches can be selected from the **Others** folder in **the Search and Compare Nodes** window. A **Vector** search is a matrix search where one operand is chosen and its cross-tabulations with a range of other operands is searched. The **Matrix** search option allows for a matrix search cross-tabulating a range of operands with a range of other operands. Other searches can be selected. Use the F1 option to explore these, or consult the software reference guidance.

Analysis?

What NVivo/N6 is able to do is allow the researcher to explore the relationships that exist within their data. What it is best able to do is to allow clearer presentation of patterns within what is often complex and tangled textual material. This is the meaning of analysis in this context. What the term 'analysis' does not mean in this context is the intellectual process of identifying what such patterns might mean and whether or not they are significant. This is still the task of the researcher.

Alternative QDA software

NVivo/N6 are certainly the most popular dedicated qualitative data analysis software. However, this does not, by definition, make it the best package for every person or for every job. Different tasks may require different tools, and different users may find different software packages more to their taste. One thing to remember is that much of the elementary work of qualitative data analysis can be done just as easily using a word-processing file as it can using a dedicated software package. If you do not want more than basic word and phrase searching, then there is little value in investing in QDA software. Similarly, if you have only a very small amount of data, analysis by means of reading and re-reading the data, making memos by hand and squint analysis followed up by written reflections upon the findings may give as much insight as any software. Still, dedicated software has its uses and here two other QDA software packages will be briefly mentioned.

ATLAS.ti

This software package is in many respects similar to the NVivo/N6 software. What makes ATLAS a little different is the emphasis given in its design to the analysis of graphical, image and audio file data. The construction of files, coding, memos and searching are all supported within ATLAS, as they are in NVivo and N6. What ATLAS focuses upon is the capacity to index a number of graphical, image, textual and/or audio files within a project for the purpose of coding, searching and analysing. NVivo/N6 files are text files in the more limited sense of the term text (that is, just written words – without scope to import even formatting conventions). Most of what NVivo/N6 is designed to allow analysis of is just plain text. NVivo, however, does allow for any document to contain hyperlinks to files which are themselves not able to be imported into NVivo itself. These documents can then be given content that describes and records the key features of the original file. And the links can be coded and assessed to bring up the picture, video and so on. This is much the same as what ATLAS enables. Through ATLAS it is possible to apply codes to specific non-text files, and then to search these codes for patterns. While this attention to the searching of non-text files is smoother in ATLAS than in NVivo/N6, it is not something that cannot be paralleled in either. The reverse is also true. ATLAS allows the researcher to carry out processes similar to the coding, memoing and searching procedures available in NVivo/N6. For further details go to www.atlasti.de.

The Ethnograph

The Ethnograph in its original format was one of the earliest QDA software packages and retains some of the earlier simplicity of formatting that sets it apart from the more complex formats of software packages that try to offer everything all in one. The Ethnograph allows the creation of projects, the importing, creation, storage and indexing of files, coding of those files, the creation of a code book of free and tree-based codes, and the searching of the project's files for patterns in the distribution of codes. It is not as complex and offers less additional functions, but is quick to learn and use. For more information go to www.scolari.co.uk/ethnograph.

Summary

Qualitative computer software enables the researcher to manage large amounts of textual data and to conduct forms of content analysis. The forms of content analysis that such software can facilitate cover the spectrum from highly deductive forms of quantitative content analysis to highly inductive forms of qualitative research. In each instance data analysis involves making a link between codes and particular instances of text within the data. Links and patterns between items coded in such a way can then be highlighted, mapped and modelled using various functions within the software. While qualitative data analysis software offers speed and efficiency in the mapping of large quantities of textual data, it is still the case that the process of coding requires that the researcher works through their data files, making the links that will then form the basis for analysis. Computer assisted qualitative data analysis is still a labour-intensive activity. In addition, while computer-assisted qualitative data analysis offers speed and efficiency in the coding and exploration of large quantities of textual data, such software cannot 'analyse' data in either the philosophical sense of drawing logical and meaningful conclusions from data, nor in the mathematical/statistical sense of providing clear, simple formulas or numerical patterns that 'sum up' the data. In so far as many qualitative researchers are suspicious of any attempt to reduce the social world down in such a way, this may not be seen as a problem. To the extent that such software may encourage the researcher to search for simplistic patterns in large quantities of data, some fear the creeping encroachment of a quantitative mentality into qualitative research. Others welcome such a move. The essential first step in such debates is to be informed enough to decide for yourself.

Keywords

Assay	Data Collection	Nodes
Attributes	Deduction	NUD*IST
Categories	Epistemology	NVivo/N6
Coding	Induction	Qualitative
Content Analysis	Matrix Display	Values
Data	Memos	
Data Analysis	Models	

Questions

1   What are the seven basic steps in the conduct of qualitative data analysis using NVivo?
2   What other qualitative data analysis software is available besides NVivo? You may wish to consult the World Wide Web to extend your answer to this question.
3   What are the strengths, limitations and dangers of using computer software packages designed to assist in the conduct of qualitative data analysis?
4   What forms of qualitative data analysis are best suited to the use of qualitative data analysis software?
5   When might it be as useful simply to use word processing packages to search through text files, rather than to use a dedicated qualitative data analysis software package?

Further reading

Bazeley, Patricia and Richards, Lyn (2000) *The NVivo Qualitative Project Book*. London: Sage.

Fielding, Nigel and Lee, Raymond (1998) *Computer Analysis and Qualitative Research*. London: Sage.

Richards, Lyn (2002a) *Using NVivo in Qualitative Research*. London: Sage.

Richards, Lyn (2002b) *Using N6 in Qualitative Research*. London: Sage.

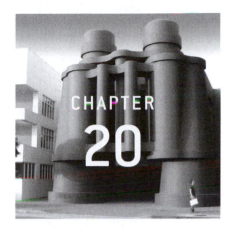

CHAPTER

20

INTRODUCTION TO
QUANTITATIVE DATA ANALYSIS

Chapter contents

By the end of this chapter you will be able to:

- Describe the data analysis process.

- Create and define new variables in SPSS.

- Understand the potential for data entry errors.

Quantitative Data Analysis

The analysis of **quantitative** data is also known as social statistics and is accompanied by a range of statistical and analytical terminology. The analysis process involves the researcher gaining an understanding of the data collected and exploring causal links between different elements of the data. It is very easy for a researcher when experiencing for the first time the process of social research to become too focused on the technical aspects of the data analysis, rather than reflect on how these aspects relate to the original purposes of the research. The application of statistical techniques should be undertaken within the understanding of the overall research aims and design. From a deductive approach this may involve the exploration of the data in relation to hypotheses established from the original research question. Alternatively, a more 'fluid' analysis strategy may be adopted that focuses on exploring the data and describing the relationships. Issues of sampling are important when using inferential statistical tests. Random or probability samples, where each unit has an equal chance of selection, will enable the calculation of population estimates of particular values from the sample data. The operationalization of concepts will have entailed the development of measurement tools and indicators. Where multiple indicators have been developed the analysis process will involve assessing each indicator in turn and possibly merging the indicators into a single scale. For example, in the case study in Chapter 5 examining rural deprivation, quantitative data was collected on a number of measures that were taken as indicators of rural deprivation. These included the availability of buses, location of post offices, household income and benefit claimants. A combination of these and other measures were then used to create indices of multiple deprivation. Both the indicators and indices provide a measure of rural deprivation for different geographical areas.

The analysis of quantitative data should not be seen solely as the preserve of a quantitative research approach. There may be occasions within qualitative research when it would be useful to collate elements of the data together for descriptive and statistical analysis.

For example, in the qualitative aspect of the research into rural deprivation, semi-structured interviews were conducted with people living in small villages. In addition to the researcher asking questions about the experience of rural daily living, information on household income and expenditure were collected. It is this data that could then be coded numerically and analysed accordingly.

The process of quantitative data analysis involves the key stages of:

- data entry;
- univariate analysis, the examination of individual variables;
- bivariate analysis, the describing and exploring of relationships between two variables;
- multivariate analysis, the expansion of the analysis to three or more variables; and
- statistical testing to enable judgements as to the generalizability of sample findings to the population.

In the quantitative data analysis chapters (20–24) a distinction will be drawn between the 'technical' or 'doing' aspects of the analysis process and the higher level understanding and reflection on why and when the analysis is appropriate. Particularly, attention shall be given to the exploration of causality when exploring relationships. The strength of relationships can be assessed by measures of associations. Inferential statistics allow the researcher to assess the likelihood of survey findings being found in the population through hypothesis and significance testing.

Quantitative data analysis software

There are a number of specialist software applications available to support quantitative data analysis. These include Minitab for Windows, **SPSS** for Windows and SAS for Windows. Details of each of these packages can be found at the company websites of www.minitab.com , www.spss.com and www.sas.com respectively. In an academic setting the choice of software package is often between SPSS and Minitab. In terms of basic analysis, there is little difference in the operational characteristics of these two. The main difference comes in the ability of SPSS to manage **variables** collected from multiple answer questions and arrange these into sets for analysis purposes. The data management techniques are also greater in SPSS, with additional modules of specialist features available. However, these additional features come at a cost, resulting in SPSS being out of the financial reach of individuals. Academic institutions are able to offer these packages for student use as part of their course of study. Contact the computing service at your host institutions for further information on availability.

SPSS is generally the software application most used by business, market reserachers and social researchers. As a result of this and the authors' belief that SPSS is the most versatile package available, in each of the following sections reference will be made to the relevant SPSS for Windows v11 commands. An overview of the structure of SPSS for Windows will be made. At the time of writing there are a number of different versions of SPSS for Windows: v9.0, v10, v10.1 and the latest v11. Essentially, these versions are almost identical so although the following instructions are written for v11 the commands will be relevant to the earlier versions. It is also likely that subsequent versions will be developed. Notwithstanding a complete overhaul of the SPSS program, it is probable that the commands in this book will still be largely relevant to future versions. Commands may alter in wording slightly or their positions in menus changed, but mostly the reader should be able intuitively to find the relevant command without difficulty.

If specialist software such as SPSS and Minitab are not available to you, it is possible to undertake much of the basic analysis outlined in this chapter using the spreadsheet package Microsoft Excel. There are a number of texts currently in print that outline Excel procedures for the following types of analysis.

Data entry

The first stage in analysing data collected from a survey is to enter the survey responses as coded data into a SPSS data file. This process requires an understanding of variables, levels of measurement and coding (Chapter 12 and 'Developing a code book' p. 181).

In primary data collection the **data entry** process consists of creating a data file. The format of the data file is that responses are entered into variables. Variables are placed in columns. A set of responses for each record, for example, an individual or household, are called **cases**. Cases are placed in rows. Variables run across the data file in columns and cases run down the data file in rows. In Table 20.1 an example of the structure of a data file is shown. The data file in Table 20.1 displays the responses of five individuals (the cases) to three questions relating to their sex, age and current primary working status (the variables). Note also that an additional variable has been included 'IdCase' that codes an identifying number for each case. It is good practice to always include such a variable in a data file as it enables entered data to be cross-checked with the original questionnaire or interview responses at a later date. Without the inclusion of the identification variable it becomes difficult to track back cases to the original response.

Table 20.1   Example data file format

Id Case	Sex	Age	Work status
1	Female	25	Full-time employed
2	Male	20	Student
3	Male	28	Full-time employed
4	Male	40	Part-time employed
5	Female	65	Retired

While it is technically possible to enter individual responses to each question as text, for example, for the variable 'sex' the responses would be 'female' or 'male', the normal practice is to numerically code the responses for each variable. Instead of entering the text 'female' a code of 1 would be entered, likewise for 'male' a code of 2 would be entered. This not only reduces the amount of time required for data entry, it also reduces the size of the data file. In addition – and the most important reason – is that by converting the responses to a numeric value it extends the range of statistical analysis procedures open to the researcher. This process of **coding** is just one of a number of aspects of quantitative research that can be uncomfortable to the social researcher as concerns are expressed over the reduction of an individual response to a numeric value. Coding data should never replace the understanding of the original question and why it was asked. The process of coding data involves the creation of a code book (see 'Developing a code book' p. 181). For categorical **variables**, nominal or ordinal, each category response is coded and entered in the data file. For **interval** variables, the numeric value is simply entered into the data file. Taking the extract of a data file shown in Table 20.1 the coded data would be entered, resulting in the data file shown in Table 20.2. The coding frame used was:

Variable: Sex, Codes: 1 = Female, 2 = Male.
Variable: Age, Codes: enter actual age value.
Variable Work, Codes: 1 = Full-time employed; 2 = Part-time employed; 3 = Retired; 4 = Student.

Table 20.2   Example coded data file

Id Case	Sex	Age	Work status
1	1	25	1
2	2	20	4
3	2	28	1
4	2	40	2
5	1	65	3

Which of the following daily newspapers have you read in the last week?

Tick all applicable

Financial Times ☐

New York Times ☐

Washington Post ☐

Melbourne Age ☐

Times of India ☐

South China Morning Post ☐

Le Monde ☐

Other ☐

(Please state) _____

Figure 20.1   Example of a multi response question

Variables for a multiple response question

Many questions will elicit a single response. For example, how old are you? The response would be recorded in years, for example, 23 years. However, some question formats may allow or require the respondent to give more than one response. An example would be a question that asks the respondent to 'tick all relevant' from the list below, or an open question that the researcher then codes after collecting the data, known as post-coding. In these instances the responses need to be clearly broken down into the appropriate number of different variables. The number of different variables required will be determined by how the responses were coded (see 'Coding for multiple response questions' p. 182). At a later stage in the process, these variables can be placed together in a **multiple response set** for analysis purposes. Figure 20.1 shows an example of a multiple response question about 'daily newspapers that were read in the last week'. For coding purposes each newspaper is given its own variable and responses are coded as 1, 'Yes' (ticked as read), and 2, 'No' (not ticked and therefore assumed not read).

These variables and corresponding codes for each case are entered into a data file, as shown in Table 20.3. As can be seen, the standard format of variables placed in columns and case responses in rows applies.

Concerns are sometimes expressed about accidentally underestimating the number of variables required for a multiple response question, particularly if one is not using the 'Yes or 'No' format. This, however, is not a problem as it is easy to insert an additional variable into a data set at a later date.

Data entry errors

It is important to be aware that during the data entry process it is possible for the researcher to make a data entry error by entering the incorrect code. Due care and attention to detail are essential. An error at the data entry stage could remain undetected or hidden

Table 20.3   Example data entry of a multiple response question

Financial Times	New York Times	Washington Post	Melbourne Age	Times of India	South China Morning Post	Le Monde	Other
2	2	1	2	2	2	1	2
2	2	2	2	2	2	2	2
1	2	2	2	2	2	2	2

until the later stages of the data analysis process, or simply never discovered.

There are a number of checks that can be undertaken once the data entry is completed to search the data for potential errors, and subsequently edit the entry. The most common, and easiest, data entry error to detect is when a code is entered that falls outside the expected range for that variable. For a nominal or ordinal variable the coding frame will state that the codes should run from a minimum value, for example, 1 for 'Male', to a maximum value, for example, 2 for 'Female', with specific missing value codes, for example –99 for 'Did not respond'. An entered value which does not meet these conditions, also known as a wild code, for example a value of 3, should trigger an investigation by the researcher. In the case of primary data collection this will involve a referral back to the original questionnaire or interview response. Other data errors may come to light because of the researcher's knowledge of the entire research project and particular sample characteristics. For example, a study of young people's voting preferences focused on a sample of 18 to 25-year-olds. The age of the respondent was recorded and for one case an age of 52 was entered, clearly incorrect if the sample complied to the age range of 18 to 25-year-olds.

Locating data entry errors that fall outside of the expected range is most easily achieved by being vigilant when entering data. As the code for each case is entered, glance at the preceding case's entry, that is, the row above.

Data entry errors that are the most difficult to detect are those that fall within the existing expected coded range but are incorrect. For example, when coding the sex of a case the entered code is 2 for Male, when in fact the respondent was female and a code of 1 should have been entered. The only way of minimizing these types of error is to double, or even triple, check your data entry. The time constraints of the research project will inevitably determine the feasibility of undertaking this type of re-checking. Beyond this, though, one can remain vigilant to the possibility of these types of entry errors by scanning the data file for inconsistencies when both entering and analysing the data. For example, in a survey focusing on the ill-health of patients attending a general practice, the sex of the respondent was recorded together with the presenting health issue. Unknown to the researcher, for one respondent the sex had been incorrectly recorded as male when it should have been female. This respondent was

presenting with a gynaecological problem. Analysis of the sex variable would not reveal this error, neither would analysis of the presenting ill-health variable. However, analysis of the relationship between the sex variable and the ill-health variable in a contingency table (see 'Contingency tables' p. 295 for further discussion) would reveal that there was one male respondent suffering from gynaecological problems. Other logical inconsistencies can occur with routing questions, for example, has someone ticked 'No' to a routing question that would then involve them not completing a number of questions, but has then completed these questions? Maybe the original routing question should have been ticked as 'Yes'.

If the researcher suspects that there may be inconsistencies in the data, then analysis of the relationships between two categorical variables using a contingency table can be carried out. Often these inconsistencies will only present after the researcher has undertaken a fair amount of analysis. Once the error is detected and corrected or removed, the change to the variable will require existing analysis to be undertaken again.

Correcting the error will involve referral back to the original data collection source, for example, a survey questionnaire. As long as each case has been given a unique identification number which has been entered as a variable (for example, Id) in the data file it is easy to relate the error back to the correct case. If the identification number of the original case has not been recorded or if access to the original data collection tool is not possible, for example, in the case of secondary data sources (see below), then the only course of action is to re-code the entry as missing data.

Using secondary data sources

When using a secondary data source, for example, a data file obtained from the Data Archive, Essex University, the process will involve obtaining the data file, which is generally in a SPSS file format, together with the relevant code book and survey information. The data file can be opened in SPSS for analysis. One should not assume that the file is 'clean' and must be alert to possible inconsistencies and errors. Although the researcher has not actually entered the data, the same process of checking the data should be undertaken. The additional benefit of doing this is that it will also familiarize the researcher with the data file before undertaking any analysis.

Where the researcher does not have access to the

original survey paperwork, data entry errors can be removed from subsequent analysis by re-coding that particular case as missing. Good practice would be to re-code such values as a new missing value in order to distinguish it from other types of missing value.

Familiarization with SPSS for Windows

This section contains a brief introduction to the key elements of SPSS for Windows v11. It is designed to familiarize you with the layout and overall structure of SPSS before proceeding to the process of creating a data file in SPSS and entering coded data. Earlier versions of SPSS for Windows are very similar to v11 and the majority of commands and instructions in this chapter will be appropriate to these versions.

Starting SPSS for Windows

If the SPSS application is stored on your own PC, you will be able to open it from the **Start** button. Alternatively, if you are using SPSS from a network service, for example, a university network, then you will need to refer to local instructions for accessing the application.

SPSS for Windows creates a number of different windows that the user will switch between depending on the data management or analysis task undertaken.

When the SPSS application is first opened the default setting is to display a new **Data editor** window. The **Data editor** is where coded survey data is inputted and stored. The data window is saved to files that are automatically given a **SAV** file extension. The data file must be retrieved at the beginning of each SPSS session in order for data management and analysis to begin. The data window itself is divided into two views: the data view contains the coded data and the variable view contains information on each of the variables in the data file.

The results of statistical and data analysis procedures are displayed in the **Viewer** window. The viewer is divided into two frames: the left frame is the index to the viewer's contents, with the actual contents displayed in the right frame. Each frame can be navigated using the respective scroll bars. Results in this window are saved to files that have a **SPO** file extension.

In addition to the **Data** editor and **Viewer** window one can also create SPSS syntax files. These windows are where files containing SPSS commands can be

compiled and are generally used when undertaking complex statistical calculations that are repeated over time. A syntax window is saved to files with a **SPS** file extension. The use of SPSS syntax files will not be covered in this text.

One can move between the different windows by selecting the required window from the taskbar or alternatively from the Window menu.

The majority of SPSS commands are contained within the menus at the top of the screen. The menus alter depending on the active or current window. A brief description of each of the menus and the window(s) they are associated with is shown in Table 20.4.

Data entry using SPSS for Windows

This section contains details on creating a new data file in SPSS. It will cover the following topics: defining a new variable, saving the data file, importing existing data files and other data file formats. If you have not already done so, open the SPSS application from the **Start** menu button. Your local set-up will determine the exact location of SPSS in the menus. SPSS will automatically open a new blank data file. If a dialog box opens asking 'What you would like to do?' click on **Cancel**.

Creating a new SPSS data file

The first step in creating a new data file is to define each of the variables. SPSS requires a **variable name** to be assigned to each variable. The name can be up to eight characters in length. It must not contain any mathematical operators (* / + - =), blank spaces or punctuation marks (/; :, .).

A **variable name** can directly reflect the variable itself, for example, Age, Gender. If there are many variables it may be advantageous to give a variable name relating to the question number, for example, Q1, Q2, Q3a, Q3b.

A **variable label** can be assigned to each variable. Unlike the variable name that is restricted to eight characters, the variable label can be longer, allowing for a more detailed description. The maximum variable label permitted is 255 characters.

The type of data can be defined and for coded data this would be numeric, but other data types including text, dates and currency are available.

The format of the data type can be defined. For

Table 20.4   Description of SPSS menus

Menu	Description
File menu (All windows)	Commands relating to Opening, Saving and Closing all types of SPSS files. Information retrieval on data files. Printing files. Exiting the SPSS program.
Edit menu (All windows)	Standard Copy, Cut and Paste commands. Search facilities. Page and Output breaks. Preferences for controlling the SPSS session.
Data menu (Data editor window only)	Commands relating to the definition of variables, file management and case selection/weighting.
Transform menu (Data editor window only)	Data transformation commands – computing new variables, re-coding values.
View menu (Viewer window only)	Commands relating to viewing the different elements in the index (left frame).
Insert menu (Viewer window only)	Enables the user to insert different elements into the viewer. For example, inserting page breaks, additional text.
Format menu (Viewer window only)	Controls the alignment of text objects, for example, left, right, centre.
Analyse menu (All windows)	Statistical commands are contained in this menu. For example, Frequencies, Crosstabulations, Descriptive Stats and so on.
Graphs menu (All windows)	A variety of graph commands including bar, line, pie, histogram.
Utilities menu (All windows)	'Other' SPSS facilities including variable information.
Windows menu (All windows)	Use this menu to move between different SPSS windows.
Help menu (All windows)	The SPSS online Help facility.

numeric data you can control the format of the data in terms of the number of decimal places and the actual size or width of the number. The default setting is to have a width of eight and two decimal places. If the codes for nominal and ordinal variables are whole numbers, then it is good practice to set the number of decimal places to zero for these variables. If codes range from 0 to 9, then the width can be set to 1. Remember that the width will need to be greater if missing values are to be included. For example, using –99 to represent missing values requires a column width of three. Other data types are also available, including dates, scientific and string formats.

For nominal and ordinal variables, value labels can be assigned to define each of the categories. While it is not essential to allocate value labels, they will appear in the results, aiding interpretation and presentation. If value labels are not assigned, the code will be displayed. Value labels should also be included for missing codes.

The format of the column refers to how wide the column appears in the **Data View**. While not essential, it can be a useful feature to maximize the number of variable columns displayed at any one time in the window.

The appropriate **level of measurement** can be assigned to each variable, scale (interval or **ratio**), ordinal or nominal.

Defining a new variable

The first stage is to define each of the variables in the data file. Switch to the **Variable View** window (Figure 20.2). Each variable will be defined in the row. For each row there are 10 columns that define the variable: name, type, width, decimals, label, values, missing, columns, align, and measure. The list order of variables in the **Variable View** will be the order that they appear in each column in the **Data View**.

To define a new variable in **Variable View**, click in the first empty cell under the **Name** column. Enter a variable name, for example, sex.

Click, or use the tab key, to move to the **Type**

column. The default setting is numeric. To alter to a different type, click on the small square with three dots that appears in the cell when you have selected the **Type** column. A **Variable Type** dialog box will be displayed; select the required type and click on **OK** to close the box. Most survey data is converted into numeric codes. It is possible in SPSS to create alphanumeric or string, currency, scientific notation, dates and times type variables.

Again click, or use the tab key, to move to the **Width** column. The width controls the maximum number of digits that can be entered for a value. For example, if the numeric codes ran from 1 to 12 with −99 as the missing value, then the minimum required width would be three: [-] [9] [9]. If the variable was storing values to two decimal places, for example, a weekly salary recorded in dollars/cents or pounds/pence sterling, was 322.45 the width required would be five: [3] [2] [2] . [4] [5].

In the **Decimals** column the number of decimal places of the code can be set. In the case of coding

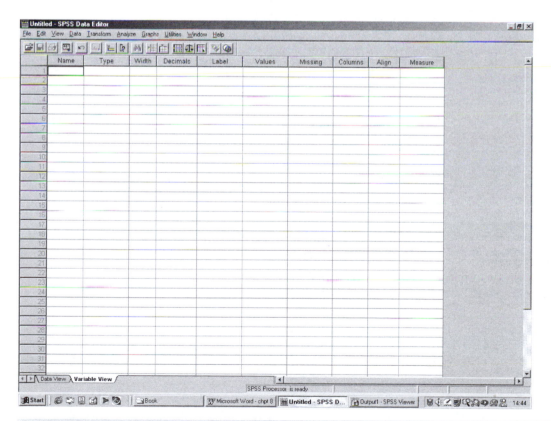

Figure 20.2   Define variable in the SPSS Variable View window

263

using only whole numbers, the decimal places can be set to zero by typing 0 into the cell. It is acceptable to leave the default setting of two decimal places as this will not affect future analysis; however, it does allow for the possibility of an accidental data entry error. For example, typing in 1.1 when 1 was required.

The column **Label** is where the variable label is entered. For example, 'sex of respondent'.

The column **Value** is where the **value labels** for categories in nominal or ordinal variables can be assigned. Value labels can be set for both valid and missing codes. To enter value labels, click on the small square that appears when you move the value column. A **Value Labels** box will appear (Figure 20.3).

To enter value labels, first click in the box next to **Value:** and enter the code of the first category, for example, 1. Next click in the box next to **Value Label:**

and enter the value label for that code, for example, Female. Now click on **Add**. Repeat this process to enter value labels for all categories in the current variable. Labels can be edited by highlighting them in the list. Edit the code or label accordingly and then click on **Change**. Labels can be deleted by highlighting the required variable and clicking once on **Remove**. Once completed, click **OK** to return to the **Variable View**. Value labels cannot be set for interval/ratio variables as the data is continuous.

The **Missing** column is used to define missing values. **Missing values** are codes that have been used to define non-response. The coding frame will contain details of the non-response codes. For the current variable, click once in the **Missing** column and then click on the **small square** that appears in the cell. The **Missing Values** box will be displayed (Figure 20.4).

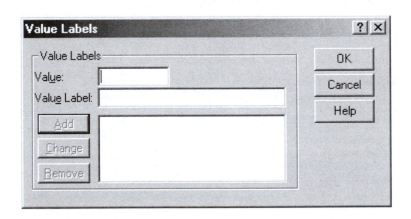

Figure 20.3   SPSS Value Labels dialog box

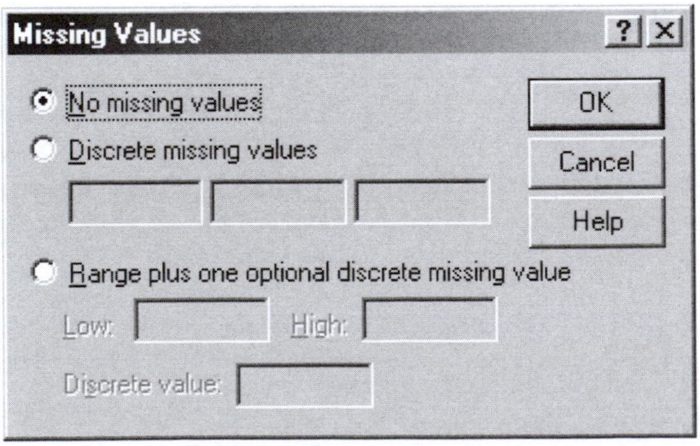

Figure 20.4   SPSS Missing Values dialog box

There are a number of options for defining missing values. The default setting is 'No missing values'. There are two different ways of defining missing values. The first is to define up to three discrete missing values. The second is to define a range of missing values that could include one discrete outside the defined range. Select the combination that best suits the type of missing codes you wish to define. Where there are one to three missing values, the first option should suffice. Where there are more than three missing values, ensure that the codes are sequential (for example, -6, -7, -8, -9) and use the second, define range, option. When the missing values have been defined, click on **OK** to return to the **Variable View**. In order to distinguish between different types of missing values in the final results, remember to assign a value label to each of the codes; see the section above on value labels.

The **Columns** and **Align** columns allow the width of the column and the alignment of the codes to be defined. It is normally sufficient to leave these on their default setting, but can be altered to aid data entry. Finally, in the **Measure** column the level of measurement for each variable can be defined by selecting the appropriate option. The options are Scale (interval/ratio), Ordinal and Nominal.

Once the variable has been set up, click on the next row down in the **Name** column to continue the variable definition process for each of the variables in the code book.

Saving the data file

To save the data file, select the **File** menu and **Save**. Alternatively, click on the floppy disk icon. In the dialog box select the directory or floppy disk in which you wish to save the data file. Enter a new file name in the **File Name** box. Click on **Save**.

Importing existing data files

Analysis of an existing data file can be undertaken in SPSS. How the data file is imported into SPSS will be determined by the format of the data file. The increasing use of SPSS as a data management and analysis tool has resulted in many data files being available as either a SPSS or SPSS portable data file format. It is, however, possible to import data that has initially been stored in other applications. SPSS has filters that will enable it to read in data from file formats that include MS Excel, symbolic link files and MS Access. Where no direct filter exists, it is often possible to write out the data from the original application into one of these file formats.

Many data archives are now able to provide data in a SPSS portable file format. This format can easily be imported into any version of SPSS. It will contain the data, together with the variable definitions. Use of secondary data files must always be undertaken in conjunction with the originator's code book and knowledge of the research objectives of the initial project. SPSS portable files can be opened in SPSS in the same way as other SPSS data files. To open a file in a different format, select the **File** menu and **Open > Data**. In the dialog box from the **Files of Type** box, alter the type to **SPSS Portable.[*.Por]**. Locate the directory or floppy disk for the file. Highlight the file and click on **Open**.

Other data file formats

In a SPSS data file the data is held in a matrix format consisting of rows containing cases and columns containing the coded data in a variable. This matrix format is common to most data files and is accepted by most of the data analysis applications available. Generic file formats accepted by SPSS include tab delimited, comma separated and space separated. A variety of file formats specific to other spreadsheet and database package formats are also accepted and include Lotus, dBase, SLK, SAS, Systat and MS Excel. SPSS v11 reads all MS Excel file formats. However, for versions MSExcel 95 and later, if there is more than one worksheet in the workbook only one worksheet can be read into a single SPSS data file.

Summary

Data entry is the initial stage in the process of analysing survey data. It requires an understanding of variables, levels of measurement and coding. The first phase of data entry in SPSS requires variables to be defined. Many survey questions require a single variable in the data file. Survey questions that produce multiple responses require more than one variable and the social researcher must allocate enough variables for these questions. The development of a thorough code book prior to using SPSS should address these issues. The second phase is the actual entering of data, normally numeric codes, into the data file. Care needs to be taken to ensure that the data entry is as accurate as possible to limit difficulties in the subsequent analysis stages.

Keywords

Case	Multiple Response Set	Value label
Coding	Nominal	Variable label
Data Entry	Ordinal	Variable Name
Interval	Quantitative	Variable
Level of Measurement	Ratio	
Missing Values	SPSS	

Questions

1 Describe the structure of a SPSS data file.
2 What are the advantages of entering survey data as numerical codes rather than as text?
3 What types of data entry errors can occur and how can you avoid them?
4 Name the different elements of a SPSS variable.

Further reading

Fielding, Jane and Gilbert, Nigel (2000) *Understanding Social Statistics*. London: Sage.

Field, Andy (2000) *Discovering Statistics using SPSS for Windows*. London: Sage.

Kinnear, Richard and Gray, Colin (2000) *SPSS for Windows Made Simple: Release 10*. Hove: Psychology Press.

Rose, David and Sullivan, Oriel (1996) *Introducing Data Analysis for Social Scientists* (2nd edn). Buckingham: Open University Press.

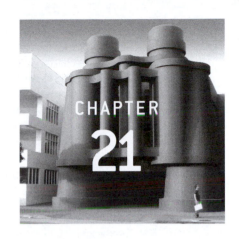

CHAPTER
21

DESCRIBING SINGLE VARIABLES

Chapter contents

By the end of this chapter you will be able to:

- Understand the univariate analysis techniques available for different levels of measurement.

- Analyse categorical variables using frequency tables.

- Use appropriate measures of central tendency and dispersion to summarize the distribution of values.

- Produce standardized scores.

- Produce graphical presentations of data using appropriate charts and graphs.

Describing single variables: univariate analysis

The first stage in the data analysis process is to be able to describe and summarize the single variables in the data set. This analysis uses **descriptive statistics**. It allows the researcher to first detect data entry errors, second to describe and report the data, and third to determine the suitability of the data for possible future statistical testing. Where the data forms a new indicator or measurement tool, the findings can be compared to the results of existing research to provide some preliminary analysis as to the reliability and validity of the measure.

At this stage the researcher should also be thinking about the subsequent analysis of relationships between the **variables**. Preliminary thoughts on these relationships between variables may change as a result of this initial examination. For example, analysis of responses to an attitudinal question may not have resulted in the range of different responses initially anticipated. Instead, the responses are all at the lower end with little variation amongst respondents. Some, though not all, of the initial univariate analysis undertaken will be suitable for inclusion in the final report. The researcher will find that the level and detail of this initial analysis for some variables may be too in-depth for inclusion in the final report, while for other variables it is at an appropriate level for inclusion. At this preliminary stage it is advisable to be thorough in the analysis of the single variables, as it will provide an overall picture from which to focus down on key variables when exploring relationships at subsequent stages.

The level of measurement of each individual variable will guide the **univariate analysis** to be undertaken. This analysis involves selecting from a range of measures including counts, percentages, measurements of distribution and spread, and graphical presentations in chart form. For categorical variables, nominal and ordinal, univariate analysis will initially involve producing a count and percentage of the number of cases that fall within each category. This summary information is presented in a **frequency** table format with the corresponding count and percentage displayed next to each of the categories in

the variable. Graphical presentation of categorical data will involve bar charts and **pie charts**.

For **interval** and **ratio** variables, univariate analysis will begin with establishing the range of values, minimum and maximum, and the calculation of the average or mean value. Appropriate graphical presentation of interval variables will be stem and leaf diagrams, box plots, histograms and line graphs.

Once the basic analysis has been undertaken, the researcher can develop the analysis to look at how the values are spread in each of the variables. For example, are values clustered around one particular value? Are there more men than women in the sample? Are individual incomes clustered within a specific range? Finally, how confident can we be that the findings in our survey, taken from a sample, are representative of the population?

Frequencies and percentages

The starting point in the process of analysing categorical variables, nominal or ordinal, is to produce a frequency count of the number of cases that responded to each of the variable categories. One would normally start by selecting variables that will enable the researcher to describe the sample. For example, gender, marital status, employment status, occupation. From this the variables relating to the key questions can be described and then finally the other variables in the data file.

For example, a frequency count of the variables 'sex' and 'marital status' may reveal that of a sample of 1,500 students, 600 were female and 900 were male; 1,200 students were single, 150 were co-habiting, 50 were married, 40 were divorced or separated and 60 students failed to answer the question, that is, missing data. Such results can be presented in a **frequency table** (see Table 21.1).

A frequency count is limiting in that it will not allow the researcher easily to make comparisons between different samples. For example, if a researcher wanted to compare the marital status distribution of their sample with a past research project which had a different sample size, calculating a percentage will enable such comparisons to be made. The formula for calculating a percentage is shown below:

$$\% = \frac{category\ count}{N} \times 100$$

N is the total number in the sample and category count is the observed value for a particular category.

Table 21.1   Example frequency tables: sex and marital status

Sex	Count		Marital Status	Count
Male	900		Single	1200
Female	600		Co-habiting	150
Total	1500		Married	50
			Divorced	40
			Missing	60

There are three types of **percentage** that can be calculated. The first is based on the total sample size; the second is based on the total number of valid cases for that variable (total sample size minus the number of missing cases for the variable); and the third is a **cumulative percentage**, which is the sum of the valid percentages as one moves down the categories. The default category order is the ascending order of the category codes.

Taking the earlier example of the marital status of the students, Table 21.2 shows the calculated total percent, valid percent and cumulative percent. Formulas for each are shown in brackets.

SPSS will calculate the count, percentage, valid percentage, and cumulative percentage using the Frequencies command.

Using SPSS to produce frequency tables

The first step when undertaking data analysis in SPSS is to open the data file.

To open a data file select the **File** menu and **Open >Data**. In the dialog box select the directory or floppy disk where the file is located. Highlight the data file and click on **Open**.

To calculate a frequency table, select the **Analyze** menu and **Descriptive Statistics > Frequencies**. A frequencies box will be displayed (Figure 21.1).

On the left-hand side of the box, all the variables contained in the opened data file will be displayed. The format shown is the variable label followed by the variable name in square brackets [].

Please note that at the beginning of a SPSS session the **Variable Display** format can be altered to display just the variable name by selecting the **Edit** menu and **Options**. From the **General** sheet under **Variable Lists** select **Display names**. Click on **OK**. Changing this format is one of individual preference and does not effect the analysis process.

The variable from which a frequency table will be produced needs to be moved from the left-hand side to the right-hand side of the box under **Variable(s)**:

Table 21.2   Marital status, count, total percentage, valid percentage and cumulative percentage

Marital status	Count	Total %	Valid %	Cumulative %
Single	1,200	80% (1,200/1,500*100)	83.3% (1,200/1,440*100)	83.3%
Co-habiting	150	10% (150/1,500*100)	10.4% (150/1,440*100)	93.7% (83.3%+10.4%)
Married	50	3.3% (50/1,500*100)	3.5% (50/1,440*100)	97.2% (83.3%+10.4%+3.5%)
Divorced	40	2.7% (40/1,500*100)	2.8% (40/1,400*100)	100% (83.3%+10.4%+3.5%+2.8%)
Missing	60	4% (60/1,500*100)	–	–
Total	1,500		1,440	

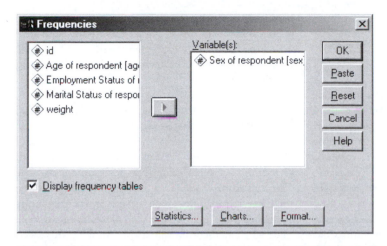

Figure 21.1   SPSS Frequencies dialog box

To move the variable, **highlight the required variable** and click once on the arrow button → to move the variable name to the section under **Variable(s):**. Click on **OK**. In Figure 21.1 the variable is 'Sex of Respondent [Sex]'.

More than one variable can be selected at a time. To select consecutive variables, click and hold on the first variable and drag down the list to highlight the other required variables. To select non-consecutive variables, click on the first variable and then hold down the **Ctrl** key before selecting the other required variables.

The **frequency table** will be calculated and displayed in the **Output Viewer.**

Table 21.3   Example of a SPSS frequency table output: sex of the respondent

Statistics
Sex of respondent

N	Valid	130
	Missing	0

Sex of respondent

		Frequency	Percent	Valid percent	Cumulative percent
Valid	Male	70	53.8	53.8	53.8
	Female	60	46.2	46.2	100.0
	Total	130	100.0	100.0	

Example of a frequency table in SPSS for Windows Viewer Window

Table 21.3 contains an example of the frequency table output in SPSS. Two tables are produced. The first table 'Statistics' displays the number of valid and missing cases for that variable; additional statistical tests, if selected, would also appear in this table.

The second table displays the count and percentages of the variable sex.

The title of the table contains the variable label. In the above example this is 'Sex of respondent'. The value labels are in the first column. In the above example these are 'Male' and 'Female'. The term 'valid' is also displayed next to the value labels to show that these are actual observations for these categories.

Interpreting each of the columns

The 'Frequency' column shows the frequency or count, that is, the number of respondents selecting each category. The 'Percent' column shows the percentage calculated on the total sample count of 130. The Valid percent column shows the percentage based on the total **valid count** excluding the number of missing cases. There are no missing cases for this variable, so the **valid percent** is identical to the percent. The 'Cumulative percent' column shows the cumulative percentage, which simply adds the valid percentages in ascending order. At the bottom of the table the number of missing cases is displayed. This information is important when using the percentage and valid percentage columns. One would normally report the valid percent in a written report.

Second example of a SPSS frequency table

In Table 21.4 there is a second example of a frequency table containing responses to the question 'Which of the following daily newspapers do you normally read?' Unlike in the previous frequency table, this variable does have some missing cases. The first statistics table shows that there are 117 valid cases and 13 missing cases. The second table shows the count, percent, valid percent and cumulative percent for each of the newspaper categories. Since there are 13 missing cases, there is a difference between the percent and valid percent. There are two types of missing data defined: 'Did not respond' and 'Do not read a daily newspaper'. Again, the valid percent would be reported in the results section of a written report.

While it is possible to produce a frequency table for an interval variable, a large sample size will result in a very long table that is difficult for the researcher to make sense of. There are alternative statistical measures that are more applicable to interval variables; these are called **measures of central tendency and dispersion**.

Measures of central tendency

Measures of Central Tendency are concerned with identifying a typical value that best summarizes the distribution of values in a variable. There are three such measures. The **mode** is the most frequently occurring value in a variable. The **median** is the middle value when all the valid values for a variable are placed in ascending order. The **mean**, commonly referred to as the average, is the value derived from adding all the values in the distribution together and dividing by the total number of values. Examples of each measure are shown below.

Table 21.4   Example of a SPSS frequency table output for 'Which of the following daily newspapers do you normally read?'

Statistics
Which of the following daily newspapers do you normally read?

N	Valid	117
	Missing	13

Which of the following daily newspapers do you normally read?

		Frequency	Percent	Valid percent	Cumulative percent
Valid	Financial Times	15	11.5	12.8	12.8
	New York Times	14	10.8	12.0	24.8
	Washington Post	13	10.0	11.1	35.9
	Melbourne Age	11	8.5	9.4	45.3
	Times of India	11	8.5	9.4	54.7
	South China Morning Post	12	9.2	10.3	65.0
	Le Monde	21	16.2	17.9	82.9
	Other	20	15.4	17.1	100.0
	Total	117	90.0	100.0	
Missing	Did not respond	7	5.4		
	Do not read a daily newspaper	6	4.6		
	Total	13	10.0		
Total		130	100.0		

The mode

In this example eleven students have been asked their age in years. The results are:

18   26   24   19   34   33   28   37   28   28   37

From looking at the distribution of values we can ascertain that the most frequently occurring age value is 28 years, recorded three times. Where there are two most frequently occurring values in a distribution, the distribution is referred to as being bi-modal. More than two modes in a distribution are called multi-modal. The use of the mode is fairly limited, due to its focus on the most frequently occurring values and not all values in the distribution.

The median

Taking the same age distribution as in the previous example, the median can be calculated by re-arranging the ages into ascending rank order:

18   19   24   26   28 | 28 | 28   33   34   37   37
                         | 6th |

The middle position in the distribution is the sixth observation as there are five observations either side.

Where there is an even number of observations in a distribution, the middle position will fall between two values. To calculate the median, add the two middle values together and divide by two. In the example below the distribution has been reduced by one to 10:

18   19   24   26 | 28   28 | 28   33   34   37
                    | 5th   6th |
                    | 28+28 /2 |
                    | = 28 |

Like the mode, the calculation of the median is not based on the entire distribution.

The mean

The mean or arithmetic mean is the most frequently used statistical measure of central tendency. In literature it is often written as $\bar{x}$. It is based on the summation of all the values in the distribution divided by the number of occurrences:

$$\bar{x} = \frac{18 + 19 + 24 + 26 + 28 + 28 + 28 + 33 + 34 + 37}{11} = 28.36$$

Using the mode, median and mean

Care should be taken when calculating the measures of central tendency. The level of measurement of the variable should guide the choice of measure. For interval and ratio variables the mode, median and mean can all be calculated, though it is normal just to use the mean. However, one must be aware that as the calculation of the mean is based on all values in the distribution, extreme values, also referred to as **outliers**, at either end of the distribution will severely impact on the mean value. If outliers are identified it may be that the median is a better representation. A common example of where outliers can affect the mean is income.

For ordinal variables the median is a useful measure of central tendency as it is itself based on placing the rank order categories. Depending on the nature of the ordinal variable, it can be appropriate to apply the measurement techniques of interval/ratio variables. These are often applied when dealing with attitudinal scales, especially if they are combined into a single index score (see Likert scales, p. 167).

SPSS will allow you to calculate a mean for a nominal variable such as 'Sex' even though it is not appropriate for this level of measurement. The calculation of the mean is based on the value codes for each category, in this case 1 = male and 2 = female. The mean will fall somewhere between these two values, for example, 1.45. Calculating a mean for a nominal variable is clearly meaningless as you cannot interpret this value. For nominal variables, the coding used for data entry is a convenience and the qualitative nature of the variable should determine the interpretation of the responses, and not just any quantitative statistical analysis that could be calculated from the codes assigned. The mode is the only appropriate measure of central tendency for nominal variables. Examining the frequency table for the category that has the highest count can easily identify the mode.

Measures of dispersion

Measures of central tendency, while providing a summary value of the most typical value in a sample, do not allow the researcher to comment on the distribution of the values. It is not possible to conclude that two samples, which have the same mean value, actually have values distributed in the same way.

Measures of dispersion provide information on how values are spread in a distribution. The following measures of dispersion can be applied to interval or ratio levels of measurement.

The range

When reporting interval/ratio variables one would be interested in the minimum, lowest, and maximum, highest, valid values recorded. From these valid values the **range** can be established. The range is simply the maximum minus the minimum value. For example, in a survey of 100 students the minimum age was 19 years and the maximum age was 55 years. The range would be 36 years (55–19).

For nominal variables the value codes, while having a numerical ascending order, are merely representing categories. Since the categories cannot be placed in any order, it does not make sense to calculate a range. For ordinal variables, the range is already known from the value codes assigned to each category. The range is limited in describing a variable, as it does not convey the most typical value or how the values are distributed within the range. An alternative approach is to calculate the inter quartile range.

The inter quartile range

The inter quartile range (IQR) provides the researcher with more information on how the values within the range are distributed. This is particularly useful for analysing interval variables. It involves placing the values in rank order from lowest to highest, as for the range. The range is then divided into four equal percentiles, or 25 per cent blocks (see Figure 21.2).

The 25th quartile (25 per cent) is Q1, the 50th quartile (50 per cent) is Q2, which is also the median, and the 75th quartile (75 per cent) is Q3. The IQRs are the values that are placed between Q1 and Q3. Unlike the range, which is calculated on the lowest and highest values, thus susceptible to extreme values, the IQR is affected less by possible extreme values. For example, in a survey of 100 students the minimum age was 19 and the maximum age was 55. All 100 ages were placed in rank order from lowest to highest. The 25th percentile was located. The value of age at this 25th percentile was 24. At the 75th percentile the value of age was 45. The IQR is calculated as the difference between 45 years and 24 years. The IQR was therefore 21 years.

Variance

Variance is a commonly used measure of dispersion. Its calculation is based on the mean and involves calculating the distance between each of the values and the mean. Since the mean is derived from these values anyway, it is hardly surprisingly that if you were to sum, or add together, all the distances of values that fall above the mean (+) with all the distances of values that fall below the mean (-), the result would be zero. The statistical fix for this is to square the distances as mathematical convention states that when two negative numbers are multiplied together they become a positive number. The effect of this is to turn all the negative distances that fall below the mean into positive numbers. The full equation for calculating variance (s^2) is:

$$s^2 = \frac{\sum (x_i - \overline{x})^2}{n}$$

x_i = observed value
$\overline{x}$ = mean
n = sample size
Σ = summation (adding all values together).

The larger the variance the further the observed values are dispersed from the mean. A variance of zero would mean that all observed values had the same value as the mean.

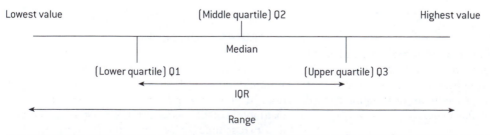

Figure 21.2   The inter quartile range

One of the difficulties with calculating the variance is that because the calculation involves squaring the differences in distance from the mean and the observed value, the resulting values are not in the same units as the original values. This makes interpretation difficult. However, if the variance is then square rooted, this returns the values to the same units. The square root of the variance is known as the 'standard deviation'.

Standard deviation

The calculation for **standard deviation** is:

$$s = \sqrt{\frac{\sum (x_i - \bar{x})^2}{n}}$$

x_i = observed value
$\bar{x}$ = mean
n = sample size
$\sum$ = summation (adding all values together)
$\sqrt{}$ = square root.

Standard deviation units are the same as the original data. For example, if the variable is age recorded in years, the calculated standard deviation can be interpreted as years. Like variance, a large standard deviation means that the data is spread out from the mean, whereas a small standard deviation means that the data is concentrated around the mean. Since variance and standard deviation are based on the mean, and consequently all the observed values for a variable, both are susceptible to extreme values that appear at either end of the distribution, known as 'outliers'. Outliers can be identified and, if appropriate, removed from the analysis.

In addition, the shape of the distribution is also a factor to be considered. If the data is skewed in a particular direction, for example, more values at the top end of the distribution than the lower, then the median may be a better measure of central tendency. Standard deviation is an important calculation in relation to the normal distribution curve (see 'The normal distribution curve and the central limit theorem' p. 311).

Measures of the shape of a distribution

There are two measures that can be calculated that will indicate the shape of the distribution of an interval or ratio variable, **skewness** and **kurtosis**. The shape of a distribution refers to the resulting trend line when the data is plotted on to a **line graph** or the shape of the distribution when the data is presented in a **histogram**. Details on producing line graphs and histograms can be found on p. 284 and p. 282 respectively. Calculating skewness will indicate the position of the lower and higher values in the distribution, which have the effect of pulling the shape of a distribution to the lower or higher ends, or tails. A negatively skewed distribution will have a greater number of observations at the higher values, pulling the distribution to the right, or higher end. A positively skewed distribution will be the opposite, with a greater number of observations at the lower values, pulling the distribution to the left (see Figure 21.3). Values that are equally distributed will be symmetrical. An example of a symmetrical distribution is the normal distribution curve as in Figure 23.1, p. 312.

Negatively skewed distributions will have a mean value that is less than the median value. Positively skewed distributions will have a mean value that is greater than the median value. It is therefore possible to assess the shape of the distribution by examining the values for the median and mean in addition to assessing the value for skewness. From the earlier section you know that the mean is susceptible to extreme values at either end of the distribution. For negatively skewed distributions the lower extreme values have the effect of pulling down or lowering the mean. For positively skewed distributions the higher extreme values pull up or raise the mean. Where distributions are greatly skewed, the median may be a more accurate measure of central tendency. As well as the measure of skewness, graphical presentations of the data allow for the distribution shape to be assessed. The most popular chart to use is the histogram. In addition, **box plots** allow the visualization of extreme values at both the lower and higher end (see 'Box plots' p. 281).

Calculating kurtosis will indicate how the values are distributed around the mode. The more tightly clustered the values around the mode, the more 'pointed' the distribution. This is known as positive kurtosis, sometimes referred to as **leptokurtic**.

The more loosely distributed values are around the mode, the distribution is flatter and wider (Figure 21.4). This is known as negative kurtosis or **platykurtic**. An even distribution is known as **mesokurtic**.

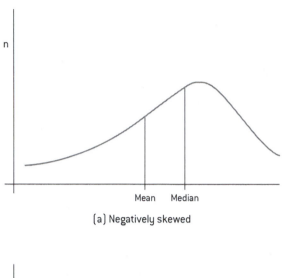

(a) Negatively skewed

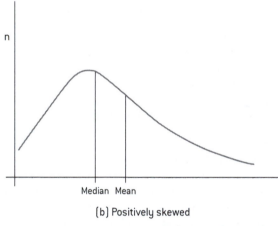

(b) Positively skewed

Figure 21.3   Skewness

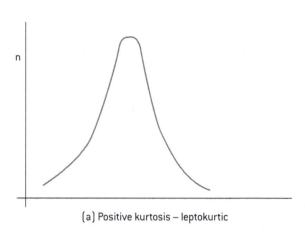

(a) Positive kurtosis – leptokurtic

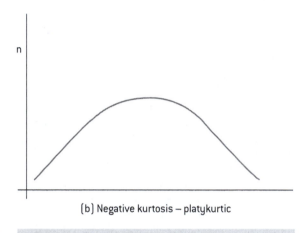

(b) Negative kurtosis – platykurtic

Figure 21.4   Kurtosis

Using SPSS to calculate measures of central tendency and dispersion

There are a number of methods for calculating measures of central tendency and dispersion in SPSS.

SPSS frequencies command

A frequency table can be produced with additional summary statistics calculated. Select the **Analyse** menu and **Descriptive Statistics >Frequencies**. **Highlight** the required variable from the left **Variable** list and click once on the arrow button → to move the variable to the section under **Variable(s):**. To calculate measures of central tendency and dispersion, click on the **Statistics** button. A

Frequencies: Statistics dialog box will be displayed (Figure 21.5).

This box is divided into sub-sections; within each there are a number of statistical options that can be selected by clicking in the corresponding box. A tick in the box states that the option has been selected. Under **Percentile Values**, the IQR values can be calculated by selecting **Quartiles**. Under **Dispersion**, the measures of standard deviation (**Std. Deviation**), variance (**Variance**), range (**Range**) and minimum and maximum (**Minimum, Maximum**) calculations can be selected. Under **Central tendency**, the mean (**Mean**), median (**Median**) and mode (**Mode**) can be selected. There is also a sum option (**Sum**) that will simply provide a total of all values for each of the selected variables. Under **Distribution**, the values of skewness (**Ske<u>w</u>ness**) and kurtosis (**<u>K</u>urtosis**) can be selected. Once the required statistics have been selected, click on **Continue** to return to the previous **Frequencies** dialog box. If a frequency table is not required, **remove the tick** next to **Display Frequency Table**. Finally, click on **OK** to execute the command. The corresponding results will be displayed in the **Viewer** window. The first summary statistics

table will now contain the additional statistics requested. An example of a summary statistics table is shown in Table 21.5.

In this example the analysis is of an interval variable, age measured in years. Measures of central tendency and dispersion appropriate for this data type were selected. The results show that there were 130 valid cases with no missing cases. The lowest age was 16 years and the maximum age 93 years. The mean age was 47.27 years and the data was slightly positively skewed with a skewness value of 0.176. Note that we can also conclude that the data is positively skewed from the calculation of the median being less than the mean. To calculate the IQR, subtract the value for percentile 25 (Quartile 1) from the value for percentile 75 (Quartile 3). From the example in Table 21.5, this would be 62.25–31.00. The interquartile range is 31.25 years.

Table 21.5   Summary statistics using SPSS

AGE	Statistics	
N	Valid	130
	Missing	0
Mean		47.27
Median		46.00
Mode		26 [a]
Std. deviation		18.326
Variance		335.842
Skewness		.176
Std. error of skewness		.212
Kurtosis		−.850
Std. error of kurtosis		.422
Range		77
Minimum		16
Maximum		93
Percentiles	25	31.00
	50	46.00
	75	62.25

[a]. Multiple modes exist; the smallest value is shown.

SPSS descriptives command

An alternative method of producing summary statistics is to use the **Descriptive Statistics** command in SPSS. This method does not produce the frequency table and the quartiles for calculating the interquartile range. Select the **A<u>n</u>alyze** menu and **De<u>s</u>criptive Statistics > <u>D</u>escriptives**. The **Descriptives** dialog box will be displayed (Figure 21.6).

As with the previous SPSS command, first highlight the required variable(s) on the left-hand side and click once on the arrow button → to move the variable across to under **Variable(s):**. To select the

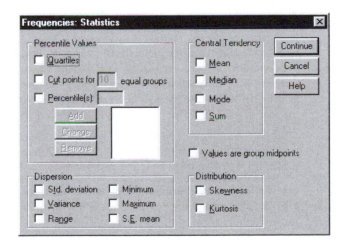

Figure 21.5   SPSS Frequencies: Statistics dialog box

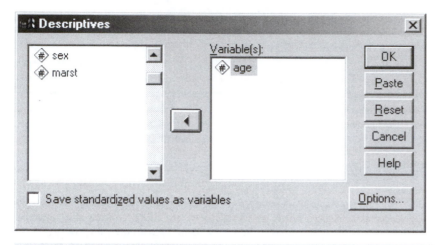

Figure 21.6 SPSS Descriptives dialog box

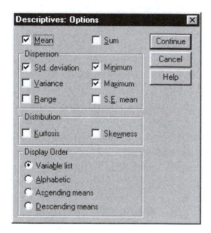

Figure 21.7 SPSS Descriptives: Options dialog box

summary statistics, click once on the **Options** button. A **Descriptive: Options** dialog box will be displayed (Figure 21.7).

This box is divided into sub-sections, each containing a number of different options. At the top there are the two options of **Mean** and **Sum**. As with previous dialog boxes, the option can be selected by clicking in the corresponding box. A tick in the box states that the option has been selected. Under **Dispersion** the standard deviation (**Std. Deviation**), variance (**Variance**), range (**Range**), minimum (**Minimum**) and maximum (**Maximum**) values can be selected. Under **Distribution**, kurtosis (**Kurtosis**) and skewness (**Skewness**) can be selected. Finally, under **Display Order** the format of the results can be altered. The

default setting is to display the results for each selected variable in the same order as the variable list (**Variable List**). Other options are to display, in alphabetical order (**Alphabetic**), an order of the smallest calculated mean (**Ascending means**) or largest mean (**Descending means**) of each variable. Unless there is a specific reason for rearranging the variable display, do not alter the default setting of **Variable List**. Other measures of central tendency, the median and mode are not available, and if required the **Frequencies** command should be used. Click on **Continue** to return to the previous **Descriptives** box and click on **OK** to execute the command. An example of the SPSS output using **Descriptives** is shown in Table 21.6.

Standardized scores

Standardized scores are particularly useful as they allow for comparisons between two interval variables with different distributions or measures. They involve calculating the distance that an observed value is from the mean and converting it into standard deviation units. Standardized scores are also called **Z scores**.

An example of using standardized scores

One student has their exam result in mathematics and a second student has their exam result in English. The second student has a higher mark than the first student; however, given that the exam marks for English and mathematics have different distributions it is not possible to say that the second student has

Table 21.6 Example of Descriptive Statistics SPSS output

	N	Range	Minimum	Maximum	Mean	Std.	Variance	Skewness		Kurtosis	
	Statistic	Statistic	Statistic	Statistic	Statistic	Statistic	Statistic	Statistic	Std. Error	Statistic	Std. Error
AGE	130	77	16	93	47.27	18.326	335.842	.176	.212	−.850	.422
Valid N (listwise)	130										

gained a higher achievement. In order to make a judgement as to whether the second student has done better than the first, we need to judge their mark according to the mean and standard deviation of each set of marks. For each value, in this case a student's exam mark, a Z score converts how far each exam mark is from the mean exam mark in units of standard deviation.

The formula for calculating Z scores is:

$$z_i = \frac{(x_i - \overline{x})}{s}$$

z_i = individual Z score
x_i = individual observed value, for example, exam mark
$\overline{x}$ = mean for the set of data
s = standard deviation.

A positive Z score means that the observed data is above the mean. A negative Z score means that the observed data is below the mean.

Below is a worked example:

Student One:
Mathematics exam mark of 60%. Mean 50%. Standard deviation = 5.6%

Student Two:
English exam mark of 70%. Mean 66%. Standard deviation = 10.5%

Student One's mathematics exam mark converted into a Z score:

$$z_{student\ 1} = \frac{60 - 50}{5.6} = 1.79$$

Student Two's English exam mark converted into a Z score:

$$z_{student\ 2} = \frac{70 - 66}{10.5} = 0.38$$

Both students have a positive Z score, which means that they both did above average in their respective exams. Student One has a higher Z score than Student Two. Although Student Two gained the higher exam mark, Student One actually did better in relation to the other students sitting the exam in mathematics.

Observations converted into standardized scores have the following properties: the mean of a standardized variable will always be zero, and the standard deviation of a standardized variable will always be one. Standardized scores are particularly useful for ranking cases based on more than one standardized variable.

Using SPSS to calculate standardized scores

Select the **Analyze** menu and **Descriptive Statistics > Descriptives**. The **Descriptives** dialog box will be displayed (Figure 21.8).

As with the previous SPSS command, first highlight the required variable(s) on the left-hand side and click once on the arrow button → to move the variable across to under **Variable(s):**. Click once in the box next to **Save standardized values as variables**. If the default settings for the statistics are not required, click on **Options** and remove the ticks from all options, then click on **Continue**. Click on **OK** to execute the command. Two new variables will be calculated and displayed in the data window. The variable names are prefixed with a z (see Figure 21.9).

If the Z variable will be required in future SPSS sessions, the data file must be saved. To save the changes in the data file, first view the data file by selecting the **Window** menu and **1** '**data file name**'. To save the changes select the **File** menu and **Save**.

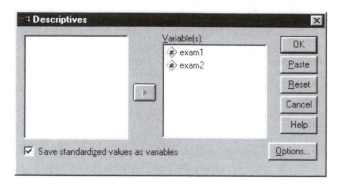

Figure 21.8   SPSS Descriptives dialog box

	exam1	exam2	zexam1	zexam2
1	58.00	60.00	.42777	-.51941
2	60.00	62.00	.63147	-.19478
3	62.00	65.00	.83517	.29217
4	64.00	58.00	1.03887	-.84405
5	61.00	61.00	.73332	-.35710
6	45.00	60.00	-.89628	-.51941
7	32.00	78.00	-2.22033	2.40228
8	55.00	69.00	.12222	.94143
9	53.00	61.00	-.08148	-.35710
10	48.00	58.00	-.59073	-.84405

Figure 21.9   Examples of Z scores calculated in SPSS

Graphical presentation of single variables

The graphical presentation of data using charts enables the researcher to get an overall feel for the data. Differences and trends can be easier to interpret when the data is presented in a chart format. The researcher can also include particular charts in the final report to both evidence the research findings and to convey a particular aspect of the data to the reader. There are different graphical techniques available according to the level of measurement or data type. This section will detail the appropriate charts for interval, ordinal and nominal variables.

Charts for interval variables

There are a number of graphic methods available that will provide a visual interpretation of the range of a variable. The following section details the flow charts most commonly used. All are easy to produce in SPSS for Windows.

Stem and leaf diagrams

Stem and leaf diagrams can be used to display interval variables that have at least two significant places. For example, currency or percentages in tens and units. The first significant unit is the stem and the second the leaf. Stem and leaf diagrams are particularly useful in identifying variables where there is more than one mode.

Table 21.7 displays a stem and leaf plot for the variable age. The stem represent units of 10 years and the leaf represents single units of 1 year. In the first line there are six observations; these are 16, 16, 17, 17, 18 and 19 years. In the second line there are eight observations; these are 20, 20, 20, 21, 21, 22, 23 and 24 years.

Box plots

Box plots represent the spread of data by placing the data in rank order. A box plot will display the median, quartiles and inter quartile range. The median is displayed as a horizontal line within a box. The lower and upper edges of the box represent the lower quartile (Q1) and upper quartile (Q3) respectively.

A box plot is shown in Figure 21.10 and represents the same variable 'age' as shown in the stem and leaf plot earlier. The position of the median line in the box provides a quick visualization of the distribution of the data. A median line that is not in the centre of the box indicates a skewed distribution. The single lines that extend beyond the box are known as the 'whiskers'. These represent the outlying values, known as 'outliers', in the distribution. Outliers greater than three box lengths from the edge of the box are displayed as points on a box plot. There are no extreme values in the box plot in Figure 21.10.

Histograms

The histogram is one of the most frequently used graphical presentations of interval or ratio data. Unlike the stem and leaf diagram, a histogram does not display the actual data. Instead it displays the count of observations (cases) that fall within a defined interval range. It involves dividing the range of values up into consecutive intervals. Each interval should not overlap with the next interval, and the number of observations that fall within each interval are counted. In a histogram each interval is displayed as one bar on the x-axis (horizontal) and each bar touches the next bar as the data is continuous. The y-axis (vertical) displays the count or frequency of cases that fall into the data range represented by the bar. An example of a histogram is shown in Figure 21.11.

Histograms should not be confused with bar charts (see 'Bar charts' p.284). In bar charts each category in the variable is represented by a bar; however, since each category is discrete, the bars do not touch.

Line graphs

Line graphs are an alternative to histograms for the presentation of interval variables. Unlike histograms, line graphs will not group the data into ranges. On the x-axis (horizontal) are the values entered in the interval variable, organized into ascending order. For every value recorded for the interval variable, the count of the number of cases with that variable is plotted against the y-axis (vertical). When all values and their frequencies have been plotted, a line is drawn between the plots to create a line graph. An example of a line graph for the age of the respondent is shown in Figure 21.12. Line graphs are not always a suitable graphical presentation for interval data as sometimes the data produces a very 'spikey' graph that is difficult to make sense of.

Using SPSS to create charts for interval variables

The following three sections detail the techniques available in SPSS for producing stem and leaf diagrams, box plots, histograms and line graphs.

Table 21.7   Example of a stem and leaf plot

AGE stem and leaf plot

Frequency	Stem & Leaf
6.00	1 . 667789
8.00	2 . 00011234
14.00	2 . 56666667778889
9.00	3 . 000113344
12.00	3 . 555568888889
12.00	4 . 000111233334
11.00	4 . 55666777999
7.00	5 . 1113444
12.00	5 . 555666677899
15.00	6 . 000222233334444
9.00	6 . 556667999
6.00	7 . 011233
4.00	7 . 6678
3.00	8 . 334
1.00	8 . 5
1.00	9 . 3

Stem width: 10

Each leaf: 1 case(s)

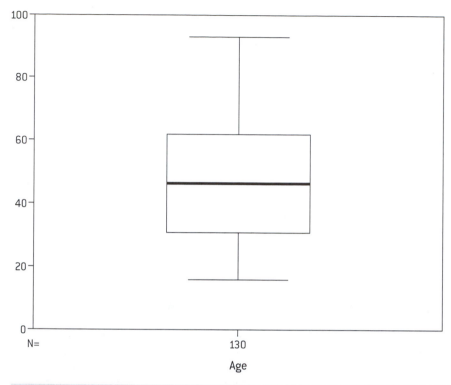

Figure 21.10   Example of a box plot

Creating stem and leaf and box plots in SPSS

The technique for producing these two charts in SPSS will also, by default, calculate the descriptive statistics that we produced by a different technique earlier. Select the **Analyze** menu and **Descriptive Statistics > Explore**. The **Explore** dialog box will be displayed (see Figure 21.13).

First **highlight** the required **Variable(s)** on the left-hand side and click once on the first arrow button → to move the variable across to the section under **Dependent List:**. In the bottom left of the dialog box under the section **Display**, check that **Both** is selected. This will produce both a stem and leaf plot and a box plot. Click on **OK** to execute the command. The **Viewer** window will display an **Explore Descriptives** table, a stem and leaf plot and a box plot. An example of the descriptive statistics produced from the **Explore** command is shown in Table 21.8. Examples of a box plot and stem and leaf diagrams for the same variable are as shown in Figure 21.10 and Table 21.7 respectively.

Creating histograms in SPSS

The easiest method to produce bar charts in SPSS is to use the **Frequencies** function. Select the **Analyze** menu and **Descriptive Statistics > Frequencies**. The **Frequencies** dialog box will be displayed. From the left-hand side highlight the interval/ratio variable(s) for which histogram(s) are required and click once on the arrow button → to move the variable across to under **Variable(s):**. Click on the **Charts . . .** button. A **Frequencies: Charts** dialog box will be displayed (see Figure 21.14).

This box is divided into two sections, each containing a number of options. Under **Chart Type** a number of different chart options are listed. A chart can be selected by clicking in the corresponding circle. Click on the circle next to **Histograms**. The second section **Chart Values** will remain grey and unavailable, as these options are not available for the histogram function. Click on **Continue** to return to the previous dialog box and then click on **OK** to execute the command.

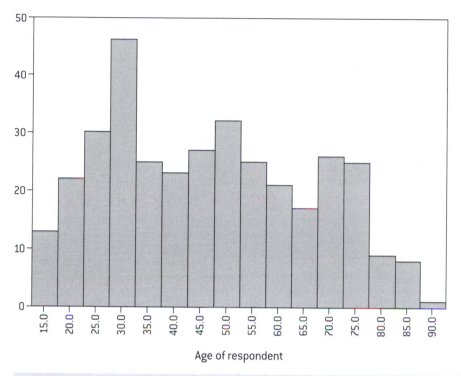

Figure 21.11   Example of a histogram

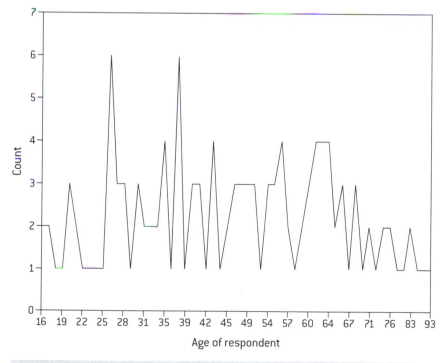

Figure 21.12   Example of a line graph

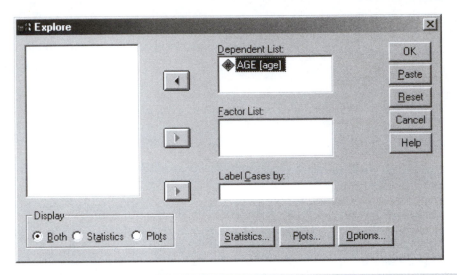

Figure 21.13   SPSS Explore dialog box

Table 21.8   Example descriptive statistics from the Explore command

Descriptives

			Statistic	Std. Error
AGE	Mean		47.27	1.607
	95% confidence	Lower bound	44.09	
	interval for mean	Upper bound	50.45	
	5% trimmed mean		46.90	
	Median		46.00	
	Variance		335.842	
	Std. deviation		18.326	
	Minimum		16	
	Maximum		93	
	Range		77	
	Interquartile range		31.25	
	Skewness		.176	.212
	Kurtosis		−.850	.422

An example of a SPSS histogram is shown in Figure 21.15. SPSS will automatically calculate the interval widths and will also display the mean, standard deviation and valid count. The histogram can be edited, titles altered, bar colour and so on; see 'Editing SPSS charts' p. 287 for details on editing.

Creating line graphs in SPSS

Select the **Graphs** menu and **Line . . .** The **Line Charts** dialog box will be displayed. Select **Simple** and click on the **Define** button. From the left-hand side highlight the interval/ratio variable for which a line graph is required and click once on the arrow button → to move the variable across to under **Category Axis:**. Under the section **Line Represents** select either **N of Cases**, to display counts, or % **of cases**, to display percentages. If you wish to include a title, click once on the **Titles . . .** button and enter an appropriate title next to **Line 1:**, then click on **Continue** to return to the previous dialog box. Finally, to ensure that any values defined as missing are excluded from the line graph, click once on the **Options . . .** button. Under **Missing Values** remove the tick next to **Display groups defined by missing values**. Click on **Continue** to return to the previous dialog box. Click on **OK** to execute the command. A line graph will be displayed in the **Viewer Window**. An example is shown in Figure 21.12. The line graph can be edited using the **Chart editor** (see 'Editing SPSS charts' p. 287 for more details).

Charts for categorical variables

Charts that are used to graphically present categorical variables, nominal or ordinal, are bar charts or pie charts.

Bar charts

A bar chart consists of two axes, x (horizontal) and y (vertical). Along the x-axis bars will be placed to represent each of the categories in the variables. Along the y-axis a measure is placed that will represent the observations for each category. The measurement can be a count, n, or a percentage of the total sample, % (see Figure 21.16).

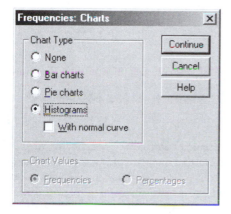

Figure 21.14   SPSS Frequencies: Charts dialog box

Pie charts

Pie charts can be used graphically to display the proportion of cases that are in each category of a single categorical variable. A pie chart is a circle that is divided into segments. Each segment represents one category in the variable. The size of the segment is calculated according to the number of cases that fall in the category. The larger the segment, the more cases in the category. Pie charts should not be used for variables that have over five or six categories or where there are a relatively small number of counts in many of the categories. In such occurrences the segment will be too narrow and impossible for the reader to assess the number of cases that fall within it. When this occurs either use a different chart, present the findings as a frequency table or, if appropriate, collapse the categories with a small number of counts into an 'Other' category; see Chapter 24 for more details on re-coding. A pie chart provides a quick visualization of the proportions of each category. An example of a Pie chart is shown in Figure 21.17.

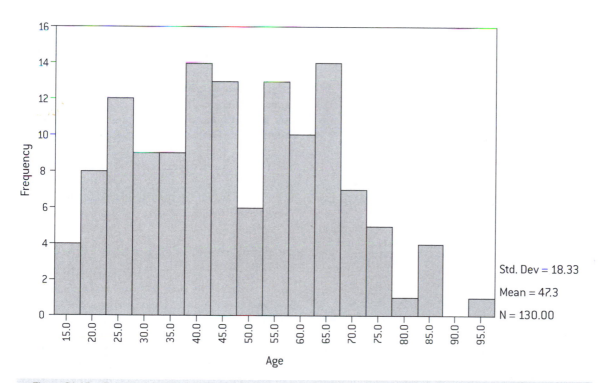

Figure 21.15   Example of a SPSS histogram displaying age distribution

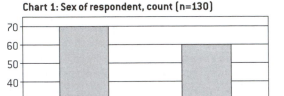

Chart 1: Sex of respondent, count (n=130)

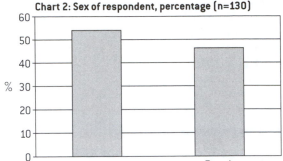

Chart 2: Sex of respondent, percentage (n=130)

Figure 21.16   Two examples of bar charts
Both charts are displaying the same data, the sex of the sample. Chart 1 is displayed as a count and Chart 2 as a percentage.

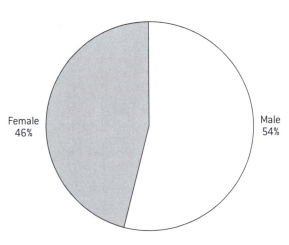

Female
46%

Male
54%

Figure 21.17   Example of a pie chart,
Sex of respondent (n = 130).

Using SPSS to create bar charts and pie charts

The following two sections detail the techniques available in SPSS for producing bar charts and pie charts.

Creating a bar chart in SPSS

The easiest method to produce **bar charts** in SPSS is to use the **Frequencies** function.

Select the **Analyze** menu and **Descriptive Statistics > Frequencies**. The Frequencies dialog box will be displayed. From the left-hand side highlight the nominal or ordinal variable(s) for which bar

charts(s) are required and click once on the arrow button → to move the variable across to under **Variable(s):**. Click on the **Charts . . .** button. A **Frequencies: Charts** dialog box will be displayed (see Figure 21.14). Under **Chart Type** click on the circle next to **Bar Charts**. The second section, **Chart Values**, is available for bar charts. Select either **Frequencies** or **Percentages**, depending on the values you wish to be displayed on the y-axis of the bar chart. Click on **Continue** to return to the **Frequencies** dialog box. One final decision to be made is whether a frequency table is required in addition to the bar chart. It is likely that in your preliminary analysis you will have already produced a frequency table, and if this is the case to stop a second table being produced click in the box next to **Display Frequency Tables**. The tick should now be removed. You will need to select this option if you wish to produce frequency tables at a later stage in the current SPSS session. Click on **OK** to execute the command. The chart will be displayed in the **Output Viewer window**.

Creating a pie chart in SPSS

The procedure for producing pie charts in SPSS is almost identical to that for bar charts. Select the **Analyze** menu and **Descriptive Statistics > Frequencies**. The **Frequencies** dialog box will be displayed. From the left-hand side highlight the nominal or ordinal variable(s) for which pie charts(s) are required and click once on the arrow button → to move the variable across to under **Variable(s):**. Click on the **Charts . . .** button. A **Frequencies: Charts** dialog box will be displayed (see Figure 21.14). Under **Chart Type** click on the circle next to **Pie Charts**. Under **Chart Values** select either **Frequencies** or **Percentages**, depending on the values you would like displayed as labels on the pie chart. Click on **Continue** to return to the **Frequencies** dialog box. If no Frequency table is required, remove the tick next to **Display Frequency Tables.** Click on **OK** to execute the command. The pie chart will be displayed in the **Viewer** window and can be edited using the **Chart Editor** (see next section).

Editing SPSS charts

Various aspects of SPSS charts can be edited using the **Chart Editor**. Common elements of SPSS charts that may require editing include the default colour schemes for bars, font types and sizes, altering line patterns, altering axis labels and categories. The type of chart and the final requirements for report and presentation purposes will determine the exact editing. This section describes some of the key features of the chart editor. The chart editor is easy and intuitive to use.

To open the **Chart Editor** switch to the **Viewer** window by selecting the **Window** menu and **2** **'Output window name'**. Locate the chart to be edited and **double-click** anywhere on the chart. This will open the chart viewer. Note also that some of the menus available have changed. An example of the **Chart Editor** is shown in Figure 21.18.

The chart can be edited using the various functions available on the toolbar and commands from the menus. The following is a brief description of some of the commands available. In the **Gallery** menu, the type of chart can be altered to a bar chart (**Bar . . .**), line graph (**Line . . .**), area chart (**Area . . .**), pie chart (**Pie . . .**), scatterplot (**Scatter . . .**) or histogram (**Histogram . . .**). The type of chart selected will depend on the level of measurement of the variable. In the **Chart** menu, commands relating to

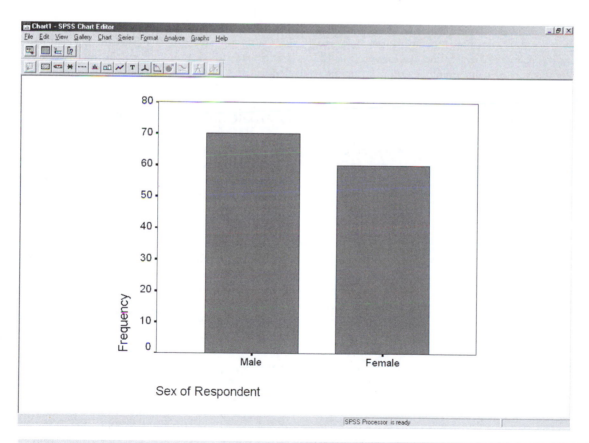

Figure 21.18   SPSS Chart Editor window

the appearance of the chart are available. They include the axis (**Axis . . .**), spacing between individual bars in bar charts (**Bar spacing . . .**), chart titles and sub-titles (**Title . . .**), notes that are appended to the bottom of the chart (**Footnotes . . .**), displaying a legend, also known as a key, to the bars in a chart (**Legend . . .**) and the placing of a solid line or box around the chart itself (**Outer frame and Inner Frame**).

The **Series** menu is where the variables displayed in the chart are selected and controlled. For *nominal* and *ordinal* variables, specific categories can be omitted (**Displayed . . .**).

The **Format** menu contains commands to edit the appearance of the chart. They require that the particular characteristic of the chart to be altered is highlighted and then the relevant command selected from the menu. For example, to alter the pattern of the bars in a bar chart first click once on one of the bars in the chart, then from the **Format** menu select **Fill Pattern . . .** and a **Fill Patterns** dialog box will open. Select the new pattern from those available and click on **Apply**. Click on **Close** to remove the dialog box.

Other options available in the **Format** menu are to change the colour of bars or lines (**Color . . .**), to alter the plot markers on a line graph (**Marker . . .**), to alter the line style on line graphs or surrounding the bars on a bar chart (**Line Style . . .**), to change the bar chart appearance from 2-D to bars with shadow or 3-D effect (**Bar Style . . .**) to apply labels on individual bars (**Bar Label Style . . .**) and to switch the x- and the y-axis (**Swap Axes).**

Once the edits are complete, return to the **Viewer** window by closing the **Chart Editor** window. Select the **File** menu and **Close**.

Exporting charts into a word processing document

Charts that are to be included in a main report will need to be placed into a word processing document. Where this is intended it is advisable to not place a chart title above the chart in SPSS and to instead type the chart title in the word processing document. The reason for this is that any chart placed into the document is likely to be re-scaled and chart title text would also be subjected to this process, possibly resulting in some very small sized titles that would be difficult to read.

There are two methods for placing charts into a word processing document. The first is to export the chart from the SPSS **Chart Editor** window and save the chart as a graphic. First view the chart to be exported in the **chart editor** window. From the **Output** window, **double-click** on the chart. To create the graphics file containing the chart, select the **File** menu and **Export Chart**. An **Export Chart** dialog box will appear. Select the directory or floppy disk in which you wish to save the data file. Next, to **Save as type:** select the required file format. A jpeg format should suffice. Then, to **File name** type enter the name of the file, for example, chart1. Click on **Save**.

The file can then be inserted as an image file into the word processing document; see the instructions of your particular word processing software for guidance.

The second method is to copy the chart from the **Output** window and to paste the chart into an open word processing document. The first stage is to have both the **Output** window with the chart showing and the word processing document open. In the **Viewer** window click once on the chart. Select the **Edit** menu and **Copy**. Using the taskbar, switch to the word processing document. Position the cursor where the chart is to appear. Select the **Edit** menu and **Paste**. The chart should now appear in the document window.

Univariate analysis for different groups

Often for comparison purposes you may wish to report on the responses of different groups. There are a number of ways of undertaking this in SPSS. One of the easiest methods is to make use of the **Split File** command. This technique involves temporarily dividing the data file into different groups. The division is defined by the categories contained in a nominal or ordinal variable in the data file. For example, if you wished to calculate the mean and standard deviation age for men and for women, the technique would involve splitting the data file into two groups, men and women. The statistics would then be calculated for each group. The groups would be defined by an existing variable; in this example, the variable 'sex'.

This technique is particularly useful when the variable to be compared between the different groups is interval, for example, age, salary. It can be utilized for other levels of measurement, though consider using the techniques discussed in Chapter 22 on bivariate analysis.

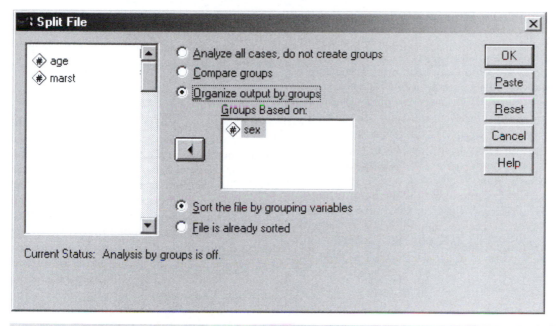

Figure 21.19   SPSS Split File dialog box

Table 21.9   Example output of descriptive statistics using Split File

Sex = Male

Descriptive Statistics[a]

	N Statistic	Range Statistic	Minimum Statistic	Maximum Statistic	Mean Statistic	Std. Statistic	Variance Statistic	Skewness Statistic	Std. Error	Kurtosis Statistic	Std. Error
AGE	70	68	16	84	46.54	19.334	373.788	.051	.287	−1.258	.566
Valid N (listwise)	70										

[a] Sex of respondent = Male

Sex = Female

Descriptive Statistics[a]

	N Statistic	Range Statistic	Minimum Statistic	Maximum Statistic	Mean Statistic	Std. Statistic	Variance Statistic	Skewness Statistic	Std. Error	Kurtosis Statistic	Std. Error
AGE	60	74	19	93	48.12	17.199	295.800	.431	.309	−.212	.608
Valid N (listwise)	60										

[a] Sex of respondent = Female

Using 'split file' in SPSS

The **split file** command can only be accessed when viewing the **Data** window. Select the **Window** menu and **1- '*filename*' SPSS Data Editor**. Select the **Data** menu and **Split File. . . .** A **Split File** dialog box will appear (see Figure 21.19). Select the option **Organize output by groups**. From the left-hand side highlight the variable whose categories will define each of the sub-groups, for example sex, and click once on the arrow button → to move the variable across to under **Groups Based on:**.

Check that the option **Sort the file by grouping variables** is selected. Click on **OK** to execute the command. In the bottom right corner of the SPSS **Data Editor** window, **Split File On** should now be displayed. Any analysis undertaken now will be divided according to the categories in the variable selected. An example of descriptive analysis of age undertaken when the **Split File** is set to 'Sex', thus dividing the results into Male and Female, is shown in Table 21.9.

Removing split file

To return to analysing all cases as one group, the **Split File** command needs to be switched off. Select the **Window** menu and **1- '*filename*' SPSS Data Editor** again. Select the **Data** menu and **Split File. . . .** From the **Split File** dialog box select the option **Analyze all cases, do not create groups**. Click on **OK** to execute the command. In the bottom right corner of the SPSS **Data Editor** window the **Split File On** should no longer be displayed.

Summary

The first stage in the analysis process is to describe and summarize single variables. This enables the social researcher to become familiar with the data and to detect any data entry errors. It is important that the analysis undertaken is appropriate for the level of measurement of the variable being analysed. Nominal variables can be summarized using a frequency table, calculating the mode and presenting the data as bar charts and pie charts. Ordinal variables can be summarized using frequency tables, the median, and again present data as bar charts or pie charts. Interval and ratio variables have a full range of statistical measures available. These include the measures of central tendency and dispersion. Interval and ratio data can be presented graphically in a histogram, stem and leaf plot, box plot and line graph.

Keywords

Bar Chart
Box Plot
Cumulative Percentage
Descriptive Statistics
Frequency
Frequency Table
Histogram
Interval
Kurtosis
Leptokurtic
Line Graph
Mean
Measures of Central Tendency

Measures of Dispersion
Median
Mesokurtic
Mode
Nominal
Ordinal
Outliers
Percentages
Platykurtic
Pie Chart
Quartiles
Range
Ratio

Skewness
Split File
Standard Deviation
Standardized Scores
Stem and Leaf diagram
Univariate Analysis
Valid Count
Valid Percentage
Variable
Variance
Z Scores

Questions

1   What are the appropriate measures of central tendency for each level of measurement and why is it important that the correct statistical measures are applied?
2   What are the appropriate means of dispersion for each level of measurement?
3   What is skewness, and how do skewed distributions influence the different measures of central tendency?
4   What are the appropriate charts for presenting nominal and ordinal data?

Further reading

Diamond, Ian and Jeffries, Julie (2000) *Beginning Statistics: An Introduction for Social Scientists*. London: Sage.

Field, Andy (2000) *Discovering Statistics using SPSS for Windows*. London: Sage.

Foster, Jeremy (1998) *Data Analysis using SPSS for Windows*. London: Sage.

Green, Samuel B., Salkind, Neil J. and Akey, Theresa M. (1999) *Using SPSS for Windows: Analyzing and Understanding Data* (2nd edn). Englewood Cliffs, NJ: Prentice Hall.

Hinton, Perry R. (1995) *Statistics Explained: A Guide for Social Science Students*. London: Routledge.

CHAPTER

22

DESCRIBING AND EXPLORING RELATIONSHIPS

Chapter contents

By the end of this chapter you will be able to:

- Analyse relationships between two variables using appropriate techniques.

- Create and interpret contingency tables in SPSS.

- Present data in a contingency table as a multiple bar chart.

- Create and interpret scatterplots.

- Calculate and interpret appropriate measures of association in SPSS.

- Calculate a simple linear regression using SPSS.

Bivariate analysis

This chapter will focus on techniques that enable the researcher to describe and explore relationships between two variables. Chapter 12 discussed the relationship between variables and how the researcher can explore and test these relationships. **Bivariate** analysis is concerned with the actual process of exploring these relationships between variables. A common problem for the first-time researcher is the sense of being overwhelmed by the data and possibilities of relationships to explore. It would be possible to explore relationships between all variables in the data set; however, the process should be driven by the original research question. If you are unclear as to what relationships to explore, return to the original research question and identify the hypotheses that state the relationships. Alternatively, if you have no firm hypotheses stated, identify possible relationships from the literature and your own views from the original research question.

This chapter will focus on describing relationships between categorical variables (nominal and ordinal) and between two interval variables. In addition to describing a relationship, measures of association can be calculated to measure the strength of the relationship. There are different measures of association available and their use is determined by the level of measurement of the two variables in the relationship. The final section of this chapter examines how the analysis of two variables can be expanded to introduce a third variable: a technique known as **elaboration**.

Contingency tables: analysing relationships between categorical variables

The most common technique used to describe and explore relationships between variables is the **contingency table** or **cross-tabulation**, reflecting that many of the variables collected by social scientists are categorical, either nominal or ordinal. Rather than describing characteristics of single variables, for example, the number of men and women in a sample

of working individuals, the number of full-time and part-time workers in the sample, cross-tabulations allow for more detailed exploration of responses by different sub-groups and exploration of hypotheses on the relationships between variables. For example, do more men than women work full-time? Can we identify variables that may affect this relationship?

The cross-tabulation or contingency table consists of placing one variable in the column and one in the row. The standard convention is to place the independent variable in the column and the dependent variable in the row. Following this convention is a matter of individual preference, there is no strong reason to adhere to it; however, it is a simple technique for ensuring that the researcher is clear as to the possible relationship between variables.

The **independent variable** is the variable that is identified in the hypothesis to be acting upon and influencing the **dependent variable**. Likewise, the dependent variable is the variable that is hypothesised as being influenced by the independent variable. Taking the earlier example of differences in employment between men and women, the hypothesis is that gender determines whether a respondent works full-time or part-time. Hence sex is the independent variable and working full-time or part-time is the dependent variable. Working full-time or part-time would not determine your sex.

A diagram of the different elements within a cross-tabulation or contingency table is shown Table 22.1.

Table 22.1 Example of a cross-tabulation: working full-time or part-time by sex, count (n=120)

Working	Male		Female		Row total (marginal)
Full-time	40	(a)	30	(b)	70
Part-time	20	(c)	30	(d)	50
Column total (marginal)	60		60		120

Counts of the number of cases that fall within each category are displayed in the cells of the table. For example, in cell (a) the count of the number of men who work full-time = 40, in cell (b) the count of the number of women who work full-time = 30. If you follow the rule of placing the dependent variable in the row and the independent variable in the column, then it will follow that the row total, often referred to as 'row marginals' (see diagram) will contain the total count for each of the categories in the dependent variable, for example, full-time and part-time. The column total, or **column marginal**, will contain the total count of the categories in the independent variable, for example, sex of respondent. As with frequency tables, a category count and total count enable a **percentage** to be calculated. Within cross-tabulations there are three different totals from which percentage can be calculated: column, row and total.

The column percentage

The **column percentage** is calculated based on the column marginal for each column in the table. The column percentage for each cell in the table is shown in Table 22.2 with corresponding calculations shown in brackets.

Interpretation of table 22.2 displaying column percentages would be as follows:

66 per cent of men worked full-time and 33 per cent of men work part-time. An equal proportion of women work full-time, 50 per cent, and part-time, 50 per cent.

Table 22.2   Example of a cross-tabulation: working full-time or part-time by sex, column percentage (n=120)

	Sex		
Working	Male	Female	Row total (marginal)
Full-time	66% (40/60*100) (a)	50% (30/60*100) (b)	58% (70/120*100) (r1)
Part-time	33% (20/60*100) (c)	50% (30/60*100) (d)	42% (50/120*100) (r2)
Column total (marginal)	100% (c1)	100% (c2)	100% (total)

The row percentage

The **row percentage** is calculated based on the **row marginal** for each row in the table. The table in Table 22.3 shows the row percentages with the corresponding calculations shown in brackets.

Table 22.3   Example of a cross-tabulation: working full-time or part-time by sex, row percentage (n=120)

	Sex		
Working	Male	Female	Row total (marginal)
Full-time	57% (40/70*100) (a)	43% (30/70*100) (b)	100% (r1)
Part-time	40% (20/50*100) (c)	60% (30/50*100) (d)	100% (r2)
Column total (marginal)	50% (60/120*100) (c1)	50% (60/120*100) (c2)	N=120 100% (total)

Interpretation of the row percentages would be of those working full-time, 57 per cent were male and 43 per cent were female, whereas 60 per cent of part-time workers were female and 40 per cent were male.

The total percentage

The **total percentage** is calculated based on the total count of valid cases in the table. This is displayed in the bottom right corner (n=120). The total percentage for each cell in the table is shown in Table 22.4 with corresponding calculations shown in brackets.

Interpretation of the table would be that of the total count of 120 individuals, 33 per cent were full-time working males, 25 per cent were full-time working females, 17 per cent were part-time working males and 25 per cent were part-time working females.

Creating contingency tables in SPSS

To produce a contingency table or cross-tabulation, first identify the two variables that are going to be examined. Open the data file containing these variables. Select the **Analyze** menu and **Descriptive Statistics > Crosstabs**. . . . A **Crosstabs** dialog box will be displayed (see Figure 22.1).

Table 22.4 Example of a cross-tabulation: working full-time or part-time by sex, total percentage (n=120)

Working	Male	Female	Row total (marginal)
	Sex		
Full-time	33% (40/120*100) (a)	25% (30/120*100) (b)	58% (70/120*100) (r1)
Part-time	17% (20/120*100) (c)	25% (30/120*100) (d)	42% (50/120*100) (r2)
Column total (marginal)	50% (60/120*100) (c1)	50% (60/120*100) (c2)	100% (total)

A contingency or cross-tabulation table consists of a number of rows and columns. To produce the table a variable needs to be allocated to both a row and column. On the right-hand side of the box there are two sections, one for row and one for column. Variables from the list need to be placed in both these sections. The independent variable should be placed in the column and the dependent variable placed in the row.

To move the first variable, dependent, into the row section, from the left-hand side highlight the nominal or ordinal variable required and click on the top arrow button → to move the variable across to under **Row(s):**. To move the second variable, independent, into the column section, from the left-hand side highlight the nominal or ordinal variable required and click on the second down arrow button → to move the variable across to under **Columns(s):**.

There are three buttons at the bottom of the **Crosstabs** box, **Statistics . . .**, **Cells . . .** and **Format. . . .** The **Statistics** button contains commands on statistical analysis techniques, including chi-square (see 'Using SPSS to calculate chi-square' p. 317). The **Format** button contains a command on controlling the category order of the row variable and it is rarely used. The **Cells** button contains commands that control the calculated data displayed in the table and enables the user to select row, column or total percentages. Click on the **Cells . . .** button.

A **Crosstabs: Cell Display** dialog box will be displayed. Under **Percentages** select one or more of the available percentages: **Row**, row percentage, **Column** column percentage and **Total**, total percentage.

Under **Counts** the default setting is **Observed** to

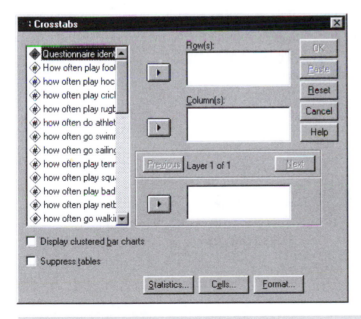

Figure 22.1 SPSS Crosstabs dialog box

display a count of the observed frequencies in each cell of the table. When calculating a chi-square the **Expected** count would also be selected. Leave the **Observed** option selected. Click on **Continue** to return to the **Crosstabs** dialog box. Click on **OK** to execute the command. The **Crosstab** table will be displayed in the **Viewer** window. An example of a **Crosstab** displaying cell counts and column percentages is shown in Table 22.5.

Interpreting the table

Interpreting a cross-tabulation will involve you analysing the percentages in the table. The table allows you to assess the evidence for the original hypothesis or your idea about the relationship between the independent and dependent variables. If the convention of placing the independent variable in the column and the dependent variable in the row is

Table 22.5   Example of a SPSS cross-tabulation

Case processing summary

	Valid		Cases Missing		Total	
	N	Percent	N	Percent	N	Percent
Which of the following daily newspapers do you normally read? Sex of respondent	117	90.0%	13	10.0%	130	100.0%

Which of the following daily newspapers do you normally read? Sex of respondent cross-tabulation

			Sex of respondent		
			Male	Female	Total
Which of the following daily newspapers do you normally read?	Financial Times	Count	5	10	15
		% within Sex of Respondent	8.3%	17.5%	12.8%
	New York Times	Count	5	9	14
		% within Sex of Respondent	8.3%	15.8%	12.0%
	Washington Post	Count	4	9	13
		% within Sex of Respondent	6.7%	15.8%	11.1%
	Melbourne Age	Count	6	5	11
		% within Sex of Respondent	10.0%	8.8%	9.4%
	Times of India	Count	6	5	11
		% within Sex of Respondent	10.0%	8.8%	9.4%
	South China Morning Post	Count	9	3	12
		% within Sex of Respondent	15.0%	5.3%	10.3%
	Le Monde	Count	9	12	21
		% within Sex of Respondent	15.0%	21.1%	17.9%
	Other	Count	16	4	10
		% within Sex of Respondent	26.7%	7.0%	17.1%
Total		Count	60	57	117
		% within Sex of Respondent	100.0%	100.0%	100.0%

followed, then you will need to compare the column per cent between each of the categories in the independent variable. Any differences in the column percentages for each row will indicate that there is a relationship between the two variables. The larger the numerical difference between the two percentages, the more strongly related the variables.

Graphical presentations of data in a contingency table

Data from a cross-tabulation can be presented as a multiple bar chart. Each category in the independent variable will have a bar for each category in the dependent variable. A legend will normally be displayed with the multiple bar chart to inform the reader as to which of the bars represent each of the dependent categories. An example of a bar chart is shown in Figure 22.2.

Producing multiple bar charts in SPSS

There are a number of methods for creating a multiple bar chart. The easiest method is to use the **Crosstab** command. Select the **Analyze** menu and **Descriptive**

Statistics>Crosstab. . . . In the **Crosstab** dialog box follow the procedure for producing cross-tabulations by placing the independent variable under column and the dependent variable under row. Place a tick next to the option **Display clustered bar charts**. If tables have already been produced or are not required, also place a tick next to **Suppress tables**. Click on **OK** to execute the command. A multiple bar chart will be displayed in the **Viewer** window and can be edited using the **Chart Editor** (see 'Editing SPSS charts' p. 287).

Measuring associations: Phi and Cramer's V

There are statistical techniques that will provide a summary statistic of the relationship between two variables. These statistics are known as **measures of association** and indicate the strength of the relationship between the two variables. There are different types of measures of association available according to the data type of the two variables in the relationship.

There are a large number of different correlation coefficients designed to take account of matters such

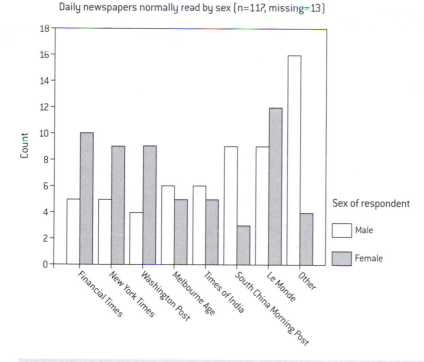

Daily newspapers normally read by sex (n=117, missing=13)

Figure 22.2 Example of a multiple bar chart

as level of measurement and the number of categories in the variables (de Vaus, 2002a: 267). A full discussion of the different types of correlation coefficient can be found in Fielding and Gilbert (2000); de Vaus (2002a); and Bryman and Cramer (2000).

The measure of association appropriate for cross-tabulations where both the independent and dependent variables are nominal are **Phi** and **Cramer's V**. Phi should be applied to cross-tabulations where both nominal variables are dichotomies. A dichotomy is a variable that has only two categories. Cramer's V can be used in cross-tabulations where one or both variables has more than two categories.

The calculation of Phi and Cramer's V is based upon the chi-square statistic. The chi-square statistic is calculated for the purposes of hypothesis testing and a discussion of chi-square can be found in 'Hypothesis testing' p. 313. The basis of the chi-square statistic, and thereby also Phi and Cramer's V, is the comparison of the observed, or actual count for each cell in the cross-tabulation compared to the expected count for each cell if there was no association between the two variables. The mathematical calculations to obtain Phi and Cramer's V are beyond this book. Since SPSS will calculate both measures of association, the important aspect is the interpretation of the statistic itself.

The value of Phi and Cramer's V will fall between 0 and 1. A value of 0 would indicate that there is no association between the two variables. A value of 1 would indicate that there is a perfect association. Rarely will values for Phi or Cramer's V of 0 or 1 be found. Instead the value will be somewhere between the two. Values closer to 0 indicate a weak or low association and values closer to 1 indicate a stronger or

high association. Bryman and Cramer (1997) suggest the following for interpreting the measures of association: 0.19 or less is very low association; 0.20 to 0.39 is low association; 0.40 to 0.69 is modest association; 0.70 to 0.89 is high association; and 0.90 to 1 is very high association.

Calculating Phi and Cramer's V in SPSS

The easiest method is to use the **Crosstab** command. Select the **Analyze** menu and **Descriptive Statistics > Crosstab. . . .** In the **Crosstab** dialog box, follow the procedure for producing cross-tabulations by placing the independent variable under column and the dependent variable under row. To calculate chi-square, click on the **Statistics . . .** button. In the section under **Nominal**, select the **Phi and Cramer's V** option in the top left corner. Click on **Continue**. Click on **OK** to execute the command. An example of the Phi and Cramer's V calculated in SPSS is shown in Table 22.6. These are the measures of association calculated for the daily newspapers read by sex table (see Table 22.5). Since this table is greater than 2 × 2, Cramer's V should be applied. The value of Cramer's V is .364. Interpretation of this value suggests that the association is low.

Analysing relationships between interval/ratio variables

The techniques discussed so far have been appropriate for analysing relationships between two nominal variables. Analysis of interval/ratio variables has been restricted to single variables or statistical measurements of interval variables between different sub-groups. The analysis of the relationship between two interval/ratio variables requires a different statistical technique called correlation. Correlation is a measure of the association. Correlation analysis involves measuring the degree to which one interval/ratio variable is related to another interval/ratio variable. Where a change in one variable is related to a change in the second variable, it is referred to as co-variance. When undertaking correlation analysis in SPSS, the dependent and independent variables need to be specified. Correlation analysis of interval/ratio variables involves the calculation of the Pearson product-moment **correlation coefficient** or Pearson's r. The value of the correlation coefficient will vary between −1.00 and +1.00 reflecting the strength and

Table 22.6   Example of Phi and Cramer's V calculated in SPSS

Symmetric measures

		Value	Approx. sig.
Nominal by Nominal	Phi	.364	.030
	Cramer's V	.364	.030
N of valid cases		117	

[a] Not assuming the null hypothesis.
[b] Using the asymptotic standard error assuming the null hypothesis.

direction of the association between the two interval variables. A correlation of +1 indicates a perfect positive association between the two interval variables. A correlation of −1 indicates a negative association between the two interval variables.

Calculation of the correlation coefficient should be undertaken in conjunction with a scatterplot of the two variables. A scatterplot allows the researcher to visualize the co-variance between the two variables. This is important, as correlation coefficients should only be calculated on linear relationships. The following two sections cover, first, calculating scatterplots using SPSS, and second, the calculation of Pearson's *r* correlation using SPSS.

Scatterplots

Scatterplots give a visual representation of the relationship between two interval variables. A scatterplot consists of two axes, x (horizontal) and y (vertical), one axis for each variable. The independent variable, x, is placed on the horizontal axis and the dependent variable, y, is placed on the vertical axis. The values of the x and y variables are plotted for each case on the respective axes of the scatterplot. The distribution of the plots will indicate the relationship between the two variables.

For a positive relationship, high values for one variable will correspond with high values for the second variable. A negative relationship would be indicated by a high value on one of the variables corresponding to a low value on the second variable (see Figure 22.3). The relationship may be linear, in a straight line, or curvilinear, in an arc. It is important to determine that the relationship is linear as only these relationships can be analysed using the correlation technique. Scatterplots will also provide a visual representation of outliers, extreme values.

Creating scatterplots in SPSS

To produce a scatterplot, select the **Graph** menu and **Scatter. . . .** In the **Scatterplot** dialog box select **Simple** and click on the **Define** button. The **Simple Scatterplot** dialog box will be displayed. From the left-hand side highlight the dependent variable and click once on the top arrow button → to move the variable across to under **Y Axis:**. Now highlight the independent variable and click once on the second arrow button → to move the variable across to under **X Axis:**. An additional option is to include a title for the scatterplot. If you wish to include a title, click on the **Titles . . .** button and type in a title in the top box. Click on **Continue** to return to the **Simple Scatterplot** dialog box. Click on **OK** to execute the command. The scatterplot will be displayed in the

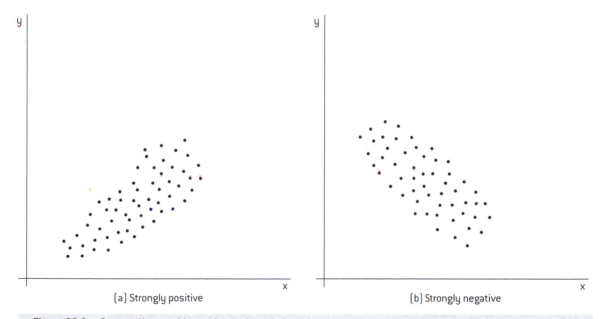

(a) Strongly positive   (b) Strongly negative

Figure 22.3   Scatterplots, positive and negative relationships

Viewer window. An example of a SPSS simple scatterplot is shown in Figure 22.4.

Interpreting the scatterplot

Interpretation of the scatterplot will involve a careful analysis of the distribution of the plots. The resulting plot can be compared to those in Figure 22.3 showing a negative and a positive relationship. The scatterplot should allow you to check for outliers and the shape of the scatterplot. Outliers appear as isolated plots that are some distance from the majority of plots and are important as they may affect any subsequent statistical analysis. Scatterplots may also reveal clusters of plots in a particular area on the plot, showing that many cases fall in a particular value range. The use of markers (see following section) may reveal intervening variables that could explain this pattern. By examining the scatterplot you may be able to visualize a line of best fit or summary line. Could a straight line be drawn or would a curved line be better suited? One of the problems with scatterplots is that it becomes difficult to assess the relationship when there are a large number of cases.

Setting markers in scatterplots

One very useful technique available in SPSS is to request that the plot marks on the scatterplot are colour coded for each case according to the characteristics of a third categorical variable. For example, a scatterplot was used to examine the relationship between an individual's income and their age. The plot markers could be set to distinguish between men and women. In order to achieve this a variable containing the categories of men and women would need to be included in the data file. In the **Scatterplot** dialog box there is a section called **Set Markers by:**. From the variable list place the distinguishing variable, for example Sex, in the box underneath.

Measuring associations: correlation coefficient

Correlation coefficients allow the researcher to summarize the relationship between two variables. The following section will focus on Pearson product-moment correlation, often referred to simply as correlation. Another way of thinking of this is how much do values of one variable associate with values in a second variable? For example, does income vary

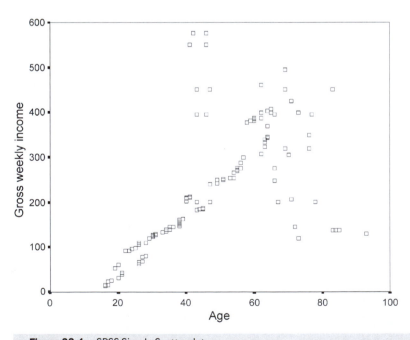

Figure 22.4 SPSS Simple Scatterplot

according to the age of the respondent? Look back to Figure 22.3 on the different relationships using scatterplots to get a visual representation of this.

Pearson's r

The Pearson product-moment correlation also known simply as Pearson's correlation, or Pearson's *r* can be used where both the independent and dependent variables are interval/ratio.

Calculating the correlation coefficient, Pearson's *r* in SPSS

Using SPSS to calculate Pearson's *r* for two interval variables, select the **Analyze** menu and **Correlate>Bivariate. . . .** The **Bivariate Correlations** dialog box will be displayed. From the left-hand side highlight the first interval variable in the relationship and click once on the arrow button → to move the variable across to under **Variables:**. Highlight the second interval variable and again click once on the arrow button → . Under **Correlation Coefficients:** check that the **Pearson** box is ticked. This is the default setting; if it is not selected, click once in the corresponding box. Under **Test of Significance** leave the default setting as **Two-tailed**. For an explanation of the meaning of two-tailed, see 'One-tailed and two-tailed tests' p. 314. Make sure that there is a tick next to the box **Flag significant correlations**. Click on **OK** to execute the command. A Correlation coefficient matrix will be displayed in the **Editor Window** and an example is shown in Table 22.7.

Interpreting Pearson's r

The Pearson's *r* correlation for the relationship between age and income is 0.632. This is a modest association. With a two-tailed significance of less than 0.05, this association is significant at the 5 per cent level. (Hypothesis testing is discussed in 'Hypothesis testing: single variables and relationships between variables' p. 313).

Analysing ordinal and interval/ratio relationships

Pearson's *r* can also be used in relationships of interval/ratio and ordinal variables if there are a large number of categories in the ordinal variable. Kanji (1999) and Blalock (1960) provide details of other correlation coefficients available for different data types or levels of measurement. Correlation co-efficients for interval and ordinal, and for two ordinal variables, include **Spearman's rank order correlation, Kendall's tau *b***, see **Kendall's tau *c*** Argyous, 2000 and Field (2000) for a full discussion of their use.

Simple linear regression analysis

The use of Pearson's correlation coefficient can be used to extend the data analysis a stage further to that of simple linear regression. Regression analysis attempts to measure the relationship between two interval or ratio variables in order to calculate a predictive equation enabling the value of the dependent variable to be determined from a given value of the independent variable.

Table 22.7   Example of a correlation coefficient matrix in SPSS

		Correlations	
		Age	Gross weekly income
Age	Pearson Correlation	1	.632**
	Sig. (2-tailed)	..	.000
	N	130	130
Gross weekly income	Pearson Correlation	.632**	1
	Sig. (2-tailed)	.000	.
	N	130	130

** Correlation is significant at the 0.01 level (two-tailed).

Regression analysis requires the two variables to be clearly defined as independent and dependent, according to the theoretical model defined by the researcher. The following presents a very basic introduction to the principles of **linear regression**. You are strongly advised to consult with one of the specialist quantitative data analysis and statistical analysis texts if you wish to undertake this analysis as there are some stringent assumptions associated with its application.

Regression is closely associated with the scatterplot and correlation coefficient. It is concerned with finding the **line of best fit** between two variables in a scatterplot.

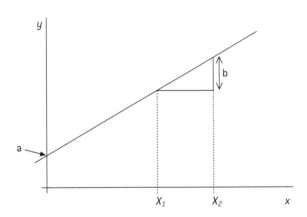

Figure 22.5   The regression line

The line of best fit is defined as a straight line that is placed on the scatterplot in a position that minimizes the distance between the line and each plot. Since it would be impossible to manually place this straight line in a position that would account for all plots and distances from the line, a regression equation is used to determine the line of best fit. The regression equation is:

$$y = a + bx$$

y is the dependent variable, **x** is the independent variable, *a* is the intercept, the point at which the line of best fit would cross the vertical, *y*, axis, *b* is the slope of the line, determined as the rate of change in *y* for a change in *x*. This is represented in Figure 22.5.

A multiple regression technique is available for use when there are more than two interval or ratio variables with more dependent variables and multiple independent variables. Additionally, it will enable you to determine which of the variables is a better predictor of the dependent variable. For details on using this technique, see Bryman and Cramer (1997); de Vaus (2002a); Rose and Sullivan (1996).

Calculating linear regression in SPSS

SPSS will calculate the regression coefficients and also provide an indicator of how well the independent variable is a predictor of the dependent variable,

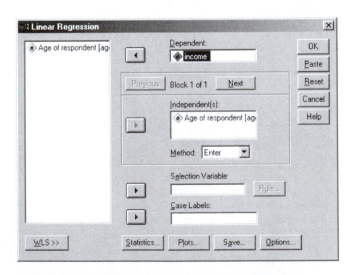

Figure 22.6   SPSS Linear Regression dialog box

reported as R^2. In addition, confidence intervals will be calculated to assess if the linear regression model is statistically significant and can be generalized to the population. The instructions on how to calculate regression using SPSS are select the **Analyze** menu and **Regression > Linear. . . .** The **Linear Regression** dialog box will be displayed (Figure 22.6).

From the left-hand side highlight the dependent variable in the relationship and click once on the arrow button → to move the variable to under **Dependent:**. Highlight the independent variable and click once on the second arrow button → to copy the variable across to under **Independent(s):**. Next to **Method:** select **Enter** from the available list. Click on the **Statistics . . .** button. In the **Linear Regression:**

Statistics dialog box check that under **Regression** coefficients **Estimates** is selected and that **Model Fit** is selected. Click on **Continue**. Click on **OK** to execute the command.

A regression model will be displayed in the **Viewer** window, and an example is shown in Table 22.8

Interpreting the output

The example output in Table 22.8 is a regression model of age and income per week. The output is quite complex and is divided into three different boxes. The key areas that you need to interpret from the SPSS output are as follows. In the **Model Summary** box under the R Square column the value is 0.4 . This

Table 22.8   SPSS Linear Regression output

Model summary

Model	R	R Square	Adjusted R Square	Std. Error of the Estimate
1	.632[a]	.400	.395	105.98893

[a] Predictors: (constant), Age.

ANOVA[b]

Model		Sum of Squares	df	Mean Square	F	Sig.
1	Regression	958558.8	1	958558.805	85.329	.000[a]
	Residual	1437908	128	11233.653		
	Total	2396466	129			

[a] Predictors: (constant), Age.
[b] Dependent variable: gross weekly income.

Coefficients[a]

Model		Unstandardized coefficients B	Std. Error	Standardized coefficients Beta	t	Sig.
1	(Constant)	8.538	25.803		.331	.741
	Age	4.704	.509	.632	9.237	.000

[a] Dependent variable: gross weekly income.

means that the regression model of age as the one variable predicting income explains 40 per cent of the variation between age and income. This means that it is a reasonable model for explaining income differences. In the **ANOVA**[b] box the statistical significance can be assessed by looking in the far right column under Sig. The value is .000 which means that the model explaining 40 per cent of the variation in income is significant at the one per cent level. There is only a one in a hundred chance of these findings occurring by chance. In the **Coefficients** box a lot of data is presented. The data that you need to determine the values of *a* and *b* are respectively, in the first row (Constant) read the data in the cell under B for *a*, and in the second row Age read the data under B for *b*. In this example *a* is £8.54 and *b* = £4.70. The regression equation would therefore be:

$$\text{Income} = £8.54 + £4.70 \times \text{Age}.$$

We know from the value of R square that this model is a reasonable predictor of income and that factors other than age contributed to income. This model could be expanded upon to build a more complex multiple regression model.

Expanding the analysis of categorical data

The techniques discussed in this chapter have focused on the description of single variables and the exploration of relationships between two variables. In order to explore and understand further the relationship between two variables, the researcher needs to think of why the relationship exists, how are the variables associated, are there any other variables that impact on the relationship? Can the relationship be applied to all cases in the data set or is it stronger or weaker in different sub-groups? Elaboration analysis is suitable for exploring such relationships in categorical, nominal or ordinal data.

Elaboration and spurious relationships

Elaboration analysis involves using a series of techniques to explore the extent to which a relationship is affected through the introduction of other variables. Does the relationship still exist, and to the same degree, when a third **control variable** is introduced? For example, if a relationship is found

between full-time and part-time work and hourly pay (grouped), is the association the same when applied to men only compared to women only? Alternatively, is the same relationship maintained when 'type of work' is applied as a third variable? Or does the relationship disappear, suggesting that type of work is the variable impacting on hourly pay?

When undertaking data analysis the researcher needs always to be alert to the presence of **spurious** relationships. Spurious simply means false. The researcher is interested in identifying and exploring relationships and an apparent relationship is said to be spurious when the association is due to a third variable, known or unknown, and is not a direct causal relationship.

The following technique for elaboration analysis involves examining the relationship between two categorical variables controlling for a third categorical variable. It is an extension of the contingency table analysis covered in the beginning of this chapter.

Elaboration techniques using SPSS: cross-tabulations

Introducing a third variable into a cross-tabulation will enable the researcher to assess the extent to which the two initial variables in the cross-tabulation are causally related. To introduce a third control variable into the contingency table, the **Crosstabs** command is used. Select the **Analyze** menu and **Descriptive Statistics > Crosstabs. . . .** A **Crosstabs** dialog box will be displayed (see Figure 22.1). Follow the same procedure as in 'Creating contingency tables in SPSS' p. 296. Place the dependent variable under **Row(s):** and the independent variable under **Column(s):**. In addition, place the third control variable in the third box under **Layer 1 or 1**. Click on the **Cells . . .** button and in the **Crosstab: Cell Display** dialog box under **Percentages** select **Column**. Column percentages are selected because the independent variable has been placed in the Column (see above page reference for more information). Click on **Continue** to return to the **Crosstabs** dialog box. Click on **OK** to execute the command. An example of a cross-tabulation controlled for a third variable is shown in Table 22.9.

You will notice from the example of using elaboration techniques that the counts for each cell in the table become extremely small as the data is divided further between the categories of the control variable.

Table 22.9   Example of a cross-tabulation controlling for a third variable

Which of the following daily newspapers do you normally read? By sex by age of respondent (grouped): under 40 years and 40 years and over (n = 117, missing = 13)

Age of respondent (grouped)				Sex of respondent		
				Male	Female	Total
Under 40 years	Which of the following daily newspapers do you normally read?	Financial Times	Count	5	1	6
			% within Sex of Respondent	19.2%	5.6%	13.6%
		New York Times	Count	2	3	5
			% within Sex of Respondent	7.7%	16.7%	11.4%
		Washington Post	Count	1	5	6
			% within Sex of Respondent	3.8%	27.8%	13.6%
		Melbourne Age	Count	3	2	5
			% within Sex of Respondent	11.5%	11.1%	11.4%
		Times of India	Count	3	1	4
			% within Sex of Respondent	11.5%	5.6%	9.1%
		South China Morning Post	Count	4	1	2
			% within Sex of Respondent	15.4%	5.6%	11.4%
		Le Monde	Count	4	3	7
			% within Sex of Respondent	15.4%	16.7%	15.9%
		Other	Count	4	2	6
			% within Sex of Respondent	15.4%	11.1%	13.6%
Total			Count	26	18	44
			% within Sex of Respondent	100.0%	100.0%	100.0%
40 years and over	Which of the following daily newspapers do you normally read?	Financial Times	Count	0	9	9
			% within Sex of Respondent	00.0%	23.1%	12.3%
		New York Times	Count	3	6	9
			% within Sex of Respondent	8.8%	15.4%	12.3%
		Washington Post	Count	3	4	7
			% within Sex of Respondent	8.8%	10.3%	9.6%
		Melbourne Age	Count	3	3	6
			% within Sex of Respondent	8.8%	7.7%	8.2%
		Times of India	Count	3	4	7
			% within Sex of Respondent	8.8%	10.3%	9.6%
		South China Morning Post	Count	5	2	7
			% within Sex of Respondent	14.7%	5.1%	9.6%
		Le Monde	Count	5	9	14
			% within Sex of Respondent	14.7%	5.1%	9.6%
		Other	Count	12	2	14
			% within Sex of Respondent	35.3%	5.1%	19.2%
Total			Count	34	39	73
			% within Sex of Respondent	100.0%	100.0%	100.0%

Summary

Bivariate analysis involves describing and exploring relationships between two variables. The analysis techniques used will depend on the level of measurement of the variables. Relationships between two categorical variables (nominal or ordinal) can be explored using contingency tables and presented graphically by using a multiple bar chart. Analysis of two interval variables requires the technique of scatterplots to produce a visual representation of the relationship which can then be described. Measures of association enable the researcher to summarize the strength of the relationship between two variables. There are different measures of association appropriate for the level of measurement of the two variables. Depending on the original research question, the social researcher may be interested in expanding the analysis to consider more complex relationships involving a third variable. Elaboration analysis involves introducing a control variable that allows the influence of this third variable to be assessed. Where the original relationship between two variables disappears on the introducing of the control variable, the relationship is said to be spurious. Linear regression has been introduced in this chapter, as it is a useful technique for predicting the influence that an independent variable has on a dependent variable.

Keywords

Bivariate Analysis	Cross-tabulation	Percentages
Column Marginal	Dependent Variable	Phi
Column Percentage	Elaboration	Regression (Simple Linear)
Contingency Tables	Independent variable	Row Marginal
Control Variable	Kendall's Tau *a*, *b* or *c*	Row Percentage
Correlation Coefficient	Line of Best Fit	Spearman's Rank Order Correlation
Count	Measures of Association	Spurious
Cramer's V	Pearson's *r*	Total Percentage

Questions

1   What type of data can be explored using contingency tables?

2   Describe the following elements of a contingency table: column marginal, row marginal and total count.

3   Identify each of the measures of association discussed in this chapter and summarize under what circumstances they can be calculated.

4   What do you understand by the term 'elaboration'?

Further reading

Argyous, George (2000) *Statistics for Social and Health Research*. London: Sage.

de Vaus, David A. (2002b) *Surveys in Social Research* (5th edn). London: UCL Press.

Field, Andy (2000) *Discovering Statistics using SPSS for Windows*. London: Sage.

Gilbert, Nigel (1993) *Analyzing Tabular Data*. London: UCL Press.

Vogt, W. Paul (1999) *Dictionary of Statistics and Methodology* (2nd edn). London: Sage.

Wright, Daniel (1997) *Understanding Statistics: An Introduction for the Social Sciences*. London: Sage.

CHAPTER

23

INFERENTIAL STATISTICS AND HYPOTHESIS TESTING

Chapter contents

By the end of this chapter you will be able to:

- Understand the importance of inferential statistics in the analysis of quantitative data.

- Calculate and analyse confidence intervals using SPSS.

- Understand what is meant by hypothesis testing.

- Analyse the relationship between two categorical variables using the chi-square test.

Inferential statistics

The focus so far has been on using descriptive statistics to describe the data. This has involved the use of techniques that have included measures of central tendency, measures of dispersion, frequency tables, cross-tabulations and charts. **Inferential statistics** focus on techniques that involve making inferences when generalizing data from a **sample** to the whole **population**. Inferential statistics can be used to estimate population characteristics, or parameters, from sample data and are also the basis of hypothesis testing.

Inferential statistics are based on the assumption that a simple random sampling technique is used to draw a sample, that is, everyone in the population has an equal chance of being selected. A discussion of different types of probability sample can be found in Chapter 13. A sample must be selected carefully to minimize sampling variability and sampling error. **Sampling variability** refers to the selecting of repeat samples from the same population which will produce different means and standard deviations.

Sampling error refers to the notion that an estimate from a sample will not be the same as the population value. Sampling error will be dependent on the size of the sample and the variability of the variable in the population.

A random sample will 'on average' have characteristics that resemble the population. Any differences between the sample and the population are there by random resulting from probability. Terminology used in inferential statistics makes the distinction between statistic, referring to the sample, and parameter when referring to the population. For example, the mean income of a sample is known as the **sample statistic**, and the mean income of the population is known as the population parameter. There are different statistical symbols used for sample and population statistics:

Sample statistics (Roman script)
Mean ($\bar{x}$), standard deviation (s), proportion (p)

Population parameters (Greek script)
Mean (μ), standard deviation (σ), proportion (π)

Where the sample has been selected by a random sampling technique, then the above can be assumed to be true. However, given the difficulties for some studies in obtaining a sampling frame, the researcher will need to make a professional judgement as to whether their sample is sufficiently representative of the population to enable the techniques in inferential statistics to be used. Details of how the sample was selected should be included in the research findings to enable the reader to assess if this is the case.

Parametric and non-parametric

Inferential statistics can be divided into two types of statistical test. Parametric tests are based on the assumptions of a normal distribution curve, as discussed below, and in using them in your analysis you are assuming that the data meets these underlying assumptions. Parametric tests are normally applied to interval data. Sometimes they are also used with ordinal data when the researcher is satisfied, or can successfully argue, that the ordinal data can be treated as if it were interval (Bryman and Cramer 1997: 117). Data that is nominal or ordinal, or where the population characteristics do not meet a normal distribution or the sample is too small, require the use of **non-parametric tests**. Non-parametric tests are based on other types of distributions.

The normal distribution curve and the central limit theorem

One of the key elements in the use of inferential statistics is the **normal distribution curve** and the **central limit theorem**. The main element of the central limit theorem is that taking repeated measures from different random samples will result in many sample means being close to the true population mean, and fewer sample means being further away from the population mean. For example, from a known sampling frame we take a 10 per cent random sample of a population of working individuals and record their income. We could then calculate the mean income of that sample. We then repeat the sampling and recording of income data for a further 100 samples taken from the same population. According to the central limit theorem, we should find that more of the calculated mean incomes will fall around the population mean income, with less samples falling a long way from this mean. This distribution of sample means will approximate to the normal distribution curve, a theoretical curve that is bell-shaped (see Figure 23.1). The shape of the normal distribution curve is the same, variations occur only in the mean and standard deviation (or spread).

The normal distribution curve has some important properties. The curve is bell-shaped and symmetrical, with the mean in the middle; 50 per cent of cases fall above the mean and 50 per cent of cases fall below the mean; 68.25 per cent of observations lie within +1 and −1 standard deviation; 95.44 per cent lie within +2 and −2 standard deviations; 95 per cent of observations lie within +1.96 and −1.96 standard deviations.

Standard error

A further feature of the central limit theorem is that if the mean is calculated from all the sample means, its value will approximately equal the population mean. If we can calculate the mean of the sample means, then we can also calculate a standard deviation. The

standard deviation of the sample means is known as the **standard error** and is expressed as SE. The central limit theorem states that the formula for the standard error of the population is:-

$$SE = \frac{SD_{population}}{\sqrt{n}}$$

The smaller the value of the standard error of the mean, the better the sample mean is as an estimate of the population mean. In practice we will not know what the SD of the population is; however, if the sample is large enough (Fielding and Gilbert (2000) cited about 100), it can be approximated using the sample standard deviation:

$$SE = \frac{SD_{sample}}{\sqrt{n}}$$

This is an important feature as it enables the researcher to assess the accuracy of a calculated sample mean. The larger SE ($\bar{x}$), then the less likely the mean from one sample is to be a good representation of the population mean.

Since the distribution of sample means approximates to the normal distribution, we can make use of some of

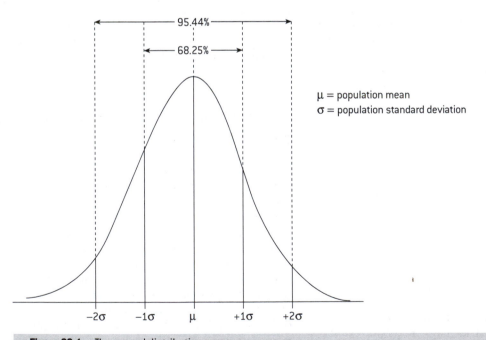

μ = population mean
σ = population standard deviation

Figure 23.1   The normal distribution curve

the properties of the normal distribution curve to calculate the likely range that the population mean will fall in estimated on the sample mean. These involve the calculation of confidence intervals.

Confidence intervals

Since the distribution of sample means approximates to the normal distribution curve, we can use the properties of the normal distribution curve to estimate how accurate the statistics drawn from our sample are, or to put it another way, how confident we can be that the findings in our sample can be generalized to the population. The normal curve states that 95 per cent of area under the curve, or cases, will fall between −1.96 and +1.96 standard deviations.

In the normal distribution of sample means we know that the sample means will fall around the true population mean μ. We know that 95 per cent of the sample means will lie within plus or minus 1.96 standard deviations from the population mean. Therefore from the population mean we could calculate the range that we would expect our sample mean to fall 95 per cent of the time. However, in research we actually want to calculate the reverse. We know the sample mean and we want to calculate the range within which we would expect the population mean to fall from our sample mean with a confidence of 95 per cent. In this case we are taking the sample mean to then infer the likely range in which the population mean would be. These ranges are called **confidence intervals**.

Manual calculation of confidence intervals for a mean

The equation for calculating the 95 per cent confidence interval for a mean is:

$$\bar{x} \pm 1.96 \times = \frac{s}{\sqrt{n}}$$

where s = standard deviation, n = count and $\bar{x}$ = sample mean.

This can be further summarized as:

$$\bar{x} \pm 1.96 \times SE(\bar{x})$$

as we take the sample mean to be the best representation of the population mean we calculated

the standard error of the mean. From this we can calculate the confidence interval at the 95 per cent level by multiplying the SE($\bar{x}$) by + and − 1.96.

The following is a worked example:

Calculating the standard error of the sample mean SE($\bar{x}$) of age from a sample of 150 individuals with a mean age of 32.5 years and standard deviation of 5.5 years, SE($\bar{x}$) was found to be 0.449 years. Taking the sample mean to be the best estimate of the population mean, we can calculate the confidence interval at the 95 per cent level:

$$32.5 \pm 1.96 \times 0.449 = 32.5 \pm 0.88$$
95% level (31.62, 33.38)

To conclude, we can be 95 per cent confident that the population mean age will lie between 31.62 years and 33.38 years.

Using SPSS to calculate standard error and confidence intervals

Select the **Analyze** menu and **Descriptive Statistics>Explore. . . .** Highlight the variable to be analysed and click on the arrow button → to move it to under **Dependent List**. Click on the **Statistics** button. The **Explore: Statistics** dialog box will open. The default **Confidence interval for the mean:** is set at 95 per cent. This should normally be sufficient, but if you are working to 99 per cent confidence alter the figure. Click on **Continue**. Under **Display** select **Statistics**, unless plots are required as well in which case leave **Both** selected. Click on **OK** to execute the command. A **Descriptives** box will be displayed containing the standard error (Std. Error), mean, and calculated 95 per cent confidence interval (Lower bound, Upper bound).

Hypothesis testing: single variables and relationships between variables

Hypothesis testing, also referred to as **significance testing**, enables researchers to make judgements as to whether there is enough evidence from the survey data to generalize the findings to a population. There are many different hypothesis tests available. Some involve comparing the observed values of a single variable from the survey data with a theoretical model about the distribution of the values in the population. For interval variables the theoretical model would be the normal distribution curve. Other hypothesis tests are available to compare the observed values in a relationship between two variables with a theoretical model of that relationship.

In order to decide which hypothesis test to use, the researcher needs three pieces of information. The first is the level of measurement, or data type, of the variable(s). The second is the number of samples. These can be one sample, two samples or many samples, often referred to in the literature as *k* samples. The third piece of information is where there are two or more samples, whether the samples are independent or dependent, also referred to as related, paired or matched. The easiest way of understanding dependent and independent samples is through illustrating the two most common occurrences in social research.

An example of two samples that are dependent is a study involving the pre-testing and post-testing of a group of individuals or cases. Here there are two samples of data collected; pre-test data values and post-test data values. The data is related since it is collected from the same cases.

An example of two samples that are independent is a cross-sectional research design that seeks to examine the relationship between two variables. When examining the relationship between two variables one variable is independent, cause, and the second variable is dependent, effect. The survey data is divided into two samples by the categories in the independent variable. For example, the variable 'sex' with two categories, male and female. The samples male and female are unrelated, since the individuals in the survey can only belong to one of the samples.

Hypothesis testing requires the establishment of two opposing hypotheses. The null hypothesis, H_0 and the alternative or research hypothesis, H_1. The **null hypothesis** is that there is no difference between observed, survey, values and those in the theoretical model. The **Alternative** or **Research hypothesis** is that there is a real difference between the observed, survey, values and those in the theoretical model.

For example, a cross-section research design collected data on two variables, the sex of the respondent, male or female, and the working status of the respondent, full-time or part-time. The null hypothesis is that there is no difference in the working status of men and women. The alternative or research hypothesis is that there is a difference in the working status of men and women.

The logic of null hypothesis testing requires that we begin by 'assuming' a particular pattern in the population. This pattern will be the opposite to that which we 'expect' (on the basis of theory and so on) to find (de Vaus, 2002a: 167).

The basis of hypothesis testing is then to test if there is enough 'evidence' from the sample data collected to reject the null hypothesis. By rejecting the null hypothesis the researcher can 'accept' the alternative or research hypothesis. The 'evidence' used to make the judgement is the level of significance of the test statistic. In Chapter 13 probability samples were discussed, and at the beginning of this chapter the issue of confidence intervals was outlined. Levels of significance, or statistical significance, allow the researcher to make a judgement as to how confident they can be about the findings in the sample data being found in the population.

If the significance level for the test statistic is less than 5 per cent (0.05), then the null hypothesis can be rejected.

Making errors in hypothesis testing

There are two possible errors to be made in hypothesis testing. A **type I error** is an incorrect rejection of the null hypothesis where the conclusion was that there was a real difference when one does not exist. The chance of this happening is the result of the significance level selected. If a 5 per cent level (0.05) is selected, then it stands that we have a one-in-twenty chance of falsely rejecting the null hypothesis. At the 1 per cent level (0.01) we would have a one-in-a-hundred chance of falsely rejecting the null hypothesis. A **type II error** is an incorrect acceptance of the null hypothesis where the conclusion was that there was no real difference when a difference did exist. The chance of a type II error is unknown.

The chances of making a type I error can be reduced by selecting a higher level of significance, 1 per cent instead of 5 per cent. However, the higher the significance level, the greater the chance of making a type II error.

There are different types of hypothesis test available for the testing of single variables and for testing the relationships between two or more variables. In both cases the hypothesis tests available are determined by the level of measurement of the variables.

One-tailed and two-tailed tests

Hypothesis testing is divided into one-tailed and two-tailed tests. The difference between these is that **one-tailed tests** impose a specific direction in the alternative hypothesis and **two-tailed tests** are non-directional in the alternative hypothesis (see Figure

23.2). For example, in a one-tailed test H_1 men have a higher monthly gross income than women. In a two-tailed test H_1 has a difference in the monthly gross incomes of men and women. In both instances H_o would be that there was no difference in the monthly gross incomes of men and women.

The researcher must have good evidence or theory to be confident of the direction that the test should be applied. If the direction is incorrect, this will result in the false acceptance of the null hypothesis. In the majority of instances the direction cannot be assumed and a two-tailed test should be employed.

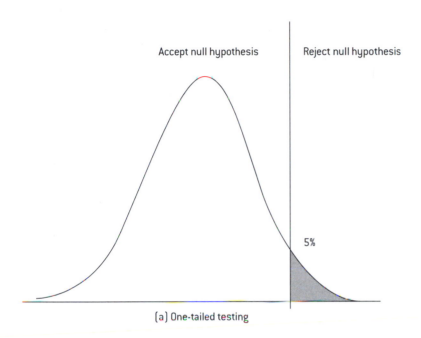

Accept null hypothesis   Reject null hypothesis

5%

(a) One-tailed testing

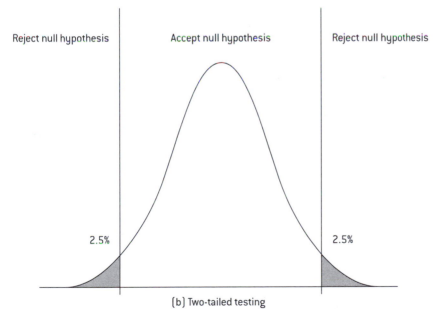

Reject null hypothesis   Accept null hypothesis   Reject null hypothesis

2.5%   2.5%

(b) Two-tailed testing

Figure 23.2   One-tailed and two-tailed testing

The chi-square test for categorical data

The most common hypothesis test used by social researchers is the **chi-square test for independence**. This is a test that is applied to a relationship between two nominal variables. It is a test that ascertains whether there is enough evidence from the survey data to state with statistical confidence that there is a relationship between two variables.

To describe the relationship between two nominal variables contingency tables can be produced in SPSS. In order for the researcher to assess whether the observed differences in the table are significant, and hence generalizable, a chi-square test can be performed, represented by χ^2. This is a non-parametric test and involves comparing the observed values with the values expected if there was no association between the two nominal variables. It enables the researcher to make a judgement as to whether the observed differences are real differences and not due to the fluctuations that occur by chance, known as 'probability', as a result of the sample selected. The formula for calculating the expected frequency count for each cell is:

$$Expected frequency = \frac{column total \times row total}{grand total}$$

Table 23.1   Contingency table examples

Car ownership by sex: count

Own a car?	Male	Female	Total
Yes	848	162	1,010
No	218	247	465
Total	1,066	409	1,475

Car Ownership by sex: expected count

Own a car?	Male	Female	Total
Yes	$\frac{1,066 \times 1,010}{1,475}$ $= 729.9$	$\frac{409 \times 1,010}{1,475}$ $= 280.1$	1,010
No	$\frac{1,066 \times 465}{1,475}$ $= 336.1$	$\frac{409 \times 465}{1,475}$ $= 128.9$	465
Total	1,066	409	1,475

Table 23.1 shows a contingency table for the relationship of car ownership by sex. The first stage in exploring this relationship is to describe the differences. A chi-square test can then be performed. The null hypothesis, H_o, is that there is no difference in car ownership between men and women. The alternative hypothesis, H_1, is that there is a difference in car ownership between men and women. The first table shows the actual count. The second table shows the **expected counts** if there was no association between the two variables, 'car ownership' and 'sex'.

Calculating chi-square

The chi-square statistic is calculated using the following formula:

$$\chi^2 = \sum \frac{(O_i - E_i)^2}{E_i}$$

O_i = observed count
E_i = expected count
$\sum$ = summation.

For each cell in the table the expected count is subtracted from the observed count. This value is squared and divided by the expected count. This is repeated for each cell in the table and the resultant values summed together. This calculation is shown in the Table 23.2.

The value of χ^2 is 218.61. If χ^2 is 'big', then there is a large difference between the observed and expected counts. However, it is difficult to assess how big 'big' is as the value of chi-square is a product of the number of cells and cell counts in the table. In order to determine this, the degrees of freedom for the table need to be calculated.

For a contingency table the degrees of freedom (df) are calculated as:

$$df = (no. of rows - 1) \times (no. of columns - 1).$$

Table 23.2   Manual calculation of chi-square

O	E	=(O-E)	(O-E)²	(O-E)²/E	
848	729.9	118.1	13947.61	19.11	
162	280.1	−118.1	13947.61	49.80	
218	336.1	−118.1	13947.61	41.50	Total
247	128.9	118.1	13947.61	108.20	218.61

In a 2×2 table the degrees of freedom would be $(2-1)\times(2-1)=1$.

If you do not have access to computing software to calculate chi-square, the next stage would be to look up on a chi-square table the critical value for 1 df. These tables are available in most data analysis texts or from specialist statistical tables texts (for example, Lindley and Scott, 1995). If χ^2 is greater than or equal to the critical value, then the null hypothesis can be rejected. If χ^2 is less than the critical value, the null hypothesis cannot be rejected. Looking up on the chi-square distribution at the 5 per cent (0.05) significance for 1 df, the critical chi-square value is 3.8415. Since the calculated chi-square, or test statistic, value is higher than this, we can reject the null hypothesis and accept the alternative or research hypothesis that there is an association between car ownership of men and women.

Using SPSS to calculate Chi-square

SPSS makes the calculating of chi-square very easy, and instead of having to look up the critical value for chi-square for the degrees of freedom in the table SPSS will calculate the level of significance for that value of chi-square based on the degrees of freedom.

To calculate chi-square in SPSS, the first stage is to select the **Crosstabs** command and place the independent variable in the column and dependent variable in the row. In the **Crosstab** dialog box calculate **the expected frequencies** by clicking on the **Cells . . .** button. The **Cells** dialog box will appear; under **Counts** select **Expected**. Click on **Continue**. To calculate chi-square click on the **Statistics . . .** button. Select the **Chi-Square** option in the top left corner. Click on **Continue**. Click on **OK** to execute the command. Table 23.3 shows an example SPSS output of a cross-tabulation and chi-square. It is based on the earlier example of car ownership by sex.

In the SPSS output the chi-square statistic is shown as 'Pearson chi-square'. The value given is 218.441. The slight variation between this and the earlier manual calculation is simply due to rounding numbers calculated to two decimal places.

The SPSS output in Table 23.3 includes a range of other calculated statistics. In instances of a 2 × 2 table SPSS will, in addition to Pearson's chi-square, also calculate a **continuity correction**. Tables that have independent and dependent variables with only two categories respectively are treated statistically as special cases. **Yates's contingency correction** can be used for

these 2 × 2 tables where the table total is more than 40, or between 20 and 40 with expected frequencies of five for each cell (Cramer, 1994: 83). The use of this correction is not widely accepted and Field (2000: 66) recommends that for this reason you do not use it.

For tables with small expected counts, where 20 per cent of the table cells have expected counts of less than five, **Fisher's exact test** can be used (Rose and Sullivan, 1996: 190). When the conditions are met, both Yates's and Fisher's are automatically calculated by SPSS. If you are unsure as to whether it is appropriate for your data to make use of Fisher's exact test or Yates's continuity correction, continue to report the chi-square statistic only.

The two-tailed significance level for Pearson's Chi-Square, Fisher's and Yates's, is displayed as .000. This means that the significance level is less than 0.01. The null hypothesis can be rejected at the 1 per cent level and the alternative hypothesis accepted.

There are some guidelines that should be applied when using chi-square. The first is that there needs to be a minimum number of expected counts in each cell of the table. The minimum expected count is five, and if more than 20 per cent of cells in the table contain an expected count of less than five, then either more data will need to be collected or re-coding techniques used to combine categories. The difficulty with the latter is that this technique reduces the sensitivity of the data.

Reporting chi-square findings

Reporting χ^2 should be in addition to an interpretation of the contingency, which would normally involve reporting the column percentages. You should clearly state the purpose of the test, the null hypothesis and research hypothesis. Report the chi-square test result, degrees of freedom and the significance level of the result. State whether these results allow you to accept or reject the null hypothesis.

From the worked example we could report that in the sample 79.5 per cent of men owned a car compared to 39.6 per cent of women. A chi-square test was performed to assess whether these observed differences are significant. Two hypotheses were established. The research hypothesis is that there is a difference in car ownership between men and women. The null hypothesis is that there is no difference in car ownership between men and women. The chi-square statistic is 218.44, the degrees of freedom are 1 and the reported significance level is .000. At the 1 per cent level the null hypothesis can be rejected. It is therefore unlikely that men and women have the same proportion of car ownership in the population, in which case we can conclude that there is an association between car ownership and sex. Note that chi-square does not tell you anything about the direction or strength of the relationship, only that it is statistically significant. The direction of the relationship can be ascertained from interpreting the column percentages in the table, and for strength the measures of association phi and Cramer's V.

Other hypothesis tests available

The chi-square test for independence is used for relationships between two nominal variables. It can also be used for a relationship between a nominal and ordinal variable, and is acceptable to use for two ordinal variables, although there are more appropriate hypothesis tests available for this and other levels of measurement. For two ordinal variables a Mann-Whitney, Wilcoxon or Kruskall-Wallis test may be undertaken. For a nominal variable, with only two categories, and an interval variable, a t-test for independence can be used. There are a number of other tests available for a nominal variable with more than two categories and an interval variable. These include Analysis of Variance (ANOVA). For further details on these and other hypothesis tests see Argyous (2000), Field (2000) or Bryman and Cramer (2000).

Table 23.3   SPSS example of cross-tabulation and chi-square

Car-owned HOHSEX cross-tabulation

| | | | HOHSEX | | |
			Male	Female	Total
Car owned	Yes	Count	848	162	1,010
		Expected count	729.9	280.1	1,010.0
		% within HOHSEX	79.5%	39.6%	68.5%
	No	Count	218	247	465
		Expected count	336.1	128.9	465.0
		% within HOHSEX	20.5%	60.4%	31.5%
Total		Count	1,066	409	1,475
		Expected count	1,066.0	409.0	1,475.0
		% within HOHSEX	100.5%	100.0%	100.0%

Chi square tests

	Value	df	Asymp. sig. (2-sided)	Exact sig. (2-sided)	Exact sig. (1-sided)
Pearson chi-square	218.441[b]	1	.000		
Continuity correction[a]	216.595	1	.000		
Likelihood ratio	209.327	1	.000		
Fisher's exact test			.000	.000	
Linear-by-linear Association	218.293	1	.000		
N of valid cases	1,475				

[a] Computed only for a 2×2 table.
[b] 0 cells (.0%) have expected count less than 5. The minimum expected count is 128.94.

Summary

Inferential statistics enable the social researcher to make generalizable claims about their research findings. Parametric tests are based on the assumptions of the normal distribution curve and are normally applied to interval data and in some cases ordinal data. Non-parametric tests are based on other types of distribution and are to be used for nominal and ordinal data or where samples are small. Both parametric and non-parametric testing require the defining of a null hypothesis and alternative or research hypothesis. The hypothesis test will involve establishing if there is enough evidence from the sample data to reject the null hypothesis. There are different hypothesis tests, depending on the level of measurement of the data and the nature of the sample data collected. An important aspect of using inferential statistics and hypothesis testing is that it is possible for the researcher to make an error by either falsely accepting or rejecting the null hypothesis.

Keywords

Alternative Hypothesis	Non-parametric Tests	Sampling Error
Central Limit Theorem	Normal Distribution Curve	Sampling Variability
Chi-square Test for Independence	Null Hypothesis	Significance Testing
Confidence Intervals	One-tailed Test	Standard Error
Continuity Correction	Parametric Tests	Two-Tailed Test
Expected Count	Population	Type I Error
Fisher's Exact Test	Research Hypothesis	Type II Error
Hypothesis	Sample	Yates's Contingency Correction
Inferential Statistics	Sample Statistic	

Questions

1 Why are inferential statistics useful to social researchers?
2 Describe the key properties of the normal distribution curve.
3 Describe the terms null hypothesis and alternative or research hypothesis.
4 When would you use a chi-square test and what does it tell you?

Further reading

Argyous, George (2000) *Statistics for Social and Health Research*. London: Sage.

Cramer, Duncan (1994) *Introducing Statistics for Social Research: Step-by-step Calculations and Computer Techniques Using SPSS*. London: Routledge.

Diamond, Ian and Jeffries, Julie (2000) *Beginning Statistics: An Introduction for Social Scientists*. London: Sage.

Field, Andy (2000) *Discovering Statistics using SPSS for Windows*. London: Sage.

Lindley, Dennis V. and Scott, William F. (1995) *New Cambridge Elementary Statistical Tables* (2nd edn). Cambridge: Cambridge University Press.

Vogt, W. Paul (1999) *Dictionary of Statistics and Methodology* (2nd edn). London: Sage.

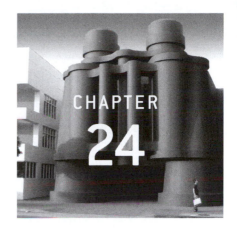

CHAPTER
24

DATA MANIPULATION

Chapter contents

By the end of this chapter you will be able to:

- Describe the different types of data manipulation used to analyse quantitative data.

- Demonstrate re-coding interval variables into categorical variables using SPSS.

- Demonstrate re-coding categorical variables using SPSS.

- Demonstrate how to create sub-sets using SPSS.

- Demonstrate how to create and analyse multiple response sets using SPSS.

The data analysis covered so far has involved analysing variables as they have been defined and entered into the data file. This chapter concentrates on introducing some data management techniques that will allow the researcher to develop and expand the analysis. These techniques can allow for a more detailed exploration of quantitative data. We will examine the following techniques:

- re-coding variables in SPSS;
- calculating new variables in SPSS;
- case selection and subsets; and
- multiple response sets.

Re-coding data – why? What are the pitfalls?

Re-coding **variables** in SPSS is a technique that is particularly useful when the original variable is not in a format that the researcher considers appropriate for the analysis. There are different types of re-coding that can be undertaken. For example, a variable 'age' coded in actual years could be re-coded into a variable 'age groups', where cases are placed into specific age groups. Alternatively, a variable on the most feared crimes against individuals lists 30 different crimes and the researcher wishes to reduce the number of categories to make the data more manageable for analysis by grouping 'like' crimes together. This technique can also be used when it has not been possible to successfully run a **chi-square** test due to more than 20 per cent of cells containing an expected cell count of less than 5. The re-coding of the test variable will involve the collapsing of **categories** together, enabling the chi-square test to be successfully applied, albeit with a reduction of variability in the variable.

There are two ways to re-code interval data into discrete groups, for example, ages into age groups. The first is to directly re-code the original variable. The second is to re-code the data from the original variable into a new variable. The first technique will result in the original data being lost from the open data file. The second procedure ensures that the original variable is left untouched and can be used for future analysis.

Consequently, always re-code a variable into a new variable.

Using SPSS to re-code variables

The process of re-coding a variable is first to note the original level of measurement of the variable to be re-coded. See 'Hierarchical order with levels of measurement' p. 145, for a full discussion. This order means that interval or ratio levels of measurement can be re-coded into an ordinal level of measurement, which in turn can be re-coded into a nominal level of measurement. Re-coding of lower order levels of measurement to higher orders is not possible. For example, it is not possible to re-code a nominal variable into an interval variable. The following is an example of re-coding an interval variable into two categorical variables: Exam scores in percentages (ratio) can be re-coded into grades A–F (ordinal), which in turn can be re-coded into a Pass/Fail (nominal).

Second, for nominal or ordinal variables refer to the original code book and frequency of counts for each category. The coding frame can be found within SPSS by selecting the **Utilities** menu and **Variables . . .**, and the category frequencies can be found by producing a frequency table (see 'Frequencies and percentages' p. 269).

In all cases of re-coding, reference to the original coding frame is essential. One must be aware of the level of measurement, coding, range of codes and the coding used for missing values. It is also strongly advisable to produce a frequency table and/or descriptive statistics of the original variable before proceeding with re-coding.

Third, the researcher must have a clear understanding of exactly how the variable data is going to be re-coded. The following sections will detail the procedures for re-coding interval data into categorical data and re-coding categorical data.

Re-coding interval data into categorical data

Re-coding an interval variable into a categorical variable, ordinal or nominal, is one of the most common data manipulation techniques. It is particularly useful where the researcher wishes to explore relationships between two variables when the dependent variable is ordinal or nominal and the independent variable in its original data type is interval. For example, the researcher wishes to explore attitudinal responses to using public transport by the age of respondents. The attitudinal variable is ordinal, coded on a scale of 1 = low usage to 5 = high usage of public transport. The age variable is coded in years and the researcher wishes to re-code the ages into age bands or ranges in order to explore possible differences in attitudes to using public transport by different age groups.

Using SPSS to re-code interval variables

The following worked example will involve re-coding the interval variable 'age' (coded in actual years) into a new variable 'age2' (ages grouped in age ranges). From earlier analysis of the original age variable, the researcher knows that the minimum age is 16 years and the maximum age is 94 years. There are no missing values. They have decided that the 'age2' variable will contain the respondents' ages grouped into the following six categories: 16–19, 20–29, 30–39, 40–49, 50–59, 60 plus. Each of the new categories will need to be given a code from 1 to 6, where 1 = 16–19 years to 6 = 60 plus years.

The **Recode** command can only be accessed when viewing the **Data Editor** window. Select the **Window** menu and **1-'filename' SPSS Data editor**. Select the **Transform** menu and select **Recode > Into Different Variables**. The **Recode into Different Variables** dialog box will appear (see Figure 24.1).

From the left-hand side highlight the variable that is to be re-coded – in this example it is the variable 'age' – and click once on the arrow button → to move the variable across to under **Input Variable ->Output Variable:**. The next stage is to define the new variable or 'output' variable. In the section **Output Variable** click in the box under **Name:** and type in the variable name **AGE2**. To assign a variable label to this new variable, click in the box under **Label:** and enter the variable label **Age of respondent recoded**. Now click once on the **Change** button to paste this information into the **Input Variable ->Output Variable: section**.

The next stage is to define the categories for the 'age2' variable. Click once on the **Old and New Values . . .** button. A **Recode into Different Variables: Old and New Values** dialog box will be displayed (see Figure 24.2). The box is divided into two halves. In the left-hand side is where the **Old value**(s) are specified and the right side is where the **New value**(s) are entered.

To recode the data for the first age category, 16–19 years, first under **Old Value** click on the first

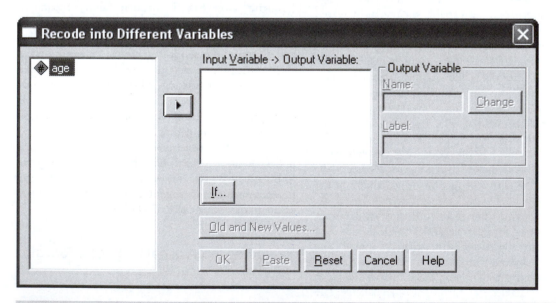

Figure 24.1   SPSS Recode into Different Variables dialog box

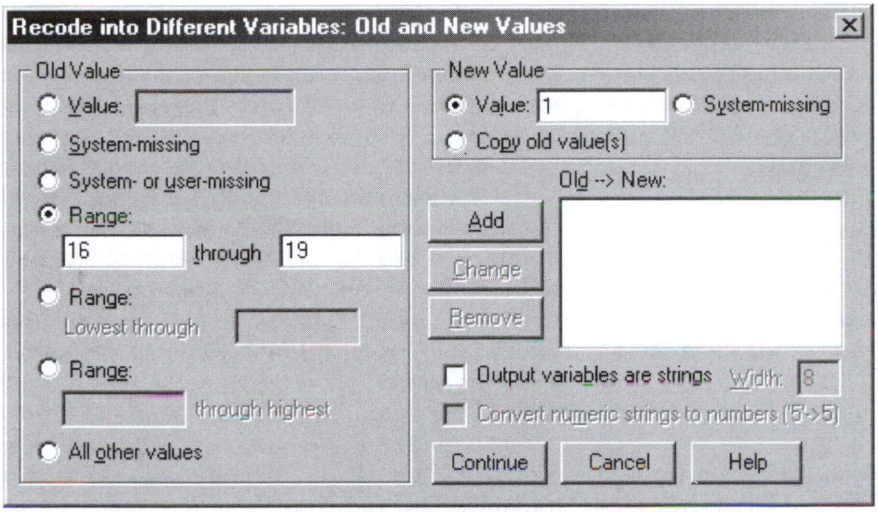

Figure 24.2   SPSS Recode into Different Variables: Old and New Values dialog box

Range option. Enter the value **16** in the left box, underneath, and the value **19** in the box to the right of **through**. Under **New Value** in the box next to **Value** enter the new code **1**. Click once on the **Add** button. In the box under **Old ->New:**, '16 thru 19 → 1' should appear. This process has defined the first age category of 16–19 years. The process now needs to be repeated for the next four age categories of 20–29 (code as 2), 30–39 (code as 3), 40–49 (code as 4), 50–59 (code as 5). For the final age category 60 plus, under **Old value** select the third **Range:** option (Range through highest). Enter **60** in the left box. There is no need to specify the highest value, 94, as this option will automatically select the highest value. Under **New Value** in the box next to **Value**, enter the new code **6**. Click once on the **Add** button.

Re-coding missing values

This variable has no missing values; see the next section for details on how to manage missing values when re-coding variables.

Once all the observed and missing values have been re-coded, click once on the **Continue** button to return to the **Re-code into Different Variables** dialog box. Click on **OK** to execute the re-code command.

The new variable 'age2' will be calculated and displayed in the **Data Editor** window. It can be located in the far right column of the **Data View** window and at the bottom of the variable list in the **Variable View** window. In the **Variable View** window,

value labels should be assigned to each of the new age categories.

The final stage of the re-coding process is to produce a frequency table for the new variable 'age2'. This will enable the researcher to check that the re-coding is correct by checking that the count and percentage for each of the age categories is as expected. The percentages for each age category should correspond to the cumulative percentage of the upper value in each age range taken from a frequency table of the original variable, 'age'.

Finally, remember to save the data file as a new variable has been created. In the **Data Editor** window select the **File** menu and **Save**.

Re-coding categorical variables

The same re-coding technique can be used to re-code a categorical variable. There may be occasions when an existing categorical variable needs to be re-coded for the purposes of the analysis you wish to undertake. You may wish to combine certain categories in a categorical variable, for example, combining categories with very small counts into one 'other' category. Alternatively, you may wish to re-code a category to 'missing' to remove it from the analysis. These techniques may also be appropriate when undertaking measures of statistical association, such as chi-square, when cells with small expected counts are problematic. The technique is essentially the same as in the earlier example of re-coding interval variables. Before undertaking the re-coding you must be absolutely sure of the code that is used for each category and which codes you wish to combine or remove. As before, you are strongly advised always to re-code to a new variable in order to preserve the original data.

Using SPSS to re-code categorical variables

In the following example the categorical variable, 'victim', contains a four-point ordinal scale of responses to the 'How worried are you about being a victim of crime?' question.

A copy of the frequency table for this variable is shown in Table 24.1.

From the frequency table and code book we know that the coding is 1 = very worried, 2 = worried, 3 = not very worried, 4 = not at all worried, and -99 = Refused to answer, missing.

In this exercise the categories 'very worried' and 'fairly worried' are going to be combined (1 and 2), the categories 'not very worried' and 'not at all worried' are going to be combined (3 and 4), and finally the 'refused to answer' (-99) category will continue to be coded as missing. The new categories will then be 1 = worried and 2 = not worried, and -99 = missing.

The **Recode** command can only be accessed when viewing the **Data** window. Select the **Window** menu and **1-'filename' SPSS Data editor**. Select the **Transform** menu and select **Recode>Into Different Variables**. The **Recode into Different Variables** dialog box will appear (see Figure 24.1). If previous re-coding has been undertaken in the current SPSS session, click once on the **Reset** button to clear the settings.

From the left-hand side highlight the variable that is to be re-coded, for example, the variable victim, and click once on the arrow button → to move the variable across to under **Input Variable ->Output Variable:**. The next stage is to define the new variable or 'Output' variable. In the section **Output Variable** click in the box under **Name:** and type in the variable name **Victim2**. To assign a variable label to this new variable, click in the box under **Label:** and enter the variable label **Victim recoded**. Now click once on the **Change** button to paste this information into the **Input Variable ->Output Variable:** section.

The next stage is to define the categories for the 'victim2' variable. Click once on the **Old and New Values . . .** button. A **Recode into Different Variables: Old and New Values** dialog box will be displayed (see Figure 24.2). The box is divided into two halves. In the left-hand side is where the **Old value**(s) are specified and the right side is where the **New value**(s) are entered.

To re-code 1[Very worried] and 2[Worried] into the first new category 1 [Worried], first under **Old Value** click on the first **Range** option. Enter the value **1** in the left box, underneath, and the value **2** in the box to the right of **through**. Under **New Value** in the box next to **Value** enter the new code **1**. Click once on the **Add** button. In the box under **Old ->New:** '1 thru 2 → 1' should appear.

Repeat this process for the second category re-coding 3 and 4 into a new category of 2 (not worried), entering the range 3 through 4 and the new value 2.

Table 24.1   Frequency table of the variable 'How worried are you about being a victim of crime?'

How worried are you about being a victim of crime?

		Frequency	Percent	Valid percent	Cumulative pecent
Valid	Very worried	100	32.8	34.5	34.5
	Worried	120	39.3	41.4	75.9
	Not very worried	60	19.7	20.7	96.6
	Not at all worried	10	3.3	3.4	100.0
	Total	290	95.1	100.0	
Missing	Refused to answer	15	4.9		
Total		305	100.0		

Table 24.2   Frequency table of the re-coded variable Victim2

How worried are you about being a victim of crime?

		Frequency	Percent	Valid percent	Cumulative pecent
Valid	Worried	220	72.1	75.9	75.9
	Not worried	70	23.0	24.1	100.0
	Total	290	95.1	100.0	
Missing	System	15	4.9		
Total		305	100.0		

Re-coding missing values

The final category from the original variable to re-code is the 'missing, refused to answer' category, coded as –99. There are two ways of dealing with this value. The first is to simply copy the existing value, -99, and in the new variable 'victim 2' set the missing value to –99. The second is to define –99 as a missing value in the **Old to New Values** dialog box.

To copy the existing value under **Old Value**, in the box next to **Value**, enter **-99**. Under **New Value** select **Copy old Value(s)**. Click once on the **Add** button. When the new variable is created, remember to set a missing value of –99 and a value label of –99 = refused to answer.

To define –99 as 'missing' under **Old Value**, in the box next to **Value** enter **–99**. Under **New Value** select **System-missing**. Click once on the **Add** button. The –99 is re-coded as a system 'missing' value and will appear as a blank entry in the data file. No value label is required.

The new variable 'victim2' will be calculated and displayed in the **Data Editor** window. It can be located in the far right column of the **Data View** window and at the bottom of the variable list in the **Variable View** window. In the **Variable View** window, value labels should be assigned to each of the new age categories.

The final stage of the re-coding process is to produce a frequency table for the new variable 'victim2'. This will enable the researcher to check that the re-coding is correct by checking that the count and percentage for each of the age categories is as expected. The frequency table for 'victim2' is shown in Table 24.2.

Finally, remember to save the data file as a new variable has been created. In the **Data Editor** window select the **File** menu and **Save**.

Calculating new variables

There are occasions when it may be advantageous for the researcher to calculate a new variable based on one or more existing variables. Common reasons for this are, first, the data the researcher would like to analyse does not exist and they need to calculate a new variable based on variables that do exist. Second, two or more variables are going to be added together to form an index, for example, taking multiple indicators and combining them into one measurement. Third, to manipulate an existing variable to give it a great weight in the analysis. For example, when creating an index based on multiple indicators, the researcher considers one of the variables to have double the weighting of other variables and it should therefore be multiplied by a factor of two. The rationale for computing a new variable must be clearly stated in the research report and, where appropriate, references to existing theories and literature to justify the data manipulation. These techniques are particularly useful when undertaking secondary analysis where the researcher is unlikely to find the variable data in the exact format required.

Using SPSS to compute a new variable

In this example the researcher is interested in creating an index of environmental awareness. The data collected does not contain a variable on environmental awareness; however, there are four variables that asked the respondent to rate on a scale of 5 (very important) to 1(not very important) the importance of the following: use of renewable energy sources; reduction in fossil fuel emissions; reduction in car journeys; and the availability of domestic recycling schemes. The responses were coded into four variables, env1, env2, env3 and env4 respectively. The researcher has decided to add the four variables together to create an overall index of the importance of environment issues. The first stage was for the researcher to check that the numerical coding was in the same direction for each of the variables. With 'very important' coded as 5 and 'not very important' coded as 1, for all variables this means that higher values in the final index will correspond with a higher overall importance value. If the coding did not run in the same direction, a re-coding procedure on the individual variable(s) would have to be undertaken before the index was computed.

To calculate the environmental importance index a new variable called 'index' is going to be created using the **Compute** command.

The compute command can only be accessed when viewing the **Data** window. Select the **Window** menu and **1-'filename' SPSS Data editor**. Select the **Transform** menu and **Compute**. The **Compute Variable** dialog box will be displayed (see Figure 24.3).

Under **Target Variable:** enter the new variable name, **Index**. Click on **Type&Label . . .** Next to **Label:** enter the variable label **Environmental Index**. Leave the **Type** set as **Numeric**. Click on **Continue** to return to the **Compute Variable** dialog box.

The variables to be combined into the 'index' variable are to be placed in the section under **Numeric Expression:**. For the index the numeric expression

will be env1 + env2 + env3 + env4. To build this expression, first highlight the variable 'env1' and then click on the arrow button → to move the variable across to the section under **Numeric Expression:**. Enter a + by either clicking on the + button from the middle section or typing in +. Now highlight the second variable 'env2' and again click on the arrow button → to move the variable across and again enter a +. Repeat this process until all the variables are entered. Click on **OK** to execute the command. A new variable 'index' will appear in the **Data Editor** window. Save the data file by selecting the **File** menu and **Save**.

Selecting cases and creating sub-sets of data

There may be occasions when undertaking data analysis that only a particular sample group of the data needs to be examined, for example, men only. More complex filtering parameters can be entered based on two or more variables. Cases that do not meet the filter conditions can be either temporarily removed or permanently removed. If the permanent option is selected, care must be taken not to overwrite the original data through saving the data file.

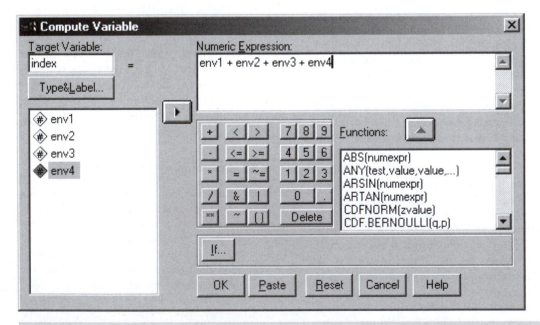

Figure 24.3   SPSS Compute Variable dialog box

Using SPSS to create sub-sets

The **Select Cases** command can only be accessed when viewing the **Data Window**. Select the **Window** menu and **1-'filename' SPSS Data editor**. Select the **Data** menu and **Select Cases. . . .** Under the **Select** section highlight the option **If condition is satisfied.** Click on the **If . . .** button. The **Select Cases:If** dialog box will be displayed (see Figure 24.4). Highlight the variable to build the selection criteria and click the arrow button → to move the variable into the right box. Next build the expression. The example in Figure 24.4 shows the expression '**sex = 1**'. This will select all cases where sex = 1 and the code 1 represents females. This expression would create a subset of females only.

The Boolean operators of AND and OR can be used to combine two or more variables. Below is an example of the expression that would select a sub-set of men aged 31–40 using the two variables 'sex', coded 1 = male, 2 = female, and age coded 1 = 16–20 years, 2 = 21–20 years, 3 = 31–40 years, 4 = 41years plus:

sex=1 AND age=3.

An expression to select a sub set of 16–20 year olds or 31–40 year olds only would be:

age=1 OR age=3.

In addition to equals to (=), the mathematical operators = >equal to or greater than, = <less than or equal to, >greater than, <less than, and, ~ = not equal to, are available.

Once the expression is complete, click on **Continue** to return to the previous **Select Cases** dialog box. In this dialog box under the section **Unselected Cases Are** select **Filtered** to temporarily remove unselected cases, or **Deleted** to permanently remove the unselected cases. Click on **OK** to execute the command. Where cases are filtered, the cases filtered out can be viewed in the **Data Editor** window as the corresponding row number has a diagonal line through it. To return to analysing all cases, remove the filter by selecting the **Data** menu and **Select Cases. . . .** Under **Select** highlight **All cases**. Click on **OK** to execute the command to return to analysing all cases.

Creating multiple response sets in SPSS

Survey questions that result in multiple responses require multiple variables to be created in SPSS. See 'Coding for multiple response questions' p. 182 and 'Different types of written report' p. 337 for more detail on creating these variables. Variables can then be placed together in a multiple response set for analysis purposes. The sets can then be analysed using multiple response frequency tables and cross-tabulations. This

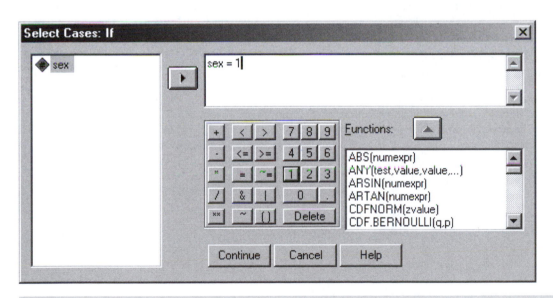

Figure 24.4   SPSS Select Cases: If dialog box

section will detail how to create multiple response sets and produce frequency tables and cross-tabulations of these sets.

The first stage of the multiple response procedure is to define the variables in a set. First, identify the variables to be merged into the set, use the coding frame for reference. Select the **Analyze** menu and **Multiple Response> Define Sets. . . .** A **Define Multiple Response Sets** dialog box will appear. Under **Set Definition**: there is a list of all variables in the current data set. One at a time highlight the variables to be included in the set and click on the arrow button → to move them to the section under **Variables in Set:**. Repeat this process until all the required variables are moved to this section. Under **Variables are Coded As:** the coding used for these variables needs to be defined. If a coding scheme of Yes/No has been used for each variable in the set, select **Dichotomies** and in the box next to **Counted Value** enter the code used for Yes, for example, **1**. Alternatively, if a coding scheme of 1 to a maximum code of n has been used for each variable in the set, select **Categories**. In the box next to **Range:** enter the lowest coded, for example, **1**, and in the box next to **through** enter the maximum coded, for example, **6**. The next stage is to create a set name. Next to **Name:** enter a multiple response set name. It can be up to seven characters in length as it will be automatically prefixed with a $ symbol. Next to **Label:** enter a multiple response set label. Click on **Add** to create the set – it will appear in the right box – and finally to remove the dialog box click on **Close**.

Producing frequency tables and cross-tabulations of multiple response sets

Frequency tables and cross-tabulations of multiple response sets cannot be created using the commands outlined in Chapters 21 and 22. Instead, the following procedure should be used.

To create a frequency table select the **Analyze** menu and **Multiple Response>Frequencies. . . .** In the **Multiple Response Frequencies** box under **Mult Response Sets:** highlight the required set and click on the arrow button → to move it to the section under **Table(s) for:**. To exclude missing values from the table under **Missing Values** select either **Exclude cases listwise within dichotomies** or **Exclude cases listwise within categories**. The selection will depend on the coding used. Click on **OK** to execute the command. A frequency table for the multiple response set will appear in the **Output Viewer**.

To create a cross-tabulation select the **Analyze** menu and **Multiple Response>Crosstabs. . . .** In the **Multiple Response Crosstabs** box both variables and mutliple response sets are displayed on the left-hand side. When exploring a relationship using multiple response sets, the set will be the dependent and the variable the independent. The conventions for placing the independent in the column and the dependent in the row can still be applied to these cross-tabulations. Highlight the required multiple response set and click on the first arrow button → to move to the section under **Row(s):**. Highlight the required independent variable and click on the second arrow button → to move to the section under **Column(s):**. The coding range for the variable will need to be defined. **Highlight the variable** under **Column(s):** and click on **Define Range**s. . . . In the dialog box enter the minimum and maximum code values. Click on **Continue**. To define the content of the cells in the table click on **Options**. Under **Cell Percentages** select the Row, Column or Total required. Under **Percentages Based On** select whether the percentages are to be based on the number of **Cases** or **Responses**. It is likely that you will require **Cases**. Click on **Continue** and click on **OK** to execute the command. A cross-tabulation will appear in the **Viewer** window.

Summary

Manipulating quantitative data enables the researcher to explore the data to greater depths. The re-coding of variables allows for improved data handling and can enable the researcher to apply hypothesis testing to variables that in their original format were not appropriate. Re-coding is particularly valuable when a nominal variable has a number of categories which contain a small number of counts, allowing for these categories to be combined into one larger category. In large data sets the technique that allows the researcher to select certain cases to create a sub-set is particularly useful when wanting to make comparisons between different groups based on more than one variable. SPSS allows the researcher to combine variables from a survey question that has multiple responses into one set. The resulting multiple response set can then be analysed as a frequency table or contingency table.

Keywords

Categories   Recode/Regroup
Chi-square test for Independence   Variable
Multiple Response Sets

Questions

1   Under what circumstances would it be appropriate to re-code an interval variable?
2   How can re-coding a categorical variable to a new variable with a smaller number of categories aid hypothesis testing?
3   In a general population survey, what variables would you require in the data set in order to produce a sub-set of cases who were single men aged over 40?
4   When is it appropriate to create multiple response sets in SPSS?

Further reading

Argyous, George (2000) *Statistics for Social and Health Research*. London: Sage.

Babbie, Earl and Halley, Fred (1998) *Adventures in Social Research: data analysis using SPSS for Windows*. Thousand Oaks, CA: Pine Forge.

Fielding, Jane and Gilbert, Nigel (2000) *Understanding Social Statistics*. London: Sage.

PART IV

PRESENTING RESEARCH FINDINGS

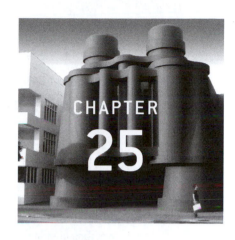

CHAPTER
25

PRODUCING A WRITTEN REPORT

Chapter contents

By the end of this chapter you will be able to:

- Produce an appropriately structured research report.

- Demonstrate how to present qualitative research findings.

- Demonstrate how to present quantitative data in appropriate tables and figures.

- Provide a written interpretation of your research findings

The written report

This chapter will consider the various issues related to presenting your research in a written report. There are many points to consider and it is important that you allocate enough time to both preparing and writing a report. You must also give careful consideration to the overall structure, content, presentation and written interpretation of your research findings.

Different types of written report

The structure of the written **report** can take a number of different forms depending upon the audience that you are writing for. The report should include details of all elements in the research process with a greater emphasis placed on some elements depending on the intended audience. A report written as part of an academic course of study is likely to have pre-defined sections and sub-sections. A report resulting from a piece of commissioned research, for example, for a local government agency or a private company, is unlikely to have a pre-defined structure with the researcher having to make decisions about the inclusion of different elements based upon the organization's requirements.

An additional consideration is the terminology and tone of the writing required for different audiences. An academic report should include a detailed discussion of the methodological approach taken and include a reflective evaluation of the research undertaken. A report for a local government agency is unlikely to require such a detailed inclusion of the methodological approach with a focus more on the research method, data collection tools and the research findings interpreted with, where applicable, policy recommendations. A report for such an agency may also benefit from the inclusion of an executive summary at the front of the report summarizing the key findings and policy recommendations.

General structure of report

Title page Containing a title that accurately reflects the research project. Including a sub-title if it helps to clarify the project. The name of the author(s), organization and a date should also be included.

Acknowledgements The Acknowledgements should contain thanks to those individuals and organizations that have enabled the research to take place. They should also contain a generic thank you to all the participants in the data collection phase of the research.

Contents page The Contents page should contain a list of the main sections, and, where appropriate, sub-sections, included in the report. The relevant page number for the start of each section and sub-section should also be included.

List of tables and figures A list of all tables and figures should be included in a separate **index**. The tables and figures should each be numbered sequentially. The relevant page number for each table and figure should be included.

Abstract The abstract is a short summary that provides a brief introduction to research problems, the methodological approach and methods adopted, and the main conclusions. It should be no longer than 150–250 words.

Introduction The purpose of this section is to briefly introduce the research problem, the aims and objectives of the study, hypotheses to be explored and so on.

Literature review This section should contain a review of the literature researched in relation to the research problem, together with a summary of previous research in the area.

Methodology and methods This should cover all the technical aspects of the research process, including the methodological approach, the research design, concepts and how they were operationalized, measurement tools developed or used, sampling, methods, data collection and the data and statistical analysis undertaken. Arising issues during the research process should also be detailed in this section. For example, where organizational constraints or gatekeepers restrict the research process. Any political or ethical considerations can also be highlighted in this section.

Research findings/research   The research findings section will detail the data collected. The structure of the research findings section will be dependent on the research aims, objectives and hypotheses, and on the quantitative or qualitative nature of the data. See 'Presenting qualitative data findings' p. 340 and 'Presenting quantitative data results' p. 344.

Discussion   The discussion section should bring together the main research findings and the key elements of the literature review. The discussion should focus on answering the original research problem, comparing the research findings with previous research in the area, and offering new insights or explanations. Reflections on the limitations of the research can also be discussed at this stage, together with recommendations for future research in the area. New literature or data should *not* be introduced in the discussion section.

Conclusions   The conclusion should summarize the main findings of the research, the debates undertaken in the discussion section and recommendations for future research. Where the research is focused on policy issues, policy recommendations can be included here.

References   A reference section should contain details of the materials that you have specifically referred to in the form of quotes in the report.

Bibliography   A bibliography should contain details of all materials that you have used during the course of the research project.

Appendices   Appendices can contain a variety of information related to the research project, but not central to the main report. For example, a copy of the survey questions, interview schedule, covering letters, interviewer prompt cards and so on. Results (charts, tables, quotes) that are omitted from the main results section may also be included.

Report layout and format

The following provides some general points for consideration when typing up a report. When presenting a report the most important element is *consistency* in the layout and format. You should refer to local guidelines for specific criteria when preparing your report.

Report sections and sub-sections   These should be numbered and the text enhanced to bold and/or italic. The most widely used format is 1, 1.1, 1.2, 1.3, 2, 2.1, 2.2, 2.3 and so on. The numbering sequence can go to a third level, for example, 1.1.1, 1.1.2, 1.1.3, however, the more levels the more complicated it becomes.

Tables   Tables contain data presented in rows and columns. Throughout the report tables must be labelled and numbered sequentially, starting at 1. For example, Table 1, Table 2, Table 3. After the table and number, the table title should be included, for example: Table 1: Sex of respondent; Table 2: Daily newspaper read by sex of respondent.

Charts   Charts are used to present data graphically. As for tables, charts should be labelled and numbered sequentially, starting at 1. The numbering of tables and charts is separate. The normal convention is to use a Figure 1, Figure 2, Figure 3 format. After the Figure and number, the chart title should be included, for example: Figure 1: Marital status of respondent.

Font, font size and line spacing   Font types are divided into two types, serif and sans serif. An example of each is **Times New Roman** and **Arial** respectively. A feature of sans serif fonts is that they are easier for some individuals to read and provide a clear image when included in a slide presentation. The normal font size for text in a report is 12pt with a line spacing of at least one and a half or double.

Report length   The length of a report will obviously vary according to the size of the research project and any local guidelines on word length, particularly for coursework-related dissertations.

Referencing sources in the bibliography

All sources, books, chapters in books, journal articles, newspaper articles and Internet sources must be referenced. There are a number of systems used for referencing; the two most common are the Harvard System and the numeric system, also known as the footnote/endnote system. The footnote system involves placing references immediately at the bottom of each page. The endnote system involves references being placed at the end of the section or book. Both the footnote and endnote system involve placing a superscript number next to the referenced text. This number then appears at the foot of the page, or at the section end/book end with the corresponding reference next to it. The number system normally starts at one.

You are advised to check with the institution, organization or publisher to whom your research report is going to be submitted for the exact format they require.

If no guidance is provided, the following section outlines some formatting suggestions based upon the Harvard system.

Book sources   These must contain the following information: the author(s) surname(s), initial, year of publication, 'title', place of publication and publisher. For example:

> May, T. (2001) *Social Research: Issues, Methods and Process* 3rd edition. Buckingham: Open University Press.

Chapters in books   For a chapter in an edited collection, the format is slightly different: chapter authors, year, chapter title, book author, book title, place of publication, publisher, page range. For example:

> Stroh, Matt (2000) 'Qualitative Interviewing', in Burton, D. (ed.), *Research Training for Social Scientists*, London: Sage. pp. 196–214.

Journal articles: Information to be presented in this order   author(s) surname(s), initial(s), year of publication, article title, journal title, volume number, part number and page range. For example:

> Bendelow, G. (1993) 'Pain perceptions, emotions and gender', *Sociology of Health and Illness*, 15, (3) 273–94.

Newspaper articles   These follow a similar format to journal articles. Where the author's name is not included in the original article, the newspaper title should be given instead: author's surname, initial or newspaper title, year, newspaper headline, newspaper title, day and month of publication, page number(s). For example:

> Guardian (2002) 'Pickets "will not stop" army', *Guardian*, 15 November, p. 2.

Internet sources   These are slightly more complex to report, given the different levels of information available about the site and author. One possible format for referencing Internet sources is to cite the author's surname, initial, (if available) year, date of page being written (if available), title of article/web page, website name, website address and date accessed. For example:

> Travis, A. (2002) '10-year-old offenders to be sent to foster homes,' Guardian Unlimited, website at http://www.guardian.co.uk/uk_news/story/0,3604, 840592,00.html. Accessed 15 November 2002.

Drafting and revisions

Writing a report can seem a daunting prospect and often the new researcher feels overwhelmed by the scale of the task. It is advisable to start writing as soon as possible during the research process. Ideas and lines of argument may alter and can be subsequently amended. We recommend that you start by producing a rough draft of how you envisage the structure of the report. The guidance on standard sections provided in the earlier part of this chapter will help you in getting started. One way to begin is to sketch out the anticipated sections and sub-sections. Within each write a few short paragraphs together with bullet points, if appropriate, that summarize the main content of those sections. It may be that you are only able to provide the most general of content guidance as you have yet to complete that section of the research process. For example, perhaps you are waiting for a particular journal article that you think may make an important contribution to the discussion in your literature review or that you are unable to provide a detailed structure for your data analysis sections as the data is still being analysed. Sketching out the various sections in this manner will enable you to see the whole structure of the report and will serve to remind you that the final report needs to be presented to the reader as a coherent whole and not several disjointed sections.

From these initial thoughts on structure you can now move on to write a first draft of the report. The order that the report is written in depends on the nature of the report and at what stage you are at in the research process. It is very rare that a researcher has the luxury of completing the research entirely before writing the report. In order to give yourself as much time as possible to review and revise the contents, start writing as early as possible. A logical approach to writing a report is to start by detailing the research aims and objectives, followed by a review of the relevant literature. The next sections would detail the methodology and methods employed in the research. Next to follow would be the presentation of the data, together with appropriate analysis and discussion of the findings. The discussion of the findings will seek to relate the research findings with the current literature, offering new thoughts and contributions to existing theories or development of new theories as appropriate. The abstract and conclusion, together with an executive summary if appropriate, will be the last of the main sections to be written.

Once you have produced a full draft report you should read through the complete report from beginning to end. Ideally you should find someone to comment on this draft. A third party should be more able to identify sections that are confusing to the reader, that require more explanation, or indeed sections that deviate from the main research aims. Sections can be revised and edited, or perhaps even deleted completely. Even if you have a third party to read through the report, you should check it carefully yourself. The most common areas that you should check for include spelling and grammar. Do not rely solely on the use of checkers supplied within word processing packages. Make sure that the text is clear and easy for the intended audience to read through. If you are not sure of the point that you are trying to convey, then it can be virtually guaranteed that your intended audience will also be mystified. While you may think what you have written makes sense, someone unfamiliar with your research area may not understand it. On this point a balance does need to be struck between making the report accessible, but at the same time not removing the theoretical and higher level discussion. Knowing your audience will guide you in this matter. If you find that sections are confusing or just simply do not make sense, try re-ordering the work or adding a suitable example. Pulling the section content apart to change the structure can often clarify matters, helping to determine the purpose of the section and the particular lines of thought or argument within it. You should not be afraid to edit your work drastically if required.

Finally, a word of warning should be offered. It is possible to spend too much time editing your report and undertaking changes that do not make a positive contribution to the final finished product. In such circumstances it is best to set a final deadline (assuming an external organization or a course work leader has not already set one) at which point all edits have to be completed and the final report presented.

Presenting qualitative data findings

Introduction: text and reduction

The most typical criticism of the presentation of qualitative data is that the audience is given a range of examples which do not allow them to comprehend whether those choice snippets represent the typical or most extreme examples from the researcher's data collection. Whilst quantitative researchers may boil down their research findings into a one-line statistical conclusion, and so be accused of excessive data reduction, the other extreme is the qualitative researcher who presents a vast array of examples and drowns their audience in seemingly undigested data. Chapters 16 to 19 sought to show the range of techniques by which a degree of qualitative data reduction can take place, even if this process will never, and does not seek to, achieve the level of reduction possible with more numerical data. This section seeks to highlight how such techniques can be usefully deployed in the presentation of findings to an audience.

The discussion of presenting quantitative data results largely hinges on the formatting of various statistical, graphical and tabular forms for inclusion in textual documents. Analysis in quantitative research is largely bound up with the production of statistical 'results' that can then be presented. These 'results' are mainly generated today using computer software. The question of presentation is that of how best to show the 'results'. In the field of qualitative data analysis, computer software does not perform this kind of analytical function. Software can enable the researcher to organize their data in various ways to enable certain relationships to be presented more clearly, both to the researcher and to any other potential audience. Recall Miles and Huberman's (1994) motto 'Think display'. This applies as much in the communication of one's findings as it does to their production.

While qualitative researchers are not able to generate statistical results to test the strength of an initial hypothesis, as has already been seen in Chapters 16 to 19, some qualitative researchers do use representational devices that mirror elements in the quantitative tradition of data presentation. The use of tables and network diagrams can identify the contents of a particular case in the same way that a frequency table and a graph might be used to map numerical data either at a particular moment or over a period of time. The production of matrix displays that map the cross-over between codes or attributes within qualitative data parallels the production of cross-tabulations in quantitative data analysis.

It is important, however, to recall that there are different ways of 'doing' qualitative data analysis. The forms of qualitative content analysis advocated by Miles and Huberman (1994) and by Berg (1998) draw heavily upon forms of data presentation that involve qualitative data being 'reduced' to units of meaning that can be counted or at least located within tables and network diagrams (see Chapters 16 to 19). Those who carry out forms of discourse analysis will very often reject the primary value of such representational devices. Such researchers prefer in-depth textual forms of analysis that rarely rely upon visual forms of data reduction (that is, tables, graphs and diagrams). Those who conduct conversation analysis once again reject the attempt to use representational devices to 'reduce' data for the purpose of either comprehension or comparison. Rather, those in the tradition of conversation analysis seek to give the most elaborate presentation of the data possible within any written or spoken presentation of analysis. It is the aim of conversation analysis never to analyse more than is presented in the article or discussion. The full transcript of the conversation being analysed must always be presented along with the analysis. There is absolutely no attempt to use presentational devices to 'reduce' data. Quite the reverse.

As such, there are different aims being pursued by different researchers. Not all qualitative researchers seek to parallel the data reduction techniques typical of more quantitative traditions and only some of these researchers use computer software to achieve this. Therefore, this section will look at a range of presentational devices. At the end of certain sections, the specific issue of transferring tables and diagrams from NVivo to word processor documents will be discussed. The labelling of these tables and diagrams should follow a similar format to those required for quantitative tables and figures. This is discussed in 'Tables' on p. 338.

Types of qualitative analysis and appropriate forms of presentation

Presenting the results of qualitative data analysis involves working with forms of textual material. Whether the data be the transcribed text of a series of recorded interviews, that of naturally occurring conversation, the notes taken by an interviewer at the time of interview, the fieldnotes taken by an ethnographer, or the contents of primary texts (such as newspapers, letters or diaries), it is fundamentally a text full of meaning. The type of text does not determine the way it should be analysed. That choice will be driven by the questions asked by the researcher. Content analysis is best able to help identify patterns of meaning across a relatively large quantity of text. Discourse analysis is best able to identify meaning in specific or small amounts of text. Conversation analysis is focused upon identifying the machinery at work in individual segments of conversation. The choice of focus determines the method of analysis to be used, though, of course there is most often a combination of motives that leads to a mixing of methods. It is the choice of data analysis methods that determines the best form of data presentation to communicate findings to a wider audience.

Conversation analysis

The golden rule when presenting analysis of conversation from a conversation analytic perspective is always to include a full transcription of the naturally occurring talk that you are going to discuss. As was shown in 'Transcription notation' p. 127, there are elaborate conventions for the presentation of talk such that the intricate machinery of pauses, intonation, interruption and turn-taking can be made manifest to those seeking to analyse the talk. Conversation analysts argue that the researcher should not draw upon inferences beyond the talk when seeking to explain it to an audience. As such, all the evidence necessary to draw the conclusions that the researcher draws should be available to the audience, whether this be the readers of a book, chapter or article, or the listeners to a spoken presentation. The audience is supposed to be able to share in the analytic process. The segment of text to be analysed is presented first, and the various dimensions of analysis (outlined in 'Doing conversation analysis' p. 216) are given after that, with each conclusion linked explicitly to the appropriate lines of text in the talk. Each line of text is numbered to facilitate this process of analytic transparency. At present there is no generally available computer software designed to facilitate the transcription of naturally occurring talk into the form used by conversation analysts.

Content analysis

The presentation of results generated by means of content analysis of qualitative data may draw upon a number of techniques designed to effect forms of data reduction that enable patterns to become apparent within large amounts of complex textual data. The three dominant forms of such reduction have been discussed in Chapters 16 to 19, both in general terms and with reference to their production within NVivo. The following discussion will outline each in turn, touching on their use and how they can be best produced for presentation purposes within NVivo. All three can be produced 'by hand' (that is, not using designated qualitative software), using paper and pencil or via other kinds of textual or graphics-based software. It is important to recall that content analysis may be used in the organization of data, elements of which can then be analysed in a more discourse analytic fashion. It is important, therefore, to think whether the use of the three techniques for presenting the findings of content analysis outlined below are to be the end of a particular presentation or merely the introduction (the contextualization) for a more detailed examination of particular sections of 'text' (see 'Discourse analysis' p. 215).

Numerical Tables within Qualitative Data Presentation

Tables in the presentation of qualitative content analysis serve much the same function as frequency tables and cross-tabulations in the presentation of quantitative data analysis. In the development of a written or spoken presentation of qualitative research, it is valuable to show the kinds of tables (that is, matrix displays) discussed in Chapter 17. Within-case displays and cross-case displays can be used to great effect in familiarizing an audience with the field or research. Context charts and checklist charts allow the audience to comprehend the characteristics of those who were researched. Time ordered displays can be used to familiarize the audience with both the research process and the events that were the subject of the research. Recall that tables should serve the purpose of communicating to the audience the findings of the research and the tables should be chosen accordingly. Do not seek to show every aspect of the data, the sample or the research process. The researcher needs to identify what is significant and select their tables in the light of this.

Using NVivo   Tables can be created within NVivo from three main sources (see Chapter 19). The first is the creation of attribute tables. The second is using various forms of matrix intersection searches within the search

tool. Finally, there is the assay function that allows numerical tables to be created that map the incidence of particular codes. Such tables need to be exported from NVivo into whatever software package is being used to write the presentation. For this to be achieved, it is necessary to transfer the NVivo file into a plain text file. With either the attribute table, matrix intersection table or assay table open, select **Export . . .** from the **File** menu at the top of the window. This opens up the **Export Profile-** window. Here it is necessary to locate where you want the new file to be stored. The default option is for the file to be re-formatted as a plain text file (**Text file (*.txt)**). The contents of this file can then be exported into a word processing file or a computer-based presentational software file. If, on the other hand, you wish to export the document into the statistical package SPSS, it is necessary to deselect the default export option and select instead the SPSS option. This allows the data to undergo more elaborate statistical investigation if that is desired.

Non-numerical code search results   It may be useful to present tables that show the incidence of particular codes and values within the data collected. This allows the audience to see whether the particular phenomenon coded for was common or rare, evenly distributed or more prevalent in some groups than in others. However, there may be more to add than just a display of numerical distribution. You may wish the audience to understand the different meanings the same phenomenon had for different groups, or the different ways in which the same outcome was achieved and so on. This will often require the presentation of textual data itself. This may be in the form of tables that contain quotes or descriptions from or of different individuals or groups about the same topic. This may be in the form of tables that contain quotes or descriptions from or of the same individuals or groups concerning a range of different topics or over a range of different times (see Chapter 17). Alternatively, the researcher may choose to select specific quotes (either from interview transcripts, fieldnotes or from primary textual sources) to illustrate their conclusions. Regarding the use of quotation as a device to illustrate a researcher's conclusion to an audience not fully familiar with the data, it is useful to recall Berg's rule of three (see p. 194). One supportive quotation does not prove anything and may not be convincing to an audience. The use of tables allows the range of findings to be presented. If this is done, then the use of a single quotation may add to the persuasiveness of the overall presentation. If tables are not used, then it is necessary to demonstrate to the audience why the selected quotation is considered representative of a more general pattern in the data. Alternatively, it is possible to say that selected quotations are illustrative of the uniqueness of particular individuals or groups. However, this claim still needs to be supported in the presentation in order to be persuasive. This can be achieved by discussion of the coding process and its outcomes. See below for discussion of this in the context of NVivo. The same principles apply when coding by hand.

Using NVivo   It is not possible to construct tables containing textual data at the points of intersection between variables within NVivo itself, but specific quotations can be cut and pasted into other document formats relatively easily. What NVivo also allows is the conduct of searches that produce textual outputs. Within NVivo the conduct of node searches, Boolean searches, text searches and proximity searches all generate textual data that can be incorporated, by cutting and pasting, into presentation formats. The conduct of such searches also makes the task of selecting those quotes that best illustrate general patterns or specific differences easier for the researcher.

Network diagrams   Diagrams that illustrate time lines (whether that of the research itself or of the lives or events being researched) or which illustrate relationships within the data are the equivalent of graphs in more numerical forms of data presentation.

Using NVivo   Models created in NVivo can be exported from NVivo in the following way. The simplest method is to select the **Export Diagram to Clipboard** option from the **Model** menu of the **Model Explorer** window. This saves a copy of the model to the clipboard and this can then be pasted directly into compatible word processing software.

Discourse analysis

Discourse analysis, as discussed in Chapter 18, takes a critical stance towards forms of data reduction that bring qualitative content analysis closer to quantitative forms of data analysis and presentation. Nevertheless, as was pointed out in Chapter 16 and 18, forms of qualitative content analysis can be usefully applied to large quantities of textual data to enable key themes to emerge that can subsequently be analysed in more

depth, using selected examples, by discourse analytic means. As such, the presentation of general characteristics about a data set in the form of tables and network diagrams may well usefully precede more discourse analytic work in a written presentation of findings. These tables and diagrams can be generated 'by hand' or using qualitative data analysis computer software packages.

For the presentation of discourse analysis itself, it is most common to use predominantly textual, that is, written, accounting techniques. More holistic descriptions of time spent in the field, of the practices, rituals and routines of a group observed, or of the life of a person interviewed, are not always usefully reduced to non-textual form. Much of the significance of a 'way of life' or 'way of seeing' would be lost in non-textual forms of data reduction. Also, the value of more open-ended forms of data collection would be lost if all the data was then packaged in more closed representational forms. The value of the more content analytic approaches to data presentation discussed above lies in enabling the researcher to identify general patterns in large amounts of data. Once done, forms of textual discourse analysis, discussed in Chapter 18, may be applied to the selected events, lives and situations. This application moves in two directions. First, specific examples can be explored in greater depth, and second, more general or holistic conclusions about the pattern of events can be presented.

Specific representational devices in discourse analytic data presentation: images, maps and notation   Much discourse analytic work is carried out on visual images and material artefacts. In presentation of research on such items it is useful to present a selection of such images or visual representations of those artefacts. A study of gender representation in advertising may deploy content analytic techniques to identify the incidence of certain characteristics. The selection of such characteristics and the attempt to understand their significance by discourse analytic means can be presented most successfully to a wide audience by means of a discussion accompanied by one or more selected examples.

Ethnographic research may use a number of representational devices to convey the meaning that those studied attach to their lives and actions. These may be drawings made by the researcher themselves, or images drawn by those studied. While time in the field allows the researcher to get to know the way those around them see the world, someone reading a discussion of that fieldwork may benefit from visual pointers such as maps, drawings and photographs from the field.

Finally, within deconstruction there is a particular notation device used to draw the attention of the reader to the analytical questioning being applied to a particular concept (or metaphor masquerading as a concept). This is to place a line through a concept or term within a text being analysed. Such a term is then said to be placed '~~under erasure~~'. It is this term that is being 'deconstructed', or taken apart.

Presenting quantitative data results

Writing descriptive accounts of quantitative results

The purpose of the results section is to convey the main findings of your research to the reader. It will form a large proportion of the overall size of the report. When writing up the results from quantitative data analysis a number of issues should be considered. The first is what are the main results that you want the reader to learn about? These should be clearly related to the original research objectives and presented in the same or broadly similar order as in the literature review and methodology sections. It is likely that through the process of exploring the data you will have collated much more data analysis than can be included in the final report. You will need to sift and sort your results accordingly. Likewise, you will need to make careful decisions about the tables and charts to be presented in the final report. A general rule is to only include those tables and charts that actually show a trend or relationship between two or more variables that relates to the original objectives. Limits on the number of tables and charts to be included in a report are sometimes suggested. The important point is that a balance must be maintained between the written interpretation and the tables/charts.

The researcher should avoid including tables and charts in reports that are not referred to in the written text. If you feel that you want to include some tables/charts that are interesting but are not a key focus of the project, consider placing them in the appendices and make a short reference to their inclusion in the write-up. The style of descriptive account could be a simple written interpretation of the summary statistics and percentages in a frequency table or contingency table. A more analytical and

contextualized explanation, offering a greater depth and possibly linking to the findings of previous research and theories from the literature review, can also be made. The key findings for the research data will inform much of the content of the subsequent discussion sections. The nature of quantitative data analysis generally requires that the written interpretations are normally undertaken in the passive voice, avoiding the use of 'I' or 'we'. There may be occasions, particularly when using multi-method or mixed-method approaches, where the use of the active voice is appropriate.

Tables

In Chapters 21 and 22 frequency tables were used to provide descriptive summaries of single variables. Contingency tables or cross-tabulations were produced to explore the relationship between two variables. For both frequency and contingency tables, the format of the table produced by SPSS is inappropriate for a formal report. The cells in the table contain a lot of data, all of which is not necessary for inclusion in the final report. SPSS row, column and total headings often fail to convey the exact meaning of the data. Tables of a suitable format can be produced within SPSS using the tables command, or alternatively the table can be reproduced using the table function in a word processing package, for example, MS Word. For both types of table the metadata, containing the accompanying titles, labels and information on missing data, must be included to allow the reader to accurately interpret the presented data. The metadata must be included for tables both from primary and secondary data sources.

A suggested format for both frequency and contingency tables is detailed below. This is only one of a number of appropriate formats and you should refer to local guidelines for your particular report. An important aspect of presenting tables is that the structure and format must be consistent throughout the report. Fink (1995c) provides some excellent guidance on how to present survey data in a report.

Frequency tables

Frequency tables summarize the data for a single variable. The basic SPSS frequency table calculates the count, percentage, valid percentage and cumulative percentage for each variable category. The most common data to present is the valid percentage for each category in that variable as this allows for comparisons between category responses to be made.

Where sample numbers are exceptionally small it may be appropriate to present the count. If there is a large number of missing data, then presenting the percentage based on the total sample size may be more appropriate. The metadata to be included with a frequency table are:

● *Table title:* The table title should start with the word Table followed by the number of the table in the report, for example, Table 1. All tables in the report should be numbered sequentially, starting from 1. This should be followed by a title that accurately reflects the frequency table data presented. It should not include the original SPSS variable name. The table title should include, either on a separate line or in brackets, the total number of valid observations for the variable, expressed as n = 100. For example: Table 1: Sex of respondents (n=100).

● *Category labels:* The labels for each category should be entered in full. Avoid replicating abbreviations that may have been used in the data entry phase, for example, *dna* for did not answer. The category labels should relate to the table title. Labels for the unit of analysis (valid percentage or count) should be entered in the appropriate column headings.

● *Footnotes:* Additional information can be placed in a footnote immediately underneath the table. Footnotes can include the number of missing cases for a variable; it is also appropriate to include where the valid percentage has been calculated and presented in the main body of the table. If presenting tables from a secondary data source, for example, aggregated data from the General Household Survey, the footnote could contain the data source and year. An example of a report-quality frequency table is shown in Table 25.1.

Table 25.1   Example of presenting a report-quality frequency table

Sex of respondents (n=100)

Sex	Percentage
Male	30
Female	70
Total	100

Missing = 10

Using SPSS to produce a report-quality frequency table
The following commands take you through the key steps involved in the Tables command to produce a report-quality frequency table. This command will calculate percentages based on the valid count and no information is provided in the final table output on the number of missing cases. It is therefore important that frequency tables using the **Descriptive Statistics** and **Frequencies** commands are produced in the first instance and **Custom Tables** only used for the final report tables. Select the **Analyze** menu and **Custom**

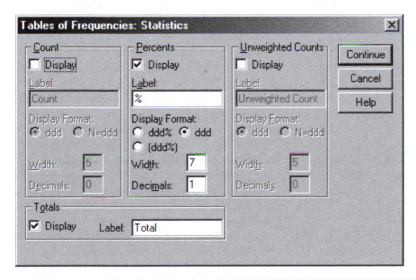

Figure 25.1   SPSS Tables of Frequencies: Statistics dialog box

Tables > **Table of Frequencies** . . .. The **Tables of Frequencies** dialog box will be displayed. Highlight the required variable from the left variable list and click once on the top arrow button → to move the variable to the section under **Frequencies for:**.

To determine the counts and/or percentages to be displayed in the final table, click on the **Statistics . . .** button. A **Tables of Frequencies: Statistics** dialog box will be displayed (see Figure 25.1). The box is divided into four sections. To create a table with percentages displayed only, under **Count** click once on **Display** to remove the default tick. Under **Percents** click once on **Display** to place a tick in the adjacent box. In the **Percents** section under **Label:** either leave as % or remove and type in 'Percentage'. In the **Percents** section under **Display Format:** select either the ddd% or ddd option. These present the data in each cell as either 10% or 10 respectively. Both of these format options are a matter of individual choice, but ones that should be consistent throughout the report. In the box next to **Decimals:** the number of decimal places that the data is displayed to can be controlled. The default is to one decimal place; if you wish it to be set to no decimal places, and rounded up to the nearest whole number, replace 1 with 0. In the section under **Totals:** click on **Display** to include a column total. Leave the default label as **Total**. Click on **Continue** to return to the previous dialog box. Other commands available include the format of empty, no observations, cells, appearing as either a zero or a blank cell (**Format . . .** button) and entering a title and footnote (**Titles . . .** button). While titles and footnotes can be entered in SPSS it is advisable to enter them in the word processed report to allow for easier text formatting. Click on **OK** to execute the command. The custom table will appear in the **Output** window. The table can be edited by **double-clicking** on any aspect of the table. The format of the table, borders, headings, font, can be edited by **right clicking** on the table and selecting **TableLooks . . .** from the menu. The procedure for placing the table into a word processing document is identical as for charts (see 'Exporting charts into a word processing document' p. 288).

Contingency tables or cross-tabulations

Contingency tables allow you to explore relationships between two variables. The standard format is that the independent variable is placed in the column and the dependent variable in the row, see 'Contingency tables' p. 295 for an in-depth discussion. Cells in the contingency table can contain a count, row percentage, column percentage or total percentage. Cells in a report-quality table will normally contain the column percentage only, since the independent variable is placed in the column. Column percentages enable the researcher to make comparisons between the different categories in the independent variable. Where the convention of placing the independent variable in the column is not followed, the cell percentage should be adjusted accordingly to row percentages.

With the independent variable in the column 'Column totals', 100 per cent should be included in the last row of the table to aid the reader in the interpretation of the table. Each column total will also need to include a count to allow the reader to see the number of observations in each of the categories in the independent variable. This will also enable the reader to calculate the individual cell counts from the column percentage. Where individual cell counts are exceptionally small, it may be more appropriate to present the count.

The metadata to be included with a contingency table are:

- *Table title*: The table should start with the words 'Table' followed by the number of the table in the report, for example, Table 2. All tables should be numbered sequentially. The format for a contingency table title is dependent variable by independent variable. The title should not include original SPSS variable names. The total number of valid observations for the variable, expressed as n = 120, should be included in brackets or on a second separate line. For example, Table 2: Working Full-Time or Part-Time by Sex (n=120).
- *Category labels for independent and dependent variables*: Labels should be entered in full, avoiding the use of abbreviations. If abbreviations are used because of limited space, a definition should be included in the table footnote. Labels for the unit of analysis (percentage or count) should be entered in the column headings, assuming the independent variable is placed in the column.
- *Footnotes*: Additional information can be placed in the footnote immediately underneath the contingency table. This information can include missing values, definitions of category labels, data source and year if using secondary data.

An example of a report-quality contingency table is shown in Table 25.2.

Table 25.2   Example of presenting a report-quality contingency table

Newspaper normally read by sex of respondent (n=120)

Employment status	Sex Male %	Female %
Full-time	66.7%	50.0%
Part-time	33.3%	50.0%
Total	100.0%	100.0%
	(n=60)	(n=60)

Using SPSS to produce a report-quality contingency table   The following commands take you through the key steps when using the **Custom Table** command in SPSS to produce report-quality contingency tables. This procedure does not provide the additional information on the number of missing cases, as produced by the **Crosstab** command, see 'Creating contingency tables in SPSS' p. 296, and consequently you should always produce an initial table using crosstabs before producing a custom table.

To produce a custom table in SPSS select the **Analyze** menu and **Custom Tables > General Tables . . ..** The **General Tables** dialog box will be displayed. From the variable list on the left side, highlight the dependent variable. Click once on the top arrow button to move this variable to the section under **Rows**:. Again from the variable list, now highlight the independent variable and click once on

the middle arrow button to move this variable to the section under **Columns**:. The default setting in SPSS is that the table will display counts in each cell. In order to produce a table that displays column per cents, a number of formatting changes need to be made. The first stage is to remove the count display in each cell followed by the second stage of selecting column per cents with the required format. To remove the count display under Rows, highlight the dependent variable and then click once on the **Edit Statistics** button. A **General Tables: Cell Statistics** box will be displayed, see Figure 25.2. This box is divided into two sections. Under **Cell Statistics**: click once on **Count** and then click on the **Remove** button. To display column per cents under **Statistics:** select **Col %**. In the bottom left corner of the dialog box there are a number of format options available to control exactly how the column per cent is displayed in the cells of the final table. Next to **Format:** a drop-down menu displays different formats for the cell data. The default setting is to display each cell value with a per cent symbol, %, next to it. For example, 50.5%. To display a cell value with no per cent symbol, select **ddd.dd** from the menu list. The second default setting that can be altered is the number of decimal places. The default decimal place setting is to display a value to one decimal place. To alter this to no decimal places, next to **Decimals:** delete 1 and type in 0. The default label for the column per cent is 'Col %'. This can be altered by editing the contents of the box next to **Labels:**. For example, changing the label to simply '%'. Once the required formatting changes have been made, click on

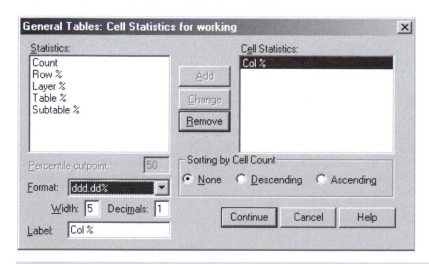

Figure 25.2   SPSS General Tables: Cell Statistics for working dialog box

the **Add** button. Finally, click on the **Continue** button to return to the **General Tables** dialog box.

To include a column total in the final row of the table, highlight the dependent variable under **Rows:** and click once on the **Insert Table** button. The variable name followed by the word 'Total' will now appear under the **Rows:** section.

The **Format** and **Titles** buttons can be used to control the appearance of empty cells and entered table titles respectively. As with the custom frequency tables earlier, it is recommend that titles be entered at the final report stage. Finally, to produce the custom table click on the **OK** button. A custom contingency table will be displayed in the **Output** window.

Charts and graphs

The presentation of **charts** and graphs in a report is fairly straightforward. Again, the charts produced by SPSS are quite basic and can be edited to improve their appearance (see 'Editing SPSS charts' p. 287). Alternatively, data from frequency tables and contingency tables can be entered into an alternative package that has a chart function within it, for example, MS Excel or MS Word. Fink (1995c) provides detailed guidance on reporting and presenting survey data. The key aspects when presenting charts in a report are:

- *Chart Title:* The chart title should follow the same format as for frequency and contingency tables for a single bar chart and multiple bar chart respectively. Charts are normally labelled as Figure 1, Figure 2 and so on.

- *Axis labels:* Edited axis labels where existing labels contain SPSS variable labels.
- *Bars:* Consider altering the bar colours and fill patterns to give a consistent appearance throughout the report. Give consideration to the colour of bars, particularly in multiple bar charts, if the report is going to be printed on a black ink only printer, or if it is going to be reproduced in grey scale. The grey scale equivalents for some colours are extremely close together, making it difficult for the reader to distinguish between bars.
- *Footnotes:* Make use of footnotes to include the number of missing cases, definitions of category labels, data source and year if using secondary data.

Writing up the results from statistical tests

The inclusion of statistical tests in a report will normally be placed after the descriptive account of the variable(s). For example, a descriptive account of the relationship between two categorical variables would be stated before proceeding to undertake a statistical test, such as chi-squared. When including the results of statistical tests in academic reports you should clearly state the purposes of the test, the null hypothesis and research hypothesis. Report the statistical tests' results in full; these include the test statistic, degrees of freedom, where applicable, and the significance level. From these finally accept or reject the null hypothesis based on these findings and the conclusions you can draw from them. An example of reporting a chi-square test can be found in 'Reporting chi-square findings' on p. 317.

Summary

This chapter has outlined the main elements of presenting your research findings in a written report. When producing a report it is vital that you consider the intended audience you are writing for. A report for an academic course is likely to have pre-defined sections with equal emphasis on methodology, methods and research findings. Reports for non-academic audiences will vary from this structure. For example, they may be less interested in the methodology and more interested in the research findings and potential policy implications. It is important that you are clear from the outset, before writing your report, that you understand these requirements and the subsequent balance between the different elements.

Keywords

Charts
Index
Report
Tables

Questions

1   Identify the key sections of a report and the information that should be included in each of the sections.

2   What information should be included when presenting a table in a report?

3   Describe the different approaches to presenting qualitative research findings

Further reading

Fink, Arlene (1995c) *How to Report on Surveys*. London: Sage.

Hague, Paul N. and Roberts, Kate (1994) *Presentations and Report Writing*. London: Kogan Page.

Robson, Colin (1993) *Real World Research*. Oxford: Blackwell.

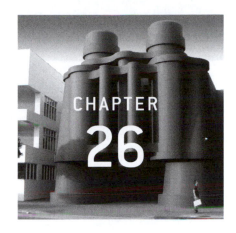

CHAPTER

26

PRESENTING RESEARCH FINDINGS TO AN AUDIENCE

Chapter contents

By the end of this chapter you will be able to:

- Prepare and undertake a verbal presentation of your research findings.

- Understand how to structure your presentation.

- Understand the different visual techniques which you can use to enhance a presentation.

The key to a successful **presentation** is to set out clearly the objectives that you wish your presentation to achieve. It is highly likely that the time allocated for a presentation will not allow you to go into every detail about the research you have undertaken and your findings. You will therefore need to make decisions as to what to include in your presentation. The audience you are addressing will in part determine the key points, or objectives, that you wish to convey. Remember that the audience expects to learn something about your research and this will be influenced by the amount of prior knowledge that they have of the process of social research and the substantive, topic, area investigated. Deciding on the level of knowledge the audience brings with them can be tricky. The more experience you gain from presenting research, the more confident you will become in making a decision as to the level of knowledge to assume. General advice when undertaking your first presentation is to assume that the audience has very little or no prior knowledge. This is particularly the case if your presentation is to a non-academic audience. Where you are presenting to an academic audience, some basic knowledge of the social research process and common concepts may be known. You can always skip over the more basic aspects of the research if it becomes clear that the audience is familiar with some aspects.

Having set the level of prior knowledge of the audience that you are going to assume, the next step is to decide on the intended objectives of the presentation itself. The audience is likely to want to know why you carried out the research, the research design, research methods used, the main findings from the data collected and how your conclusions inform or relate to current understanding and theory.

Organizing the material

Organizing your material is a fairly straightforward process, as the presentation will follow a similar structure to a written report. The structure is likely to be:

- State background to the research project.
- Research aims/questions.

- Research design and methods employed.
- Key findings.
- Discussion of key findings in relation to existing literature and theory.
- Conclusions.

You will need to tailor the structure and content to the allocated time that you have for the presentation. If you do not have time to present the entire research project, select a number of key findings and focus on those. You will be able to assess the constraints of the time allocation by practising your talk.

Delivery of a presentation

There are a number of elements to successfully delivering a presentation.

- Use of visual aids.
- Content of visual aids.
- Body language and eye contact.
- Clarity and tone of voice.

Use of visual aids

There are a variety of **visual aids** available including flip charts/whiteboards, overhead projectors, computer LCD projectors, video and audio recorders.

Flip charts and whiteboards tend to be used more in situations where discussion and small group work is taking place. They can be used for presentations where no other visual aids are available. The use of flip charts and whiteboards requires the presenter to have a supply of suitable marker pens and board erasers.

Overhead projectors and computer LCD projectors allow the presenter to prepare in advance OHPs or a computer-based slideshow. Where a slide show is prepared it is always advisable to have a back-up of the slides printed on ordinary OHP transparency sheets.

Content of visual aids

Keep the content of slides, OHP or computer-based presentation simple:

- Use bullet point lists to highlight key points.
- Do not clutter the slide with too much text.
- The text should be at least 14 point. Remember that it needs to be seen by those sitting at the back of the room.
- Include graphs and tables as appropriate.
- Avoid the use of large tables. In these instances it is better to report the content of 'key' cells.

When using a computer slideshow do not over-use the 'additional features' available through the templates. Flashing graphics, additional noise, over-use of multiple colour schemes and graphics can detract from the content of your research.

Video and audio materials can provide a useful addition to a presentation. A short piece of video footage can be included to illustrate a particular point. Alternatively, some audio from an interview or group discussion can add context and life to the presentation. The use of video and audio materials also breaks up the presentation and gives the presenter a few welcome minutes of rest from speaking.

When designing the use of video or audio materials make sure that:

- the selected materials are appropriate; and
- the video or audio clip is not too long.

Body language and eye contact

It is important that you build a rapport with the audience to increase your own confidence and reinforce to the audience that you have something important to say and they should listen to you. The easiest way to achieve this is to engage with the audience through eye contact. Look around the audience and remember to smile, even if you are feeling very nervous. In addition, eye contact with the audience will provide you with feedback on how your presentation is going – does the audience understand what you are saying? Finally, avoid annoying habits such as fumbling with a pen or jewellery.

Clarity and tone of voice

Speak clearly and confidently. If you are concerned that your nervousness will show through in your voice tone, try taking some deep breaths to calm your nerves. Try to avoid repeating phrases, for example, OK, right, cool. You will probably not notice them, but your audience will! You will need to speak at a slightly slower pace than your normal speaking rate. The more nervous you are, the more likely you are to speak quickly, resulting in the audience becoming confused and the talk becoming shorter than originally anticipated.

Presenting the research

One of the most pressing issues for the presenter is whether they should read a pre-prepared script or try to remember everything they want to say. Neither of these two extremes is advantageous. A person who reads from a script runs the risk of disengaging from the audience as they read with their head buried in the paper they are holding. Likewise, unless the presenter is extremely confident, calm and has an excellent memory, the latter is also likely to fail. The reality will be somewhere in between. When first presenting it is likely that you will want to have detailed notes in front of you, and as experience grows the notes are likely to become briefer. When preparing your speaking notes, consider the following:

- Make use of headers and sub-headers to divide your talk into manageable sections. These may correspond with the key words on your visual aids.
- Consider the use of index cards as they are smaller and easier to manage than large sheets of paper.

And finally, it is advisable to practise your talk to a group of supportive friends or colleagues. Practising the talk will enable you to judge whether the information you wish to present is possible within the allocated presentation time.

Summary

A successful presentation is achieved by setting clear objectives as to the purpose of the presentation. The researcher needs to decide upon the elements of the research that they wish to share with the audience, as inevitably there will be time restrictions limiting discussion of all areas relating to the research. This will involve organizing the material appropriately and developing a structure that has a number of sections and subsections. The use of visual aids can enhance a presentation, give a professional look and give the presenter an additional confidence boost. It will be the confidence of the presenter that will ultimately determine the success of the presentation. Body language, clarity and tone of voice will convey how important your research is and that it makes a positive contribution to the subject area.

Keywords

Presentation
Visual Aids

Questions

1   Identify the key sections of a presentation and the information that should be included in each of the sections.
2   How can visual aids improve your presentation?
3   What other elements can improve your presentation?

Further reading

Bradbury, Andrew (2000) *Successful Presentations* (2nd edn). London: Kogan Page.
Byram, Lynda (1999) *Being Successful in Presentations*. London: Blackhall.

Abstracts and Indexes: Abstracts are summaries that sum up the content of a journal article (or other *Text*). Abstracts used to be collected into large bound volumes that could be searched for using parallel volumes of 'Indexes' (alphabetical lists by author, title and subject matter). Now, much of this searching can be done on electronic abstracting and indexing services.

Action Research: Research designed not simply to know the world, but to enable change. Action research is more than just policy driven research, it seeks to implement policy through the research itself. See also *Evaluation Research* and *Participant Action Research*.

Actors: While an actor is said to engage in action, machines, plants, objects and so on only display behaviour (the position of animals is controversial in this spectrum). Action requires a consciousness capable of reflecting upon a course of action. While behaviour can be studied simply in terms of causal mechanisms, understanding action requires a knowledge of what the actor intended to achieve by their action, even if this is not the whole story. The capacity for self-reflection is seen by some as grounds for saying an actor is 'morally' responsible for their actions in the way that, for example, a thunderbolt is not responsible for its behaviour. This view is premised upon the belief that if an action was 'chosen', in the course of 'reflection', the actor could have chosen not to take that course of action. In other words, some believe that actors are at least in part able to determine (cause) their own actions and therefore should be held accountable for those actions. Others prefer to use the term 'subject' to refer to the human individual (consciousness as well as physical being) so as to avoid this attribution of something close to 'free will'. The term 'actor' is closely associated with the term 'agency', which again is often used to attribute self-determination to human beings, rather than seeing them as outcomes of the social arrangements they are a part of. Once again, critics highlight the fact that such a term assumes some kind of freedom of the will, something that cannot be proven, and is almost impossible to conceptualize, except in the base sense of feeling the urge to blame and punish (itself a form of social causation that justifies itself in the language of responsible actors).

Adjacency Pairs: *Conversation Analytic* term referring to forms of talk where the first speaker's talk elicits a predictable response. The expectation built into such pairs is what is significant. Speakers can choose to deviate, but the expectation is still present. See also *Turn-Taking*.

Advocacy: In a research context, advocacy describes the situation when the researcher role becomes merged with that of supporting the group being studied in a political or other sense. While *Action Research* refers to research that seeks to change those being researched, research as advocacy is more focused at changing the way others see or treat those being researched. This distinction is not rigid.

Aggregated Data: Data that has been previously manipulated and summarized into *Tables*.

Aide-mémoire: List of themes, questions and keywords that an *Open-Ended* interviewer keeps with them during an *Interview*. The purpose is to remind the interviewer of things to bring into the *Interview*, or ways of developing a line of questioning, not as a strict script (which would be an *Interview Schedule*).

Alternative Hypothesis: (Also called *Research Hypothesis*. Used in hypothesis testing. It asserts that there is a real difference between observed values and those expected in the theoretical model as stated in the *Null Hypothesis*.

Anonymity: Anonymity is where the identity of a research participant is not recorded for the purposes of research, or where records are destroyed once data collected has been recorded. Anonymity is not the same as confidentiality (see *Confidentiality*).

Archive/Archival Research: Research based on existing *Data* and other *Textual* materials. This may mean working from a formal library or from the archives of organizations or individuals. Government records and personal letters and diaries may form the subject of archival research. Archival research now includes working with material held electronically, or which can be located electronically, but which has then to be located in physical archives.

Artefact: Any product of human cultural production. In social research the word is used in two senses. First, Artefact can refer to any cultural product recorded or collected for analysis by the researcher. Examples might include diaries, photographs, items of clothing or jewellery, cooking implements and/or newspapers. Second, Artefact can refer to any research outcome that might be said to have been biased by the research process itself. If the researcher's questions, appearance, behaviour or simply their presence leads to distortions in results, these distorted results are referred to as research artefacts, rather than valid representations of reality.

Assay: Originally 'to assay' was to analyse the mineral content of a substance, such as in assessing the gold content. In social research an assay table sets out the number of times selected *Codes* occur within selected cases.

Attributes: Attributes are general properties possessed by one or more persons or objects. Recording and comparing attributes enables patterns to be identified if underlying similarities exist within or between groups.

Autobiographical Method: Use of the researcher's own life story as a subject of research.

Availability Sampling: See *Opportunity Sampling*.

Axial Codes: Axial *Codes* are *Codes* that the researcher selects to represent and to highlight what they perceive to be the core issues or themes within the *Text* they are analysing. Distinguished from *Systematic Coding*.

Balancing: When developing rank order categories for *Closed-ended Questions*, ensure that there are equal numbers of positive and negative categories.

Bar Chart: A graphical presentation of data appropriate for nominal or ordinal variables. Consists of a series of bars on the X (horizontal) axis with a count or percentage displayed on the Y (vertical) axis. Each bar represents the count or percentage of observations in a category.

Baseline: An established point from which to measure changes over time or between locations. The term can be used to refer to highly *Quantitative* measures. For example, changes in unemployment in all OECD countries can be compared by translating each country's unemployment figure in a given year into the figure 100 and then calculating changes in each country year by year in relation to that standardized baseline *Statistic*. More *Qualitative* use of the term baseline refers to the collection of data on attitudes and beliefs at one point in time to be compared with results gathered later (often after a particular policy initiative or programme).

Before and After Design: A research design in which all subjects are measured, pre-test, before being subjected to the manipulation of an *Independent Variable*. The subjects are then measured again, post-test. Pre-test and post-test findings are then compared. There is no control group.

Biased: Bias occurs when *Sample* characteristics are different to those found in a *Population*.

Biographical Method: The use of written accounts of lives as a source of *Data*. Biographical method can be distinguished from *Life History* interviewing, where the researcher interviews rather than reads accounts of lives. However, this distinction is not always maintained and the terms have become in part interchangeable.

Bivariate Analysis: Analysis of *Quantitative Data* that describes and explores the relationship between two *Variables*.

Box Plot: A graphical presentation for *Interval* variables. Graphically represents the *Median* and first and third *Quartiles* as a box.

Breaching: An *Ethnomethodological* term referring to deliberate attempts by the researcher to break social conventions in order to see how people cope and react to someone who does not conform to expected patterns. Such research is typically *Covert*.

Case: An individual unit being studied. A case could be a person, institution, household, organization and so on.

Case Study/Case Study Method: Research that is non-*Comparative*. A case study may focus on one individual, one area, one group or one organization. It is not designed to compare one individual or group to another. Though it is possible to conduct a series of case studies, each study would not be designed specifically to enable comparison with others.

Categorical Variables: A term used for *Nominal* and *Ordinal* variables. The attributes of the data can be categorized.

Categories: The grouping of *Data* in a unit, each member of which shares one or more characteristics. Categories require the ability to specify their boundaries. This involves criteria of *Internal Homogeneity* and *External Discretion*.

Causality: see *Causation*.

Causation: In simple terms, causation is the process that makes an outcome happen. Causation is something more than just the fact that certain things happen regularly in a sequence. However, outcomes rarely have only one potential cause, and particular causal factors do not always lead to the same outcome. *Mediations*, as well as *Necessary* and *Sufficient Conditions* are important aspects of causal accounting. When testing a *Hypothesis* the researcher tries to test the extent to which variation in one or more *Independent Variables* causes variation in one or more *Dependent Variables*.

Census: A survey of all cases in a population.

Central Limit Theorem: A mathematical theorem that states that repeated sample means, taken using a random sampling technique, will approximate to a *Normal Distribution Curve*. It is used as the basis for *Inferential Statistics* and *Hypothesis Testing* (also called *Significance Testing*).

Charts: A form of visual display in which time/sequence, size, quantity, relationships or causal processes are represented. Bar or pie charts, histograms and scatterplots are examples of *Quantitative* charts, while Gant charts and cognitive maps are examples of more *Qualitative* charts.

Chi-Square Test for Independence: A *Non-parametric Hypothesis* test used to assess the statistical significance of findings. Enables the researcher to assess if sample findings can be *Generalized* to a population. This is a suitable test for a relationship between two categorical variables. Involves comparing the *Expected* values of no relationship between the two variables (*Null Hypothesis*) with the observed values (*Alternative* or *Research Hypothesis*).

Classic Experimental Design: In a classic experimental design, subjects are randomly allocated to two groups, the experimental group and the control group. Pre-test observations are made on both groups. Only the experimental group is then subjected to stimuli. Observations are then taken again on both groups, known as post-test.

Classification: A classification system is a set of categories, often arranged in a scale, into which every member of the population can be located. See also *Attributes*.

Closed-ended Questions: Also called *Standardized Questions*.

Cluster Sample: A sampling method where a number of locations are selected from which individual units are then selected by *Random Sampling* or *Non-Probability Based Sampling* techniques.

Code Book: (Also called *Coding Frame*.) Contains a list of the variables and coding for each variable in the survey data set.

Codes: See *Coding*.

Coding: The identification and application of *Codes* to *Data*. In *Quantitative Data* coding refers to the application of numerical values to the different possible responses (see *Variable* and *Values*) to questions in a *Questionnaire*, for example. In *Qualitative* research, coding refers to the selection and application of *Codes* to segments of *Textual* material so that all segments associated with a code can then be analysed together and patterns identified.

Coding Frame: This is a list of all *Codes* being used in a coding based *Qualitative Data Analysis* exercise.

Cognitive Maps: These can be either mental maps held by those the researcher is investigating, or *Charts* designed by the researcher to represent the mental maps of those being researched. Sometimes the researcher can use maps made by the researched.

Cohort studies: A *Research Design* that involves *Data Collection* on the same subjects at two or more periods in time.

Column Marginal: The column totals in a *Contingency Table*.

Column percentage: A percentage calculated in a *Contingency Table* where the percentage of a cell count is calculated according to the *Column Marginal* (also called column total).

Community Studies: Research aiming to understand the 'way of life' of a particular community, often involving *Field Research* and *Life History* interviewing.

Comparative Analysis: This is where *Data* from different locations or groups is analysed to identify similarities and differences at a given time.

Comparative Design: A *Research Design* that focuses on identifying differences and similarities between two or more groups.

Concept: A theoretical unit that needs to be translated from an abstract idea into something that can be identified and measured if it is to be researched.

Confidence Intervals: Based on the *Central Limit Theorem* and the properties of the *Normal Distribution Curve*. They enable the researcher to estimate the accuracy of the sample statistics and whether the findings can be generalized to the population.

Confidentiality: Where personal information is collected by a researcher, confidentiality refers to the non-disclosure of that information to parties other than the research team (or in some cases specified others). Confidentiality is not the same as anonymity (see *Anonymity*).

Consequentialist Ethics: *Ethical* view that it can be legitimate to infringe on the *Ethical* rights of those researched (such as deception or non-full disclosure of the researcher's intentions), in cases where a greater good is achieved. This view contrasts with the *De-ontological (or Transcendentalist) Ethical* view.

Constant Comparison: The *Grounded Theory* technique of building theory by continually comparing the latest round of *Data Collection* with ideas generated in previous rounds of *Data Collection* for the purpose of testing emerging ideas that might lead the research to be taken in new and fruitful directions.

Construct Validity: A *Validity* that is used to assess how well the measurement conforms to the theoretical model.

Constructionism: (Also called *Social Constructionism*.) See *Phenomenology*. Some writers distinguish constructionism from a more radical Social Constructivism, but often the terms are used interchangeably. Constructionism focuses upon how people create their social reality through interaction with each other.

Content Analysis: The technique of *Coding Textual Data* so that all instances where the same *Code* has been applied can be either counted (in *Quantitative* content analysis) or compared and further analysed (in *Qualitative* content analysis).

Content Validity: A *validity* that is used to assess how well the measurement tool measures the different dimensions of a *Concept*.

Contingency Table: (Also called *Cross-tabulation*.) A two-way table that displays the relationship between two *Categorical Variables*. Each cell in the table displays the observations. The independent variable is normally placed in the column and the dependent variable in the row. *Row Percentages*, *Column Percentages* and *Total Percentages* can be calculated for each cell in the table.

Continuity Correction (also called *Yates's Contingency Correction*): A hypothesis test used to test the significance of the findings between two *Categorical Variables*. Can be used in place of the *Chi-square Test for Independence* in 2X2 tables with small cell counts.

Control variable: A variable that influences the relationship between the *Independent* and *Dependent Variables*. Referred to as the 'Z' variable in mathematical notation.

Controlled Conditions: Research procedures designed to allow only those *Variables* that the researcher is interested in to vary, allowing relations between those variables to be studied more rigorously.

Controlled conditions may distort the actions of those researched and critics suggest *Naturalistic* research conditions are often more *Valid*.

Convenience Sampling: See *Opportunity Sampling*.

Conversation Analysis: Research tradition focused upon the collecting, *Transcription* and analysis of naturally occurring talk. Conversation analysis aims to provide an account of the machinery in operation within talk by means of fine-grain analysis of talk without reference to context or motive, unless those things are explicitly deployed in the talk itself. Conversation analysis has developed a highly sophisticated form of *Transcription Notation* to facilitate this goal.

Correlation: Pattern of association between variables or the statistical measure used to identify such patterns. Correlations may be positive (increases in one variable are associated with increases in the other) or negative (increases in one are associated with decreases in the other). Correlations may be strong, weak or non-existent. A correlation may indicate a *Causal* relationship, but not all correlations are causal.

Correlation Coefficient: A measure of association that summarizes how two variables co-vary. There are different measures of association for the levels of measurement of the two variables. *Pearson's r* is used for measuring the association between two *Interval Variables*. *Phi* and *Cramer's V* are used for the measurement of association between two *nominal variables*. *Kendall's Tau a, b or c* are used for measuring the association between two *ordinal variables*.

Count: The frequency of observations.

Covering Letter: A letter that accompanies a *Self-completion Survey* detailing the nature of the research project, completion and return instructions.

Covert Research: Research where those being researched are not aware, or not fully aware, of the researcher's role. This may be by means of hidden *Observation*, the recording of *Non-Intrusive Data*, or by covert *Participant Observation*.

Cramer's V: A measure of association used for examining the relationship between two *Categorical Variables*. Cramer's V is used in tables that are larger than 2x2. Normally interpreted in conjunction with a *Contingency Table*.

Criterion Validity: Criterion validity refers to the checking of the performance of a *Measurement Tool* or *Indicator*. The researcher performs some initial analysis on a *Measurement Tool* or *Indicator* to check that it returns results that would be expected.

Cross-case Displays: Graphical devices (*Tables, Charts* and so on) designed to highlight the existence or non-existence of patterns between cases, as distinct from *Within-Case Displays*. There are both *Quantitative* and *Qualitative* forms of such devices.

Cross-sectional Design: A *Research Design* that involves collecting data from a sample at one point in time. Variations in particular characteristics of the sample are used to describe and explore relationships.

Cross-Tabulation: See *Contingency Table*.

Cumulative Percentage: A *Percentage* that is derived from adding together the frequency percentage of *Values* or *Categories* in a *Frequency Table*.

Data: Numerical or *Textual* material generated and recorded in the research process for the purpose of analysis. *Data* is not 'out there' waiting to be collected. *Data* is the product of the research itself and is determined by the research process.

Data Analysis: The analysis of research data.

Data Collection: The period in the research project that involves engaging with a target sample or population from whom data is collected.

Data Entry: Occuring after a period of *Data Collection*, data entry involves inputting data into an appropriate data file. For *Quantitative* data this could be a SPSS data file. For *Qualitative* data this could be the transcribing of interviews and their importation into an analysis package such as NVivo.

Data Reduction: Forms of representational and analytical device used to reduce large amounts of numerical or *Textual* material to forms from which patterns or the lack of patterns can be identified.

Data Saturation: A technique proposed within *Grounded Theory* to enable the researcher to identify when enough *Data* has been collected. Through *Constant Comparison* of *Data* and emerging theories the researcher is able to make tentative predictions (or emergent *Hypotheses*) about what new rounds of *Data Collection* will generate. When these predictions are continually confirmed the researcher can conclude that enough *Data* has been collected.

Data Set: All *Data* collected by one or more projects and integrated for the purpose of analysis.

Data Type See *Level of Measurement*.

Deconstruction: Form of *Discourse Analysis* focused upon the highlighting of multiple meanings within the seemingly coherent concepts deployed in literary, political, philosophical and other *Texts*. Deconstruction challenges the view that authors deploy language. Rather, language is seen to flow through its 'users'.

Deduction: The generation of logical conclusions from rational premises. Forms a key step in *Hypothetico-deductive methods* (*Hypothesis* testing) of research and is the opposite of *Induction*.

Deductive Coding: The generation of the *Codes* to be used in coding *Data* prior to any analysis of the *Data* itself.

Delphi Group: *Focus Group* in which the participants are selected for being experts in the field to be discussed.

De-ontological (or Transcendentalist) Ethics: *Ethical* stance opposed to the *Consequentialist* view that the *Ethical* rights of those being researched can be legitimately violated if the consequence is to bring about a greater good. The de-ontological view argues that *Ethical* rights cannot be traded.

Dependent Variable: *Variable* that a researcher predicts will be affected by the variation of another variable (this other *Variable* being called the *Independent Variable*). Referred to as the Y variable in mathematical notation.

Depth Validity: See *Validity (Internal)*.

Description: Mode of *Data* presentation that does not seek to 'explain' why things are as they are, only to show what is going on. See also *Descriptive Statistics*.

Descriptive Statistics: Statistics that enable the researcher to identify and explore patterns in the data collected, as distinct from *Inferential Statistics*.

Dichotomy (also called Dichotomies): A categorical variable that has only two response categories. For example: Yes/No, Male/Female, True/False.

Discourse Analysis: Form of *Qualitative Data Analysis* focused upon the meaning of *Textual Data*. Discourse analysis is critical of more *Quantitative* forms of *Content Analysis* that seek to count the incidence of particular units of meaning within a *Text*. *Semiotics*, *Deconstruction* and *Narrative* analysis are forms of discourse analysis.

Elaboration: Process of analysing relationships between the *Independent Variable* and *Dependent Variable* which seeks to uncover the effects of a *Control Variable*. Seeks to uncover *Spuriousness*.

Emergence: Term drawn from *Grounded Theory*, and used widely in *Qualitative* research, to refer to the technique of concept selection, formation and refinement that builds up from *Data Collection*. The researcher seeks to allow useful key terms to 'emerge' from relatively open-ended early rounds of data collection. This use of *Induction* is then followed by more *Deductive* forms of data collection that seek to evaluate the significance of the newly identified concepts.

Empirical: Reference to the collection of *data* (by various means), rather than drawing conclusions only from the manipulation of theoretical propositions.

Epistemology: The branch of Philosophy dealing with the grounds by which knowledge about the world can be gained and assessed. See also *Ontology*, *Methodology* and *Method*.

Ethics: Branch of Philosophy and field of everyday thinking dealing with questions of what is morally right and wrong.

Ethnographic/Ethnography: Research tradition based upon forms of *Naturalistic Data Collection*. Commonly associated with anthropological *Fieldwork*, that is, time spent 'living' with a community. Ethnography draws upon a wide range of *Data Collection* methods, but its rationale lies in the premise that the researcher should go to those they research, rather than for the researched to enter contrived research conditions set up by the researcher.

Ethnomethodology: Research tradition established by Harold Garfinkel and others, focused upon identifying the methods used by people to establish and maintain a sense of social order through forms of social interaction. Ethnomethodology rejects social structural accounts of social order and is keen to show how such 'fictions' are maintained and deployed in everyday life.

Evaluation Research: Research oriented towards measuring organizational performance, whether against *Quantitative* standards or in terms of more *Qualitative Indicators* of satisfaction.

Exclusiveness: When developing *Categories* for *Closed-Ended Questions* the researcher needs to ensure that respondents can only select one of the *Categories*. Particular care needs to be taken with *Categories* that represent numerical ranges. For example, with age ranges ensure that there are no overlaps in the age *Categories*.

Exhaustiveness: The available *Categories* in *Closed-Ended Questions* need to contain an appropriate range of responses. Where appropriate, exhaustiveness can be ensured by included a final 'Other – please state' category.

Expected Count (also called *Expected Frequency*): The expected value if there were no association between two *Categorical Variables*. Should be calculated for the *Chi-square Test for Independence*. The expected counts are the values expected if the *Null Hypothesis* were true.

Experimental Research: Research designed to test a *Hypothesis*, usually through the establishment of *Controlled Conditions* and the manipulation of

Independent Variables to measure changes in *Dependent Variables*.

Explanation: Account that suggests a *Causal* process behind *Data* collected.

Exploration: Research that is designed not to test a *Hypothesis* by *Deductive* means, but which instead aims to explore a field in a more *Inductive* way.

External Discretion: What makes the contents of one *Category* distinct from the contents of another *Category*. If a *Case* could be placed in more than one *Category*, then those *Categories* do not display external discretion. See also *Internal Homogeneity*.

External Validity: The extent to which research findings can be generalized to the population and different social settings.

Face-to-face Interview: See *Interview*.

Face Validity: Refers to the assessment of whether the *Measurement Tool* is a suitable measure of a concept.

Facilitator: Person who leads a focus group. Sometimes called *Moderator*. The Facilitator's job is to frame the discussion, ask initial questions, and 'manage' the flow of conversation. Depending upon the goals of the research and the dynamics of the group, the Facilitator may wish to encourage less vocal members of the group to participate, or allow more vocal participants to 'lead'/'dominate' discussion.

Facts: Real things in the world or statements about reality that are 'True'. Facts are supposedly neutral with regard to whether such things are morally right or wrong. The idea that factual statements can be made that do not contain value judgements has been questioned by some.

Feminist Method: Research methods building upon the principles of feminist theory and ethics, and therefore designed to avoid detachment, domination and exploitation in the conduct of research, and to promote women's consciousness and empowerment in society. Feminist Method is primarily *Qualitative* and often *Participant Action* oriented. Some advocates and critics have, however, questioned the assumptions that qualitative methods are intrinsically more suited to women and that qualitative approaches are always the best methods for highlighting, and therefore challenging, the subordination of women in society.

Field Research/Fieldwork: Research carried out in naturally occurring settings rather than in controlled conditions. See also *Ethnography*.

Fisher's Exact Test: A *Hypothesis* or *Significance Test* appropriate for exploring the relationship between two *Categorical Variables* that are *Dichotomies* (2x2 tables) where the *Expected Counts* are small (<5 per cell).

Focus Group Interview: *Interview* with a group of people at the same time, and usually in the same place (though forms of tele-conferencing can also be used). Distinct from the one-to-one *Interview* format, the focus group may be geared to assessing group dynamics, but is more often interested in generating a range of opinions. Many forms of focus group exist.

Frequency See **Count**.

Frequency Tables: Tables presenting the distribution of *Values* within a single *Quantitative Variable*.

Gatekeepers: Persons within a research process, whose assistance enables the researcher to access those they want to research or others they want to research if the gatekeeper is themself part of the researcher's sample. Gatekeepers may hold formal positions of responsibility within the accessing process or they may be well connected and helpful 'locals' within the environment the researcher enters.

Generalizability: also known as *External Validity*. The extent to which findings from the researcher's *Sample* can be claimed to accurately reflect the characteristics of a wider *Population* of those groups the researcher *Sampled* from. Factors affecting generalizability are the quality and quantity of the *Sample* and the *Variance* within the *Sample* collected. Statistical measures of *Significance* are designed to test these characteristics.

Genre: Literary styles, often deployed in everyday *Text* and talk, that frame specific content within a more general form of story-telling (for example tragedy, comedy, thriller, political drama, soap-opera).

Graphs: Visual representations of *Data*.

Grounded Theory: Approach developed by Barney Glaser and Anselm Strauss (1967) by which theory emerges from exploration of a field rather than in advance. Theories emerging from the field are then tested by *Constant Comparison* in subsequent rounds of *Data Collection* until a point of *Saturation* is reached.

Hermeneutics: The study of meaningful objects or actions. Originally, the term was used in biblical study, but in the modern age has come to be applied to the more general study of literature and culture. Hermeneutics is associated with *qualitative* social research in general, and with *Phenomenology* in particular.

Histogram: A graphical presentation for use with *interval variables*. *Variable values* are divided into ranges and these ranges are displayed as adjoining bars on a *Chart*. Histograms should not be confused with *Bar Charts* that are for *Categorical Variables*.

Hypothesis Testing: (also called *Significance Testing*). A statistical technique that allows for *generalizations* to be made from a *sample* to the wider *population*. It involves developing an *alternative hypothesis* and a *null hypothesis*. The collected sample data is then tested to see if there is sufficient evidence to enable the null hypothesis to be rejected, and thereby the alternative hypothesis can be accepted. There are different hypothesis tests for different *levels of measurement*. (See *Chi-Square Test for Independence*.)

Hypothesis: Tentative theory that makes a prediction which can then be tested. See also *Deduction* and *Hypothetico-deductive Method*. Hypothesis testing is the opposite of *Induction*.

Hypothetico-Deductive Method: Research method in which theory (that is, prior literature on the subject) is used to generate a *Hypothesis*, which is then tested by *Empirical* means.

Independent Variable: Often referred to as the cause (see *causation*), assumed to be the variable influencing changes in the *dependent variable*. Referred to as the 'X' variable in mathematical notation.

In-Depth Interviews: *Interviews* that use *open-ended* and often relatively unstructured questioning to explore a topic in significant detail from the interviewee's perspective.

Index: See *Indicators*.

Indicators: *Empirically* measurable *Variables* that are used to gauge the extent of an underlying phenomenon. Often a range of *Variables* are combined to create a more sophisticated indicator (for example, income, housing tenure, access to transport and so on would all be part of a 'Rural Poverty' indicator).

Induction: Philosphical field of generating conclusions where pure logical relationships between premises are insufficient. In social research inductive methods are those that generate theory from evidence, rather than generating testable theory from rational extensions from existing theory. Opposite of *Deduction*.

Inductive Codes: When *Coding*, such as in *Content Analysis*, *Codes* that the researcher chooses on the basis of reading the *Data* are called inductive codes. See *Induction*.

Inferential Statistics: Statistics that allow the researcher to make inferences on the likelihood of the sample findings being replicated in the population. Involves *Hypothesis Testing*.

Informed Consent: Consent refers to the express willingness of those being researched to participate. Informed consent is consent that is based upon a full disclosure by the researcher, in terms those being researched can understand, of the aims, methods and intended uses of the research.

Internal Homogeneity: The extent to which all those assigned to a particular *Category* are the same, or sufficiently similar, at least in the terms specified by the *Operationalization* of that *Category*.

Internal Validity: Internal validity is concerned with establishing whether no other factors, on which *Data* may or may not have been recorded, could explain the research findings. Sampling technique and *Measurement Tools* can compromise internal validity.

Internet Self-completion survey: A self-completion survey that is distributed via the Internet. Can be sent by e-mail to respondents or placed on a Web page.

Inter Quartile Range: The middle 50 per cent of values in a *Range*. Values should be placed in ascending order, from lowest to highest. Calculated by taking the upper (75th) *Quartile* value from the lower (25th) quartile value.

Interval: A *Level of Measurement* where *Data* is measured on a continuous scale. Interval *Data* is also a term that may be used to refer to both interval and *Ratio Data*. *Data* can be placed in rank order and can be subjected to mathematical calculations. Interval data does not have a *True Zero Point*. Ratio Interval data does have a *True Zero Point*.

Interview: Traditionally a face-to-face talk based on the *Data Collection* method, though telephone and computer interviewing are also popular. Interviews may be one-to-one or group-based, and may be more or less formal/*Structured* (that is, with a rigid set of questions in a specified sequence: set out in an *Interview Schedule*) or informal/*un-structured* (less rigid and based upon a more loose *Aide-mémoire*). *Standardized* interview questions require an answer that is one of a selected series of options. *Un-Standardized Questions* require more *open-ended* answers. See also *Interviewer Effect/Interviewer Bias*.

Interview Schedule: Written outline of the questions to be asked in an *Interview*. A highly *Structured* and *Standardized* interview schedule would be more or less the same as a *Questionnaire*, except that the interviewer would be the one to ask the questions and record the answers.

Interviewer Effect/Interviewer Bias: Potential for the social characteristics and behaviour of the interviewer to distort the responses of the interviewee.

In Vivo Codes: When *Coding Textual Data* by reading the *Text* before generating the *Codes*. *Codes* that are actual words or phrases used in the *Data* itself are called *in vivo* codes.

Kendall's Tau *a, b* or *c*: A measure of association used to summarize the relationship between two *Ordinal Variables*. There are three versions of this measure: Tau *a*, tau *b*, and tau *c*.

Keywords: Search terms used when conducting a *Literature Search*. These are rather like *Codes* used in analysis of *Textual Data*. Keywords may emerge prior to the *Literature Search*, or in the process of the *Literature Review* of previously found materials.

Kurtosis: A statistical measure that indicates how *Values* are distributed around the *Mode*. Positive kurtosis indicates that *Values* are more tightly clustered around the *Mode*. Negative kurtosis indicates that *Values* are more loosely distributed.

Latent Codes: Codes used in the analysis of *Textual Data* that do not refer to particular surface characteristics in the *Text*, but to underlying phenomena the researcher believes exist beneath the range of surface terms being used in the *Text*. The researcher may believe a range of different terms being used all relate to an underlying theme.

Level of Measurement: *Variables* can be distinguished in terms of the level of mathematical scaling that can be carried out on that *Data*. *Nominal Data* has no mathematical sequence. *Ordinal Data* can be arranged in an order, but levels of difference between units cannot be specified. *Interval Data* is ordered and the difference between the units can be numerically specified. *Ratio Data* is similar to *Interval Data*, with the added feature that the numerical scale on which units are located has a true point. This means that the difference between unit *Values* can be calculated in proportion (5 metres is half of 10 metres). *Level of Measurement* determines the *Statistical* tests that can be carried out on the *Data*.

Leptokurtic: A term used to describe positive *kurtosis* where a distribution is tall and peaked.

Life History: *Interview* form in which the focus is the life story of the person being interviewed. Such *Interviews* tend to be structured around the life course, but are otherwise relatively *Open-ended*.

Likert Scales: An attitudinal *Scale* used in survey questions. Involves the construction of a number of statements with the same *Scale* responses, for example, a 5-point strongly agree to strongly disagree *Scale*. The *Scale* responses are then scored and can be combined into one total score.

Linear Regression: A technique used to describe the relationship between two *Variables* based on calculating the line of best fit. Both the *Independent* and *Dependent* variables need to be *Interval* or *Ratio*.

Line Graph: A graphical presentation for *Interval Data*. The frequency of *Observations* for each *Interval Value* is plotted on to a graph. Particularly useful for representing trends, especially economic trends.

Line of Best Fit: A predicted line that best summarizes the co-variance between two *Interval Variables*. Used in *Correlation* and *Regression* analyses.

Literature Review: The process of evaluating the output from a *Literature Search*. Of course, identifying a *Text* as being relevant to the researcher requires that searching involves a degree of reviewing. The two are never fully separate.

Literature Search: The process of identifying and locating existing published research and theory on the subject the researcher is interested in researching. See also *Literature Review*.

Longitudinal Design: A *Research Design* that involves collecting *Data* on *Cases* over an extended period.

Mail or postal survey: A Self-Completion survey that is distributed via the postal service.

Manifest Codes: *Codes* generated for the analysis of *Textual Data* which are themselves directly linked to the expressed content of the *Data*. Opposite of *Latent Codes* and often the same as *In vivo Codes* (but not always).

Matrix Display (grid): Table used for representing the incidence of cross-over between *Codes* and *Attributes* (that is, general *Codes*), between *Codes*, or between *Codes* and particular units (individuals, groups or organizations). Matrix *Tables* can be structured around time.

Matrix Questions: Individual questions that have the same response *Categories* can be organized into a Table. Particularly useful in the design of *Self-completion Surveys*.

Mean: A *Measure of Central Tendency*. All the *Values* in a distribution are added together and divided by the number of *Observations*. The mean is affected by extreme *values*.

Measurement Tools: See *Indicators*.

Measures of Association: Statistical measures that summarize the relationship between two *Variables*. There are different measures of association according to the *Levels of Measurement* of the two *Variables*. See *Correlation, Pearson's r, Kendall's Tau a, b or c, Spearman's Rank Order Correlation (rho), Phi* and *Cramer's V*.

Measures of Central Tendency: A single *Statistical* measure that summarizes the distribution of *Values* in a *Variable*. There are different measures of

central tendency according to the *Level of Measurement* of the *Data*. See *Mean, Mode, Median*.

Measures of Dispersion: A *Statistical* measure that summarizes the amount of spread or variation in the distribution of *Values* in a *Variable*. See *Standard Deviation* and *Variance*.

Measures of Significance: see *Hypothesis Testing*.

Median: A *Measure of Central Tendency*. Scores are placed in rank order, from lowest to highest. The *Value* in the middle position is the median. Where two *Values* occupy the middle position, they should be added together and divided by 2. Used for *Ordinal Variables* and sometimes *Interval Variables*. Unlike the *Mean*, the median is not sensitive to extreme *Values*.

Mediations: Intervening *Variables* that impact upon the influence of *Independent Variables* and *Dependent Variables*. Mediations may inhibit, enhance, change or cancel out *Causal* mechanisms at work between other *Variables*.

Memos: Notes made by the researcher in the process of *Data Collection* and/or *Data Analysis*. Memos may be separate, linked to particular *Data*, or collected to form a research diary (an account of the research process itself).

Mesokurtic: A term used to describe *Kurtosis* where the distribution is symmetrical.

Method: The actual process used to collect *Data*. See also *Ontology, Epistemology* and *Methodology*.

Methodology: General principles and traditions of *Data Collection*. See also *Ontology, Epistemology* and *Method*.

Missing Values: *Data* that has not been recorded.

Mixed Methods: (Also called *Multi-method*.) *Research Design* using more than one *Data Collection* technique. This may or may not involve the mixing of *Qualitative* and *Quantitative Data*.

Mode: A *Measure of Central Tendency*. It is the most frequently occurring *Value* in a distribution of scores.

Models: Mapping devices designed to represent the relationship between key elements in a field of study. Models may be *Predictive, Causal* or *Descriptive*, and may be discursive, mathematical or graphical.

Moderator: See *Facilitator*.

Monographs: Term used to refer to a book devoted to outlining a single research project. In its narrower usage the term refers to a single book devoted to outlining the conduct and findings of a particular ethnographic or case study project.

Multi-method: See *Mixed Methods*.

Multiple Response Questions: *Survey* questions that ask respondents to select more than one item from a

Category list are known as multiple response questions.

Multiple Response Sets: *SPSS* allows for *Variables* derived from *Multiple Response Questions* to be combined for analysis purposes into a multiple response set.

Multi-stage Sampling: A sampling technique that involves *Case* selection at different stages. For example, a *Random Sample* of universities is selected. Within this university sample, a further *Random Sample* of students is selected.

Mutually Exclusive: Phrase used to refer to *Categories* whose content does not overlap.

Myth: *Semiotic* term for when a sign becomes the *Signifier* for a deeper meaning (such as SNAKE standing for Evil). See Also, *Semiotics/Semiology*.

Narrative: The construction of process/sequence within a text. Narrative Analysis seeks to study the textual devices at work in such constructions.

Narrative Analysis: Form of *Discourse Analysis* dealing with the construction of *Narrative* sequence within *Text*.

Nation-state: A state that is characterized by defined geographical borders and a government that has sovereign power.

Naturalism/Naturalistic: Research that takes place outside of *Controlled Conditions*.

Necessary Condition: A factor that is essential to an outcome. See also *Sufficient Condition*.

Network Diagram (flows and links): Graphic representational model designed to show links between *Variables* or *Codes* within a *Data Set*.

Nodes: Term referring to *Coding* terms in *NVivo* (*Qualitative Data Analysis* software). Nodes can be organized into trees, sets or *Cases*, or they can remain as free nodes.

Nominal: A level of measurement where response *Categories* cannot be placed into any specific order and no judgement can be made about the relative size or distance of one *Category* to another.

Non-equivalent Control Group: A quasi-experimental *Research Design* in which subjects are divided into experimental and control groups according to naturally occurring features.

Non-experimental Research Design: *Research Designs* that do not adhere to the experimental designs that originated from the natural sciences.

Non-intrusive Data Collection: Collection of *Data* that does not involve interaction with those to whom the *Data* refers. Examples might be forms of hidden *Observation*, collection of *Official Statistics*, or analysing the contents of people's rubbish/trash bins.

Non-parametric Tests: Non-parametric tests are *Statistical* tests that are based on distributions other than the *Normal Distribution Curve*. They are used where the population characteristics do not meet the normal curve and/or the *Sample Size* is small.

Non-Probability Based Sampling: Sampling methods that do not select *Cases* randomly from a *Sampling Frame* (of all members of the target *Population*). See also *Snowball Sampling, Opportunity Sampling* and *Theoretical Sampling*.

Non-response: Failure of a *Case* to provide a response to a question. Non-response can occur for a number of reasons poor question construction can mean that the respondent is unable to answer; the question is not applicable; or refusal to answer. Non-response is recorded as missing data.

Normal Distribution Curve: The normal distribution curve is a theoretical curve whose properties are that it is bell-shaped with the *Population Mean* in the middle.

Normative: A statement containing or based upon an *Ethical* judgement. Opposite of *Positive*.

NUD*IST: See *NVivo/N6*.

Null Hypothesis: Used in *Hypothesis* testing. States that there is no difference between the observed *Values* and those found in the stated theoretical model.

NVivo/N6: *Qualitative Data Analysis* software packages descended from *NUD*IST* (Non-Numerical Unstructured Data * Interpretation, Structuring and Theorizing).

Objective/Objectivity: A proposition that is not biased or distorted by particular motives is said to be objective. Science seeks to present the 'truth'. Objectivity is the lack of a *Standpoint*. Not every social researcher accepts that this detachment is either possible or desirable.

Observation: Form of *Data Collection* based upon recording observable events, whether in *Controlled Conditions* (such as in an experiment) or in *Naturalistic Field* conditions. Observation may be *Overt* or *Covert, Participant*-based or not.

Official Statistics: Numerical *Data* collected by government agencies and departments. A valuable source for *Secondary Research*.

One-tailed Test: A directional *Statistical* test that states the direction of a test. For example, in a survey of males' and females' weekly income, a one-tailed test would state that one group, males, had a higher weekly income than the second group, females.

Ontology/Ontological: Branch of Philosophy concerned with questions of what exists, or questions of being. See also *Epistemology, Methodology* and *Method*.

Open Coding: *Coding* of *Textual Data* whereby the researcher reads through the *Text* (of either *Open-ended Questioning* or of *Primary Texts*), *Coding* what they consider to be significant items as they go along. After this the researcher may choose to re-organize their *Coding Frame* by other forms of *Coding*. Open coding is the opposite of *Prescriptive Coding*.

Open-ended observation: Observation-based data collection method where the researcher seeks to allow important issues to emerge from time spent observing, rather than beginning with a fully pre-structured set of things to look for, count or focus attention upon. As such, open-ended observation is a form of *Induction*-based *Data Collection*.

Open-ended Questions: Questions that do not require the respondent to choose between a prescribed set of answers.

Operationalization: The 'translation' of theoretical *Concepts* into measurable *Categories* and *Variables*.

Opportunity Sampling: (Also called *Convenience* or *Availability Sampling*.) Selecting members of a *Sample* as and when such members present themselves, such as stopping people in the street. Such *Sampling* often involves *Quota Sampling*.

Ordinal: An ordinal level of measurement is applied to *Categorical Variables* whose response *Categories* can be placed into a rank order of importance. For example, *Rating Scales*. No mathematical calculations can be made in relation to the distance between the *Categories*.

Outliers: *Values* in an *Interval Variable* that are at the extreme lower or upper end of a distribution. Outliers will influence the *Mean* value.

Overt Research: Research where those being researched are aware that the researcher is collecting *Data*. Opposite of *Covert Research*.

Panel Studies: A research study that surveys representatative *Samples* at two or more points in time.

Parameter: A parameter is a *Statistic* that is calculated from the *Population*.

Parametric Tests: Statistical tests that are based on the assumptions of the *Normal Distribution Curve*. They are normally applied to *Interval Data*.

Participant Observation: *Naturalistic Fieldwork* based research where the researcher takes up a role within the group they are researching. This may be *Covert* or *Overt*.

Participant Action Research: Research where the researcher becomes involved in seeking to facilitate the goals of those being researched and those being researched become involved in the design and conduct of the research.

Pattern Codes/Specific Codes: *Coding* focused upon drawing out the specific characteristics of the *Texts*

being analysed, as distinct from *Summary Codes* that focus upon generic characteristics, such as who, what, when, where and so on.

Pearson's r: A *measure of association* used to explore the association between two *Interval Variables*. The measure will vary between −1 to 0 to +1. A value of 0 means no association, a value of −1 means a negative association and a value of +1 a positive association.

Percentages: A percentage is the proportion of *Observations* for a certain *Value* in a *Variable* divided by the total number of *Observations* for that *Variable*. This Value is then multiplied by 100 to give a percentage.

Phenomenology: Tradition of social research and theory that attends to the experience of the world from the point of view of people, and which is critical of claims that external *Causal* processes operate to generate social reality. The social world is seen as a social construction, and an achievement of people. Closely associated with *Constructionism* and opposed to *Realism* and *Positivism*.

Phi: A *Measure of Association* used when exploring the association between two *Categorical Variables* that are *Dichotomies*. Calculated for 2x2 tables. *Values* will vary between 0 and 1. A *Value* of 0 means no association and a *Value* of 1 means a perfect association.

Pie Chart: A graphical presentation suitable for *Nominal* or *Ordinal Variables*. The circle, or pie, is divided into a number of slices. The size of each slice is determined by the number of *Observations* in each *Category*.

Pilot/Piloting: Pre-testing of research instruments such as *Questionnaires* or *Interview Schedules* to a small sub-*Sample* of the target *Population* to identify weaknesses within the *Data Collection* instrument.

Platykurtic: A term used to describe negative *Kurtosis* where a distribution is flat.

Pluralism: See *Mixed Methods/Triangulation*.

Poetics: Linguistic devices used to generate rhetorical effects within language. Often used as a means of persuasion in everyday language and in research writing. The poetics of language is therefore both a topic to be studied and a source of bias.

Polysemy: Polysemy is the notion that texts can be interpreted in a variety of ways (often referred to in the context of media/*Discourse Analysis*).

Population: All members of the category under investigation. Sometimes, for practical purposes, the population is defined as all members of the *Sampling Frame* available, but this excludes the hidden population (those not identified within the sampling frame). Where there is no reasonably comprehensive sampling frame to draw a *Random Sample* of the population from, the researcher will need to use a *Non-probability Sample* to access members of the population they are interested in.

Positive/Positivism: Focus upon *Facts* without reference to *Ethical* judgements about them. A positive statement is non-*Normative*. Positivism is the belief that knowledge of the world can be detached from *Ethical* evaluation.

Post-coding: The numerical *Coding* of responses to *Open-ended Questions*.

Post-Primary Research: *Data Collection* conducted after a first round of *Data Collection*, either by similar methods or by alternative methods. Often conducted for the purpose of checking the *Validity* of *Primary Research* findings.

Prediction: A statement about the future that can be tested if stated in a rigorous form (that is, as a *Hypothesis*).

Predictive Validity: Research findings that make predictions about future events are said to have predictive validity if the predicted events are measured at a subsequent point in time.

Prescriptive Coding/Pre-emptive Coding: *Codes* developed from the review of prior research and theory in a *Field* and not from the *Data* collected. If research is designed to test a *Hypothesis*, *Codes* will often need to have been specified in advance.

Presentation: To deliver verbally the details and findings from a piece of research.

Primary Research: *Data Collection* carried out by the researcher or research team that will analyse it. Distinct from *Secondary Data*.

Primary Sources: *Textual* (and sometimes numerical) sources that were not produced originally for research purposes. Letters, newspaper articles and diaries would be examples of this.

Probability Sampling: A *Sampling* technique where it is known the probability or likelihood that a *Sampling Unit* will be selected from a *Sampling Frame*. Usually associated with a *Random Sampling Technique*.

Purposive Sampling: *Sampling* based on the researcher's understanding of the *Field* and emergent interests in it. Non-*Random* (that is, *Non-Probability*) based *Sampling* method often associated with *Grounded Theory* and other *Qualitative* methods.

Qualitative: Refers to forms of *Data*, *Data Collection* and *Data Analysis* that give priority to one or more of the following: meanings over numerical measurement, *Induction* over *Deduction*, *Constructionism/Phenomenology* (attention to small group interaction) over *Objectivism/Realism* (attention to *Social Structures* and Constraints), and to *Depth* over *Generalizability*.

Quantitative: Refers to forms of *Data*, *Data Collection* and *Data Analysis* that give priority to one or more of the following: numerical measurement over meanings, *Deduction* over *Induction*, *Objectivism/Realism* (attention to *Social Structures* and Constraints) over *Constructionism/Phenomenology* (attention to small group interaction), and to *Generalizability* over *Depth*.

Quartiles: The *Values* in a distribution are placed into rank order and then divided into four equal parts or quartiles.

Quasi-experimental Design: A *Research Design* that is often used when a classic experimental design is not achievable. There are many variations of quasi-experimental design. The main feature is that test groups are allocated according to naturally occurring features.

Questionnaire: (Also called *Self-completion Surveys*) A question-based *Data Collection* instrument designed to be distributed and filled in by the person responding without the presence of an interviewer. Questionnaires are *Structured* but can have a degree of variation in the level to which expected answers are *Standardized*.

Questionnaire Survey: See *Survey*.

Quota Sampling: Form of *Opportunity/Convenience/Availability Sampling* where the researcher seeks to fill certain quotas of different types of people from those they meet, such as on the street.

Random Sampling: *Sampling* based on the random selection of units from a *Sampling Frame* of the whole target *Population* (or as near to this as possible). This method is designed to give each member of the *Population* an equal chance of being selected and so to minimize *Sampling error*/bias.

Range: The difference between the highest *Value* and lowest value in a distribution.

Ranking Questions: Questions that ask a respondent to assign a rank order to a series of *Categories*. For example, placing a list of different foods into order of preference from 1 = lowest preference to 5 = highest preference.

Rating Scales: Response *Categories* that require the respondent to position their response on a *Scale*. For example, the 5-point rating *Scale* of strongly agree, agree, neutral, disagree, and strongly disagree.

Ratio: A *Level of Measurement* for continuous data that has a *True Zero Point*. Often combined with and referred to as *Interval Data*.

Realism: Approach to the study of the natural and physical world which holds that beneath appearances there are *Causal* mechanisms at work. Opposed to both *Positivism* and *Phenomenology/Constructionism*.

Recode/Regroup: Values taken from one *Variable* are re-classified into a new *Variable*. For example, an *Interval Variable* recording age in years is re-coded into age groups.

Regression (Simple Linear): Simple linear regression allows the researcher to build a model of the relationship between an *Independent* and a *Dependent Variable*. It is concerned with finding the line of best fit between two *Interval Variable*s on a *Scatterplot*.

Relationship: Term used to refer to an association between *Variables, Concepts* or *Categories*. Relationships may be *Causal* in nature, but the identification of a relationship may not be sufficient grounds to demonstrate or identify a *Causal* process.

Reliability: When a *Data Collection* instrument records the same phenomenon, it is said to be reliable. This does not mean consistency of results every time, only the consistency in the way, for example, a question is understood by interviewees. If a question was interpreted differently each time it was asked, or an experimental set of conditions were experienced differently by different participants, the responses generated would not be said to be reliable. Reliability can be tested during *Piloting*.

Report: To deliver the details and findings from a piece of research in a written format.

Research Design: Provides the framework for the research process involving the collection and analysis of data.

Research Hypothesis: See *Alternative Hypothesis*.

Research Methods: Research techniques employed to collect data.

Research Question: Term used to refer to the focus of a research topic. A research question may form the broad agenda within which a researcher develops a *Hypothesis* in order to test a prediction by *Deduction*. Alternatively, where the researcher does not choose to test a *Hypothesis*, the term research question is used to refer to the alternative strategy of *Induction*, where research is designed to *Explore* a theme, rather than test a prediction.

Routing or Funnelling Questions: Questions that direct a respondent to answer specific questions in a survey.

Row Marginal: The row totals in a *contingency table*.

Row Percentage: A percentage calculated in a *Contingency Table* where the percentage of a cell count is calculated according to the row marginal (also called row total).

Sample: A sub-section of the total target *Population* selected to participate in the research. Sampling methods (see *Random Sampling, Snowball Sampling, Opportunity Sampling, Cluster Sampling, Sampling Frame, Stratified Sampling, Probability* and *Non-Probability Sampling*) seek to gain an accurate cross-section of the *Population* but differences in the nature of *Populations* require different techniques in particular circumstances.

Sample Size: The total number of *Sampling Units*, or *Cases*, selected from the *Sampling Frame*.

Sample Statistic: A statistical measure that is calculated from the *Sample Data*. For example, the *Mean* age of a *Sample* of 100 men.

Sampling: See *Sample*.

Sampling Error: The difference between the *Population Parameter* and the *Sample Statistic*. The smaller the sampling error, the more representative the *Sample* of the *Population*. Sampling error is determined by the *Sample Size* and the variability of the *Variable* being collected in the *Population*.

Sampling Frame: Database of all members of a target *Population*, or as near to that goal as is possible. A sampling frame may already exist for some *Populations*, or it may have to be created by the researcher in other cases. In some situations, no sampling frame can be generated and the researcher needs to adopt *Non-Probability Sampling* methods. Using a sampling frame allows the researcher to *Randomly* select a *Sample* such that each member of the *Population* has an equal chance of being selected.

Sampling Units: *Cases* that are selected for inclusion in the *Sample* to be surveyed.

Sampling Variability: *Samples* drawn from the same *Population* will produce different *Sample Statistics*. For example, repeated *Random Samples* from the same *Population* will produce different *Means* and *Standard Deviations*.

Saturation: See *Data Saturation*.

Scale: An alternative term for *Interval* or *Ratio Levels* of *Measurement*.

Scatterplot: A graphical presentation of the relationship between two *Interval Variables*. For each case a position plot is marked according to the values for the X, *Independent Variable*, and Y, *Dependent Variable*. The X, *Independent Variable* is the horizontal axis and the Y, *Dependent Variable*, is on the vertical axis.

Schedules: A timetable that details the order of planned events.

Score: The number of observed occurrences of a particular event or response. Also known as a *Count*.

Secondary Data: See *Secondary Sources*.

Secondary Data Analysis: Research based upon the re-analysis of data collected during previous research projects. See also *Secondary Research*. As there is no *Primary Research* stage in secondary data analysis, the terms secondary research and secondary data analysis are often used to mean the same thing; though in the strict sense the former term covers the wider aspects of *Research Design* and selection/accessing data sources and *Archives*.

Secondary Research: Research where the researcher uses the *Primary Research* of others to carry out secondary *Data Analysis* of their own. Also called *Secondary Data Analysis*.

Secondary Sources: Existing *Data*, whether numerical or *Textual*, that was gathered by others at some prior time for the purpose of research. Diaries and letters would not count. Also called *Secondary Data*.

Self-Completion Survey: A *Quantitative* research method that consists of a series of pre-determined questions that are answered by a respondent. Normally consists of a mixture of *closed-ended questions* and *open-ended questions*.

Semantic Differential Scales: A *Scale* that requires a respondent to indicate their position on an issue on a numerical *Scale* between two extremes. The end of each *Scale* represents an extreme position. For example, dull to fun with the 10-point *Scale* of 0 to 9.

Semiology/Semiotics: The science of *Signs*, semiology studies the organization of meaning within language. A *Sign* is the combination of a *Signifier* and a *Signified*. When a *Sign* becomes a *Signifier* for another deeper meaning, this is referred to as *Myth* or mythic language.

Sign: A meaningful linguistic unit.

Significance Testing: See *Hypothesis Testing*.

Signified: A concept.

Signifier: A word/image or other representational unit.

Skewness: A *Statistical* measure that indicates the position of lower and higher *Values* of a distribution. A positively skewed distribution will have a greater number of *Observations* at the higher *Values*. Negatively skewed distributions will have a greater number of *Observations* at the lower *Values*.

Snowball Sampling: Identifying subsequent members of a *Sample* by asking current members of the *Sample* to identify other participants with the required characteristics. Often used where no *Sampling Frame* can be identified or constructed. See also *Non-Probability Based Sampling*.

Social Constructionism: See *Constructionism*.

Social Constructivism: See *Constructionism*.

Social Structures: Architectural/biographical metaphor seeking to highlight the objective constraints imposed upon individuals by social institutions such as the family, school, state or market.

Social Survey: A generic term used to describe *Self-completion Surveys* and *Structured Interview* methods.

Sociological Codes: Codes that are based on theoretical concepts, not the language of those who generated the *Texts* being analysed. The researcher may want to highlight theoretical links beneath the diversity of descriptions of what they believe to be the same thing. Opposite of *Open Coding* and of *In vivo Coding*.

Spearman's Rank Order Correlation: Can also be referred to us Spearman's rho. A *Measure of Association* used where the relationship is between two *Ordinal Variables* or an *Interval* and *Ordinal Variable*. A *value* of 0 means no association, a *Value* of −1 means a negative association, and a *Value* of +1 a positive association.

Split File: A technique in *SPSS* for dividing the *Data* into groups according to the *Categories* in a nominal or *Ordinal Variable*. For example, grouping *Cases* according to whether they are male or female.

SPSS: Statistical Products and Service Solutions. A *Data* and *Statistical* analysis software program.

Spurious: also called Spuriousness. Occurs where a relationship between an *Independent* and a *Dependent Variable* is either altered or removed by the introduction of a third, control, *Variable*. Spuriousness is detected through the process of *Elaboration*.

Standard Deviation: A *Measure of Dispersion* that summarizes the spread of *Scores* in a distribution. See also *Variance*.

Standard Error: The *Standard Deviation* of the *Sample Means*.

Standardized Questions: Questions, whether in an *Interview* or *Questionnaire*, which require the respondent to select from a prescribed set of responses. Opposite of *Open-ended Questions* (otherwise called un-standardized questions) and *Open Coding* at the *Data Analysis* stage.

Standardized Scores: Also called Z scores. The conversion of an *Interval Value* into a standard *Score*. The resulting score is expressed in units of *Standard Deviation*. It is useful when comparing an individual's *Score* on two measures where each has a different *Mean* and *Standard Deviation*.

Standpoint: A perspective from which to see the world and which influences the way you see things. *Objectivists* seek to detach science from such a position. Standpoint theorists have rejected this view, seeing *Objectivity* as the ideology of the social engineer's standpoint.

Statistic: A numeric summary of a range of *Values*.

Stem and Leaf Diagram-A technique for exploring the *Values* in an *Interval Variable*. Unlike other techniques for *Interval Variables* (*Histogram, Box Plot, Line Graph*), the stem and leaf diagram displays the actual *Data*.

Stratified Sampling: Selecting in advance to represent particular social groups or strata within the *Sample* and in particular proportions (often based on prior knowledge or estimations of the distribution of those strata within the target *Population*). A useful technique when seeking to target for selection small groups whose representation within a *Random Sample* may be statistically insignificant, but whose characteristics are of particular interest to the researcher.

Structured Interview: An *Interview* where the interviewer asks a series of pre-determined questions to the interviewee.

Structured Questions: A *Data Collection* instrument (*Questionnaire* or *Interview*) where the wording and sequence of the questions is prescribed. Opposite of the unstructured *Interview* (which is rare). Semi-*Structured Interviews* involve a degree of flexibility in wording and sequence.

Sufficient Condition: Factor whose presence is sufficient to bring about a particular outcome. There is no such thing as a singular sufficient condition. Often a factor may be a *Necessary Condition*, but other factors will also be necessary. Confusing necessary and sufficient conditions is a common logical error.

Summary Codes: See *Pattern Codes/Specific Codes*.

Survey: A specific approach to collecting social data. It involves collecting the same data from all *Cases* in a *Sample* or from all *Cases* in a *Census*. The data collection techniques associated with the survey include the *questionnaire*, the *telephone interview* and the *structured interview*.

Systematic Codes: Systematic coding involves going through the *Text* to be analysed and identifying all the emerging themes that the researcher can find. Distinct from *Axial Coding*.

Systematic Sampling: A *Probability Sampling* technique involving the selection of *Sampling Units* from a *Sampling Frame* according to the proportion of the *Sample Size* to the total units in the *Sampling Frame*. For example, if a *Sample* of 10 per cent is required from a *Sampling Frame* of 1,000, every tenth unit would be selected.

Tables: Representational device used to present *Frequencies* and *Cross-tabulations* in the field of *Quantitative Data* and which are also used in the presentation of *Qualitative Data* (either for highlighting numerical aspects of *Textual Data* or in presenting selected *Textual* materials). See also *Matrix Displays*.

Telephone Interview: A survey conducted using a telephone.

Tendencies: Where a significant, but not constant, relationship is observed between a preceding factor and a consequent 'outcome', a tendency is said to exist. While some poor people are healthy and some wealthy people unhealthy, it is still true that there is a tendency for income to be positively associated with health.

Text/Textual: Any representational device that carries meaning. Text in the more restricted meaning refers to forms of writing, but has been extended in the form of textual analysis to refer to anything that can be 'read' (such as an advertisement, a piece of music or a film). This approach sees all social phenomena as 'text'. See also *Discourse Analysis, Genre, Narrative* analysis and *Semiology*.

Theoretical Sampling: See *Purposive Sampling*.

Time-ordered Display: When exploring a relationship between two *Variables* the researcher needs to ensure that the *Independent Variable* naturally occurs in time before the *Dependent Variable*.

Total Percentage: A percentage calculated in a *Contingency Table* where the percentage of a cell count is calculated according to the total count of *Observations* in the *Table*.

Transcendentalist: See *De-ontological*.

Transcription: The transfer of spoken words into written *Text*. Today this is usually from a recording device into a computer file.

Transcription Notation: Highly complex form of *Transcription* developed by *Conversation Analysts* to capture the many subtle pauses, cross-overs and changes of intonation characteristic of talk, but which are not easily conveyed within the normal conventions of transcription.

Triangulation: Approaching the same topic from a number of different approaches, triangulation may involve the use of more that one researcher or research team, more than one round of *Data Collection*, different types of *Data Collection* or different theoretical frameworks.

True Zero Point: The defining characteristic of a *Ratio Variable*. A true zero point allows for the following type of calculations to be made: if person A is aged 20 years and person B is aged 40 years, person B is twice the age of person A.

Turn-taking: The focus of attention in *Conversation*

Analysis where the expectation is built into talk that one person speaks after another. From this seemingly trivial *Observation*, *Conversation Analysis* develops interesting accounts of hidden expectations that are the machinery within talk.

Two-tailed Test: Non-directional *Statistical* tests that do not impose a specific direction on the tests. For example, in a survey of males' and females' weekly incomes, a two-tailed test would test to see if there were a significant difference in the incomes of men and women. It would not state if males earned more than females, only that there was a difference.

Type I Error: The incorrect rejection of the *Null Hypothesis*, where the conclusion was that there was a real difference when one did not exist. Used in *Hypothesis* testing.

Type II Error: The incorrect acceptance of the *Null Hypothesis* concluding that there was no real difference when, in fact, a real difference did exist.

Univariate analysis: Analysis of *Quantitative Data* that describes and summarizes a single variable.

Unstandardized Questions: (see **Open-ended questions**).

Valid Count: The total number of valid responses made to a question and recorded in a single *Variable*. The valid count is derived from the total count in a sample minus the count of missing data.

Valid Percentage: A *Percentage* that is calculated based on the total *Valid Count*.

Validity (External/Internal): External validity refers to the degree to which *Data* from a *Sample* can be *Generalized* to the wider target *Population*. Internal validity refers to the extent to which *Data* collected accurately reflects the reality of the beliefs or behaviours of those from whom that *Data* was collected.

Value Freedom: Belief commonly held in the natural sciences that there are no meaningful *Ethical* issues regarding the nature or use of its subject matter, the physical and natural world, and that research in those fields can be purely *Objective*. This view is not common in the Social Sciences.

Value Label: A descriptive label that is applied to the coded response *Categories* of *Nominal* or *Ordinal Variables* in *SPSS*.

Value Neutrality: The proposition that while any choice to research one topic rather than another contains a *Value*-based element, once chosen it is possible and necessary to detach *Values* from *Objective Data Collection* and *Analysis*.

Values (as distinct from Facts): *Normative* or *Ethical* positions held either by a researcher or by those being researched. Values in this sense may be the subject of the research, the motivation behind research, or a potential source of bias in research. Some would argue that certain biases are 'correct', and are not therefore distortions.

Values (within a Variable): If a *Variable* is any unit (characteristic, *Code* or *Attribute*) whose value can vary, values are a range of possible variations available to that *Variable*.

Variable: Any unit of *Data Collection* whose *Value* can vary. See *Levels of Measurement*.

Variable Label: A descriptive label that is applied to all *Variables* in *SPSS*.

Variable Name: A name applied to a *Variable* in SPSS.

Variance: The square of *Standard Deviation*.

Visual Aids: Equipment that the researcher can use to enhance a *Presentation*. For example, using an overhead projector to present transparencies.

Visual Data: *Data* that is non-numerical and non-*Textual* in the sense of simply words (though often images are read as meaningful *Texts*). Increasingly, film, photography, digital imagery and drawing is being used as *Data*.

Visual Reduction: The use of representational devices (*Tables*, diagrams, maps and graphs) to allow patterns within complex *Textual* or numerical *Data* to stand out.

Within-case Display: Graphical devices (*Tables*, *Charts* and so on) designed to highlight the existence or non-existence of patterns within *Cases*, as distinct from *Cross-case Displays*.

Yates's Contingency Correction: See *Continuity Correction*.

Z Scores: See *Standardized Scores*.

REFERENCES

Aldridge, Alan and Levine, Ken (2001) *Surveying the Social World: Principles and Practice in Survey Research.* Buckingham: Open University Press.

Allan, S., Adam, B. and Carter, C. (eds) (1999) *Environmental Risks and the Media.* London: Routledge.

Anderson, A. (1997) *Media, Culture and the Environment.* London: UCL.

Arber, S. (2001) 'Secondary analysis of survey data', in N. Gilbert (ed.), *Researching Social Life* (2nd edn). London: Sage. pp. 269–86.

Argyous, G. (2000) *Statistics for Social and Health Research.* London: Sage.

Atkinson, J.M. (1978) *Discovering Suicide: Studies in the Social Organisation of Sudden Death.* Basingstoke: Macmillan.

Atkinson, J.M. and Heritage, John (1984) *Structures of Social Action: Studies in Conversation Analysis.* Cambridge: Cambridge University Press.

Atkinson, P. (1992) *Understanding Ethnographic Texts.* London, Sage.

Atkinson, R. (1998) *The Life Story Interview.* London: Sage.

Atkinson, R. and Flint, J. (2001) *Accessing Hidden and Hard-to-Reach Populations: Snowball Research Strategies.* Social Research Update Issue 33. University of Surrey.

Babbie, E. and Halley, F. (1998) *Adventures in Social Research: Data Analysis Using SPSS for Windows.* Thousand Oaks, CA: Pine Forge.

Ball, S., Davies, J., David, M. and Reay, D. (2002) 'Classification and Judgement: social class and the 'cognitive structures' of choice of Higher Education', *British Journal of Sociology of Education*, 23 (1): 51–72.

Balnaves, M. and Caputi, P. (2001) *Introduction to Quantitative Research Methods: An Investigative Approach.* London: Sage.

Banks, M. (2001) *Visual Methods in Social Research.* London: Sage.

Barr, H., Hammick, M., Koppel, I. and Reeves, S. (1999) 'Evaluating Interprofessional Education: two systematic reviews', *British Educational Research Journal*, 25 (4): 533–45.

Barthes, R. (1967) *Elements of Semiology.* London: Cape.

Barthes, R. (1973) *Mythologies.* London: Paladin.

Bauman, Z. and May, T. (2001) *Thinking Sociologically.* Oxford: Blackwell.

Bazeley, P. and Richards, L. (2000) *The NVivo Qualitative Project Book.* London: Sage.

Becker, H. (1967) 'Whose side are we on?', *Social Problems,* 14: 239–47.

Becker, H. and Geer, B.(1960) 'Participant observation: the analysis of qualitative field data', in R.N. Adams and J. J. Preiss (eds), *Human Organization Research.* Homewood, IL: Dorsey.

Becker, Howard (1986) *Writing for Social Scientists.* Chicago, IL: University of Chicago Press.

Becker, H. Geer, B., Hughes, E.C. and Strauss, A.L. (1961) *Boys in White: Student Culture in Medical School.* Chicago, IL: University of Chicago Press.

Bell, Colin and Newby, Howard (1971) *Community Studies: An Introduction to the Sociology of the Local Community.* London: Allen and Unwin.

Belson, William A. (1981) *The Design and Understanding of Survey Questions.* London: Gower.

Benson, Douglas and Hughes, John (1991) 'Evidence and Inference', in Graham Button (ed.), *Ethnomethodology and the Human Sciences.* Cambridge: Cambridge University Press. pp. 109–136.

Berelson, B. (1952) *Content Analysis in Communication Research.* New York: Hafner.

Berg, Bruce L. (1998) *Qualitative Research Methods for the Social Sciences.* Needham Heights, MA: Allyn and Bacon.

Bergner, M., Bobbitt, A., Carter W.B. and Gilson, B.S. (1981) 'The Sickness Impact Profile: development and final version of a health status measure', *Medical Care*, 19: 787–805.

Beveridge, W. (1942) *Social Insurance and Allied Services.* London: HMSO.

Black, D. (1992) *Inequalities in Health: The Black Report.* London: Penguin.

Black, T. (1999) *Doing Quantitative Research in the Social Sciences: An Integrated Approach to Research Design, Measurement and Statistics.* London: Sage.

Blalock, H. (1960) *Social Statistics* (2nd edn). Boston, MA: McGraw-Hill.

Bouma, Gary D. and Atkinson, G.B.J. (1995) *A Handbook of Social Science Research.* Oxford: Oxford University Press.

Bradbury, Andrew (2000) *Successful Presentations* (2nd edn). London: Kogan Page.

Brewer, John (2000) *Ethnography*. Buckingham: Open University Press.

Bryant, L., Evans, J., Sutton, C. and Beer, J. (2002) *The Experience of Deprivation and Exclusion*. Plymouth: Social Research and Regeneration Unit, University of Plymouth.

Bryant, L., Sutton, C. and Bunyard, T. (2000) *The Integration of Sea Service: Evaluation Study*. Plymouth: Social Research and Regeneration Unit, University of Plymouth.

Bryman, Alan (1988) *Quantity and Quality in Social Research*. London: Routledge.

Bryman, Alan (2001) *Social Research Methods*. Oxford: Oxford University Press.

Bryman, Alan and Cramer, Duncan (1997) *Quantitative Data Analysis with SPSS for Windows: A Guide for Social Scientists*. London: Routledge.

Bryman, Alan and Cramer, Duncan (2000) *Quantitative Data Analysis with SPSS for Windows Release 10: A Guide for Social Scientists*. London: Routledge.

Bulmer, Martin (1984) *The Chicago School of Sociology: Industrialization, diversity, and the rise of sociological research*. Chicago, IL: University of Chicago Press.

Burgess, Robert G. (1984) *In the Field*. London: Allen and Unwin.

Burgess, Robert (ed.) (1993) *Education Research and Evaluation: For Policy and Practice?* London: Falmer.

Burton, Dawn (ed.) (2000) *Research Training for Social Scientists*. London: Sage.

Button, Graham (1990) 'Going up a blind alley - conflating conversation analysis and computational modelling', in Pauline M. Luff (ed.), *Computers and Conversation*. London: Academic Press. pp.67–90.

Button, Graham, (ed.) (1991) *Ethnomethodology and the Human Sciences*. Cambridge: Cambridge University Press.

Byram, Lynda (1999) *Being Successful in Presentations*. London: Blackhall.

Calder, B.T. (1977) 'Focus groups and the nature of qualitative marketing research', *Journal of Marketing Research*, 42: 702–37.

Carmichael, S. and Hamilton, C.V. (1968) *Black Power: The Politics of Liberation in America*. London: Jonathan Cape.

Cicourel, Aaron (1968), *Method and Measurement in Sociology*. New York: Free Press.

Clarke, Alan and Dawson, Ruth (1999) *Evaluation Research: An Introduction to Principles, Methods and Practice*. London: Sage.

Clegg, Frances (1982) *Simple Statistics: A Course Book for the Social Sciences*. Cambridge: Cambridge University Press.

Clifford, James (1986) 'Introduction: partial truths', in J.

Clifford and G.E. Marcus (eds), *Writing Culture: The Poetics and Politics of Ethnography*. Berkeley, CA: University of California Press.

Collins, Harry and Pinch, Trevor (1998) *The Golem at Large: What You Should Know About Technology*. Cambridge: Cambridge University Press.

Coomber, Ross (1997) 'Using the Internet for social research', *Sociological Research Online*, 2 (2): <http://www.socresonline.org.uk/socresonline/2/2/2.htm>

Cottle, S. (1993) *TV News, Urban Conflict and the Inner City*. Leicester: Leicester University Press.

Cottle, S. (1999) 'TV news, lay voices and the visualisation of environmental risks', in S. Allan, B. Adam and C. Carter (eds), *Environmental Risks and the Media*. London: Routledge. pp. 29–44.

Countryside Agency (2000) *Rural Services in 2000: Working for People and Places in Rural England*. Northampton: Countryside Agency.

Countryside Agency (1999) *Working for People and Places in Rural England*. Northampton: Countryside Agency.

Cramer, D. (1994) *Introducing Statistics for Social Research: Step-by-step Calculations and Computer Techniques Using SPSS*. London: Routledge.

Crompton, R., Gallie, D. and Purcell, K. (eds) (1996), *Changing Forms of Employment: Organisations, Skills and Gender*. London: Routledge.

Dale, Angela, Arber, Sara and Procter, Michael (1988) *Doing Secondary Analysis*. London: Unwin Hyman.

David, Matthew (2002) 'Problems of participation: the limits of action research', *International Journal of Social Research Methodology: Theory and Practice*, 5 (1): 11–17.

David, Matthew (2003), 'The politics of communication: information technology, local knowledge and social exclusion', in *Telematics and Informatics*, 20 (3): 235–53.

David, Matthew and Zeitlyn, David (1996) 'What are they doing? Dilemmas in analysing bibliographic searching: cultural and technical networks in academic life', *Sociological Research Online*, 1 (4): <http://www.socresonline.org.uk/socresonline/1/4/2.html>

Deacon, D., Pickering, M., Golding, P. and Murdock, G. (1999) *Researching Communications: A Practical Guide to Methods in Media and Cultural Analysis*. London: Arnold.

Delbridge, R. (1998) *Life on the Line in Contemporary Manufacturing*. Oxford: Oxford University Press.

Derrida, Jacques (1972) 'Structure, sign and play in the discourse of the human sciences', in R. Machsey and E. Donato (eds), *The Structuralist Controversy*. London: Johns Hopkins University Press.

DETR – Department of the Environment, Transport and the Regions (2000) *Indices of Deprivation 2000*.

Regeneration Research Summary, Number 31.

de Vaus, David (1996) *Surveys in Social Research*. London: UCL Press.

de Vaus, David (2001) *Research Design in Social Research*. London: Sage.

de Vaus, D.A. (2002a) *Analysing Social Science Data: 50 Key Problems in Data Analysis*. London: Sage.

de Vaus, D.A. (2002b) *Surveys in Social Research* (5th edition). London: UCL Press.

Diamond, I. and Jeffries, J. (2000) *Beginning Statistics: An Introduction for Social Scientists*. London: Sage.

Durkheim, E. (1952) *Suicide: A Study in Sociology*. London: Routledge.

Ellen, Roy F. (1984) *Ethnographic Research – A Guide to General Conduct*. New York: Harcourt Brace.

Ellis, Lee (1994) *Research Methods in the Social Sciences*. Madison, WI: WCB Brown and Benchmark.

Emmison, Michael and Smith, Philip (2000) *Researching the Visual: Images, Objects, Contexts and Interactions in Social and Cultural Inquiry*. London: Sage.

Ericson, R.V., Baranek, P.M. and Chan, J.B.L. (1991) *Representing Order: Crime, Law and Justice in the News Media*. Buckingham: Open University Press.

Fairclough, R. (1995) *Media Discourse*. London: Edward Arnold.

Fern, E.F. (1982) 'The use of focus groups for idea generation: the effects of group size, acquaintanceship, and moderator on response quantity and quality', *Journal of Marketing Research*, 19: 1–13.

Ferrie, J., Martikainen, P., Shipley, M., Marmot, M., Stansfeld, S. and Davey-Smith, G. (2001) 'Employment status and health after privatisation in white collar civil servants: prospective cohort study', *British Medical Journal*, 322: 1–7.

Fetterman, David (1998) *Ethnography: Step by Step* (2nd edn). London: Sage.

Field, A. (2000) *Discovering Statistics using SPSS for Windows*. London: Sage.

Fielding, Jane and Gilbert, Nigel (2000) *Understanding Social Statistics*. London: Sage.

Fielding, Nigel (1981) *The National Front*. London: Routledge.

Fielding, Nigel (1995) 'Ethnography', in N. Gilbert (ed.) *Researching Social Life*. London: Sage. pp. 154–71.

Fielding, Nigel and Lee, Raymond (1998) *Computer Analysis and Qualitative Research*. London: Sage.

Fink, Arlene (1995a) *The Survey Kit: How to Ask Survey Questions*. Thousand Oaks, CA: Sage.

Fink, Arlene (1995b) *The Survey Kit: How to Sample in Surveys*. Thousand Oaks, CA: Sage.

Fink, Arlene (1995c) *How to Report on Surveys*. London: Sage.

Foddy, William (1993) *Constructing Questions for Interviews and Questionnaires: Theory and Practice in Social Research*. Cambridge: Cambridge University Press.

Foster, Jeremy (1998) *Data Analysis Using SPSS for Windows*. London: Sage.

Fowler, Floyd (1988) *Survey Research Methods*. London: Sage.

Fowler, Floyd (1995) *Improving Survey Questions: Design and Evaluation*. London: Sage.

Fuller, Steve (2000) *The Governance of Science*. Buckingham: Open university Press.

Garfinkel, Harold (1984) *Studies in Ethnomethodology*. Cambridge: Polity.

Geertz, C. (ed.) (1973) *The Interpretation of Culture*. New York: Basic Books.

Gellner, Ernest (1992) *Postmodernism, Reason and Religion*. London: Routledge.

Giarchi, G. (1999) *The Overshadowed Districts of East Cornwall*. Plymouth: University of Plymouth.

Giddens, A. (1984) *The Constitution of Society*. Cambridge: Polity.

Gilbert, Nigel (1993) *Analyzing Tabular Data*. London: UCL.

Gilbert, Nigel (ed.) (2001) *Researching Social Life* (2nd edn). London: Sage.

Gillborn, D. (1990) *'Race', Ethnicity and Education*. London: Unwin Hyman.

Glaser, Barney (1992) *Emergence vs Forcing: Basics of Grounded Theory Analysis*. Mill Valley, CA: Sociology Press.

Glaser, Barney and Strauss, Anselm (1967) *The Discovery of Grounded Theory: Strategies for Qualitative Research*. Chicago, IL: Aldine.

Goffman, Erving (1959) *The Presentation of Self in Everyday Life*. Harmondsworth: Penguin.

Goffman, Erving (1968) *Asylums: Essays on the Social Situation of Mental Patients and Other Inmates*. London: Pelican.

Goffman, Erving (1990) *Stigma: Notes on the Management of Spoiled Identity*. London, Penguin.

Gold, R.L. (1958) 'Roles in Sociological Fieldwork', *Social Forces*, 36: 217–23.

Government Statistical Service (1998) *Harmonised Concepts and Questions for Government Social Surveys: Update December 1997*. London: Office for National Statistics.

Gouldner, Alvin (1979) *The Future of Intellectuals and the Rise of the New Class*. New York. MacMillan.

Green, S., Salkind, N. and Akey, T. (1999) *Using SPSS for Windows: Analyzing and Understanding Data* (2nd edn). Englewood Cliffs, NJ: Prentice Hall.

Griffiths, P., Gossop, M., Powis, B. and Strang, J. (1993) 'Reaching hidden populations of drug users by privileged access interviewers: methodological and practical issues', *Addiction*, 88: 1617–26.

Guardian (2002) 'Internet usage soars'. Monday, 10 June 2002. <*http://media.guardian.co.uk/newmedia/story/0,7496,730906,00.html*>

Hague, Paul N. and Roberts, Kate (1994) *Presentations and Report Writing*. London: Kogan Page.

Hakim, Catherine (1982) *Secondary Analysis in Social Research: A Guide to Data Sources and with Examples*. London: Harper Collins.

Hakim, Catherine (2000) *Research Design: Successful Designs for Social and Economic Research* (2nd edn). London: Routledge.

Halliday, J. (1998) *Developing Rural Indicators: Findings from a Project in the Blackdown Hills*. Exeter: Devon County Council.

Hammersley, Martyn (1995) *The Politics of Social Research*. London: Sage.

Hammersley, Martyn (1998) *Reading Ethnographic Research* (2nd edn). London: Longman.

Hammersley, Martyn (2000) *Taking Sides in Social Research: Essays on Partisanship and Bias*. London: Routledge.

Hammersley, Martyn and Atkinson, Paul (1995) *Ethnography: Principles in Practice* (2nd edn). London: Routledge.

Hansen, A., Cottle, S., Negrine, R. and Newbold, C. (1998) *Mass Communication Research Methods*. Basingstoke: Macmillan.

Harding, Sandra (1986) *The Science Question in Feminism*. Buckingham: Open University Press.

Harries-Jones, Peter (1991) *Making Knowledge Count*. London: McGill Queens University Press.

Hart, Chris (1998) *Doing a Literature Review*. London: Sage.

Hart, Chris (2001) *Doing a Literature Search*. London: Sage.

Heritage, John (1997) 'Conversation analysis and institutional talk: analysing data', in David Silverman (ed.), *Qualitative Research: Theory, Methods and Practice*. London: Sage. pp. 161–82.

Hinton, P.R. (1995) *Statistics Explained: A Guide for Social Science Students*. London: Routledge.

Homan, Roger (1991) *The Ethics of Social Research*. Harlow: Longman.

Humphries, Laud (1970) *The Tea Room Trade*. London: Duckworth.

Husserl, E. (1962) *Ideas: General Introduction to Pure Phenomenology*. New York: Collier.

Jenkinson, Crispin (ed.) (1994) *Measuring Health and Medical Outcomes*. London: UCL.

Junker, B. (1960) *Fieldwork*. Chicago, IL: University of Chicago Press.

Kanji, G.K. (1999) *100 Statistical Tests* (2nd edn). London: Sage.

Keefer, Jane (1993) 'The hungry rats syndrome: information literacy, and the academic reference process', *RQ*, 32 (3): 333–9.

Kinnear, Richard and Gray, Colin (2000) *SPSS for Windows Made Simple: Release 10*. Hove: Psychology Press.

Kmietowicz, Z.W. and Yannoulis, Y. (1998) *Statistical Tables for Economic, Business and Social Studies*. Harlow: Longman Scientific and Technical.

Kohler-Riessman, Catherine (1993) *Narrative Analysis*. London: Sage.

Kuper, Adam (1973), *Anthropology and Anthropologists*. London: Allen Lane.

Lawson, Tony and Garrod, Joan (1994) *The Complete A–Z Sociology Handbook*. London: Hodder and Stoughton Educational.

Lee, Raymond (1993) *Doing Research on Sensitive Topics*. London: Sage.

Lee, Raymond (2000) *Unobtrusive Methods in Social Research*. Buckingham: Open University Press.

Lévi-Strauss, Claude (1979) *Myth and Meaning*. New York: Schocken.

Lindley, D.V. and Scott, W.F. (1995) *New Cambridge Elementary Statistical Tables* (2nd edn). Cambridge: Cambridge University Press.

Lofland, John (1996) 'Analytic ethnography: features, failings, and futures', *Journal of Contemporary Ethnography*, 24 (1): 30–67.

McDowell, Ian and Newell, Claire (1996) *Measuring Health : A Guide to Rating Scales and Questionnaires*. New York: Oxford University Press.

Macpherson, William (1999) *The Stephen Lawrence Inquiry: Report of an Inquiry by Sir William Macpherson of Cluny*. London: Home Office. Cm 4262-I.

Mann, Chris and Stewart, Fiona (2000) *Internet Communication and Qualitative Research: A Handbook for Researching Online*. London: Sage.

Manning, Peter and Cullum-Swan, Betsy (1998) 'Narrative, content and semiotic analysis', in Norman K. Denzin and Yvonna S. Lincoln (eds), *Collecting and Interpreting Qualitative Materials*. London: Sage. pp. 246–73.

Marsh, Catherine (1988) *Exploring Data: An Introduction to Data Analysis for Social Scientists*. Cambridge: Polity.

Mason, David (1982) 'After Scarman: a note on the concept of institutional racism', *New Community*, 10 (1): 123–33.

Mason, David (2000) *Race and Ethnicity in Modern Britain* (2nd edn). Oxford: Oxford University Press.

May, Tim (1997) *Social Research: Issues, Methods and Processes* (2nd edn). Buckingham: Open University Press.

May, Tim (2001) *Social Research: Issues, Methods and Process* (third edition). Buckingham: Open University Press.

Mayhew, Henry (1961) *London Labour and the London Poor* (Four Volumes). London: Griffin.

Maynard, Mary (1998) 'Feminists' knowledge, and the knowledge of feminisms: epistemology, theory, methodology and method', in Tim May and Malcolm Williams (eds), *Knowing the Social World*. Buckingham, Open University Press. pp. 120–37.

Menard, S. (1991) *Longitudinal Research*. Newbury Park, CA: Sage.

Miles, Matthew and Huberman, A. Michael (1994) *Qualitative Data Analysis*. London: Sage.

Morgan, David L. (1997) *Focus Groups as Qualitative Research*. London: Sage.

Morgan, David L. (1998) *The Focus Group Guidebook*. London: Sage.

Morley, David (1980) *The 'Nationwide' Audience: Structure and Decoding*. London: British Film Institute.

Moser, C.A. and Kalton, G. (1971) *Survey Methods in Social Investigation* (2nd edn). London: Heinemann.

Mullins, A., McCluskie, J. and Taylor-Browne, J. (2001) *Challenging the Rural Idyll: Children and Families speak Out about Life in Rural England in the 21st century*. NCH Report on behalf of the Countryside Agency.

Murphy, R. and Torrance, H. (eds) (1987) *Evaluating Education: Issues and Methods*. Buckingham: Open University Press.

Nettleton, S. and Burrows, R. (1998) 'Mortgage debt, insecure home ownership and health: an exploratory analysis', in M. Bartley, D. Blane and G. Davey-Smith (eds) *The Sociology of Health Inequalities*. Oxford: Blackwell.

Nettleton, S. and Burrows, R. (2000) 'When a capital investment becomes an emotional loss: the health consequences of the experience of mortgage possession in England', *Housing Studies*, 15 (3): 463–79.

Norris, Christopher (1982) *Deconstruction: Theory and Practice*. London: Methuen.

Norris, Christopher (1987) *Jacques Derrida*. London: Fontana.

Norris, N. (1990) *Understanding Educational Evaluation*. London: Kogan Page.

Oakley, Ann (1981) 'Interviewing women: a contradiction in terms?', in H. Roberts (ed.), *Doing Feminist Research*. London: Routledge.

Oakley, Ann (2000) *Experiments in Knowing: Gender and Method in the Social Sciences*. Cambridge: Polity.

Oppenheim, A.N. (1992) *Questionnaire Design, Interviewing and Attitude Measurement* (2nd edn). London: Pinter.

Outhwaite, William and Bottomore, Tom (1993) *The Blackwell Dictionary of Twentieth Century Thought*. London: Blackwell.

Pallant, J. (2001) *SPSS Survival Manual*. Buckingham: Open University Press.

Pawson, Ray and Tilley, Nick (1997) *Realistic Evaluation*. London: Sage.

Payne, J. in collaboration with Hyde, M., Giarchi, G. and Payne, G. (1995) *Regional Profile of the South West with Special Reference to Disadvantage and Poverty*. Community Research Centre, University of Plymouth and National Lotteries Charities Board South West.

Pilnick, Alison (2002) What 'most people' do: Exploring the ethical implications of genetic counselling', *New Genetics and Society*, 21 (3): 339–50.

Pink, Sarah (2001) *Doing Visual Ethnography*. London: Sage.

Porter, Sam (2002) 'Critical Realist Ethnography', in Tim May (ed.), *Qualitative Research in Action*. London: Sage. pp. 53–72.

Potter, Jonathan (1997) 'Discourse Analysis as a way for analysing naturally occurring talk', in David Silverman (ed.), *Qualitative Research: Theory, Methods and Practice*. London: Sage. pp. 144–60.

Potter, Jonathan and Wetherell, Margaret (1994) 'Analysing discourse', in Alan Bryman and Robert Burgess (eds), *Analysing Qualitative Data*. London: Routledge. pp. 47–65.

Psathas, George (1995) *Conversation Analysis: The Study of Talk-in-Interaction*. London: Sage.

Punch, K. (1998) *Introduction to Social Research: Quantitative and Qualitative Approaches*. London: Sage.

Regan de Bere, S. (2003) 'Evaluating the implications of complex interprofessional education for improvements in collaborative practice: a multidimensional model', *British Educational Research Journal*, 29 (1): 105–124.

Regan de Bere, S., Annandale, S. and Natrass, H. (2000) 'Achieving health improvements through interprofessional learning in south west England', *International Journal of Interprofessional Care*, 14 (2): 161–74.

Renzetti, Claire M. and Lee, Raymond M. (1993) *Researching Sensitive Topics*. London: Sage.

Richards, Lyn (2002a) *Using NVivo in Qualitative Research*. London: Sage.

Richards, Lyn (2002b) *Using N6 in Qualitative Research*. London: Sage.

Robson, C. (1993) *Real World Research*. Oxford: Blackwell.

Robson, C. (2002) *Real World Research: A Resource for Social Scientists and Practitioner-Researchers* (2nd edn). Oxford: Blackwell.

Rohlf, James F. and Sokal, Robert (1995) *Statistical Tables*. New York: Freeman.

Rose, D. and Sullivan, O. (1996) *Introducing Data Analysis for Social Scientists* (2nd edn). Buckingham: Open University Press.

Rossi, P.H., Freeman, H.E. and Lipsey, M.W. (1999) *Evaluation: A Systematic Approach* (6th edn). London: Sage.

Rowntree, S. (1901/1980) *Poverty: A study of Town Life*. New York: Garland.

Ruspini, E. (2000) *Longitudinal Research in the Social Sciences*. Social Research Update Issue 28. University of Surrey.

Sacks, Harvey (1992) *Lectures on Conversation*. Oxford: Blackwell.

Sapsford, Roger (1999) *Survey Research*. London: Sage.

Sarantakos, Sotirios (1998) *Social Research* (2nd edition). Basingstoke: Macmillan.

Sayer, Andrew (1992) *Method in Social Science: A Realist Approach*. London: Routledge.

Schlesinger, P. and Tumber, H. (1994) *Reporting Crime: The Media Politics of Criminal Justice*. London: Clarendon.

Schutt, Russell (2001) *Investigating the Social World* (3rd edn). Thousand Oaks, CA: Pine Forge.

Schutz, Alfred (1972) *The Phenomenology of the Social World*. London: Heinemann.

Scott, A. (1994) *Willing Slaves? British Workers Under Human Resource Management*. Cambridge: Cambridge University Press.

Scott, John (1990) *A Matter of Record: Documentary Sources in Social Research*. Cambridge: Polity.

Shucksmith, M., Roberts, D., Scott, D., Chapman, P. and Conway, E. (1996) *Disadvantages in Rural Areas*. Rural Research Report 29. London: Rural Development Commission.

Silverman, David (1993) *Interpreting Qualitative Data*. London: Sage.

Silverman, David (1998) *Harvey Sacks: Social Science and Conversation Analysis*. Cambridge: Polity.

Silverman, David (2000a) 'Analysing talk and text', in Norman K. Denzin and Yvonna S. Lincoln (eds), *Handbook of Qualitative Research* (2nd edn). London: Sage. pp. 821–34.

Silverman, David (2000b) *Doing Qualitative Research – A Practical Handbook*. London: Sage.

Simmons, R. (2001) 'Questionnaires', in N. Gilbert (ed.), *Researching Social Life* (2nd edn). London: Sage. pp. 85–104.

Spitzer, W.O., Dobson, A.J. and Hall, J. (1981) 'Measuring the quality of life of cancer patients: a concise QL-Index for use by physicians', *Journal of Chronic Diseases*, 34: 585–97.

Stake, R. (1998) 'Case Studies', in N. Denzin and Y. Lincoln (eds), *Strategies of Qualitative Inquiry*. London: Sage.

Stanley, L. and Wise, S. (1983) *Breaking Out: Feminist Consciousness and Feminist Research*. London: Routledge.

Strauss, Anselm and Corbin, Juliet (1990) *Basics of Qualitative Research: Grounded Theory Procedures and Techniques*. London: Sage.

Sutton, Carole (1994) 'Piloting a study of the medical condition Vulvar Vestibulitis'. MSc. thesis, University of Plymouth.

Thomas, R. and Purdon, S. (1994) *Telephone Methods for Social Surveys*. Social Research Update Issue 8. University of Surrey.

Townsend, P. (1979) *Poverty in the United Kingdom*. London: Allen Lane.

Turkle, Sherry (1996) *Life on the Screen: Identity in the Age of the Internet*. New York: Simon and Schuster.

UK Data Archive, The (2002) www.data-archive.co.uk. Essex: University of Essex.

Vogt, W. (1999) *Dictionary of Statistics and Methodology* (2nd edn). London: Sage.

Ware, J.E. and Sherbourne, C.D. (1992) 'The MOS 36-item short-form health survey (SF-36) I: Conceptual framework and item selection', *Medical Care*, 30 (6): 473–83.

Weber, Max (1930/original 1905) *The Protestant Ethic and the Spirit of Capitalism*. London: Unwin Hyman.

Weber, Max (1949) *The Methodology of the Social Sciences*. New York: Free Press.

Weber, W. (1975) *Roscher and Knies: The Logical Problems of Historical Economics*. New York: Free Press.

Whyte, William Foote (ed.) (1991a) *Participatory Action Research*. London: Sage.

Whyte, William Foote (1991b) *Social Theory for Action: How Individuals and Organizations Learn to Change*. London: Sage.

Wilkinson, Sue (1998) 'Focus groups in feminist research: power, interaction and the co-production of meaning', *Women's Studies International Forum*, 21 (1): 111–25.

Wight, D. (1994) 'Boys' thoughts and talk about sex in a working class locality of Glasgow', *Sociological Review*, 42: 702–37.

Williams, J. (1985) 'Redefining Institutional Racism' *Ethnic and Racial Studies*, 8(3): 323–48.

Williams, Malcolm (2002) 'Generalization in interpretive research', in Tim May (ed.), *Qualitative Research in Action*. London: Sage. pp. 125–43.

Williams, Malcolm and May, Tim (1996) *Introduction to the Philosophy of Social Research*. London: UCL.

Wolcott, H.F. (1973) *The Man in the Principal's Office: An Ethnography*. Prospect Heights, IL: Waveland.

Wright, D. (1997) *Understanding Statistics: An Introduction for the Social Sciences*. London: Sage.

Wright, Erik Olin (1997) *Class Counts: Comparative Studies in Class Analysis*. Cambridge: Cambridge University Press.

Yin, Robert K. (1994) *Case Study Research: Design and Methods* (2nd edn). London: Sage.

Zeitlyn, David, David, Matthew and Bex, Jane (1999) *Knowledge Lost in Information*. London: British Humanities Press.

Zeller, R.A. (1993) 'Combining qualitative and quantitative techniques to develop culturally sensitive measures', in D.G. Ostrow and R.C. Kessler (eds), *Methodological Issues in AIDS Behavioral Research*. New York: Plenum. pp. 95–116.